Microsoft®
Visual Basic® .NET: RELOADED

Diane Zak

THOMSON
™
COURSE TECHNOLOGY

Australia • Canada • Mexico • Singapore • Spain • United Kingdom • United States

THOMSON

COURSE TECHNOLOGY

Microsoft® Visual Basic® .NET: RELOADED

by Diane Zak

Managing Editor:
Jennifer Muroff

Senior Product Manager:
Tricia Boyle

Acquisitions Editor:
Roberts Apse

Marketing Manager:
Brian Berkeley

Associate Product Manager:
Mirella Misiaszek

Editorial Assistant:
Amanda Piantedosi

Production Editor:
Melissa Panagos

Cover Designer:
Steve Deschene

Interior Designer:
Ann Small

Compositor:
GEX Publishing Services

Manufacturing Coordinator:
Laura Burns

Title Editor:
Linda Linardos

Disclaimer
Course Technology reserves the right to revise this publication and make changes from time to time in its content without notice.

ISBNs 0-619-21287-X
0-619-21565-8

Contents

CHAPTER 4

Making Decisions in a Program 117

CHAPTER 7
Sub and Function Procedures 249

CHAPTER 8
Sequential Access Files and Error Handling 283

Preface

Microsoft Visual Basic .NET: RELOADED uses Visual Basic .NET, an object-oriented language, to teach programming concepts. This book is designed for a beginning programming course; however, it assumes students have learned basic Windows skills and file management from one of Course Technology's other books that covers the Microsoft Windows operating system.

WHY RELOADED?

You may be asking yourself, "What is the significance of RELOADED in the title?" When we began development of this text, we knew it was going to be different. We planned to create a book about Visual Basic that set itself apart from the other books out there. It was important that we express this in the title. It seemed that RELOADED was perfect for what we were trying to express—a feeling of rejuvenation, boldness, and currency. As you proceed through the chapters and continue your endeavor to learn Visual Basic. NET, we hope you also find that the text possesses all of these qualities.

ORGANIZATION AND COVERAGE

Microsoft Visual Basic .NET: RELOADED contains 13 chapters and 4 appendices. In the chapters, students with no previous programming experience learn how to plan and create their own interactive Windows applications. By the end of the book, students will have learned how to use TOE charts, pseudocode, and flowcharts to plan an application. They also will learn how to work with controls and write If...Then...Else, Select Case, Do...Loop, and For...Next statements, as well as how to create and manipulate variables, constants, sequential access files, structures, classes, and arrays. Students also will learn how to manipulate strings, use ADO.NET to connect to a database, and use ASP.NET to create a Web-based application. The text also introduces students to OOP concepts and terminology.

Initially, the Visual Studio .NET IDE can seem overwhelming to a student. To alleviate this problem, Appendix A takes the student on a step-by-step tour of the IDE.

Appendix B summarizes the GUI design rules that are covered in the chapters, and Appendix C lists the basic tools available when creating Windows applications. Finally, Appendix D teaches students how to create simple reports using Crystal Reports.

APPROACH

There are many different approaches to teaching programming with Visual Basic .NET, and it's difficult to write one book that fits all of these approaches. Some instructors, for example, prefer a tutorial-style book, while others prefer a book that focuses on programming concepts only. *Microsoft Visual Basic .NET: RELOADED* is designed to fit the latter approach.

However, some instructors prefer a book that combines programming concepts and tutorials, and allows the student to determine how much "tutorial-help" he or she needs to understand a particular concept. *Microsoft Visual Basic .NET: RELOADED* can fill that need as well, if used with its optional Lab Manual.

The optional Lab Manual contains 13 chapters, each corresponding to a chapter in the book. Each chapter in the Lab Manual consists of 4 labs. Try out *Microsoft Visual Basic .NET: RELOADED – Lab Manual* to accompany this text!

FEATURES

Microsoft Visual Basic .NET: RELOADED is an exceptional textbook because it also includes the following features:

- **Read This Before You Begin** This section is consistent with Course Technology's unequaled commitment to helping instructors introduce technology into the classroom. Technical considerations and assumptions about hardware, software, and default settings are listed in one place to help instructors save time and eliminate unnecessary aggravation.

- **Full color interior** Interior design displays features of text in vibrant color for better illustration of important topics.

- **How To boxes** The How To boxes in each chapter summarize important concepts and provide a quick reference for students. For example, How To boxes show the steps for performing a task, such as starting Microsoft Visual Studio .NET 2003. Additionally, each time a new control is introduced, its most commonly used properties are listed in a How To box. Similarly, when a new statement is covered, its syntax is shown in a How To box along with examples of using the syntax.

HOW TO...

Use the For Each...Next Statement

Syntax
For Each *element* **In** *group*
    [*statements*]
Next *element*

Example
```
Dim strMonths() As String = {"JAN", "FEB", "MAR", "APR", _
        "MAY", "JUN", "JUL", "AUG", "SEP", "OCT", "NOV", "DEC"}
Dim strElement As String

For Each strElement In strMonths
     Me.lblMonths.Text = Me.lblMonths.Text & strElement _
          & ControlChars.NewLine
Next strElement
```
displays the contents of the strMonths array in the lblMonths control

---

- **Tip** Tips provide additional information about a procedure—for example, an alternative method of performing the procedure. They also relate the OOP terminology learned in Chapter 1 to applications created in Visual Basic .NET.

- **GUI Design Tip** GUI Design Tips contain guidelines and recommendations for designing applications that follow Windows standards.

- **Complete Programming Examples** At the end of each chapter is an example of a completed program. The Programming Example shows the TOE chart and pseudocode used to plan the program, as well as the user interface, Objects/Properties/Settings chart, and Visual Basic .NET code. The Programming Example demonstrates the concepts learned in the chapter.

PROGRAMMING EXAMPLE

PAO Application

During July and August of each year the Political Awareness Organization (PAO) sends a questionnaire to the voters in their district. The questionnaire asks the voter to provide his or her political party (Democrat, Republican, or Independent) and age. From the returned questionnaires, the organization's secretary tabulates the number of Democrats, Republicans, and Independents in the district. Create an application that allows the organization's secretary to enter the political party and age, and also save this information to a sequential access file. The application also should calculate and display the number of voters in each political party. Name the solution PAO Solution. Name the project PAO Project. Name the form file PAO Form.vb.

- **Quick Review** Following the Programming Example in each chapter is a Quick Review, which recaps the concepts covered in the chapter.

- **Key Terms** Following the Quick Review in each chapter is a collection of all the key terms found throughout the chapter. Definitions are also included in sentence format.

Key Terms

An application writes information to an **output file**, and reads information from an **input file**.

A **sequential access file** is composed of lines of text that are both stored and retrieved sequentially. A sequential access file is often referred to as a **text file**.

A **StreamWriter object** is used to write a sequence of characters to a sequential access file.

- **Review Questions and Exercises** Each chapter concludes with meaningful, conceptual Questions that test students' understanding of what they learned in the chapter. The Questions are followed by Exercises, which provide students with additional practice of the skills and concepts they learned in the chapter.

- **Discovery Exercises** The Windows environment allows students to learn by exploring and discovering what they can do. The Discovery Exercises are designated by a "discovery" icon in the margin. They encourage students to challenge and independently develop their own programming skills while exploring the capabilities of Visual Basic .NET.

- **Debugging Exercises** One of the most important programming skills a student can learn is the ability to find and fix problems in an existing application. The Debugging Exercises are designated by the "debugging" icon in the margin and provide an opportunity for students to detect and correct errors in an existing application.

- **Case Projects** At the end of each chapter are four Case Projects. The Case Projects give the student the opportunity to independently synthesize and evaluate information, examine potential solutions, and make recommendations.

- **Think Tank Case Projects** The last Case Project in each chapter is designated by the "Think Tank" icon. The Think Tank Case Projects are more challenging than the other Case Projects.

- **Glossary** A glossary is included at the end of the book listing all the key terms in alphabetical order, along with definitions.

ONLINE COMPANION

Take advantage of the online companion to accompany *Microsoft Visual Basic .NET: RELOADED!* The online companion contains:

- **Chapter Summaries** outlining the primary topics covered in the chapter.

- **Key terms** from each chapter listed with their definitions.

- **Quizzes** offering 30 brand new multiple choice questions not found in the book.

- **Exercises** providing 2 brand new exercises, not found in the book, written by a subject matter expert.

- **Web links** containing general information related to Visual Basic .NET such as links to sites with data about programming careers, newsgroup sites, or FAQs.

    The online companion can be found at **www.course.com/zakreloaded**.

TEACHING TOOLS

The following supplemental materials are available when this book is used in a classroom setting. All of the teaching tools available with this book are provided to the instructor on a single CD-ROM. Many can also be found at the Course Technology Web site (**www.course.com**).

- **Electronic Instructor's Manual**—The Instructor's Manual that accompanies this textbook includes additional instructional material to assist in class preparation, including Sample Syllabi, Chapter Outlines, Technical Notes, Lecture Notes, Quick Quizzes, Teaching Tips, Discussion Topics, and Key Terms.

- **ExamView®** This textbook is accompanied by ExamView, a powerful testing software package that allows instructors to create and administer printed, computer (LAN-based), and Internet exams. ExamView includes hundreds of questions that correspond to the topics covered in this text, enabling students to generate detailed study guides that include page references for further review. The computer-based and Internet testing components allow students to take exams at their computers, and also save time for the instructor by grading each exam automatically.

- **PowerPoint Presentations** This book comes with Microsoft PowerPoint slides for each chapter. These are included as a teaching aid for classroom presentation, to make available to students on the network for chapter review, or to be printed for classroom distribution. Instructors can add their own slides for additional topics they introduce to the class.

- **Data Files** Data Files, which are necessary for completing many of the end-of-chapter Exercises, are provided on the Teaching Tools CD-ROM and may also be found on the Course Technology Web site at **www.course.com**.

- **Solution Files** Solutions to end-of-chapter Review Questions, Exercises, and Case Projects are provided on the Teaching Tools CD-ROM and may also be found on the Course Technology Web site at **www.course.com**. The solutions are password protected.

- **Distance Learning** Course Technology is proud to present online courses in WebCT and Blackboard, to provide the most complete and dynamic learning experience possible. When you add online content to one of your courses, you're adding a lot: self tests, links, glossaries, and, most of all, a gateway to the 21st century's most important information resource. We hope you will make the most of your course, both online and offline. For more information on how to bring distance learning to your course, contact your local Course Technology sales representative.

ACKNOWLEDGMENTS

Writing a book is a team effort rather than an individual one. I would like to take this opportunity to thank my team, especially Jennifer Muroff (Managing Editor), Tricia Boyle (Senior Product Manager), Melissa Panagos (Production Editor), and Shawn Day (Quality Assurance). Thank you for your support, enthusiasm, patience, and hard work. I could not have completed this project without you. Last, but certainly not least, I want to thank the following reviewers for their invaluable ideas and comments:

James J. Ball, Indiana State University; Clifford Brozo, Monroe College; Lenore Horowitz, Schenectady County Community College; Rachelle Kristof Hippler, Bowling Green State University – Firelands; Patricia Mayer Milligan, Baylor University; Elaine Seeman, East Carolina University.

Diane Zak

Read This Before You Begin

TO THE USER

Data Files

To complete some of the exercises in this book, you will need data files that have been created for this book. Your instructor will provide the data files to you. You also can obtain the files electronically from the Course Technology Web site by connecting to **www.course.com**, and then searching for this book title.

Each chapter in this book has its own set of data files, which are stored in a separate folder within the VbDotNet folder; the only exception to this is Chapter 13. For example, the files for Chapter 1 are stored in the VbDotNet\Chap01 folder. Similarly, the files for Chapter 2 are stored in the VbDotNet\Chap02 folder. The files for Chapter 13 are stored in the Inetpub\wwwroot\Chap13 folder. Throughout this book, you will be instructed to open files from or save files to these folders.

You can use a computer in your school lab or your own computer to complete the Programming Examples, Exercises, and Case Projects in this book.

Using Your Own Computer

To use your own computer to complete the material in this book, you will need the following:

- A 486-level or higher personal computer running Microsoft Windows. This book was written and Quality Assurance tested using Microsoft Windows XP.

- Microsoft Visual Studio .NET 2003 Professional Edition or Enterprise Edition, or Microsoft Visual Basic .NET 2003 Standard Edition must be installed on your computer. This book was written using Microsoft Visual Studio .NET 2003 Professional and Quality Assurance tested using Microsoft Visual Basic .NET 2003 Standard Edition.

   If you purchased this copy of the text, then you also received Microsoft Visual Basic .NET 2003 Standard Edition contained on a set 5 CD-ROMs.

- **Data files.** You will not be able to complete some of the Exercises in this book using your own computer unless you have the data files. You can get the data files from your instructor, or you can obtain the data files electronically from the Course Technology Web site by connecting to **www.course.com**, and then searching for this book title.

Figures

The figures in this book reflect how your screen will look if you are using a Microsoft Windows XP system. Your screen may appear slightly different in some instances if you are using another version of Microsoft Windows.

Visit Our World Wide Web Site

Additional materials designed especially for you might be available for your course on the World Wide Web. Go to **www.course.com**. Periodically search this site for more details.

TO THE INSTRUCTOR

To complete some of the Exercises in this book, your users must use a set of data files. These files are included in the Instructor's Resource Kit. They also may be obtained electronically through the Course Technology Web site at **www.course.com**. Follow the instructions in the Help file to copy the data files to your server or standalone computer. You can view the Help file using a text editor such as WordPad or Notepad. Once the files are copied, you should instruct your users how to copy the files to their own computers or workstations.

The Programming Examples, Exercises, and Case Projects in this book were Quality Assurance tested using Microsoft Visual Basic .NET 2003 Standard Edition on a Microsoft Windows XP operating system.

Course Technology Data Files

You are granted a license to copy the data files to any computer or computer network used by individuals who have purchased this book.

An Introduction to Visual Basic .NET

- Explain the history of programming languages
- Define the terminology used in object-oriented programming languages
- Create a Visual Basic .NET Windows-based application
- Manage the windows in the IDE
- Set the properties of an object
- Add a control to a form
- Use the Label and Button tools
- Enter code in the Code Editor window
- Save a solution
- Start and end an application
- Print a project's code
- Close a solution
- Open an existing solution

PROGRAMMERS

Although computers appear to be amazingly intelligent machines, they cannot yet think on their own. Computers still rely on human beings to give them directions. The directions are called **programs**, and the people who write the programs are called **programmers**. Programmers make it possible for us to communicate with our personal computers; without them, we wouldn't be able to use the computer to write a letter or play a game.

Typical tasks performed by a computer programmer include analyzing a problem statement or project specification, planning an appropriate solution, and converting the solution to a language that the computer can understand. According to the career Web site *WetFeet.com*, successful programmers are analytical thinkers; they are able to approach a problem in many different ways and identify the strengths and weaknesses of each approach. Patience, strong writing and communication skills, and the ability to work well in a team are also important characteristics of successful programmers. "The most successful programmers are not only competent code writers, but well liked among their peers."

The U.S. Department of Labor's Bureau of Labor Statistics ranks computer programming as the fastest growing occupation between the years 2000 and 2010: the number of jobs is expected to increase from 380,000 to 760,000. Depending on geographical location, the median salary of programmers ranges from $46,000 to $81,000.

A BRIEF HISTORY OF PROGRAMMING LANGUAGES

Just as human beings communicate with each other through the use of languages such as English, Spanish, Hindi, and Chinese, programmers use a variety of special languages, called **programming languages**, to communicate with the computer. Some popular programming languages are Visual Basic .NET, Visual C# .NET, C++, Visual C++ .NET, Java, Perl (Practical Extraction and Report Language), C, and COBOL (Common Business Oriented Language). In the next sections, you follow the progression of programming languages from machine languages to assembly languages, and then to high-level languages.

Machine Languages

Within a computer, all data is represented by microscopic electronic switches that can be either off or on. The off switch is designated by a 0, and the on switch is designated by a 1. Because computers can understand only these on and off switches, the first programmers had to write the program instructions using nothing but combinations of 0s and 1s; for example, a program might contain the instruction 00101 10001 10000. Instructions written in 0s and 1s are called **machine language** or **machine code**. The machine languages (each type of machine has its own language) represent the only way to communicate directly with the computer. As you can imagine, programming in machine language is very tedious and error-prone and requires highly trained programmers.

Assembly Languages

Slightly more advanced programming languages are called **assembly languages**. The assembly languages simplify the programmer's job by allowing the programmer to use mnemonics in place of the 0s and 1s in the program. **Mnemonics** are memory aids—in this case, alphabetic abbreviations for instructions. For example, most assembly languages use the mnemonic ADD to represent an add operation and the mnemonic MUL to represent a multiply operation. An example of an instruction written in an assembly language is MUL b1, ax.

Programs written in an assembly language require an **assembler**, which also is a program, to convert the assembly instructions into machine code—the 0s and 1s the computer can understand. Although it is much easier to write programs in assembly language than in machine language, programming in assembly language still is tedious and requires highly trained programmers.

High-Level Languages

High-level languages represent the next major development in programming languages. High-level languages are a vast improvement over machine and assembly languages, because they allow the programmer to use instructions that more closely resemble the English language. An example of an instruction written in a high-level language is grossPay = hours * rate.

Programs written in a high-level language require either an interpreter or a compiler to convert the English-like instructions into the 0s and 1s the computer can understand. Like assemblers, both interpreters and compilers are separate programs. An **interpreter** translates the high-level instructions into machine code, line by line, as the program is running, whereas a **compiler** translates the entire program into machine code before running the program.

Like their predecessors, the first high-level languages were used to create procedure-oriented programs. When writing a **procedure-oriented program**, the programmer concentrates on the major tasks that the program needs to perform. A payroll program, for example, typically performs several major tasks, such as inputting the employee data, calculating the gross pay, calculating the taxes, calculating the net pay, and outputting a paycheck. The programmer must instruct the computer every step of the way, from the start of the task to its completion. In a procedure-oriented program, the programmer determines and controls the order in which the computer processes the instructions. In other words, the programmer must determine not only the proper instructions to give the computer, but the correct sequence of those instructions as well. Examples of high-level languages used to create procedure-oriented programs include COBOL, BASIC (Beginner's All-Purpose Symbolic Instruction Code), and C.

Recently, more advanced high-level languages have emerged; these languages are used to create object-oriented programs. Different from a procedure-oriented program, which focuses on the individual tasks the program must perform, an **object-oriented program** requires the programmer to focus on the objects that the program can use to accomplish its goal. The objects can take on many different forms. For example, programs written for the Windows environment typically use objects such as check boxes, list boxes, and buttons. A payroll program, on the other hand, might utilize objects found in the real world, such as a time card object, an employee object, and a check object. Because each object is viewed as an independent unit, an object can be used in more than one program, usually with little or no modification. A check object used in a payroll program, for example, also can be used in a sales revenue program (which receives checks from customers) and an accounts payable program (which issues checks to creditors). The ability to use an object for more than one purpose saves programming time and money—an advantage that contributes to the popularity of object-oriented programming. Examples of high-level languages used to create object-oriented programs include Visual Basic .NET, Java, C++, Visual C++ .NET, and Visual C# .NET.

In this book, you learn how to create object-oriented programs using the Visual Basic .NET language. Although you may have either heard or read that object-oriented programs are difficult to write, do not be intimidated. Admittedly, creating object-oriented programs does take some practice. However, you already are familiar with many of the concepts upon which object-oriented programming is based. Much of the anxiety of object-oriented programming stems from the terminology used when discussing it. Many of the terms are unfamiliar, because they typically are not used in everyday conversations. The next section will help to familiarize you with the terms used in discussions about object-oriented programming. Do not be concerned if you do not understand everything right away; you will see further explanations and examples of these terms throughout this book.

OOP TERMINOLOGY

When discussing object-oriented programs, you will hear programmers use the terms OOP (pronounced like *loop*) and OOD (pronounced like *mood*). **OOP** is an acronym for object-oriented programming and simply means that you are using an object-oriented language to create a program that contains one or more objects. OOD, on the other hand, is an acronym for object-oriented design. Like top-down design, which is used to plan procedure-oriented programs, **OOD** also is a design methodology, but it is used to plan object-oriented programs. Unlike top-down design, which breaks up a problem into one or more tasks, OOD divides a problem into one or more objects.

An **object** is anything that can be seen, touched, or used; in other words, an object is nearly any *thing*. As mentioned earlier, the objects used in an object-oriented program can take on many different forms. The menus, check boxes, and buttons included in most Windows programs are objects. An object also can represent something encountered in real life—such as a wristwatch, a car, a credit card receipt, and an employee.

Every object has attributes and behaviors. The **attributes**, also called **properties**, are the characteristics that describe the object. When you tell someone that your wristwatch is a Farentino Model 35A, you are describing the watch (an object) in terms of some of its attributes—in this case, its maker and model number. A watch also has many other attributes, such as a crown, dial, hour hand, minute hand, and movement.

An object's **behaviors**, also called **methods**, are the operations (actions) that the object is capable of performing. A watch, for example, can keep track of the time. Some watches also can keep track of the date. Still others can illuminate their dials when a button on the watch is pushed.

You also will hear the term "class" in OOP discussions. A **class** is a pattern or blueprint used to create an object. Every object used in an object-oriented program comes from a class. A class contains—or, in OOP terms, it **encapsulates**—all of the attributes and behaviors that describe the object the class creates. The blueprint for the Farentino Model 35A watch, for example, encapsulates all of the watch's attributes and behaviors. Objects created from a class are referred to as **instances** of the class, and are said to be "instantiated" from the class. All Farentino Model 35A watches are instances of the Farentino Model 35A class.

"Abstraction" is another term used in OOP discussions. **Abstraction** refers to the hiding of the internal details of an object from the user; hiding the internal details helps prevent the user from making inadvertent changes to the object. The internal mechanism of a watch, for example, is enclosed (hidden) in a case

TIP

The class itself is not an object; only an instance of the class is an object.

TIP

The term "encapsulate" means "to enclose in a capsule." In the context of OOP, the "capsule" is a class.

to protect the mechanism from damage. Attributes and behaviors that are not **hidden** are said to be **exposed** to the user. Exposed on a Farentino Model 35A watch are the crown used to set the hour and minute hands, and the button used to illuminate the dial. The idea behind abstraction is to expose to the user only those attributes and behaviors that are necessary to use the object, and to hide everything else.

Another OOP term, **inheritance**, refers to the fact that you can create one class from another class. The new class, called the **derived class**, inherits the attributes and behaviors of the original class, called the **base class**. For example, the Farentino company might create a blueprint of the Model 35B watch from the blueprint of the Model 35A watch. The Model 35B blueprint (the derived class) will inherit all of the attributes and behaviors of the Model 35A blueprint (the base class), but it then can be modified to include an additional feature, such as an alarm.

Finally, you also will hear the term "polymorphism" in OOP discussions. **Polymorphism** is the object-oriented feature that allows the same instruction to be carried out differently depending on the object. For example, you open a door, but you also open an envelope, a jar, and your eyes. You can set the time, date, and alarm on a Farentino watch. Although the meaning of the verbs "open" and "set" are different in each case, you can understand each instruction because the combination of the verb and the object makes the instruction clear. Figure 1.1 uses the wristwatch example to illustrate most of the OOP terms discussed in this section.

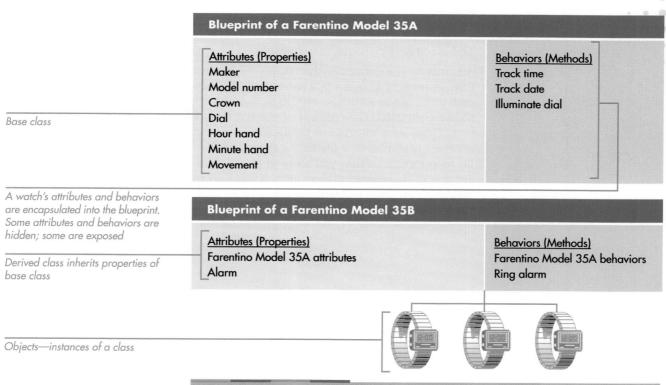

FIGURE 1.1   Illustration of OOP terms

Visual Basic .NET, which is the programming language you will use in this book, is available as a stand-alone product or as part of Visual Studio .NET.

VISUAL STUDIO .NET

Visual Studio .NET is Microsoft's newest integrated development environment. An **integrated development environment (IDE)** is an environment that contains all of the tools and features you need to create, run, and test your programs. For example, an IDE contains an editor for entering your program instructions, and a compiler for running and testing the program.

Included in Visual Studio .NET are the Visual Basic .NET, Visual C++ .NET, Visual C# .NET, and Visual J# .NET programming languages. You can use the languages available in Visual Studio .NET to create Windows-based or Web-based programs, referred to as **applications**. A **Windows-based application** has a Windows user interface and runs on a desktop computer. A **user interface** is what you see and interact with when using an application. Graphics programs, data-entry systems, and games are examples of Windows-based applications. A **Web-based application**, on the other hand, has a Web user interface and runs on a server. You access a Web-based application using your computer's browser. Examples of Web-based applications include e-commerce applications available on the Internet and employee handbook applications accessible on a company's intranet.

Applications created in Visual Studio .NET are composed of solutions, projects, and files.

Solutions, Projects, and Files

A **solution** is a container that stores the projects and files for an entire application. A **project** also is a container, but it stores files associated with only a specific piece of the solution. Although the idea of solutions, projects, and files may sound confusing, the concept of placing things in containers is nothing new to you. Think of a solution as being similar to a drawer in a filing cabinet. A project then is similar to a file folder that you store in the drawer, and a file is similar to a document that you store in the file folder. You can place many file folders in a filing cabinet drawer, just as you can place many projects in a solution. You also can store many documents in a file folder, similar to the way you can store many files in a project. Figure 1.2 illustrates this analogy.

TIP

Microsoft licenses the Visual Studio .NET IDE to other vendors, who also can add languages to the IDE.

TIP

Projects stored in the same solution can be written in different .NET languages.

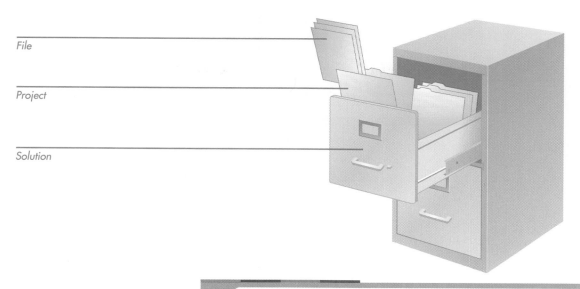

File

Project

Solution

FIGURE 1.2   Illustration of a solution, project, and file

Starting Microsoft Visual Studio .NET

Figure 1.3 shows the steps you follow to start Microsoft Visual Studio .NET 2003, which is the version of Visual Studio .NET used in this book. If you are using a previous version of Microsoft Visual Studio .NET, your steps will be slightly different than the ones shown in Figure 1.3.

Note: As mentioned in the Read This Before You Begin section of this book, you are not expected to follow the steps listed in the How To boxes right now. The How To boxes provide a quick reference that you can use when completing the Programming Example, Exercises, and Case Projects found at the end of the chapter.

HOW TO...

Start Microsoft Visual Studio .NET 2003

1. Click the Start button on the taskbar.
2. Point to All Programs, then point to Microsoft Visual Studio .NET 2003.
3. Click Microsoft Visual Studio .NET 2003.

FIGURE 1.3   How to start Microsoft Visual Studio .NET 2003

When you start Visual Studio .NET 2003, your screen will appear similar to Figure 1.4; however, your Projects tab might include project names and dates. (If you are using a previous version of Visual Studio .NET, your startup screen will look different than the one shown in Figure 1.4.)

Solution Explorer window

Server Explorer window

Toolbox window

Class View window

Dynamic Help window

Start Page window

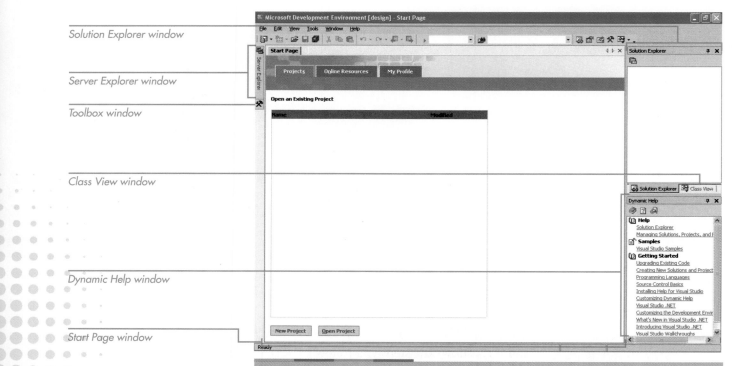

FIGURE 1.4   Visual Studio .NET 2003 startup screen

As Figure 1.4 indicates, the IDE contains six windows: Start Page, Server Explorer, Toolbox, Solution Explorer, Class View, and Dynamic Help. Figure 1.5 briefly describes the purpose of each window.

Window	Purpose
Class View	display the classes, methods, and properties included in a solution
Dynamic Help	display links to context-sensitive help
Server Explorer	display data connections and servers
Solution Explorer	display the names of projects and files included in a solution
Start Page	create and open projects, access Visual Studio .NET information online, customize various program settings in the IDE
Toolbox	display items that you can use when creating a project

FIGURE 1.5   Purpose of the windows included in the IDE

CREATING A VISUAL BASIC .NET WINDOWS-BASED APPLICATION

Figure 1.6 shows the steps you follow to create a Visual Basic .NET Windows-based application, and Figure 1.7 shows an example of a completed New Project dialog box. (You learn how to create a Web-based application in a subsequent chapter.)

HOW TO...

Create a Visual Basic .NET Windows-Based Application

1. Start Visual Studio .NET, then click File on the menu bar.
2. Point to New, then click Project to open the New Project dialog box.
3. Click Visual Basic Projects in the Project Types list box.
4. Click Windows Application in the Templates list box.
5. Enter an appropriate name and location in the Name and Location text boxes, respectively.
6. If necessary, click the More button.
7. Select the Create directory for Solution check box.
8. Enter an appropriate name in the New Solution Name text box.
9. Click the OK button.

FIGURE 1.6   How to create a Visual Basic .NET Windows-based application

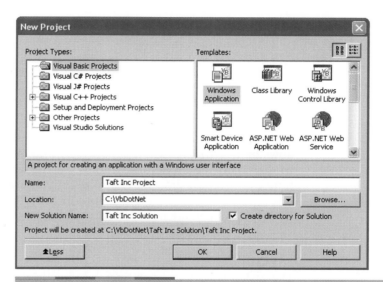

FIGURE 1.7   Completed New Project dialog box

TIP

A template is a pattern that Visual Studio .NET uses to create solutions and projects. Each template listed in the Templates list box includes a set of standard folders and files appropriate for the solution or project. The folder and files are automatically created on your computer's hard disk when you click the OK button in the New Project dialog box.

When you click the OK button in the New Project dialog box, Visual Studio .NET creates a solution and adds a Visual Basic .NET project to the solution, as shown in Figure 1.8.

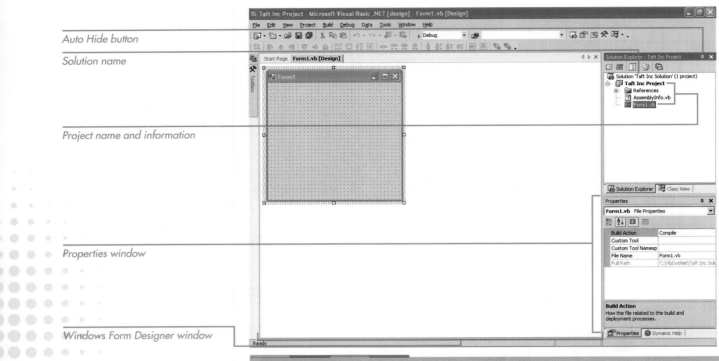

Auto Hide button

Solution name

Project name and information

Properties window

Windows Form Designer window

FIGURE 1.8   Solution and project created by Visual Studio .NET

Notice that, in addition to the six windows discussed earlier, two new windows appear in the development environment: the Windows Form Designer window and the Properties window. Having eight windows open at the same time can be confusing, especially when you are first learning the IDE. In most cases, you will find it easier to work in the IDE if you either close or auto-hide the windows you are not currently using.

Managing the Windows in the IDE

The easiest way to close an open window in the IDE is to click the Close button on the window's title bar. In most cases, the View menu provides an appropriate option for opening a closed window. To open the Toolbox window, for instance, you click View on the menu bar, and then click Toolbox on the menu. The options for opening the Start Page and Dynamic Help windows, however, are located on the Help menu rather than on the View menu.

You can use the Auto Hide button (see Figure 1.8) on a window's title bar to auto-hide a window. When you auto-hide a window and then move the mouse pointer away from the window, the window is minimized and appears as a tab on the edge of the IDE. Additionally, the vertical pushpin on the Auto Hide button is replaced by a horizontal pushpin, which indicates that the window is auto-hidden. The Server Explorer and Toolbox windows shown in Figure 1.8 are examples of auto-hidden windows.

To temporarily display a window that has been auto-hidden, you simply place your mouse pointer on the window's tab; doing so slides the window into view. You can permanently display an auto-hidden window by clicking the Auto Hide button on the window's title bar. When you do so, the horizontal pushpin on the button is replaced by a vertical pushpin, which indicates that the window is not auto-hidden. Figure 1.9 summarizes what you learned in this section.

HOW TO...

Manage the Windows in the IDE

- To close an open window, click its Close button.
- To open a window, use the View menu or the Help menu (for the Start Page and Dynamic Help windows).
- To auto-hide a window, click its Auto Hide button.
- To temporarily display an auto-hidden window, place your mouse pointer on the window's tab.
- To permanently display an auto-hidden window, click its Auto Hide button.

FIGURE 1.9   How to manage the windows in the IDE

In the next several sections, you take a closer look at the Dynamic Help, Windows Form Designer, Solution Explorer, Properties, and Toolbox windows. You also look at a new window, called the Code Editor window. (The Server Explorer and Class View windows are covered in subsequent chapters in this book.)

THE DYNAMIC HELP WINDOW

Figure 1.10 shows the **Dynamic Help window**, which is a context-sensitive system. As you are working in the IDE, the window is constantly being updated with links pertaining to whatever is appropriate for what you are doing at the time.

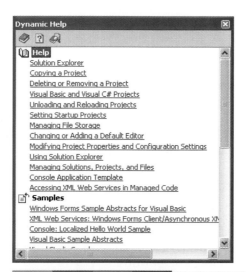

FIGURE 1.10   Dynamic Help window

An advantage of keeping the Dynamic Help window open is that it allows you to conveniently access help as you are working in the IDE. A disadvantage is that an open Dynamic Help window consumes computer memory and processor time, both of which are required to keep the window updated. In most instances, it is better to close the Dynamic Help window while you are working in the IDE.

THE WINDOWS FORM DESIGNER WINDOW

Figure 1.11 shows the **Windows Form Designer window**, where you create (or design) the graphical user interface, referred to as a **GUI**, for your project. Recall that a user interface is what you see and interact with when using an application.

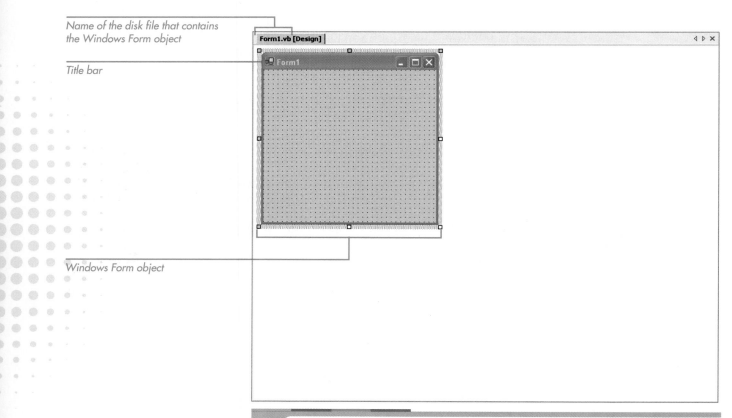

Name of the disk file that contains the Windows Form object

Title bar

Windows Form object

FIGURE 1.11   Windows Form Designer window

Only a Windows Form object appears in the designer window shown in Figure 1.11. A **Windows Form object**, or **form**, is the foundation for the user interface in a Windows-based application. You create the user interface by adding other objects, such as buttons and text boxes, to the form. Dots are displayed in the form to assist you in aligning the objects. The dots will not be visible when you run the application.

Notice that a title bar appears at the top of the Windows Form object. The title bar contains a default caption—in this case, Form1—as well as Minimize, Maximize, and Close buttons.

At the top of the designer window is a tab labeled Form1.vb [Design]. [Design] identifies the window as the designer window. Form1.vb is the name of the file (on your computer's hard disk) that contains the Visual Basic .NET instructions required to create a Windows Form object. Recall that all objects in an object-oriented program come from—or, in OOP terms, are instances of—a class. The Windows Form object, for example, is an instance of the Windows Form class. The form object is automatically instantiated for you when you create a Windows-based application.

THE SOLUTION EXPLORER WINDOW

The **Solution Explorer window** displays a list of the projects contained in the current solution, and the items contained in each project. Figure 1.12 shows the Solution Explorer window for the Taft Inc Solution.

FIGURE 1.12   Solution Explorer window

The Solution Explorer window indicates that the Taft Inc Solution contains one project named Taft Inc Project. Within the Taft Inc Project are a References folder and two files named AssemblyInfo.vb and Form1.vb. Figure 1.13 shows the contents of the References folder for the Taft Inc Project.

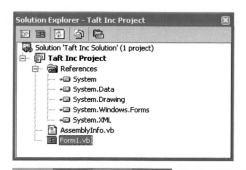

FIGURE 1.13   Contents of the References folder

The References folder contains **references**, which are simply addresses of memory cells within the computer's internal memory; each reference points to a namespace. You can picture a namespace as a block of internal memory cells. A **namespace** contains the code that defines a group of related classes. The System.Windows.Forms namespace, for instance, contains the definition of the Windows Form class, which is the class used to create a Windows Form object. When a project contains a reference to a namespace, it can use the classes that are defined in the namespace to create objects.

Recall that the Taft Inc Project also contains two files named AssemblyInfo.vb and Form1.vb. The .vb on both filenames indicates that the files are "Visual Basic" source files. A **source file** is a file that contains program instructions, called **code**. The AssemblyInfo.vb file stores the code needed to deploy (install and configure) the project. The Form1.vb file contains the code that creates (instantiates) the Windows Form object displayed in the designer window. As you add objects (such as buttons and text boxes) to the form, the code to instantiate those objects is automatically added to the Form1.vb file. The file also will contain the Visual Basic .NET instructions you enter to tell the objects how to respond when they are clicked, double-clicked, scrolled, and so on. You enter the instructions in the Code Editor window, which you view later in this chapter.

The source file containing the code to create the Windows Form object is referred to as a **form file**, because it contains the code associated with the form. The code associated with the first Windows Form object included in a project is automatically stored in a form file named Form1.vb. The code associated with the second Windows Form object in the same project is stored in a form file named Form2.vb, and so on. Because a project can contain many Windows Form objects and, therefore, many form files, it is a good practice to give each form file a more meaningful name; this will help you keep track of the various form files in the project. You can use the Properties window to change the filename.

THE PROPERTIES WINDOW

As is everything in an object-oriented language, a file is an object. Each object has a set of attributes that determine its appearance and behavior. The attributes, called properties, are listed in the **Properties window**. In the context of OOP, the Properties window exposes the object's properties to the programmer.

When an object is created, a default value is assigned to each of its properties. The Properties window shown in Figure 1.14, for example, lists the default values assigned to the properties of the Form1.vb file contained in the Taft Inc Project.

TIP

To display the Form1.vb properties, you first must click Form1.vb in the Solution Explorer window.

Object box

Properties list

Settings box

Description pane

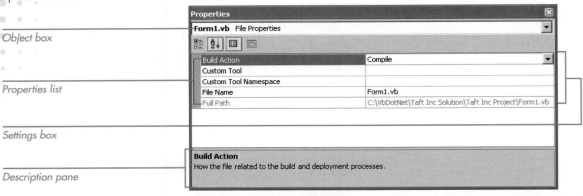

FIGURE 1.14   Properties window showing the properties of the Form1.vb file object

As indicated in Figure 1.14, the Properties window includes an Object box and a Properties list. The Object box is located immediately below the Properties window's title bar. The **Object box** contains the name of the selected object; in this case, it contains Form1.vb, which is the name of the form file object. When an object is selected, its properties appear in the Properties window.

The **Properties list** has two columns. The left column displays the names of the properties associated with the selected object. You can use the Alphabetic or Categorized buttons, which are located below the Object box, to display the property names either alphabetically or by category. The right column in the Properties list is called the **Settings box** and displays the current value, or setting, of each of the properties. For example, the current value of the Build Action property shown in Figure 1.14 is Compile. Notice that a brief description of the selected property appears in the Description pane located at the bottom of the Properties window.

TIP

You also can change the File Name property by right-clicking Form1.vb in the Solution Explorer window, and then clicking Rename on the context menu.

Depending on the property, you can change the default value by selecting the property in the Properties list, and then either typing a new value in the Settings box or selecting a predefined value from a list or dialog box. For example, to change the value of the File Name property, you click File Name in the Properties list and then type the new filename in the Settings box. However, to change the value of the Build Action property, you click Build Action in the Properties list, then click the list arrow button in the Settings box, and then click one of the predefined settings that appears in a drop-down list.

Like a file object, a Windows Form object also has a set of properties.

Properties of a Windows Form Object

To display the properties of a Windows Form object in the Properties window, you first must select the object. You select the Windows Form object by clicking it in the designer window.

The Properties window in Figure 1.15 shows a partial listing of the properties of a Windows Form object. The vertical scroll bar on the Properties window indicates that there are more properties to view.

Class

Location of the Windows Form object class

Windows Form object name

Windows Form object

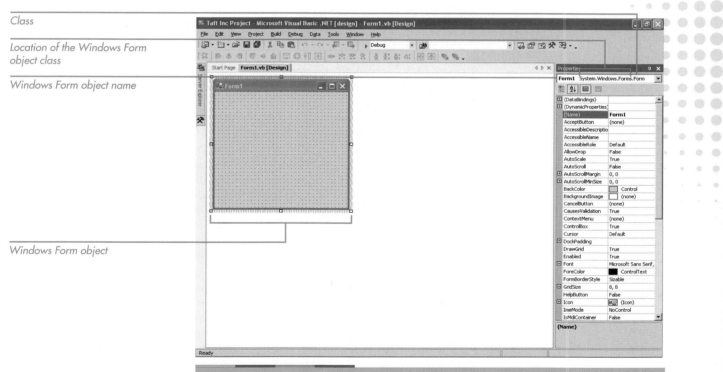

FIGURE 1.15   Windows Form object properties listed in the Properties window

Notice that Form1 System.Windows.Forms.Form appears in the Object box. Form1 is the name of the Windows Form object. The name is automatically assigned to the form when the form is created—or, in OOP terms, instantiated. System.Windows.Forms.Form is the name (Form) and location (System.Windows.Forms) of the class used to instantiate the Windows Form object. The period that separates each word in the name is called the **dot member access operator**. Similar to the backslash (\) in a folder path, the dot member access operator indicates a hierarchy, but of namespaces rather than folders. In other words, the backslash in the path C:\VbDotNet\Taft Inc Solution\Taft Inc Project\Form1.vb indicates that the Form1.vb file is contained in (or is a member of) the Taft Inc Project folder, which is a member of the Taft Inc Solution folder, which is a member of the VbDotNet folder, which is a member of the C: drive. Likewise, the name System.Windows.Forms.Form indicates that the Form class is a member of the Forms namespace, which is a member of the Windows namespace, which is a member of the System namespace. The dot member access operator allows the computer to locate the Form class in the computer's internal memory, similar to the way the backslash (\) allows the computer to locate the Form1.vb file on your computer's hard disk.

As you did with the form file object, you should assign a more meaningful name to the Windows Form object; this will help you keep track of the various forms in a project. Unlike a form file object, the Windows Form object has a Name property rather than a File Name property. You use the name entered in an object's **Name property** to refer to the object in code. The name must begin with a letter and contain only letters, numbers, and the underscore character. You cannot use punctuation characters or spaces in the name. One popular naming convention is to have the first three characters in the name represent the object's type (form, button, and so on), and the remainder of the name represent the object's purpose. For example, a descriptive name for a form used to calculate commission amounts is frmCommission. The "frm" identifies the object as a form, and "Commission" reminds you of the form's purpose. Similarly, a form used to access an employee database might be named frmEmployee or frmPersonnel. Keep in mind that the names of the forms within the same project must be unique.

In addition to changing the Form object's Name property, you also should change its **Text property**, which controls the caption displayed in the form's title bar. The caption also is displayed on the application's button on the taskbar while the application is running. The default caption, Form1, is automatically assigned to the first form in a project. Better, more descriptive captions include "Commission Calculator" and "Employee Information".

The Name and Text properties of a Form object always should be changed to more meaningful values. At times, you also may want to change the Form object's StartPosition property. You use the **StartPosition property** to determine where the form is positioned when the application is run and the form first appears on the screen. A form that represents a splash screen, for example, always should appear in the middle of the screen. As you may know, a **splash screen** is the first image that appears when an application is run. It is used to introduce the application and to hold the user's attention while the application is being read into the computer's memory. To display a Form object in the middle of the screen, you change its StartPosition property from WindowsDefaultLocation to CenterScreen.

Figure 1.16 lists the names and uses of several properties of a Windows Form object.

TIP

The Name property is used by the programmer, whereas the Text property is read by the user.

HOW TO...

Use a Windows Form Object

Property	Use to
AcceptButton	specify a default button that will be "clicked" when the user presses the Enter key
BackColor	specify the background color of the form
BackgroundImage	display a graphic as the background of the form
CancelButton	specify a cancel button that will be "clicked" when the user presses the Esc key
ContextMenu	specify a shortcut menu that displays when the user right-clicks the form
Font	specify the font type and size to use for text (usually set to Tahoma)
FormBorderStyle	control the border of the form
Name	give the form a meaningful name that begins with "frm"
StartPosition	specify the starting position of the form
Text	specify the caption that appears in the form's title bar and on the taskbar

FIGURE 1.16   How to use a Windows Form object

Recall that you can add other objects, such as text boxes and buttons, to a form; you add the objects using the Toolbox window.

THE TOOLBOX WINDOW

TIP

Appendix C lists the basic tools and provides a brief description of each.

The **Toolbox window**, or **toolbox**, contains the tools and other components you use when creating your application. The contents of the toolbox vary depending on the designer in use. The toolbox shown in Figure 1.17 appears when you are using the Windows Form designer.

The Windows Forms tab on the toolbox contains 47 basic tools that you can use when designing your application's user interface. Each tool is identified by both an icon and a name. The up and down arrow buttons on the tab allow you to scroll the list of tools.

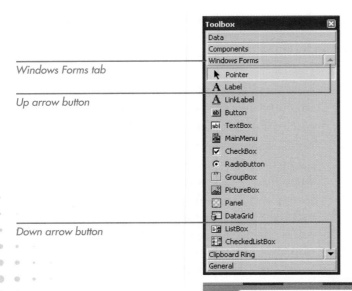

Windows Forms tab

Up arrow button

Down arrow button

FIGURE 1.17   Toolbox window

In the context of OOP, each tool in the toolbox represents a class—a pattern from which one or more objects are instantiated. The object's attributes (properties) and behaviors (methods) are encapsulated (combined) in the tool. The tools allow you to instantiate objects such as text boxes, list boxes, and radio buttons. These objects, called **controls**, are displayed on the form. Figure 1.18 lists the steps you follow to add a control to a form.

HOW TO...

Add a Control to a Form

1. Click a tool on the Windows Forms tab in the toolbox, but do not release the mouse button.
2. Hold down the mouse button as you drag the mouse pointer to the form. As you drag the mouse pointer, both an outline of a rectangle and a plus box follow the mouse pointer.
3. Release the mouse pointer.

FIGURE 1.18   How to add a control to a form

TIP

You also can add a control to the form by clicking the control's tool in the toolbox and then clicking the form. Additionally, you can click the control's tool in the toolbox, then place the mouse pointer on the form, and then press the left mouse button and drag the mouse pointer until the control is the desired size.

Controls on a form can be selected, sized, moved, deleted, or locked and unlocked. The easiest way to select a control is to click it in the designer window; however, you also can use the list arrow button in the Properties window's Object box to select a control. You size a control using the sizing handles that appear around it when it is selected. You move a control by dragging it to the desired location, and you delete it by clicking it and then pressing the Delete key on your keyboard. To lock the controls in place, which prevents them from being inadvertently moved, you click the form (or any control on the form), then click Format on the menu bar, and then click Lock Controls; you follow the same procedure to unlock the controls.

In this chapter, you learn about the Label tool and the Button tool.

The Label Tool

You use the **Label tool** to instantiate a label control. The purpose of a **label control** is to display text that the user is not allowed to edit while the application is running. Label controls are used in an interface to identify other controls and also display program output. The form shown in Figure 1.19, for example, includes three identifying labels and one display label.

Displays program output

Identifies a list box

Identifies a text box

Identifies a label control

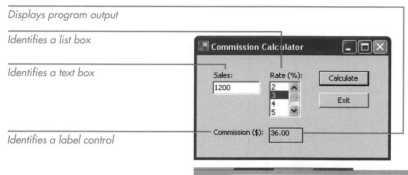

FIGURE 1.19   Label controls on a form

TIP

The label controls shown in Figure 1.19 are instances of the Label class.

The "Sales:" label in Figure 1.19 tells the user the type of information to enter in the text box located below it, and the "Rate (%):" label describes the numbers listed in the list box. The "Commission ($):" label identifies the contents of the label control located to its right; in this case, the label control displays a commission amount.

Figure 1.20 lists the names and uses of several properties of a label control. As with all controls, you use the Name property to give the control a more meaningful name, and you use the Text property to specify the text to display inside the control.

HOW TO...

Use a Label Control

Property	Use to
AutoSize	automatically size the label control to fit its current contents
BorderStyle	specify whether the label control has a visible border (identifying labels should not have a visible border)
ContextMenu	specify a shortcut menu that displays when the user right-clicks the label control
Font	specify the font type and size to use for text (usually set to Tahoma)
Name	give the label control a meaningful name that begins with "lbl"
Text	specify the caption that appears inside the label control

FIGURE 1.20   How to use a label control

Some programmers assign meaningful names to all of the label controls in an interface, while others do so only for label controls that display program output; in this book, you follow the latter convention. As Figure 1.20 indicates, label control names should begin with "lbl". For example, you might assign the name lblCommission to the label control that displays the commission amount in Figure 1.19.

The Button Tool

You use the **Button tool** to instantiate a button control. In Windows applications, a **button control** is used to perform an immediate action when clicked. The OK and Cancel buttons are examples of button controls found in most Windows applications.

The form shown in Figure 1.21 contains two button controls labeled Calculate and Exit. The text that appears on each button's face is entered in the button's Text property.

Button controls

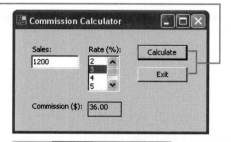

FIGURE 1.21   Button controls on a form

TIP

The button controls shown in Figure 1.21 are instances of the Button class.

Figure 1.22 lists the names and uses of several properties of a button control.

HOW TO...

Use a Button Control

Property	Use to
ContextMenu	specify a shortcut menu that displays when the user right-clicks the button control
Enabled	indicate whether the button control can respond to an event (such as clicking)
Font	specify the font type and size to use for text (usually set to Tahoma)
Image	indicate the image to display on the face of the button control
Name	give the button control a meaningful name that begins with "btn"
Text	specify the caption that appears inside the button control

FIGURE 1.22   How to use a button control

You should assign meaningful names to the button controls in an interface, and the names should begin with "btn". Good names for the Calculate and Exit button controls shown in Figure 1.21 are btnCalc and btnExit.

After creating your application's user interface, you then write the Visual Basic .NET instructions that tell the objects how to respond when they are clicked, double-clicked, and so on. You enter the instructions in the Code Editor window, which is the last window you view in this chapter.

THE CODE EDITOR WINDOW

Think about the Windows environment for a moment. Did you ever wonder why the OK and Cancel buttons respond the way they do when you click them, or how the Exit option on the File menu knows to close the application? The answer to these questions is very simple: a programmer gave the buttons and menu option explicit instructions on how to respond to the actions of the user. Those actions—such as clicking, double-clicking, and scrolling—are called **events**. The set of Visual Basic .NET instructions, or code, that tells an object how to respond to an event is called an **event procedure**. You enter an event procedure's code in the Code Editor window. Figure 1.23 shows various ways of opening the Code Editor window, and Figure 1.24 shows the Code Editor window opened in the IDE.

HOW TO...

Open the Code Editor Window

*   Right-click the form, and then click View Code on the context menu.
*   Verify that the designer window is the active window, then click View on the menu bar, and then click Code.
*   Verify that the designer window is the active window, then press the F7 key on your keyboard.

FIGURE 1.23   How to open the Code Editor window

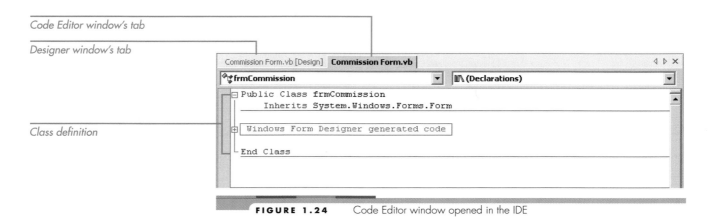

Code Editor window's tab

Designer window's tab

Class definition

FIGURE 1.24   Code Editor window opened in the IDE

The Code Editor window shown in Figure 1.24 contains some Visual Basic .NET code (instructions). As indicated in the figure, the block of code that begins with the `Public Class frmCommission` instruction and ends with the `End Class` instruction is a class definition. A **class definition** is a block of code that specifies (or defines) the attributes and behaviors of an object. The frmCommission class definition, for example, specifies the attributes and behaviors of a frmCommission object. When you start the application, Visual Basic .NET uses the class definition to create the object.

Notice the `Inherits System.Windows.Forms.Form` instruction included in the frmCommission class definition. As you learned earlier in this chapter, you can create one class (called the derived class) from another class (called the base class). The derived class inherits all of the attributes and behaviors of the base class, but then can be modified to, for instance, include an additional feature. The `Inherits System.Windows.Forms.Form` instruction allows the frmCommission class (the derived class) to inherit the attributes and behaviors of the Form class (the base class), which is provided by Visual Studio .NET and defined in the System.Windows.Forms namespace. In other words, rather than you having to write all of the code necessary to create a Windows Form object, Visual Studio .NET provides the basic code in the Form class. As you add controls to your Windows Form object, the Windows Form designer makes the appropriate modifications to the derived class. You can view the additional code generated by the designer by clicking the plus box next to the `Windows Form Designer generated code` entry in the Code Editor window. Figure 1.25 shows some of the code generated by the designer. Do not be overwhelmed by the code shown in the figure. In most cases, you do not need to concern yourself with this code.

Method Name list box

Class Name list box

Instantiates the btnCalc control

Assigns Calculate to the btnCalc control's Text property

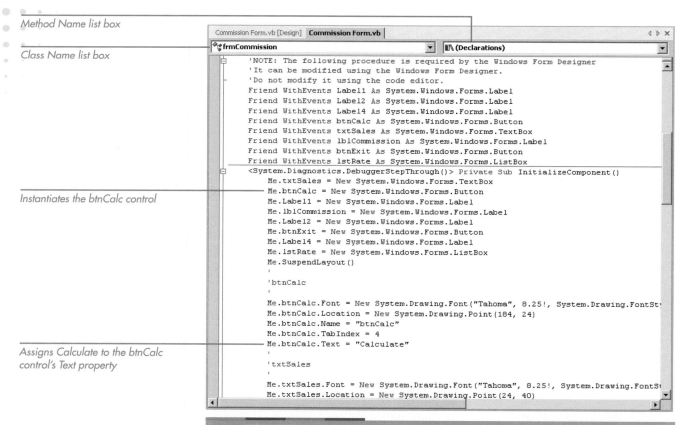

FIGURE 1.25   Some of the code generated by the Windows Form designer

TIP

To collapse the code generated by the designer, you click the minus box next to the **Windows Form Designer generated code** entry in the Code Editor window.

TIP

The Code Editor window exposes an object's behaviors to the programmer.

Each time you add a control to the frmCommission form and then set the control's properties, the designer enters the appropriate code in the frmCommission class definition. For example, when you use the toolbox to add the btnCalc control to the form, the designer enters the instruction `Me.btnCalc = New System.Windows.Forms.Button` in the frmCommission class definition. The `Me` in the instruction refers to the current form, which, in this case, is frmCommission. Similarly, when you set the btnCalc control's Text property to Calculate in the Properties window, the designer records the instruction `Me.btnCalc.Text = "Calculate"` in the frmCommission class definition. The instruction, called an **assignment statement**, assigns the word "Calculate" to the Text property of the btnCalc control on the frmCommission form.

As Figure 1.25 indicates, the Code Editor window also contains a Class Name list box and a Method Name list box. The **Class Name list box** lists the names of the objects included in the user interface. The **Method Name list box**, on the other hand, lists the events to which the selected object is capable of responding. In OOP, the events are considered behaviors, because they represent actions that the object can have performed on it.

You use the Class Name and Method Name list boxes to select the object and event, respectively, that you want to code. For example, to code the btnExit object's Click event, you select btnExit in the Class Name list box and select Click in the Method Name list box. When you do so, a code template for the btnExit object's Click event procedure appears in the Code Editor window, as shown in Figure 1.26. The first line in the code template is called the **procedure header**, and the last line is called the **procedure footer**.

Procedure header

Procedure footer

FIGURE 1.26 Code template for the btnExit object's Click event procedure

The procedure header begins with the two keywords `Private Sub`. A **keyword** is a word that has a special meaning in a programming language. The `Sub` keyword is an abbreviation of the term **sub procedure**, which, in programming terminology, refers to a block of code that performs a specific task. The `Private` keyword indicates that the procedure can be used only within the class in which it is defined—in this case, only within the frmCommission class.

Following the `Sub` keyword is the name of the object (`btnExit`), an underscore (`_`), the name of the event (`Click`), and parentheses containing `ByVal sender as Object, ByVal e As System.EventArgs`. The items within the parentheses are called parameters and represent information that is passed to the procedure when it is invoked. For now, you do not need to worry about the parameters; you learn more about parameters later in this book.

Following the items in parentheses in the procedure header is `Handles btnExit.Click`. This part of the procedure header indicates that the procedure handles (or is associated with) the btnExit object's Click event. In other words, the procedure will be processed when the btnExit object is clicked. As you learn later in this book, you can associate the same procedure with more than one event. To do so, you list each event, separated by commas, in the `Handles` section of the procedure header.

The code template ends with the procedure footer, which contains the keywords `End Sub`. You enter your Visual Basic .NET instructions at the location of the insertion point, which appears between the `Private Sub` and `End Sub` lines in Figure 1.26. The Code Editor automatically indents the line between the procedure header and footer. Indenting the lines within a procedure makes the instructions easier to read and is a common programming practice.

Notice that the keywords in the code appear in a different color from the rest of the code. The Code Editor window displays keywords in a different color to help you quickly identify these elements. In this case, the color-coding helps you easily locate the procedure header and footer.

When the user clicks the Exit button shown earlier in Figure 1.21, it indicates that he or she wants to end the application. You stop an application by entering the `Me.Close` method in the button's Click event procedure.

The Me.Close Method

You use the **Me.Close method** to instruct the computer to terminate the current application. A **method** is a predefined Visual Basic .NET procedure that you can call (or invoke) when needed. You call the `Me.Close` method by entering the instruction `Me.Close()` in a procedure. Notice the empty set of parentheses after the method's name in the instruction. The parentheses are required when calling any of Visual Basic .NET's methods; however, depending on the method, the parentheses may or may not be empty. Figure 1.27 shows the `Me.Close` method entered in the btnExit object's Click event procedure.

TIP

If you forget to enter the parentheses after a method's name, the Code Editor will enter them for you when you move the insertion point to another line in the Code Editor window.

```
Private Sub btnExit_Click(ByVal sender As Object, ByVal e As System.EventArgs) Handles btnExit.Click
    Me.Close()

End Sub
End Class
```

FIGURE 1.27   `Me.Close` method entered in the btnExit object's Click event procedure

When the user clicks the Exit button, the computer processes the instructions shown in Figure 1.27 one after another in the order in which they appear in the procedure. In programming, this is referred to as **sequential processing** or as the **sequence structure**. (You learn about two other programming structures [selection and repetition] in future chapters.)

It is a good practice to save the current solution every 10 or 15 minutes so that you will not lose a lot of work if the computer loses power.

SAVING A SOLUTION

Figure 1.28 shows two ways that you can use to save a solution. When you save a solution, the computer saves any changes made to the files included in the solution.

HOW TO...

Save a Solution

- Click File on the menu bar, and then click Save All.
- Click the Save All button 🖫 on the Standard toolbar.

FIGURE 1.28   How to save a solution

When you are finished coding the application, you need to start it to verify that it is working correctly.

STARTING AND ENDING AN APPLICATION

Before you start an application for the first time, you need to specify the name of the **startup form**, which is the form that the computer automatically displays. You select the name from the Startup object list box in the Property Pages dialog box. Figure 1.29 shows the steps you follow to specify the startup form's name, and Figure 1.30 shows the Property Pages dialog box for the Taft Inc Project.

HOW TO...

Specify the Startup Form

1. Right-click the project name in the Solution Explorer window, and then click Properties to open the Property Pages dialog box.
2. If necessary, click the Common Properties folder to open it, and then click General.
3. Click the Startup object list arrow in the dialog box, and then click the appropriate form name in the list.
4. Click the OK button.

FIGURE 1.29   How to specify the startup form

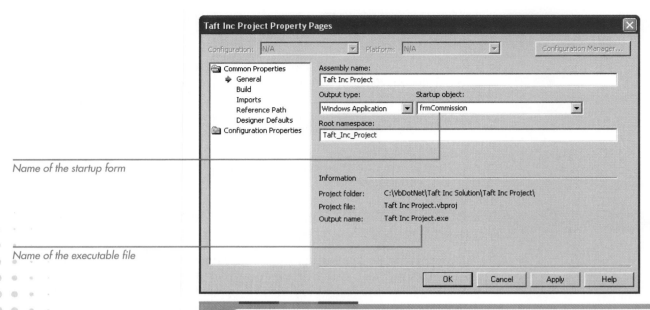

Name of the startup form

Name of the executable file

FIGURE 1.30   Taft Inc Project Property Pages

Figure 1.31 shows two ways that you can use to start an application, and Figure 1.32 shows the result of starting the Taft Inc Commission Calculator application. Notice that the computer automatically displays the startup form, which in this case is the frmCommission form. (At this point, you do not need to be concerned about the windows that appear at the bottom of the screen in Figure 1.32.)

HOW TO...

Start an Application

- Save the solution. Click Debug on the menu bar, and then click Start.
- Save the solution, then press the F5 key on your keyboard.

FIGURE 1.31   How to start an application

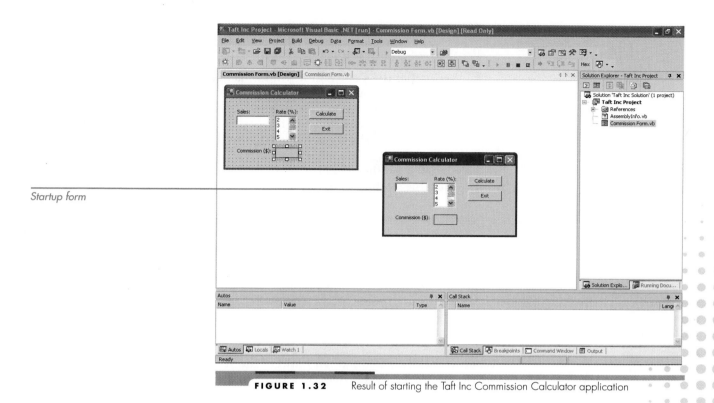

Startup form

FIGURE 1.32   Result of starting the Taft Inc Commission Calculator application

When you start a Visual Basic .NET application, the computer automatically creates a file that can be run outside of the Visual Studio .NET IDE; for example, it can be run from the Run dialog box in Windows. The file, referred to as an **executable file**, has the same name as the project, but with an .exe filename extension. As Figure 1.30 indicates, the name of the executable file for the Taft Inc Project is Taft Inc Project.exe. The computer stores the executable file in the project's bin folder. In this case, for example, the Taft Inc Project.exe file is stored in the VbDotNet\Taft Inc Solution\Taft Inc Project\bin folder.

The way you end (or close) an application depends on the application's interface. For example, you can close the Commission Calculator application shown in Figure 1.32 by clicking either the Exit button in the interface or the Close button on the application's title bar. Many applications, such as Visual Studio .NET and Microsoft Word, provide an Exit option on a File menu for this purpose.

Next, you learn how to print the code entered in the Code Editor window.

PRINTING YOUR CODE

You always should print a copy of your application's code, because the printout will help you understand and maintain the application in the future. Figure 1.33 shows the steps you follow to print the code. (Only the code that is not collapsed in the Code Editor window will be sent to the printer for printing.)

HOW TO...

Print Your Application's Code

1. Verify that the Code Editor window is the active window.
2. Verify that the only plus box in the Code Editor window appears next to the `Windows Form Designer generated code` entry. If a plus box appears anywhere else in the Code Editor window, click the plus box. (You typically do not need to print the code generated by the designer.)
3. Click File on the menu bar, and then click Print.
4. Click the OK button to begin printing.

FIGURE 1.33   How to print your application's code

In the remainder of this chapter, you learn how to close the current solution, and how to open an existing solution.

CLOSING THE CURRENT SOLUTION

When you close a solution, all projects and files contained in the solution also are closed. If unsaved changes were made to the solution, project, or form, a dialog box opens and prompts you to save the appropriate files. Figure 1.34 shows the steps you follow to close a solution.

HOW TO...

Close a Solution

1. Click File on the menu bar.
2. Click Close Solution.

FIGURE 1.34   How to close a solution

OPENING AN EXISTING SOLUTION

Figure 1.35 shows the steps you follow to open an existing solution. If a solution is already open in the IDE, it is closed before another solution is opened. In other words, only one solution can be open in the IDE at any one time.

HOW TO...

Open an Existing Solution

1. Click File on the menu bar, and then click Open Solution.
2. Locate and then click the solution filename, which has a .sln filename extension. (The .sln stands for "solution.")
3. Click the Open button.
4. If the Windows Form Designer window is not displayed, click View on the menu bar, and then click Designer.

FIGURE 1.35   How to open an existing solution

PROGRAMMING EXAMPLE

State Capitals

Create a Visual Basic .NET application that displays the capital of the state in a label when a button with the state's name is clicked. Use the following states: Alabama, Alaska, Arizona, and Arkansas. Use button and label controls in the interface. Name the solution State Capital Solution. Name the project State Capital Project. Name the form file State Capital Form.vb. Save the files in the VbDotNet\Chap01 folder.

User Interface:

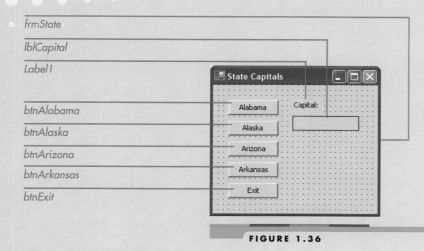

FIGURE 1.36

Objects, Properties, and Settings

Object	Property	Setting
frmState	Name	frmState (be sure to change the startup form to this name)
	Text	State Capitals
	StartPosition	CenterScreen
	Font	Tahoma
btnAlabama	Name	btnAlabama
	Text	Alabama
btnAlaska	Name	btnAlaska
	Text	Alaska
btnArizona	Name	btnArizona
	Text	Arizona
btnArkansas	Name	btnArkansas
	Text	Arkansas
btnExit	Name	btnExit
	Text	Exit
Label1	AutoSize	True
	Text	Capital:
lblCapital	Name	lblCapital
	BorderStyle	FixedSingle
	Text	(empty) (Hint: delete the text that appears in the Settings box in the Properties window.)

FIGURE 1.37

Code:

```
Public Class frmState
    Inherits System.Windows.Forms.Form

Windows Form Designer generated code

    Private Sub btnAlabama_Click(ByVal sender As Object, ByVal e As System.EventArgs) Handles btnAlabama.Click
        Me.lblCapital.Text = "Montgomery"

    End Sub

    Private Sub btnAlaska_Click(ByVal sender As Object, ByVal e As System.EventArgs) Handles btnAlaska.Click
        Me.lblCapital.Text = "Juneau"

    End Sub

    Private Sub btnArizona_Click(ByVal sender As Object, ByVal e As System.EventArgs) Handles btnArizona.Click
        Me.lblCapital.Text = "Phoenix"

    End Sub

    Private Sub btnArkansas_Click(ByVal sender As Object, ByVal e As System.EventArgs) Handles btnArkansas.Click
        Me.lblCapital.Text = "Little Rock"

    End Sub

    Private Sub btnExit_Click(ByVal sender As Object, ByVal e As System.EventArgs) Handles btnExit.Click
        Me.Close()

    End Sub
End Class
```

FIGURE 1.38

Quick Review

- The directions given to a computer are called programs and are written by programmers using a variety of programming languages.
- Programming languages have progressed from machine languages to assembly languages, and then to high-level languages.
- An assembler translates assembly language programs into machine language.
- Programs written in a high-level language require either an interpreter or a compiler to convert the program instructions into machine language.
- Procedure-oriented programs focus on tasks, whereas object-oriented programs focus on objects.
- An object is anything that can be seen, touched, or used. All objects have attributes (properties) and behaviors (methods).
- A class is a pattern from which an object can be instantiated (created). A class encapsulates the object's attributes and behaviors. Some attributes and behaviors are hidden, while others are exposed.
- You can create one class (the derived class) from another class (the base class). The derived class inherits the attributes and behaviors of the base class.
- Applications created in Visual Studio .NET are composed of solutions, projects, and files.
- The Dynamic Help window allows you to access context-sensitive help.
- You create your application's GUI in the Windows Form Designer window.
- A form is the foundation for the user interface in a Windows-based application.
- A Windows Form object is an instance of the Windows Form class.
- The Solution Explorer window displays the names of projects and files contained in the current solution.
- The Properties window exposes an object's properties to the programmer.
- The dot member access operator indicates a hierarchy of namespaces.
- You use the value stored in an object's Name property to refer to the object in code.
- The value stored in the form's Text property displays in the form's title bar and on the taskbar when the application is running.
- The value stored in a control's Text property displays inside the control.
- Controls on a form can be selected, sized, moved, deleted, or locked and unlocked.
- A label control displays text that the user is not allowed to edit while the application is running.
- You use a button control to perform an immediate action when clicked.
- You tell an object how to respond to an event by coding an event procedure. You enter the code in the Code Editor window.
- The System.Windows.Forms namespace contains the Form class definition. The forms you create inherit the attributes and behaviors of the Form class.
- When you add a control to a form and then set the control's properties, the Windows Forms designer enters the appropriate code in the Code Editor window.
- You use the Class Name and Method Name list boxes in the Code Editor window to select the object and event, respectively, that you want to code.
- In OOP, events to which an object can respond are considered behaviors.
- The Code Editor provides a code template for each of an object's event procedures. The code template begins with the `Private Sub` line and ends with the `End Sub` line. You enter your Visual Basic .NET instructions between those lines.

- You use the `Me.Close` method to terminate an application.
- You should save the solution every 10 or 15 minutes.
- Before you start an application for the first time, you need to specify the name of the startup form.
- When you start a Visual Basic .NET application, the computer automatically creates an executable file.
- You should print an application's code, because the printout will help you understand and maintain the application in the future.

Key Terms

The directions given to computers are called **programs**.

The people who write programs are called **programmers**.

Programmers use **programming languages** to communicate with the computer.

Computer instructions written in 0s and 1s are called **machine language** or **machine code**.

Assembly languages were developed after machine languages and allow the programmer to use mnemonics in place of the 0s and 1s in a program.

The alphabetic abbreviations used to represent instructions in assembly languages are called **mnemonics**.

An **assembler** is a program that converts assembly instructions into machine code.

High-level languages were developed after assembly languages and allow the programmer to use computer instructions that more closely resemble the English language.

An **interpreter** is a program that translates high-level instructions into machine code, line by line, as the program is running.

A **compiler** is a program that translates all of a program's high-level instructions into machine code before running the program.

When writing a **procedure-oriented program**, the programmer concentrates on the major tasks that the program needs to perform.

When writing an **object-oriented program**, the programmer concentrates on the objects that the program can use to accomplish its goal.

OOP is an acronym for object-oriented programming and means that you are using an object-oriented language to create a program that contains one or more objects.

OOD is an acronym for object-oriented design—the design methodology used to plan object-oriented programs.

An **object** is anything that can be seen, touched, or used.

Attributes, also called **properties**, are the characteristics that describe an object.

Behaviors, also called **methods**, are the operations (actions) that an object is capable of performing.

A **class** is a pattern or blueprint used to create an object.

A class **encapsulates** (contains) all of the attributes and behaviors that describe the object the class creates.

Objects created from a class are referred to as **instances** of the class.

Abstraction refers to the hiding of the internal details of an object from the user.

Some attributes and behaviors of an object are **hidden** from the user, while others are **exposed** to the user.

Inheritance refers to the fact that you can create one class from another class. The new class is called the **derived class**, and the original class is called the **base class**.

Polymorphism is the object-oriented feature that allows the same instruction to be carried out differently depending on the object.

An **integrated development environment (IDE)** is an environment that contains all of the tools and features you need to create, run, and test your programs.

Application is another name for program.

A **Windows-based application** has a Windows user interface and runs on a desktop computer, whereas a **Web-based application** has a Web user interface and runs on a server..

A **user interface** is what you see and interact with when using an application.

A **solution** is a container that stores the projects and files for an entire application.

A **project** is a container that stores files associated with only a specific piece of a solution.

The **Dynamic Help window** is a context-sensitive system that is constantly being updated as you are working in the IDE.

You use the **Windows Form Designer window** to create your application's GUI.

GUI stands for graphical user interface.

A **Windows Form object**, or **form**, is the foundation for the user interface in a Windows-based application.

The **Solution Explorer window** displays a list of the projects contained in the current solution, and the items contained in each project.

References are addresses of memory cells within the computer's internal memory; each reference points to a namespace.

A **namespace** is an area in the computer's internal memory that contains the code definitions for a group of related classes.

A **source file** is a file that contains code.

Code is another name for program instructions.

A **form file** contains the code associated with a Windows Form object.

An object's attributes (properties) are listed in the **Properties window**.

The **Object box** in the Properties window contains the name of the selected object.

The left column of the **Properties list** displays the names of the properties associated with the selected object. The right column is called the **Settings box** and displays the current value (setting) of each of the properties.

The **dot member access operator**, which is a period, indicates a hierarchy of namespaces.

You use the name entered in an object's **Name property** to refer to the object in code.

The **Text property** of a form displays in the form's title bar and on the taskbar while the application is running. The **Text property** of a control appears inside the control.

You use the **StartPosition property** to determine where the form is positioned when the application is run and the form first appears on the screen.

A **splash screen** is the first image that appears when an application is run. It is used to introduce the application and hold the user's attention while the application is being read into the computer's internal memory.

The **Toolbox window**, or **toolbox**, contains the tools and other components you use when creating your application. Each tool represents a class.

A **control** is an object displayed on a form.

You use the **Label tool** to instantiate a **label control**, which displays text that the user is not allowed to edit while the application is running.

You use the **Button tool** to instantiate a button control. In a Windows application, a **button control** is used to perform an immediate action when clicked.

Events are actions performed by a user and recognized by an object. Examples include clicking, double-clicking, and scrolling.

An **event procedure** is a set of Visual Basic .NET instructions that tells an object how to respond to an event.

A **class definition** is a block of code that specifies (or defines) the attributes and behaviors of an object.

An **assignment statement** is an instruction that assigns a value to something, such as a property of a control.

The **Class Name list box** in the Code Editor window lists the names of the objects included in the user interface.

The **Method Name list box** in the Code Editor window lists the events to which the selected object is capable of responding.

The first line in the code template is called the **procedure header**, and the last line is called the **procedure footer**.

A **keyword** is a word that has a special meaning in a programming language.

The term **sub procedure** refers to a block of code that performs a specific task.

The **Me.Close method** instructs the computer to terminate the current application.

A **method** is a predefined Visual Basic .NET procedure that you can call (or invoke) when needed.

The computer processes a procedure's instructions, one after another, in the order in which they appear in the procedure. This is referred to as **sequential processing** or as the **sequence structure**.

The **startup form** is the form that is automatically displayed when an application is started.

An **executable file** is a file that can be run outside of the Visual Studio .NET IDE.

Review Questions

1. The set of directions given to a computer is called _____.
   a. computerese
   b. commands
   c. instructions
   d. a program

2. Instructions written in 0s and 1s are called _____.
   a. assembly language
   b. booleans
   c. machine code
   d. mnemonics

3. A(n) _____ translates the entire high-level program into machine code before running the program.
   a. assembler
   b. compiler
   c. interpreter
   d. translator

4. In procedure-oriented programs, the emphasis is on the major tasks needed to accomplish the program's goal.
   a. True
   b. False

5. In object-oriented programs, the emphasis is on objects needed to accomplish the program's goal.
   a. True
   b. False

6. A(n) _____ is a pattern or blueprint.
   a. attribute
   b. behavior
   c. class
   d. instance

7. The object that you create from a class is called a(n) _____.
   a. abstraction
   b. attribute
   c. instance
   d. subclass

8. In the context of OOP, the combining of an object's attributes and behaviors into one package is called _____.
   a. abstraction
   b. combining
   c. encapsulation
   d. inheritance

9. In the context of OOP, the hiding of the internal details of an object from the user is called _____.
   a. abstraction
   b. combining
   c. encapsulation
   d. inheritance

10. Alcon Toys manufactures several versions of a basic doll. Assume that the basic doll is called Model A and the versions are called Models B, C, and D. In the context of OOP, the Model A doll is called the _____ class; the other dolls are called the _____ class.
    a. base, derived
    b. base, inherited
    c. derived, base
    d. inherited, derived

11. In the context of OOP, _____ refers to the fact that you can create one class from another class.
    a. abstraction
    b. combining
    c. encapsulation
    d. inheritance

12. A _____ is a container that stores the projects and files for an entire application.
    a. form file
    b. profile
    c. solution
    d. template

13. The _____ window lists the projects and files included in a solution.
    a. Object
    b. Project
    c. Properties
    d. Solution Explorer

14. You use the _____ window to set the characteristics that control an object's appearance and behavior.
    a. Characteristics
    b. Object
    c. Properties
    d. Toolbox

15. Which of the following instructions instantiates a label control named lblCommission?
    a. `Me.lblCommission = New System.Windows.Forms.Label`
    b. `Me.Label = New System.Windows.Forms.lblCommission`
    c. `Me.Label = New System.Windows.Forms.Label.lblCommission`
    d. `Me.lblCommission =`
       `New System.Windows.Forms.lblCommission`

16. Which of the following instructions displays the caption "Sales:" in a label control named Label1?
    a. `Me.Label1.Caption = "Sales:"`
    b. `Me.Label1.Text = "Sales:"`
    c. `Me.Label1.Name = "Sales:"`
    d. `Me.Label1.Label = "Sales:"`

17. The _____ method terminates the current application.
    a. `Me.Close`
    b. `Me.Done`
    c. `Me.Finish`
    d. `Me.Stop`

18. The caption that appears on the face of a button control is stored in the control's _____ property.
   a. Caption
   b. Command
   c. Label
   d. Text

19. Actions such as clicking and double-clicking are called _____.
   a. actionEvents
   b. events
   c. happenings
   d. procedures

20. The _____ list box in the Code Editor window lists the events to which the selected object is capable of responding.
   a. Event Name
   b. Method Name
   c. Object Name
   d. Procedure Name

Exercises

1. Define the following terms:
   a. OOP
   b. OOD
   c. attribute
   d. behavior

2. Explain the difference between assembly languages and high-level languages.

3. Explain the difference between a Windows-based application and a Web-based application.

4. Explain the difference between a Windows Form object's Text property and its Name property.

5. Explain the difference between a form file object and a Windows Form object.

6. Define the terms "reference" and "namespace".

7. What does the dot member access operator indicate in the text System.Windows.Forms.Label?

8. In this exercise, you modify this chapter's Programming Example.
   a. Create the State Capitals application shown in this chapter's Programming Example. Save the application in the VbDotNet\Chap01 folder.
   b. Add another label control to the form. Modify the application so that it displays a message that indicates the state's U.S. Constitution signing order. For example, when the user clicks the Alabama button, the button's Click event procedure should display the message "Alabama was the 22nd state to sign the U.S. Constitution." (Alaska was the 49th state to sign the Constitution, Arizona was the 48th state, and Arkansas was the 25th state.)
   c. Save the solution, then start and test the application. Close the solution.
   d. Locate the application's .exe file. Run the file from the Run dialog box in Windows.

9. In this exercise, you add label and button controls to a form. You also change the properties of the form and its controls.
   a. Open the Mechanics Solution (Mechanics Solution.sln) file, which is contained in the VbDotNet\Chap01\Mechanics Solution folder.
   b. Assign the filename Mechanics Form.vb to the form file object.
   c. Assign the name frmMechanics to the Windows Form object.
   d. The Windows Form object's title bar should say IMA. Set the appropriate property.
   e. The Windows Form object should be centered on the screen when it first appears. Set the appropriate property.
   f. Add a label control to the form. Change the label control's name to lblCompany.
   g. The label control should stretch to fit its current contents. Set the appropriate property.
   h. The label control should display the caption "International Mechanics Association" (without the quotation marks). Set the appropriate property.
   i. Display the label control's text in italics using the Tahoma font. Change the size of the text to 12 points.
   j. Center the label control horizontally and vertically on the form.
   k. Add a button control to the form. Change the button control's name to btnExit.
   l. The button control should display the caption "Exit" (without the quotation marks). Set the appropriate property.
   m. Display the button control's caption using the Tahoma font. Change the size of the text to 12 points.
   n. The Exit button should terminate the application when it is clicked. Enter the appropriate code in the Code Editor window.
   o. Change the project's startup form to frmMechanics.
   p. Save the solution, then start and test the application. Close the solution.

10. In this exercise, you add label and button controls to a form. You also change the properties of the form and its controls.
   a. Create the user interface shown in Figure 1.39. Name the solution Costello Solution. Name the project Costello Project. Name the form file object Costello Form.vb. Save the application in the VbDotNet\Chap01 folder.

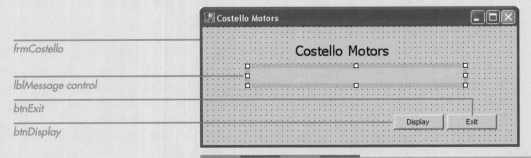

frmCostello

lblMessage control

btnExit

btnDisplay

FIGURE 1.39

b. The Exit button should terminate the application when it is clicked. Enter the appropriate code in the Code Editor window.

c. When the Display button is clicked, it should display the message "We have the best deals in town!" in the lblMessage control. Enter the appropriate code in the Code Editor window.

d. Change the project's startup form to frmCostello.

e. Save the solution. Start and then test the application. Close the solution.

11. In this exercise, you use the Description pane in the Properties window to research two properties of a Windows Form object.

a. Open either a new or an existing solution, then view the properties of the Form object.

b. What property allows you to remove the dots (referred to as the positioning grid) from the form?

c. What property determines whether the value stored in the form's Text property appears on the Windows taskbar when the application is running?

d. Close the solution.

12. In this exercise, you find and correct an error in an application. The process of finding and correcting errors is called debugging.

a. Open the Debug Solution (Debug Solution.sln) file, which is contained in the VbDotNet\Chap01\Debug Solution folder.

b. Start the application. Click the Exit button. Notice that the Exit button does not end the application.

c. Click the Close button on the form's title bar to end the application.

d. Open the Code Editor window. Locate and then correct the error.

e. Save the solution, then start and test the application. Close the solution.

Case Projects

Castle's Ice Cream Parlor

Create an application that displays the price of an item in a label when a button with the item's name is clicked.

Item	Price
Banana Split	1.79
Sundae	.99
Milkshake	2.25

Use button and label controls in the interface. Include a button control that allows the user to terminate the application. Be sure to assign meaningful names to the form, the button controls, and the label control that displays the price.

Allen School District

Create an application that displays the name of the principal and the school's phone number in labels when a button with the school's name is clicked.

School	Principal	Phone number
Primary Center	June Davis	111-9999
Lewis Middle School	Matt Hayes	111-8888
Kaufman Junior High	Sandy Jenkins	111-8978
Allen High School	Perry Thomas	111-2222

Use button and label controls in the interface. Include a button control that allows the user to terminate the application. Be sure to assign meaningful names to the form, the button controls, and the label controls that display the name and phone number.

Elvira Learning Center

Create an application that displays the equivalent Spanish word in a label when a button with an English word is clicked.

English	Spanish
Hello	Hola
Good-bye	Adios
Love	Amor
Cat	Gato
Dog	Perro

Use button and label controls in the interface. Include a button control that allows the user to terminate the application. Be sure to assign meaningful names to the form, the button controls, and the label control that displays the Spanish word.

Mary Golds Flower Shop

Create an eye-catching splash screen for the flower shop. You can use the tools you learned about in this chapter, or you can experiment with other tools from the toolbox, such as the PictureBox tool. You also can use the graphics files that come with Visual Studio .NET; the files are located in the Program Files\Microsoft Visual Studio .NET 2003\Common7\Graphics folder on your computer's hard disk. Many of the graphics in these files can be displayed on a form, button control, or picture box control.

Creating a User Interface

After studying Chapter 2, you should be able to:

- Plan an application
- Complete a TOE chart
- Use a text box control
- Explain the difference between a primary window and a dialog box
- Follow the Windows standards regarding the layout and labeling of controls
- Align and size controls
- Follow the Windows standards regarding the use of graphics, fonts, and color
- Assign access keys to controls
- Set the tab order
- Designate a default button and a cancel button

PLANNING AN APPLICATION

Before you can create the user interface for your application, you need to plan the application. The plan should be developed jointly with the user to ensure that the application meets the user's needs. It cannot be stressed enough that the only way to guarantee the success of an application is to actively involve the user in the planning phase. Figure 2.1 lists the steps you follow when planning an application.

HOW TO...

Plan an Application

1. Identify the tasks the application needs to perform.
2. Identify the objects to which you will assign those tasks.
3. Identify the events required to trigger an object into performing its assigned tasks.
4. Design the user interface.

FIGURE 2.1   How to plan an application

You can use a TOE (Task, Object, Event) chart to record the application's tasks, objects, and events, which are identified in the first three steps of the planning phase. In the next several sections, you complete a TOE chart for the Skate-Away Sales Company.

SKATE-AWAY SALES

Skate-Away Sales sells skateboards by phone. The skateboards are priced at $100 each and are available in two colors—yellow and blue. The company employs 20 salespeople to answer the phones. The salespeople record each order on a form that contains the customer's name, address, and the number of blue and yellow skateboards ordered. The salespeople then calculate the total number of skateboards ordered and the total price of the skateboards, including a 5% sales tax. The company's sales manager, Jacques Cousard, feels that having the salespeople manually perform the necessary calculations is much too time-consuming and prone to errors. He wants you to create a computerized application that will solve the problems of the current order-taking system. The first step in planning this application is to identify the application's tasks.

Identifying the Application's Tasks

Realizing that it is essential to involve the user when planning the application, you meet with the sales manager of Skate-Away Sales, Mr. Cousard, to determine his requirements. You ask Mr. Cousard to bring the form the salespeople currently use to record the orders. Viewing the current forms and procedures will help you gain a better understanding of the application. You also can use the current form as a guide when designing the user interface. Figure 2.2 shows the current order form used by Skate-Away Sales.

Skate-Away Sales Order Form:

Customer name: _____

Address: _____

City: _____ State: _____ ZIP: _____

Number of blue skateboards ordered:	Number of yellow skateboards ordered:	Total number of skateboards ordered:	Total price:

ACCT. # _____   Grand total:

FIGURE 2.2   Current order form used by Skate-Away Sales

When identifying the tasks an application needs to perform, it is helpful to ask the following questions:

- What information, if any, will the application need to display on the screen and/or print on the printer?
- What information, if any, will the user need to enter into the user interface to display and/or print the desired information?
- What information, if any, will the application need to calculate to display and/or print the desired information?
- How will the user end the application?
- Will previous information need to be cleared from the screen before new information is entered?

The answers to these questions will help you identify the application's major tasks. The answers for each question for the Skate-Away Sales application are as follows.

What information, if any, will the application need to display on the screen and/or print on the printer? (Notice that "display" refers to the screen, and "print" refers to the printer.) The Skate-Away Sales application should display the customer's name, street address, city, state, ZIP code, the number of blue skateboards ordered, the number of yellow skateboards ordered, the total number of skateboards ordered, and the total price of the order. In this case, the application does not need to print anything on the printer.

What information, if any, will the user need to enter into the user interface to display and/or print the desired information? In the Skate-Away Sales application, the salesperson (the user) must enter the customer's name, street address, city, state, ZIP code, and the number of blue and yellow skateboards ordered.

What information, if any, will the application need to calculate to display and/or print the desired information? The Skate-Away Sales application needs to calculate the total number of skateboards ordered and the total price of the order.

TIP

You can draw a TOE chart by hand, or you can use the table feature in a word processor (such as Microsoft Word) to draw one.

How will the user end the application? All applications should give the user a way to exit the program. The Skate-Away Sales application will use an Exit button for this task.

Will previous information need to be cleared from the screen before new information is entered? After Skate-Away's salesperson enters and calculates an order, he or she will need to clear the order's information from the screen before entering the next order.

Figure 2.3 shows the Skate-Away Sales application's tasks listed in a TOE chart. The tasks in a TOE chart do not need to be listed in any particular order. In this case, the data entry tasks are listed first, followed by the calculation tasks, display tasks, application ending task, and screen clearing task.

Task	Object	Event
Get the following order information from the user: Customer's name Street address City State ZIP code Number of blue skateboards ordered Number of yellow skateboards ordered		
Calculate the total skateboards ordered and the total price		
Display the following information: Customer's name Street address City State ZIP code Number of blue skateboards ordered Number of yellow skateboards ordered Total skateboards ordered Total price		
End the application		
Clear the screen for the next order		

FIGURE 2.3   Tasks entered in a TOE chart

Next, identify the objects that will perform the tasks listed in the TOE chart.

Identifying the Objects

After completing the Task column of the TOE chart, you then assign each task to an object in the user interface. For this application, the only objects you will use, besides the Windows form itself, are the button, label, and text box controls. As you learned in Chapter 1, you use a label control to display information that you do not want the user to change while your application is running, and you use a button control to perform an action immediately after the user clicks it. You use a **text box** to give the user an area in which to enter data. You instantiate (create) a text box using the **TextBox tool** in the toolbox. Figure 2.4 lists the names and uses of several properties of a text box. Notice that the names of text boxes usually begin with "txt".

HOW TO...

Use a Text Box

Property	Use to
CharacterCasing	indicate whether the text should be left alone or converted to uppercase or lowercase
ContextMenu	specify a shortcut menu that displays when the user right-clicks the text box
Font	specify the font type and size to use for text (usually set to Tahoma)
MaxLength	specify the maximum number of characters that can be entered
Name	give the text box a meaningful name that begins with "txt"
PasswordChar	specify the character to display for password input
Text	specify the text that appears inside the text box
TextAlign	indicates how the text should be aligned within the text box

FIGURE 2.4   How to use a text box

Now assign each of the tasks in the TOE chart shown in Figure 2.3 to an object. The first task listed in the figure is to get the order information from the user. For each order, the salesperson will need to enter the customer's name, address, city, state, and ZIP code, as well as the number of blue skateboards ordered and the number of yellow skateboards ordered. Because you need to provide the salesperson with areas in which to enter the information, you assign the first task to seven text boxes—one for each item of information. The names of the text boxes will be txtName, txtAddress, txtCity, txtState, txtZip, txtBlue, and txtYellow.

The second task listed in the TOE chart is to calculate both the total number of skateboards ordered and the total price. So that the salesperson can calculate these amounts at any time, you assign the task to a button named btnCalc.

The third task listed in the TOE chart is to display the order information, the total number of skateboards ordered, and the total price. The order information will be displayed automatically when the user enters that information in the seven text boxes. The total skateboards ordered and the total price, however, are not entered by the user; rather, those amounts are calculated by the btnCalc control. Because the user should not be allowed to change the calculated results, you will have the btnCalc control display the total skateboards ordered and the total price in two label controls named lblTotalBoards and lblTotalPrice. Recall from Chapter 1 that a user cannot access the contents of a label control while the application is running. Notice that the task of displaying the total skateboards ordered involves two objects (btnCalc and lblTotalBoards). The task of displaying the total price also involves two objects (btnCalc and lblTotalPrice).

The last two tasks listed in the TOE chart are "End the application" and "Clear the screen for the next order." You assign these tasks to buttons so that the user has control over when the tasks are performed. You name the buttons btnExit and btnClear. Figure 2.5 shows the TOE chart with the Task and Object columns completed.

Task	Object	Event
Get the following order information from the user: Customer's name Street address City State ZIP code Number of blue skateboards ordered Number of yellow skateboards ordered	 txtName txtAddress txtCity txtState txtZip txtBlue txtYellow	
Calculate the total skateboards ordered and the total price	btnCalc	
Display the following information: Customer's name Street address City State ZIP code Number of blue skateboards ordered Number of yellow skateboards ordered Total skateboards ordered Total price	 txtName txtAddress txtCity txtState txtZip txtBlue txtYellow btnCalc, lblTotalBoards btnCalc, lblTotalPrice	
End the application	btnExit	
Clear the screen for the next order	btnClear	

FIGURE 2.5   Tasks and objects entered in a TOE chart

After defining the application's tasks and assigning those tasks to objects in the user interface, you then determine which objects need an event (such as clicking or double-clicking) to occur for the object to do its assigned task. Identify the events required by the objects listed in Figure 2.5's TOE chart.

Identifying the Events

The seven text boxes listed in the TOE chart in Figure 2.5 are assigned the task of getting and displaying the order information. Text boxes accept and display information automatically, so no special event is necessary for them to do their assigned task.

The two label controls listed in the TOE chart are assigned the task of displaying the total number of skateboards ordered and the total price of the order. Label controls automatically display their contents so, here again, no special event needs to occur. (Recall that the two label controls will get their values from the btnCalc control.)

The remaining objects listed in the TOE chart are the three buttons: btnCalc, btnClear, and btnExit. You will have the buttons perform their assigned tasks when the user clicks them. Figure 2.6 shows the TOE chart with the tasks, objects, and events necessary for the Skate-Away Sales application.

TIP

Not all objects in a user interface will need an event to occur in order for the object to perform its assigned tasks.

Task	Object	Event
Get the following order information from the user:		
Customer's name	txtName	None
Street address	txtAddress	None
City	txtCity	None
State	txtState	None
ZIP code	txtZip	None
Number of blue skateboards ordered	txtBlue	None
Number of yellow skateboards ordered	txtYellow	None
Calculate the total skateboards ordered and the total price	btnCalc	Click
Display the following information:		
Customer's name	txtName	None
Street address	txtAddress	None
City	txtCity	None
State	txtState	None
ZIP code	txtZip	None
Number of blue skateboards ordered	txtBlue	None
Number of yellow skateboards ordered	txtYellow	None
Total skateboards ordered	btnCalc, lblTotalBoards	Click, None
Total price	btnCalc, lblTotalPrice	Click, None
End the application	btnExit	Click
Clear the screen for the next order	btnClear	Click

FIGURE 2.6   Completed TOE chart ordered by task

If the application you are creating is small, as is the Skate-Away Sales application, you can use the TOE chart in its current form to help you write the Visual Basic .NET code. When the application you are creating is large, however, it is helpful to rearrange the TOE chart so that it is ordered by object instead of by task. To do so, you simply list all of the objects in the Object column, being sure to list each object only once. Then list the tasks you have assigned to each object in the Task column, and list the event in the Event column. Figure 2.7 shows the rearranged TOE chart, ordered by object rather than by task.

Task	Object	Event
1. Calculate the total skateboards ordered and the total price 2. Display the total skateboards ordered and the total price in lblTotalBoards and lblTotalPrice	btnCalc	Click
Clear the screen for the next order	btnClear	Click
End the application	btnExit	Click
Display the total skateboards ordered (from btnCalc)	lblTotalBoards	None
Display the total price (from btnCalc)	lblTotalPrice	None
Get and display the order information	txtName, txtAddress, txtCity, txtState, txtZip, txtBlue, txtYellow	None

FIGURE 2.7   Completed TOE chart ordered by object

After completing the TOE chart, the next step is to design the user interface.

DESIGNING THE USER INTERFACE

Although the TOE chart lists the objects you need to include in the application's user interface, it does not tell you *where* to place those objects in the interface. While the design of an interface is open to creativity, there are some guidelines to which you should adhere so that your application is consistent with the Windows standards. This consistency will make your application easier to both learn and use, because the user interface will have a familiar look to it. The guidelines are referred to as GUI guidelines, because they pertain to Graphical User Interfaces. The first GUI guideline you learn in this chapter relates to the form itself.

Most Windows applications consist of a main window, possibly some other primary windows, and one or more secondary windows, called dialog boxes. The primary viewing and editing of your application's data takes place in a **primary window**. The primary window shown in Figure 2.8, for example, allows you to view and edit documents created using the Notepad application. **Dialog boxes** are used to support and supplement a user's activities in the primary windows. The Font dialog box shown in Figure 2.8, for instance, allows you to specify the font of the text selected in the primary window.

Font dialog box

Notepad's primary window

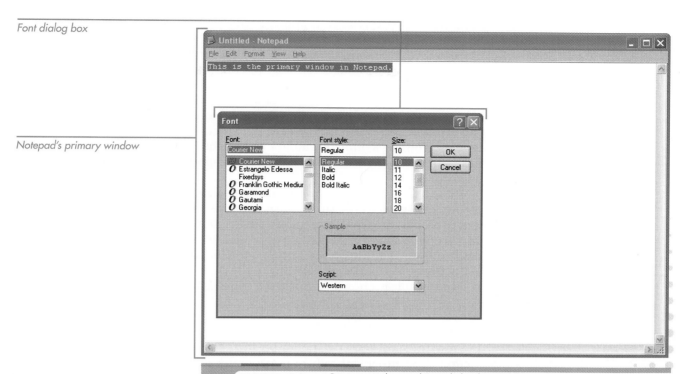

FIGURE 2.8   Primary window and Font dialog box in Notepad

Primary windows can be resized, minimized, maximized, and closed by the user. To resize a primary window, the user simply drags the window's border. To minimize, maximize, or close a primary window, the user clicks the Minimize, Maximize, or Close buttons that appear on the window's title bar. Unlike primary windows, dialog boxes can be closed only; the only buttons that appear in a dialog box's title bar are the Close button and, in some cases, the Help button.

In Visual Basic .NET, you use a Windows Form object, or form, to create both primary windows and dialog boxes. You specify the border style of the window or dialog box using the form's **FormBorderStyle property**. Figure 2.9 lists the valid settings for the FormBorderStyle property and provides a brief description of the border provided by each setting.

FormBorderStyle setting	Description of the border
Fixed3D	fixed, three-dimensional
FixedDialog	fixed, thick dialog-style
FixedSingle	fixed, thin line
FixedToolWindow	fixed, tool window style
None	no border
Sizable	sizable, normal style (default setting)
SizableToolWindow	sizable, tool window style

FIGURE 2.9   FormBorderStyle settings

If the form represents a primary window, you typically leave the form's FormBorderStyle property at its default setting, Sizable. When the FormBorderStyle property is set to Sizable, the user can drag the form's borders to change the form's size while the application is running. You also leave the form's MinimizeBox and MaximizeBox properties set at their default setting, True. This allows the user to minimize and maximize the form using the Minimize and Maximize buttons on the form's title bar. The user always should be able to minimize a primary window and, in most cases, also maximize it. However, if you want to prevent the user from maximizing a primary window, you set the form's MaximizeBox property to False; doing this makes the Maximize button appear dimmed (grayed-out) on the title bar.

If the form represents a dialog box, you usually set the form's FormBorderStyle property to FixedDialog. The FixedDialog setting draws a fixed, thick dialog-style border around the form. Recall that a dialog box should not have the Minimize and Maximize buttons on its title bar. You remove the Minimize and Maximize buttons from the title bar by setting both the MinimizeBox and MaximizeBox properties of the form to False.

Next, you learn how to arrange the controls in an interface.

Arranging the Controls

In Western countries, you should organize the user interface so that the information flows either vertically or horizontally, with the most important information always located in the upper-left corner of the screen. In a vertical arrangement the information flows from top to bottom; the essential information is located in the first column of the screen, while secondary information is placed in subsequent columns. In a horizontal arrangement, on the other hand, the information flows from left to right; the essential information is placed in the first row of the screen, with secondary information placed in subsequent rows. You can use white (empty) space, a group box control, or a panel control to group related controls together.

Figures 2.10 and 2.11 show two different interfaces for the Skate-Away Sales application. In Figure 2.10, the information is arranged vertically, and white space is used to group related controls together. In Figure 2.11, the information is arranged horizontally, and related controls are grouped together using a group box control and a panel control.

TIP

You instantiate group box and panel controls using the GroupBox and Panel tools, respectively, in the toolbox. The difference between a panel control and a group box control is that, unlike a group box, a panel control can have scroll bars. Additionally, a group box control, unlike a panel control, has a Text property. You learn more about group box and panel controls by completing Discovery Exercise 10 at the end of this chapter.

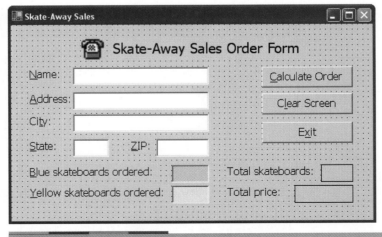

FIGURE 2.10   Vertical arrangement of the Skate-Away Sales interface

Group box control

Panel control

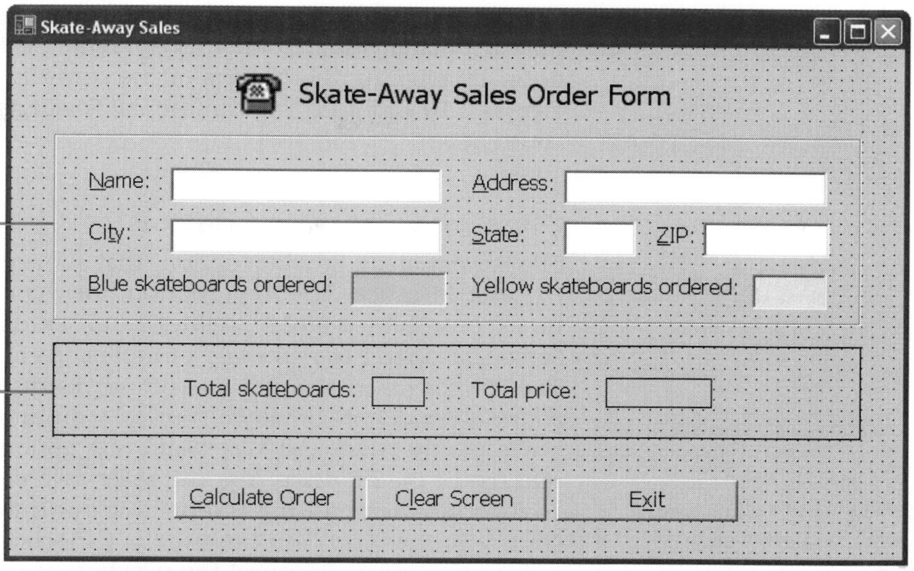

FIGURE 2.11   Horizontal arrangement of the Skate-Away Sales interface

Notice that each text box and button control in the interface is labeled so the user knows the control's purpose. Labels that identify text boxes should be left-aligned and positioned either above or to the left of the text box. As you learned in Chapter 1, buttons are identified by a caption that appears on the button itself. Identifying labels and captions should be from one to three words only, and each should appear on one line. Labels and captions should be meaningful. The label identifying a text box, for example, should tell the user the type of information to enter. A button's caption, on the other hand, should indicate the action the button will perform when it is clicked.

A text box's identifying label should end with a colon (:), as shown in Figures 2.10 and 2.11. The colon distinguishes an identifying label from other text in the user interface, such as the heading text "Skate-Away Sales Order Form". The Windows standard is to use sentence capitalization for identifying labels. **Sentence capitalization** means you capitalize only the first letter in the first word and in any words that are customarily capitalized. The Windows standard for button captions is to use book title capitalization. When using **book title capitalization**, you capitalize the first letter in each word, except for articles, conjunctions, and prepositions that do not occur at either the beginning or the end of the caption.

When positioning the controls, be sure to maintain a consistent margin from the edge of the form; two or three dots is recommended. For example, notice in Figure 2.11 that three dots separate the bottom border of the three buttons from the bottom edge of the form. Also notice that three dots appear between the left edge of the form and the left border of the group box and panel controls.

Related controls typically are placed on succeeding dots. Controls that are not part of any logical grouping may be positioned from two to four dots away from other controls.

Always size the buttons in the interface relative to each other. When the buttons are positioned horizontally, as they are in Figure 2.11, all the buttons should be the same height; their widths, however, may vary if necessary. If the buttons are stacked vertically, as they are in Figure 2.10, all the buttons should be the same height and the same width.

When laying out the controls in the interface, try to minimize the number of different margins so that the user can more easily scan the information. You can do so by aligning the borders of the controls wherever possible, as shown in Figures 2.10 and 2.11. You can use the Format menu to align (and also size) the controls.

Aligning and Sizing Controls

The Format menu provides options that allow you to manipulate the controls in the user interface. The Align option, for example, allows you to align two or more controls by their left, right, top, or bottom borders. You can use the Make Same Size option to make two or more controls the same width and/or height. The Format menu also has a Center in Form option that centers one or more controls either horizontally or vertically on the form.

To use the Align and Make Same Size options, two or more controls must be selected in the interface. You can select two controls at a time by clicking one control and then pressing and holding down the Ctrl key as you click the other control in the form. You can use the Ctrl+click method to select as many controls as you want. To cancel the selection of one of the selected controls, press and hold down the Ctrl key as you click the control. To cancel the selection of all of the selected controls, release the Ctrl key, then click the form or an unselected control on the form.

When you are finished selecting the controls, you will notice that the sizing handles on the last control selected are black, whereas the sizing handles on the other selected controls are white, as shown in Figure 2.12. (If the controls are locked on the form, the last control selected will have a black border; the other selected controls will have a white border.)

TIP

You also can select a group of controls on the form by placing the mouse pointer slightly above and to the left of the first control you want to select, then pressing the left mouse button and dragging. A dotted rectangle appears as you drag. When all of the controls you want to select are within (or at least touched by) the dotted rectangle, release the mouse button. All of the controls surrounded or touched by the dotted rectangle will be selected.

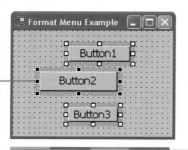

The last control selected has black sizing handles

FIGURE 2.12   Controls selected in an interface

The Align and Make Same Size options on the Format menu use the control with the black sizing handles as the reference control when aligning and sizing the selected controls. In other words, if you use the Make Same Size option to make the three controls in Figure 2.12 the same size, the height and width of the controls with the white sizing handles will be changed to match the height and width of the reference control. Likewise, if you use the Align option to align the selected controls by their left borders, the left borders of the controls with the white sizing handles will be aligned with the left border of the reference control, as shown in Figure 2.13.

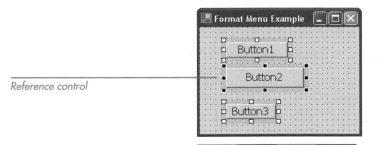

Reference control

FIGURE 2.13   Result of aligning the selected controls by their left borders

When building the user interface, keep in mind that you want to create a screen that no one notices. Snazzy interfaces may get "oohs" and "aahs" during their initial use, but they become tiresome after a while. The most important point to remember is that the interface should not distract the user from doing his or her work. Unfortunately, it is difficult for some application developers to refrain from using the many different colors, fonts, and graphics available in Visual Basic .NET; actually, using these elements is not the problem—overusing them is. So that you do not overload your user interfaces with too much color, too many fonts, and too many graphics, the next three sections provide some guidelines to follow regarding these elements. Consider the graphics first.

Including Graphics in the User Interface

The human eye is attracted to pictures before text, so include a graphic only if it is necessary to do so. Graphics typically are used to either emphasize or clarify a portion of the screen. You also can use a graphic for aesthetic purposes, as long as the graphic is small and placed in a location that does not distract the user. For example, the small graphic in the Skate-Away Sales interfaces (shown earlier in Figures 2.10 and 2.11) is included for aesthetics only. The graphic is purposely located in the upper-left corner of the interface, which is where you want the user's eye to be drawn first anyway. The graphic adds a personal touch to the Skate-Away Sales order form without being distracting to the user.

Next, you learn some guidelines pertaining to the use of different fonts in the interface.

Including Different Fonts in the User Interface

You can use an object's **Font property** to change the type, style, and size of the font used to display the text in the object. A **font** is the general shape of the characters in the text; Tahoma, Courier, and Microsoft Sans Serif are examples of font types. Font styles include regular, bold, and italic. The numbers 8, 10, and 18 are examples of font sizes, which typically are measured in points, with one **point** equaling 1/72 of an inch.

Some fonts are serif, and some are sans serif. A **serif** is a light cross stroke that appears at the top or bottom of a character. The characters in a serif font have the light strokes, whereas the characters in a sans serif font do not. ("Sans" is a French word meaning "without.") Books use serif fonts, because those fonts are easier to read on the printed page. Sans serif fonts, on the other hand, are easier to read on the screen, so you should use a sans serif font for the text in a user interface. For applications that will run on systems running Windows 2000 or Windows XP, it is recommended that you use the Tahoma font, because it offers improved readability and globalization support. You should use only one font type for all of the text in the interface. The Skate-Away Sales interfaces, for example, use only the Tahoma font.

You can use 8-, 9-, 10-, 11-, or 12-point fonts for the elements in the user interface; however, text displayed using a 12-point font is easier to read at high screen resolutions. Be sure to limit the number of font sizes used to either one or two. The Skate-Away Sales interfaces (shown earlier in Figures 2.10 and 2.11) use two font sizes: 16 point for the heading at the top of the interface, and 12 point for everything else.

Visual Basic .NET automatically assigns the value Microsoft Sans Serif, 8.25 point to a form's Font property when the form is created. When you add a control to the form, the form's Font property value is automatically assigned to the control's Font property. Therefore, if you want to change the font used in an interface—perhaps to Tahoma, 12 point—you should change the form's Font property before adding any controls to the form. This will ensure that all of the controls on the form use the same font, and you will not need to set each control's Font property separately.

Avoid using italics and underlining in an interface, because both make text difficult to read. Additionally, limit the use of bold text to titles, headings, and key items that you want to emphasize.

In addition to overusing graphics and fonts, many application developers make the mistake of using either too much color or too many different colors in the user interface. In the next section you learn some guidelines pertaining to the use of color.

Including Color in the User Interface

Just as the human eye is attracted to graphics before text, it also is attracted to color before black and white, so use color sparingly. It is a good practice to build the interface using black, white, and gray first, then add color only if you have a good reason to do so. Keep the following four points in mind when deciding whether to include color in an interface:

1. Some users will be working on monochrome monitors.
2. Many people have some form of either color-blindness or color confusion, so they will have trouble distinguishing colors.
3. Color is very subjective; a pretty color to you may be hideous to someone else.
4. A color may have a different meaning in a different culture.

Usually, it is best to use black text on a white, off-white, or light gray background. Because dark text on a light background is the easiest to read, never use a dark color for the background or a light color for the text; a dark background is hard on the eyes, and light-colored text can appear blurry.

If you are going to include color in the interface, limit the number of colors to three, not including white, black, and gray. Be sure that the colors you choose complement each other.

Although color can be used to identify an important element in the interface, you should never use it as the only means of identification. For example, in the Skate-Away Sales interfaces, the blue and yellow text boxes help the salesperson quickly identify where to enter the order for blue and yellow skateboards, respectively. However, color is not the only means of identifying those areas in the interfaces; the labels to the left of the text boxes also tell the user where to enter the orders for blue and yellow skateboards.

Looking closely at the Skate-Away Sales interfaces shown earlier in Figures 2.10 and 2.11, you will notice that the captions for many of the controls contain an underlined letter. The underlined letter is called an access key.

ASSIGNING ACCESS KEYS

An **access key** allows the user to select an object using the Alt key in combination with a letter or number. For example, you can select Visual Basic .NET's File menu by pressing Alt+F, because the letter "F" is the File menu's access key. Access keys are not case sensitive—in other words, you can select the File menu by pressing either Alt+F or Alt+f. Similarly, you can select the Calculate Order button in the interface shown in Figure 2.14 by pressing either Alt+C or Alt+c.

Access key

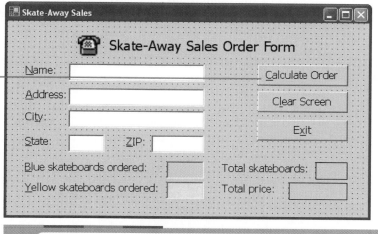

FIGURE 2.14   Skate-Away Sales interface

You should assign access keys to each of the controls (in the interface) that can accept user input. Examples of such controls include text boxes and buttons, because the user can enter information in a text box and he or she can click a button. It is important to assign access keys to these controls for the following three reasons:

1. Access keys allow a user to work with the application even if the mouse becomes inoperative.
2. Access keys allow users who are fast typists to keep their hands on the keyboard.
3. Access keys allow people with disabilities, which may prevent them from working with a mouse, to use the application.

You assign an access key by including an ampersand (&) in the control's caption or identifying label. For example, to assign an access key to a button, you include the ampersand in the button's Text property, which is where a button's caption is stored. To assign an access key to a text box, on the other hand, you include the ampersand in the Text property of the label control that identifies the text box. (As you learn later in this chapter, you also must set the identifying label's TabIndex property to a value that is one number less than the value stored in the text box's TabIndex property.) You enter the ampersand to the immediate left of the character you want to designate as the access key. For example, to assign the letter C as the access key for the Calculate Order button, you enter &Calculate Order in the button's Text property. To assign the letter N as the access key for the txtName control, you enter &Name: in the Text property of its identifying label control.

Each access key appearing in the interface should be unique. The first choice for an access key is the first letter of the caption or identifying label, unless another letter provides a more meaningful association. For example, the letter X typically is the access key for an Exit button, because the letter X provides a more meaningful association than does the letter E. If you can't use the first letter (perhaps because it already is used as the access key for another control) and no other letter provides a more meaningful association, then use a distinctive consonant in the caption or label. The last choices for an access key are a vowel or a number.

Most times, the order in which controls are added to a form does not represent the desired tab order, which is the order that each control should receive the focus when the user presses the Tab key. You specify the desired order using the TabIndex property.

SETTING THE TABINDEX PROPERTY

The **TabIndex property** determines the order in which a control receives the focus when the user presses either the Tab key or an access key while the application is running. A control having a TabIndex of 2, for instance, will receive the focus immediately after the control whose TabIndex is 1. Likewise, a control with a TabIndex of 18 will receive the focus immediately after the control whose TabIndex is 17. When a control has the **focus**, it can accept user input.

When you add to a form a control that has a TabIndex property, Visual Basic .NET sets the control's TabIndex property to a number that represents the order in which the control was added to the form. The TabIndex property for the first control added to a form is 0 (zero), the TabIndex property for the second control is 1, and so on. In most cases, you will need to change the TabIndex values of the controls, because the order in which controls are added to a form rarely represents the desired tab order.

To determine the appropriate TabIndex settings for an interface, you first make a list of the controls (in the interface) that can accept user input. The list should reflect the order in which the user will want to access the controls. For example, in the Skate-Away Sales interface shown in Figure 2.14, the user typically will want to access the txtName control first, then the txtAddress control, the txtCity control, and so on. If a control that accepts user input is identified by a label control, you also include the label control in the list. (A text box is an example of a control that accepts user input and is identified by a label control.) You place the name of the label control immediately above the name of the control it identifies. For example, in the Skate-Away Sales interface, the Label2 control (which contains Name:) identifies the txtName control; therefore, Label2 should appear immediately above txtName in the list. The names of controls that do not accept user input, and those that are not identifying controls, should be listed at the bottom of the list; these names do not need to appear in any specific order.

After listing the controls, you then assign each control in the list a TabIndex value, beginning with the number 0. Figure 2.15 shows the list of controls for the Skate-Away Sales interface shown in Figure 2.14, along with the appropriate TabIndex values. Rows pertaining to controls that accept user input are shaded in the figure.

TIP

When a box has the focus, an insertion point appears inside it. When a button has the focus, its border is highlighted and a dotted rectangle appears around its caption.

Controls that accept user input, along with their identifying label controls	TabIndex setting
Label2 (Name:)	0
txtName	1
Label3 (Address:)	2
txtAddress	3
Label4 (City:)	4
txtCity	5
Label5 (State:)	6
txtState	7
Label6 (ZIP:)	8
txtZip	9
Label7 (Blue skateboards ordered:)	10
txtBlue	11
Label8 (Yellow skateboards ordered:)	12
txtYellow	13
btnCalc	14
btnClear	15
btnExit	16
Other controls	**TabIndex setting**
Label1 (Skate-Away Sales Order Form)	17
Label9 (Total skateboards:)	18
Label10 (Total price:)	19
lblTotalBoards	20
lblTotalPrice	21
PictureBox1	This control does not have a TabIndex property.

Identifying label

Text box

FIGURE 2.15   List of controls and TabIndex settings

TIP

If a control does not have a TabIndex property, you do not assign it a TabIndex value. You can tell if a control has a TabIndex property by viewing its Properties list.

As Figure 2.15 indicates, 10 controls in the Skate-Away Sales interface—seven text boxes and three buttons—can accept user input. Notice that each text box in the list is associated with an identifying label control, whose name appears immediately above the text box name in the list. Also notice that the TabIndex value assigned to each text box's identifying label control is one number less than the value assigned to the text box itself. For example, the Label2 control has a TabIndex value of 0, and its corresponding text box (txtName) has a TabIndex value of 1. Likewise, the Label3 control and its corresponding text box have TabIndex values of 2 and 3, respectively. For a text box's access key (which is defined in the identifying label) to work appropriately, you must be sure to set the identifying label control's TabIndex property to a value that is one number less than the value stored in the text box's TabIndex property.

You can use the Properties list to set the TabIndex property of each control; or, you can use the Tab Order option on the View menu. When you use the Tab Order option, the current TabIndex value for each control (except controls that do not have a TabIndex property) appears in blue boxes on the form. You begin specifying the desired tab order by placing the mouse pointer on the first control you want in the tab order; in this case, you place the mouse pointer on the Label2 control, which contains the text Name:. A rectangle surrounds the control and the mouse pointer becomes a crosshair, as shown in Figure 2.16.

Crosshair

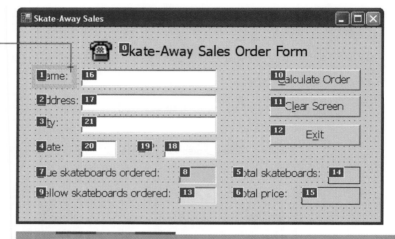

FIGURE 2.16   Crosshair positioned on the Name: label

You then click the control; when you do, the number 0 appears in the blue box, and the color of the box changes from blue to white to indicate that you have set the TabIndex value of that control. You then click the next control you want in the tab order, and so on. When you have finished setting all of the TabIndex values, the color of the boxes will automatically change from white to blue, as shown in Figure 2.17.

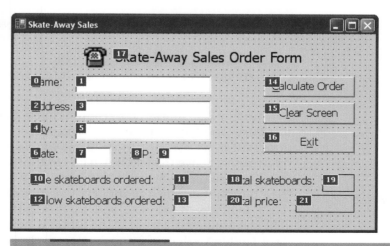

FIGURE 2.17   Correct TabIndex values shown in the form

You remove the TabIndex boxes from the form by pressing the Esc key on your keyboard; alternatively, you can click View, and then click Tab Order.

In many interfaces, one of the buttons is designated as the default button, and another is designated as the cancel button.

DESIGNATING DEFAULT AND CANCEL BUTTONS

As you already know from using Windows applications, you can select a button by clicking it or by pressing the Enter key when the button has the focus. If you make a button the **default button**, you also can select it by pressing the Enter key even when the button does not have the focus. When a button is selected, the computer processes the code contained in the button's Click event procedure.

An interface does not have to have a default button. However, if one is used, it should be the button that is most often selected by the user, except in cases where the tasks performed by the button are both destructive and irreversible. For example, a button that deletes information should not be designated as the default button. If you assign a default button in an interface, it typically is the first button, which means that it is on the left when the buttons are positioned horizontally on the screen, and on the top when the buttons are stacked vertically.

You specify the default button (if any) by setting the form's **AcceptButton property** to the name of the button. For example, to make the Calculate Order button the default button in the Skate-Away Sales interface, you set the form's AcceptButton property to btnCalc. The default button in an interface has a darkened border, as shown in Figure 2.18.

The default button has a darkened border

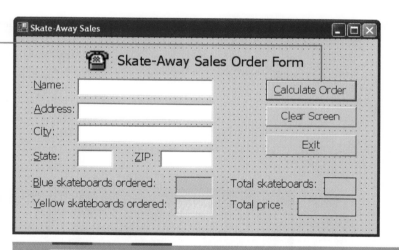

FIGURE 2.18   Default button shown in the interface

TIP

A form can have only one default button and one cancel button.

You also can designate a cancel button in an interface. Unlike the default button, the **cancel button** is automatically selected when the user presses the Esc key. You specify the cancel button (if any) by setting the form's **CancelButton property** to the name of the button. For example, to make the Exit button the cancel button in the Skate-Away Sales interface, you set the form's CancelButton property to btnExit.

PROGRAMMING EXAMPLE

Moonbucks Coffee

Create a user interface that allows the user to enter the following customer information: name, address, city, state, ZIP code, the number of pounds of regular coffee ordered, and the number of pounds of decaffeinated coffee ordered. The interface will need to display the total number of pounds of coffee ordered and the total price of the order. Name the solution Moonbucks Solution. Name the project Moonbucks Project. Name the form file Moonbucks Form.vb. Save the files in the VbDotNet\Chap02 folder.

TOE Chart:

Task	Object	Event
1. Calculate the total pounds of coffee ordered and the total price of the order 2. Display the total pounds of coffee ordered and the total price of the order in lblTotalPounds and lblTotalPrice	btnCalc	Click
Clear the screen for the next order	btnClear	Click
End the application	btnExit	Click
Display the total pounds of coffee ordered (from btnCalc)	lblTotalPounds	None
Display the total price of the order (from btnCalc)	lblTotalPrice	None
Get and display the order information	txtName, txtAddress, txtCity, txtState, txtZip, txtRegular, txtDecaf	None

FIGURE 2.19

User Interface:

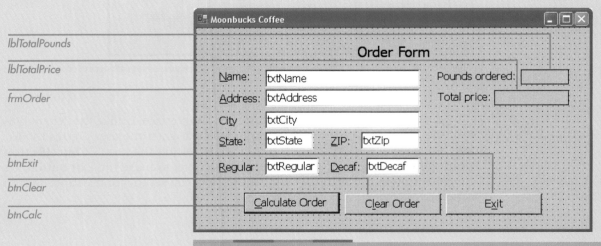

FIGURE 2.20

Objects, Properties, and Settings

Object	Property	Setting
frmOrder	Name	frmOrder (be sure to change the startup form to this name)
	AcceptButton	btnCalc
	CancelButton	btnExit
	Font	Tahoma, 12 point (change this before adding any controls)
	Size	600, 344
	StartPosition	CenterScreen
	Text	Moonbucks Coffee
Label1	AutoSize	True
	Font	Tahoma, 16 point
	Text	Order Form
		Use the Format menu to center this label horizontally
Label2	AutoSize	True
	Text	&Name:
Label3	AutoSize	True
	Text	&Address:
Label4	AutoSize	True
	Text	Ci&ty:
Label5	AutoSize	True
	Text	&State:
Label6	AutoSize	True
	Text	&ZIP:
Label7	AutoSize	True
	Text	&Regular:
Label8	AutoSize	True
	Text	&Decaf:
Label9	AutoSize	True
	Text	Pounds ordered:
Label10	AutoSize	True
	Text	Total price:
lblTotalPounds	Name	lblTotalPounds
	BorderStyle	FixedSingle
	Text	(empty)
lblTotalPrice	Name	lblTotalPrice
	BorderStyle	FixedSingle
	Text	(empty)

(Table is continued on next page)

Object	Property	Setting
txtName	Name Text	txtName (empty)
txtAddress	Name Text	txtAddress (empty)
txtCity	Name Text	txtCity (empty)
txtState	Name Text	txtState (empty)
txtZip	Name Text	txtZip (empty)
txtRegular	Name Text	txtRegular (empty)
txtDecaf	Name Text	txtDecaf (empty)
btnCalc	Name Text	btnCalc &Calculate Order
btnClear	Name Text	btnClear C&lear Order
btnExit	Name Text	btnExit E&xit

FIGURE 2.21

Tab Order:

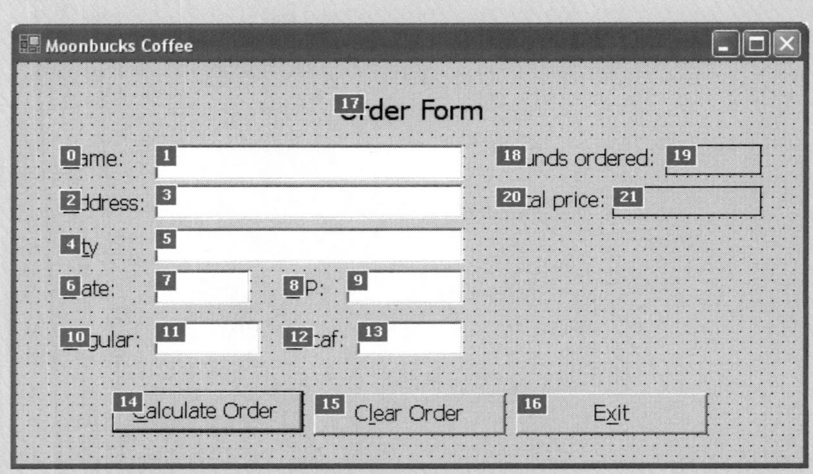

FIGURE 2.22

Code:

```
Public Class frmOrder
    Inherits System.Windows.Forms.Form

    Windows Form Designer generated code

    Private Sub btnExit_Click(ByVal sender As Object, ByVal e As System.EventArgs) Handles btnExit.Click
        Me.Close()

    End Sub
End Class
```

FIGURE 2.23

Quick Review

- You should plan an application jointly with the user to ensure that the application meets the user's needs.
- Planning an application requires that you identify the tasks, objects, and events. You then build the interface.
- You can use a TOE chart to record an application's tasks, objects, and events.
- You use a text box control to give the user an area in which to enter data.
- The primary viewing and editing of your application's data takes place in a primary window.
- Dialog boxes are used to support and supplement a user's activities in a primary window.
- Primary windows can be resized, minimized, maximized, and closed by the user. The user can only close dialog boxes.
- You use the form's FormBorderStyle property to specify the border style of a primary window or dialog box.
- In Western countries, you should organize the user interface so that the information flows either vertically or horizontally, with the most important information always located in the upper-left corner of the screen.
- Labels that identify text boxes should be left-aligned and positioned either above or to the left of the text box. They also should end with a colon and be entered using sentence capitalization.
- Identifying labels and button captions should be from one to three words only, and each should appear on one line.
- Identifying labels and button captions should be meaningful. Button captions should be entered using book title capitalization.
- When positioning the controls, you should maintain a consistent margin from the edge of the form; two or three dots is recommended.
- Related controls typically are placed on succeeding dots. Controls that are not part of any logical grouping may be positioned from two to four dots away from other controls.
- When buttons are positioned horizontally on the screen, all the buttons should be the same height; their widths, however, may vary if necessary. When buttons are stacked vertically on the screen, all the buttons should be the same height and the same width.
- Align the borders of the controls wherever possible to minimize the number of different margins used in the interface.
- You can use the Format menu to align, size, and center the controls in an interface.

- To select more than one control at a time, click one of the controls that you want to select, then Ctrl+click the remaining controls you want to select. You cancel the selection of a selected control by Ctrl+clicking the control. To cancel the selection of all of the selected controls, release the Ctrl key, then click the form or an unselected control on the form.
- When you select more than one control at a time, the last control selected has black sizing handles and is used as the reference control for the options on the Format menu.
- Graphics and color should be used sparingly in an interface.
- You can use an object's Font property to change the type, style, and size of the font used to display the text in the object. It is recommended that you use the Tahoma font for applications that will run on systems running Windows 2000 or Windows XP.
- You can use 8-, 9-, 10-, 11-, or 12-point fonts for the text in an interface. Avoid using italics and underlining in an interface, and limit the use of bold text to titles, headings, and key items that you want to emphasize.
- You should assign access keys to each of the controls (in the interface) that can accept user input—such as text boxes and buttons. You assign an access key by including an ampersand (&) in the control's caption or identifying label.
- The TabIndex property determines the order in which a control receives the focus when the user presses either the Tab key or an access key. The TabIndex property of a text box should be set to a value that is one number more than the value stored it the TabIndex property of its identifying label.
- You use the form's AcceptButton property to designate a default button, and its CancelButton property to designate a cancel button.

Key Terms

You use a **text box** to give the user an area in which to enter data. A text box is instantiated using the **TextBox tool**.

A **primary window** is a window in which the primary viewing and editing of your application's data takes place.

A **dialog box** is a window that supports and supplements a user's activities in a primary window.

The form's **FormBorderStyle property** allows you to specify the border style of the form.

Sentence capitalization means you capitalize only the first letter in the first word and in any words that are customarily capitalized.

Book title capitalization means you capitalize the first letter in each word, except for articles, conjunctions, and prepositions that do not occur at either the beginning or the end of the caption.

An object's **Font property** allows you to change the type, style, and size of the font used to display the text in the object.

A **font** is the general shape of the characters in the text.

A **point** is a font measurement and is equal to 1/72 of an inch.

A **serif** is a light cross stroke that appears at the top or bottom of a character.

An **access key** is the underlined character in an object's identifying label caption. An access key allows the user to select the object using the Alt key in combination with the character.

The **TabIndex property** determines the order in which a control receives the focus when the user presses either the Tab key or an access key while the application is running.

When a control has the **focus**, it can accept user input.

A **default button** can be selected by pressing the Enter key even when the button does not have the focus. You specify the default button (if any) by setting the form's **AcceptButton property**.

A **cancel button** can be selected by pressing the Esc key. You specify the cancel button (if any) by setting the form's **CancelButton property**.

Review Questions

1. You use a _____ control to accept or display information that can be changed while the application is running.
   a. entry
   b. label
   c. text box
   d. word processing

2. When designing a user interface, you should organize the information _____.
   a. either horizontally or vertically
   b. horizontally only
   c. vertically only

3. When designing a user interface, the most important information should be placed in the _____ of the screen.
   a. center
   b. lower-left corner
   c. upper-left corner
   d. upper-right corner

4. You can use _____ to group related controls together in an interface.
   a. a group box control
   b. a panel control
   c. white space
   d. All of the above.

5. Which of the following statements is false?
   a. A button's caption should appear on one line.
   b. A button's caption should be from one to three words only.
   c. A button's caption should be entered using book title capitalization.
   d. A button's caption should end with a colon (:).

6. The labels that identify text boxes should be entered using _____.
   a. book title capitalization
   b. sentence capitalization
   c. either a or b

7. Which of the following statements is false?
   a. Labels that identify text boxes should be aligned on the left.
   b. An identifying label should be positioned either above or to the left of the text box it identifies.
   c. Labels that identify text boxes should be entered using book title capitalization.
   d. Labels that identify text boxes should end with a colon (:).

8. The _____ property determines the order in which a control receives the focus when the user presses the Tab key or an access key.
   a. OrderTab
   b. SetOrder
   c. TabIndex
   d. TabOrder

9. When placing controls on a form, you should maintain a consistent margin of _____ dots from the edge of the window.
   a. one or two
   b. two or three
   c. two to five
   d. three to 10

10. If the buttons are positioned horizontally on the screen, then each button should be _____.
    a. the same height
    b. the same width
    c. the same height and the same width

11. If the buttons are stacked vertically on the screen, then each button should be _____.
    a. the same height
    b. the same width
    c. the same height and the same width

12. When building an interface, always use _____.
    a. dark text on a dark background
    b. dark text on a light background
    c. light text on a dark background
    d. light text on a light background

13. You use the _____ character to assign an access key to a control.
    a. &
    b. *
    c. @
    d. ^

14. You assign an access key using a control's _____ property.
    a. Access
    b. Caption
    c. KeyAccess
    d. Text

15. Use a _____ font for the text in the user interface.
    a. sans serif
    b. serif

16. The human eye is attracted to _____.
    a. color before black and white
    b. graphics before text
    c. text before graphics
    d. both a and b

17. You use the _____ property to designate a default button in the interface.
    a. button's AcceptButton
    b. button's DefaultButton
    c. form's AcceptButton
    d. form's DefaultButton

18. If a text box has a TabIndex value of 7, its identifying label should have a TabIndex value of _____.
    a. 6
    b. 7
    c. 8
    d. 9

19. A dialog box can be _____ by the user.
    a. closed
    b. maximized
    c. minimized
    d. All of the above.

20. A primary window can be _____ by the user.
    a. closed
    b. maximized
    c. minimized
    d. All of the above.

Exercises

1. Define the following terms:
   a. book title capitalization
   b. sentence capitalization

2. List the four steps you should follow when planning a Visual Basic .NET application.

3. Explain the procedure for choosing a control's access key.

4. Explain how you give users keyboard access to a text box.

5. In this exercise, you modify this chapter's Programming Example.
   a. Create the Moonbucks Coffee application shown in this chapter's Programming Example. Save the application in the VbDotNet\ Chap02 folder.
   b. Modify the user interface so that it displays the total number of pounds of coffee ordered, the price of the order without sales tax, the sales tax amount, and the total price of the order. Be sure to reset the tab order.
   c. Also modify the TOE chart shown in Figure 2.19 and the OPS (Object, Property, Setting) chart shown in Figure 2.21.
   d. Save the solution, then start the application. Click the Exit button, then close the solution.

6. In this exercise, you modify an existing application's user interface so that the interface follows the design guidelines you learned in this chapter.
   a. Open the Time Solution (Time Solution.sln) file, which is contained in the VbDotNet\Chap02\Time Solution folder.
   b. Lay out and organize the interface so that it follows all of the design guidelines specified in this chapter.
   c. Save the solution, then start the application. Click the Exit button, then close the solution.

7. In this exercise, you prepare a TOE chart and build an interface.

    Scenario: Sarah Brimley is the accountant at Paper Products. The salespeople at Paper Products are paid a commission, which is a percentage of the sales they make. (In other words, if you have sales totaling $2,000 and your commission rate is 10%, then your commission is $200.) Sarah wants you to create an application that will compute the commission after she enters the salesperson's name, sales, and commission rate.
    a. Prepare a TOE chart ordered by object.
    b. Build an appropriate interface. Name the solution, project, and form file Paper Solution, Paper Project, and Paper Form.vb, respectively. Save the solution in the VbDotNet\Chap02 folder.

8. In this exercise, you prepare a TOE chart and build an interface.

    Scenario: RM Sales divides its sales territory into four regions: North, South, East, and West. Robert Gonzales, the sales manager, wants an application in which he can enter the current year's sales for each region and the projected increase (expressed as a percentage) in sales for each region. He then wants the application to compute the following year's projected sales for each region. (For example, if Robert enters 10000 as the current sales for the South region, and then enters a 10% projected increase, the application should display 11000 as next year's projected sales.)
    a. Prepare a TOE chart ordered by object.
    b. Build an appropriate interface. Name the solution, project, and form file RMSales Solution, RMSales Project, and RMSales Form.vb, respectively. Save the solution in the VbDotNet\Chap02 folder.

9. In this exercise, you learn how to bypass a control in the tab order when the user is tabbing.
    a. Open the Johnson Solution (Johnson Solution.sln) file, which is contained in the VbDotNet\Chap02\Johnson Solution folder.
    b. Start the application. Press the Tab key several times and notice where the focus is placed each time. Click the Exit button.
    c. Assume that most of Johnson's customers are located in California. Enter CA in the txtState control's Text property.
    d. Find a way to bypass (skip over) the txtState control when the user is tabbing. If the user needs to place the focus in the txtState control—perhaps to change the control's contents—he or she will need to click or double-click the control, or use its access key.
    e. Save the solution, then start and test the application. Click the Exit button, then close the solution.

10. In this exercise, you learn about the group box and panel controls.
    a. Open the GroupPanel Solution (GroupPanel Solution.sln) file, which is contained in the VbDotNet\Chap02\GroupPanel Solution folder.
    b. Use the GroupBox tool to add a group box control to the form. Change the group box control's Text property to Shirts. Change its Size property to 200, 136, and its Location property to 40, 24.
    c. Drag four label controls and two text boxes into the group box. Give three of the label controls the following captions: Red:, Green:, and Total:. Set the AutoSize property of these label controls to True. The remaining label control should be empty. Name the empty label control lblTotal. The two text boxes should be empty. Name the text boxes txtRed and txtGreen. Align and size the label and text box controls appropriately within the group box control.

d. Use the Panel tool to add a panel control to the form. Change the panel control's BorderStyle property to FixedSingle. Change its Size property to 200, 64, and its Location property to 40, 168.

e. Drag two button controls into the panel control. Name the buttons btnCalc and btnExit. Give the buttons the following captions: <u>C</u>alculate and E<u>x</u>it. Align and size the buttons appropriately with the panel control.

f. Click View on the menu bar, and then click Tab Order. Click the group box control, the <u>R</u>ed: label, the txtRed control, the <u>G</u>reen: label, the txtGreen control, the Total: label, and the lblTotal control. What values appear in the tab order boxes for these controls?

g. Click the panel control, the btnCalc control, and the btnExit control. What values appear in the tab order boxes for these controls?

h. Press the Esc key on your keyboard.

i. Code the Exit button so that it ends the application.

j. Save the solution, then start the application. Verify that the tab order and access keys work correctly.

k. Click the Exit button, then close the solution.

11. In this exercise, you find and correct an error in an application. The process of finding and correcting errors is called debugging.

a. Open the Debug Solution (Debug Solution.sln) file, which is contained in the VbDotNet\Chap02\Debug Solution folder.

b. Start the application. Test all of the access keys in the interface. Notice that one or more of them are not working. Stop the application.

c. Locate and then correct any errors.

e. Save the solution, then start and test the access keys again. Click the Exit button, then close the solution.

Case Projects

Crispies Bagels and Bites

Create a TOE chart and a user interface for an application that allows the user to enter the number of bagels, donuts, and cups of coffee a customer orders. The application should display the total price of the order. Use button, label, and text box controls in the interface. Include a button control that allows the user to terminate the application. Be sure to assign meaningful names to the form, the button controls, the text boxes, and the label control that displays the total price. Name the solution, project, and form file Crispies Solution, Crispies Project, and Crispies Form.vb, respectively. Save the solution in the VbDotNet\Chap02 folder.

Perry Primary School

Create a TOE chart and a user interface for an application that allows the user to enter two numbers. The application should display the sum of and difference between both numbers. Use button, label, and text box controls in the interface. Include a button control that allows the user to terminate the application. Be sure to assign meaningful names to the form, the button controls, the text boxes, and the label controls that display the sum and difference. Name the solution, project, and form file Perry Solution, Perry Project, and Perry Form.vb, respectively. Save the solution in the VbDotNet\Chap02 folder.

Jasper Health Foods

Create a TOE chart and a user interface for an application that allows the user to enter the sales amounts for four states: Illinois, Indiana, Kentucky, and Ohio. The application should display the total sales and the sales commission earned. Use button, label, and text box controls in the interface. Include a button control that allows the user to terminate the application. Be sure to assign meaningful names to the form, the button controls, the text boxes, and the label controls that display the total sales and commission. Name the solution, project, and form file Jasper Solution, Jasper Project, and Jasper Form.vb, respectively. Save the solution in the VbDotNet\Chap02 folder.

Sophia's Italian Deli

Sophia's offers the following items on its lunch menu: Italian sub, meatball sandwich, slice of pizza, sausage sandwich, meatball/sausage combo, chicken fingers, ravioli plate, lasagna plate, bowl of soup, Caesar salad, calamari, spumoni, and cheesecake. Create a TOE chart and a user interface for an application that allows the user to enter a customer's lunch order. The application should display the price of the order without sales tax, the sales tax amount, and the total price of the order. Name the solution, project, and form file Sophia Solution, Sophia Project, and Sophia Form.vb, respectively. Save the solution in the VbDotNet\Chap02 folder.

Variables, Constants, Methods, and Calculations

After studying Chapter 3, you should be able to:

- Declare both a variable and a named constant
- Write an assignment statement
- Use the Convert class methods to convert data to the appropriate type
- Write arithmetic expressions
- Understand the scope of both a variable and a named constant
- Include internal documentation in the code
- Use the Option Explicit and Option Strict statements
- Use a TOE chart to code an application
- Use pseudocode and a flowchart to plan an object's code
- Send the focus to a control
- Explain the difference between syntax error and logic errors
- Format an application's numeric output

VARIABLES

Variables are computer memory locations where programmers can temporarily store data. The data may be entered by the user at the keyboard, or it may be read from a file, or it may be the result of a calculation made by the computer. The memory locations are called variables because the contents of the locations can change as the application is running.

Every variable has a name, data type, scope, and lifetime. You learn how to select an appropriate data type first.

Selecting a Data Type for a Variable

Each variable (memory location) used in an application must be assigned a data type by the programmer. The **data type** determines the type of data the variable can store. Figure 3.1 describes the basic data types available in Visual Basic .NET.

Type	Stores	Memory required	Values
Boolean	logical value	2 bytes	True, False
Byte	binary number	1 byte	0 to 255 (unsigned)
Char	one Unicode character	2 bytes	one Unicode character
Date	date and time information	8 bytes	dates from January 1, 0001 to December 31, 9999, and times from 0:00:00 to 23:59:59
Decimal	fixed-point number	16 bytes	+/-79,228,162,514,264,337,593,543, 950,335 number with no decimal point; +/-7.9228162514264337593543 43950335 with a decimal point; smallest non-zero number is +/- 0.0000000000000000000000000001
Double	floating-point number	8 bytes	+/- 4.94065645841247E-324 to 1.79769313486231E308
Integer	integer	4 bytes	-2,147,483,648 to 2,147,483,647
Long	integer	8 bytes	-9,223,372,036,854,775,808 to 9,223,372,036,854,775,807
Object	object reference	4 bytes	N/A
Short	integer	2 bytes	-32,768 to 32,767
Single	floating-point number	4 bytes	+/- 1.401298E-45 to 3.402823E38
String	text	varies	0 to approximately 2 billion characters

FIGURE 3.1   Basic data types in Visual Basic .NET

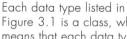

TIP

Each data type listed in Figure 3.1 is a class, which means that each data type is a pattern from which one or more objects—in this case, variables—are created (instantiated).

As Figure 3.1 indicates, variables assigned the Integer, Long, or Short data type can store **integers**, which are whole numbers—numbers without any decimal places. The differences among these three data types are in the range of integers each type can store and the amount of memory each type needs to store the integer.

Figure 3.1 indicates that Single and Double variables can store a **floating-point number**, which is a number that is expressed as a multiple of some power of 10. Floating-point numbers are written in E (exponential) notation, which is similar to scientific notation. For example, the number 3,200,000 written in E (exponential) notation is 3.2E6; written in scientific notation it is 3.2×10^6. Notice that exponential notation simply replaces "$X\ 10^6$" with the letter E followed by the power number—in this case, 6. Floating-point numbers also can have a negative number after the E. For example, 3.2E-6 means 3.2 divided by 10 to the sixth power, or .0000032.

Floating-point numbers are used to represent both extremely small and extremely large numbers. The differences between the Single and Double types are in the range of numbers each type can store and the amount of memory each type needs to store the numbers. Although a Double variable can store numbers in a Single variable's range, a Double variable takes twice as much memory to do so.

Variables declared using the Decimal data type store numbers with a fixed decimal point. Unlike floating-point numbers, fixed-point numbers are not expressed as a multiple of some power of 10. For example, the number 32000 expressed as a floating-point number is 3.2E4, but that same number expressed as a fixed-point number is simply 32000. Calculations involving fixed-point numbers are not subject to the small rounding errors that may occur when floating-point numbers are used. In most cases, these small rounding errors do not create any problems in an application. One exception, however, is when the application contains complex equations dealing with money, where you need accuracy to the penny. In those cases, the Decimal data type is the best type to use.

Also listed in Figure 3.1 are the Char data type, which can store one Unicode character, and the String data type, which can store from zero to approximately two billion characters.

You use a Boolean variable to store the Boolean values True and False, and a Date variable to store date and time information. The Byte data type is used to store binary numbers.

If you do not assign a specific data type to a variable, Visual Basic .NET assigns the Object type to it. Unlike other variables, an Object variable can store many different types of data, and it also can freely change the type of stored data while the application is running. For example, you can store the number 40 in an Object variable at the beginning of the application and then, later on in the application, store the text "John Smith" in that same variable. Although the Object data type is the most flexible data type, it is less efficient than the other data types. At times it uses more memory than necessary to store a value and, because the computer has to determine which type of data is currently stored in the variable, your application will run more slowly.

In this book, you will use the Integer data type to store integers. You will use the Decimal data type for numbers that contain decimal places and are used in calculations. You will use the String data type for text and numbers not used in calculations.

In addition to assigning a data type to the variables used in an application, the programmer also must assign a name to each variable.

TIP

Unicode is the universal character-encoding scheme for characters and text. It assigns a unique numeric value and name to each character used in the written languages of the world. For more information, see The Unicode Standard at *www.unicode.org*.

Selecting a Name for a Variable

You should assign a descriptive name to each variable used in an application. The name should help you remember the variable's data type and purpose. One popular naming convention is to have the first three characters in the name represent the data type, and the remainder of the name represent the variable's purpose. This is the naming convention used in this book. Figure 3.2 lists the three characters typically associated with the Visual Basic .NET data types.

Type	ID
Boolean	bln
Byte	byt
Char	cha
Date	dtm
Decimal	dec
Double	dbl
Integer	int
Long	lng
Object	obj
Short	shr
Single	sng
String	str

FIGURE 3.2   Data types and their three-character IDs

In addition to the three-character ID, many programmers also include the lowercase letter "m"—which stands for "module scope"—at the beginning of module-level variable names, because this helps to distinguish the module-level variables from variables having a more narrow scope, such as procedure-level and block-level variables. For example, you would use intScore to name a procedure-level Integer variable, but use mintScore to name a module-level Integer variable. You learn about the scope of a variable later in this chapter.

It is a common practice to type the letter m and the three-character ID using lowercase letters, and then use Pascal-case for the remainder of the variable's name. Using **Pascal-case**, you capitalize the first letter in each word in the name. For example, a good name for a variable that stores a sales amount is decSalesAmount. Although S also could be used as the variable's name, it is not as descriptive as the name decSalesAmount. In the latter case, the name reminds you that the variable is a Decimal variable that stores a sales amount.

TIP

Pascal is a programming language that was created by Niklaus Wirth in the late 1960s. It was named in honor of the seventeenth-century French mathematician Blaise Pascal, and is used to develop scientific applications.

In addition to being descriptive, the name that a programmer assigns to a variable must follow several specific rules, which are listed in Figure 3.3. Also included in the figure are examples of valid and invalid variable names.

Rules for naming variables

1. The name must begin with a letter.

2. The name must contain only letters, numbers, and the underscore character. No punctuation characters or spaces are allowed in the name.

3. The name cannot contain more than 16383 characters. (Thirty-two characters is the recommended maximum number of characters to use.)

4. The name cannot be a reserved word, such as Print.

Valid variable names	Invalid variable names	
blnPrint	Print	(the name cannot be a reserved word)
dec2002Sales	2002SalesDec	(the name must begin with a letter)
intRegionWest	intRegion West	(the name cannot contain a space)
mstrFirstName	mstrFirst.Name	(the name cannot contain punctuation)

FIGURE 3.3   Rules for variable names along with examples of valid and invalid names

Now that you know how to select an appropriate data type and name for a variable, you can learn how to declare a variable in code. Declaring a variable tells Visual Basic .NET to set aside a small section of the computer's internal memory.

DECLARING A VARIABLE

You use a declaration statement to declare, or create, a variable. Figure 3.4 shows the syntax of a declaration statement and includes several examples of declaring variables.

HOW TO...

Declare a Variable

Syntax
accessibility variablename [**As** *datatype*][= *initialvalue*]

Examples
```
Dim intHours As Integer
```
declares an Integer variable named intHours; the variable is automatically initialized to 0

```
Dim decPrice As Decimal
Dim decDiscount As Decimal
```
declares two Decimal variables (with module scope) named decPrice and decDiscount; the variables are automatically initialized to 0

```
Private mblnDataOk As Boolean = True
```
declares a Boolean variable (with module scope) named mblnDataOk and initializes it using the keyword **True**

```
Dim strName As String
Dim intAge As Integer
```
declares a String variable named strName and an Integer variable named intAge; the String variable is automatically initialized to **Nothing**, and the Integer variable is automatically initialized to 0

FIGURE 3.4   How to declare a variable

In the syntax shown in Figure 3.4, *accessibility* is typically either the keyword `Dim` or the keyword `Private`; the appropriate keyword to use depends on the scope of the variable. You use the `Dim` keyword to declare variables having either block-level or procedure-level scope. However, you use the `Private` keyword to declare variables having module-level scope. As mentioned earlier, you learn about the scope of variables later in this chapter.

Variablename in the syntax is the variable's name, and *datatype* is the variable's data type. *Initialvalue* is the value you want stored in the variable when it is created in the computer's internal memory.

Although the "**As** *datatype*" part of a declaration statement is optional, as indicated by the square brackets in the syntax, you always should assign a specific data type to each variable you declare. If you do not assign a data type to a variable, Visual Basic .NET assigns the Object type to the variable, which is not the most efficient data type.

Notice that the "= *initialvalue*" part of a declaration statement also is optional. If you do not assign an initial value to a variable when it is declared, Visual Basic .NET stores a default value in the variable; the default value depends on the variable's data type. A variable declared using one of the numeric data types is automatically initialized to—in other words, given a beginning value of—the number 0. Visual Basic .NET automatically initializes a Boolean variable using the keyword **False**, and a Date variable to 12:00 AM January 1, 0001. Object and String variables are automatically initialized using the keyword **Nothing**. Variables initialized to **Nothing** do not actually contain the word "Nothing"; rather, they contain no data at all.

After a variable is created, you can use an assignment statement to store other data in the variable.

TIP

A variable is considered an object in Visual Basic .NET and is an instance of the class specified in the *datatype* information. The **Dim intHours As Integer** statement, for example, creates an object named intHours, which is an instance of the Integer class.

TIP

Dim comes from the word "dimension", which is how programmers in the 1960s referred to the process of allocating the computer's memory.

ASSIGNING DATA TO AN EXISTING VARIABLE

You use an **assignment statement**, which is one of several types of Visual Basic .NET instructions, to assign a value to a variable while an application is running. Figure 3.5 shows the syntax of an assignment statement that assigns a value to a variable; the figure also includes several examples of assignment statements. The equal sign (=) that appears in an assignment statement is referred to as the **assignment operator**.

HOW TO...

Assign a Value to a Variable

Syntax
variablename = value

Examples
```
intNumber = 500
```
assigns the integer 500 to an Integer variable named intNumber

```
strName = "Mary"
```
assigns the string "Mary" to a String variable named strName

```
dblRate = .03
```
assigns the Double number .03 to a Double variable named dblRate

```
decRate = .03D
```
converts the number .03 from Double to Decimal, and then assigns the result to a Decimal variable named decRate

```
strState = Me.txtState.Text
```
assigns the string contained in the txtState control's Text property to a String variable named strState

```
decSales = Convert.ToDecimal(Me.txtSales.Text)
```
converts the contents of the txtSales control's Text property to Decimal, and then assigns the result to a Decimal variable named decSales

```
strAge = Convert.ToString(intAge)
```
converts the contents of the Integer variable named intAge to a string, and then assigns the result to a String variable named strAge

FIGURE 3.5   How to assign a value to a variable

When the computer processes an assignment statement, the value that appears on the right side of the assignment operator is assigned to (or stored in) the variable whose name appears on the left side of the assignment operator. The data type of the value should be the same data type as the variable. For example, the `intNumber = 500` assignment statement shown in Figure 3.5 stores the number 500, which is an integer, in an Integer variable named intNumber. Similarly, the `strName = "Mary"` assignment statement stores the string

TIP

When the computer processes an assignment statement that assigns a string to a String variable, it assigns only the characters that appear between the quotation marks; the computer does not store the quotation marks themselves in the variable.

TIP

The I in the `intHours = 40I` example in Figure 3.6 is not necessary because Visual Basic .NET treats a numeric literal constant that does not have a decimal place as an Integer number, unless the number is large enough to be a Long number.

"Mary" in a String variable named strName. A **string** is simply a group of characters enclosed in quotation marks.

The number 500 and the string "Mary" are called literal constants. A **literal constant** is an item of data whose value does not change while the application is running. The number 500 is a numeric literal constant, and the string "Mary" is a string literal constant. Notice that you can store literal constants in variables. Also notice that string literal constants are enclosed in quotation marks, but numeric literal constants and variable names are not. The quotation marks differentiate a string from both a number and a variable name. In other words, "500" is a string, but 500 is a number. Similarly, "Mary" is a string, but Mary (without the quotation marks) would be interpreted by Visual Basic .NET as the name of a variable.

In Visual Basic .NET, a numeric literal constant that has a decimal place is automatically treated as a Double number. Therefore, the `dblRate = .03` assignment statement in Figure 3.5 assigns the Double number .03 to a Double variable named dblRate. The next assignment statement in the figure, `decRate = .03D`, shows how you can convert a numeric literal constant of the Double type to the Decimal data type, and then assign the result to a Decimal variable. The D that follows the number .03 in the statement is one of the literal type characters in Visual Basic .NET. A **literal type character** forces a literal constant to assume a data type other than the one its form indicates. In this case, the D forces the Double number .03 to assume the Decimal data type. Figure 3.6 lists the literal type characters in Visual Basic .NET. You append a literal type character to the end of the literal constant.

Literal type character	Data type	Example
S	Short	shrAge = 35S
I	Integer	intHours = 40I
L	Long	lngPopulation = 20500L
D	Decimal	decRate = .03D
F	Single	sngRate = .03F
R	Double	dblSales = 2356R
C	Char	chaInitial = "A"C

FIGURE 3.6   Literal type characters

In Visual Basic .NET, the content of a control's Text property is automatically treated as a string. Therefore, the `strState = Me.txtState.Text` assignment statement shown in Figure 3.5 assigns the string contained in the txtState control's Text property to a String variable named strState. The next assignment statement in the figure, `decSales = Convert.ToDecimal(Me.txtSales.Text)`, shows how you use one of the methods defined in the Visual Basic .NET Convert class to convert the string contained in a control's Text property to a Decimal number, and then assign the result to a Decimal variable.

Using the Convert Class

Recall that a class is a group of instructions used to create an object. The instructions in the **Convert class**, for example, create an object that is either a number or a string, depending on the method used. A method is a specific portion of the class instructions, and its purpose is to perform a task for the class. The methods in the Convert class, for instance, convert a value to a specified data type, and then return the result of doing so.

Figure 3.7 lists the most commonly used methods contained in the Convert class. Notice that you use a period to separate the class name (`Convert`) from the method name (`ToDouble`, `ToInt16`, `ToInt32`, `ToSingle`, and `ToString`). As you learned in Chapter 1, the period is called the dot member access operator, and it indicates that what appears to the right of the operator is a member of what appears to the left of the operator. In this case, the dot member access operator indicates that the `ToDouble`, `ToInt16`, `ToInt32`, `ToSingle`, and `ToString` methods are members of the Convert class.

Method	Purpose
`Convert.ToDouble` (*value*)	convert *value* to the Double data type
`Convert.ToInt16` (*value*)	convert *value* to the Short data type
`Convert.ToInt32` (*value*)	convert *value* to the Integer data type
`Convert.ToSingle` (*value*)	convert *value* to the Single data type
`Convert.ToString` (*value*)	convert *value* to the String data type

FIGURE 3.7   Most commonly used methods contained in the Convert class

The last assignment statement shown earlier in Figure 3.5 is `strAge = Convert.ToString(intAge)`. The assignment statement uses the `Convert.ToString` method to convert the integer stored in the intAge variable to a string. The assignment statement then assigns the result to a String variable named strAge.

It is important to remember that a variable can store only one item of data at any one time. When you use an assignment statement to assign another item to the variable, the new data replaces the existing data. For example, assume that a button's Click event procedure contains the following three lines of code:

```
Dim intNumber As Integer
intNumber = 500
intNumber = intNumber * 2
```

When you run the application and click the button, the three lines of code are processed as follows:

- The Dim statement creates the intNumber variable in memory and automatically initializes it to the number 0.
- The `intNumber = 500` assignment statement removes the zero from the intNumber variable and stores the number 500 there instead. The variable now contains the number 500 only.

- The `intNumber = intNumber * 2` assignment statement first multiplies the contents of the intNumber variable (500) by the number 2, giving 1000. The assignment statement then replaces the current contents of the intNumber variable (500) with 1000. Notice that the calculation appearing on the right side of the assignment operator (=) is performed first, and then the result is assigned to the variable whose name appears on the left side of the assignment operator.

As you can see, after data is stored in a variable, you can use the variable in calculations. When a statement contains the name of a variable, the computer uses the value stored inside the variable to process the statement.

Next, you learn how to write arithmetic expressions in Visual Basic .NET.

WRITING ARITHMETIC EXPRESSIONS

Most applications require the computer to perform one or more calculations. You instruct the computer to perform a calculation by writing an arithmetic expression that contains one or more arithmetic operators. Figure 3.8 lists the arithmetic operators available in Visual Basic .NET, along with their precedence numbers. The **precedence numbers** indicate the order in which Visual Basic .NET performs the operation in an expression. Operations with a precedence number of 1 are performed before operations with a precedence number of 2, which are performed before operations with a precedence number of 3, and so on. However, you can use parentheses to override the order of precedence, because operations within parentheses always are performed before operations outside of parentheses.

Operator	Operation	Precedence number
^	exponentiation (raises a number to a power)	1
–	negation	2
*, /	multiplication and division	3
\	integer division	4
Mod	modulus arithmetic	5
+, –	addition and subtraction	6

Important Note: You can use parentheses to override the order of precedence. Operations within parentheses are always performed before operations outside parentheses.

FIGURE 3.8   Arithmetic operators and their order of precedence

Notice that some operators shown in Figure 3.8 have the same precedence number. For example, both the addition and subtraction operators have a precedence number of 6. If an expression contains more than one operator having the same priority, those operators are evaluated from left to right. In the expression 3 + 12 / 3 – 1, for instance, the division (/) is performed first, then the addition (+), and then the subtraction (–). In other words, the computer first divides 12 by 3, then adds the result of the division (4) to 3, and then subtracts 1 from the result of the addition (7). The expression evaluates to 6.

TIP

The difference between the negation and subtraction operators shown in Figure 3.8 is that the negation operator is unary, whereas the subtraction operator is binary. Unary and binary refer to the number of operands required by the operator. Unary operators require one operand; binary operators require two operands.

You can use parentheses to change the order in which the operators in an expression are evaluated. For example, the expression 3 + 12 / (3 – 1) evaluates to 9, not 6. This is because the parentheses tell the computer to subtract 1 from 3 first, then divide the result of the subtraction (2) into 12, and then add the result of the division (6) to 3.

Two of the arithmetic operators listed in Figure 3.8 might be less familiar to you; these are the integer division operator (\) and the modulus arithmetic operator (Mod). You use the **integer division operator** (\) to divide two integers, and then return the result as an integer. For example, the expression 211\4 results in 52—the integer result of dividing 211 by 4. (If you use the standard division operator [/] to divide 211 by 4, the result is 52.75 rather than simply 52.)

The modulus arithmetic operator also is used to divide two numbers, but the numbers do not have to be integers. After dividing the numbers, the **modulus arithmetic operator** returns the remainder of the division. For example, 211 Mod 4 equals 3, which is the remainder of 211 divided by 4. One use for the modulus arithmetic operator is to determine whether a year is a leap year—one that has 366 days rather than 365 days. As you may know, if a year is a leap year, then its year number is evenly divisible by the number 4. In other words, if you divide the year number by 4 and the remainder is 0 (zero), then the year is a leap year. You can determine whether the year 2004 is a leap year by using the expression 2004 Mod 4. This expression evaluates to 0 (the remainder of 2004 divided by 4), so the year 2004 is a leap year. Similarly, you can determine whether the year 2005 is a leap year by using the expression 2005 Mod 4. This expression evaluates to 1 (the remainder of 2005 divided by 4), so the year 2005 is not a leap year.

When entering an arithmetic expression in code, you do not enter the dollar sign ($) or the percent sign (%). If you want to enter a percentage in an arithmetic expression, you first must change the percentage to its decimal equivalent; for example, you would change 5% to .05. Figure 3.9 shows examples of arithmetic expressions in assignment statements.

HOW TO...

Include Arithmetic Expressions in Assignment Statements

```
decBonus = Convert.ToDecimal(Me.txtSales.Text) * .05D
```
converts both the txtSales control's Text property and the numeric literal constant to Decimal before multiplying both amounts, then assigns the result to a Decimal variable named decBonus

```
intAge = intAge + 1
```
adds the integer 1 to the contents of an Integer variable named intAge, then assigns the result to the intAge variable

```
strAverage = Convert.ToString(decSum / intCount)
```
divides the contents of a Decimal variable named decSum by the contents of an Integer variable named intCount, then converts the result to a string before assigning it to a String variable named strAverage

FIGURE 3.9   How to include arithmetic expressions in assignment statements

You now know how to use a variable declaration statement to declare a variable; recall that the statement allows you to assign a name, data type, and initial value to the variable you are declaring. You also know how to use an assignment statement to store literal constants and the result of arithmetic expressions in an existing variable. There are just two more things about variables that you need to learn: in addition to a name and a data type, recall that every variable also has both a scope and a lifetime.

THE SCOPE AND LIFETIME OF A VARIABLE

A variable's **scope** indicates where in the application's code the variable can be used, and its **lifetime** indicates how long the variable remains in the computer's internal memory. Most of the variables used in an application will have procedure scope; however, some may have module scope or block scope. The scope is determined by where you declare the variable—in other words, where you enter the variable's declaration statement. Typically, you enter the declaration statement either in a procedure, such as an event procedure, or in the Declarations section of a form.

When you declare a variable in a procedure, the variable is called a **procedure-level variable** and is said to have **procedure scope**, because only that procedure can use the variable. For example, if you enter the `Dim intNumber As Integer` statement in the btnCalc control's Click event procedure, only the btnCalc control's Click event procedure can use the intNumber variable. No other procedures in the application are allowed to use the intNumber variable. As a matter of fact, no other procedures in the application will even know that the intNumber variable exists. Procedure-level variables remain in the computer's internal memory only while the procedure in which they are declared is running; they are removed from memory when the procedure ends. In other words, a procedure-level variable has the same lifetime as the procedure that declares it. As mentioned earlier, most of the variables in your applications will be procedure-level variables.

Figure 3.10 shows two procedures that declare procedure-level variables. It is customary to enter the variable declaration statements at the beginning of the procedure, as shown in the figure. For now, do not worry about the lines of green text that appear in the figure. The lines, called comments, are used to internally document a program. You learn about comments later in this chapter.

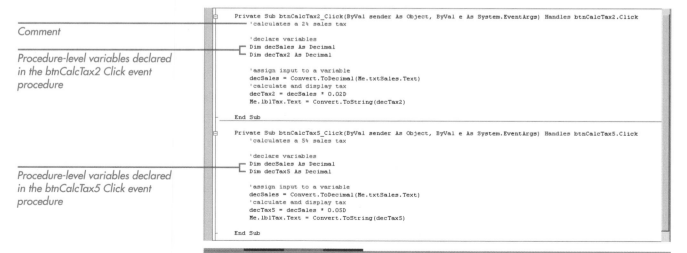

Comment

Procedure-level variables declared in the btnCalcTax2 Click event procedure

Procedure-level variables declared in the btnCalcTax5 Click event procedure

FIGURE 3.10　Procedure-level variables declared in two procedures

Both procedures shown in Figure 3.10 declare two procedure-level Decimal variables. In the btnCalcTax2_Click event procedure, the variables are named decSales and decTax2; only the btnCalcTax2_Click event procedure can use these variables. The variables in the btnCalcTax5_Click event procedure are named decSales and decTax5 and can be used only by the btnCalcTax5_Click event procedure. Notice that both procedures declare a variable named decSales. When you use the same name to declare a variable in more than one procedure, each procedure creates its own variable when the procedure is invoked. Each procedure also destroys its own variable when the procedure ends. In other words, although the decSales variables in the two procedures have the same name, they are not the same variable; rather, each is created and destroyed independently from the other.

In addition to declaring a variable in a procedure, you also can declare a variable in the form's Declarations section, which begins with the `Public Class` statement and ends with the `End Class` statement. When you declare a variable in the form's Declarations section, the variable is called a **module-level variable** and is said to have **module scope**. A module-level variable can be used by all of the procedures in the form, including the procedures associated with the controls contained on the form. For example, if you enter the `Private mintNumber As Integer` statement in a form's Declarations section, every procedure in the form can use the mintNumber variable. Module-level variables retain their values and remain in the computer's internal memory until the application ends. In other words, a module-level variable has the same lifetime as the application itself. Figure 3.11 shows a module-level variable declared in the form's Declarations section. Notice that you place the declaration statement after the `[Windows Form Designer generated code]` entry in the section, but before the first `Private Sub` statement.

frmSales form's Declarations section

Module-level variable declared in the Declarations section

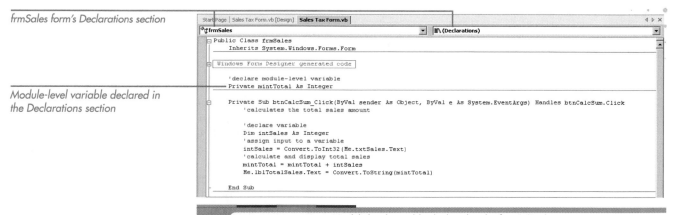

FIGURE 3.11   Module-level variable declared in the form's Declarations section

As mentioned earlier, variables also can have **block scope**; such variables are called **block-level variables**. Block-level variables are declared within specific blocks of code, such as within `If...Then...Else` statements or `For...Next` statements. A block-level variable can be used only by the block of code in which it is declared. You learn more about block-level variables in Chapter 4.

In addition to literal constants and variables, you also can use named constants in your code.

NAMED CONSTANTS

Like a variable, a **named constant** is a memory location inside the computer. However, unlike a variable, the contents of a named constant cannot be changed while the application is running. You create a named constant using the **Const statement**. Figure 3.12 shows the syntax of the `Const` statement and includes several examples of declaring named constants.

HOW TO...

Declare a Named Constant

Syntax
Const *constantname* [**As** *datatype*] = *expression*

Examples
`Const decPI As Decimal = 3.141593D`
declares decPI as a Decimal named constant; converts the Double number 3.141593 to Decimal and stores the result in decPI

`Const intMAX_HOURS As Integer = 40`
declares intMAX_HOURS as an Integer named constant; initializes intMAX_HOURS to the integer 40

`Private Const mstrTITLE As String = "ABC Company"`
declares mstrTITLE as a String named constant; initializes mstrTITLE to the string "ABC Company"

FIGURE 3.12   How to declare a named constant

In the syntax shown in Figure 3.12, *constantname* and *datatype* are the constant's name and data type, respectively, and *expression* is the value you want assigned to the named constant. The *expression* can be a literal constant or another named constant; it also can contain arithmetic and logical operators. (You learn about logical operators in Chapter 4.) The *expression* cannot, however, contain variables.

The square brackets in the `Const` statement's syntax indicate that the "**As** *datatype*" portion is optional. If you do not assign a data type to a constant, Visual Basic .NET assigns a data type based on the *expression*. For example, if you create a named constant for the number 45.6 and do not assign a data type to the constant, Visual Basic .NET assigns the Double data type to it, because a numeric literal constant having a decimal place is assumed to be a Double number. It is a good programming practice to include the "**As** *datatype*" portion in a constant declaration statement, because doing so gives you control over the constant's data type.

The rules for naming a named constant are the same as for naming a variable. However, the customary practice is to capitalize the part of the name following the ID, as in decPI, intMAX_HOURS, and mstrTITLE. Doing this helps to distinguish the named constants from the variables used in an application.

Similar to creating variables, you create a procedure-level constant by entering the `Const` statement in the appropriate procedure, and you create a module-level constant by entering the `Const` statement in the form's Declarations section.

Named constants make code more self-documenting and, therefore, easier to modify, because they allow you to use meaningful words in place of values that are less clear. The named constant decPI, for example, is much more meaningful than is the number 3.141593, which is the value of pi rounded to six decimal places. Once you create a named constant, you then can use the constant's name rather than its value in the code. Unlike variables, named constants cannot be inadvertently changed while your program is running. Figure 3.13 shows a named constant declared and used in a procedure.

Named constant

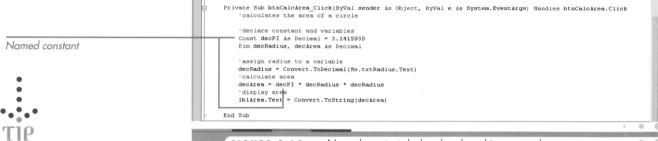

FIGURE 3.13   Named constant declared and used in a procedure

Recall that the lines of green text shown in Figure 3.13 are called comments. It is a good practice to leave yourself some comments as reminders in the Code Editor window. Programmers refer to comments as **internal documentation**.

INTERNALLY DOCUMENTING THE PROGRAM CODE

Visual Basic .NET provides an easy way to document a program internally. You simply place an apostrophe (') before the text you want treated as a comment. Visual Basic .NET ignores everything that appears after the apostrophe on that line.

It is a good programming practice to use a comment to document each procedure's purpose. You enter the comment at the beginning of the procedure, below the `Private Sub` line. Many programmers follow the comment with a blank line. You also should include comments that explain various sections of the program's code, because comments make the program instructions more readable and easier to understand by anyone viewing the program.

Many programmers also use comments to document the project's name and purpose, as well as the programmer's name and the date the code was either created or modified. Such comments typically are placed at the beginning of the application's code, above the `Public Class` statement. The area above the `Public Class` statement in the Code Editor window is called the General Declarations section; Figure 3.14 shows comments typically entered in this section.

General Declarations section

Comments

FIGURE 3.14   Comments typically entered in the General Declarations section

You also should enter two Option statements in the General Declarations section.

OPTION EXPLICIT AND OPTION STRICT

Earlier in the chapter you learned that it is important to declare the variables and named constants used in an application; by doing so you have control over their data type. Unfortunately, in Visual Basic .NET you can create variables "on the fly," which means that if your code contains the name of an undeclared variable—a variable that does not appear in either a `Dim` or a `Private` statement—Visual Basic .NET creates one for you and assigns the Object data type to it. Recall that the Object type is not a very efficient data type. Because it is so easy to forget to declare a variable—and so easy to misspell a variable's name while coding, thereby inadvertently creating an undeclared variable—Visual Basic .NET provides a way that will prevent you from using undeclared variables in your code. You simply enter the statement `Option Explicit On` in the General Declarations section of the Code Editor window. Then if your code contains the name of an undeclared variable, Visual Basic .NET informs you of the error.

In this chapter you also learned that the data type of the value that appears on the right side of the assignment operator in an assignment statement should be the same as the data type of the variable that appears on the left side of the assignment operator. If the value's data type does not match the memory location's data type, the computer uses a process called **implicit type conversion** to convert the value to fit the memory location. For example, if you assign the integer 9 to a Decimal memory location, which stores fixed-point numbers, the computer converts the integer to a fixed-point number before storing the value in the memory location; it does so by appending a decimal point and the number 0 to the end of the integer. In this case, for example, the integer 9 is converted to the fixed-point number 9.0, and it is the fixed-point number 9.0 that is assigned to the Decimal memory location. If the memory location is used subsequently in a calculation, the results of the calculation will not be adversely affected by the implicit conversion of the number 9 to the number 9.0.

However, if you inadvertently assign a Double number—such as 3.2—to a memory location that can store only integers, the computer converts the Double number to an integer before storing the value in the memory location. It does so by rounding the number to the nearest whole number and then truncating (dropping off) the decimal portion of the number. In this case, the computer converts the Double number 3.2 to the integer 3. As a result, the number 3, rather than the number 3.2, is assigned to the memory location. If the memory location is used subsequently in a calculation, the results of the calculation probably will be adversely affected by the implicit conversion of the number 3.2 to the number 3; more than likely, the conversion will cause the calculated results to be incorrect.

With implicit type conversions, data loss can occur when the value of one data type (for example, Double) is converted to a data type with less precision or smaller capacity (for example, Integer). You can eliminate the problems that occur as a result of implicit type conversions by entering the `Option Strict On` statement in the General Declarations section of the Code Editor window.

When the `Option Strict On` statement appears in an application's code, Visual Basic .NET uses the following type conversion rules:

- Strings will not be implicitly converted to numbers.
- Numeric data types will be implicitly converted to less restrictive types. For example, a Short will be implicitly converted to an Integer or Long, and a Single will be implicitly converted to a Double.
- Implicit conversion to more restrictive types will cause a syntax error. For example, a Double will not be implicitly converted to a Single. Similarly, a Long will not be implicitly converted to an Integer or Short.

Figure 3.15 shows both Option statements entered in the General Declarations section. The statements typically are entered below the comments that document the project's name, the project's purpose, the programmer's name, and the date the code was either created or modified.

General Declarations section

Option statements

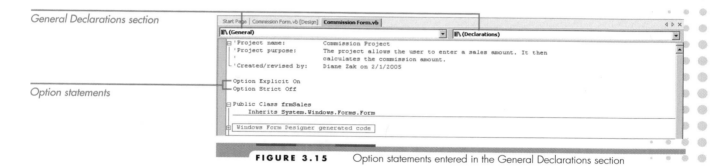

FIGURE 3.15 Option statements entered in the General Declarations section

Next, you will use what you learned in this chapter to code the Skate-Away Sales application.

CODING THE SKATE-AWAY SALES APPLICATION

In Chapter 2, you learned how to plan an application. Recall that planning an application requires you to

1. Identify the tasks the application needs to perform.
2. Identify the objects to which you will assign those tasks.
3. Identify the events required to trigger an object into performing its assigned tasks.
4. Design the user interface.

After planning an application, you then can begin coding the application so that the objects in the interface perform their assigned tasks when the appropriate event occurs. The objects and events that need to be coded are listed in the application's TOE chart, along with the tasks assigned to each object and event.

In Chapter 2, you created a TOE chart and a user interface for the Skate-Away Sales application. As you may remember, Skate-Away Sales sells skateboards by phone. The skateboards are priced at $100 each and are available in two colors— yellow and blue. Recall that the salespeople enter the order information using the interface shown in Figure 3.16.

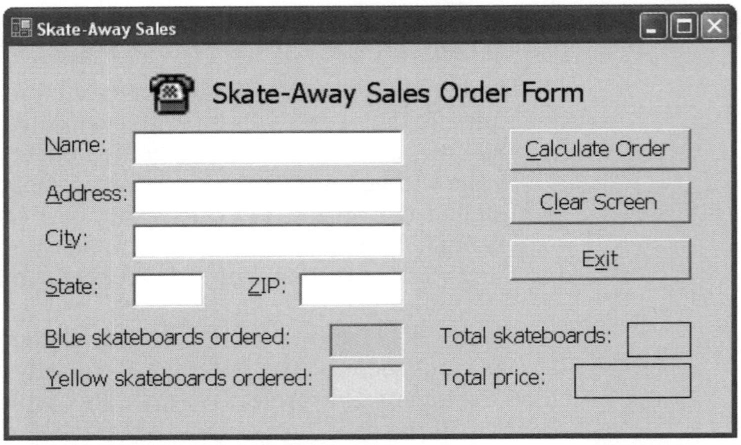

FIGURE 3.16 Skate-Away Sales user interface

The Skate-Away Sales application should calculate and display the total number of skateboards ordered and the total price of the skateboards, including a 5% sales tax. Figure 3.17 shows the TOE chart created in Chapter 2.

Task	Object	Event
1. Calculate the total skateboards ordered and the total price 2. Display the total skateboards ordered and the total price in lblTotalBoards and lblTotalPrice	btnCalc	Click
Clear the screen for the next order	btnClear	Click
End the application	btnExit	Click
Display the total skateboards ordered (from btnCalc)	lblTotalBoards	None
Display the total price (from btnCalc)	lblTotalPrice	None
Get and display the order information	txtName, txtAddress, txtCity, txtState, txtZip, txtBlue, txtYellow	None

FIGURE 3.17 TOE chart for the Skate-Away Sales application

According to the TOE chart shown in Figure 3.17, only the three buttons require coding, as they are the only objects with an event—in this case, the Click event—listed in the third column of the chart. Before you begin coding an object's event procedure, you should plan the procedure. Programmers commonly use either pseudocode or a flowchart when planning a procedure's code.

Using Pseudocode to Plan a Procedure

Pseudocode uses short phrases to describe the steps a procedure needs to take to accomplish its goal. Even though the word *pseudocode* might be unfamiliar to you, you already have written pseudocode without even realizing it. Think about the last time you gave directions to someone. You wrote each direction down on paper, in your own words; your directions were a form of pseudocode. Figure 3.18 shows the pseudocode for the procedures that need to be coded in the Skate-Away Sales application.

---

btnCalc Click Event Procedure (pseudocode)

1. calculate total skateboards ordered = blue skateboards ordered + yellow skateboards ordered

2. calculate total price = total skateboards ordered * skateboard price * (1 + sales tax rate)

3. display total skateboards ordered and total price in lblTotalBoards and lblTotalPrice

---

btnClear Click Event Procedure (pseudocode)

1. clear the Text property of the txtName, txtAddress, txtCity, txtState, txtZip, txtBlue, and txtYellow controls

2. clear the Text property of the lblTotalBoards and lblTotalPrice controls

3. send the focus to txtName

---

btnExit Click Event Procedure (pseudocode)

1. end the application

FIGURE 3.18   Pseudocode for the Skate-Away Sales application

As the pseudocode indicates, the btnCalc control's Click event procedure is responsible for calculating the total skateboards ordered and the total price, and then displaying the calculated results in the appropriate label controls in the interface. The btnClear control's Click event procedure will prepare the screen for the next order by removing the contents of the text boxes and two label controls, and then sending the focus to the txtName control. The btnExit control's Click event procedure will simply end the application.

Using a Flowchart to Plan a Procedure

Unlike pseudocode, which consists of short phrases, a **flowchart** uses standardized symbols to show the steps a procedure must follow to reach its goal. Figure 3.19 shows the flowcharts for the procedures that need to be coded in the Skate-Away Sales application. Notice that the logic pictured in the flowcharts is the same as the logic shown in the pseudocode.

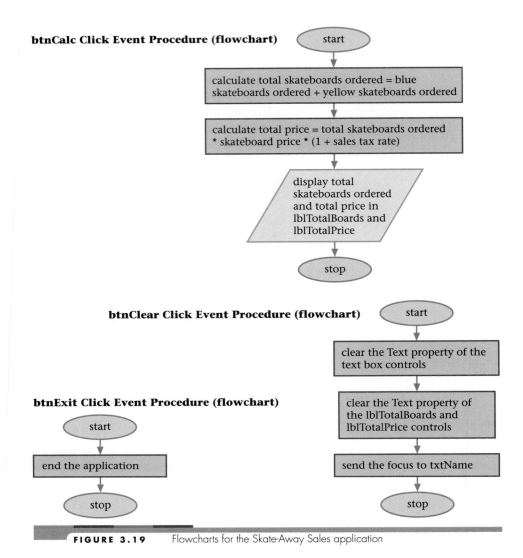

FIGURE 3.19   Flowcharts for the Skate-Away Sales application

TIP

In Chapters 4 and 5, you learn the purpose of another flowchart symbol: the diamond.

The flowcharts shown in Figure 3.19 contain three different symbols: an oval, a rectangle, and a parallelogram. The symbols are connected with lines, called **flowlines**. The oval symbol is called the **start/stop symbol**. The start oval indicates the beginning of the flowchart, and the stop oval indicates the end of the flowchart. The rectangles that appear between the start and the stop ovals are called **process symbols**. You use the process symbol to represent tasks such as making calculations.

The parallelogram in a flowchart is called the **input/output symbol** and is used to represent input tasks (such as getting information from the user) and output tasks (such as displaying information). The parallelogram shown in Figure 3.19 represents an output task.

When planning a procedure, you do not need to create both a flowchart and pseudocode; you need to use only one of these planning tools. The tool you use is really a matter of personal preference. For simple procedures, pseudocode works just fine. When a procedure becomes more complex, however, the procedure's steps may be easier to understand in a flowchart. In this book, you usually will use pseudocode when planning procedures.

TIP

As you learned in Chapter 1, you use the `Me.Close()` statement to terminate an application.

The programmer uses either the procedure's pseudocode or its flowchart as a guide when coding the procedure. For example, according to the pseudocode and flowchart shown in Figures 3.18 and 3.19, the btnExit control's Click event procedure has one task, and that is to end the application. The task is accomplished by the `Me.Close()` statement shown in Figure 3.20.

```
Private Sub btnExit_Click(ByVal sender As Object, ByVal e As System.EventArgs) Handles btnExit.Click
    'ends the application
    Me.Close()

End Sub
```

FIGURE 3.20 btnExit control's Click event procedure

Next, you learn how to code the btnClear control's Click event procedure.

CODING THE BTNCLEAR CONTROL'S CLICK EVENT PROCEDURE

According to the TOE chart shown earlier in Figure 3.17, the btnClear control's Click event procedure is assigned the task of clearing the screen for the next order. The procedure's pseudocode, shown in Figure 3.21, indicates that the task involves clearing the Text property of the text box and label controls in the interface, and then sending the focus to the txtName control.

btnClear Click Event Procedure (pseudocode)
1. clear the Text property of the txtName, txtAddress, txtCity, txtState, txtZip, txtBlue, and txtYellow controls
2. clear the Text property of the lblTotalBoards and lblTotalPrice controls
3. send the focus to txtName

FIGURE 3.21 Pseudocode for the btnClear control's Click event procedure

First, you learn how to clear the contents of a control's Text property while an application is running.

Assigning a Value to the Property of a Control

While an application is running, you can clear the Text property of a control by assigning a zero-length string to it. As you learned earlier, a string is a group of characters enclosed in quotation marks. The word "Jones", for example, is a string. Likewise, "45" is a string, but 45 is not; 45 is a number. "Jones" is a string with a length of five, because there are five characters between the quotation marks. "45" is a string with a length of two, because there are two characters between the quotation marks. Following this logic, a **zero-length string**, also called an **empty string**, is a set of quotation marks with nothing between them, like this: "". Assigning a zero-length string to the Text property of a control while an application is running removes the contents of the control.

Similar to the way you use an assignment statement to assign a value to a variable, you also use an assignment statement to assign a value to the property of a control. Figure 3.22 shows the syntax of an assignment statement that assigns a value to an object's property. The figure also includes several examples of assignment statements.

HOW TO...

Assign a Value to the Property of an Object

Syntax
[**Me.**]*object.property* = *expression*

Examples
```
Me.txtName.Text = ""
```
assigns a zero-length string to the txtName control's Text property

```
Me.lblBonus.Text = Convert.ToString(decSales * .05D)
```
multiplies the contents of the decSales variable by .05 (treated as a Decimal number), and then converts the product to a String and assigns the result to the lblBonus control's Text property

```
Me.lblTotalBoards.Text =
Convert.ToString(Convert.ToInt32(Me.txtBlue.Text) +
Convert.ToInt32(Me.txtYellow.Text))
```
converts the Text properties of the txtBlue and txtYellow controls to Integer, then adds together both integers, then converts the sum to a String and assigns the result to the lblTotalBoards control's Text property

```
Me.lblTotalBoards.Text = Convert.ToString(intBlue +
intYellow)
```
adds together the contents of the intBlue and intYellow variables, then converts the sum to a String and assigns the result to the lblTotalBoards control's Text property

FIGURE 3.22   How to assign a value to the property of an object

TIP

The dot member access operator in the assignment statement `Me.txtName.Text` indicates that the Text property is a member of the txtName control, which is a member of the current form.

The `Me.` in the syntax shown in Figure 3.22 refers to the current form and is optional, as indicated by the square brackets ([]) in the syntax. *Object* and *property* are the names of the object and property, respectively, to which you want the value of the *expression* assigned. Notice that you use the dot member access operator to separate the form reference (`Me`) from the object name, and the object name from the property name. Also notice that you use the assignment operator (=) to separate the [**Me.**]*object.property* information from the *expression*.

When the assignment statements shown in Figure 3.22 are encountered in a program, the computer assigns the value of the expression appearing on the right side of the assignment operator to the object and property that appears on the left side of the assignment operator. For example, the assignment statement `Me.txtName.Text = ""` assigns a zero-length string to the Text property of the txtName control. Similarly, the assignment statement `Me.lblBonus.Text = Convert.ToString(decSales * .05D)` multiplies the contents of the decSales variable by .05 and assigns the product (treated as a String) to the Text property of the lblBonus control.

The `Me.lblTotalBoards.Text = Convert.ToString(Convert.ToInt32 (Me.txtBlue.Text) + Convert.ToInt32(Me.txtYellow.Text))` statement in Figure 3.22 first converts the contents of the txtBlue and txtYellow controls to integers. The statement then adds together the two integers and assigns the sum, converted to a string, to the Text property of the lblTotalBoards control. The last assignment statement shown in the figure, `Me.lblTotalBoards.Text = Convert.ToString(intBlue + intYellow)`, first adds together the contents of the intBlue and intYellow variables. The statement then assigns the sum, converted to a string, to the Text property of the lblTotalBoards control.

The last step in the pseudocode shown in Figure 3.21 is to send the focus to the txtName control. You can accomplish this using the `Focus` method. As you learned in Chapter 1, a method is a predefined Visual Basic .NET procedure that you can call (or invoke) when needed.

Using the `Focus` Method

The **Focus method** allows you to move the focus to a specified control while the application is running. As you learned in Chapter 2, when a control has the focus, it can accept user input. Figure 3.23 shows the syntax of the `Focus` method and includes two examples of using the method.

HOW TO...

Use the Focus method

Syntax
[**Me.**]*object*.**Focus()**

Examples
```
Me.txtName.Focus()
```
sends the focus to the txtName control

```
Me.btnClear.Focus()
```
sends the focus to the btnClear control

FIGURE 3.23   How to use the Focus method

In the syntax shown in Figure 3.23, `Me.` is optional, as indicated by the square brackets in the syntax. *Object* is the name of the object to which you want the focus sent. For example, to send the focus to the txtName control, you use the statement `Me.txtName.Focus()`. However, to send the focus to the btnClear control, you use the statement `Me.btnClear.Focus()`. Figure 3.24 shows the code for the btnClear control's Click event procedure.

```
Private Sub btnClear_Click(ByVal sender As Object, ByVal e As System.EventArgs) Handles btnClear.Click
    'prepares the screen for the next order

    'clear the screen
    Me.txtAddress.Text = ""
    Me.txtBlue.Text = ""
    Me.txtCity.Text = ""
    Me.txtName.Text = ""
    Me.txtState.Text = ""
    Me.txtYellow.Text = ""
    Me.txtZip.Text = ""
    Me.lblTotalBoards.Text = ""
    Me.lblTotalPrice.Text = ""

    'set the focus
    Me.txtName.Focus()

End Sub
```

FIGURE 3.24   Code for the btnClear control's Click event procedure

The btnCalc control's Click event procedure is the only procedure that still needs to be coded.

CODING THE BTNCALC CONTROL'S CLICK EVENT PROCEDURE

According to the TOE chart shown earlier in Figure 3.17, the btnCalc control's Click event procedure is responsible for calculating both the total number of skateboards ordered and the total price of the order, and then displaying the calculated amounts in the lblTotalBoards and lblTotalPrice controls. The procedure's pseudocode is shown in Figure 3.25.

btnCalc Click Event Procedure (pseudocode)
1. calculate total skateboards ordered = blue skateboards ordered + yellow skateboards ordered
2. calculate total price = total skateboards ordered * skateboard price * (1 + sales tax rate)
3. display total skateboards ordered and total price in lblTotalBoards and lblTotalPrice

FIGURE 3.25   Pseudocode for the btnCalc control's Click event procedure

The first step listed in the pseudocode shown in Figure 3.25 is to calculate the total number of skateboards ordered. This is accomplished by adding the number of blue skateboards ordered to the number of yellow skateboards ordered. Recall that the number of blue skateboards ordered is recorded in the txtBlue control's Text property as the user enters that information in the interface. Likewise, the number of yellow skateboards ordered is recorded in the txtYellow control's Text property.

The next step listed in the pseudocode is to calculate the total price of the order; you do this by multiplying the total number of skateboards ordered by the skateboard price ($100), and then adding a 5% sales tax to the result. Step 3 in the pseudocode indicates that the total skateboards ordered and the total price should be displayed in the lblTotalBoards and lblTotalPrice controls in the interface. Figure 3.26 shows two of the many ways of writing the code for the btnCalc control's Click event procedure.

Version 1

```
Dim intTotalSkateboards As Integer
Dim decTotalPrice As Decimal

'calculate total skateboards and total price
intTotalSkateboards = Convert.ToInt32(Me.txtBlue.Text) + Convert.ToInt32(Me.txtYellow.Text)
decTotalPrice = (intTotalSkateboards * 100D) * (1 + .05D)

'display calculated results
Me.lblTotalBoards.Text = Convert.ToString(intTotalSkateboards)
Me.lblTotalPrice.Text = Convert.ToString(decTotalPrice)
```

Version 2

```
Const decTAXRATE As Decimal = 0.05D
Const decSKATEBOARD_PRICE As Decimal = 100D
Dim intBlue As Integer
Dim intYellow As Integer
Dim intTotalSkateboards As Integer
Dim decTotalPrice As Decimal

'assign input to variables
intBlue = Convert.ToInt32(Me.txtBlue.Text)
intYellow = Convert.ToInt32(Me.txtYellow.Text)

'calculate total skateboards and total price
intTotalSkateboards = intBlue + intYellow
decTotalPrice = (intTotalSkateboards * decSKATEBOARD_PRICE) * (1 + decTAXRATE)

'display calculated results
Me.lblTotalBoards.Text = Convert.ToString(intTotalSkateboards)
Me.lblTotalPrice.Text = Convert.ToString(decTotalPrice)
```

FIGURE 3.26 Two versions of the code for the btnCalc control's Click event procedure

Notice that Version 1's code uses two variables, while Version 2's code uses four variables and two named constants. Although Version 2's code is longer than Version 1's code, the variables and named constants in Version 2's code make the calculation statements easier to understand.

Figure 3.27 shows the completed code for the Skate-Away Sales application.

```
'Project name:          Skate Away Project
'Project purpose:       The project allows the user to enter a name, address, city,
'                       state, ZIP, the number of blue skateboards ordered, and the
'                       number of yellow skateboards ordered. The project
'                       calculates the total number of skateboards ordered and the
'                       total price.
'Created/revised by:    Diane Zak on 2/1/2005

Option Explicit On
Option Strict On

Public Class frmOrder
    Inherits System.Windows.Forms.Form

[Windows Form Designer generated code]

    Private Sub btnExit_Click(ByVal sender As Object, ByVal e As System.EventArgs)
Handles btnExit.Click
        'ends the application
        Me.Close()

    End Sub

    Private Sub btnClear_Click(ByVal sender As Object, ByVal e As System.EventArgs)
Handles btnClear.Click
        'prepares the screen for the next order

        'clear the screen
        Me.txtAddress.Text = ""
        Me.txtBlue.Text = ""
        Me.txtCity.Text = ""
        Me.txtName.Text = ""
        Me.txtState.Text = ""
        Me.txtYellow.Text = ""
        Me.txtZip.Text = ""
        Me.lblTotalBoards.Text = ""
        Me.lblTotalPrice.Text = ""

        'set the focus
        Me.txtName.Focus()

    End Sub

    Private Sub btnCalc_Click(ByVal sender As Object, ByVal e As System.EventArgs)
Handles btnCalc.Click
        'calculates the total number of skateboards ordered and the total price
```

(Figure is continued on next page)

```
      'declare constants and variables
      Const decTAXRATE As Decimal = 0.05D
      Const decSKATEBOARD_PRICE As Decimal = 100D
      Dim intBlue As Integer
      Dim intYellow As Integer
      Dim intTotalSkateboards As Integer
      Dim decTotalPrice As Decimal

      'assign input to variables
      intBlue = Convert.ToInt32(Me.txtBlue.Text)
      intYellow = Convert.ToInt32(Me.txtYellow.Text)

      'calculate total skateboards and total price
      intTotalSkateboards = intBlue + intYellow
      decTotalPrice = (intTotalSkateboards * decSKATEBOARD_PRICE) * (1 + decTAXRATE)

      'display calculated results
      Me.lblTotalBoards.Text = Convert.ToString(intTotalSkateboards)
      Me.lblTotalPrice.Text = Convert.ToString(decTotalPrice)

   End Sub
End Class
```

FIGURE 3.27   Completed code for the Skate-Away Sales application

After coding an application, you then need to test the application to verify that the code works correctly. If the code contains an error, called a **bug**, you need to correct the error before giving the application to the user.

TESTING AND DEBUGGING THE APPLICATION

You test an application by starting it and entering some sample data. You should use both valid and invalid test data. **Valid data** is data that the application is expecting. For example, the Skate-Away Sales application is expecting the user to enter a numeric value as the number of blue skateboards ordered. **Invalid data**, on the other hand, is data that the application is not expecting. The Skate-Away Sales application, for example, is not expecting the user to enter a letter for the number of either blue or yellow skateboards ordered. You should test the application as thoroughly as possible, because you don't want to give the user an application that ends abruptly when invalid data is entered.

Debugging refers to the process of locating errors in the program. Program errors can be either syntax errors or logic errors. Most **syntax errors** are simply typing errors that occur when entering instructions; for example, typing `Me.Clse()` instead of `Me.Close()` results in a syntax error. The Code Editor detects most syntax errors as you enter the instructions. An example of a much more difficult type of error to find, and one that the Code Editor cannot detect, is a logic error. You create a **logic error** when you enter an instruction that does not give you the expected results. An example of a logic error is the instruction `decAverage = decNum1 + decNum2 / 2`, which is supposed to calculate the average of two numbers. Although the instruction is syntactically correct, it is logically incorrect. The instruction to calculate the average of two numbers, written correctly, is `decAverage = (decNum1 + decNum2) / 2`. Because division has a higher precedence number than does addition, you must place parentheses around the `decNum1 + decNum2` part of the equation.

First, you will test the Skate-Away Sales application using valid data. Assume that you start the application and then enter your name, address, city, state, and ZIP code. You also enter 5 as the number of blue skateboards ordered and 10 as the number of yellow skateboards ordered. After clicking the Calculate Order button, the interface will appear similar to the one shown in Figure 3.28.

FIGURE 3.28   Result of testing the application using valid data

The interface shown in Figure 3.28 indicates that a total of 15 skateboards were ordered at a cost of 1575.00; both amounts are correct.

Now you will test the Skate-Away Sales application using invalid data—more specifically, you will enter a letter as the number of yellow skateboards ordered. In this test, assume that you start the application and then enter your name, address, city, state, and ZIP code. You also enter 5 as the number of blue skateboards ordered, but you inadvertently enter the letter "t" as the number of yellow skateboards ordered. After clicking the Calculate Order button, and then waiting several seconds, an error message appears in a dialog box, as shown in Figure 3.29.

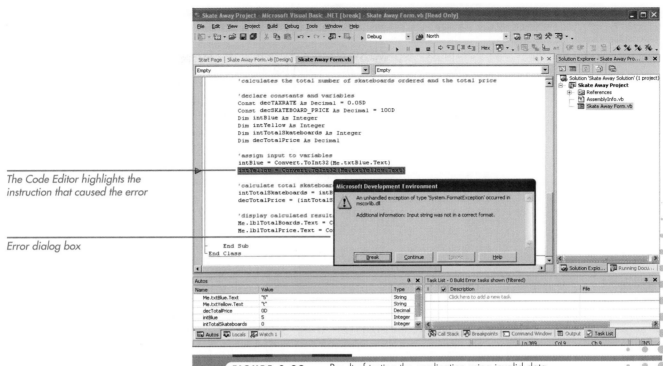

The Code Editor highlights the instruction that caused the error

Error dialog box

FIGURE 3.29   Result of testing the application using invalid data

The error message indicates that an "unhandled exception occurred" and that the "Input string was not in the correct format." The Code Editor highlights the instruction that caused the error—in this case, the error occurred when the computer was processing the `intYellow = Convert.ToInt32 (Me.txtYellow.Text)` instruction. The error occurred because the `Convert.ToInt32` method cannot convert a letter to an integer. You also will find that the Convert.ToInt32 method cannot convert the contents of an empty text box to an integer. Therefore, you will get the same error message if you click the Calculate Order button when either (or both) text boxes are empty. You learn how to handle these errors, called exceptions, later in this book. For now, just be aware that the applications you create in this chapter will probably not work with invalid data.

To return to Design mode after an error occurs, you click the Break button in the error dialog box to close the dialog box. You then click Debug on the menu bar, and then click Stop Debugging.

The last topic covered in this chapter is how to format an application's numeric output.

FORMATTING NUMERIC OUTPUT

Numbers representing monetary amounts typically are displayed with either zero or two decimal places and usually include a dollar sign and a thousand separator. Similarly, numbers representing percentage amounts usually are displayed with zero or more decimal places and a percent sign. Specifying the number of decimal places and the special characters to display in a number is called **formatting**. Figure 3.30 shows the syntax you use to format a number. The figure also includes several examples of formatting numbers.

HOW TO...

Format a Number

Syntax
*variablename.***ToString**(*formatString*)

Examples
```
Me.lblCommission.Text = decCommission.ToString("C")
```
assuming that the decCommission variable contains the number 1250, the statement assigns the string "$1,250.00" to the Text property of the lblCommission control

```
Me.lblTotal.Text = decTotal.ToString("N2")
```
assuming that the decTotal variable contains the number 123.675, the statement assigns the string "123.68" to the Text property of the lblTotal control

```
Me.lblRate.Text = decRate.ToString("P")
```
assuming that the decRate variable contains the number .06, the statement assigns the string "6%" to the Text property of the lblRate control

FIGURE 3.30   How to format a number

In the syntax shown in Figure 3.30, *variablename* is the name of a numeric variable, and *formatString* is a string that specifies the format you want to use. The *formatString* argument, which must be enclosed in double quotation marks, takes the form *Axx*, where *A* is an alphabetic character called the **format specifier**, and *xx* is a sequence of digits called the **precision specifier**. The format specifier must be one of the built-in format characters; the most commonly used format characters are listed in Figure 3.31. The precision specifier controls the number of significant digits or zeros to the right of the decimal point in the formatted number.

Format specifier	Name	Description
C or c	Currency	displays a number with a dollar sign; the precision specifier indicates the desired number of decimal places; if appropriate, displays a number with a thousand separator; negative numbers are enclosed in parentheses
D or d	Decimal	formats only integers; the precision specifier indicates the minimum number of digits desired; if required, the number is padded with zeros to its left to produce the number of digits specified by the precision specifier; if appropriate, displays a number with a thousand separator; negative numbers are preceded by a minus sign
F or f	Fixed-point	the precision specifier indicates the desired number of decimal places; negative numbers are preceded by a minus sign
N or n	Number	the precision specifier indicates the desired number of decimal places; if appropriate, displays a number with a thousand separator; negative numbers are preceded by a minus sign
P or p	Percent	the precision specifier indicates the desired number of decimal places; multiplies the number by 100 and displays the number with a percent sign; negative numbers are preceded by a minus sign

FIGURE 3.31   *Most commonly used format specifiers*

Notice that you can use either an uppercase letter or a lowercase letter as the format specifier. Figure 3.32 shows examples of how various *formatStrings* format numeric values.

formatString	Value	Result
C	3764	$3,764.00
C0	3764	$3,764
C2	3764	$3,764.00
C2	456.783	$456.78
C2	456.785	$456.79
C2	-75.31	($75.31)
D	3764	3764
D	-53	-53
D3	8	008
D3	15	015
F	3764	3764.00
F0	3764	3764
F2	3764	3764.00
F2	456.783	456.78
F2	456.785	456.79
F2	-75.31	-75.31
N	3764	3,764.00
N0	3764	3,764
N2	3764	3,764.00
N2	456.783	456.78
N2	456.785	456.79
N2	-75.31	-75.31
P	.364	36.40%
P	-.05	-5.00%
P1	.3645	36.5%
P2	1.1	110.00%

FIGURE 3.32   Examples of how various *formatStrings* format numeric values

TIP

To learn how to create custom *formatStrings*, click Help on the menu bar, and then click Index. Click either Visual Basic or Visual Studio in the Filtered by list box, then type *custom numeric format strings* in the Look for text box, and then press Enter.

Recall that the Skate-Away Sales application displays the total price of the order in the lblTotalPrice control. To include a dollar sign, thousand separator, and two decimal places when displaying the total price, you need simply to change the `Me.lblTotalPrice.Text = Convert.ToString(decTotalPrice)` statement in the btnCalc_Click event procedure to `Me.lblTotalPrice.Text = decTotalPrice.ToString("C2")`. You also could use the statement `Me.lblTotalPrice.Text = decTotalPrice.ToString("C")`, because the default precision specifier for the Currency format is two decimal places.

PROGRAMMING EXAMPLE

Currency Calculator

Create a Visual Basic .NET application that allows the user to enter the number of American dollars that he or she wants to convert to both British pounds and Mexican pesos. The application should make the appropriate calculations and then display the results on the screen. Name the solution Currency Calculator Solution. Name the project Currency Calculator Project. Name the form file Currency Calculator Form.vb. Save the application in the VbDotNet\Chap03 folder.

TOE Chart:

Task	Object	Event
1. Convert the American dollars to British pounds 2. Convert the American dollars to Mexican pesos 3. Display the number of British pounds and the number of Mexican pesos in lblBritish and lblMexican 4. Send the focus to txtAmerican	btnCalc	Click
End the application	btnExit	Click
Display the number of British pounds (from btnCalc)	lblBritish	None
Display the number of Mexican pesos (from btnCalc)	lblMexican	None
Get and display the number of American dollars	txtAmerican	None

FIGURE 3.33

User Interface:

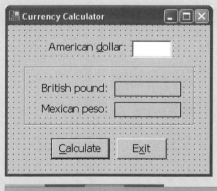

FIGURE 3.34

Objects, Properties, and Settings

Object	Property	Setting
frmCalculator	Name	frmCalculator (be sure to change the startup form to this name)
	AcceptButton	btnCalc
	Font	Tahoma, 12 point (be sure to change the form's font before adding the controls)
	Size	312, 264
	StartPosition	CenterScreen
	Text	Currency Calculator
Label1	AutoSize	True
	Text	American &dollar:
Label2	AutoSize	True
	Text	British pound:
Label3	AutoSize	True
	Text	Mexican peso:
lblBritish	Name	lblBritish
	BorderStyle	FixedSingle
	Text	(empty)
lblMexican	Name	lblMexican
	BorderStyle	FixedSingle
	Text	(empty)
txtAmerican	Name	txtAmerican
	Text	(empty)
btnCalc	Name	btnCalc
	Text	&Calculate
btnExit	Name	btnExit
	Text	E&xit

FIGURE 3.35

Tab Order:

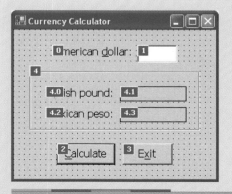

FIGURE 3.36

Pseudocode:

btnExit Click event procedure

1. close application

btnCalc Click event procedure

1. assign input value to a variable
2. calculate number of British pounds by multiplying American dollars by .626881
3. calculate number of Mexican pesos by multiplying American dollars by 10.392
4. display number of British pounds and number of Mexican pesos in lblBritish and lblMexican
5. send the focus to the txtAmerican text box

Code:

```
'Project name:        Currency Calculator Project
'Project purpose:     The project converts the number of American dollars entered by the
'                     user to the number of British pounds and the number of Mexican pesos
'Created/revised by:  Diane Zak on 2/1/2005

Option Explicit On
Option Strict On

Public Class frmCalculator
    Inherits System.Windows.Forms.Form

[Windows Form Designer generated code]

    Private Sub btnExit_Click(ByVal sender As Object, ByVal e As System.EventArgs)
Handles btnExit.Click
        'ends the application
        Me.Close()

    End Sub

    Private Sub btnCalc_Click(ByVal sender As Object, ByVal e As System.EventArgs)
Handles btnCalc.Click
        'converts American dollars to British pounds and Mexican pesos

        'declare constants and variables
        Const decBRITISH_RATE As Decimal = 0.626881D
        Const decMEXICAN_RATE As Decimal = 10.392D
        Dim decAmericanDollars As Decimal
        Dim decBritishPounds As Decimal
        Dim decMexicanPesos As Decimal

        'assign input to variable
        decAmericanDollars = Convert.ToDecimal(Me.txtAmerican.Text)

        'calculate British pounds and Mexican pesos
        decBritishPounds = decAmericanDollars * decBRITISH_RATE
        decMexicanPesos = decAmericanDollars * decMEXICAN_RATE
```

(Figure is continued on next page)

```
        'display British pounds and Mexican pesos
        Me.lblBritish.Text = Convert.ToString(decBritishPounds)
        Me.lblMexican.Text = Convert.ToString(decMexicanPesos)


        'set the focus
        Me.txtAmerican.Focus()
    End Sub
End Class
```

FIGURE 3.37

Quick Review

- Variables and named constants are computer memory locations that store data. The contents of a variable can change while the application is running; however, the contents of a named constant cannot change while the application is running.
- All variables and named constants have a name, data type, scope, and lifetime.
- The name assigned to a variable or named constant should help you remember the memory location's data type and purpose.
- The letter "m" at the beginning of a memory location's name indicates that the memory location has module scope.
- You use a declaration statement to declare a variable. If the variable has either block or procedure scope, you begin the declaration statement with the keyword Dim. If the variable has module scope, you begin the declaration statement with the keyword Private.
- You can use an assignment statement to assign a value to an existing variable while the application is running. The data type of the value should be the same as the data type of the variable.
- The equal sign (=) in an assignment statement is called the assignment operator.
- Unlike variables and named constants, which are computer memory locations, a literal constant is an item of data. The value of a literal constant does not change while the application is running.
- String literal constants are enclosed in quotation marks (""), whereas numeric literal constants are not enclosed in quotation marks.
- A literal type character is a letter that is appended to the end of a literal constant. You use a literal type character to specify the data type of a literal constant.
- The Convert class contains methods that convert values to a specified data type.
- A variable can store only one item of data at any one time.
- The integer division operator divides two integers, and then returns the result.
- The modulus arithmetic operator divides two numbers, and then returns the remainder.
- A procedure-level memory location can be used only by the procedure in which it is declared. A module-level memory location can be used by all of the procedures in the form. A block-level memory location can be used only within the block of code in which it is declared.

- You use the Const statement to declare a named constant.
- It is a good programming practice to use comments to internally document your application's code. Comments begin with the apostrophe.
- The Option Explicit On statement tells the computer to warn you if your code contains the name of an undeclared variable.
- The Option Strict On statement tells the computer not to perform any implicit type conversions that may lead to a loss of data. The computer also should not implicitly convert strings to numbers.
- Programmers commonly use either pseudocode (short phrases) or a flowchart (standardized symbols) when planning a procedure's code.
- You can use an assignment statement to assign a value to the property of an object while the application is running. The data type of the value should be the same as the data type of the property.
- You can use the Focus method to move the focus to a control while the application is running.
- After coding an application, you should test the application (with both valid and invalid data) to verify that the code works correctly.
- You can format an application's numeric output so that it displays special characters (such as dollar signs and percent signs) and the desired number of decimal places.

Key Terms

A **variable** is a computer memory location where programmers can temporarily store data.

A variable's **data type** determines the type of data the variable can store.

An **integer** is a whole number—that is, a number without any decimal places.

A **floating-point number** is a number that is expressed as a multiple of some power of 10.

Pascal-case, which is used when entering variable names, means that you capitalize the first letter in each word in the variable name.

You use an **assignment statement** to assign a value to a variable or to the property of an object while an application is running.

The equal sign (=) in an assignment statement is referred to as the **assignment operator**.

A **string** is a group of characters enclosed in quotation marks.

A **literal constant** is an item of data whose value does not change while an application is running.

You can use a **literal type character** to convert a literal constant to a different data type.

The **Convert class** contains methods that return the result of converting a value to a specified data type.

The **precedence numbers** for the arithmetic operators indicate the order in which Visual Basic .NET performs the arithmetic operation in an expression.

The **integer division operator** (\) divides two integers, and then returns the result as an integer.

The **modulus arithmetic operator** (Mod) returns the remainder of a division.

A variable's **scope** indicates where in the application's code the variable can be used.

A variable's **lifetime** indicates how long the variable remains in the computer's internal memory.

Procedure-level variables are declared in a procedure and have **procedure scope**.

Module-level variables are declared in the form's Declarations section and have **module scope**.

Block-level variables are declared within a specific block of code and have **block scope**.

A **named constant** is a computer memory location whose contents cannot be changed while the application is running. You create a named constant using the **Const statement**.

The comments in a program are called **internal documentation**.

Implicit type conversion is the process by which a value is automatically converted to fit the memory location to which it is assigned.

Pseudocode uses phrases to describe the steps a procedure needs to take to accomplish its goal.

A **flowchart** uses standardized symbols to show the steps a procedure needs to take to accomplish its goal.

The lines connecting the symbols in a flowchart are called **flowlines**.

The oval symbol in a flowchart is called the **start/stop symbol**.

The rectangle symbol in a flowchart is called the **process symbol**.

The parallelogram in a flowchart is called the **input/output symbol**.

A **zero-length string**, also called an **empty string**, is a set of quotation marks with nothing between them.

You use the **Focus method** to move the focus to a control while the application is running.

An error in a program is called a **bug**.

Valid data is data that the application is expecting.

Invalid data is data that the application is not expecting.

Debugging refers to the process of locating errors in the program.

Most **syntax errors** are typing errors that occur when entering instructions.

A **logic error** occurs when you enter an instruction that is syntactically correct, but does not give you the expected results.

Specifying the number of decimal places and the special characters to display in a number is called **formatting**.

When formatting a number, the **format specifier** determines the special characters that will appear in the formatted number. The **precision specifier** controls the number of significant digits or zeros to the right of the decimal point in the formatted number.

Review Questions

1. _____ are memory locations in which you store information, temporarily.
   a. Literal constants
   b. Named constants
   c. Variables
   d. both b and c

2. Which of the following are valid variable names?
   a. dec94Income
   b. decInc_94
   c. decIncomeTax
   d. All of the above.

3. A(n) _____ variable is known only to the procedure in which it is declared.
   a. block-level
   b. module-level
   c. procedure-level
   d. open-level

4. A _____ is a data item whose value does not change while the program is running.
   a. literal constant
   b. literal variable
   c. named constant
   d. variable

5. A _____ is a memory location whose value can change while the program is running.
   a. literal constant
   b. literal variable
   c. named constant
   d. variable

6. If you do not provide a data type in a variable declaration statement, Visual Basic .NET assigns the _____ data type to the variable.
   a. Decimal
   b. Integer
   c. Object
   d. String

7. Many programmers begin a module-level variable's name with the _____.
   a. letter m
   b. letters mod
   c. letters mlev
   d. None of the above.

8. Which of the following declares a procedure-level String variable?
   a. `Dim strCity`
   b. `Dim strCity As String`
   c. `Private strCity`
   d. `Private strCity As String`

9. Which of the following assigns the number 2.89 to a Decimal variable named decPrice? (Assume that the application contains the `Option Strict On` statement.)
   a. `decPrice = 2.89`
   b. `decPrice = 2.89D`
   c. `decPrice = D2.89`
   d. None of the above.

10. Which of the following assigns the contents of the txtSales control to a Single variable named sngSales? (Assume that the application contains the `Option Strict On` statement.)
   a. `sngSales = Me.txtSales.Text`
   b. `sngSales = Me.txtSales.Text.Convert.ToSingle`
   c. `sngSales = Convert(Me.txtSales.Text).ToSingle`
   d. `sngSales = Convert.ToSingle(Me.txtSales.Text)`

11. Which of the following declares a Double named constant?
   a. `Const dblRATE As Double = .09`
   b. `Const dblRATE As Double = .09D`
   c. `Constant dblRATE = .09`
   d. both a and b

12. Which of the following assigns the sum of two Integer variables to the Text property of the lblTotal control? (Assume that the application contains the `Option Strict On` statement.)
   a. `Me.lblTotal.Text = Convert.ToInteger(intNum1 + intNum2)`
   b. `Me.lblTotal.Text = Convert.ToInt32(intNum1 + intNum2)`
   c. `Me.lblTotal.Text = Convert.ToString(intNum1) + Convert.ToString(intNum2)`
   d. None of the above.

13. Comments in an application's code begin with the _____ character.
   a. apostrophe (')
   b. asterisk (*)
   c. caret (^)
   d. None of the above.

14. Most of the variables used in an application are _____.
   a. block-level
   b. module-level
   c. procedure-level
   d. variable-level

15. The _____ statement prevents data loss due to implicit type conversions.
   a. `Option Explicit On`
   b. `Option Strict On`
   c. `Option Implicit Off`
   d. `Option Convert Off`

16. Which of the following sends the focus to the txtNumber control?
   a. `Me.txtNumber.Focus()`
   b. `Me.txtNumber.SendFocus()`
   c. `Me.txtNumber.SetFocus()`
   d. `SetFocus(Me.txtNumber)`

17. Which of the following is a valid assignment statement?
    a. `Me.txtName = 'Jones'`
    b. `Me.txtName.Caption = 'Jones'`
    c. `Me.txtName.Text = "Jones"`
    d. `Me.txtName.Text = 'Jones'`

18. The statement `decTotal = decNumber + decNum2 * 3`, which should multiply by 3 the sum of `decNum1` and `decNum2` and then assign the result to the `decTotal` variable, is an example of _____.
    a. a logic error
    b. a syntax error
    c. a correct instruction

19. The statement `decJanSales + decFebSales = decTotalSales`, which should add together the January and February sales amounts and then assign the result to the `decTotalSales` variable, is an example of _____.
    a. a logic error
    b. a syntax error
    c. a correct instruction

20. Assume that the decSales variable contains the number 12345.89. Which of the following displays the number as 12,345.89?
    a. `Me.lblSales.Text = decSales.ToString("C2")`
    b. `Me.lblSales.Text = decSales.ToString("N2")`
    c. `Me.lblSales.Text = decSales.ToString("D2")`
    d. `Me.lblSales.Text = decSales.ToString("F2")`

Exercises

1. Assume a procedure needs to store an item's name and its price. The price may have a decimal place. Write the appropriate Dim statements to create the necessary procedure-level variables.

2. Assume a procedure needs to store the name of an item in inventory and its height and weight. The height may have decimal places; the weight will be whole numbers only. Write the appropriate Dim statements to create the necessary procedure-level variables.

3. Write an assignment statement that assigns Miami to an existing variable named strCity.

4. Write an assignment statement that adds the contents of the decSales1 variable to the contents of the decSales2 variable, and then assigns the sum to an existing variable named decTotalSales.

5. Write an assignment statement that multiplies the contents of the decSalary variable by the number 1.5, and then assigns the result to the decSalary variable.

6. Assume a form contains two buttons named btnSalary and btnBonus. Both buttons' Click event procedures need to use the mstrEmpName variable. Write the appropriate statement to declare the mstrEmpName variable. Also specify where you will need to enter the statement and whether the variable is a procedure-level or module-level variable.

7. Write the statement to declare a procedure-level named constant named decTAX_RATE whose value is .05.

8. In this exercise, you modify this chapter's Programming Example.
   a. Create the Currency Calculator application shown in this chapter's Programming Example. Save the application in the VbDotNet\ Chap03 folder.
   b. Modify the application so that it also displays the number of Canadian dollars and the number of Japanese yen. Use the following conversion rates:

   1 American dollar = 1.3874 Canadian dollar
   1 American dollar = 118.24 Japanese yen

   c. Modify the application so that it displays the number of pounds, pesos, Canadian dollars, and yen using three decimal places only. Be sure to modify the TOE chart and pseudocode before modifying the code. Also be sure to modify the comments contained in the Code Editor window.
   d. Save the solution, then start and test the application. Close the application, then close the solution.

9. In this exercise, you complete the application from Chapter 2's Exercise 6.
   a. Copy the Time Solution folder from VbDotNet\Chap02 to VbDotNet\Chap03.
   b. Open the Time Solution (Time Solution.sln) file, which is contained in the VbDotNet\Chap03\Time Solution folder.
   c. Open the Code Editor window and enter the appropriate comments at the beginning of the code. Also enter the Option Explicit On and Option Strict On statements.
   d. The application should calculate and display the total number of weekday hours and the total number of weekend hours. Write the appropriate pseudocode, then code the application. Use variables to temporarily store the input and calculated values.
   e. Save the solution, then start and test the application. Close the application, then close the solution.

10. In this exercise, you complete the application from Chapter 2's Exercise 7.
    a. Copy the Paper Solution folder from VbDotNet\Chap02 to VbDotNet\Chap03.
    b. Open the Paper Solution (Paper Solution.sln) file, which is contained in the VbDotNet\Chap03\Paper Solution folder.
    c. Open the Code Editor window and enter the appropriate comments at the beginning of the code. Also enter the Option Explicit On and Option Strict On statements.
    d. Use the TOE chart you created in Chapter 2's Exercise 7 to write the appropriate pseudocode, then code the application. Use variables to temporarily store the sales amount, commission rate, and commission amount. Display the commission amount with a dollar sign and two decimal places.
    e. Save the solution, then start the application. Test the application using your name, 2000 as the sales amount, and 10 as the commission rate. The commission should be $200.00.
    f. Close the application, then close the solution.

11. In this exercise, you complete the application from Chapter 2's Exercise 8.
    a. Copy the RMSales Solution folder from VbDotNet\Chap02 to VbDotNet\Chap03.
    b. Open the RMSales Solution (RMSales Solution.sln) file, which is contained in the VbDotNet\Chap03\RMSales Solution folder.
    c. Open the Code Editor window and enter the appropriate comments at the beginning of the code. Also enter the `Option Explicit On` and `Option Strict On` statements.
    d. Use the TOE chart you created in Chapter 2's Exercise 8 to write the appropriate pseudocode, then code the application. Use variables to temporarily store the sales amounts, projected increase rates, and projected sales amounts. Display the projected sales amounts with a dollar sign and zero decimal places.
    e. Save the solution, then start the application. Test the application using the following sales amounts and rates:

Region	Sales	Projected Increase (%)
North	25000	5
South	30000	7
East	10000	4
West	15000	11

    f. Close the application, then close the solution.

12. Scenario: John Lee wants an application in which he can enter the following three pieces of information: his cash balance at the beginning of the month, the amount of money he earned during the month, and the amount of money he spent during the month. He wants the application to compute his ending balance.
    a. Prepare a TOE chart ordered by object.
    b. Build an appropriate interface. Name the solution JohnLee Solution. Name the project JohnLee Project. Save the application in the VbDotNet\Chap03 folder.
    c. Write the pseudocode, then code the application.
    d. Save the solution, then start the application. Test the application using the following data.
    Beginning cash balance: 5000   Earnings: 2500   Expenses: 3000
    e. Close the application, then close the solution.

13. Scenario: Jackets Unlimited is having a 25% off sale on all its merchandise. The store manager asks you to create an application that requires the clerk simply to enter the original price of a jacket. The application should then compute the discount and new price.
    a. Prepare a TOE chart ordered by object.
    b. Build an appropriate interface. Name the solution Jackets Solution. Name the project Jackets Project. Save the application in the VbDotNet\Chap03 folder.
    c. Write the pseudocode, then code the application. Display a dollar sign and two decimal places in the discount and new price amounts.
    d. Test the application using the following data.
    Jacket's original price: 50
    e. Close the application, then close the solution.

14. Scenario: Colfax Industries needs an application that allows the shipping clerk to enter the quantity of an item in inventory and the number of the items that can be packed in a box for shipping. When the shipping clerk clicks a button, the application should compute and display the number of full boxes that can be packed and how many of the item are left over.
   a. Prepare a TOE chart ordered by object.
   b. Build an appropriate interface. Name the solution Colfax Solution. Name the project Colfax Project. Save the application in the VbDotNet\Chap03 folder.
   c. Write the pseudocode, then code the application.
   d. Test the application using the following information. Colfax has 45 skateboards in inventory. If six skateboards can fit into a box for shipping, how many full boxes could the company ship, and how many skateboards will remain in inventory?
   e. Close the application, then close the solution.

15. Scenario: Management USA, a small training center, plans to run two full-day seminars on December 1. The seminars are called "How to Be an Effective Manager" and "How to Run a Small Business." Each seminar costs $200. Registration for the seminars will be done by phone. When a company calls to register its employees, the phone representative will ask for the following information: the company's name, address (including city, state, and ZIP code), the number of employees registering for the "How to Be an Effective Manager" seminar, and the number of employees registering for the "How to Run a Small Business" seminar. Claire Jenkowski, the owner of Management USA, wants the application to calculate the total number of employees the company is registering and the total cost.
   a. Prepare a TOE chart ordered by object.
   b. Build an appropriate interface. Name the solution Management Solution. Name the project Management Project. Save the application in the VbDotNet\Chap03 folder. (*Hint*: The state entry should appear in uppercase. See Figure 2.4 in Chapter 2 for the appropriate property.)
   c. Write the pseudocode, then code the application.
   d. Test the application using the following data.
   Company Name: ABC Company
   Address: 345 Main St.
   City, State, ZIP: Glen, TX 70122
   Registrants for "How to Be an Effective Manager": 10
   Registrants for "How to Run a Small Business": 5
   e. Close the application, then close the solution.

16. In this exercise, you learn how to declare a Static variable.
   a. Open the Static Solution (Static Solution.sln) file, which is contained in the VbDotNet\Chap03\Static Solution folder.
   b. Start the application. Click the Count button. The message indicates that you have pressed the Count button once, which is correct.
   c. Click the Count button several more times. Each time you click the Count button, the message changes to indicate the number of times the button was clicked.
   d. Click the Exit button to end the application.
   e. Open the Code Editor window and study the code. Notice that the code uses a module-level variable to keep track of the number of times the Count button is clicked. Rather than using a module-level variable for this purpose, you also can use a Static variable.

f. Modify the code so that it uses a Static variable rather than a module-level variable.

g. Save the solution, then start the application. Click the Count button several times. Each time you click the Count button, the message should change to indicate the number of times the button was clicked.

h. Click the Exit button to end the application, then close the solution.

17. In this exercise, you find and correct an error in an application. The process of finding and correcting errors is called debugging.

a. Open the Debug Solution (Debug Solution.sln) file, which is contained in the VbDotNet\Chap03\Debug Solution folder.

b. Start the application, then test the application.

c. Locate and then correct any errors.

e. Save the solution, then start and test the application. When the application is working correctly, close the solution.

Case Projects

Willow Pools

Create an application that allows the user to enter the length, width, and height of a rectangle. The application should calculate and display the volume of the rectangle. Test the application using the following data. The swimming pool at a health club is 100 feet long, 30 feet wide, and 4 feet deep. How many cubic feet of water will the pool contain?

Builder's Inc.

Create an application that allows the user to enter both the diameter of a circle and the price of railing material per foot. The application should calculate and display the circumference of the circle and the total price of the railing material. Test the application using the following information. Jack Jones, one of Builders Inc.'s customers, is building a railing around a circular deck having a diameter of 36 feet. The railing material costs $2 per foot. What is the circumference of the deck and the total price of the railing material?

Tile Limited

Create an application allows the user to enter the length and width (in feet) of a rectangle, and the price of a square foot of tile. The application should calculate and display the area of the rectangle and the total price of the tile. Test the application using the following data. Susan Caper, one of Tile Limited's customers, is tiling a floor in her home. The floor is 12 feet long and 14 feet wide. The price of a square foot of tile is $1.59. What is the area of the floor and how much will the tile cost?

Quick Loans

Create an application that allows the user to enter the amount of a loan, the interest rate, and the term of the loan (in years). The application should calculate and display the total amount of interest and the total amount to be repaid. (*Hint*: Visual Basic .NET has a function that you can use to calculate a loan payment. You can use the Help menu to find the appropriate function and then display its Help window.) Test the application using the following data. You visit Quick Loans because you want to borrow $9000 to buy a new car. The loan is for three years at an annual interest rate of 12%. How much will you pay in interest over the three years, and what is the total amount you will repay?

Making Decisions in a Program

THE SELECTION STRUCTURE

The applications you created in the previous three chapters used the sequence programming structure only, where a procedure's instructions are processed, one after another, in the order in which each appears in the procedure. In many applications, however, the next instruction processed depends on the result of a decision or comparison that the program must make. For example, a payroll program typically needs to compare the number of hours the employee worked with the number 40 to determine whether the employee should receive overtime pay in addition to regular pay. Based on the result of that comparison, the program then selects either an instruction that computes regular pay only or an instruction that computes regular pay plus overtime pay.

You use the **selection structure**, also called the **decision structure**, when you want a program to make a decision or comparison and then select one of two paths, depending on the result of that decision or comparison. Although the idea of using the selection structure in a program is new, the concept of the selection structure is already familiar to you, because you use it each day to make hundreds of decisions. For example, every morning you have to decide if you are hungry and, if you are, what you are going to eat. Figure 4.1 shows other examples of selection structures you might use today.

Condition

Condition

Example 1	Example 2

if *it is raining*
    wear a raincoat
    bring an umbrella
	if *you have a test tomorrow*
	    study tonight
	otherwise
	    watch a movie

FIGURE 4.1   Selection structures you might use today

In the examples shown in Figure 4.1, the portion in *italics*, called the **condition**, specifies the decision you are making and is phrased so that it results in either a true or false answer only. For example, either it is raining (true) or it is not raining (false); either you have a test tomorrow (true) or you do not have a test tomorrow (false).

If the condition is true, you perform a specific set of tasks. If the condition is false, on the other hand, you might or might not need to perform a different set of tasks. For instance, look at the first example shown in Figure 4.1. If it is raining (a true condition), then you will wear a raincoat and bring an umbrella. Notice that you do not have anything in particular to do if it is not raining (a false condition). Compare this with the second example shown in Figure 4.1. If you have a test tomorrow (a true condition), then you will study tonight. However, if you do not have a test tomorrow (a false condition), then you will watch a movie.

TIP

As you may remember from Chapter 1, the selection structure is one of the three programming structures. The other two programming structures are sequence (which you used in the previous chapters) and repetition (which is covered in Chapter 5).

Like you, the computer also can evaluate a condition and then select the appropriate tasks to perform based on that evaluation. When using the selection structure in a program, the programmer must be sure to phrase the condition so that it results in either a true or a false answer only. The programmer also must specify the tasks to be performed when the condition is true and, if necessary, the tasks to be performed when the condition is false.

Visual Basic .NET provides four forms of the selection structure: If, If/Else, If/ElseIf/Else, and Case. First you learn about the If and If/Else selection structures.

WRITING PSEUDOCODE FOR THE IF AND IF/ELSE SELECTION STRUCTURES

An **If selection structure** contains only one set of instructions, which are processed when the condition is true. An **If/Else selection structure**, on the other hand, contains two sets of instructions: one set is processed when the condition is true and the other set is processed when the condition is false. Figure 4.2 shows examples of both the If and the If/Else selection structures written in pseudocode.

If selection structure

Condition

True path

1. get the part number and price
2. if *the part number is "AB203"*
   calculate the price by multiplying the price by 1.1
   display "Price increase" message
   end if
3. display the part number and price

If/Else selection structure

Condition

True path

False path

1. get the sales amount
2.
3. if *the sales amount is greater than 1500*
   calculate the commission by multiplying the sales amount by .02
   else
   calculate the commission by multiplying the sales amount by .01
   end if
4. display the commission

FIGURE 4.2   Examples of the If and If/Else selection structures written in pseudocode

Although pseudocode is not standardized—every programmer has his or her own version—you will find some similarities among the various versions. For example, many programmers begin the selection structure with the word "if" and end the structure with the two words "end if"; they also use the word "else" to designate the instructions to be performed when the condition is false.

In the examples shown in Figure 4.2, the italicized portion of the instruction indicates the condition to be evaluated. Notice that each condition results in either a true or a false answer only. In Example 1, either the part number is "AB203" or it isn't. In Example 2, either the sales amount is greater than the number 1500 or it isn't.

When the condition is true, the set of instructions following the condition is selected for processing. The instructions following the condition are referred to as the **true path**—the path you follow when the condition is true. The true path ends when you come to the "else" or, if there is no "else", when you come to the end of the selection structure (the "end if"). After the true path instructions are processed, the instruction following the "end if" is processed. In the examples shown in Figure 4.2, the display instructions are processed after the instructions in the true path.

The instructions processed when the condition is false depend on whether the selection structure contains an "else". When there is no "else", as in the first example shown in Figure 4.2, the selection structure ends when its condition is false, and processing continues with the instruction following the "end if". In the first example, for instance, the "display the part number and price" instruction is processed when the part number is not "AB203." In cases where the selection structure contains an "else", as in the second example shown in Figure 4.2, the instructions between the "else" and the "end if"—referred to as the **false path**—are processed before the instruction after the "end if" is processed. In the second example, the "calculate the commission by multiplying the sales amount by .01" instruction is processed first, followed by the "display the commission" instruction.

Recall from Chapter 3 that, in addition to using pseudocode to plan the code for a procedure, programmers also use flowcharts.

FLOWCHARTING THE IF AND IF/ELSE SELECTION STRUCTURES

Unlike pseudocode, which consists of short phrases, a flowchart uses standardized symbols to show the steps the computer must take to accomplish a task. Figure 4.3 shows Figure 4.2's examples in flowchart form.

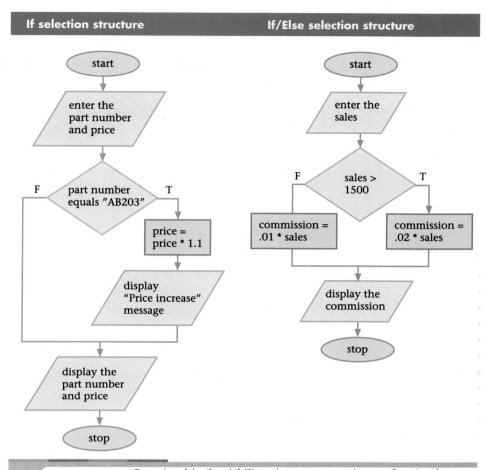

FIGURE 4.3   Examples of the If and If/Else selection structures drawn in flowchart form

TIP

You also can mark the flowlines leading out of the diamond with a "Y" and an "N" (for yes and no).

As you learned in Chapter 3, the oval in the figure is the start/stop symbol, the rectangle is the process symbol, and the parallelogram is the input/output symbol. The new symbol in the flowcharts, the diamond, is called the **selection/repetition symbol**, because it is used to represent both the selection and repetition structures. In Figure 4.3's flowcharts, the diamonds represent the selection structure. (You learn how to use the diamond to represent the repetition structure in Chapter 5.) Notice that inside each diamond is a comparison that evaluates to either true or false only. Each diamond also has one flowline entering the symbol and two flowlines leaving the symbol. The two flowlines leading out of the diamond should be marked so that anyone reading the flowchart can distinguish the true path from the false path. You mark the flowline leading to the true path with a "T" (for true), and you mark the flowline leading to the false path with an "F" (for false).

Next, you learn how to code the If and If/Else selection structures in Visual Basic .NET.

CODING THE IF AND IF/ELSE SELECTION STRUCTURES

You use the **If...Then...Else statement** to code the If and If/Else selection structures in Visual Basic .NET. Figure 4.4 shows the syntax of the If...Then...Else statement and includes two examples of using the statement.

HOW TO...

Use the If...Then...Else Statement to Code the If and If/Else Selection Structures

Syntax
If *condition* **Then**
    statement block containing one or more statements to be processed when the condition is true
[Else
    statement block containing one or more statements to be processed when the condition is false]
End If

Examples
```
If strPart = "AB203" Then
     decPrice = decPrice * 1.1D
     Me.lblMessage.Text = "Price increase"
End If
```
If the strPart variable contains the string "AB203", the first instruction in the true path multiplies the contents of the decPrice variable by 1.1 and assigns the result to the decPrice variable. The second instruction in the true path displays the message "Price increase" in the lblMessage control.

```
If decSales > 1500D Then
     decCommission = .02D * decSales
Else
     decCommission = .01D * decSales
End If
```
If the decSales variable contains a number that is greater than 1500, the instruction in the true path multiplies the contents of the decSales variable by .02; otherwise, the instruction in the false path multiplies the contents of the decSales variable by .01.

FIGURE 4.4   How to use the If...Then...Else statement to code the If and If/Else selection structures

The items in square brackets in the syntax are optional. For example, you do not always need to include the Else portion of the syntax, referred to as the **Else clause**, in an If...Then...Else statement. Words in **bold**, however, are essential components of the statement. The words If, Then, and End If, for instance, must be included in the If...Then...Else statement. The word Else must be included only if the statement uses the Else clause.

Items in *italics* in the syntax indicate where the programmer must supply information pertaining to the current application. For instance, the programmer must supply the *condition* to be evaluated. The *condition* must be a Boolean expression, which is an expression that results in a Boolean value (True or False). In addition to supplying the *condition*, the programmer also must supply the statements to be processed when the *condition* evaluates to true and, optionally, when the *condition* evaluates to false. The set of statements contained in the true path, as well as the set of statements contained in the false path, are referred to as a **statement block**.

The If...Then...Else statement's *condition* can contain variables, literal constants, named constants, properties, methods, arithmetic operators, comparison operators, and logical operators. You already know about variables, literal constants, named constants, properties, methods, and arithmetic operators. You learn about comparison operators and logical operators in this chapter.

TIP

In Visual Basic .NET, a statement block is a set of statements terminated by an Else, End If, Loop, or Next clause.

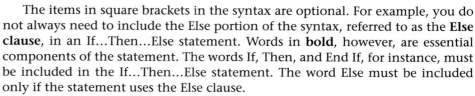

COMPARISON OPERATORS

Visual Basic .NET provides nine **comparison operators**, also referred to as **relational operators**. Figure 4.5 lists the six most commonly used comparison operators and includes examples of using the operators in the If...Then...Else statement's *condition*.

Notice that the expression contained in each *condition* shown in Figure 4.5 evaluates to one of two Boolean values—either True or False. All expressions containing a comparison operator will result in an answer of either True or False only.

TIP

The other comparison operators are Is, TypeOf...Is, and Like. You use the Is operator to determine whether two object references refer to the same object. You use the TypeOf...Is operator to determine whether an object is a specified type. The Like operator allows you to use pattern matching to determine whether one string is equal to another string.

HOW TO...

Use the Most Commonly Used Comparison Operators

Operator	Operation
=	equal to
>	greater than
>=	greater than or equal to
<	less than
<=	less than or equal to
<>	not equal to

Examples

`If intNum1 = intNum2 Then`
Compares the contents of the intNum1 variable to the contents of the intNum2 variable. The *condition* evaluates to True if the contents of both variables are equal; otherwise, it evaluates to False.

`If intWeight > 190 Then`
Compares the contents of the intWeight variable to the number 190. The *condition* evaluates to True if the intWeight variable contains a number that is greater than 190; otherwise, it evaluates to False.

`If intAge >= 21 Then`
Compares the contents of the intAge variable to the number 21. The *condition* evaluates to True if the intAge variable contains a number that is greater than or equal to 21; otherwise, it evaluates to False.

`If decPrice < 45.75D Then`
Compares the contents of the decPrice variable to the number 45.75. The *condition* evaluates to True if the decPrice variable contains a number that is less than 45.75; otherwise, it evaluates to False.

`If decPrimeRate <= decRate Then`
Compares the contents of the decPrimeRate variable to the contents of the decRate variable. The *condition* evaluates to True if the decPrimeRate variable contains a number that is less than or equal to the number stored in the decRate variable; otherwise, it evaluates to False.

`If strState <> "MA" Then`
Compares the contents of the strState variable to the string "MA". The *condition* evaluates to True if the strState variable does not contain the string "MA"; otherwise, it evaluates to False.

FIGURE 4.5   How to use the most commonly used comparison operators

Unlike arithmetic operators, comparison operators do not have an order of precedence in Visual Basic .NET. If an expression contains more than one comparison operator, Visual Basic .NET evaluates the comparison operators from left to right in the expression. Keep in mind, however, that comparison operators are evaluated after any arithmetic operators in the expression. For example, in the expression 12 / 2 * 3 < 7 + 4, the three arithmetic operators (/, *, +) are evaluated before the comparison operator (<) is evaluated. The result of the expression is the Boolean value False, as shown in Figure 4.6.

Evaluation steps	Result
Original expression	12 / 2 * 3 < 7 + 4
12 / 2 is evaluated first	6 * 3 < 7 + 4
6 * 3 is evaluated second	18 < 7 + 4
7 + 4 is evaluated third	18 < 11
18 < 11 is evaluated last	False

FIGURE 4.6   Evaluation steps for an expression containing arithmetic and comparison operators

Next, you view two examples of procedures that contain comparison operators in an If...Then...Else statement. The first procedure uses the If selection structure, and the second procedure uses the If/Else selection structure.

Using Comparison Operators – Example 1

Assume you want to create a procedure that displays both the lowest and highest of two numbers entered by the user. Figure 4.7 shows the pseudocode and flowchart for a procedure that will accomplish this task, and Figure 4.8 shows the corresponding Visual Basic .NET code. Figure 4.9 shows a sample run of the application that contains the procedure.

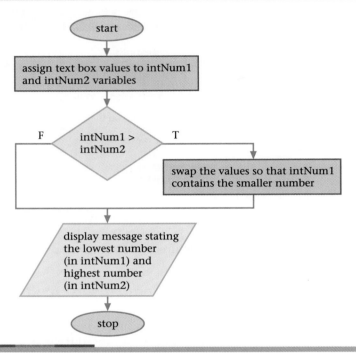

btnDisplay Click Event Procedure (pseudocode and flowchart)

1. assign text box values to intNum1 and intNum2 variables
2. if the number contained in intNum1 is greater than the number contained in intNum2
      swap the numbers so that intNum1 contains the smaller number
   end if
3. display (in the lblMessage control) a message stating the lowest number and the highest number

FIGURE 4.7   Pseudocode and flowchart showing the If selection structure

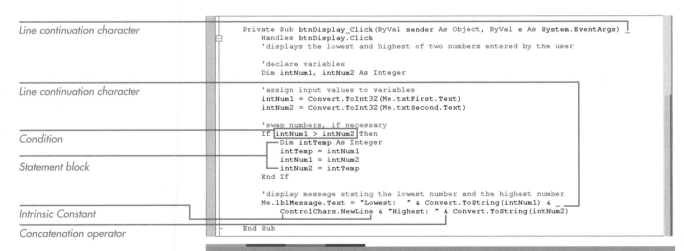

Line continuation character
Line continuation character
Condition
Statement block
Intrinsic Constant
Concatenation operator

```
Private Sub btnDisplay_Click(ByVal sender As Object, ByVal e As System.EventArgs) _
    Handles btnDisplay.Click
    'displays the lowest and highest of two numbers entered by the user

    'declare variables
    Dim intNum1, intNum2 As Integer

    'assign input values to variables
    intNum1 = Convert.ToInt32(Me.txtFirst.Text)
    intNum2 = Convert.ToInt32(Me.txtSecond.Text)

    'swap numbers, if necessary
    If intNum1 > intNum2 Then
        Dim intTemp As Integer
        intTemp = intNum1
        intNum1 = intNum2
        intNum2 = intTemp
    End If

    'display message stating the lowest number and the highest number
    Me.lblMessage.Text = "Lowest:   " & Convert.ToString(intNum1) & _
        ControlChars.NewLine & "Highest:  " & Convert.ToString(intNum2)
End Sub
```

FIGURE 4.8   Visual Basic .NET code showing the If selection structure

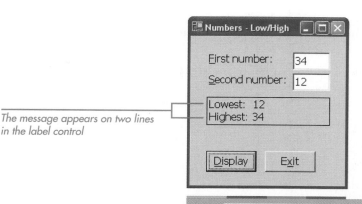

The message appears on two lines in the label control

FIGURE 4.9   Sample run of the application that contains the procedure

Notice that the code shown in Figure 4.8 first declares two procedure-level Integer variables named intNum1 and intNum2; it then assigns the contents of two text boxes to the variables. The `intNum1 > intNum2` condition in the If...Then...Else statement tells the computer to compare the contents of the intNum1 variable to the contents of the intNum2 variable. If the condition evaluates to True, it means that the value in the intNum1 variable is greater than the value in the intNum2 variable. In that case, the four instructions contained in the If...Then...Else statement's true path swap the values contained in those variables. Swapping the values places the smaller number in the intNum1 variable, and the larger number in the intNum2 variable. If the `intNum1 > intNum2` condition evaluates to False, on the other hand, the true path instructions are skipped over. The instructions do not need to be processed because the intNum1 variable already contains a number that is smaller than the one stored in intNum2. The last statement in the procedure displays a message that indicates the lowest number (which is contained in intNum1) and the highest number (which is contained in intNum2).

Study closely the instructions used to swap the values stored in the intNum1 and intNum2 variables. The first instruction, `Dim intTemp As Integer`, declares a variable named intTemp. Like the variables declared at the beginning of a procedure, variables declared within a statement block remain in memory until the procedure ends. However, unlike variables declared at the beginning of a procedure, variables declared within a statement block have block scope rather than procedure scope. Recall that when a variable has procedure scope, it can be used anywhere within the procedure. A variable that has **block scope**, on the other hand, can be used only within the statement block in which it is declared. In this case, for example, the intNum1 and intNum2 variables can be used anywhere within the btnDisplay control's Click event procedure, but the intTemp variable can be used only within the If...Then...Else statement's true path. You may be wondering why the intTemp variable was not declared at the beginning of the procedure, along with the intNum1 and intNum2 variables. Although that would have been correct, the intTemp variable is not needed unless a swap is necessary, so there is no reason to create the variable until it is needed.

The second instruction in the If...Then...Else statement's true path, `intTemp = intNum1`, assigns the value in the intNum1 variable to the intTemp variable. The intTemp variable is necessary to store the contents of the intNum1 variable temporarily so that the swap can be made. If you did not store the intNum1 variable's value in the intTemp variable, the intNum1 variable's value would be lost when the computer processes the next statement, `intNum1 = intNum2`, which replaces the contents of the intNum1 variable with the contents of the intNum2 variable. Finally, the `intNum2 = intTemp` instruction assigns the value in the intTemp variable to the intNum2 variable. Figure 4.10 illustrates the concept of swapping, assuming the user entered the numbers eight and four in the txtFirst and txtSecond controls, respectively.

	intTemp	intNum1	intNum2
values stored in the variables immediately before the `intTemp = intNum1` instruction is processed	0	8	4
result of the `intTemp = intNum1` instruction	8	8	4
result of the `intNum1 = intNum2` instruction	8	4	4
result of the `intNum2 = intTemp` instruction, which completes the swapping process	8	4	8

Values were swapped

FIGURE 4.10   Illustration of the swapping concept

The code shown in Figure 4.8 contains three items that were not covered in the previous three chapters: the line continuation character, the concatenation operator, and the `ControlChars.NewLine` constant. You use the **line continuation character**, which is a space followed by an underscore, to break up a long instruction into two or more physical lines in the Code Editor window; breaking up an instruction in this manner makes the instruction easier to read and understand. The code shown in Figure 4.8 contains two line continuation characters: one appears at the end of the first line in the procedure, and the other appears at the end of the line entered below the last comment.

You use the **concatenation operator**, which is the ampersand (&), to concatenate (connect or link) strings together. When concatenating strings, you must be sure to include a space before and after the ampersand; otherwise, Visual Basic .NET will not recognize the ampersand as the concatenation operator. Figure 4.11 shows some examples of string concatenation. As the last example shows, you do not need to use the `Convert.ToString` method when concatenating a numeric value to a string. This is because Visual Basic .NET automatically converts, to a string, a numeric value preceded by the concatenation operator.

TIP

You also can use the plus sign (+) to concatenate strings. To avoid confusion, however, you should use the plus sign for addition and the ampersand for concatenation.

HOW TO...

Concatenate Strings

Assume you have the following variables:

Variables	Data type	Contents
strFirstName	String	Sue
strLastName	String	Chen
intAge	Integer	21

Using the above variables, this concatenated string:	Would result in:
`strFirstName & strLastName`	SueChen
`strFirstName & " " & strLastName`	Sue Chen
`strLastName & ", " & strFirstName`	Chen, Sue
`"She is " & Convert.ToString(intAge) & "!"`	She is 21!
`"She is " & intAge & "!"`	She is 21!

FIGURE 4.11   How to concatenate strings

The concatenation operator appears four times in the `Me.lblMessage.Text = "Lowest: " & Convert.ToString(intNum1) & ControlChars.NewLine & "Highest: " & Convert.ToString(intNum2)` statement, which is included in the code shown in Figure 4.8. The statement concatenates five strings: the string "Lowest: ", the contents of the intNum1 variable converted to a string, the `ControlChars.NewLine` constant, the string "Highest: ", and the contents of the intNum2 variable converted to a string. The **ControlChars.NewLine constant** in the statement advances the insertion point to the next line in the lblMessage control and is the reason that the "Highest: 34" text appears on the second line in the control, as shown in Figure 4.9.

Using Comparison Operators – Example 2

Now assume you want to give the user the option of displaying either the sum of two numbers that he or she enters, or the difference between the two numbers. Figure 4.12 shows the pseudocode and flowchart for a procedure that will accomplish this task, and Figure 4.13 shows the corresponding Visual Basic .NET code. Figure 4.14 shows a sample run of the application that contains the procedure.

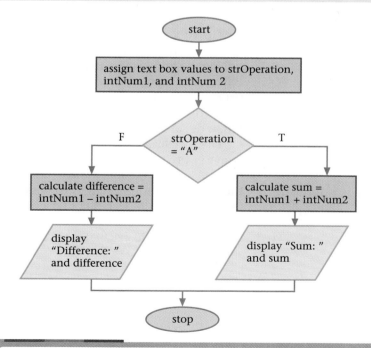

btnCalc Click Event Procedure (pseudocode and flowchart)

1. assign text box values to strOperation, intNum1, and intNum2 variables
2. if the strOperation variable contains "A"
   calculate the sum by adding together the numbers contained in intNum1 and intNum2
   display (in the lblAnswer control) the message "Sum:" and the sum
   else
   calculate the difference by subtracting the number contained in intNum2 from the number contained in intNum1
   display (in the lblAnswer control) the message "Difference:" and the difference
   end if

FIGURE 4.12   Pseudocode and flowchart showing the If/Else selection structure

```
Private Sub btnCalc_Click(ByVal sender As Object, ByVal e As System.EventArgs) _
    Handles btnCalc.Click
    'calculates the sum of or difference between two numbers

    'declare variables
    Dim strOperation As String
    Dim intNum1, intNum2, intAnswer As Integer

    'assign input values to variables
    strOperation = Me.txtOperation.Text
    intNum1 = Convert.ToInt32(Me.txtNum1.Text)
    intNum2 = Convert.ToInt32(Me.txtNum2.Text)

    'calculate and display sum or difference
    If strOperation = "A" Then
        intAnswer = intNum1 + intNum2
        Me.lblAnswer.Text = "Sum: " & intAnswer
    Else
        intAnswer = intNum1 - intNum2
        Me.lblAnswer.Text = "Difference: " & intAnswer
    End If

End Sub
```

Assigns the Text property, which contains one uppercase character, to the strOperation variable

Compares the one uppercase character stored in the strOperation variable to the uppercase letter A

FIGURE 4.13   Visual Basic .NET code showing the If/Else selection structure

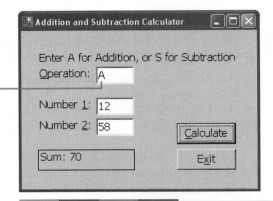

The txtOperation control's MaxLength and CharacterCasing properties are set to 1 and Upper, respectively, in the Properties window

FIGURE 4.14   Sample run of the application that contains the procedure

TIP

As you learned in Chapter 2, a text box's MaxLength property specifies the maximum number of characters that can be entered in the text box, and its CharacterCasing property indicates whether the text should be left alone or converted to uppercase or lowercase.

The code shown in Figure 4.13 first declares four procedure-level variables: a String variable named strOperation and three Integer variables named intNum1, intNum2, and intAnswer. The `strOperation = Me.txtOperation.Text` statement assigns the contents of the txtOperation control's Text property to the strOperation variable. In this case, the Text property contains one uppercase character; this is because the txtOperation control's MaxLength and CharacterCasing properties are set to 1 and Upper, respectively, in the Properties window.

The `intNum1 = Convert.ToInt32(Me.txtNum1.Text)` and `intNum2 = Convert.ToInt32(Me.txtNum2.Text)` statements convert the contents of the txtNum1 and txtNum2 text boxes to integers, assigning the results to the intNum1 and intNum2 variables. The `strOperation = "A"` condition in the If...Then...Else statement tells the computer to compare the contents of the strOperation variable to the uppercase letter "A". If the condition is true, the selection structure calculates and displays the sum of the two numbers entered

The uppercase letter A is stored in the computer's internal memory using the eight bits 01000001 (ASCII code 65), whereas the lowercase letter a is stored using the eight bits 01100001 (ASCII code 97). ASCII stands for American Standard Code for Information Interchange and is the coding scheme used by microcomputers to represent the numbers, letters, and symbols on the keyboard.

by the user. If the condition is false, on the other hand, the selection structure calculates and displays the difference between the two numbers.

Now assume that the txtOperation control's CharacterCasing property is not set to Upper, but is left at its default value, Normal. If the user enters an uppercase letter "A" in the text box, the `strOperation = Me.txtOperation.Text` statement will assign an uppercase letter "A" to the strOperation variable, and the `strOperation = "A"` condition in the selection structure will evaluate to True. As a result, the selection structure's true path will calculate and display the sum of the numbers entered by the user, which is correct. However, if the user enters a lowercase letter "a" in the text box, the `strOperation = Me.txtOperation.Text` statement will assign a lowercase letter "a" to the strOperation variable, and the `strOperation = "A"` condition in the selection structure will evaluate to False; this is because string comparisons in Visual Basic .NET are case-sensitive. As a result, the selection structure's false path will calculate and display the difference between the numbers entered by the user, which is incorrect.

Visual Basic .NET provides two methods that you can use to solve the case problems that occur when comparing strings: ToUpper and ToLower.

USING THE TOUPPER AND TOLOWER METHODS

As is true in most programming languages, string comparisons in Visual Basic .NET are case-sensitive, which means that the string "Yes" is not the same as the string "YES" or the string "yes". A problem occurs when you need to include a string, either entered by the user or read from a file, in a comparison, because you cannot always control the case of the string. Although you can set a text box's CharacterCasing property to Upper or Lower, you may not want to change the case of the user's entry as he or she is typing it. And it's entirely possible that you may not be aware of the case of strings that are read from a file. Before using a string in a comparison, you can convert it to either uppercase or lowercase, and then use the converted string in the comparison.

You use the **ToUpper method** to convert a string to uppercase, and the **ToLower method** to convert a string to lowercase. Figure 4.15 shows the syntax of both methods and includes several examples of using the methods.

HOW TO...

Use the ToUpper and ToLower Methods

Syntax
string.ToUpper()
string.ToLower()

Examples
```
If strLetter.ToUpper() = "P" Then
```
compares the uppercase version of the string stored in the strLetter variable to the uppercase letter "P"

```
If strState.ToLower() = "ca" Then
```
compares the lowercase version of the string stored in the strState variable to the lowercase letters "ca"

```
If strItem1.ToUpper() <> strItem2.ToUpper() Then
```
compares the uppercase version of the string stored in the strItem1 variable to the uppercase version of the string stored in the strItem2 variable

```
If "reno" = Me.txtCity.Text.ToLower() Then
```
compares the lowercase letters "reno" to the lowercase version of the string stored in the txtCity control

```
Me.lblName.Text = strName.ToUpper()
```
assigns the uppercase version of the string stored in the strName variable to the Text property of the lblName control

```
strName = strName.ToUpper()
```
changes the contents of the strName variable to uppercase

FIGURE 4.15 How to use the ToUpper and ToLower methods

In each syntax shown in Figure 4.15, *string* typically is the name of a String variable that contains the string you want to convert; however, as the fourth example shows, *string* also can be the property of an object. Both methods temporarily convert the string to the appropriate case. For example, `strLetter.ToUpper()` temporarily converts the contents of the strLetter variable to uppercase, and `strState.ToLower()` temporarily converts the contents of the strState variable to lowercase.

You also can use the `ToUpper` or `ToLower` methods to permanently convert the contents of a String variable or property to uppercase or lowercase. To do so, you simply include the variable or property, along with the appropriate method, in an assignment statement. For example, to permanently change the contents of the strName variable to uppercase, you use the assignment statement `strName = strName.ToUpper()`. You use the assignment statement `Me.txtName.Text = Me.txtName.Text.ToLower()` to convert the contents of the txtName control's Text property to lowercase.

When using the `ToUpper` method in a comparison, be sure that everything you are comparing is uppercase. In other words, the clause `If strLetter.ToUpper() = "p"` Then will not work correctly: the *condition* will always evaluate to False, because the uppercase version of a letter will never be equal to its lowercase counterpart. Likewise, when using the `ToLower` method in a comparison, be sure that everything you are comparing is lowercase.

As mentioned earlier, if the CharacterCasing property of the txtOperation control (shown earlier in Figure 4.14) was left at its default value, Normal, the code shown in Figure 4.13 would not work correctly if the user enters a lowercase letter "a" in the text box. Recall that the code will calculate and display the difference between, rather than the sum of, the two numbers entered by the user. Figures 4.16 and 4.17 show two different ways of using the `ToUpper` method to fix this problem. In Figure 4.16, the `ToUpper` method is included in the statement that assigns the text box value to the strOperation variable. In Figure 4.17, the `ToUpper` method is included in the selection structure's condition. The assignment statement in Figure 4.16 will permanently change the value in the strOperation variable to uppercase, while the condition in Figure 4.17 will change the value to uppercase only temporarily. In this instance, neither way is better than the other; both simply represent two different ways of performing the same task.

ToUpper method

```
Private Sub btnCalc_Click(ByVal sender As Object, ByVal e As System.EventArgs) _
    Handles btnCalc.Click
    'calculates the sum of or difference between two numbers

    'declare variables
    Dim strOperation As String
    Dim intNum1, intNum2, intAnswer As Integer

    'assign input values to variables
    strOperation = Me.txtOperation.Text.ToUpper()
    intNum1 = Convert.ToInt32(Me.txtNum1.Text)
    intNum2 = Convert.ToInt32(Me.txtNum2.Text)

    'calculate and display sum or difference
    If strOperation = "A" Then
        intAnswer = intNum1 + intNum2
        Me.lblAnswer.Text = "Sum: " & intAnswer
    Else
        intAnswer = intNum1 - intNum2
        Me.lblAnswer.Text = "Difference: " & intAnswer
    End If

End Sub
```

FIGURE 4.16   Code showing the ToUpper method in the assignment statement

ToUpper method

```
Private Sub btnCalc_Click(ByVal sender As Object, ByVal e As System.EventArgs) _
    Handles btnCalc.Click
    'calculates the sum of or difference between two numbers

    'declare variables
    Dim strOperation As String
    Dim intNum1, intNum2, intAnswer As Integer

    'assign input values to variables
    strOperation = Me.txtOperation.Text
    intNum1 = Convert.ToInt32(Me.txtNum1.Text)
    intNum2 = Convert.ToInt32(Me.txtNum2.Text)

    'calculate and display sum or difference
    If strOperation.ToUpper() = "A" Then
        intAnswer = intNum1 + intNum2
        Me.lblAnswer.Text = "Sum: " & intAnswer
    Else
        intAnswer = intNum1 - intNum2
        Me.lblAnswer.Text = "Difference: " & intAnswer
    End If

End Sub
```

FIGURE 4.17   Code showing the ToUpper method in the selection structure's condition

Recall that you also can use logical operators in the If...Then...Else statement's *condition*.

LOGICAL OPERATORS

Logical operators, sometimes referred to as **Boolean operators**, allow you to combine two or more *conditions* into one compound *condition*. Visual Basic .NET has six logical operators, which are listed along with their order of precedence in Figure 4.18. The figure also contains examples of using logical operators in the If…Then…Else statement's *condition*.

HOW TO...

Use the Logical Operators

Operator	Operation	Precedence number
Not	reverses the value of the *condition*; True becomes False, and False becomes True	1
And	all conditions must be true for the compound condition to be true	2
AndAlso	same as the And operator, except performs short-circuit evaluation	2
Or	only one of the conditions must be true for the compound condition to be true	3
OrElse	same as the Or operator, except performs short-circuit evaluation	3
Xor	one and only one condition can be true for the compound condition to be true	4

Examples
```
If Not blnInsured Then
```
The *condition* evaluates to True if the blnInsured variable contains the Boolean value False; otherwise, it evaluates to False.

```
If intHours > 0 And intHours <= 40 Then
```
The compound *condition* evaluates to True if the intHours variable contains a number that is greater than zero, but less than or equal to 40; otherwise, it evaluates to False.

```
If strState = "TN" AndAlso decSales > 50000D Then
```
The compound *condition* evaluates to True if the strState variable contains the letters "TN" and, at the same time, the decSales variable contains a number that is greater than 50000; otherwise, it evaluates to False.

```
If strRating = "A" Or strRating = "B" Then
```
The compound *condition* evaluates to True if the strRating variable contains either the letter "A" or the letter "B"; otherwise, it evaluates to False.

(Figure is continued on next page)

```
If strState = "TN" OrElse decSales > 50000D Then
```
The compound *condition* evaluates to True if the strState variable contains the letters "TN" or if the decSales variable contains a number that is greater than 50000; otherwise, it evaluates to False.

```
If strCoupon1 = "USED" Xor strCoupon2 = "USED" Then
```
The compound *condition* evaluates to False if neither or both variables contain the string "USED"; otherwise, it evaluates to True.

FIGURE 4.18   How to use the logical operators

The tables shown in Figure 4.19, called **truth tables**, summarize how Visual Basic .NET evaluates the logical operators in an expression. Like expressions containing comparison operators, expressions containing logical operators always evaluate to a Boolean value.

Truth table for the Not operator

value of *condition*	value of Not *condition*
True	False
False	True

Truth table for the And operator

value of *condition 1*	value of *condition2*	value of *condition 1* And *condition2*
True	True	True
True	False	False
False	True	False
False	False	False

Truth table for the AndAlso operator

value of *condition 1*	value of *condition2*	value of *condition 1* AndAlso *condition2*
True	True	True
True	False	False
False	(not evaluated)	False

Truth table for the Or operator

value of *condition 1*	value of *condition2*	value of *condition 1* Or *condition2*
True	True	True
True	False	True
False	True	True
False	False	False

Truth table for the OrElse operator

value of *condition 1*	value of *condition2*	value of *condition 1* OrElse *condition2*
True	(not evaluated)	True
False	True	True
False	False	False

(Table is continued on next page)

Truth table for the Xor operator

value of *condition1*	value of *condition2*	value of *condition1* Xor *condition2*
True	True	False
True	False	True
False	True	True
False	False	False

FIGURE 4.19 Truth tables for the logical operators

As Figure 4.19 indicates, the Not operator reverses the truth-value of the *condition*. If the value of the *condition* is True, then the value of Not *condition* is False. Likewise, if the value of the *condition* is False, then the value of Not *condition* is True.

Now look at the truth tables for the And and AndAlso logical operators. When you use the And or AndAlso operators to combine two conditions, the resulting compound condition is True only when both conditions are True. If either condition is False or if both conditions are False, then the compound condition is False. The difference between the And and AndAlso operators is that the And operator always evaluates both conditions, while the AndAlso operator performs a **short-circuit evaluation**, which means that it does not always evaluate *condition2*. Because both conditions combined with the AndAlso operator need to be True for the compound condition to be True, the AndAlso operator does not evaluate *condition2* if *condition1* is False. Although the And and AndAlso operators produce the same results, the AndAlso operator is more efficient.

Now look at the truth tables for the Or and OrElse logical operators. When you combine conditions using the Or or OrElse operators, the compound condition is False only when both conditions are False. If either condition is True or if both conditions are True, then the compound condition is True. The difference between the Or and OrElse operators is that the Or operator always evaluates both conditions, while the OrElse operator performs a short-circuit evaluation. Because only one of the conditions combined with the OrElse operator needs to be True for the compound condition to be True, the OrElse operator does not evaluate *condition2* if *condition1* is True. Although the Or and OrElse operators produce the same results, the OrElse operator is more efficient.

Finally, look at the truth table for the Xor operator. When you combine conditions using the Xor operator, the compound condition is True only when one and only one condition is True. If both conditions are True or both conditions are False, then the compound condition is False. In the next section, you use the truth tables to determine which logical operator is appropriate for the If...Then...Else statement's compound condition.

Using the Truth Tables

Assume that you want to pay a bonus to every A-rated salesperson whose monthly sales total more than $10,000. To receive a bonus, the salesperson must be rated A and he or she must sell more than $10,000 in product. Assuming the two variables strRating and decSales contain the salesperson's rating and sales amount, you can phrase *condition1* as `strRating = "A"` and *condition2* as `decSales > 10000D`. Now the question is, which logical operator should you use to combine both conditions into one compound condition? You can use the truth tables shown in Figure 4.19 to answer this question.

For a salesperson to receive a bonus, remember that both *condition1* (strRating = "A") and *condition2* (decSales > 10000D) must be True at the same time. If either condition is False, or if both conditions are False, then the compound condition should be False, and the salesperson should not receive a bonus. According to the truth tables, the And, AndAlso, Or, and OrElse operators evaluate the compound condition as True when both conditions are True. However, only the And and AndAlso operators evaluate the compound condition as False when either one or both of the conditions are False. The Or and OrElse operators, you will notice, evaluate the compound condition as False only when *both* conditions are False. Therefore, the correct compound condition to use here is either strRating = "A" And decSales > 10000D or strRating = "A" AndAlso decSales > 10000D. Recall, however, that the AndAlso operator is more efficient than the And operator.

Now assume that you want to send a letter to all A-rated salespeople and all B-rated salespeople. Assuming the rating is stored in the strRating variable, you can phrase *condition1* as strRating = "A" and *condition2* as strRating = "B". Now which operator do you use?

At first it might appear that either the And or the AndAlso operator is the correct one to use, because the example says to send the letter to "all A-rated salespeople and all B-rated salespeople." In everyday conversations, you will find that people sometimes use the word *and* when what they really mean is *or*. Although both words do not mean the same thing, using *and* instead of *or* generally does not cause a problem because we are able to infer what another person means. Computers, however, cannot infer anything; they simply process the directions you give them, word for word. In this case, you actually want to send a letter to all salespeople with either an A or a B rating (a salesperson cannot have both an A rating and a B rating), so you will need to use either the Or or the OrElse operator. As the truth tables indicate, the Or and OrElse operators are the only operators that evaluate the compound condition as True if one or more of the conditions is True. Therefore, the correct compound condition to use here is either strRating = "A" Or strRating = "B" or strRating = "A" OrElse strRating = "B". Recall, however, that the OrElse operator is more efficient than the Or operator.

Finally, assume that, when placing an order, a customer is allowed to use only one of two coupons. Assuming the program uses the variables strCoupon1 and strCoupon2 to keep track of the coupons, you can phrase *condition1* as strCoupon1 = "USED" and *condition2* as strCoupon2 = "USED". Now which operator should you use to combine both conditions? According to the truth tables, the Xor operator is the only operator that evaluates the compound condition as True when one and only one condition is True. Therefore, the correct compound condition to use here is strCoupon1 = "USED" Xor strCoupon2 = "USED".

Figure 4.20 shows the order of precedence for the arithmetic, comparison, and logical operators you have learned so far.

Operator	Operation	Precedence number
^	exponentiation	1
−	negation	2
*, /	multiplication and division	3
\	integer division	4
Mod	modulus arithmetic	5
+, −	addition and subtraction	6
&	concatenation	7
=, >, >=, <, <=, <>	equal to, greater than, greater than or equal to, less than, less than or equal to, not equal to	8
Not	reverses truth value of condition	9
And, AndAlso	all conditions must be true for the compound condition to be true	10
Or, OrElse	only one condition needs to be true for the compound condition to be true	11
Xor	one and only one condition can be true for the compound condition to be true	12

FIGURE 4.20   Order of precedence for arithmetic, comparison, and logical operators

Notice that logical operators are evaluated after any arithmetic operators or comparison operators in an expression. In other words, in the expression 12 > 0 AndAlso 12 < 10 * 2, the arithmetic operator (*) is evaluated first, followed by the two comparison operators (> and <), followed by the logical operator (AndAlso). The expression evaluates to True, as shown in Figure 4.21.

Evaluation steps	Result
Original expression	12 > 0 AndAlso 12 < 10 * 2
10 * 2 is evaluated first	12 > 0 AndAlso 12 < 20
12 > 0 is evaluated second	True AndAlso 12 < 20
12 < 20 is evaluated third	True AndAlso True
True AndAlso True is evaluated last	True

FIGURE 4.21   Evaluation steps for an expression containing arithmetic, comparison, and logical operators

In the next section, you view the Visual Basic .NET code for a procedure that contains a logical operator in an If...Then...Else statement.

Using Logical Operators in an If...Then...Else Statement

Assume you want to create a procedure that calculates and displays an employee's gross pay. To keep this example simple, assume that no one at the company works more than 40 hours per week, and everyone earns the same hourly rate, $10.65. Before making the gross pay calculation, the procedure should verify that the number of hours entered by the user is greater than or equal to zero, but less than or equal to 40. Programmers refer to the process of verifying that the input data is within the expected range as **data validation**. In this case, if the number is valid, the procedure should calculate and display the gross pay; otherwise, it should display an error message alerting the user that the input data is incorrect. Figure 4.22 shows two ways of writing the Visual Basic .NET code for this procedure. Notice that the If...Then...Else statement in the first example uses the AndAlso logical operator, whereas the If...Then...Else statement in the second example uses the OrElse logical operator.

Example 1: using the AndAlso operator

```
Dim decHours, decGross As Decimal
decHours = Convert.ToDecimal(Me.txtHours.Text)
If decHours >= 0D AndAlso decHours <= 40D Then
     decGross = decHours * 10.65D
     Me.lblResult.Text = decGross.ToString("C2")
Else
     Me.lblResult.Text = "Input Error"
End If
```

Example 2: using the OrElse operator

```
Dim decHours, decGross As Decimal
decHours = Convert.ToDecimal(Me.txtHours.Text)
If decHours < 0D OrElse decHours > 40D Then
     Me.lblResult.Text = "Input Error"
Else
     decGross = decHours * 10.65D
     Me.lblResult.Text = decGross.ToString("C2")
End If
```

FIGURE 4.22 AndAlso and OrElse logical operators in the If...Then...Else statement

The compound condition in the first example shown in Figure 4.22 tells the computer to determine whether the value stored in the decHours variable is greater than or equal to the number 0 and, at the same time, less than or equal to the number 40. If the compound condition evaluates to True, then the selection structure calculates and displays the gross pay; otherwise, it displays the "Input Error" message.

The compound condition in the second example shown in Figure 4.22 tells the computer to determine whether the value stored in the decHours variable is less than the number 0 or greater than the number 40. If the compound condition evaluates to True, then the selection structure displays the "Input Error" message; otherwise, it calculates and displays the gross pay. Both If...Then...Else statements shown in Figure 4.22 produce the same results, and simply represent two different ways of performing the same task.

You can use what you have learned so far to fix the problem that occurred when testing the Skate-Away Sales application in Chapter 3.

MODIFYING THE SKATE-AWAY SALES APPLICATION

In Chapter 3, you created an application for Skate-Away Sales, a company that sells skateboards by phone. Figure 4.23 shows the application's user interface.

FIGURE 4.23   User interface for the Skate-Away Sales application

As you may remember, you tested the application using the following valid data: your name, address, city, state, ZIP code, 5 as the number of blue skateboards ordered, and 10 as the number of yellow skateboards ordered. When you clicked the Calculate Order button after entering the data, the application showed that a total of 15 skateboards were ordered at a cost of 1575.00; both amounts were correct.

You also tested the application using invalid data for the number of yellow skateboards ordered; more specifically, you entered the letter "t' rather than a number. When you clicked the Calculate Order button, an error message appeared in a dialog box. The error message indicated that an "unhandled exception occurred" and that the "Input string was not in the correct format." Recall that the `intYellow = Convert.ToInt32(Me.txtYellow.Text)` statement caused the error, because the `Convert.ToInt32` method cannot convert a letter to an integer. As mentioned in Chapter 3, you also will find that the `Convert.ToInt32` method cannot convert the contents of an empty text box to an integer. Therefore, you will get the same error message if you click the Calculate Order button when either (or both) text boxes are empty. (Keep in mind that it is possible that a customer might order either blue skateboards only or yellow skateboards only.) Although the error message that appeared in the dialog box may be meaningful to a programmer, it is not very meaningful to the user. One way of solving the "unfriendly error message" problem is to prevent the error message from appearing in the first place. You can do so by using the If and If/Else forms of the selection structure to validate the data entered in the txtBlue and txtYellow controls.

TIP

The `Convert.ToInt32` method also cannot convert special characters—such as a dollar sign or a comma—to an integer. You learn how to remove special characters from a string in Chapter 6.

Figure 4.24 shows the modified pseudocode and code for the btnCalc control's Click event procedure. Changes made to the original pseudocode and code are shaded in the figure.

btnCalc Click Event Procedure (pseudocode)

1. if the txtBlue text box is empty
       assign 0 to the txtBlue text box
   end if
2. if the txtYellow text box is empty
       assign 0 to the txtYellow text box
   end if
3. if the txtBlue and txtYellow text boxes contain numbers
       calculate total skateboards ordered = blue skateboards ordered + yellow skateboards ordered
       calculate total price = total skateboards ordered * skateboard price * (1 + sales tax rate)
       display total skateboards ordered and total price in lblTotalBoards and lblTotalPrice
   else
       display a message indicating that the user should enter one or more valid numbers
   end if

btnCalc Click event procedure (Visual Basic .NET code)

```
Private Sub btnCalc_Click(ByVal sender As Object, ByVal e As System.EventArgs) _
        Handles btnCalc.Click
        'calculates the total number of skateboards ordered and the total price

        'declare constants and variables
        Const decTAXRATE As Decimal = 0.05D
        Const decSKATEBOARD_PRICE As Decimal = 100D
        Dim intBlue As Integer
        Dim intYellow As Integer
        Dim intTotalSkateboards As Integer
        Dim decTotalPrice As Decimal

        'check whether text boxes are empty
        If Me.txtBlue.Text = "" Then
            Me.txtBlue.Text = 0
        End If
        If Me.txtYellow.Text = "" Then
            Me.txtYellow.Text = 0
        End If
```

(Figure is continued on next page)

```
'check whether text boxes contain numbers
If IsNumeric(Me.txtBlue.Text) AndAlso IsNumeric(Me.txtYellow.Text) Then
    'assign input to variables
    intBlue = Convert.ToInt32(Me.txtBlue.Text)
    intYellow = Convert.ToInt32(Me.txtYellow.Text)

    'calculate total skateboards and total price
    intTotalSkateboards = intBlue + intYellow
    decTotalPrice = (intTotalSkateboards * decSKATEBOARD_PRICE) * (1 + decTAXRATE)

    'display calculated results
    Me.lblTotalBoards.Text = Convert.ToString(intTotalSkateboards)
    Me.lblTotalPrice.Text = Convert.ToString(decTotalPrice)
Else
    MessageBox.Show("Please enter one or more valid numbers.", _
        "Skate-Away Sales", MessageBoxButtons.OK, MessageBoxIcon.Information, _
        MessageBoxDefaultButton.Button1)
End If
```

FIGURE 4.24   Modified pseudocode and code for the btnCalc control's Click event procedure

TIP

As you learned in Chapter 3, "" is a zero-length string, also called an empty string.

The first two selection structures in the code determine whether the user entered any data in the txtBlue and txtYellow controls. If the txtBlue control is empty, the first selection structure assigns a zero to the control's Text property. Similarly, the second selection structure assigns a zero to the txtYellow control's Text property if the txtYellow control is empty. Notice that neither of these selection structures has an Else clause.

The third selection structure in the code uses the `IsNumeric` function, along with the AndAlso logical operator, to determine whether the txtBlue and txtYellow controls contain numeric values.

The `IsNumeric` Function

A **function** is a predefined procedure that performs a specific task and then returns a value after completing the task. The **IsNumeric function**, for example, checks if an *expression* can be converted to a number, and then returns the Boolean value True if it can be converted or the Boolean value False if it can't be converted. Figure 4.25 shows the syntax and several examples of the `IsNumeric` function.

HOW TO...

How to Use the IsNumeric Function

Syntax
IsNumeric(*expression*)

Examples

Function	Returns
IsNumeric("5")	True
IsNumeric("$45")	True
IsNumeric("3,678.55")	True
IsNumeric("")	False
IsNumeric("AB")	False
IsNumeric("5%")	False
IsNumeric(Me.txtBlue.Text)	True if the value stored in the Text property can be converted to a number; otherwise, False

FIGURE 4.25 How to use the IsNumeric function

TIP

In previous versions of Visual Basic, programmers used the **CInt** function to convert an expression to an integer. Unlike the **Convert.ToInt32** method, the **CInt** function will convert an expression containing a dollar sign or a comma to a number. The **CInt** function is also available in Visual Basic .NET. However, the advantage of learning the Convert methods is that, unlike the **CInt** function, the Convert methods can be used in any .NET language.

Notice that the `IsNumeric` function returns the Boolean value False if the *expression* contains the empty string, letters, or the percent sign. The function returns the Boolean value True, on the other hand, if the *expression* contains a number only, or if it contains a number with a dollar sign, a comma, or a period. Keep in mind that, although the `IsNumeric` function evaluates an *expression* that contains a dollar sign or a comma as a number, the `Convert.ToInt32` method cannot convert values containing either of those characters to an integer. If your code tries to use the `Convert.ToInt32` method to convert an *expression* containing a dollar sign or a comma, Visual Basic .NET will display an error message. In Chapter 6, you will learn how to remove the dollar sign and comma from an *expression* before using the `Convert.ToInt32` method. For now, just be sure not to enter any dollar signs or commas in your input data. In this chapter and the next, you will be using the `IsNumeric` function only to verify that the *expression* does not contain any letters.

If the `IsNumeric(Me.txtBlue.Text) AndAlso IsNumeric(Me.txtYellow.Text)` compound condition shown in Figure 4.24 evaluates to True, it means that both text boxes contain values that can be converted to numbers. In that case, the instructions in the selection structure's true path convert the contents of both text boxes to integers, and store the results in the intBlue and intYellow variables. The procedure then calculates and displays the total skateboards ordered and the total price, and then the procedure ends.

If the `IsNumeric(Me.txtBlue.Text) AndAlso IsNumeric(Me.txtYellow.Text)` compound condition evaluates to False, on the other hand, it means that at least one of the text boxes contains a value that cannot be converted to a number. In that case, the instruction in the selection structure's false path uses the `MessageBox.Show` method to display an appropriate message to the user.

The MessageBox.Show Method

You can use the **MessageBox.Show method** to display a message box that contains text, one or more buttons, and an icon. Figure 4.26 shows the syntax of the `MessageBox.Show` method. It also lists the meaning of each argument used by the method, and includes two examples of using the method to create a message box.

HOW TO...

Use the MessageBox.Show Method

Syntax
MessageBox.Show(*text, caption, buttons, icon*[, *defaultButton*])

Argument	Meaning
text	text to display in the message box
caption	text to display in the title bar of the message box

buttons	buttons to display in the message box; can be one of the following constants:
	`MessageBoxButtons.AbortRetryIgnore`
	`MessageBoxButtons.OK`
	`MessageBoxButtons.OKCancel`
	`MessageBoxButtons.RetryCancel`
	`MessageBoxButtons.YesNo`
	`MessageBoxButtons.YesNoCancel`

icon	icon to display in the message box; typically, one of the following constants:
	`MessageBoxIcon.Exclamation`
	`MessageBoxIcon.Information`
	`MessageBoxIcon.Stop`

defaultButton	button automatically selected when the user presses Enter; can be one of the following constants:
	`MessageBoxDefaultButton.Button1` (default setting)
	`MessageBoxDefaultButton.Button2`
	`MessageBoxDefaultButton.Button3`

Examples
```
MessageBox.Show("Record deleted.", "Payroll", _
     MessageBoxButtons.OK, MessageBoxIcon.Information)
```
displays an informational message box that contains the message "Record deleted."

```
MessageBox.Show("Delete this record?", "Payroll", _
     MessageBoxButtons.YesNo, MessageBoxIcon.Exclamation, _
     MessageBoxDefaultButton.Button2)
```
displays a warning message box that contains the message "Delete this record?"

FIGURE 4.26   How to use the `MessageBox.Show` method

As Figure 4.26 indicates, the *text* argument specifies the text to display in the message box. The *text* argument can be a String literal constant, String named constant, or String variable. The message in the *text* argument should be concise but clear, and should be entered using sentence capitalization. You should avoid using the words "error," "warning," or "mistake" in the message, as these words imply that the user has done something wrong.

The *caption* argument specifies the text to display in the title bar of the message box, and typically is the application's name. Like the *text* argument, the *caption* argument can be a String literal constant, String named constant, or String variable. Unlike the *text* argument, however, the *caption* argument is entered using book title capitalization.

The *buttons* argument indicates the buttons to display in the message box and can be one of six different constants. For example, a *buttons* argument of `MessageBoxButtons.AbortRetryIgnore` displays the Abort, Retry, and Ignore buttons in the message box. A *buttons* argument of `MessageBoxButtons.OK`, on the other hand, displays only the OK button in the message box.

The *icon* argument specifies the icon to display in the message box and typically is one of the following constants: `MessageBoxIcon.Exclamation`, `MessageBoxIcon.Information`, or `MessageBoxIcon.Stop`. A message box's icon indicates the type of message being sent to the user. The `MessageBoxIcon.Exclamation` constant, for example, displays the Warning Message icon, which alerts the user to a condition or situation that requires him or her to make a decision before the application can proceed. The message to the user can be phrased as a question, such as "Save changes to the document?"

The `MessageBoxIcon.Information` constant displays the Information Message icon. The Information Message icon indicates that the message in the message box is for information only and does not require the user to make a decision. An example of an informational message is "The changes were saved." A message box with an Information Message icon should contain only an OK button; in other words, you always use `MessageBoxButtons.OK` for the *buttons* argument when using `MessageBoxIcon.Information` for the *icon* argument. The user acknowledges the informational message by clicking the OK button.

The `MessageBoxIcon.Stop` constant displays the Stop Message icon, which alerts the user to a serious problem that requires intervention or correction before the application can continue. You would use the Stop Message icon in a message box that alerts the user that the disk in the disk drive is write-protected.

The *defaultButton* argument in the `MessageBox.Show` method identifies the default button, which is the button that is selected automatically when the user presses the Enter key on his or her keyboard. To designate the first button in the message box as the default button, you either set the *defaultButton* argument to `MessageBoxDefaultButton.Button1`, or you simply omit the argument. To have the second or third button be the default button, you set the *defaultButton* argument to `MessageBoxDefaultButton.Button2` or `MessageBoxDefaultButton.Button3`, respectively. The default button should be the button that represents the user's most likely action, as long as that action is not destructive.

Study closely the two examples shown in Figure 4.26. In the first example, the `MessageBox.Show("Record deleted.", "Payroll", MessageBoxButtons.OK, MessageBoxIcon.Information)` instruction displays the informational message box shown in Figure 4.27. Similarly, the `MessageBox.Show("Delete this record?", "Payroll", MessageBoxButtons.YesNo, MessageBoxIcon.Exclamation, MessageBoxDefaultButton.Button2)` instruction in the second example displays the warning message box shown in Figure 4.28.

FIGURE 4.27   Message box displayed by the first example shown in Figure 4.26

Default button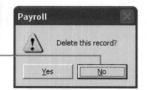

FIGURE 4.28   Message box displayed by the second example shown in Figure 4.26

After displaying the message box, the `MessageBox.Show` method waits for the user to choose one of the buttons displayed in the message box. It then closes the message box and returns an integer that indicates which button the user chose.

Sometimes you are not interested in the value returned by the `MessageBox.Show` method. This is the case when the message box is for informational purposes only, like the message box shown in Figure 4.27. Recall that the only button in an informational message box is the OK button. Many times, however, the button selected by the user determines the next task performed by an application. For example, selecting the Yes button in the message box shown in Figure 4.28 tells the application to delete the record; selecting the No button tells the application not to delete the record.

Figure 4.29 lists the integer values returned by the `MessageBox.Show` method; each integer is associated with a button that can appear in a message box. The figure also lists the constant values assigned to each integer, and the meaning of the integers and constants. Additionally, the figure contains three examples of using the value returned by the `MessageBox.Show` method.

HOW TO...

Use the Value Returned by the MessageBox.Show Method

Number	Constant	Meaning
1	DialogResult.OK	user chose the OK button
2	DialogResult.Cancel	user chose the Cancel button
3	DialogResult.Abort	user chose the Abort button
4	DialogResult.Retry	user chose the Retry button
5	DialogResult.Ignore	user chose the Ignore button
6	DialogResult.Yes	user chose the Yes button
7	DialogResult.No	user chose the No button

Examples
```
Dim intButton As Integer
intButton = MessageBox.Show("Delete this record?", _
            "Payroll", MessageBoxButtons.YesNo, _
            MessageBoxIcon.Exclamation, _
            MessageBoxDefaultButton.Button2)
If intButton = DialogResult.Yes Then
    instructions to delete the record
End If


If MessageBox.Show("Delete this record?", _
        "Payroll", MessageBoxButtons.YesNo, _
        MessageBoxIcon.Exclamation, _
        MessageBoxDefaultButton.Button2) _
        = DialogResult.Yes Then
        instructions to delete the record
End If


Dim intButton As Integer
intButton = MessageBox.Show("Play another game?", _
            "Math Monster", MessageBoxButtons.YesNo, _
            MessageBoxIcon.Exclamation)
If intButton = DialogResult.Yes Then
    instructions to start another game
Else  'DialogResult.No
    instructions to close the game application
End If
```

FIGURE 4.29   How to use the value returned by the MessageBox.Show method

As Figure 4.29 indicates, the MessageBox.Show method returns the integer 6 when the user selects the Yes button. The integer 6 is represented by the constant DialogResult.Yes. When referring to the MessageBox.Show method's return value in code, you should use the constants listed in Figure 4.29 rather than the integers, because the constants make the code easier to understand.

Look closely at the three examples shown in Figure 4.29. In the first example, the value returned by the `MessageBox.Show` method is assigned to an Integer variable named intButton. If the user selects the Yes button in the message box, the integer 6 is stored in the intButton variable; otherwise, the integer 7 is stored in the variable to indicate that the user selected the No button. The selection structure in the example compares the contents of the intButton variable to the constant `DialogResult.Yes`. If the intButton variable contains the integer 6, which is the value of the `DialogResult.Yes` constant, then the instructions to delete the record are processed; otherwise, the deletion instructions are skipped.

You do not have to store the value returned by the `MessageBox.Show` method in a variable, although doing so can make your code more readable. For instance, in the second example shown in Figure 4.29, the method's return value is not stored in a variable. Instead, the method appears in the selection structure's condition, where its return value is compared to the `DialogResult.Yes` constant.

The selection structure shown in the third example in Figure 4.29 performs one set of tasks when the user selects the Yes button, and another set of tasks when the user selects the No button. It is a good programming practice to document the Else portion of the selection structure as shown in the figure, because it makes it clear that the Else portion is processed only when the user selects the No button.

As you learned earlier, you use the selection structure when you want a procedure to make a decision and then select one of two paths—either the true path or the false path—based on the result of that decision. Both paths in a selection structure can include instructions that declare variables, perform calculations, and so on; both also can include other selection structures, called nested selection structures.

NESTED SELECTION STRUCTURES

When either a selection structure's true path or its false path contains another selection structure, the inner selection structure is referred to as a **nested selection structure**, because it is contained (nested) within the outer selection structure. You use a nested selection structure when more than one decision must be made before the appropriate action can be taken. For example, assume you want to create a procedure that determines voter eligibility and displays one of three messages. The messages and the criteria for displaying each message are shown in the following chart:

Message	Criteria
"You are too young to vote."	person is younger than 18 years old
"You can vote."	person is at least 18 years old and is registered to vote
"You need to register before you can vote."	person is at least 18 years old but is not registered to vote

As the chart indicates, the person's age and voter registration status determine the appropriate message to display. If the person is younger than 18 years old, the procedure should display the message "You are too young to vote." However, if the person is at least 18 years old, the procedure should display one of two different messages. The correct message to display is determined by the person's voter registration status. If the person is registered, then the appropriate message is "You can vote."; otherwise, it is "You need to register before you can vote." Notice that determining the person's voter registration status is important only *after* his or her age is determined. You can think of the decision regarding the age as being the **primary decision**, and the decision regarding the registration status as being the **secondary decision**, because whether the registration decision needs to be made depends on the result of the age decision. The primary decision is always made by the outer selection structure, while the secondary decision is always made by the inner (nested) selection structure.

Figure 4.30 shows the pseudocode and Visual Basic .NET code for the voter eligibility procedure, and Figure 4.31 shows the corresponding flowchart. In both figures, the outer selection structure determines the age (the primary decision), and the nested selection structure determines the voter registration status (the secondary decision). Notice that the nested selection structure appears in the outer selection structure's true path in both figures.

TIP

The lines connecting the selection structures in the pseudocode and code shown in Figure 4.30 are included in the figure to help you see which clauses are related to each other.

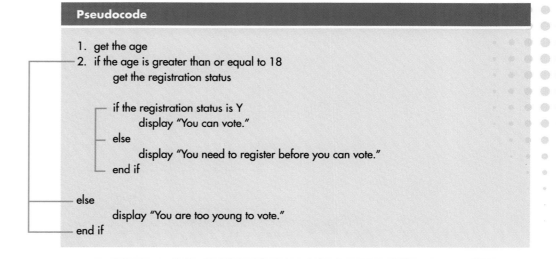

Pseudocode

1. get the age
2. if the age is greater than or equal to 18
       get the registration status

       if the registration status is Y
            display "You can vote."
       else
            display "You need to register before you can vote."
       end if

   else
       display "You are too young to vote."
   end if

Visual Basic .NET code

```
Dim intAge As Integer, strStatus As String
intAge = Convert.ToInt32(Me.txtAge.Text)
If intAge >= 18 Then
    strStatus = Me.txtStatus.Text.ToUpper()

    If strStatus = "Y" Then
        Me.lblMessage.Text = "You can vote."
    Else
        Me.lblMessage.Text = "You need to register before
        you can vote."
    End If

Else
    Me.lblMessage.Text = "You are too young to vote."
End If
```

FIGURE 4.30 Pseudocode and Visual Basic .NET code showing the nested selection structure in the true path

Flowchart

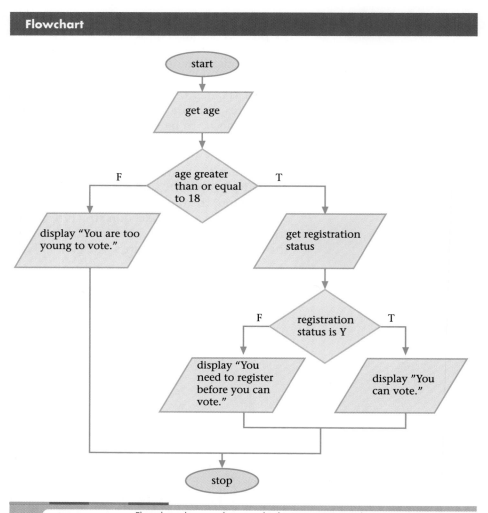

FIGURE 4.31   Flowchart showing the nested selection structure in the true path

Look closely at the code shown in Figure 4.30. The code declares two variables named intAge and strStatus. It then converts the contents of the txtAge control to an integer and assigns the result to the intAge variable. The condition in the outer selection structure checks whether the age stored in the intAge variable is greater than or equal to 18. If the condition is false, it means that the person is not old enough to vote. In that case, only one message—the "You are too young to vote." message—is appropriate. After the message is displayed, both the outer selection structure and the procedure end.

If the outer selection structure's condition is true, on the other hand, it means that the person *is* old enough to vote. Before displaying the appropriate message, the instructions in the outer selection structure's true path first convert the contents of the txtStatus control to uppercase, and then assign the result to the strStatus variable. A nested selection structure is used to determine whether the person is registered. If he or she is registered, the instruction in the nested selection structure's true path displays the message "You can vote."; otherwise, the instruction in the nested selection structure's false path displays the message "You need to register before you can vote." After the appropriate message is displayed, both selection structures and the procedure end. Notice that the nested selection structure in this procedure is processed only when the outer selection structure's condition is true.

Figures 4.32 and 4.33 show the pseudocode, Visual Basic .NET code, and flowchart for a different version of the voter eligibility procedure. As in the previous version, the outer selection structure in this version determines the age (the primary decision), and the nested selection structure determines the voter registration status (the secondary decision). In this version of the procedure, however, the nested selection structure appears in the false path of the outer selection structure.

Pseudocode

1. get the age
2. if the age is less than 18
       display "You are too young to vote."
   else
       get the registration status

       if the registration status is Y
            display "You can vote."
       else
            display "You need to register before you can vote."
       end if

   end if

Visual Basic .NET code

```
Dim intAge As Integer, strStatus As String
intAge = Convert.ToInt32(Me.txtAge.Text)
If intAge < 18 Then
    Me.lblMessage.Text = "You are too young to vote."
Else
    strStatus = Me.txtStatus.Text.ToUpper()

    If strStatus = "Y" Then
         Me.lblMessage.Text = "You can vote."
    Else
         Me.lblMessage.Text = "You need to register before
         you can vote."
    End If

End If
```

FIGURE 4.32   Pseudocode and Visual Basic .NET code showing the nested selection structure in the false path

Flowchart

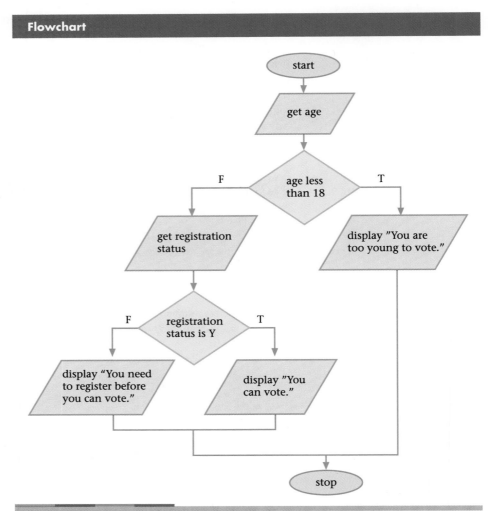

FIGURE 4.33   Flowchart showing the nested selection structure in the false path

Like the version shown earlier, this version of the voter eligibility procedure first declares the intAge and strStatus variables, and then assigns the contents of the txtAge control (converted to an integer) to the intAge variable. However, rather than checking whether the age stored in the intAge variable is greater than or equal to 18, the outer selection structure in this version checks whether the age is less than 18. If the condition is true, the instruction in the outer selection structure's true path displays the message "You are too young to vote." If the condition is false, the instructions in the outer selection structure's false path assign the contents of the txtStatus control (converted to uppercase) to the strStatus variable, and then use a nested selection structure to determine whether the person is registered. If the person is registered, the instruction in the nested selection structure's true path displays the message "You can vote."; otherwise, the instruction in the nested selection structure's false path displays the message "You need to register before you can vote." Unlike in the previous version, the nested selection structure in this version of the procedure is processed only when the outer selection structure's condition is false.

Notice that both versions of the voter eligibility procedure produce the same results. Neither version is better than the other; each simply represents a different way of solving the same problem.

In addition to the If and If/Else forms of the selection structure, Visual Basic .NET also provides the If/ElseIf/Else and Case forms. The If/ElseIf/Else and Case forms of the selection structure are commonly referred to as **extended selection structures** or **multiple-path selection structures**.

THE IF/ELSEIF/ELSE SELECTION STRUCTURE

At times, you may need to create a selection structure that can choose from several alternatives. For example, assume you are asked to create a procedure that displays a message based on a letter grade that the user enters. The valid letter grades and their corresponding messages are shown in the following chart.

Letter grade	Message
A	Excellent
B	Above Average
C	Average
D	Below Average
F	Below Average

As the chart indicates, when the letter grade is an A, the procedure should display the message "Excellent." When the letter grade is a B, the procedure should display the message "Above Average," and so on. Figure 4.34 shows two versions of the Visual Basic .NET code for the grade procedure. The first version uses nested If/Else structures to display the appropriate message, while the second version uses the If/ElseIf/Else structure. As you do with the If/Else selection structure, you use the If...Then...Else statement to code the If/ElseIf/Else selection structure.

Version 1 – nested If/Else structures	Version 2 – If/ElseIf/Else structure

```
Dim strGrade As String
strGrade = Me.txtGrade.Text.ToUpper()

If strGrade = "A" Then
  Me.lblMsg.Text = "Excellent"
Else
  If strGrade = "B" Then
    Me.lblMsg.Text = "Above Average"
  Else
    If strGrade = "C" Then
      Me.lblMsg.Text = "Average"
    Else
      If strGrade = "D" OrElse _
          strGrade = "F" Then
        Me.lblMsg.Text = "Below Average"
      Else
        Me.lblMsg.Text = "Error"
      End If
    End If
  End If
End If
```

```
Dim strGrade As String
strGrade = Me.txtGrade.Text.ToUpper()

If strGrade = "A" Then
    Me.lblMsg.Text = "Excellent"
ElseIf strGrade = "B" Then
    Me.lblMsg.Text = "Above Average"
ElseIf strGrade = "C" Then
    Me.lblMsg.Text = "Average"
ElseIf strGrade = "D" OrElse _
        strGrade = "F" Then
    Me.lblMsg.Text = "Below Average"
Else
    Me.lblMsg.Text = "Error"
End If
```

You need only one End If statement to mark the end of the entire If/ElseIf/Else selection structure

You need four End If statements to mark the end of the entire If/Else selection structure

FIGURE 4.34   Two versions of the Visual Basic .NET code for the grade procedure

Although you can write the grade procedure using either nested If/Else selection structures (as shown in Version 1) or the If/ElseIf/Else selection structure (as shown in Version 2), the **If/ElseIf/Else structure** provides a much more convenient way of writing a multiple-path selection structure.

Next, you learn about the Case form of the selection structure.

THE CASE SELECTION STRUCTURE

It is often simpler and clearer to use the Case form of the selection structure, rather than the If/ElseIf/Else form, in situations where the selection structure has many paths from which to choose. Figure 4.35 shows the pseudocode and flowchart for the grade procedure, using the Case selection structure.

Pseudocode

1. get grade
2. grade value:

A	display "Excellent"
B	display "Above Average"
C	display "Average"
D, F	display "Below Average"
Other	display "Error"

Flowchart

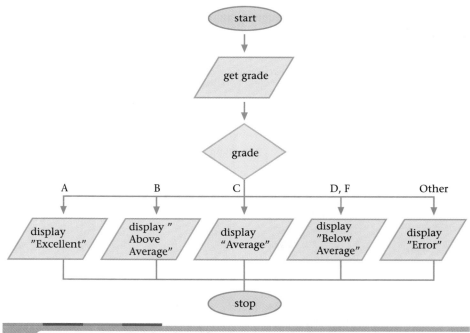

FIGURE 4.35   Pseudocode and flowchart showing the Case selection structure

Notice that the flowchart symbol for the Case form of the selection structure is the same as the flowchart symbol for the If, If/Else, and If/ElseIf/Else forms—a diamond. However, unlike the diamonds used in the other selection structures, the Case diamond does not contain a condition requiring a true or false answer. Instead, the Case diamond contains an expression—in this case, grade—whose value determines which path is chosen.

Like the If, If/Else, and If/ElseIf/Else diamond, the Case diamond has one flowline leading into the symbol. Unlike the other diamonds, however, the Case diamond has many flowlines leading out of the symbol. Each flowline represents a possible path for the selection structure. The flowlines must be marked appropriately, indicating which value(s) are necessary for each path to be chosen.

Figure 4.36 shows the syntax of the **Select Case statement**, which is used to code the Case selection structure in Visual Basic .NET. It also shows how to use the Select Case statement to code the grade procedure.

HOW TO...

Use the Select Case Statement

Syntax
Select Case *selectorExpression*
      Case *expressionList1*
           [instructions for the first Case]
      [**Case** *expressionList2*
           [instructions for the second Case]]
      [**Case** *expressionListn*
           [instructions for the nth case]]
      [**Case Else**
           [instructions for when the selectorExpression does not match any of the expressionLists]]
End Select

Example
```
Dim strGrade As String
strGrade = Me.txtGrade.Text.ToUpper()

Select Case strGrade
    Case "A"
        Me.lblMsg.Text = "Excellent"
    Case "B"
        Me.lblMsg.Text = "Above Average"
    Case "C"
        Me.lblMsg.Text = "Average"
    Case "D", "F"
        Me.lblMsg.Text = "Below Average"
    Case Else
        Me.lblMsg.Text = "Error"
End Select
```

FIGURE 4.36 How to use the Select Case statement

TIP

It is customary to indent each Case clause, as well as the instructions within each Case clause, as shown in Figure 4.29.

The Select Case statement begins with the Select Case clause and ends with the two words End Select. Between the Select Case clause and the End Select are the individual Case clauses. Each Case clause represents a different path that the selection structure can follow. You can have as many Case clauses as necessary in a Select Case statement. If the Select Case statement includes a Case Else clause, the Case Else clause must be the last clause in the statement.

Notice that the Select Case clause must include a *selectorExpression*. The *selectorExpression* can contain any combination of variables, constants, methods, operators, and properties. In the grade procedure shown in Figure 4.36, the *selectorExpression* is a String variable named strGrade.

Each of the individual Case clauses, except the Case Else clause, must contain an *expressionList*, which can include one or more expressions. To include more than one expression in an *expressionList*, you simply separate each expression with a comma, as in the *expressionList* Case "D", "F". The data type of the expressions must be compatible with the data type of the *selectorExpression*. In other words, if the *selectorExpression* is numeric, the expressions in the Case clauses should be numeric. Likewise, if the *selectorExpression* is a string, the expressions should be strings. In the grade procedure shown in Figure 4.36, the *selectorExpression* (strGrade) is a string, and so are the expressions—"A", "B", "C", "D", and "F"—as the quotation marks indicate.

When processing the Select Case statement, the computer first compares the value of the *selectorExpression* with the values listed in *expressionList1*. If a match is found, the computer processes the instructions for the first Case, stopping when it reaches either another Case clause (including the Case Else clause) or the End Select (which marks the end of the selection structure). It then skips to the instruction following the End Select. If a match is not found in *expressionList1*, the computer skips to the second Case clause, where it compares the *selectorExpression* with the values listed in *expressionList2*. If a match is found, the computer processes the instructions for the second Case clause and then skips to the instruction following the End Select. If a match is not found, the computer skips to the third Case clause, and so on. If the *selectorExpression* does not match any of the values listed in any of the *expressionLists*, the computer then processes the instructions listed in the Case Else clause or, if there is no Case Else clause, it processes the instruction following the End Select. Keep in mind that if the *selectorExpression* matches a value in more than one Case clause, only the instructions in the first match are processed.

You also can specify a range of values in an *expressionList*—such as the values 1 through 4, and values greater than 10. You do so using the keywords To and Is.

TIP

The *selectorExpression* needs to match only one of the expressions listed in an *expressionList*.

Using To and Is in an ExpressionList

You can use either the keyword To or the keyword Is to specify a range of values in a Case clause's *expressionList*. You use the To keyword when you know both the upper and lower bounds of the range, and you use the Is keyword when you know only one end of the range—either the upper or lower end. For example, assume that the price of an item sold by ABC Corporation depends on the number of items ordered, as shown in the following chart:

Number of items ordered	Price per item
1 – 5	$ 25
6 – 10	$ 23
More than 10	$ 20

TIP

Because intNumOrdered is an Integer variable, you also can write the third Case clause shown in Figure 4.37 as **Case Is >= 11**.

TIP

If you neglect to type the keyword **Is** in an expression, the Code Editor types it in for you. In other words, if you enter **Case > 10**, the Code Editor changes the clause to **Case Is > 10**.

TIP

When you use the **To** keyword, the value preceding the **To** always must be less than the value following the **To**; in other words, **10 To 6** is not a correct expression. Visual Basic .NET will not display an error message if the value preceding the **To** is greater than the value following the **To**. Instead, the Select Case statement simply will not give the correct results. This is another reason why it always is important to test your code thoroughly.

Figure 4.37 shows the Visual Basic .NET code for a procedure that assigns the appropriate price per item to the intItemPrice variable, and then displays the price in a label control.

Visual Basic .NET code

```
Dim intNumOrdered, intItemPrice As Integer
intNumOrdered = Convert.ToInt32(Me.txtNumOrdered.Text)
Select Case intNumOrdered
    Case 1 To 5
        intItemPrice = 25
    Case 6 To 10
        intItemPrice = 23
    Case Is > 10
        intItemPrice = 20
    Case Else
        'processed when the user enters zero or a negative number
        intItemPrice = 0
End Select
Me.lblPrice.Text = intItemPrice.ToString("C0")
```

FIGURE 4.37   Example of using the **To** and **Is** keywords in a Select Case statement

According to the ABC Corporation's price chart, the price for one to five items is $25 each. You could, therefore, have written the first **Case** clause as **Case 1, 2, 3, 4, 5**. However, a more convenient way of writing that range of numbers is to use the keyword **To** in the **Case** clause, but you must follow this syntax to do so: **Case** *smallest value in the range* **To** *largest value in the range*. The expression **1 To 5** in the first **Case** clause, for example, specifies the range of numbers from one to five, inclusive. The expression **6 To 10** in the second **Case** clause specifies the range of numbers from six to 10, inclusive. Notice that both **Case** clauses state both the lower (1 and 6) and upper (5 and 10) ends of each range.

The third **Case** clause in Figure 4.37, **Case Is > 10**, contains the **Is** keyword rather than the **To** keyword. Recall that you use the **Is** keyword when you know only one end of the range of values—either the upper or lower end. In this case, for example, you know only the lower end of the range, 10. You always use the **Is** keyword in combination with one of the following comparison (relational) operators: =, <, <=, >, >=, <>. The **Case Is > 10** clause, for example, specifies all numbers that are greater than the number 10.

The **Case Else** clause shown in Figure 4.37 is processed only when the intNumOrdered variable contains a value that is not included in any of the previous **Case** clauses—namely, a zero or a negative number.

PROGRAMMING EXAMPLE

Fat Calculator

Create a Visual Basic .NET application that allows the user to enter the total number of calories and grams of fat contained in a specific food. The application should calculate and display two values: the food's fat calories (the number of calories attributed to fat) and its fat percentage (the ratio of the food's fat calories to its total calories). Additionally, the application should display the message "This food is high in fat." if the fat percentage is over 30%; otherwise, it should display the message "This food is not high in fat." Name the solution Fat Calculator Solution. Name the project Fat Calculator Project. Name the form file Fat Calculator Form.vb. Save the application in the VbDotNet\Chap04 folder.

TOE Chart:

Task	Object	Event
1. Calculate the fat calories 2. Calculate the fat percentage 3. Display the fat calories and fat percentage in lblFatCals and lblFatPercent 4. Display (in a message box) either the "This food is high in fat." message or the "This food is not high in fat." message 5. Display (in a message box) the message "The calories and fat grams must be numbers." when the Text properties of the txtCalories and txtFatGrams controls are not numeric	btnCalc	Click
End the application	btnExit	Click
Display the fat calories (from btnCalc)	lblFatCals	None
Display the fat percentage (from btnCalc)	lblFatPercent	None
Get and display the calories and fat grams	txtCalories, txtFatGrams	None

FIGURE 4.38

User Interface:

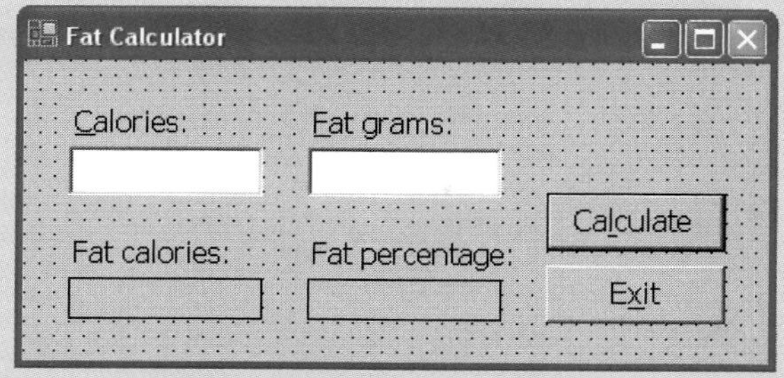

FIGURE 4.39

Objects, Properties, and Settings

Object	Property	Setting
frmFatCalc	Name	frmFatCalc (be sure to change the startup form to this name)
	AcceptButton	btnCalc
	Font	Tahoma, 12 point (be sure to change the form's font before adding the controls)
	Size	408, 200
	StartPosition	CenterScreen
	Text	Fat Calculator
Label1	AutoSize	True
	Text	&Calories:
Label2	AutoSize	True
	Text	&Fat grams:
Label3	AutoSize	True
	Text	Fat calories:
Label4	AutoSize	True
	Text	Fat percentage:
lblFatCals	Name	lblFatCals
	BorderStyle	FixedSingle
	Text	(empty)
	TextAlign	MiddleCenter
lblFatPercent	Name	lblFatPercent
	BorderStyle	FixedSingle
	Text	(empty)
	TextAlign	MiddleCenter

(Table is continued on next page)

Object	Property	Setting
txtFatGrams	Name	txtFatGrams
	Text	(empty)
txtCalories	Name	txtCalories
	Text	(empty)
btnCalc	Name	btnCalc
	Text	Ca&lculate
btnExit	Name	btnExit
	Text	E&xit

FIGURE 4.40

Tab Order:

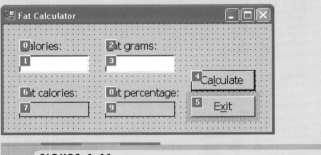

FIGURE 4.41

Pseudocode:

btnExit Click event procedure

1. close application

btnCalc Click event procedure

1. if the txtCalories and txtFatGrams controls contain numbers
        assign the numbers to variables
        calculate the fat calories by multiplying the total calories by 9
        calculate the fat percentage by dividing the fat calories by the total calories
        display the fat calories and fat percentage in lblFatCals and lblFatPercent
        if the fat percentage is over 30%
                display the "This food is high in fat." message in a message box
                    else
                display the "This food is not high in fat." message in a message box
                    end if
   else
        display the "The calories and fat grams must be numbers." message in a message box
     end if

Code:

```
'Project name:          Fat Calculator Project
'Project purpose:       The project allows the user to enter the number of
'                       calories and grams of fat contained in a specific food.
'                       It then calculates the food's fat calories and its
'                       fat percentage.
'Created/revised by:    Diane Zak on 2/1/2005

Option Explicit On
Option Strict On

Public Class frmFatCalc
    Inherits System.Windows.Forms.Form

[Windows Form Designer generated code]

    Private Sub btnExit_Click(ByVal sender As Object, ByVal e As System.EventArgs)
Handles btnExit.Click
        'ends the application
        Me.Close()

    End Sub

    Private Sub btnCalc_Click(ByVal sender As Object, ByVal e As System.EventArgs)
Handles btnCalc.Click
        'calculates a food's fat calories and its fat percentage

        'declare variables
        Dim intCalories, intFatGrams, intFatCalories As Integer
        Dim decFatPercent As Decimal, strMessage As String

        'determine whether the text boxes contain numbers
        If IsNumeric(Me.txtCalories.Text) AndAlso IsNumeric(Me.txtFatGrams.Text) Then
            'assign input values to variables
            intCalories = Convert.ToInt32(Me.txtCalories.Text)
            intFatGrams = Convert.ToInt32(Me.txtFatGrams.Text)

            'calculate fat calories and fat percentage
            intFatCalories = intFatGrams * 9
            decFatPercent = Convert.ToDecimal(intFatCalories) / _
                Convert.ToDecimal(intCalories)

            'display fat calories and fat percentage
            Me.lblFatCals.Text = Convert.ToString(intFatCalories)
            Me.lblFatPercent.Text = decFatPercent.ToString("P2")
```

(Table is continued on next page)

```
        'assign appropriate message to variable
        If decFatPercent > 0.3D Then
            strMessage = "This food is high in fat."
        Else
            strMessage = "This food is not high in fat."
        End If

        'display the message
        MessageBox.Show(strMessage, "Fat Calculator", _
            MessageBoxButtons.OK, MessageBoxIcon.Information, _
            MessageBoxDefaultButton.Button1)

    Else     'one or both of the text boxes does not contain a number
        MessageBox.Show("The calories and fat grams must be numbers.", _
            "Fat Calculator", MessageBoxButtons.OK, MessageBoxIcon.Information, _
            MessageBoxDefaultButton.Button1)
    End If

    End Sub
End Class
```

FIGURE 4.42

Quick Review

- The selection structure allows a program to make a decision or comparison and then select one of two paths, depending on the result of that decision or comparison.
- Visual Basic .NET provides four forms of the selection structure: If, If/Else, If/ElseIf/Else, and Case.
- In a flowchart, you use the diamond, called the selection/repetition symbol, to represent the selection structure's condition.
- In Visual Basic .NET, you use the If...Then...Else statement to code the If, If/Else, and If/ElseIf/Else forms of the selection structure.
- All expressions containing a comparison operator will result in an answer of either True or False only.
- Comparison operators do not have an order of precedence in Visual Basic .NET. Rather, they are evaluated from left to right in an expression, and are evaluated after any arithmetic operators in the expression.
- Variables declared in either the true or false path of a selection structure have block scope.
- You use the line continuation character to break up a long instruction into two or more physical lines in the Code Editor window.
- You connect (or link) strings together using the concatenation operator.
- The `ControlChars.NewLine` constant advances the insertion point to the next line in a control.
- String comparisons in Visual Basic .NET are case-sensitive. When comparing strings, you can use either the `ToUpper` method or the `ToLower` method to temporarily convert the strings to uppercase or lowercase, respectively.

- You use logical operators to create compound conditions. All expressions containing a logical operator will result in an answer of either True or False only.
- Like arithmetic operators, logical operators have an order of precedence and are evaluated after any arithmetic and comparison operators in an expression.
- The Convert.ToInt32 method cannot convert a letter, a special character (such as a dollar sign or a comma), or the contents of an empty text box to an integer.
- You can use the IsNumeric function to verify that an expression can be converted to a number.
- The MessageBox.Show method allows you to communicate with the user by displaying a message box.
- The MessageBox.Show method returns an integer that indicates which message box button the user chose. You should use the constant associated with the button when referring to the integer in code.
- Use sentence capitalization for the *text* argument in the `MessageBox.Show` method, but book title capitalization for the *caption* argument. The name of the application typically appears in the *caption* argument.
- Avoid using the words "error," "warning," or "mistake" in the `MessageBox.Show` method's message, as these words imply that the user has done something wrong.
- Display the Warning Message icon in a message box that alerts the user that he or she must make a decision before the application can continue. You can phrase the message as a question.
- Display the Information Message icon in a message box that displays an informational message along with an OK button only.
- Display the Stop Message icon when you want to alert the user of a serious problem that must be corrected before the application can continue.
- The default button in the message box should be the one that represents the user's most likely action, as long as that action is not destructive.
- You can nest selection structures, which means that you can place one selection structure in either the true or false path of another selection structure.
- The primary decision is always made by the outer selection structure. The secondary decision is always made by the inner (nested) selection structure.
- Typically, you use the If/ElseIf/Else and Case forms of the selection structure when the structure must choose from several alternatives.
- In Visual Basic .NET, you use the Select Case statement to code the Case form of the selection structure.
- You use the keyword `To` in a `Case` clause's *expressionList* when you know both the upper and lower bounds of the range you want to specify. You use the keyword `Is` when you know only one end of the range.

Key Terms

The **selection structure**, also called the **decision structure**, allows a program to make a decision or comparison and then select the appropriate path, depending on the result of that decision or comparison.

The **condition** in a selection structure specifies the decision you are making and must be phrased so that it results in either a true or false answer only.

An **If selection structure** contains only one set of instructions, which are processed when the condition is true.

An **If/Else selection structure** contains two sets of instructions: one set is processed when the condition is true and the other set is processed when the condition is false.

The **true path** in a selection structure contains the instructions that are processed when the condition evaluates to True.

The **false path** in a selection structure contains the instructions that are processed when the condition evaluates to False.

The diamond in a flowchart is called the **selection/repetition** symbol.

You use the **If...Then...Else statement** to code the If, If/Else, and If/ElseIf/Else forms of the selection structure in Visual Basic .NET.

The **Else clause** in an If...Then...Else statement contains the instructions that are processed when the condition evaluates to False.

A **statement block** is a set of statements terminated by an Else, End If, Loop, or Next statement.

Comparison operators, also called **relational operators**, allow you to compare values in a selection structure's condition.

A variable that has **block scope** can be used only within the statement block in which it is declared.

The **line continuation character** is a space followed by an underscore. It is used to enter a long instruction on two or more physical lines in the Code Editor window.

The **concatenation operator** is the ampersand (&). It is used to concatenate strings together.

The **ControlChars.NewLine constant** advances the insertion point to the next line in a control.

The **ToUpper method** temporarily converts a string to uppercase.

The **ToLower method** temporarily converts a string to lowercase.

Logical operators, sometimes referred to as **Boolean operators**, allow you to combine two or more *conditions* into one compound *condition*.

Truth tables summarize how Visual Basic .NET evaluates the logical operators in an expression.

The AndAlso and OrElse logical operators perform **short-circuit evaluation**, which means that they do not always evaluate the second condition in a compound condition.

Data validation is the process of verifying that a program's input data is within the expected range.

A **function** is a predefined procedure that performs a specific task and then returns a value after completing the task.

The **IsNumeric function** checks if an *expression* can be converted to a number, and then returns either the Boolean value True or the Boolean value False.

The **MessageBox.Show method** displays a message box that contains text, one or more buttons, and an icon.

In a nested selection structure, the **primary decision** is always made by the outer selection structure. The **secondary decision**, which depends on the result of the primary decision, is always made by the inner (nested) selection structure.

The **If/ElseIf/Else** and **Case** forms of the selection structure are commonly referred to as **extended selection structures** or **multiple-path selection structures**, because they have several alternatives from which to choose.

In Visual Basic .NET, you use the **Select Case statement** to code the Case selection structure.

Review Questions

1. Which of the following is a valid condition for an If...Then...Else statement?
   a. `Convert.ToInt32(Me.lblPrice.Text) > 0 AndAlso < 10`
   b. `decSales > 500D OrElse < 800D`
   c. `intNum > 100 AndAlso intNum <= 1000`
   d. `strState.ToUpper() = "Alaska" OrElse strState.ToUpper() = "Hawaii"`

2. Assume you want to compare the string contained in the Text property of the txtName control with the name Bob. Which of the following conditions should you use in the If...Then...Else statement? (Be sure the condition will handle Bob, BOB, bob, and so on.)
   a. `Me.txtName.Text = ToUpper("BOB")`
   b. `Me.txtName.Text.ToUpper() = "Bob"`
   c. `Me.txtName.Text.ToUpper() = "BOB"`
   d. `ToUpper(Me.txtName.Text) = "BOB"`

3. The expression 3 > 6 AndAlso 7 > 4 evaluates to _____.
   a. True
   b. False

4. The expression 4 > 6 OrElse 10 < 2 * 6 evaluates to _____.
   a. True
   b. False

5. The expression 7 >= 3 + 4 Or 6 < 4 And 2 < 5 evaluates to _____.
   a. True
   b. False

Use the following code to answer Questions 6 through 9.

```
If intId = 1 Then
        Me.lblName.Text = "Janet"
ElseIf intId = 2 OrElse intId = 3 Then
        Me.lblName.Text = "Paul"
ElseIf intId = 4 Then
        Me.lblName.Text = "Jerry"
Else
        Me.lblName.Text = "Sue"
End If
```

6. What will the preceding code display if the intId variable contains the number 2?
   a. Janet
   b. Jerry
   c. Paul
   d. Sue

7. What will the preceding code display if the intId variable contains the number 4?
   a. Janet
   b. Jerry
   c. Paul
   d. Sue

8. What will the preceding code display if the intId variable contains the number 3?
   a. Janet
   b. Jerry
   c. Paul
   d. Sue

9. What will the preceding code display if the intId variable contains the number 8?
   a. Janet
   b. Jerry
   c. Paul
   d. Sue

10. A nested selection structure can appear in _____ of another selection structure.
    a. only the true path
    b. only the false path
    c. either the true path or the false path

11. If the *selectorExpression* used in the Select Case statement is an Integer variable named intCode, which of the following Case clauses is valid?
    a. `Case Is > 7`
    b. `Case 3, 5`
    c. `Case 1 To 4`
    d. All of the above.

Use the following Select Case statement to answer Questions 12 through 14.

```
Select Case intId
      Case 1
            Me.lblName.Text = "Janet"
      Case 2 To 4
            Me.lblName.Text = "Paul"
      Case 5, 7
            Me.lblName.Text = "Jerry"
      Case Else
            Me.lblName.Text = "Sue"
End Select
```

12. What will the preceding Select Case statement display if the intId variable contains the number 2?
    a. Janet
    b. Jerry
    c. Paul
    d. Sue

13. What will the preceding Select Case statement display if the intId variable contains the number 3?
    a. Janet
    b. Jerry
    c. Paul
    d. Sue

14. What will the preceding Select Case statement display if the intId variable contains the number 6?
    a. Janet
    b. Jerry
    c. Paul
    d. Sue

15. Which of the following constants can be used to advance the insertion point to the next line in the lblAnswer control?
    a. `Advance.NewLine`
    b. `ControlChars.NewLine`
    c. `NewLine.Advance`
    d. None of the above.

16. Assuming the strPrice variable contains $5.65, what will the `IsNumeric(strPrice)` function return?
    a. True
    b. False
    c. 5.65
    d. an error message

17. If the user clicks the OK button in a message box displayed by the `MessageBox.Show` method, the message box returns the number 1, which is equivalent to which constant?
    a. `DialogResult.OK`
    b. `DialogResult.OKButton`
    c. `MessageBox.OK`
    d. `MessageResult.OK`

18. Which of the following is the line continuation character?
    a. a space followed by an ampersand
    b. a space followed by an asterisk
    c. a space followed by a hyphen
    d. None of the above.

19. Assume the strCity variable contains the string "Boston" and the strState variable contains the string "MA". Which of the following will display the string "Boston, MA" (the city, a comma, a space, and the state) in the lblAddress control?
    a. `Me.lblAddress.Text = "strCity" & ", " & "strState"`
    b. `Me.lblAddress.Text = strCity $ ", " $ strState`
    c. `Me.lblAddress.Text = strCity & ", " & strState`
    d. `Me.lblAddress.Text = "strCity," & "strState"`

20. Assume that a Select Case statement's *selectorExpression* is an Integer variable. Which of the following `Case` clauses tells the computer to process the instructions when the Integer variable contains one of the following numbers: 1, 2, 3, 4, or 5?
    a. `Case 1, 2, 3, 4, And 5`
    b. `Case 1 To 5`
    c. `Case 5 To 1`
    d. Both a and b.

Exercises

1. The six logical operators are listed below. Indicate their order of precedence by placing a number (1, 2, and so on) on the line to the left of the operator. (If two or more operators have the same precedence, assign the same number to each.)

    _____ Xor
    _____ And
    _____ Not
    _____ Or
    _____ AndAlso
    _____ OrElse

2. An expression can contain arithmetic, comparison, and logical operators. Indicate the order of precedence for the three types of operators by placing a number (1, 2, or 3) on the line to the left of the operator type.

    _____ Arithmetic
    _____ Logical
    _____ Comparison

Use the following selection structure to answer Questions 3 and 4:

```
If intNumber <= 100 Then
    intNumber = intNumber * 2
Else
    intNumber = intNumber * 3
End If
```

3. Assume the intNumber variable contains the number 90. What value will be in the intNumber variable after the above selection structure is processed?

4. Assume the intNumber variable contains the number 1000. What value will be in the intNumber variable after the above selection structure is processed?

5. Assume that you need to create a procedure that displays the appropriate fee to charge a golfer. The fee is based on the following fee schedule:

Fee	Criteria
0	Club members
15	Non-members golfing on Monday through Thursday
25	Non-members golfing on Friday through Sunday

    In this procedure, which is the primary decision and which is the secondary decision? Why?

6. Draw the flowchart that corresponds to the following pseudocode.

    if hours are greater than 40
            display "Overtime pay"
    else
            display "Regular pay"
    end if

7. Write an If...Then...Else statement that displays the string "Pontiac" in the lblCarMake control if the txtCar control contains the string "Grand Am" (in any case).

8. Write an If...Then...Else statement that displays the string "Entry error" in the lblMessage control if the intUnits variable contains a number that is less than 0; otherwise, display the string "Valid Number".

9. Write an If...Then...Else statement that displays the string "Reorder" in the lblMessage control if the decPrice variable contains a number that is less than 10; otherwise, display the string "OK".

10. Write an If...Then...Else statement that assigns the number 10 to the decBonus variable if the decSales variable contains a number that is less than or equal to $250; otherwise, assign the number 15.

11. Write an If...Then...Else statement that displays the number 25 in the lblShipping control if the strState variable contains the string "Hawaii" (in any case); otherwise, display the number 50.

12. Assume you want to calculate a 3% sales tax if the strState variable contains the string "Colorado" (in any case); otherwise, you want to calculate a 4% sales tax. You can calculate the sales tax by multiplying the tax rate by the contents of the decSales variable. Display the sales tax in the lblSalesTax control. Draw the flowchart, then write the Visual Basic .NET code.

13. Assume you want to calculate an employee's gross pay. Employees working more than 40 hours should receive overtime pay (time and one-half) for the hours over 40. Use the variables decHours, decRate, and decGross. Display the contents of the decGross variable in the lblGross control. Write the pseudocode, then write the Visual Basic .NET code.

14. Write the If...Then...Else statement that displays the string "Dog" in the lblAnimal control if the strAnimal variable contains the letter "D" (in any case); otherwise, display the string "Cat". Draw the flowchart, then write the Visual Basic .NET code.

15. Assume you want to calculate a 10% discount on desks sold to customers in Colorado. Use the variables strItem, strState, decSales, and decDiscount. Format the discount using the "C2" format and display it in the lblDiscount control. Write the pseudocode, then write the Visual Basic .NET code.

16. Assume you want to calculate a 2% price increase on all red shirts, but a 1% price increase on all other items. In addition to calculating the price increase, also calculate the new price. You can use the variables strColor, strItem, decOrigPrice, decIncrease, and decNewPrice. Format the original price, price increase, and new price using the "N2" format. Display the original price, price increase, and new price in the lblOriginal, lblIncrease, and lblNew controls, respectively. Write the Visual Basic .NET code.

17. Write the Visual Basic .NET code that swaps the values stored in the decMarySales and decJeffSales variables, but only if the value stored in the decMarySales variable is less than the value stored in the decJeffSales variable.

18. Write the Visual Basic .NET code that displays the message "Highest honors" if a student's test score is 90 or above. If the test score is 70 through 89, display the message "Good job". For all other test scores, display the message "Retake the test". Use the If/ElseIf/Else selection structure. The test score is stored in the intScore variable. Display the appropriate message in the lblMsg control.

19. Write the Visual Basic .NET code that compares the contents of the intQuantity variable to the number 10. If the intQuantity variable contains a number that is equal to 10, display the string "Equal" in the lblMsg control. If the intQuantity variable contains a number that is greater than 10, display the string "Over 10". If the intQuantity variable contains a number that is less than 10, display the string "Not over 10". Use the If/ElseIf/Else selection structure.

20. Write the Visual Basic .NET code that corresponds to the flowchart shown in Figure 4.43. Store the salesperson's code, which is entered in the txtCode control, in an Integer variable named intCode. Store the sales amount, which is entered in the txtSales control, in a Decimal variable named decSales. Display the result of the calculation, or the error message, in the lblMsg control.

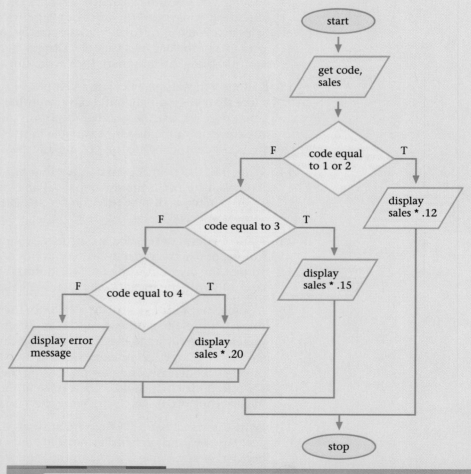

FIGURE 4.43

21. Write the Visual Basic .NET code that corresponds to the flowchart shown in Figure 4.44. Store the salesperson's code, which is entered in the txtCode control, in an Integer variable named intCode. Store the sales amount, which is entered in the txtSales control, in a Decimal variable named decSales. Display the result of the calculation, or the error message, in the lblMsg control.

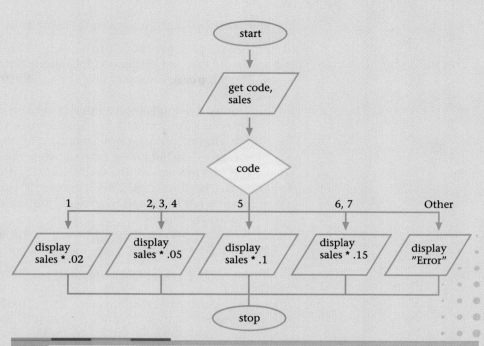

FIGURE 4.44

22. Assume that a procedure needs to display a shipping charge based on the state name stored in the strState variable. (You can assume that the state name is stored using uppercase letters.) Write a Select Case statement that assigns the shipping charge to the decShip variable. Use the following table to determine the appropriate shipping charge.

State entered in the strState variable	Shipping charge
HAWAII	$25.00
OREGON	$30.00
CALIFORNIA	$32.50

Display an appropriate message in the lblMsg control if the strState variable contains a value that does not appear in the table. Also assign the number 0 to the decShip variable.

23. Rewrite the code from Exercise 22 using an If…Then…Else statement.

24. The price of a concert ticket depends on the seat location stored in the strSeat variable. (You can assume that the seat location is stored using uppercase letters.) Write a Select Case statement that displays the price in the lblPrice control. Use the following table to determine the appropriate price.

Seat location	Concert ticket price
BOX	$75.00
PAVILION	$30.00
LAWN	$21.00

Display an appropriate message in the lblPrice control if the strSeat variable contains a value that does not appear in the table.

25. Rewrite the code from Exercise 24 using an If...Then...Else statement.

26. In this exercise, you modify this chapter's Programming Example.
    a. Create the Fat Calculator application shown in this chapter's Programming Example. Save the application in the VbDotNet\Chap04 folder.
    b. Modify the application so that it displays the message "The calories entry must be numeric." in a message box when the Text property of the txtCalories control is not numeric. The application should display the message "The fat grams entry must be numeric." in a message box when the Text property of the txtFatGrams control is not numeric. (You no longer need to display the message "The calories and fat grams must be numbers.") Be sure to modify the TOE chart and pseudocode before modifying the code.
    c. Save the solution, then start and test the application. Click the Exit button to end the application, then close the solution.

27. In this exercise, you code an application that swaps two values entered by the user.
    a. Create the interface shown earlier in Figure 4.9. Name the solution Numbers Solution. Name the project Numbers Project. Save the application in the VbDotNet\Chap04 folder.
    b. Open the Code Editor window and enter the appropriate comments at the beginning of the code. Also enter the Option Explicit On and Option Strict On statements.
    c. Code the btnExit Click event procedure so that it ends the application.
    d. Enter the code for the btnDisplay Click event procedure, which is shown in Figure 4.8.
    e. Save the solution, then start the application. Test the application by entering the two values 10 and 7, and then clicking the Display button. Then test it by entering the two values 5 and 9, and then clicking the Display button. Click the Exit button to end the application.
    f. Modify the btnDisplay Click event procedure so that it displays an appropriate message (in a message box) if any of the text boxes are either empty or contain a nonnumeric value.
    g. Save the solution, then start the application. Test the application.
    h. Click the Exit button to end the application, then close the solution.

28. In this exercise, you code an application that either adds or subtracts two numbers.
    a. Create the interface shown earlier in Figure 4.14. Name the solution Arithmetic Solution. Name the project Arithmetic Project. Save the application in the VbDotNet\Chap04 folder.
    b. Open the Code Editor window and enter the appropriate comments at the beginning of the code. Also enter the Option Explicit On and Option Strict On statements.
    c. Code the btnExit Click event procedure so that it ends the application.
    d. Enter the code for the btnCalc Click event procedure, which is shown in Figure 4.13.
    e. Save the solution, then start the application. Test the application by entering the letter a and the two numbers 23 and 13, and then clicking the Calculate button. Then test it by entering the letter X and the two values 5 and 9, and then clicking the Calculate button. Although you entered the letter X rather than the letter S, notice that the application displays the difference between the two numbers. Click the Exit button to end the application.

f. Modify the btnCalc Click event procedure so that it displays (in a message box) an appropriate message if the user does not enter either the letter A (in any case) or the letter S (in any case). Also display an appropriate message if the Text properties of the txtNum1 and txtNum2 controls are either empty or contain a nonnumeric value.

g. Save the solution, then start the application. Test the application.

h. Click the Exit button to end the application, then close the solution.

29. In this exercise, you modify the application created in Exercise 28.

a. Use Windows to make a copy of the Arithmetic Solution folder, which is contained in the VbDotNet\Chap04 folder. Rename the folder Arithmetic Solution — Modified.

b. Open the Arithmetic Solution (Arithmetic Solution.sln) file contained in the Arithmetic Solution — Modified folder.

c. If the user enters a letter other than A, a, S, or s, use the MessageBox.Show method to display a message box that asks the user if he or she intended to enter the letter A. Include Yes and No buttons in the message box. if the user clicks the Yes button, the application should display the sum of the two numbers. If the user clicks the No button, the application should assume that the user wants to display the difference between the two numbers. (You will no longer need to display a message if the user does not enter either the letter A or the letter S.) As before, the application also should verify that the txtNum1 and txtNum2 controls contain numbers.

d. Save the solution, then start the application. Test the application.

e. Click the Exit button to end the application, then close the solution.

30. In this exercise, you complete two procedures that display a message based on a code entered by the user.

a. Open the Animal Solution (Animal Solution.sln) file, which is contained in the VbDotNet\Chap04\Animal Solution folder.

b. Open the Code Editor window. Complete the If...Then...Else button's Click event procedure by writing an If...Then...Else statement that displays the string "Dog" if the intAnimal variable contains the number 1. Display the string "Cat" if the intAnimal variable contains the number 2. Display the string "Bird" if the intAnimal variable contains anything other than the number 1 or the number 2. Display the appropriate string in the lblMsg control.

c. Save the solution, then start the application. Test the If...Then...Else button three times, using the numbers 1, 2, and 5.

d. Click the Exit button to end the application.

e. Complete the Select Case button's Click event procedure by writing a Select Case statement that displays the string "Dog" if the strAnimal variable contains either the letter "D" or the letter "d". Display the string "Cat" if the strAnimal variable contains either the letter "C" or the letter "c". Display the string "Bird" if the strAnimal variable contains anything other than the letters "D", "d", "C", or "c". Display the appropriate string in the lblMsg control.

f. Save the solution, then start the application. Test the Select Case button three times, using the letters D, c, and x.

g. Click the Exit button to end the application, then close the solution.

31. In this exercise, you code an application that calculates a bonus.

a. Open the Bonus Solution (Bonus Solution.sln) file, which is contained in the VbDotNet\Chap04\Bonus Solution folder.

b. The user will enter the sales amount in the txtSales control. The sales amount will always be an integer. Code the btnCalc Click event procedure so that it calculates the salesperson's bonus. Display the bonus, formatted with a dollar sign and two decimal places, in the lblBonus control. The following rates should be used when calculating the bonus:

Sales amount ($)	Bonus
0–5000	1% of the sales amount
5001–10000	3% of the sales amount
Over 10000	7% of the sales amount

Display an appropriate message if the sales amount is negative or not numeric.

c. Save the solution, then start the application. Test the application with both valid and invalid data.

d. Click the Exit button to end the application, then close the solution.

32. In this exercise, you complete a procedure that calculates and displays the total amount owed by a company.

a. Open the Seminar Solution (Seminar Solution.sln) file, which is contained in the VbDotNet\Chap04\Seminar Solution folder.

b. Open the Code Editor window. Assume you offer programming seminars to companies. Your price per person depends on the number of people the company registers. (For example, if the company registers seven people, then the total amount owed is $560, which is calculated by multiplying the number 7 by the number 80.) Display the total amount owed in the lblTotal control. Use the Select Case statement and the following table to complete the Calculate button's Click event procedure.

Number of registrants	Criteria
1 – 4	$100 per person
5 – 10	$ 80 per person
11 or more	$ 60 per person
Less than 1	$ 0 per person

Display an appropriate message if the number registered is not numeric.

c. Save the solution, then start the application. Test the application four times, using the following data: 7, 4, 11, and –3.

d. Click the Exit button to end the application, then close the solution.

33. In this exercise, you create an application for Golf Pro, a U.S. company that sells golf equipment both domestically and abroad. Each of Golf Pro's salespeople receives a commission based on the total of his or her domestic and international sales. The application you create should allow the user to enter the amount of domestic sales and the amount of international sales. It then should calculate and display the commission. Use the following information to code the application:

Sales	Commission
1 – 100,000	2% * sales
100,001 – 400,000	2,000 + 5% * sales over 100,000
400,001 and over	17,000 + 10% * sales over 400,000

a. Build an appropriate interface. Name the solution Golf Pro Solution. Name the project Golf Pro Project. Save the application in the VbDotNet\Chap04 folder.

b. Code the application. Keep in mind that the sales amounts may contain decimal places.

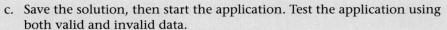

c. Save the solution, then start the application. Test the application using both valid and invalid data.

d. End the application, then close the solution.

34. In this exercise, you learn about the SelectAll method and a text box control's Enter event.

a. Open the Name Solution (Name Solution.sln) file, which is contained in the VbDotNet\Chap04\Name Solution folder.

b. Start the application. Type your first name in the First text box, then press Tab. Type your last name in the Last text box, then click the Concatenate Name button. Your full name appears in the lblFullName control.

c. Press Tab twice to move the focus to the First text box. Notice that the insertion point appears after your first name in the text box. It is customary in Windows applications to have a text box's existing text selected (highlighted) when the text box receives the focus. You can select a text box's existing text by entering the SelectAll method in the text box's Enter event.

d. Click the Exit button to end the application.

e. Open the Code Editor window. Enter the SelectAll method in the Enter event procedures for the txtFirst and txtLast controls.

f. Save the solution, then start the application. Type your first name in the First text box, then press Tab. Enter your last name in the Last text box, then click the Concatenate Name button. Your full name appears in the lblFullName control.

g. Press Tab twice to move the focus to the First text box. Notice that your first name is selected in the text box. Press Tab to move the focus to the Last text box. Notice that your last name is selected in the text box.

h. Click the Exit button to end the application, then close the solution.

35. In this exercise, you find and correct an error in an application. The process of finding and correcting errors is called debugging.

a. Open the Debug Solution (Debug Solution.sln) file, which is contained in the VbDotNet\Chap04\Debug Solution folder.

b. Open the Code Editor window. Review the existing code. The btnCalc Click event procedure should calculate a 10% bonus if the code entered by the user is either 1 or 2 and, at the same time, the sales amount is greater than $10,000. Otherwise, the bonus rate is 5%.

c. Start the application. Type the number 1 in the Code text box. Type 200 in the Sales amount text box, then click the Calculate Bonus button. A message box appears and indicates that the bonus amount is $20.00 (10% of $200), which is incorrect; it should be $10.00 (5% of $200).

d. Click the OK button to close the message box. Click the Exit button to end the application.

e. Make the appropriate change to the btnCalc control's Click event procedure.

f. Save the solution, then start the application. Type the number 1 in the Code text box. Type 200 in the Sales amount text box, then click the Calculate Bonus button. The message box correctly indicates that the bonus amount is $10.00.

g. Click the Exit button to end the application, then close the solution.

Case Projects

Allenton Water Department

Create an application that calculates a customer's water bill. The user will enter the current meter reading and the previous meter reading. The application should calculate and display the gallons of water used and the total charge for the water. The charge for water is $1.75 per 1000 gallons, or .00175 per gallon. Before making the calculations, verify that the meter readings entered by the user are valid. To be valid, both meter readings must be numeric, and the current meter reading must be greater than or equal to the previous meter reading. Display appropriate messages if the meter readings are not valid.

Professor Juarez

Create an application that displays a letter grade based on the average of three test scores entered by Professor Juarez. Each test is worth 100 points. Verify that the test scores entered by the professor are numeric. Use the following information to complete the procedure:

Test average	Grade
90–100	A
80–89	B
70–79	C
60–69	D
below 60	F

Barren Community Center

Create an application that displays a seminar fee, which is based on the membership status and age entered by the user. Verify that the data entered by the user is valid. Use the following information to code the application:

Seminar fee	Criteria
10	Club member younger than 65 years old
5	Club member at least 65 years old
20	Non-member

Willow Health Club

Create an application that displays the number of daily calories needed to maintain your current weight. Use the following information to code the application:

Moderately active female: total calories per day = weight multiplied by 12 calories per pound

Relatively inactive female: total calories per day = weight multiplied by 10 calories per pound

Moderately active male: total calories per day = weight multiplied by 15 calories per pound

Relatively inactive male: total calories per day = weight multiplied by 13 calories per pound

Repeating Program Instructions

After studying Chapter 5, you should be able to:

- Include the repetition structure in pseudocode and in a flowchart
- Write a For…Next statement
- Calculate a periodic payment using the Pmt function
- Write a Do…Loop statement
- Initialize and update counters and accumulators
- Display a dialog box using the InputBox function

THE REPETITION STRUCTURE

As you learned in Chapter 1, the three programming structures are sequence, selection, and repetition. Every program contains the sequence structure, in which the program instructions are processed, one after another, in the order in which each appears in the program. Most programs also contain the selection structure, which you learned about in Chapter 4. Recall that programmers use the selection structure when they need the computer to make a decision and then take the appropriate action based on the result of that decision.

In addition to including the sequence and selection structures, many programs also include the repetition structure. Programmers use the **repetition structure**, referred to more simply as a **loop**, when they need the computer to repeatedly process one or more program instructions until some condition is met, at which time the repetition structure ends. For example, you may want to process a set of instructions—such as the instructions to calculate net pay—for each employee in a company. Or, you may want to process a set of instructions until the user enters a negative sales amount, which indicates that he or she has no more sales amounts to enter.

A repetition structure can be either a pretest loop or a posttest loop. In both types of loops, the condition is evaluated with each repetition, or iteration, of the loop. In a **pretest loop**, the evaluation occurs before the instructions within the loop are processed, while in a **posttest loop**, the evaluation occurs after the instructions within the loop are processed. Depending on the result of the evaluation, the instructions in a pretest loop may never be processed. The instructions in a posttest loop, however, always will be processed at least once. Of the two types of loops, the pretest loop is the most commonly used.

You code a repetition structure (loop) in Visual Basic .NET using one of the following statements: For...Next, Do...Loop, and For Each...Next. You learn about the For...Next and Do...Loop statements in this chapter. The For Each...Next statement is covered in Chapter 9.

THE FOR...NEXT STATEMENT

You can use the **For...Next statement** to code a loop whose instructions you want processed a precise number of times. The loop created by the For...Next statement is a pretest loop, because the loop's condition is evaluated before the instructions in the loop are processed. Figure 5.1 shows the syntax of the For...Next statement and includes two examples of using the statement.

TIP

As with the sequence and selection structures, you already are familiar with the repetition structure. For example, shampoo bottles typically include a direction that tells you to repeat the "apply shampoo to hair," "lather," and "rinse" steps until your hair is clean.

TIP

Pretest and posttest loops also are called top-driven and bottom-driven loops, respectively.

TIP

You do not need to specify the name of the *counter* variable in the Next clause in a For...Next statement. However, doing so is highly recommended, because it makes your code more self-documenting.

HOW TO...

Use the For...Next Statement

Syntax
For *counter* = *startvalue* **To** *endvalue* [**Step** *stepvalue*]
      [*statements*]
Next *counter*

Examples
```
Dim intNum, intNumSquared As Integer
For intNum = 1 To 3
    intNumSquared = intNum * intNum
    MessageBox.Show(Convert.ToString(intNum) & " squared is " _
        & Convert.ToString(intNumSquared), "Number Squared", _
        MessageBoxButtons.OK, MessageBoxIcon.Information)
Next intNum
```
displays the squares of the numbers 1, 2, and 3 in message boxes

```
Dim intNum, intNumSquared As Integer
For intNum = 3 To 1 Step -1
    intNumSquared = intNum * intNum
    MessageBox.Show(Convert.ToString(intNum) & " squared is " _
        & Convert.ToString(intNumSquared), "Number Squared", _
        MessageBoxButtons.OK, MessageBoxIcon.Information)
Next intNum
```
displays the squares of the numbers 3, 2, and 1 in message boxes

FIGURE 5.1   How to use the For...Next statement

TIP

You can use the **Exit For** statement to exit the For...Next statement prematurely—in other words, to exit it before it has finished processing. You may need to do so if the loop encounters an error when processing its instructions.

TIP

You can nest For...Next statements, which means that you can place one For...Next statement within another For...Next statement.

The For...Next statement begins with the For clause and ends with the Next clause. Between the two clauses, you enter the instructions you want the loop to repeat.

In the syntax for the For...Next statement, *counter* is the name of the numeric variable that the computer will use to keep track of the number of times it processes the loop instructions. The *startvalue*, *endvalue*, and *stepvalue* items control how many times the loop instructions are processed. The *startvalue* tells the computer where to begin, the *endvalue* tells the computer when to stop, and the *stepvalue* tells the computer how much to add to (or subtract from if the *stepvalue* is a negative number) the *counter* variable each time the loop is processed. If you omit the *stepvalue*, a *stepvalue* of positive 1 is used. In the first example shown in Figure 5.1, the *startvalue* is 1, the *endvalue* is 3, and the *stepvalue* (which is omitted) is 1. Those values tell the computer to start counting at 1 and, counting by 1s, stop at 3—in other words, count 1, 2, and then 3. The computer will process the loop instructions shown in the first example three times.

The For clause's *startvalue*, *endvalue*, and *stepvalue* must be numeric and can be either positive or negative, integer or non-integer. If *stepvalue* is positive, then *startvalue* must be less than or equal to *endvalue* for the loop instructions to be processed. In other words, the instruction `For intNum = 1 To 3` is correct, but the instruction `For intNum = 3 To 1` is not correct, because you cannot count from 3 (the *startvalue*) to 1 (the *endvalue*) by adding increments of 1 (the *stepvalue*). If, on the other hand, *stepvalue* is negative, then *startvalue* must be greater than or equal to *endvalue* for the loop instructions to be processed. For example, the instruction For intNum = 3 To 1 Step -1 is correct, but the instruction For intNum = 1 To 3 Step -1 is not correct, because you cannot count from 1 to 3 by subtracting increments of 1.

When processing the For...Next statement, the computer performs the following three tasks:

1. The computer initializes the numeric *counter* variable to the *startvalue*. This is done only once, at the beginning of the loop.
2. If the *stepvalue* is positive, the computer checks whether the value in the *counter* is greater than the *endvalue*. (Or, if the *stepvalue* is negative, the computer checks whether the value in the *counter* is less than the *endvalue*.) If it is, the computer stops processing the loop; processing continues with the statement following the Next clause. If it is not, the computer processes the instructions within the loop, and then the next task, task 3, is performed. (Notice that the computer evaluates the loop condition before processing the statements within the loop.)
3. The computer adds the *stepvalue* to the *counter*. It then repeats tasks 2 and 3 until the *counter* is greater than (or less than, if the *stepvalue* is negative) the *endvalue*.

Figure 5.2 describes how the computer processes the code shown in the first example in Figure 5.1. Notice that when the For...Next statement in that example ends, the value stored in the intNum variable is 4.

Processing steps for the first example in Figure 5.1

1. The computer creates and initializes the intNum and intNumSquared variables in memory.
2. The computer initializes the *counter*, intNum, to 1 (*startvalue*).
3. The computer checks whether the value in intNum is greater than 3 (*endvalue*). It's not.
4. The assignment statement multiplies the value in intNum by itself and assigns the result to intNumSquared.
5. The MessageBox.Show method displays the message "1 squared is 1".
6. The computer processes the Next clause, which adds 1 (*stepvalue*) to intNum, giving 2.
7. The computer checks whether the value in intNum is greater than 3 (*endvalue*). It's not.
8. The assignment statement multiplies the value in intNum by itself and assigns the result to intNumSquared.
9. The MessageBox.Show method displays the message "2 squared is 4".
10. The computer processes the Next clause, which adds 1 (*stepvalue*) to intNum, giving 3.
11. The computer checks whether the value in intNum is greater than 3 (*endvalue*). It's not.
12. The assignment statement multiplies the value in intNum by itself and assigns the result to intNumSquared.
13. The MessageBox.Show method displays the message "3 squared is 9".
14. The computer processes the Next clause, which adds 1 (*stepvalue*) to intNum, giving 4.
15. The computer checks whether the value in intNum is greater than 3 (*endvalue*). It is, so the computer stops processing the For...Next statement. Processing continues with the statement following the Next clause.

FIGURE 5.2 Processing steps for the code shown in the first example in Figure 5.1

Figure 5.3 shows the pseudocode and flowchart corresponding to the first example in Figure 5.1.

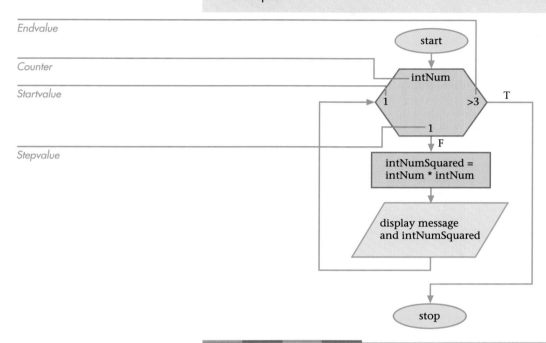

Pseudocode and flowchart for the first example in Figure 5.1

1. repeat for intNum = 1 to 3
    calculate intNumSquared by multiplying intNum by intNum
    display message and intNumSquared
end repeat

Endvalue

Counter

Startvalue

Stepvalue

FIGURE 5.3   Pseudocode and flowchart for the first example shown in Figure 5.1

TIP

If the *stepvalue* is a negative number, a less-than sign (<) should precede the *endvalue* in the hexagon, as a loop with a negative *stepvalue* stops when the value in the *counter* variable is less than the *endvalue*.

The For…Next loop is represented in a flowchart by a hexagon, which is a six-sided figure. Four values are recorded inside the hexagon: the name of the *counter* variable, the *startvalue*, the *stepvalue*, and the *endvalue*. Notice that the *endvalue* in the hexagon shown in Figure 5.3 is preceded by a greater-than sign (>); this is done to remind you that the loop stops when the value in the *counter* variable is greater than the *endvalue*.

Before viewing the Payment Calculator application, which uses the For…Next statement to calculate and display the monthly payments on a loan amount, you learn about the Visual Basic .NET Pmt function. ("Pmt" stands for "Payment.")

THE PMT FUNCTION

You can use the Visual Basic .NET **Pmt function** to calculate a periodic payment on either a loan or an investment. Figure 5.4 shows the syntax of the Pmt function and lists the meaning of each argument included in the function. The figure also includes three examples of using the function.

HOW TO...

Use the Pmt function

Syntax
Pmt(*Rate, NPer, PV*[, *FV, Due*])

Argument	Meaning
Rate	interest rate per period
NPer	total number of payment periods (the term)
PV	present value of the loan or investment; the present value of a loan is the loan amount, whereas the present value of an investment is zero
FV	future value of the loan or investment; the future value of a loan is zero, whereas the future value of an investment is the amount you want to accumulate; if omitted, the number 0 is assumed
Due	due date of payments; can be either the constant `DueDate.EndOfPeriod` or the constant `DueDate.BegOfPeriod`; if omitted, `DueDate.EndOfPeriod` is assumed

Example 1 – Calculates the annual payment for a loan of $9,000 for 3 years at 5% interest. The payments are due at the end of each period (year).
Rate: .05
NPer: 3
PV: 9000
FV: 0
Due: `DueDate.EndOfPeriod`
Function: `Pmt(.05, 3, 9000, 0, DueDate.EndOfPeriod)`
              or
          `Pmt(.05, 3, 9000)`
Annual payment (rounded to the nearest cent): -3,304.88

Example 2 – Calculates the monthly payment for a loan of $12,000 for 5 years at 6% interest. The payments are due at the beginning of each period (month).
Rate: .06/12
NPer: 5 * 12
PV: 12000
FV: 0
Due: `DueDate.BegOfPeriod`
Function: `Pmt(.06/12, 5 * 12, 12000, 0, DueDate.BegOfPeriod)`
Monthly payment (rounded to the nearest cent): -230.84

Example 3 – Calculates the amount you need to save each month to accumulate $40,000 at the end of 20 years. The interest rate is 6%, and deposits are due at the beginning of each period (month).
Rate: .06/12
NPer: 20 * 12
PV: 0
FV: 40000
Due: `DueDate.BegOfPeriod`
Function: `Pmt(.06/12, 20 * 12, 0, 40000, DueDate.BegOfPeriod)`
Monthly payment (rounded to the nearest cent): -86.14

FIGURE 5.4   How to use the Pmt function

Notice that the Pmt function contains five arguments. Three of the arguments (*Rate*, *NPer*, and *PV*) are required, and two (*FV* and *Due*) are optional. If the *FV* (future value) argument is omitted, the Pmt function uses the default value, 0. If the *Due* argument is omitted, the Pmt function uses the constant `DueDate.EndOfPeriod` as the default value. The `DueDate.EndOfPeriod` constant indicates that payments are due at the end of each period.

Study closely the three examples shown in Figure 5.4. Example 1 uses the Pmt function to calculate the annual payment for a loan of $9,000 for 3 years at 5% interest, where payments are due at the end of each period; in this case, a period is a year. As the example indicates, the annual payment returned by the Pmt function and rounded to the nearest cent is -3,304.88. In other words, if you borrow $9,000 for 3 years at 5% interest, you would need to make three annual payments of $3,304.88 to pay off the loan. Notice that the Pmt function returns a negative number. To change the negative number to a positive number, you can precede the Pmt function with the negation operator, like this: `-Pmt(.05, 3, 9000, 0, DueDate.EndOfPeriod)`. The **negation operator** reverses the sign of a number: a negative number becomes a positive number and vice versa.

When calculating an annual payment, the *Rate* argument should specify the annual interest rate, and the *NPer* argument should specify the life of the loan or investment in years. In Example 1, the *Rate* argument is .05, which is the annual interest rate, and the *NPer* argument is the number 3, which is the number of years you have to pay off the loan. As the example indicates, you can use the function `Pmt(.05, 3, 9000, 0, DueDate.EndOfPeriod)` to calculate the annual payment. You also can use the function `Pmt(.05, 3, 9000)`, because the default values for the optional *FV* and *Due* arguments are 0 and `DueDate.EndOfPeriod`, respectively.

The Pmt function shown in Example 2 in Figure 5.4 calculates the monthly payment for a loan of $12,000 for 5 years at 6% interest, where payments are due at the beginning of each period; in this case, a period is a month. Notice that the *Rate* and *NPer* arguments are expressed in monthly terms rather than in annual terms. The monthly payment for this loan, rounded to the nearest cent, is -230.84.

In addition to using the Pmt function to calculate the payments required to pay off a loan, you also can use the Pmt function to calculate the amount you would need to save each period to accumulate a specific sum. The function `Pmt(.06/12, 20 * 12, 0, 40000, DueDate.BegOfPeriod)` shown in Example 3 in Figure 5.4, for instance, indicates that you need to save 86.14 (rounded to the nearest cent) each month to accumulate $40,000 at the end of 20 years, assuming a 6% interest rate and the appropriate amount deposited at the beginning of each period.

Next, you view the Payment Calculator application, which uses the For...Next statement and the Pmt function.

The Payment Calculator Application

Herman Juarez has been shopping for a new car and has asked you to create an application that he can use to calculate and display his monthly car payment, using annual interest rates of 5%, 6%, 7%, 8%, 9%, and 10% and a term of five years. Figure 5.5 shows the Visual Basic .NET code for a procedure that performs this task, and Figure 5.6 shows a sample run of the Payment Calculator application that contains the procedure.

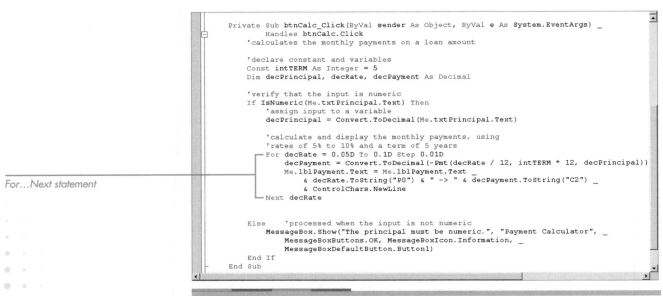

```
Private Sub btnCalc_Click(ByVal sender As Object, ByVal e As System.EventArgs) _
    Handles btnCalc.Click
    'calculates the monthly payments on a loan amount

    'declare constant and variables
    Const intTERM As Integer = 5
    Dim decPrincipal, decRate, decPayment As Decimal

    'verify that the input is numeric
    If IsNumeric(Me.txtPrincipal.Text) Then
        'assign input to a variable
        decPrincipal = Convert.ToDecimal(Me.txtPrincipal.Text)

        'calculate and display the monthly payments, using
        'rates of 5% to 10% and a term of 5 years
        For decRate = 0.05D To 0.1D Step 0.01D
            decPayment = Convert.ToDecimal(-Pmt(decRate / 12, intTERM * 12, decPrincipal))
            Me.lblPayment.Text = Me.lblPayment.Text _
                & decRate.ToString("P0") & " -> " & decPayment.ToString("C2") _
                & ControlChars.NewLine
        Next decRate

    Else    'processed when the input is not numeric
        MessageBox.Show("The principal must be numeric.", "Payment Calculator", _
            MessageBoxButtons.OK, MessageBoxIcon.Information, _
            MessageBoxDefaultButton.Button1)
    End If
End Sub
```

For...Next statement

FIGURE 5.5   Code for the btnCalc Click event procedure

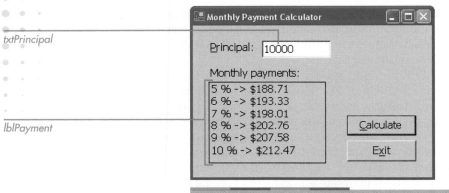

txtPrincipal

lblPayment

FIGURE 5.6   Sample run of the application that contains the procedure

The code shown in Figure 5.5 begins by declaring a named constant for the term and initializing it to the number five, which is the number of years Herman has to pay off the loan. The code also declares three variables to store the principal, rate, and payment amounts. The code then uses the IsNumeric function to verify that the principal amount, which the user enters in the txtPrincipal control, is numeric. If it's not numeric, an appropriate message is displayed in a message box. However, if it is numeric, the contents of the txtPrincipal control is converted to Decimal and stored in the decPrincipal variable.

The For...Next statement in the procedure repeats its instructions six times, using annual interest rates of .05, .06, .07, .08, .09, and .1. The first instruction in the For...Next statement uses the Pmt function to calculate the monthly payment.

Notice that the negation operator precedes the Pmt function; this changes the negative number returned by the Pmt function to a positive number. Also notice that the For...Next statement's *counter* variable (decRate), which keeps track of the annual interest rates, is divided by 12 and used as the *Rate* argument in the Pmt function. It is necessary to divide the annual interest rate by 12 to get a monthly rate, because you want to display monthly payments rather than an annual payment. The intTERM constant, on the other hand, is multiplied by 12 to get the number of monthly payments; this result is used as the *NPer* argument in the Pmt function. Lastly, the decPrincipal variable, which stores the principal entered by the user, is used as the *PV* argument in the function.

The second instruction in the For...Next statement is an assignment statement that concatenates the current contents of the lblPayment control to the following items: the annual interest rate converted to a string and formatted to a percentage with zero decimal places, the string " -> " (a space, a hyphen, a greater than sign, and a space), the monthly payment amount converted to a string and formatted with a dollar sign and two decimal places, and the `ControlChars.NewLine` constant. As you learned in Chapter 4, the `ControlChars.NewLine` constant advances the insertion point to the next line in a control. Figure 5.6 shows the output displayed by the btnCalc_Click procedure when the user clicks the Calculate button after entering 10000 in the txtPrincipal control.

Recall that you also can use the Do...Loop statement to code a repetition structure in Visual Basic .NET.

THE DO...LOOP STATEMENT

Unlike the For...Next statement, the **Do...Loop statement** can be used to code both a pretest loop and a posttest loop. Figure 5.7 shows two slightly different versions of the Do...Loop statement's syntax. You use the first version to code a pretest loop, and the second version to code a posttest loop. Figure 5.7 also includes an example of using each syntax to display the numbers 1, 2, and 3 in a message box.

HOW TO...

Use the Do...Loop Statement

Do...Loop syntax (pretest loop)
Do {While | Until} *condition*
    [instructions to be processed either while the condition is true or until the condition becomes true]
Loop

Do...Loop syntax (posttest loop)
Do
    [instructions to be processed either while the condition is true or until the condition becomes true]
Loop {While | Until} *condition*

Pretest loop example
```
Dim intNum As Integer = 1
Do While intNum <= 3
      MessageBox.Show(Convert.ToString(intNum), "Numbers", _
          MessageBoxButtons.OK, MessageBoxIcon.Information)
      intNum = intNum + 1
Loop
```

Posttest loop example
```
Dim intNum As Integer = 1
Do
      MessageBox.Show(Convert.ToString(intNum), "Numbers", _
          MessageBoxButtons.OK, MessageBoxIcon.Information)
      intNum = intNum + 1
Loop Until intNum > 3
```

FIGURE 5.7   How to use the Do...Loop statement

TIP

You can use the **Exit Do** statement to exit the Do...Loop statement prematurely—in other words, to exit it before the loop has finished processing. You may need to do so if the loop encounters an error when processing its instructions.

TIP

You can nest Do...Loop statements, which means that you can place one Do...Loop statement within another Do...Loop statement.

TIP

As both examples shown in Figure 5.7 indicate, you do not type the braces ({}) or the pipe symbol (|) when entering the Do...Loop statement.

Notice that the Do...Loop statement begins with the Do clause and ends with the Loop clause. Between both clauses, you enter the instructions you want the computer to repeat.

The **{While | Until}** portion of each syntax shown in Figure 5.7 indicates that you can select only one of the keywords appearing within the braces; in this case, you can choose either the keyword `While` or the keyword `Until`. You follow the keyword with a *condition*, which can contain variables, constants, properties, methods, and operators. Like the *condition* used in the If...Then...Else statement, the *condition* used in the Do...Loop statement also must evaluate to a Boolean value—either True or False. The *condition* determines whether the computer processes the loop instructions. The keyword `While` indicates that the loop instructions should be processed while the *condition* is true. The keyword `Until`, on the other hand, indicates that the loop instructions should be processed until the *condition* becomes true. Notice that the keyword (either `While` or `Until`) and the *condition* appear in the Do clause in a pretest loop, but in the Loop clause in a posttest loop.

Figure 5.8 describes how the computer processes the code shown in the examples in Figure 5.7.

Processing steps for the pretest loop example in Figure 5.7

1. The computer creates the intNum variable and initializes it to 1.
2. The computer processes the Do clause, which checks whether the value in intNum is less than or equal to 3. It is.
3. The `MessageBox.Show` method displays 1 (the contents of the intNum variable).
4. The `intNum = intNum + 1` statement adds 1 to intNum, giving 2.
5. The computer processes the Loop clause, which returns processing to the Do clause (the beginning of the loop).
6. The computer processes the Do clause, which checks whether the value in intNum is less than or equal to 3. It is.
7. The `MessageBox.Show` method displays 2 (the contents of the intNum variable).
8. The `intNum = intNum + 1` statement adds 1 to intNum, giving 3.
9. The computer processes the Loop clause, which returns processing to the Do clause (the beginning of the loop).
10. The computer processes the Do clause, which checks whether the value in intNum is less than or equal to 3. It is.
11. The `MessageBox.Show` method displays 3 (the contents of the intNum variable).
12. The `intNum = intNum + 1` statement adds 1 to intNum, giving 4.
13. The computer processes the Loop clause, which returns processing to the Do clause (the beginning of the loop).
14. The computer processes the Do clause, which checks whether the value in intNum is less than or equal to 3. It isn't, so the computer stops processing the Do...Loop statement. Processing continues with the statement following the Loop clause.

Processing steps for the posttest loop example in Figure 5.7

1. The computer creates the intNum variable and initializes it to 1.
2. The computer processes the Do clause, which marks the beginning of the loop.
3. The `MessageBox.Show` method displays 1 (the contents of the intNum variable).
4. The `intNum = intNum + 1` statement adds 1 to intNum, giving 2.
5. The computer processes the Loop clause, which checks whether the value in intNum is greater than 3. It isn't, so processing returns to the Do clause (the beginning of the loop).
6. The `MessageBox.Show` method displays 2 (the contents of the intNum variable).
7. The `intNum = intNum + 1` statement adds 1 to intNum, giving 3.
8. The computer processes the Loop clause, which checks whether the value in intNum is greater than 3. It isn't, so processing returns to the Do clause (the beginning of the loop).
9. The `MessageBox.Show` method displays 3 (the contents of the intNum variable).
10. The `intNum = intNum + 1` statement adds 1 to intNum, giving 4.
11. The computer processes the Loop clause, which checks whether the value in intNum is greater than 3. It is, so the computer stops processing the Do...Loop statement. Processing continues with the statement following the Loop clause.

FIGURE 5.8   Processing steps for the code shown in the examples in Figure 5.7

Figure 5.9 shows the flowcharts associated with the examples in Figure 5.7; the pseudocode for each example is shown in Figure 5.10.

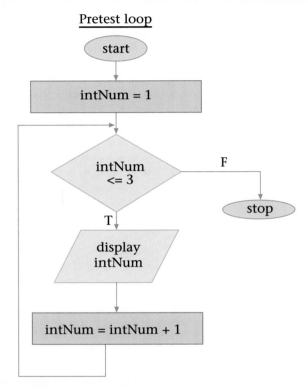

Flowchart for the pretest loop example

(Figure is continued on next page)

Flowchart for the posttest loop example

Posttest loop

start

intNum = 1

display
intNum

intNum = intNum + 1

intNum > 3   T

stop

F

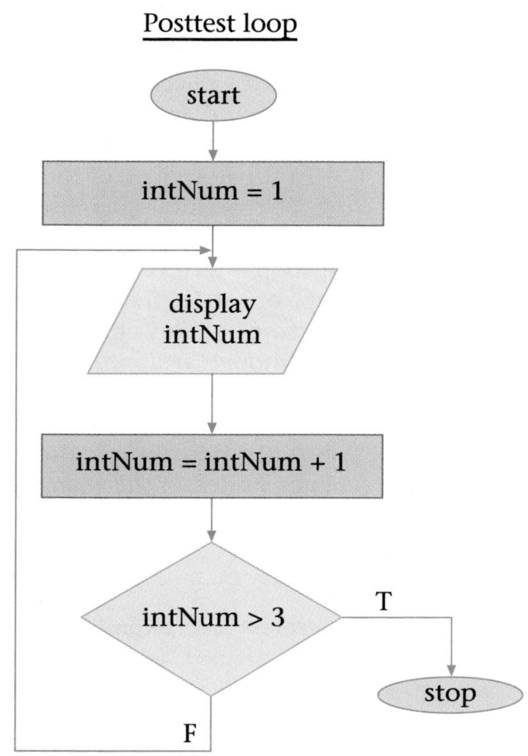

FIGURE 5.9   Flowcharts for the examples shown in Figure 5.7

Pseudocode for the pretest loop example

1. assign 1 to intNum variable
2. repeat while intNum < = 3
    display intNum
    add 1 to intNum
    end repeat

Pseudocode for the posttest loop example

1. assign 1 to intNum variable
2. repeat
    display intNum
    add 1 to intNum
    end repeat until intNum > 3

FIGURE 5.10   Pseudocode for the examples shown in Figure 5.7

Notice that a diamond represents the loop condition in both flowcharts shown in Figure 5.9. As with the selection structure diamond, which you learned about in Chapter 4, the repetition structure diamond contains a comparison that evaluates to either True or False only. The result of the comparison determines whether the computer processes the instructions within the loop.

Like the selection diamond, the repetition diamond has one flowline entering the diamond and two flowlines leaving the diamond. The two flowlines leaving the diamond should be marked with a "T" (for True) and an "F" (for False).

In the flowchart of the pretest loop shown in Figure 5.9, the flowline entering the repetition diamond, as well as the symbols and flowlines within the True path, form a circle or loop. In the posttest loop's flowchart shown in Figure 5.9, the loop is formed by all of the symbols and flowlines in the False path. It is this loop, or circle, that distinguishes the repetition structure from the selection structure in a flowchart.

Although it appears that the pretest and posttest loops produce the same results—in this case, for example, both examples shown in Figure 5.7 display the numbers 1 through 3—that will not always be the case. In other words, the two loops are not always interchangeable. The difference between both loops is demonstrated in the examples shown in Figure 5.11.

Examples and processing steps

Pretest loop example

```
Dim intNum As Integer = 10
Do While intNum <= 3
    MessageBox.Show(Convert.ToString(intNum), "Numbers", _
        MessageBoxButtons.OK, MessageBoxIcon.Information)
    intNum = intNum + 1
Loop
```

Processing steps for the pretest loop

1. The computer creates the intNum variable and initializes it to 10.
2. The computer processes the Do clause, which checks whether the value in intNum is less than or equal to 3. It isn't, so the computer stops processing the Do...Loop statement. Processing continues with the statement following the Loop clause.

Posttest loop example

```
Dim intNum As Integer = 10
Do
    MessageBox.Show(Convert.ToString(intNum), "Numbers", _
        MessageBoxButtons.OK, MessageBoxIcon.Information)
    intNum = intNum + 1
Loop Until intNum > 3
```

Processing steps for the posttest loop

1. The computer creates the intNum variable and initializes it to 10.
2. The computer processes the Do clause, which marks the beginning of the loop.
3. The `MessageBox.Show` method displays 10 (the contents of the intNum variable).
4. The `intNum = intNum + 1` statement adds 1 to intNum, giving 11.
5. The computer processes the Loop clause, which checks whether the value in intNum is greater than 3. It is, so the computer stops processing the Do...Loop statement. Processing continues with the statement following the Loop clause.

FIGURE 5.11   Examples showing that the pretest and posttest loops do not always produce the same results

Comparing the processing steps shown in both examples in Figure 5.11, you will notice that the instructions in the pretest loop are not processed; this is because the `intNum <= 3` condition, which is evaluated *before* the instructions are processed, evaluates to False. The instructions in the posttest loop, on the other hand, are processed one time; this is because the `intNum > 3` condition is evaluated *after* (rather than *before*) the loop instructions are processed.

Many times an application will need to display a subtotal, a total, or an average. You calculate this information using a repetition structure that includes a counter, or an accumulator, or both.

USING COUNTERS AND ACCUMULATORS

Counters and accumulators are used within a repetition structure to calculate subtotals, totals, and averages. A **counter** is a numeric variable used for counting something—such as the number of employees paid in a week. An **accumulator** is a numeric variable used for accumulating (adding together) something—such as the total dollar amount of a week's payroll.

Two tasks are associated with counters and accumulators: initializing and updating. **Initializing** means to assign a beginning value to the counter or accumulator. Typically, counters and accumulators are initialized to zero; however, they can be initialized to any number, depending on the value required by the application. The initialization task is done before the loop is processed, because it needs to be done only once.

Updating, also called **incrementing**, means adding a number to the value stored in the counter or accumulator. The number can be either positive or negative, integer or non-integer. A counter is always incremented by a constant value—typically the number 1—whereas an accumulator is incremented by a value that varies. The assignment statement that updates a counter or an accumulator is placed within the loop in a procedure, because the update task must be performed each time the loop instructions are processed. You use both a counter and an accumulator, as well as a repetition structure, in the Sales Express application, which you view next.

TIP

Counters are used to answer the question, "How many?"—for example, "How many salespeople live in Virginia?" Accumulators are used to answer the question, "How much?"—for example, "How much did the salespeople sell this quarter?"

THE SALES EXPRESS APPLICATION

Assume that Sales Express wants an application that the sales manager can use to display the average amount the company sold during the prior year. The sales manager will enter the amount of each salesperson's sales. The application will use a counter to keep track of the number of sales amounts entered by the sales manager, and an accumulator to total those sales amounts. After all of the sales amounts are entered, the application will calculate the average sales amount by dividing the value stored in the accumulator by the value stored in the counter; it then will display the average sales amount on the screen. Figure 5.12 shows the pseudocode for a possible solution to the Sales Express problem.

Pseudocode for the Sales Express application

Priming read

1. get a sales amount from the user
2. repeat while the user entered a sales amount
        if the sales amount is numeric
                add 1 to the counter variable
                add the sales amount to the accumulator variable
        else
                display an appropriate message in a message box
        end if
        get a sales amount from the user
    end repeat
3. if the counter variable contains a value that is greater than zero
        calculate the average sales by dividing the accumulator variable by the counter
        variable
        display the average sales in the lblAverage control
    else
        display the number 0 in the lblAverage control
        display an appropriate message in a message box
    end if

FIGURE 5.12   Pseudocode for the Sales Express application

Step 1 in the pseudocode shown in Figure 5.12 is to get a sales amount from the user. Step 2 is a pretest loop whose instructions are processed as long as the user enters a sales amount. The first instruction in the loop is a selection structure that checks whether the sales amount entered by the user is numeric. If it is numeric, the counter variable is incremented by one and the accumulator variable is incremented by the sales amount; otherwise, an appropriate message is displayed in a message box. After the selection structure within the loop is processed, the application requests another sales amount from the user. It then checks whether a sales amount was entered to determine whether the loop instructions should be processed again. When the user has finished entering sales amounts, the loop ends and processing continues with Step 3 in the pseudocode.

Step 3 in the pseudocode is a selection structure that checks whether the counter variable contains a value that is greater than zero. Before using a variable as the divisor in an expression, you always should verify that the variable does not contain the number zero because, as in math, division by zero is not mathematically possible. Dividing by zero in a program will cause the program to end abruptly with an error.

As Step 3 indicates, if the counter variable contains a value that is greater than zero, the average sales amount is calculated and then displayed in the lblAverage control; otherwise, the number zero is displayed in the lblAverage control and an appropriate message is displayed in a message box.

Notice that "get a sales amount from the user" appears twice in the pseudocode shown in Figure 5.12: immediately above the loop and also within the loop. The "get a sales amount from the user" entry that appears above the loop is referred to as the **priming read**, because it is used to prime (prepare or set up) the loop. In this case, the priming read gets only the first salesperson's sales amount from the user. Because the loop in Figure 5.12 is a pretest loop, this first value determines whether the loop instructions are processed at all. The "get a sales amount from the user" entry that appears within the loop gets the sales amounts for the remaining salespeople (if any) from the user.

Before viewing the code for the Sales Express application, you learn about the InputBox function. The application will use the InputBox function to get the sales amounts from the user.

The InputBox Function

The **InputBox function** displays one of Visual Basic .NET's predefined dialog boxes. The dialog box contains a message, along with an OK button, a Cancel button, and an input area in which the user can enter information. Figure 5.13 shows an example of a dialog box created by the InputBox function.

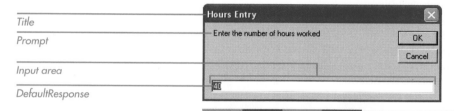

Title
Prompt
Input area
DefaultResponse

FIGURE 5.13 Example of a dialog box created by the InputBox function

The message that you display in the dialog box should prompt the user to enter the appropriate information in the input area of the dialog box. The user then needs to click either the OK button or the Cancel button to continue working in the application. Figure 5.14 shows the syntax of the InputBox function and includes several examples of using the function.

HOW TO...

Use the InputBox Function

Syntax
InputBox(*prompt*[, *title*][, *defaultResponse*])

Examples
```
strName = InputBox("Enter your name")
```
Displays a dialog box that shows "Enter your name" as the prompt, the project's name as the title, and an empty input area. Assigns the user's response to the strName variable.

```
strCity = InputBox("City name", "City")
```
Displays a dialog box that shows "City name" as the prompt, "City" as the title, and an empty input area. Assigns the user's response to the strCity variable.

```
strState = InputBox("State name", "State", "Alaska")
```
Displays a dialog box that shows "State name" as the prompt, "State" as the title, and "Alaska" in the input area. Assigns the user's response to the strState variable.

```
strState = InputBox("State name",, "Alaska")
```
Displays a dialog box that shows "State name" as the prompt, the project's name as the title, and "Alaska" in the input area. Assigns the user's response to the strState variable.

```
strRate = InputBox(strPROMPT, strTITLE, "0.0")
```
Displays a dialog box that shows the contents of the strPROMPT constant as the prompt, the contents of the strTITLE constant as the title, and "0.0" in the input area. Assigns the user's response to the strRate variable.

FIGURE 5.14   How to use the InputBox function

TIP

InputBox Function's Prompt and Title Capitalization
In the InputBox function, use sentence capitalization for the *prompt*, and book title capitalization for the *title*.

TIP

The InputBox function's syntax also includes *XPos* and *YPos* arguments, which allow you to specify the horizontal and vertical position of the dialog box on the screen. Both arguments are optional; if omitted, the dialog box appears centered on the screen.

TIP

You learned about both sentence and book title capitalization in Chapter 2.

GUI Design

In the syntax for the InputBox function, *prompt* is the message you want displayed inside the dialog box, *title* is the text you want displayed in the dialog box's title bar, and *defaultResponse* is the text you want displayed in the input area of the dialog box. In Figure 5.13, "Enter the number of hours worked" is the *prompt*, "Hours Entry" is the *title*, and "40" is the *defaultResponse*.

When entering the InputBox function in the Code Editor window, the *prompt*, *title*, and *defaultResponse* arguments must be enclosed in quotation marks, unless that information is stored in a named constant or variable. The Windows standard is to use sentence capitalization for the *prompt*, but book title capitalization for the *title*. The capitalization (if any) you use for the *defaultResponse* depends on the text itself.

Notice that the *title* and *defaultResponse* arguments are optional, as indicated by the square brackets in the syntax. If you omit the *title*, the project name appears in the title bar. If you omit the *defaultResponse* argument, a blank input area appears when the dialog box opens.

As you learned in Chapter 4, a function is a predefined procedure that performs a specific task and then returns a value after completing the task. The task performed by the InputBox function is to display a dialog box. The value returned by the InputBox function depends on whether the user clicks the dialog box's OK button, Cancel button, or Close button. If the user clicks the OK button, the InputBox function returns the value contained in the input area of the dialog box; this value is always treated as a string. However, if the user clicks either the Cancel button in the dialog box or the Close button on the dialog box's title bar, the InputBox function returns a zero-length (or empty) string.

Now that you know how to use the InputBox function, you can view the code for the Sales Express application.

Code for the Sales Express Application

Figure 5.15 shows the Visual Basic .NET code corresponding to the pseudocode shown earlier in Figure 5.12.

Code corresponding to the pseudocode shown in Figure 5.12

```
Dim strSales As String
Dim intSalesCount As Integer   'counter
Dim decSalesTotal As Decimal   'accumulator
Dim decSalesAverage As Decimal

'get first sales amount from the user
strSales = InputBox("Enter a sales amount. Click Cancel to end.", _
    "Sales Entry", "0")

'repeat as long as the user entered a numeric sales amount
Do While strSales <> ""
    If IsNumeric(strSales) Then
        'update counter and accumulator
        intSalesCount = intSalesCount + 1
        decSalesTotal = decSalesTotal + Convert.ToDecimal(strSales)
    Else
        MessageBox.Show("The sales amount must be numeric." _
            "Sales Express", MessageBoxButtons.OK, _
            MessageBoxIcon.Information)
    End If
    'get next sales amount from the user
    strSales = InputBox("Enter a sales amount. Click Cancel to end.", _
        "Sales Entry", "0")
Loop

'calculate and display average if intSalesCount > 0
If intSalesCount > 0 Then
    decSalesAverage = decSalesTotal / intSalesCount
    Me.lblAverage.Text = decSalesAverage.ToString("C2")
Else
    Me.lblAverage.Text = "0"
    MessageBox.Show("No sales amounts were entered.", "SalesExpress", _
        "Sales Express", MessageBoxButtons.OK,
        MessageBoxIcon.Information)
End If
```

Priming read

FIGURE 5.15   Code for the Sales Express application

TIP

If you forget to enter the
`strSales =`
`InputBox("Enter a`
`sales amount. Click`
`Cancel to end.",`
`"Sales Entry", "0")`
instruction within the loop, you
will create an endless or infinite
loop. To stop an endless loop,
click Debug on the menu bar,
and then click Stop Debugging.

The code begins by declaring four variables: strSales, intSalesCount, decSalesTotal, and decSalesAverage. The strSales variable will store the sales amounts entered by the user. The intSalesCount variable is the counter variable that will keep track of the number of sales amounts entered. The decSalesTotal variable is the accumulator variable that the computer will use to total the sales amounts. The remaining variable, decSalesAverage, will store the average sales amount after it has been calculated.

Recall that counters and accumulators must be initialized, or given a beginning value; typically, the beginning value is the number zero. Because the Dim statement automatically assigns a zero to Integer and Decimal variables when the variables are created, you do not need to enter any additional code to initialize the intSalesCount counter or the decSalesTotal accumulator. If you want to initialize a counter or an accumulator to a value other than zero, however, you can do so either in the Dim statement that declares the variable or in an assignment statement. For example, to initialize the intSalesCount counter variable to the number one, you could use either the declaration statement `Dim intSalesCount As Integer = 1` or the assignment statement `intSalesCount = 1` in your code. (To use the assignment statement, the variable must already be declared.)

After the variables are declared, the InputBox function in the code displays a dialog box that prompts the user to either enter a sales amount or click the Cancel button, which indicates that the user has no more sales amounts to enter. As you learned earlier, the value returned by the InputBox function depends on whether the user clicks the dialog box's OK button, Cancel button, or Close button. In this case, if the user enters a sales amount and then clicks the OK button in the dialog box, the InputBox function returns (as a string) the sales amount contained in the input area of the dialog box. However, if the user clicks either the dialog box's Cancel button or its Close button, the function returns a zero-length string (""). The assignment statement that contains the InputBox function assigns the function's return value to the strSales variable.

Next, the computer evaluates the loop *condition* in the Do...Loop statement to determine whether the loop instructions should be processed. In this case, the `strSales <> ""` *condition* compares the contents of the strSales variable to a zero-length string. If the strSales variable does not contain a zero-length string, the loop *condition* evaluates to True and the computer processes the loop instructions. If, on the other hand, the strSales variable contains a zero-length string, the loop *condition* evaluates to False and the computer skips over the loop instructions.

Now take a closer look at the instructions within the loop. The first instruction in the loop is a selection structure that determines whether the value stored in the strSales variable is numeric. If the value is not numeric, the `MessageBox.Show` method in the selection structure's false path displays an appropriate message. However, if the value is numeric, the two instructions in the selection structure's true path are processed. The first instruction, `intSalesCount = intSalesCount + 1`, updates the counter variable by adding a constant value of one to it. Notice that the counter variable, intSalesCount, appears on both sides of the assignment operator. The statement tells the computer to add one to the contents of the intSalesCount variable, then place the result back in the intSalesCount variable. The intSalesCount variable's value will be incremented by one each time the loop is processed. The second instruction in the true path, `decSalesTotal = decSalesTotal + Convert.ToDecimal(strSales)`, updates the accumulator variable by adding a sales amount to it. Notice that the accumulator variable, decSalesTotal, also appears on both sides of the assignment operator. The statement tells the computer to add the contents of the strSales variable (converted to Decimal) to the contents of the decSalesTotal variable, then place the result back in the decSalesTotal variable. The decSalesTotal variable's value will be incremented by a sales amount, which will vary, each time the loop is processed.

After the selection structure in the loop is processed, the InputBox function displays a dialog box that prompts the user for another sales amount. Notice that the `strSales = InputBox ("Enter a sales amount. Click Cancel to end.", "Sales Entry", "0")` instruction appears twice in the code—before the Do...Loop statement and within the Do...Loop statement. Recall that the `strSales = InputBox("Enter a sales amount. Click Cancel to end.", "Sales Entry", "0")` instruction located above the loop is referred to as the priming read, and its task is to get only the first sales amount from the user. The `strSales = InputBox("Enter a sales amount. Click Cancel to end.", "Sales Entry", "0")` instruction located within the loop gets each of the remaining sales amounts (if any) from the user.

After the user enters another sales amount, the computer returns to the Do clause, where the loop *condition* is tested again. If the *condition* evaluates to True, the loop instructions are processed again. If the *condition* evaluates to False, the loop stops and the instruction after the Loop clause is processed. That instruction is a selection structure that determines whether the counter variable, intSalesCount, contains a value that is greater than zero. Recall that before using a variable as the divisor in an expression, you first should verify that the variable does not contain the number zero, because division by zero is mathematically impossible and will cause the program to end with an error. In this case, if the counter variable is greater than zero, the instructions in the selection structure's true path calculate the average sales amount and assign the result to the decAverageSales variable, and then display the contents of the variable in the lblAverage control. However, if the counter variable is not greater than zero, the instructions in the selection structure's false path display the number zero in the lblAverage control and display an appropriate message in a message box.

PROGRAMMING EXAMPLE

Grade Calculator

Create a Visual Basic .NET application that allows the user to enter the points a student earns on four projects and two tests. Each project is worth 50 points, and each test is worth 100 points. The application should total the points earned and then assign the appropriate grade, using the following chart:

Total points earned	Grade
360 – 400	A
320 – 359	B
280 – 319	C
240 – 279	D
below 240	F

After assigning the grade, the application should display the total points earned and the grade. Name the solution Grade Calculator Solution. Name the project Grade Calculator Project. Name the form file Grade Calculator Form.vb. Save the application in the VbDotNet\Chap05 folder.

TOE Chart:

Task	Object	Event
1. Get points earned on four projects and two tests 2. Display an appropriate message if the points earned are not numeric 3. Calculate the total points earned 4. Display the total points earned in lblTotalPoints 5. Display the grade in lblGrade	btnAssignGrade	Click
End the application	btnExit	Click
Display the total points earned (from btnAssignGrade)	lblTotalPoints	None
Display the grade (from btnAssignGrade)	lblGrade	None

FIGURE 5.16

User Interface:

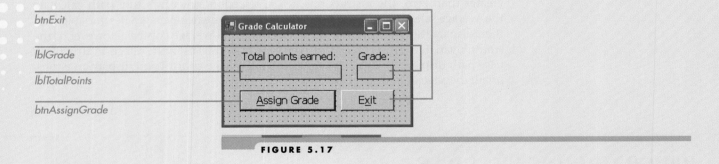

btnExit

lblGrade

lblTotalPoints

btnAssignGrade

Grade Calculator

Total points earned: Grade:

Assign Grade   Exit

FIGURE 5.17

Objects, Properties, and Settings

Object	Property	Setting
frmGrade	Name	frmGrade (be sure to change the startup form to this name)
	AcceptButton	btnAssignGrade
	Font	Tahoma, 12 point (be sure to change the form's font before adding the controls)
	Size	288, 176
	StartPosition	CenterScreen
	Text	Grade Calculator
(Table is continued on next page)		

Object	Property	Setting
Label1	AutoSize	True
	Text	Total points earned:
Label2	AutoSize	True
	Text	Grade:
lblTotalPoints	Name	lblTotalPoints
	BorderStyle	FixedSingle
	Text	(empty)
	TextAlign	MiddleCenter
lblGrade	Name	lblGrade
	BorderStyle	FixedSingle
	Text	(empty)
	TextAlign	MiddleCenter
btnAssignGrade	Name	btnAssignGrade
	Text	&Assign Grade
btnExit	Name	btnExit
	Text	E&xit

FIGURE 5.18

Tab Order:

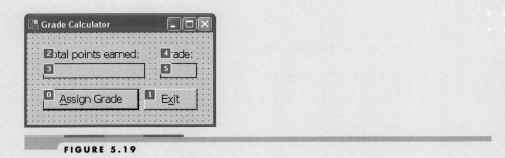

FIGURE 5.19

Pseudocode:

btnExit Click event procedure

1. close application

btnAssignGrade Click event procedure

1. repeat while the number of projects counter is less than 5
       get the points earned on the project
       if the points earned is numeric
          add the project points to the total points accumulator
          add 1 to the number of projects counter
    else
          display an appropriate message in a message box
    end if
  end repeat

2. repeat while the number of tests counter is less than 3
> get the points earned on the test
> if the points earned is numeric
>> add the test points to the total points accumulator
>> add 1 to the number of tests counter
> else
>> display an appropriate message in a message box
> end if
end repeat

3. assign the grade based on the total points earned value:

>= 360	assign A as the grade
>= 320	assign B as the grade
>= 280	assign C as the grade
>= 240	assign D as the grade
< 240	assign F as the grade

4. display the total points earned in lblTotalPoints
5. display the grade in lblGrade

Code:

```
'Project name:        Grade Calculator Project
'Project purpose:     The project calculates the total points earned on four projects
'                     and two tests. It also displays the total points earned and
'                     the appropriate grade.
'Created/revised by:  Diane Zak on 2/1/2005

Option Explicit On
Option Strict On

Public Class frmGrade
    Inherits System.Windows.Forms.Form

[Windows Form Designer generated code]

    Private Sub btnExit_Click(ByVal sender As Object, ByVal e As System.EventArgs) _
        Handles btnExit.Click
        'ends the application
        Me.Close()
    End Sub

    Private Sub btnAssignGrade_Click(ByVal sender As Object, ByVal e As System.EventArgs) _
        Handles btnAssignGrade.Click
        'calculates the total points earned, displays the total points earned
        'and the grade

        'declare variables
        Dim intProjectNum As Integer = 1    'counter-keeps track of the number of projects
        Dim intTestNum As Integer = 1       'counter-keeps track of the number of tests
        Dim intTotalPoints As Integer       'accumulator-keeps track of the total points
        Dim strProjectPoints, strTestPoints, strGrade As String
```

(Figure is continued on next page)

```
        'get and accumulate project points
        Do While intProjectNum < 5
            strProjectPoints = InputBox("Enter the points earned on project " _
                & intProjectNum, "Grade Calculator", "0")
            If IsNumeric(strProjectPoints) Then
                intTotalPoints = intTotalPoints + Convert.ToInt32(strProjectPoints)
                intProjectNum = intProjectNum + 1
            Else
                MessageBox.Show("Please enter a valid number.", "Grade Calculator", _
                    MessageBoxButtons.OK, MessageBoxIcon.Information, _
                    MessageBoxDefaultButton.Button1)
            End If
        Loop

        'get and accumulate test points
        Do While intTestNum < 3
            strTestPoints = InputBox("Enter the points earned on test " _
                & intTestNum, "Grade Calculator", "0")
            If IsNumeric(strTestPoints) Then
                intTotalPoints = intTotalPoints + Convert.ToInt32(strTestPoints)
                intTestNum = intTestNum + 1
            Else
                MessageBox.Show("Please enter a valid number.", "Grade Calculator", _
                    MessageBoxButtons.OK, MessageBoxIcon.Information, _
                    MessageBoxDefaultButton.Button1)
            End If
        Loop

        'assign grade
        Select Case intTotalPoints
            Case Is >= 360
                strGrade = "A"
            Case Is >= 320
                strGrade = "B"
            Case Is >= 280
                strGrade = "C"
            Case Is >= 240
                strGrade = "D"
            Case Else
                strGrade = "F"
        End Select

        'display total points earned and grade
        Me.lblTotalPoints.Text = Convert.ToString(intTotalPoints)
        Me.lblGrade.Text = strGrade

    End Sub
End Class
```

FIGURE 5.20

Quick Review

- The three programming structures are sequence, selection, and repetition.
- The repetition structure, also called a loop, allows a program to repeatedly process one or more program instructions.
- A repetition structure can be either a pretest loop or a posttest loop.
- Depending on the loop condition, the instructions in a pretest loop may never be processed.
- The instructions in a posttest loop are always processed at least once.
- You can use the For...Next statement to code a pretest loop whose instructions you want processed a precise number of times.
- Typically, a hexagon is used in a flowchart to represent a repetition structure that is coded using the For...Next statement.
- You can use the Do...Loop statement to code either a pretest loop or a posttest loop.
- The Pmt function calculates a periodic payment on either a loan or an investment.
- The *condition* used in the Do...Loop statement must evaluate to a Boolean value.
- When used in the Do...Loop statement, the keyword `While` indicates that the loop instructions should be processed while the *condition* is true. The keyword `Until`, on the other hand, indicates that the loop instructions should be processed until the *condition* becomes true.
- A diamond is used in a flowchart to represent the *condition* in a Do...Loop statement.
- You use a counter and/or an accumulator to calculate subtotals, totals, and averages.
- Counters and accumulators must be initialized and updated. The initialization is done outside of the loop that uses the counter, and the updating is done within the loop.
- The InputBox function displays a dialog box that contains a message, an OK button, a Cancel button, and an input area. The function returns a string.
- In the InputBox function, you should use sentence capitalization for the *prompt*, and book title capitalization for the *title*.
- Before using a variable as the divisor in an expression, you first should verify that the variable does not contain the number zero. Dividing by zero is mathematically impossible and will cause the program to end with an error.

Key Terms

The **repetition structure** is also called a **loop**. You use a loop to repeatedly process one or more program instructions until some condition is met, at which time the loop ends.

In a **pretest loop**, the loop condition is evaluated before the instructions within the loop are processed.

In a **posttest loop**, the loop condition is evaluated after the instructions within the loop are processed.

The **For...Next statement** can be used to code a pretest loop whose instructions must be processed a precise number of times.

You can use the **Pmt function** to calculate a periodic payment on either a loan or an investment.

The **negation operator** reverses the sign of a number: a negative number becomes a positive number and vice versa.

The **Do...Loop statement** can be used to code both a pretest loop and a posttest loop.

A **counter** is a numeric variable used for counting something and allows you to answer the question "How many?".

An **accumulator** is a numeric variable used for accumulating (adding together) something and allows you to answer the question "How much?".

Initializing means to assign a beginning value to a variable, such as a counter variable or an accumulator variable.

Updating, also called **incrementing**, means adding a number to the value stored in a counter or accumulator variable.

The **priming read** prepares the loop for processing.

The **InputBox function** displays a dialog box that contains a message, OK and Cancel buttons, and an input area.

Review Questions

1. Which of the following flowchart symbols represents the *condition* in a Do...Loop statement?
   a. diamond
   b. hexagon
   c. parallelogram
   d. rectangle

2. Assuming intCount is a numeric variable, how many times will the `MessageBox.Show` method be processed?

   ```
   For intCount = 4 To 11 Step 2
           MessageBox.Show("Hello")
   Next intCount
   ```

   a. 3
   b. 4
   c. 5
   d. 8

3. What is the value of intCount when the loop in Question 2 stops?
   a. 10
   b. 11
   c. 12
   d. 13

4. When the *stepvalue* in a For...Next statement is positive, the instructions within the loop are processed only when the *counter* is _____ the *endvalue*.
   a. greater than
   b. greater than or equal to
   c. less than
   d. less than or equal to

5. Which of the following is a valid For clause?
   a. `For intTemp = 5 To 1 Step .25`
   b. `For intTemp = 1 To 3 Step -1`
   c. `For intTemp = 3 To 1`
   d. `For intTemp = 1 To 10`

6. When processing the For...Next statement, the computer performs three tasks, as shown below. Put these tasks in their proper order by placing the numbers 1 through 3 on the line to the left of the task.

   _____ Adds the *stepvalue* to the *counter*.

   _____ Initializes the *counter* to the *startvalue*.

   _____ Checks whether the value in the *counter* is greater (less) than the *endvalue*.

7. Assume you do not know the precise number of times the loop instructions should be processed. You can use the _____ statement to code this loop.
   a. Do...Loop
   b. For...Next
   c. either a or b

8. Assume you know the precise number of times the loop instructions should be processed. You can use the _____ statement to code this loop.
   a. Do...Loop
   b. For...Next
   c. either a or b

9. The _____ loop processes the loop instructions at least once, whereas the _____ loop instructions might not be processed at all.
   a. posttest, pretest
   b. pretest, posttest

10. Which of the following clauses stops the loop when the value in the intAge variable is less than the number 0?
    a. `Do While intAge >= 0`
    b. `Do Until intAge < 0`
    c. `Loop While intAge >= 0`
    d. All of the above.

11. How many times will the `MessageBox.Show` method be processed?

```
Dim intCount As Integer
Do While intCount > 3
        MessageBox.Show("Hello")
        intCount = intCount + 1
Loop
```

    a. 0
    b. 1
    c. 3
    d. 4

12. How many times will the `MessageBox.Show` method be processed?

```
Dim intCount As Integer
Do
        MessageBox.Show("Hello")
        intCount = intCount + 1
Loop While intCount > 3
```

a. 0
b. 1
c. 3
d. 4

Refer to Figure 5.21 to answer Questions 13 through 16.

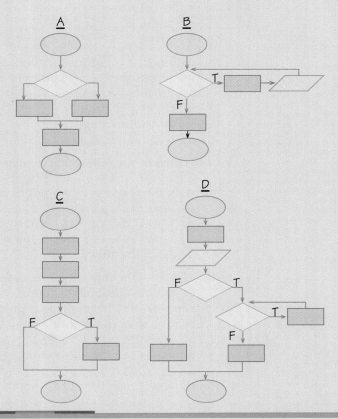

FIGURE 5.21

13. Which of the following programming structures are used in flowchart A in Figure 5.21? (Select all that apply.)
    a. sequence
    b. selection
    c. repetition

14. Which of the following programming structures are used in flowchart B in Figure 5.21? (Select all that apply.)
    a. sequence
    b. selection
    c. repetition

15. Which of the following programming structures are used in flowchart C in Figure 5.21? (Select all that apply.)
    a. sequence
    b. selection
    c. repetition

16. Which of the following programming structures are used in flowchart D in Figure 5.21? (Select all that apply.)
    a. sequence
    b. selection
    c. repetition

17. Assume a procedure allows the user to enter one or more values. The first input instruction will get the first value only and is referred to as the _____ read.
    a. entering
    b. initializer
    c. priming
    d. starter

18. Assume the InputBox function is used to display a dialog box. When the user clicks the Cancel button in the dialog box, the function returns _____.
    a. the number zero
    b. the empty string
    c. an error message
    d. None of the above.

19. Which of the following calculates the monthly payment on a loan of $5,000 for 2 years at 4% interest? Payments are due at the end of the month and should be expressed as a positive number.
    a. `-Pmt(.04/12, 2 * 12, 5000)`
    b. `-Pmt(.04/12, 24, 5000)`
    c. `-Pmt(.04/12, 24, 5000, 0, DueDate.EndOfPeriod)`
    d. All of the above.

20. Which of the following calculates the amount you need to save each month to accumulate $50,000 at the end of 10 years? The interest rate is 3% and deposits, which should be expressed as a positive number, are due at the beginning of the month.
    a. `-Pmt(.03/12, 10 * 12, 0, 50000, DueDate.BegOfPeriod)`
    b. `-Pmt(.03/12, 10 * 12, 50000, 0)`
    c. `Pmt(.03/12, 10 * 12, 50000, 0, DueDate.BegOfPeriod)`
    d. `-Pmt(.03/12, 120, 50000, 0, DueDate.BegOfPeriod)`

Exercises

1. Create a chart (similar to the one in Figure 5.2) that lists the processing steps for the code shown in the second example in Figure 5.1.

2. Write a Visual Basic .NET Do clause that processes the loop instructions as long as the value in the intQuantity variable is greater than the number 0. Use the `While` keyword.

3. Rewrite the Do clause from Exercise 2 using the `Until` keyword.

4. Write a Visual Basic .NET Do clause that stops the loop when the value in the intStock variable is less than or equal to the value in the intReorder variable. Use the Until keyword.

5. Rewrite the Do clause from Exercise 4 using the While keyword.

6. Write a Visual Basic .NET Loop clause that processes the loop instructions as long as the value in the strLetter variable is either Y or y. Use the While keyword.

7. Rewrite the Loop clause from Exercise 6 using the Until keyword.

8. Write a Visual Basic .NET Do clause that processes the loop instructions as long as the value in the strName variable is not "Done" (in any case). Use the While keyword.

9. Rewrite the Do clause from Exercise 8 using the Until keyword.

10. Write a Visual Basic .NET assignment statement that updates the intQuantity counter variable by 2.

11. Write a Visual Basic .NET assignment statement that updates the intTotal counter variable by –3.

12. Write a Visual Basic .NET assignment statement that updates the intTotalPurchases accumulator variable by the value stored in the intPurchases variable.

13. Write a Visual Basic .NET assignment statement that subtracts the contents of the decReturns variable from the decSales accumulator variable.

14. What will the following code display in message boxes?

```
Dim intX As Integer
Do While intX < 5
    MessageBox.Show(Convert.ToString(intX))
    intX = intX + 1
Loop
```

15. What will the following code display in message boxes?

```
Dim intX As Integer
Do
    MessageBox.Show(Convert.ToString(intX))
    intX = intX + 1
Loop Until intX > 5
```

16. An instruction is missing from the following code. What is the missing instruction and where does it belong in the code?

```
Dim intNum As Integer = 1
Do While intNum < 5
    MessageBox.Show(Convert.ToString(intNum))
Loop
```

17. An instruction is missing from the following code. What is the missing instruction and where does it belong in the code?

```
Dim intNum As Integer = 10
Do
    MessageBox.Show(Convert.ToString(intNum))
Loop Until intNum = 0
```

18. What will the following code display in message boxes?

```
Dim intTotEmp As Integer
Do While intTotEmp <= 5
    MessageBox.Show(Convert.ToString(intTotEmp))
    intTotEmp = intTotEmp + 2
Loop
```

19. What will the following code display in message boxes?

```
Dim intTotEmp As Integer = 1
Do
    MessageBox.Show(Convert.ToString(intTotEmp))
    intTotEmp = intTotEmp + 2
Loop Until intTotEmp >= 3
```

20. Write the Visual Basic .NET code that corresponds to the flowchart shown in Figure 5.22. (Display the calculated results on separate lines in the lblResults control.)

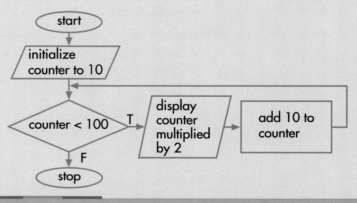

FIGURE 5.22

21. In this exercise, you code three procedures that display the even integers between 1 and 9 in a label control.
    a. Open the Even Number Solution (Even Number Solution.sln) file, which is contained in the VbDotNet\Chap05\Even Number Solution folder.
    b. Code the For...Next button's Click event procedure so that it displays the even integers between 1 and 9 in the lblEvenNums control; display each even integer on a separate line in the control. Use the For...Next statement.
    c. Code the Do...Loop Pretest button's Click event procedure so that it displays the even integers between 1 and 9 in the lblEvenNums control; display each even integer on a separate line in the control. Use a pretest loop coded with the Do...Loop statement.
    d. Code the Do...Loop Posttest button's Click event procedure so that it displays the even integers between 1 and 9 in the lblEvenNums control; display each even integer on a separate line in the control. Use a posttest loop coded with the Do...Loop statement.
    e. Save the solution, then start the application. Test each button in the interface.
    f. Click the Exit button to end the application, then close the solution.

22. In this exercise, you code a procedure that displays the squares of the even integers from 2 through 12 in a label control.
    a. Open the Even Squares Solution (Even Squares Solution.sln) file, which is contained in the VbDotNet\Chap05\Even Squares Solution folder.
    b. Code the Display button's Click event procedure so that it displays the squares of the even integers from 2 through 12 in the lblSquares control; display each square on a separate line in the control. Use the For...Next statement.
    c. Save the solution. Start and then test the application.
    d. Click the Exit button to end the application, then close the solution.

23. In this exercise, you code an application for Gwen Industries. The application calculates and displays the total sales and bonus amounts.
    a. Open the Gwen Solution (Gwen Solution.sln) file, which is contained in the VbDotNet\Chap05\Gwen Solution folder.
    b. Code the Calculate button's Click event procedure so that it allows the user to enter as many sales amounts as he or she wants to enter. Use the InputBox function to get the sales amounts. When the user has completed entering the sales amounts, the procedure should display the total sales in the lblTotalSales control. It also should display a 10% bonus in the lblBonus control.
    c. Save the solution, then start the application. Test the application using the following six sales amounts: 600.50, 4500.75, 3500, 2000, 1000, and 6500. Then test it again using the following four sales amounts: 75, 67, 88, and 30.
    d. Click the Exit button to end the application, then close the solution.

24. In this exercise, you code an application for Colfax Industries. The application calculates and displays the total company sales.
    a. Open the Colfax Solution (Colfax Solution.sln) file, which is contained in the VbDotNet\Chap05\Colfax Solution folder.
    b. Code the Add button's Click event procedure so that it adds the amount entered in the txtSales control to an accumulator variable, and then displays the contents of the accumulator variable in the lblTotalSales control. Display the total sales with a dollar sign and two decimal places.
    c. Save the solution, then start the application. Test the application using the following sales amounts: 1000, 2000, 3000, and 4000.
    d. Click the Exit button to end the application, then close the solution.

25. In this exercise, you create an application for Premium Paper. The application allows the sales manager to enter the company's income and expense amounts. The number of income and expense amounts may vary each time the application is started. For example, the user may enter five income amounts and three expense amounts. Or, he or she may enter 20 income amounts and 30 expense amounts. The application should calculate and display the company's total income, total expense, and profit (or loss). Use the InputBox function to get the individual income and expense amounts.
    a. Name the solution Premium Solution. Name the project Premium Project. Save the application in the VbDotNet\Chap05 folder.
    b. Design an appropriate interface. Use label controls to display the total income, total expenses, and profit (loss). Display the calculated amounts with a dollar sign and two decimal places. If the company experienced a loss, display the amount of the loss using a red font; otherwise, display the profit using a black font. (*Hint*: Set the label control's ForeColor property to either `Color.Red` or `Color.Black`.)

c. Code the application. Keep in mind that the income and expense amounts may contain decimal places.

d. Save the solution, then start the application. Test the application twice, using the following data:

First test: Income amounts: 57.75, 83.23
                         Expense amounts: 200
Second test: Income amounts: 5000, 6000, 35000, 78000
                         Expense amounts: 1000, 2000, 600

e. Stop the application, then close the solution.

26. In this exercise, you create an application that allows the user to enter a series of integers. The application then displays the sum of the odd integers and the sum of the even integers.

a. Build an appropriate interface. Name the solution SumOddEven Solution. Name the project SumOddEven Project. Save the application in the VbDotNet\Chap05 folder.

b. Code the application.

c. Save the solution, then start the application. Test the application using the following integers: 45, 2, 34, 7, 55, 90, and 32. The sum of the odd integers should be 107, and the sum of the even integers should be 158. Then test it again using the following integers: 5, 7, and 33.

d. Stop the application, then close the solution.

27. In this exercise, you create an application that allows the user to enter two integers. The application then displays all of the odd numbers between both integers and all of the even numbers between both integers.

a. Build an appropriate interface. Name the solution OddEven Solution. Name the project OddEven Project. Save the application in the VbDotNet\Chap05 folder.

b. Code the application.

c. Save the solution, then start the application. Test the application using the following integers: 6 and 25. The application should display the following odd numbers: 7, 9, 11, 13, 15, 17, 19, 21, and 23. It also should display the following even numbers: 8, 10, 12, 14, 16, 18, 20, 22, and 24. Then test it again using the following integers: 10 and 3.

d. Stop the application, then close the solution.

28. In this exercise, you modify this chapter's Programming Example.

a. Create the Grade Calculator application shown in this chapter's Programming Example. Save the application in the VbDotNet\ Chap05 folder.

b. Modify the application so that it allows the user to display the grade for any number of students. (*Hint*: You will need to add another loop to the program.) Be sure to modify the TOE chart and pseudocode before modifying the code.

c. Save the solution, then start and test the application. Close the application, then close the solution.

29. In this exercise, you find and correct an error in an application. The process of finding and correcting errors is called debugging.

a. Open the Debug Solution (Debug Solution.sln) file, which is contained in the VbDotNet\Chap05\Debug Solution folder.

b. Open the Code Editor window. Review the existing code.

c. Start and then test the application. Click the Exit button to end the application.

d. Correct any errors in the code.

e. Save the solution, then start and test the application again.

f. Click the Exit button to end the application, then close the solution.

Case Projects

Caldwell Middle School

Create an application that displays a multiplication table similar to the one shown in Figure 5.23, where x is a number entered by the user and y is the result of multiplying x by the numbers from 1 through 9.

Multiplication Table
$x * 1 = y$
$x * 2 = y$
$x * 3 = y$
$x * 4 = y$
$x * 5 = y$
$x * 6 = y$
$x * 7 = y$
$x * 8 = y$
$x * 9 = y$

FIGURE 5.23

Franklin University

Create an application that allows the user to enter the gender (either F or M) and GPA for one or more students. The application should calculate the average GPA for all students, the average GPA for male students, and the average GPA for female students.

Edmonton Bank

Create an application that allows the user to enter the amount a customer plans to deposit in a savings account at the end of each year. Assume that the bank is paying a 10% interest, compounded annually and paid on the last day of each year. The application should calculate and display the value of the account at the end of 5 years, 10 years, 15 years, 20 years, 25 years, and 30 years. You can use the Visual Basic .NET FV (Future Value) function to make the calculations. The syntax of the FV function is **FV**(*Rate, Nper, Pmt*).

Math Is Fun Inc.

Create an application that displays the first 10 Fibonacci numbers (1, 1, 2, 3, 5, 8, 13, 21, 34, and 55). Notice that, beginning with the third number in the series, each Fibonacci number is the sum of the prior two numbers. In other words, 2 is the sum of 1 plus 1, 3 is the sum of 1 plus 2, 5 is the sum of 2 plus 3, and so on.

String Manipulation

After studying Chapter 6, you should be able to:

- Determine the number of characters contained in a string
- Remove characters from a string
- Determine whether a string begins or ends with one or more specific characters
- Access characters contained in a string
- Replace one or more characters in a string
- Insert characters in a string
- Search a string for one or more characters
- Compare strings using the Like operator

MANIPULATING STRINGS IN VISUAL BASIC .NET

Many times, an application will need to manipulate (process) string data. For example, an application may need to verify that an inventory part number begins with a specific letter; or, it may need to determine whether the last three characters in an employee number are valid. In this chapter, you learn several ways of manipulating strings in Visual Basic .NET. You begin by learning how to determine the number of characters contained in a string.

DETERMINING THE NUMBER OF CHARACTERS CONTAINED IN A STRING

In many applications, it is necessary to determine the number of characters contained in a string. For example, an application that expects the user to enter a 10-digit phone number needs to verify that the user entered the required number of characters. You can use a string's **Length property** to determine the number of characters contained in the string. Figure 6.1 shows the syntax of the Length property and includes several examples of using the property.

In the first example in Figure 6.1, the `intNumChars = Me.txtZip.Text.Length` statement assigns to the intNumChars variable the number of characters contained in the txtZip control's Text property. (Recall that the Text property of a control is treated as a string.) Assuming the user enters the ZIP code 60111 in the txtZip control, the statement assigns the number five to the intNumChars variable.

The `Dim strName As String = "Paul Blackfeather"` statement in the second example assigns the string "Paul Blackfeather" to a String variable named strName. The `intNumChars = strName.Length` statement then uses the strName variable's Length property to determine the number of characters contained in the variable, assigning the result to the intNumChars variable. In this case, the number 17 will be assigned, because the strName variable contains 17 characters.

The pretest loop shown in the third example in Figure 6.1 processes the loop instruction, which prompts the user to enter a phone number, until the phone number entered contains 10 characters, at which time the loop ends. The code shown in the last example prompts the user to enter a part number, and stores the user's response in a String variable named strPart. The selection structure in the code then determines whether the strPart variable contains at least four characters.

HOW TO...

Use the Length Property of a String

Syntax
To determine the number of characters contained in a string: *string*.**Length**

Examples
```
Dim intNumChars As Integer
intNumChars = Me.txtZip.Text.Length
```
assigns to the intNumChars variable the number of characters contained in the txtZip control's Text property

```
Dim intNumChars As Integer
Dim strName As String = "Paul Blackfeather"
intNumChars = strName.Length
```
assigns the number 17 to the intNumChars variable

```
Dim strPhone As String
strPhone = InputBox("10-digit phone number", "Phone")
Do While strPhone.Length <> 10
      strPhone = InputBox("10-digit phone number", "Phone")
Loop
```
gets a phone number from the user until the number of characters contained in the phone number is equal to the number 10

```
Dim strPart As String
strPart = InputBox("Part number", "Part Number")
If strPart.Length >= 4 Then
      instructions to process when the condition evaluates to True
Else
      instructions to process when the condition evaluates to False
End If
```
gets a part number from the user, and then determines whether the part number contains at least four characters

FIGURE 6.1   How to use the Length property of a string

Next, you learn how to remove characters from a string.

REMOVING CHARACTERS FROM A STRING

At times, an application may need to remove one or more characters from an item of data entered by the user. For example, an application may need to remove a dollar sign from the beginning of a sales amount; or, it may need to remove a percent sign from the end of a tax rate.

You can use the **TrimStart method** to remove one or more characters from the beginning of a string, and the **TrimEnd method** to remove one or more characters from the end of a string. To remove one or more characters from both the beginning and end of a string, you use the **Trim method**. Each method returns a string with the appropriate characters removed (trimmed).

Figure 6.2 shows the syntax of the TrimStart, TrimEnd, and Trim methods and includes several examples of using each method.

HOW TO...

Use the TrimStart, TrimEnd, and Trim Methods

Syntax
To remove characters from the beginning of a string:
string.**TrimStart**([*trimChars*])
To remove characters from the end of a string: *string*.**TrimEnd**([*trimChars*])
To remove characters from both the beginning and end of a string:
string.**Trim**([*trimChars*])

Examples
```
Dim strName As String
strName = Me.txtName.Text.TrimStart()
```
assigns the contents of the txtName control's Text property, excluding any leading spaces, to the strName variable

```
Me.txtName.Text = Me.txtName.Text.TrimStart()
```
removes any leading spaces from the txtName control's Text property

```
Dim strName As String
strName = Me.txtName.Text.TrimEnd()
```
assigns the contents of the txtName control's Text property, excluding any trailing spaces, to the strName variable

```
Dim strRate As String, decRate As Decimal
strRate = InputBox("Rate:", "Rate")
decRate = Convert.ToDecimal(strRate.TrimEnd("%"c, " "c))
```
assigns the contents of the strRate variable, excluding any trailing percent signs and spaces, to the decRate variable

```
Me.txtName.Text = Me.txtName.Text.Trim()
```
removes any leading and trailing spaces from the txtName control's Text property

```
Dim strNum As String
strNum = InputBox("Number:", "Number")
strNum = strNum.Trim("$"c, " "c, "%"c)
```
removes any leading and trailing dollar signs, spaces, and percent signs from the strNum variable

FIGURE 6.2   How to use the TrimStart, TrimEnd, and Trim methods

In each syntax, *trimChars* is a comma-separated list of characters that you want removed (trimmed) from the *string*. Notice that the *trimChars* argument is optional in each syntax. If you omit the *trimChars* argument, Visual Basic .NET assumes that you want to remove one or more spaces from the beginning and/or end of the *string*. In other words, the default value for the *trimChars* argument is the space character (" ").

Study closely the examples shown in Figure 6.2. When processing the `strName = Me.txtName.Text.TrimStart()` statement, which is shown in the first example, the computer first makes a temporary copy of the string stored in the txtName control's Text property. It then removes any leading spaces from the temporary copy of the string, and assigns the resulting string to the strName variable. Assuming the user enters the string " Karen" (two spaces followed by the name Karen) in the txtName control, the statement assigns the name "Karen" to the strName variable; however, the txtName control's Text property still contains " Karen" (two spaces followed by the name Karen). After the statement is processed, the computer removes the temporary copy of the string from its internal memory.

Notice that the `strName = Me.txtName.Text.TrimStart()` statement does not remove the leading spaces from the txtName control's Text property. To remove the leading spaces from the Text property, you use the statement shown in the second example in Figure 6.2: `Me.txtName.Text = Me.txtName.Text.TrimStart()`.

When processing the statement shown in the third example in Figure 6.2, `strName = Me.txtName.Text.TrimEnd()`, the computer first makes a temporary copy of the string stored in the txtName control's Text property. It then removes any trailing spaces from the copied string, assigning the result to the strName variable. After the statement is processed, the computer removes the copied string from its internal memory. Assuming the user enters the string "Ned Yander   " (the name Ned Yander followed by four spaces) in the txtName control, the statement assigns the name "Ned Yander" to the strName variable; however, the statement does not change the contents of the txtName control's Text property.

When processing the `decRate = Convert.ToDecimal(strRate. TrimEnd("%"c, " "c))` statement shown in the fourth example in Figure 6.2, the computer first makes a copy of the string stored in the strRate variable. It then removes any trailing percent signs and spaces from the copied string, and assigns the resulting string, treated as a Decimal number, to the decRate variable. For example, if the strRate variable contains the string "3 %" (the number 3, a space, and a percent sign), the statement assigns the number 3 to the decRate variable, but it does not change the value stored in the strRate variable. Likewise, if the strRate variable contains the string "15% " (the number 15, a percent sign, and two spaces), the statement assigns the number 15 to the decRate variable, but leaves the contents of the strRate variable unchanged. The letter c that appears after each string in the *trimChars* argument is one of the literal type characters you learned about in Chapter 3. Recall that a literal type character forces a literal constant to assume a different data type—in this case, the c forces each string in the *trimChars* argument to assume the Char (character) data type.

You can use the `Me.txtName.Text = Me.txtName.Text.Trim()` statement, which is shown in the fifth example in Figure 6.2, to remove any leading and trailing spaces from the txtName control's Text property. Likewise, you can use the `strNum = strNum.Trim("$"c, " "c, "%"c)` statement, which is shown in the last example, to remove any leading and trailing dollar signs, spaces, and percent signs from the strNum variable.

Next, you learn how to use the Remove method to remove characters that are not located at the beginning or end of a string.

TIP

The literal type characters are listed in Figure 3.6 in Chapter 3.

The Remove Method

You can use the **Remove method** to remove one or more characters located anywhere in a string. Figure 6.3 shows the syntax of the Remove method and includes several examples of using the method. Like the TrimStart, TrimEnd, and Trim methods, the Remove method returns a string with the appropriate characters removed.

HOW TO...

Use the Remove Method

Syntax
To remove characters from anywhere in a string:
string.**Remove**(*startIndex*, *count*)

Examples
```
Dim strName As String = "John Cober"
Me.txtName.Text = strName.Remove(0, 5)
```
assigns the string "Cober" to the txtName control's Text property

```
Dim strName As String = "John"
Me.txtName.Text = strName.Remove(2, 1)
```
assigns the string "Jon" to the txtName control's Text property

```
Dim strName As String = "Janis"
strName = strName.Remove(3, 2)
```
assigns the string "Jan" to the strName variable

FIGURE 6.3   How to use the Remove method

Each character in a string is assigned a unique number, called an **index**, that indicates the character's position in the string. The first character in a string has an index of zero, the second character has an index of one, and so on. In the Remove method's syntax, *startIndex* is the index of the first character you want removed from the *string*, and *count* is the number of characters you want removed. For example, to remove only the first character from a string, you use the number zero as the *startIndex*, and the number one as the *count*. To remove the fourth through eighth characters, you use the number three as the *startIndex*, and the number five as the *count*.

Study closely the three examples shown in Figure 6.3. When processing the Me.txtName.Text = strName.Remove(0, 5) statement shown in the first example, the computer makes a copy of the string stored in the strName variable. It then removes the first five characters from the copied string; in this case, the computer removes the letters J, o, h, and n, and the space character. The computer then assigns the resulting string ("Cober") to the txtName control's Text property before removing the copied string from its internal memory. The contents of the strName variable are not changed as a result of processing the Me.txtName.Text = strName.Remove(0, 5) statement.

When processing the Me.txtName.Text = strName.Remove(2, 1), statement, which is shown in the second example in Figure 6.3, the computer makes a copy of the string stored in the strName variable. It then removes one character, beginning with the character whose index is 2, from the copied string. The character with an index of 2 is the third character in the string—in this case, the letter h. The computer then assigns the resulting string ("Jon") to the txtName control's Text property. Here again, the statement does not change the string stored in the strName variable.

You can use the `strName = strName.Remove(3, 2)` statement shown in the last example in Figure 6.3 to remove two characters, beginning with the character whose index is 3, from the string stored in the strName variable. In this case, the letters i and s are removed, changing the contents of the strName variable from "Janis" to "Jan".

Next, you learn how to determine whether a string begins or ends with a specific sequence of characters.

DETERMINING WHETHER A STRING BEGINS OR ENDS WITH A SPECIFIC SEQUENCE OF CHARACTERS

In many applications, it is necessary to determine whether a string begins or ends with a specific character or characters. For example, an application may need to determine whether a phone number entered by the user begins with area code "312". Or, an application may need to determine whether a tax rate entered by the user ends with a percent sign.

Visual Basic .NET provides the **StartsWith method** for determining whether a specific sequence of characters occurs at the beginning of a string, and provides the **EndsWith method** for determining whether a specific sequence of characters occurs at the end of a string. Figure 6.4 shows the syntax of the StartsWith and EndsWith methods along with examples of using each method.

HOW TO...

Use the StartsWith and EndsWith Methods

Syntax
To determine whether a specific sequence of characters occurs at the beginning of a string: *string*.**StartsWith**(*subString*)
To determine whether a specific sequence of characters occurs at the end of a string: *string*.**EndsWith**(*subString*)

Examples
```
Dim strPay As String
strPay = InputBox("Pay rate", "Pay")
If strPay.StartsWith("$") Then
     strPay = strPay.TrimStart("$"c)
End If
```
determines whether the string stored in the strPay variable begins with the dollar sign; if it does, the dollar sign is removed from the string

```
Dim strPhone As String
strPhone = InputBox("10-digit phone number", "Phone")
Do While strPhone.StartsWith("312")
     MessageBox.Show(strPhone)
     strPhone = InputBox("10-digit phone number", "Phone")
Loop
```
determines whether the string stored in the strPhone variable begins with "312"; if it does, the contents of the strPhone variable are displayed in a message box and the user is prompted to enter another phone number

(Figure is continued on next page)

```
Dim strCityState As String = Me.txtCityState.Text.ToUpper()
If strCityState.EndsWith("CA") Then
     Me.lblState.Text = "California customer"
End If
```
determines whether the string stored in the strCityState variable ends
with "CA"; if it does, the string "California customer" is displayed in the
lblState control

```
Dim strName As String
strName = InputBox("Your name:", "Name")
strName = strName.ToUpper()
If Not strName.EndsWith("SMITH") Then
     Me.lblName.Text = strName
End If
```
determines whether the string stored in the strName variable ends with
"SMITH"; if it does not, the variable's value is displayed in the lblName
control

```
Dim strName As String
strName = InputBox("Your name:", "Name")
If Not strName.ToUpper().EndsWith("SMITH") Then
     Me.lblName.Text = strName
End If
```
determines whether the string stored in the strName variable ends with
"SMITH"; if it does not, the variable's value is displayed in the lblName
control

FIGURE 6.4   How to use the StartsWith and EndsWith methods

In the syntax for the StartsWith and EndsWith methods, *subString* is a string that
represents the sequence of characters you want to search for either at the beginning
or end of the *string*. The StartsWith method returns the Boolean value True if
subString is located at the beginning of *string*; otherwise, it returns the Boolean value
False. Likewise, the EndsWith method returns the Boolean value True if *subString* is
located at the end of *string*; otherwise, it returns the Boolean value False.

In the first example shown in Figure 6.4, the `If strPay.StartsWith("$")`
`Then` clause determines whether the string stored in the strPay variable begins
with the dollar sign. If it does, the `strPay = strPay.TrimStart("$"c)` statement removes the dollar sign from the variable's contents. You also can write the
If clause in this example as `If strPay.StartsWith("$") = True Then`.

Notice that, in the first example, `"$"` is used as the *subString* argument in the
StartsWith method, but `"$"c` is used as the *trimChars* argument in the TrimStart
method. This is because the *subString* argument must be a string, while the
trimChars argument must be a listing of one or more characters.

In the second example shown in Figure 6.4, the `Do While strPhone.StartsWith("312")` clause determines whether the string stored in the strPhone variable begins with "312". If it does, the contents of the variable are displayed in a message box and the user is prompted to enter another phone number. You also can write the Do clause in this example as `Do While strPhone.StartsWith("312") = True`.

In the third example shown in Figure 6.4, the code displays the string "California customer" in the lblState control if the string stored in the strCityState variable ends with "CA". Here again, you also can write the If clause in this example as `If strCityState.EndsWith("CA") = True Then`.

The `strName = strName.ToUpper()` statement shown in the fourth example in Figure 6.4 changes the contents of the strName variable to uppercase. The `If Not strName.EndsWith("SMITH") Then` clause then compares the contents of the strName variable to the string "SMITH". If the strName variable does not end with the string "SMITH", the `Me.lblName.Text = strName` statement displays the contents of the strName variable in the lblName control. You also can write the If clause in this example as `If strName.EndsWith("SMITH") = False Then`.

The code shown in the last example in Figure 6.4 is similar to the code shown in the fourth example, except the ToUpper method is included in the If clause rather than in an assignment statement. When processing the `If Not strName.ToUpper().EndsWith("SMITH") Then` clause shown in the last example, the computer first makes a copy of the string stored in the strName variable; it then converts the copied string to uppercase. The computer then determines whether the copied string ends with the string "SMITH". Notice that the computer processes the methods from left to right; in other words, it processes the ToUpper method before processing the EndsWith method. If the copied string does not end with the string "SMITH", the `Me.lblName.Text = strName` statement displays the contents of the strName variable in the lblName control. Unlike the code in the fourth example, the code in this example does not permanently change the contents of the strName variable to uppercase. The If clause in this example also can be written as `If strName.ToUpper().EndsWith("SMITH") = False Then`.

Next you learn how to access characters contained in a string.

ACCESSING CHARACTERS CONTAINED IN A STRING

At times, an application may need to access one or more characters contained in a string. For example, an application may need to determine whether the letter K appears as the third character in a string; or, it may need to display only the string's first five characters. You can use the **Substring method** to access any number of characters in a string. Figure 6.5 shows the syntax of the Substring method and includes several examples of using the method.

HOW TO...

Use the Substring Method

Syntax
To access one or more characters contained in a string:
string.**Substring**(*startIndex*[, *count*])

Examples
```
Dim strName As String = "Peggy Ryan"
strFirst = strName.Substring(0, 5)
strLast = strName.Substring(6)
```
assigns "Peggy" to the strFirst variable, and assigns "Ryan" to the strLast variable

```
Dim strSales As String
strSales = Me.txtSales.Text
If strSales.StartsWith("$") Then
    strSales = strSales.Substring(1)
End If
```
determines whether the string stored in the strSales variable begins with the dollar sign; if it does, assigns the contents of the variable, excluding the dollar sign, to the strSales variable

```
Dim strRate As String, decRate As Decimal
strRate = InputBox("Enter rate", "Tax Rate")
If strRate.EndsWith("%") Then
    decRate = Convert.ToDecimal(strRate.Substring(0, _
        strRate.Length - 1))
Else
    decRate = Convert.ToDecimal(strRate)
End If
```
determines whether the string stored in the strRate variable ends with the percent sign; if it does, assigns the contents of the strRate variable, excluding the percent sign and treated as a Decimal number, to the decRate variable; otherwise, assigns the contents of the strRate variable, treated as a Decimal number, to the decRate variable

FIGURE 6.5   How to use the Substring method

The Substring method contains two arguments: *startIndex* and *count*. *StartIndex* is the index of the first character you want to access in the *string*. As you learned earlier, the first character in a string has an index of zero, the second character has an index of one, and so on. The *count* argument, which is optional, specifies the number of characters you want to access. The Substring method returns a string that contains *count* number of characters, beginning with the character whose index is *startIndex*. If you omit the *count* argument, the Substring method returns all characters from the *startIndex* position through the end of the string.

Study closely the three examples shown in Figure 6.5. In the first example, the `strFirst = strName.Substring(0, 5)` statement assigns the first five characters contained in the strName variable ("Peggy") to the strFirst variable. The `strLast = strName.Substring(6)` statement assigns all of the characters contained in the strName variable, beginning with the character whose index is 6, to the strLast variable. In this case, the statement assigns "Ryan" to the strLast variable.

The code shown in the second example in Figure 6.5 uses the StartsWith method to determine whether the string stored in the strSales variable begins with the dollar sign. If it does, the `strSales = strSales.Substring(1)` statement assigns all of the characters from the strSales variable, beginning with the character whose index is 1, to the strSales variable. The `strSales = strSales.Substring(1)` statement is equivalent to the statement `strSales = strSales.Remove(0, 1)`, as well as to the statement `strSales = strSales.TrimStart("$"c)`.

The code shown in the last example in Figure 6.5 uses the EndsWith method to determine whether the string stored in the strRate variable ends with the percent sign. If it does, the statement `decRate = Convert.ToDecimal(strRate.Substring(0, strRate.Length - 1))` assigns all of the characters contained in the strRate variable, excluding the last character (which is the percent sign), to the decRate variable. The `decRate = Convert.ToDecimal(strRate.Substring(0, strRate.Length - 1))` statement is equivalent to the statement `decRate = Convert.ToDecimal(strRate.Remove(strRate.Length - 1, 1))`, as well as to the statement `decRate = Convert.ToDecimal(strRate.TrimEnd("%"c))`.

Next, you learn how to replace a sequence of characters in a string with another sequence of characters.

REPLACING CHARACTERS IN A STRING

You can use the **Replace method** to replace a sequence of characters in a string with another sequence of characters. For example, you can use the Replace method to replace area code "800" with area code "877" in a phone number. Or, you can use it to replace the dashes in a Social Security number with the empty string. Figure 6.6 shows the syntax of the Replace method and includes several examples of using the method.

HOW TO...

Use the Replace Method

Syntax
To replace all occurrences of a sequence of characters in a string with another sequence of characters: *string*.**Replace**(*oldValue, newValue*)

Examples
```
Dim strPhone As String = "1-800-111-0000"
Dim strNewPhone As String
strNewPhone = strPhone.Replace("800", "877")
```
assigns the string "1-877-111-0000" to the strNewPhone variable

```
Dim strSocial As String = "000-11-9999"
strSocial = strSocial.Replace("-", "")
```
assigns the string "000119999" to the strSocial variable

```
Dim strWord As String = "latter"
strWord = strWord.Replace("t", "d")
```
assigns the string "ladder" to the strWord variable

FIGURE 6.6   How to use the Replace method

TIP

If the strPhone variable shown in the first example in Figure 6.6 contained "1-800-111-0800", the string "1-877-111-0877" would be assigned to the strNewPhone variable, because the Replace method replaces all occurrences of *oldValue* with *newValue*.

In the syntax, *oldValue* is the sequence of characters that you want to replace in the *string*, and *newValue* is the replacement characters. The Replace method returns a string with all occurrences of *oldValue* replaced with *newValue*.

When processing the `strNewPhone = strPhone.Replace("800", "877")` statement, which is shown in the first example in Figure 6.6, the computer first makes a copy of the string stored in the strPhone variable. It then replaces "800" with "877" in the copied string, and then assigns the result—in this case, "1-877-111-0000"—to the strNewPhone variable.

In the second example shown in Figure 6.6, the `strSocial = strSocial.Replace("-", "")` statement replaces each dash (hyphen) in the string stored in the strSocial variable with a zero-length (empty) string. After the statement is processed, the strSocial variable contains the string "000119999".

In the last example in Figure 6.6, the `strWord = strWord.Replace ("t", "d")` statement replaces each letter "t" in the string stored in the strWord variable with the letter "d". The statement changes the contents of the strWord variable from "latter" to "ladder".

The Replace method replaces all occurrences of *oldValue* with *newValue*. At times, however, you may need to replace only a specific occurrence of *oldValue* with *newValue*; for this, you use the Mid statement rather than the Replace method.

The Mid Statement
You can use the **Mid statement** to replace a specified number of characters in a string with characters from another string. Figure 6.7 shows the syntax of the Mid statement and includes several examples of using the statement.

HOW TO...

Use the Mid Statement

Syntax
To replace a specific number of characters in a string with characters from another string: **Mid(***targetString, start* [, *count*]**) =** *replacementString*

Examples
```
Dim strName As String = "Rob Smith"
Mid(strName, 7, 1) = "y"
```
changes the contents of the strName variable to "Rob Smyth"

```
Dim strName As String = "Rob Smith"
Mid(strName, 7) = "y"
```
changes the contents of the strName variable to "Rob Smyth"

```
Dim strName As String = "Ann Johnson"
Mid(strName, 5) = "Paul"
```
changes the contents of the strName variable to "Ann Paulson"

```
Dim strName As String = "Earl Cho"
Mid(strName, 6) = "Liverpool"
```
changes the contents of the strName variable to "Earl Liv"

FIGURE 6.7   How to use the Mid statement

In the Mid statement's syntax, *targetString* is the string in which you want characters replaced, and *replacementString* contains the replacement characters. *Start* is the character position of the first character you want replaced in the *targetString*. The first character in the *targetString* is in character position one, the second is in character position two, and so on. (Notice that the character position is not the same as the index, which begins with zero.) The *count* argument, which is optional in the Mid statement, specifies the number of characters to replace in the *targetString*. If *count* is omitted, the Mid statement replaces the lesser of either the number of characters in the *replacementString*, or the number of characters in the *targetString* from position *start* through the end of the *targetString*.

Study closely the examples shown in Figure 6.7. In the first example, the `Mid(strName, 7, 1) = "y"` statement replaces the letter "i", which is located in character position seven in the strName variable, with the letter "y". After the statement is processed, the strName variable contains the string "Rob Smyth".

You also can omit the *count* argument and use the `Mid(strName, 7) = "y"` statement, which is shown in the second example in Figure 6.7, to replace the letter "i" in the strName variable with the letter "y". Recall that when the *count* argument is omitted from the Mid statement, the statement replaces the lesser of either the number of characters in the *replacementString* (in this case, one) or the number of characters in the *targetString* from position *start* through the end of the *targetString* (in this case, three).

The `Mid(strName, 5) = "Paul"` statement in the third example in Figure 6.7 replaces four characters in the strName variable, beginning with the character located in character position five in the variable (the letter J). Here again, because the *count* argument is omitted from the Mid statement, the statement replaces the lesser of either the number of characters in the *replacementString* (in this case, four) or the number of characters in the *targetString* from position *start* through the end of the *targetString* (in this case, seven). After the statement is processed, the strName variable contains the string "Ann Paulson".

The `Mid(strName, 6) = "Liverpool"` statement in the last example in Figure 6.7 replaces three characters in the strName variable, beginning with the character located in character position six in the variable (the letter C). Here again, because the *count* argument is omitted from the Mid statement, the statement replaces the lesser of either the number of characters in the *replacementString* (in this case, nine) or the number of characters in the *targetString* from position *start* through the end of the *targetString* (in this case, three). After the statement is processed, the strName variable contains the string "Earl Liv".

Now you learn how to insert characters at the beginning and end of a string.

INSERTING CHARACTERS AT THE BEGINNING AND END OF A STRING

You can use the PadLeft and PadRight methods to pad a string with a character until the string is a specified length; both methods return the padded string. The **PadLeft method** pads the string on the left—in other words, it inserts the padded characters at the beginning of the string; doing so right-aligns the characters within the string. The **PadRight method**, on the other hand, pads the string on the right, which inserts the padded characters at the end of the string and left-aligns the characters within the string. Figure 6.8 shows the syntax of the PadLeft and PadRight methods and includes several examples of using the methods.

In each syntax, *length* is an integer that represents the desired length of the *string*—in other words, the total number of characters you want the *string* to contain. The *character* argument is the character that each method uses to pad the *string* until it reaches the desired *length*. Notice that the *character* argument is optional in each syntax; if omitted, the default *character* is the space character.

HOW TO...

Use the PadLeft and PadRight Methods

Syntax
To insert characters at the beginning of a string:
string.**PadLeft**(*length*[, *character*])
To insert characters at the end of a string: *string*.**PadRight**(*length*[, *character*])

Examples
```
Dim intNum as Integer = 42
Dim strNum As String
strNum = Convert.ToString(intNum)
strNum = strNum.PadLeft(5)
```
assigns "   42" (three spaces and the string "42") to the strNum variable

```
Dim intNum as Integer = 42
Dim strNum As String
strNum = intNum.ToString().PadLeft(5)
```
assigns "   42" (three spaces and the string "42") to the strNum variable

```
Dim decNetPay As Decimal = 767.89D
Dim strNet As String
strNet = decNetPay.ToString("C2").PadLeft(15, "*"c)
```
assigns "********$767.89" to the strNet variable

```
Dim strName As String = "Sue"
Dim strNewName As String
strNewName = strName.PadRight(10)
```
assigns "Sue   " (the string "Sue" and seven spaces) to the strNewName variable

```
Dim strName As String = "Sue"
strName = strName.PadRight(10)
```
assigns "Sue   " (the string "Sue" and seven spaces) to the strName variable

FIGURE 6.8   How to use the PadLeft and PadRight methods

The code shown in the first two examples in Figure 6.8 produces the same results; both assign five characters—three space characters, the character 4, and the character 2—to the strNum variable. However, the first example uses two assignment statements to accomplish the task, while the second example uses one assignment statement. The first assignment statement in the first example, `strNum = Convert.ToString(intNum)`, assigns the contents of the intNum variable, converted to a String, to the strNum variable. When processing the second assignment statement in the first example, `strNum = strNum.PadLeft(5)`, the computer first makes a copy of the string stored in the strNum variable. It then pads the copied string with space characters until the string contains exactly five characters. In this case, the computer uses three space characters, which it inserts at the beginning of the string. The computer then assigns the resulting string—"   42"—to the strNum variable.

When processing the `strNum = intNum.ToString().PadLeft(5)` assignment statement in the second example, the computer first makes a copy of the value stored in the intNum variable. It then converts the copied value to a string, then inserts space characters at the beginning of the string until the string has exactly five characters, and then assigns the result to the strNum variable. Here again, notice that when two methods appear in an expression, the computer processes the methods from left to right. In this case, the computer processes the ToString method before processing the PadLeft method.

When processing the `strNet = decNetPay.ToString("C2").PadLeft(15, "*"c)` statement shown in the third example in Figure 6.8, the computer first makes a copy of the number stored in the decNetPay variable. It then converts the number to a string and formats it with a dollar sign and two decimal places. The computer then pads the string with asterisks until the string contains exactly 15 characters. In this case, the computer inserts eight asterisks at the beginning of the string. The computer assigns the resulting string ("*********$767.89") to the strNet variable.

When processing the `strNewName = strName.PadRight(10)` statement shown in the fourth example in Figure 6.8, the computer first makes a copy of the string stored in the strName variable. It then pads the copied string with space characters until the string contains exactly 10 characters. In this case, the computer uses seven space characters, which it inserts at the end of the string. The computer then assigns the resulting string—"Sue   "—to the strNewName variable. The `strNewName = strName.PadRight(10)` statement does not change the contents of the strName variable. To assign "Sue   " to the strName variable, you would need to use the `strName = strName.PadRight(10)` statement shown in the last example in Figure 6.8.

The PadLeft and PadRight methods can be used to insert characters only at the beginning or end of a string; neither can be used to insert characters within a string. Visual Basic .NET provides the Insert method for inserting characters anywhere within a string.

Inserting Characters within a String

You can use the **Insert method** to insert characters within a string. For example, you can use the Insert method to insert an employee's middle initial within his or her name. Or, you can use it to insert parentheses around the area code in a phone number. Figure 6.9 shows the syntax of the Insert method and includes two examples of using the method.

HOW TO...

Use the Insert Method

Syntax
To insert characters within a string: *string*.**Insert**(*startIndex, value*)

Examples
```
Dim strName As String = "Rob Smith"
Dim strNewName As String
strNewName = strName.Insert(4, "T. ")
```
assigns the string "Rob T. Smith" to the strNewName variable

```
Dim strPhone As String = "3120501111"
strPhone = strPhone.Insert(0, "(")
strPhone = strPhone.Insert(4, ")")
strPhone = strPhone.Insert(8, "-")
```
changes the contents of the strPhone variable to "(312)050-1111"

FIGURE 6.9   How to use the Insert method

In the Insert method's syntax, *startIndex* specifies where in the *string* you want the *value* inserted. To insert the *value* at the beginning of the *string*, you use the number zero as the *startIndex*. To insert the *value* as the second character in the *string*, you use the number one as the *startIndex*, and so on. The Insert method returns a string with the appropriate characters inserted.

When processing the `strNewName = strName.Insert(4, "T. ")` statement shown in the first example in Figure 6.9, the computer first makes a copy of the string stored in the strName variable, and then inserts the *value* "T. " (the letter T, a period, and a space) in the copied string. The letter T is inserted in *startIndex* position 4, which makes it the fifth character in the string. The period and space are inserted in *startIndex* positions 5 and 6, making them the sixth and seventh characters in the string. After the statement is processed, the strNewName variable contains the string "Rob T. Smith"; however, the strName variable still contains "Rob Smith".

In the second example shown in Figure 6.9, the `strPhone = strPhone.Insert(0, "(")` statement changes the contents of the strPhone variable from "3120501111" to "(3120501111". The `strPhone = strPhone.Insert(4, ")")` statement then changes the contents of the variable from "(3120501111" to "(312)0501111", and the `strPhone = strPhone.Insert(8, "-")` statement changes the contents of the variable from "(312)0501111" to "(312)050-1111".

Next, you learn how to search a string to determine whether it contains a specific sequence of characters.

SEARCHING A STRING

You can use the **IndexOf method** to search a string to determine whether it contains a specific sequence of characters. For example, you can use the IndexOf method to determine whether the area code "312" appears in a phone number, or whether the street name "Elm Street" appears in an address. Figure 6.10 shows the syntax of the IndexOf method and includes several examples of using the method.

HOW TO...

Use the IndexOf Method

Syntax
To search a string to determine whether it contains a specific sequence of characters: *string*.**IndexOf**(*value*[, *startIndex*])

Examples
```
Dim strMsg As String = "Have a nice day"
Dim intIndex As Integer
intIndex = strMsg.IndexOf("nice", 0)
```
assigns the number 7 to the intIndex variable

```
Dim strMsg As String = "Have a nice day"
Dim intIndex As Integer
intIndex = strMsg.IndexOf("nice")
```
assigns the number 7 to the intIndex variable

```
Dim strMsg As String = "Have a nice day"
Dim intIndex As Integer
intIndex = strMsg.IndexOf("Nice")
```
assigns the number -1 to the intIndex variable

```
Dim strMsg As String = "Have a nice day"
Dim intIndex As Integer
intIndex = strMsg.ToUpper().IndexOf("NICE")
```
assigns the number 7 to the intIndex variable

```
Dim strMsg As String = "Have a nice day"
Dim intIndex As Integer
intIndex = strMsg.IndexOf("nice", 5)
```
assigns the number 7 to the intIndex variable

```
Dim strMsg As String = "Have a nice day"
Dim intIndex As Integer
intIndex = strMsg.IndexOf("nice", 8)
```
assigns the number -1 to the intIndex variable

FIGURE 6.10   How to use the IndexOf method

In the syntax, *value* is the sequence of characters for which you are searching in the *string*, and *startIndex* is the index of the character at which the search should begin—in other words, *startIndex* specifies the starting position for the search. Recall that the first character in a string has an index of zero, the second character has an index of one, and so on. Notice that the *startIndex* argument is optional in the IndexOf method's syntax. If you omit the *startIndex* argument, the IndexOf method begins the search with the first character in the *string*.

The IndexOf method searches for *value* within *string*, beginning with the character whose index is *startIndex*. If the IndexOf method does not find the *value*, it returns the number -1; otherwise, it returns the index of the starting position of *value* within *string*.

You can use either the `intIndex = strMsg.IndexOf("nice", 0)` statement shown in the first example in Figure 6.10, or the `intIndex = strMsg.IndexOf("nice")` statement shown in the second example, to search for the word "nice" in the strMsg variable, beginning with the first character in the variable. In each case, the word "nice" begins with the eighth character in the variable. The eighth character has an index of seven, so both statements assign the number seven to the intIndex variable.

The IndexOf method performs a case-sensitive search, as the third example in Figure 6.10 indicates. In this example, the `intIndex = strMsg.IndexOf("Nice")` statement assigns the number -1 to the intIndex variable, because the word "Nice" is not contained in the strMsg variable.

You can use the `intIndex = strMsg.ToUpper().IndexOf("NICE")` statement shown in the fourth example in Figure 6.10 to perform a case-insensitive search for the word "nice". The ToUpper method in the statement is processed first and temporarily converts the string stored in the strMsg variable to uppercase. The IndexOf method then searches the uppercase string for the word "NICE". The statement assigns the number seven to the intIndex variable because, ignoring case, the word "nice" begins with the character whose index is seven.

The `intIndex = strMsg.IndexOf("nice", 5)` statement shown in the fifth example in Figure 6.10 searches for the word "nice" in the strMsg variable, beginning with the character whose index is five; that character is the second letter "a". The statement assigns the number seven to the intIndex variable, because the word "nice" begins with the character whose index is seven.

The `intIndex = strMsg.IndexOf("nice", 8)` statement shown in the last example in Figure 6.10 searches for the word "nice" in the strMsg variable, beginning with the character whose index is eight; that character is the letter "i". Notice that the word "nice" does not appear anywhere in the "ice day" portion of the string stored in the strMsg variable. Therefore, the statement assigns the number -1 to the intIndex variable.

In Chapter 4, you learned how to compare two values using the >, >=, <, <=, =, and <> comparison operators. When comparing two strings, you also can use the Like comparison operator.

THE LIKE OPERATOR

The **Like operator** allows you to use pattern-matching characters to determine whether one string is equal to another string. Figure 6.11 shows the syntax of the Like operator and includes a listing of the operator's pattern-matching characters. The figure also shows several examples of using the Like operator.

HOW TO...

Use the Like operator

Syntax
To use pattern-matching characters to determine whether one string is equal to another string: *string* **Like** *pattern*

Pattern-matching characters	Matches in string
?	any single character
*	zero or more characters
#	any single digit (0-9)
[*charlist*]	any single character in the *charlist* (for example, [a-z] matches any lowercase letter)
[!*charlist*]	any single character not in the *charlist* (for example, [!a-z] matches any character that is not a lowercase letter)

Examples
```
strName.ToUpper() Like "B?LL"
```
evaluates to True if the string stored in the strName variable begins with the letter B, followed by one character and then the two letters LL; otherwise, it evaluates to False

```
strState Like "K*"
```
evaluates to True if the string stored in the strState variable begins with the letter K, followed by zero or more characters; otherwise, it evaluates to False

```
strId Like "###*"
```
evaluates to True if the string stored in the strId variable begins with three digits, followed by zero or more characters; otherwise, it evaluates to False

```
strName.ToUpper() Like "T[OI]M"
```
evaluates to True if the string stored in the strName variable begins with the letter T, followed by either the letter O or the letter I, followed by the letter M; otherwise, it evaluates to False

```
strLetter Like "[a-z]"
```
evaluates to True if the character stored in the strLetter variable is a lowercase letter; otherwise, it evaluates to False

```
For intX = 0 to strName.Length - 1
   If strName.Substring(intX, 1) _
     Like "[!a-zA-Z]" Then
        MessageBox.Show("Not a letter")
   Else
        MessageBox.Show("Letter")
   End If
Next intX
```
evaluates to True if the current character in the strName variable is not a letter; otherwise, it evaluates to False

FIGURE 6.11   How to use the Like operator

In the Like operator's syntax, both *string* and *pattern* must be String expressions; however, *pattern* can contain one or more of the pattern-matching characters described in Figure 6.11. The Like operator evaluates to True if *string* matches *pattern*; otherwise it evaluates to False.

Study closely each example shown in Figure 6.11. The `strName.ToUpper()` `Like "B?LL"` expression shown in the first example contains the question mark (?) pattern-matching character, which is used to match one character in the *string*. Examples of *strings* that would make this expression evaluate to True include "Bill", "Ball", "bell", and "bull". Examples of *strings* for which the expression would evaluate to False include "BPL", "BLL", and "billy".

The `strState Like "K*"` expression shown in the second example uses the asterisk (*) pattern-matching character to match zero or more characters. Examples of *strings* that would make this expression evaluate to True include "KANSAS", "Ky", and "Kentucky". Examples of *strings* for which the expression would evaluate to False include "kansas" and "ky".

In the third example, the `strId Like "###*"` expression contains two different pattern-matching characters: the number sign (#), which matches a digit, and the asterisk (*), which matches zero or more characters. Examples of *strings* that would make this expression evaluate to True include "178" and "983Ab". Examples of *strings* for which the expression would evaluate to False include "X34" and "34Z".

In the fourth example, the `strName.ToUpper() Like "T[OI]M"` expression contains a *charlist* (character list)—in this case, the two letters O and I—enclosed in square brackets ([ ]). The expression evaluates to True if the string stored in the strName variable is either "Tom" or "Tim" (entered in any case). If the strName variable does not contain "Tom" or "Tim"—for example, if it contains "Tam" or "Tommy"—the expression evaluates to False.

The expression shown in the fifth example in Figure 6.11, `strLetter Like "[a-z]"`, also contains a *charlist* enclosed in square brackets; however, the *charlist* represents a range of values—in this case, the lowercase letters "a" through "z". Notice that you use a hyphen (-) to specify a range of values. In this case, if the character stored in the strLetter variable is a lowercase letter, then the expression evaluates to True; otherwise, it evaluates to False.

The `strName.Substring(intX, 1) Like "[!a-zA-Z]"` expression shown in the last example in Figure 6.11 also contains a *charlist* that specifies a range of values; however, the *charlist* is preceded by an exclamation point (!), which stands for "not". The expression evaluates to True if the current character in the strName variable is *not* a letter; otherwise, it evaluates to False.

Figure 6.12 summarizes the string manipulation techniques you learned in this chapter.

TIP

When using the hyphen to specify a range of values, the value on the left side of the hyphen must have a lower ASCII value than the value on the right side of the hyphen. For example, you must use [a-z], and not [z-a], to specify the lowercase letters of the alphabet. As you may remember from Chapter 4, ASCII stands for American Standard Code for Information Interchange and is the coding scheme used by microcomputers to represent the numbers, letters, and symbols on the keyboard. To view the ASCII values, click Help on the menu bar and then click Index. Type ASCII characters in the Look for box, and then click ASCII character set in the list.

Technique	Syntax	Purpose
EndsWith method	*string*.**EndsWith**(*subString*)	determine whether a string ends with a specific sequence of characters
IndexOf method	*string*.**IndexOf**(*value*[, *startIndex*])	search a string to determine whether it contains a specific sequence of characters
Insert method	*string*.**Insert**(*startIndex*, *value*)	insert characters within a string
Length property	*string*.**Length**	determine the number of characters in a string
Like operator	*string* **Like** *pattern*	use pattern-matching characters to determine whether one string is equal to another string
Mid statement	**Mid**(*targetString*, *start* [, *count*]) = *replacementString*	replace a specific number of characters in a string with characters from another string
PadLeft method	*string*.**PadLeft**(*length*[, *character*])	pads the beginning of a string with a character until the string is a specified length
PadRight method	*string*.**PadRight**(*length*[, *character*])	pads the end of a string with a character until the string is a specified length
Remove method	*string*.**Remove**(*startIndex*, *count*)	remove characters from anywhere in a string
Replace method	*string*.**Replace**(*oldValue*, *newValue*)	replace all occurrences of a sequence of characters in a string with another sequence of characters
StartsWith method	*string*.**StartsWith**(*subString*)	determine whether a string begins with a specific sequence of characters
Substring method	*string*.**Substring**(*startIndex*[, *count*])	access one or more characters contained in a string
Trim method	*string*.**Trim**([*trimChars*])	remove characters from both the beginning and end of a string
TrimEnd method	*string*.**TrimEnd**([*trimChars*])	remove characters from the end of a string
TrimStart method	*string*.**TrimStart**([*trimChars*])	remove characters from the beginning of a string

FIGURE 6.12   String manipulation techniques

PROGRAMMING EXAMPLE

Hangman Game

On days when the weather is bad and the students cannot go outside to play, Mr. Mitchell, who teaches second grade at Hinsbrook School, spends recess time playing a simplified version of the Hangman game with his class. The game requires two people to play. Currently, Mr. Mitchell thinks of a word that has five letters. He then draws five dashes on the chalkboard—one for each letter in the word. One student then is chosen to guess the word, letter by letter. If the student guesses a correct letter, Mr. Mitchell replaces the appropriate dash or dashes with the letter. For example, if the original word is *moose* and the student guesses the letter *o*, Mr. Mitchell changes the fives dashes on the chalkboard to -oo--. The game is over when the student guesses all of the letters in the word, or when he or she makes ten incorrect guesses, whichever comes first. Create a Visual Basic .NET application that simulates Mr. Mitchell's version of the Hangman game. Name the solution Hangman Solution. Name the project Hangman Project. Name the form file Hangmen Form.vb. Save the application in the VbDotNet\Chap06 folder.

TOE Chart:

Task	Object	Event
1. Get a five-letter word from player 1 2. Display five dashes in the lblWord control 3. Clear the lblIncorrectGuesses control 4. Get a letter from player 2 5. Search the word for the letter 6. If the letter is contained in the word, replace the appropriate dash(es) 7. If the letter is not contained in the word, add 1 to the number of incorrect guesses 8. If all of the dashes have been replaced, the game is over, so display the message "Great guessing!" in a message box 9. If the user makes 10 incorrect guesses, the game is over, so display the message "Sorry, the word is" and the word in a message box, and display the "Game Over" message in the lblWord control	btnPlay	Click
End the application	btnExit	Click
Display dashes, letters, "Game Over" message (from btnPlay)	lblWord	None
Display the number of incorrect guesses (from btnPlay)	lblIncorrectGuesses	None

FIGURE 6.13

User Interface:

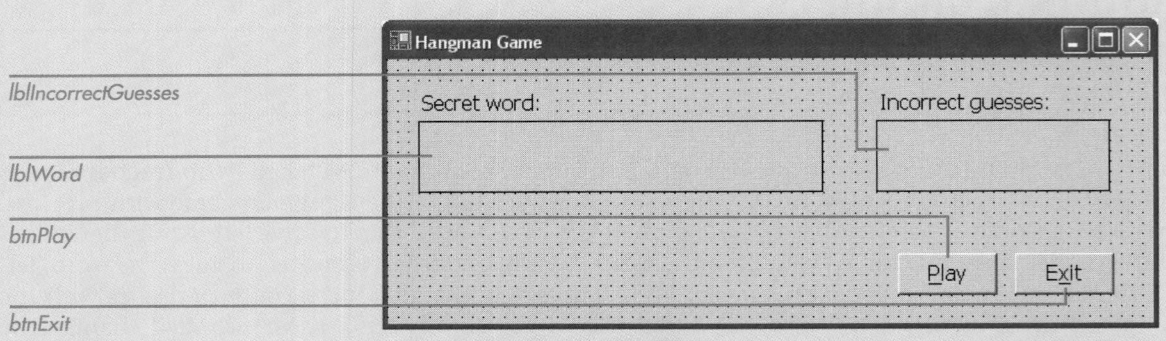

lblIncorrectGuesses

lblWord

btnPlay

btnExit

FIGURE 6.14

Objects, Properties, and Settings

Object	Property	Setting
frmHangman	Name	frmHangman (be sure to change the startup form to this name)
	Font	Tahoma, 12 point (be sure to change the form's font before adding the controls)
	Size	584, 240
	StartPosition	CenterScreen
	Text	Hangman Game
Label1	AutoSize	True
	Text	Secret word:
Label2	AutoSize	True
	Text	Incorrect guesses:
lblWord	Name	lblWord
	BorderStyle	FixedSingle
	Font	Tahoma, 36 point
	Text	(empty)
	TextAlign	MiddleCenter
lblIncorrectGuesses	Name	lblIncorrectGuesses
	BorderStyle	FixedSingle
	Font	Tahoma, 36 point
	Text	(empty)
	TextAlign	MiddleCenter
btnPlay	Name	btnPlay
	Text	&Play
btnExit	Name	btnExit
	Text	E&xit

FIGURE 6.15

Tab Order:

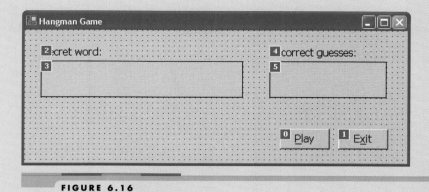

FIGURE 6.16

Pseudocode:

btnExit Click event procedure

1. close application

btnPlay Click event procedure

1. get a 5-letter word from player 1
2. repeat while the word does not contain 5 letters
   get a 5-letter word from the user
   end repeat
3. convert word to uppercase
4. display five dashes in the lblWord control
5. clear the lblIncorrectGuesses control
6. repeat while the game is not over
   get a letter from player 2, then convert letter to uppercase
   repeat for each character in the word
      if the current character is equal to the letter entered by player 2
         replace the appropriate dash in the lblWord control
         set the blnDashReplaced variable to True
      end if
   end repeat
   if a dash was replaced in the lblWord control
      if the lblWord control does not contain any dashes
         set the blnGameOver variable to True
         display the "Great guessing!" message in a message box
      else
         reset the blnDashReplaced variable to False
      end if
   else
      add 1 to the intIncorrectGuesses counter variable
      display the intIncorrectGuesses variable's value in the lblIncorrectGuesses control
      if the user made 10 incorrect guesses
         set the blnGameOver variable to True
         display the "Game Over" message in the lblWord control
         display the "Sorry, the word is" message and the word in a message box
      end if
   end if
end repeat

Code:

```vb
'Project name:          Hangman Project
'Project purpose:       The project simulates the Hangman game.
'Created/revised by:    Diane Zak on 2/1/2005

Option Explicit On
Option Strict On

Public Class frmHangman
    Inherits System.Windows.Forms.Form

[Windows Form Designer generated code]

    Private Sub btnExit_Click(ByVal sender As Object, ByVal e As System.EventArgs) _
        Handles btnExit.Click
        'ends the application
        Me.Close()
    End Sub

    Private Sub btnPlay_Click(ByVal sender As Object, ByVal e As System.EventArgs) _
        Handles btnPlay.Click
        'simulates the Hangman game

        'declare variables
        Dim strWord As String               'stores the word to be guessed
        Dim strLetter As String             'stores the letter guesses
        Dim blnDashReplaced As Boolean      'indicates if a dash was replaced
        Dim blnGameOver As Boolean          'indicates if the game is over
        Dim intIncorrectGuesses As Integer  'counts the number of incorrect guesses
        Dim intIndex As Integer             'keeps track of the indexes

        'get a 5-letter word from the first player
        strWord = InputBox("Enter a 5-letter word:", "Word")
        Do While strWord.Length <> 5
            strWord = InputBox("Enter a 5-letter word:", "Word")
        Loop

        'convert word to uppercase
        strWord = strWord.ToUpper()

        'display five dashes in lblWord control
        Me.lblWord.Text = "-----"

        'clear the lblIncorrectGuesses control
        Me.lblIncorrectGuesses.Text = ""

        'allow the second player to guess a letter
        'the game is over when either the word has been guessed or
        'the second player makes 10 incorrect guesses
        Do While Not blnGameOver
            'get a letter from the second player
            strLetter = InputBox("Enter a letter:", "Letter", "", 500, 400)

            'convert letter to uppercase
            strLetter = strLetter.ToUpper()
```

(Figure is continued on next page)

```
        'search the word for the letter
        For intIndex = 0 To strWord.Length - 1
            If strWord.Substring(intIndex, 1) = strLetter Then
                'replace appropriate dash in the lblWord control
                Mid(Me.lblWord.Text, intIndex + 1) = strLetter
                'indicate that a replacement was made
                blnDashReplaced = True
            End If
        Next intIndex

        'determine whether a replacement was made
        If blnDashReplaced Then
            'if the word does not contain any dashes, then
            'the user guessed the word, so the game is over
            If Me.lblWord.Text.IndexOf("-") = -1 Then
                blnGameOver = True
                MessageBox.Show("Great guessing!", "Hangman Game", _
                    MessageBoxButtons.OK, MessageBoxIcon.Information, _
                    MessageBoxDefaultButton.Button1)
            Else    'reset the blnDashReplaced variable
                blnDashReplaced = False
            End If

        Else   'processed when the word contains at least one dash
            'update the counter variable, then display the result
            intIncorrectGuesses = intIncorrectGuesses + 1
            Me.lblIncorrectGuesses.Text = Convert.ToString(intIncorrectGuesses)
            'determine whether the user has made 10 incorrect guesses
            If intIncorrectGuesses = 10 Then
                'if the user made 10 incorrect guesses, the game is over
                blnGameOver = True
                Me.lblWord.Text = "Game Over"
                MessageBox.Show("Sorry, the word is " & strWord, "Hangman Game", _
                    MessageBoxButtons.OK, MessageBoxIcon.Information, _
                    MessageBoxDefaultButton.Button1)
            End If
        End If
    Loop

    End Sub
End Class
```

FIGURE 6.17

Quick Review

- You can use a string's Length property to determine the number of characters contained in the string.
- The TrimStart method removes one or more characters from the beginning of a string, and the TrimEnd method removes one or more characters from the end of a string. The Trim method removes one or more characters from both the beginning and end of a string. The TrimStart, TrimEnd, and Trim methods return a string with the appropriate characters removed (trimmed).

- You can use the Remove method to remove one or more characters from anywhere in a string. The Remove method returns a string with the appropriate characters removed.
- The StartsWith method determines whether a string begins with a specific sequence of characters. The method returns either the Boolean value True or the Boolean value False.
- The EndsWith method determines whether a string ends with a specific sequence of characters. The method returns either the Boolean value True or the Boolean value False.
- The Substring method allows you to access one or more characters contained in a string. The method returns a string that contains the specified number of characters.
- You can use the Replace method to replace all occurrences of a sequence of characters in a string with another sequence of characters. The method returns a string with all occurrences of the old value replaced with the new value.
- The Mid statement allows you to replace a specific number of characters in a string with characters from another string.
- The PadLeft method allows you to insert characters at the beginning of a string, until the string is a specified length. The PadRight method allows you to insert characters at the end of a string, until the string is a specified length. Both methods return a string with the appropriate characters inserted.
- You can use the Insert method to insert characters within a string. The method returns a string with the appropriate characters inserted.
- The IndexOf method allows you to search a string to determine whether it contains a specific sequence of characters. The method returns the number -1 if the sequence of characters is not contained in the portion of the string being searched; otherwise, it returns the index of the starting position of the characters within the string.
- The Like comparison operator allows you to use pattern-matching characters to determine whether one string is equal to another string.

Key Terms

A string's **Length property** stores an integer that represents the number of characters contained in the string.

The **TrimStart, TrimEnd, Trim,** and **Remove methods** remove one or more characters from a string, and then return a string with the appropriate characters removed.

The unique number assigned to each character in a string is called an **index**.

The **StartsWith** and **EndsWith methods** return the Boolean value True if a specific sequence of characters occurs at the beginning and end, respectively, of a string; otherwise, they return the Boolean value False.

The **Substring method** returns characters from a string.

The **Replace method** returns a string with all occurrences of a sequence of characters replaced with another sequence of characters.

The **Mid statement** replaces a portion of a string with another string.

The **PadLeft, PadRight,** and **Insert methods** return a string with the appropriate characters inserted.

The **IndexOf method** searches a *string* for a *value*, and returns the number –1 if the *value* is found in the *string*; otherwise, it returns the index of the starting position of *value* within *string*.

The **Like operator** allows you to use pattern-matching characters to determine whether one string is equal to another string.

Review Questions

1. You can use the _____ to determine the number of characters in a string.
   a. Length method
   b. Length property
   c. NumChars property
   d. Size property

2. Assume that the strAmount variable contains the string "$56.55". Which of the following removes the dollar sign from the variable's contents?
   a. `strAmount = strAmount.Remove("$")`
   b. `strAmount = strAmount.Remove(0, 1)`
   c. `strAmount = strAmount.TrimStart("$"c)`
   d. Both b and c.

3. Assume that the strState variable contains the string "MI   " (the letters M and I followed by three spaces). Which of the following removes the three spaces from the variable's contents?
   a. `strState = strState.Remove(2, 3)`
   b. `strState = strState.Remove(3, 3)`
   c. `strState = strState.TrimEnd(2, 3)`
   d. Both a and c.

4. Which of the following removes any dollar signs and percent signs from the beginning and end of the string stored in the strAmount variable?
   a. `strAmount = strAmount.Trim("$"c, "%"c)`
   b. `strAmount = strAmount.Trim("$, %"c)`
   c. `strAmount = strAmount.TrimAll("$"c, "%"c)`
   d. `strAmount = strAmount.TrimAll("$, %"c)`

5. Which of the following can be used to determine whether the string stored in the strPart variable begins with the letter A?
   a. `strPart.BeginsWith("A")`
   b. `strPart.Starts("A")`
   c. `strPart.StartsWith("A")`
   d. `strPart.StartsWith = "A"`

6. Which of the following can be used to determine whether the string stored in the strPart variable ends with either the letter B or the letter b?
   a. `strPart.Ends("B, b")`
   b. `strPart.Ends("B", "b")`
   c. `strPart.EndsWith("B", "b")`
   d. `strPart.ToUpper().EndsWith("B")`

7. Which of the following assigns the first three characters in the strPart variable to the strCode variable?
   a. `strCode = strPart.Assign(0, 3)`
   b. `strCode = strPart.Sub(0, 3)`
   c. `strCode = strPart.Substring(0, 3)`
   d. `strCode = strPart.Substring(1, 3)`

8. Assume that the strWord variable contains the string "Bells". Which of the following changes the contents of the strWord variable to "Bell"?
   a. `strWord = strWord.Remove(strWord.Length - 1, 1)`
   b. `strWord = strWord.Substring(0, strWord.Length - 1)`
   c. `strWord = strWord.Replace("s", "")`
   d. All of the above.

9. Which of the following changes the contents of the strZip variable from "60121" to "60323"?
   a. `Replace(strZip, "1", "3")`
   b. `strZip.Replace("1", "3")`
   c. `strZip = strZip.Replace("1", "3")`
   d. `strZip = strZip.Replace("3", "1")`

10. Which of the following changes the contents of the strZip variable from "60537" to "60536"?
    a. `Mid(strZip, "7", "6")`
    b. `Mid(strZip, 4, "6")`
    c. `strZip = Mid(strZip, 4, "6")`
    d. None of the above.

11. Which of the following changes the contents of the strWord variable from "men" to "mean"?
    a. `strWord = strWord.AddTo(2, "a")`
    b. `strWord = strWord.Insert(2, "a")`
    c. `strWord = strWord.Insert(3, "a")`
    d. `strWord = strWord.Replace(2, "a")`

12. Assuming that the strMsg variable contains the string "Happy holidays", the `strMsg.IndexOf("day")` method returns _____.
    a. -1
    b. 0
    c. 10
    d. 11

13. Assume that the strMsg variable contains the string "Good morning". The statement `Mid(strMsg, 6) = "night"` changes the contents of the strMsg variable to _____.
    a. Good mnight
    b. Good mnightg
    c. Good night
    d. Good nightng

14. Which of the following If clauses can be used to determine whether the strAmount variable contains a comma?
    a. `If strAmount.Contains(",") Then`
    b. `If strAmount.Substring(",") Then`
    c. `If strAmount.IndexOf(",") = 0 Then`
    d. `If strAmount.IndexOf(",") > -1 Then`

15. Which of the following can be used to assign the fifth character in the strWord variable to the strLetter variable?
    a. `strLetter = strWord.Substring(4)`
    b. `strLetter = strWord.Substring(5, 1)`
    c. `strLetter = strWord(5).Substring`
    d. None of the above.

16. If the strWord variable contains the string "Irene Turner", the `strWord.IndexOf("r")` method returns _____.
    a. -1
    b. 2
    c. 3
    d. None of the above.

17. Which of the following can be used to determine whether the strPartNum variable contains two characters followed by a digit?
    a. `If strPartNum Like "??#" Then`
    b. `If strPartNum Like "**?" Then`
    c. `If strPartNum Like "##?" Then`
    d. None of the above.

18. Which of the following can be used to determine whether the strItem variable contains either the word "shirt" or the word "skirt"? You can assume that the strItem variable contains uppercase letters only.
    a. `If strItem = "SHIRT" AndAlso strItem = "SKIRT" Then`
    b. `If strItem = "S[HK]IRT" Then`
    c. `If strItem Like "S[HK]IRT" Then`
    d. `If strItem Like "S[H-K]IRT" Then`

19. Assume that the strState variable contains the string "Florida". Which of the following assigns six spaces followed by the contents of the strState variable to the strState variable?
    a. `strState = strState.Pad(13)`
    b `strState = strState.PadLeft(6)`
    c. `strState = strState.PadLeft(13)`
    d. `strState = strState.PadRight(6)`

20. Assume that the strMsg variable contains the string "Great job". Which of the following assigns the contents of the strMsg variable followed by four exclamation points (!) to the strNewMsg variable?
    a. `strNewMsg = strMsg.PadLeft(4, "!"c)`
    b. `strNewMsg = strMsg.PadLeft(13, "!")`
    c. `strNewMsg = strMsg.PadRight(4, "!")`
    d. `strNewMsg = strMsg.PadRight(13, "!"c)`

Exercises

1. Write the Visual Basic .NET statement that displays in the lblSize control the number of characters contained in the strMsg variable.

2. Write the Visual Basic .NET statement that removes the leading spaces from the strCity variable.

3. Write the Visual Basic .NET statement that removes the leading and trailing spaces from the strNum variable.

4. Write the Visual Basic .NET statement that removes any trailing spaces, commas, and periods from the strAmount variable.

5. Write the Visual Basic .NET statement that uses the Remove method to remove the first two characters from the strName variable.

6. Write the Visual Basic .NET code that uses the EndsWith method to determine whether the string stored in the strRate variable ends with the percent sign. If it does, the code should use the TrimEnd method to remove the percent sign from the variable's contents.

7. Assume that the strPart variable contains the string "ABCD34G". Write the Visual Basic .NET statement that assigns the number 34 in the strPart variable to the strCode variable.

8. Assume that the strAmount variable contains the string "3,123,560". Write the Visual Basic .NET statement that assigns the contents of the variable, excluding the commas and treated as a Decimal number, to the decAmount variable.

9. Write the Mid statement that changes the contents of the strWord variable from "mouse" to "mouth".

10. Write the Visual Basic .NET statement that uses the Insert method to change the contents of the strWord variable from "mend" to "amend".

11. Write the Visual Basic .NET statement that uses the IndexOf method to determine whether the strAddress variable contains the street name "Elm Street" (entered in uppercase, lowercase, or a combination of uppercase and lowercase). Begin the search with the first character in the strAddress variable, and assign the method's return value to the intIndex variable.

12. In this exercise, you modify this chapter's Programming Example.
    a. Create the Hangman Game application shown in this chapter's Programming Example. Save the application in the VbDotNet\ Chap06 folder.
    b. Modify the application so that it allows the first player to enter a word that contains any number of characters. The number of incorrect guesses the user is allowed to make should be twice as many as the number of characters in the word. For example, if the word contains seven characters, allow the user to make fourteen incorrect guesses. Similarly, if the word contains three letters, allow the user to make six incorrect guesses. Be sure to modify the TOE chart and pseudocode before modifying the code.
    c. Save the solution, then start and test the application. Click the Exit button to end the application, then close the solution.

13. In this exercise, you complete an application that displays a shipping charge based on the ZIP code entered by the user.
    a. Open the Zip Solution (Zip Solution.sln) file, which is contained in the VbDotNet\Chap06\Zip Solution folder.
    b. The Display Shipping Charge button's Click event procedure should display the appropriate shipping charge based on the ZIP code entered by the user. To be valid, the ZIP code must contain exactly five digits, and the first three digits must be either "605" or "606". All ZIP codes beginning with "605" have a $25 shipping charge. All ZIP codes beginning with "606" have a $30 shipping charge. All other ZIP codes are invalid and the procedure should display an appropriate message. Code the procedure appropriately.

c. Save the solution, then start the application. Test the application using the following ZIP codes: 60677, 60511, 60344, and 7130.

d. Click the Exit button to end the application, then close the solution.

14. In this exercise, you complete an application that displays the name of the month corresponding to three letters entered by the user.

a. Open the Month Solution (Month Solution.sln) file, which is contained in the VbDotNet\Chap06\Month Solution folder.

b. The user will enter the first three characters of the month's name in the txtMonth text box. The Display Month button's Click event procedure should display the name of the month corresponding to the characters entered by the user. For example, if the user enters the three characters "Jan" (in any case), the procedure should display the string "January" in the lblMonth control. If the user enters "Jun", the procedure should display "June". If the three characters entered by the user do not match any of the 12 months, or if the user does not enter exactly three characters, the procedure should display an appropriate message.

c. Save the solution, then start the application. Test the application using the following data: jun, dec, xyz, july.

d. Click the Exit button to end the application, then close the solution.

15. In this exercise, you code an application that displays the color of an item.

a. Open the Color Solution (Color Solution.sln) file, which is contained in the VbDotNet\Chap06\Color Solution folder.

b. The Display Color button's Click event procedure should display the color of the item whose item number is entered by the user. All item numbers contain exactly five characters. All items are available in four colors: blue, green, red, and white. The third character in the item number indicates the item's color, as follows:

Character	Color
B or b	Blue
G or g	Green
R or r	Red
W or w	White

For example, if the user enters 12b45, the procedure should display the word "Blue" in the lblColor control. If the item number does not contain exactly five characters, or if the third character is not one of the characters listed above, the procedure should display an appropriate message in a message box.

c. Save the solution, then start the application. Test the application using the following item numbers: 12x, 12b45, 99G44, abr55, 78w99, and 23abc.

d. Click the Exit button to end the application, then close the solution.

16. In this exercise, you code an application that allows the user to enter a name (the first name followed by a space and the last name). The application then displays the name (the last name followed by a comma, a space, and the first name).

a. Build an appropriate interface. Name the solution Reverse Name Solution. Name the project Reverse Name Project. Save the application in the VbDotNet\Chap06 folder.

b. Code the application.

c. Save the solution, and then start the application. Test the application using the following names: Carol Smith, Jose Martinez, Sven Miller, and Susan.

d. Stop the application, then close the solution.

17. In this exercise, you modify the application that you created in Exercise 16 so that it displays the names using proper case.
    a. Use Windows to make a copy of the Reverse Name Solution folder, which is contained in the VbDotNet\Chap06 folder. Rename the folder Proper Case Solution.
    b. Open the Reverse Name Solution (Reverse Name Solution.sln) file contained in the Proper Case Solution folder.
    c. Modify the application so that it displays the first and last names in proper case. In other words, the first and last names should begin with an uppercase letter, and the remaining letters should be lowercase.
    d. Save the solution, then start the application. Test the application using jAke millEr as the name. The application should display Miller, Jake.
    e. Stop the application, then close the solution.

18. In this exercise, you code an application that allows the user to enter a phone number. The application then removes any hyphens, spaces, and parentheses from the phone number before displaying the phone number.
    a. Build an appropriate interface. Name the solution Phone Solution. Name the project Phone Project. Save the application in the VbDotNet\Chap06 folder.
    b. Code the application.
    c. Save the solution, then start the application. Test the application using the following phone numbers: (555) 111-1111, 555-5555, and 123-456-1111.
    d. Stop the application, then close the solution.

19. In this exercise, you code an application that displays a message indicating whether a portion of a string begins with another string.
    a. Open the String Solution (String Solution.sln) file, which is contained in the VbDotNet\Chap06\String Solution folder.
    b. The application allows the user to enter a name (first name followed by a space and the last name) and the search text. If the last name (entered in any case) begins with the search text (entered in any case), the Display Message button's Click event procedure should display the message "The last name begins with" followed by a space and the search text. If the characters in the last name come before the search text in the ASCII coding scheme, display the message "The last name comes before" followed by a space and the search text. Finally, if the characters in the last name come after the search text in the ASCII coding scheme, display the message "The last name comes after" followed by a space and the search text.
    c. Save the solution, then start the application. To test the application, enter Helga Swanson as the name, then use the following strings for the search text: g, ab, he, s, SY, sw, swan, and wan.
    d. Click the Exit button to end the application, then close the solution.

20. In this exercise, you find and correct an error in an application. The process of finding and correcting errors is called debugging.
    a. Open the Debug Solution (Debug Solution.sln) file, which is contained in the VbDotNet\Chap06\Debug Solution folder.
    b. Open the Code Editor window. Review the existing code.
    c. Start the application. Enter Tampa, Florida in the Address text box, then click the Display City button. The button displays the letter T in a message box, which is incorrect; it should display the word Tampa. Click the OK button to close the dialog box, then click the Exit button to end the application.

   d. Correct the application's code, then save the solution and start the application.

   e. Enter Tampa, Florida in the Address text box, then click the Display City button. The button should display the word Tampa in a message box. Close the dialog box.

   f. Click the Exit button to end the application, then close the solution.

Case Projects

Georgetown Credit

Credit card companies typically assign a special digit, called a check digit, to the end of each customer's credit card number. Many methods for creating the check digit have been developed. One simple method is to multiply every other number in the credit card number by two, then add the products to the remaining numbers to get the total. You then take the last digit in the total and append it to the end of the number, as illustrated in Figure 6.18.

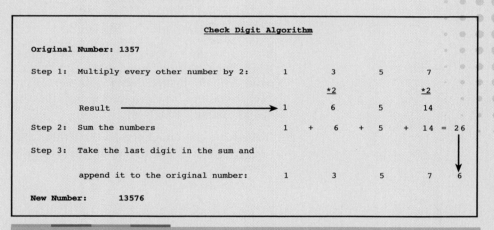

FIGURE 6.18

Create an application that allows the user to enter a five-digit credit card number; assume that the fifth digit is the check digit. The application should use the method illustrated in Figure 6.18 to verify that the credit card number is valid. Display appropriate messages indicating whether the credit card number is valid or invalid.

Jacobson Finance

Create an application that allows the user to enter a password that contains five, six, or seven characters. The application then should create and display a new password as follows:

1. Replace all vowels (A, E, I, O, and U) with the letter X.

2. Replace all numbers with the letter Z.

3. Reverse the characters in the password.

BobCat Motors

Each salesperson at BobCat Motors is assigned an ID number, which consists of four characters. The first character is either the letter F or the letter P. The letter F indicates that the salesperson is a full-time employee; the letter P indicates that he or she is a part-time employee. The middle two characters are the salesperson's initials, and the last character is either a 1 or a 2. A 1 indicates that the salesperson sells new cars, and a 2 indicates that the salesperson sells used cars. Create an application that allows the sales manager to enter a salesperson's ID and the number of cars the salesperson sold during the month. The application should allow the sales manager to enter this information for as many salespeople as needed. The application should calculate and display the total number of cars sold by each of the following four categories of employees: full-time employees, part-time employees, employees selling new cars, and employees selling used cars.

Pig Latin Is Challenging

Create an application that allows the user to enter a word. The application should display the word in pig Latin form. The rules for converting a word into pig Latin form are as follows:

1. If the word begins with a vowel (A, E, I, O, or U), then add the string "-way" (a dash followed by the letters w, a, and y) to the end of the word. For example, the pig Latin form of the word "ant" is "ant-way".

2. If the word does not begin with a vowel, first add a dash to the end of the word. Then continue moving the first character in the word to the end of the word until the first character is the letter A, E, I, O, U, or Y. Then add the string "ay" to the end of the word. For example, the pig Latin form of the word "Chair" is "air-Chay".

3. If the word does not contain the letter A, E, I, O, U, or Y, then add the string "-way" to the end of the word. For example, the pig Latin form of "56" is "56-way".

7

Sub and Function Procedures

After studying Chapter 7, you should be able to:

- Explain the difference between a Sub procedure and a Function procedure
- Create a Sub procedure
- Create a procedure that receives information passed to it
- Explain the difference between passing data *by value* and passing data *by reference*
- Create a Function procedure

PROCEDURES

A **procedure** is a block of program code that performs a specific task. Programmers use procedures for two reasons. First, procedures allow the programmer to avoid duplicating code in different parts of a program. If a program needs to perform the same task several times, it is more efficient to enter the appropriate code once, in a procedure, and then call the procedure to perform its task when needed. Second, procedures allow large and complex applications, which typically are written by a team of programmers, to be broken into small and manageable tasks; each member of the team can be assigned one of the tasks to code as a procedure. When each programmer has completed his or her procedure, all of the procedures are gathered together into one application.

Procedures in Visual Basic .NET can be either Sub procedures or Function procedures. The difference between both types of procedures is that a **Function procedure** returns a value after performing its assigned task, whereas a **Sub procedure** does not return a value. Although you have been using Sub procedures since Chapter 1, this chapter provides a more in-depth look into their creation and use. After exploring the topic of Sub procedures, you then learn how to create and use Function procedures.

SUB PROCEDURES

There are two types of Sub procedures in Visual Basic .NET: event procedures and independent Sub procedures. The procedures that you coded in previous chapters were event procedures. An event procedure is simply a Sub procedure that is associated with a specific object and event, such as a button's Click event. Recall that the computer automatically processes an event procedure when the event occurs. An **independent Sub procedure**, on the other hand, is a collection of code that can be invoked from one or more places in an application. Unlike an event procedure, an independent Sub procedure is independent of any object and event, and is processed only when called, or invoked, from code.

Figure 7.1 shows the syntax you use to create an independent Sub procedure. It also includes an example of an independent Sub procedure, and the steps you follow to enter an independent Sub procedure in the Code Editor window.

HOW TO...

Procedure header

Procedure footer

Create an Independent Sub Procedure

Syntax
Private Sub *procedurename*([*parameterlist*])
      [*statements*]
End Sub

Example
```
Private Sub ClearLabels()
    'removes the contents of the label controls
    'that display the regular pay, overtime pay,
    'and gross pay

    Me.lblRegularPay.Text = ""
    Me.lblOvertimePay.Text = ""
    Me.lblGrossPay.Text = ""
End Sub
```

Steps for entering an independent Sub procedure in the Code Editor window

1. Open the Code Editor window.
2. Click a blank line in the Code Editor window. The blank line can be anywhere between the [`Windows Form Designer generated code`] entry and the `End Class` statement; however, it must be outside of any other Sub or Function procedure.
3. Type the Sub procedure header and press the Enter key on your keyboard. When you press the Enter key, the Code Editor will automatically enter the Sub procedure footer (`End Sub`) for you.

FIGURE 7.1   How to create an independent Sub procedure

TIP

An independent Sub procedure also can begin with the keywords **Public**, **Protected**, **Friend**, or **Protected Friend**.

As do all procedures, independent Sub procedures have both a procedure header and procedure footer. In most cases, the procedure header begins with the keyword `Private`, which indicates that the procedure can be used only by the other procedures in the current form. Following the `Private` keyword in the procedure header is the keyword `Sub`, which identifies the procedure as a Sub procedure—one that does not return a value after performing its assigned task. After the `Sub` keyword is the *procedurename*. The rules for naming an independent Sub procedure are the same as those for naming variables and constants. (The naming rules are listed in Figure 3.3 in Chapter 3.) You should select a descriptive name for the Sub procedure—one that indicates the task the procedure performs. It is a common practice to begin the name with a verb. For example, a good name for a Sub procedure that clears the contents of the label controls in an interface is ClearLabels.

Following the *procedurename* in the procedure header is a set of parentheses that contains an optional *parameterlist*. The *parameterlist* lists the data type and name of memory locations used by the procedure to store the information passed to it when it is invoked. As you may remember from Chapter 1, these memory locations are referred to as **parameters**. The *parameterlist* also specifies how each parameter is passed—either *by value* or *by reference*. You learn more about the *parameterlist*, and about passing information *by value* and *by reference*, later in this chapter.

Unlike the procedure header, which varies with each procedure, the procedure footer for a Sub procedure is always `End Sub`. Between the procedure header and procedure footer, you enter the instructions you want the computer to process when the procedure is invoked. For example, when the ClearLabels procedure shown in Figure 7.1 is invoked, the computer will process the three assignment statements entered in the procedure.

You can invoke an independent Sub procedure using the **Call statement**. Figure 7.2 shows the syntax of the Call statement and includes an example of using the statement to invoke the ClearLabels procedure shown in Figure 7.1.

HOW TO...

Call an Independent Sub Procedure

Syntax
Call *procedurename*([*argumentlist*])

Example
```
Call ClearLabels()
```

FIGURE 7.2   How to call an independent Sub procedure

In the Call statement's syntax, *procedurename* is the name of the procedure you are invoking (calling), and *argumentlist* (which is optional) is a comma-separated list of arguments you want passed to the procedure. If you have no information to pass to the procedure that you are calling, as is the case in the ClearLabels procedure, you simply include an empty set of parentheses after the *procedurename*, as shown in Figure 7.2.

Next, you view an application that uses the ClearLabels procedure.

The Gladis Antiques Application

The manager at Gladis Antiques wants an application that he can use to calculate an employee's regular pay, overtime pay, and gross pay. Employees are paid on an hourly basis and are given time and one-half for the hours worked over 40. Figure 7.3 shows a sample run of the Gladis Antiques application, and Figure 7.4 shows the application's code.

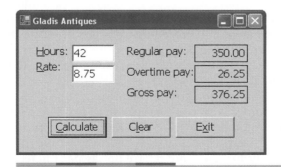

FIGURE 7.3   Sample run of the Gladis Antiques application

```
'Project name:          Gladis Antiques Project
'Project purpose:       The project calculates an employee's regular pay,
'                       overtime pay, and gross pay.
'Created/revised by:    Diane Zak on 2/1/2005

Option Explicit On
Option Strict On

Public Class frmGladis
    Inherits System.Windows.Forms.Form

[Windows Form Designer generated code]

    Private Sub ClearLabels()
        'removes the contents of the label controls
        'that display the regular pay, overtime pay,
        'and gross pay

        Me.lblRegularPay.Text = ""
        Me.lblOvertimePay.Text = ""
        Me.lblGrossPay.Text = ""
    End Sub

    Private Sub btnClear_Click(ByVal sender As Object, _
        ByVal e As System.EventArgs) Handles btnClear.Click
        'prepares the screen for the next calculation

        'clear the text boxes and label controls
        Me.txtHours.Text = ""
        Me.txtRate.Text = ""
        Call ClearLabels()
    End Sub

    Private Sub btnCalc_Click(ByVal sender As Object, _
        ByVal e As System.EventArgs) Handles btnCalc.Click
        'calculates the gross pay

        'declare variables
        Dim strHoursWorked As String
        Dim strPayRate As String
        Dim decHoursWorked As Decimal
        Dim decPayRate As Decimal
        Dim decRegularPay As Decimal
        Dim decOvertimePay As Decimal
        Dim decGrossPay As Decimal

        If IsNumeric(Me.txtHours.Text) AndAlso IsNumeric(Me.txtRate.Text) Then
            'assign input to variables
            decHoursWorked = Convert.ToDecimal(Me.txtHours.Text)
            decPayRate = Convert.ToDecimal(Me.txtRate.Text)

            If decHoursWorked <= 40D Then
                'calculate regular pay
                decRegularPay = decHoursWorked * decPayRate
            Else
                'calculate regular pay and overtime pay
                decRegularPay = 40 * decPayRate
                decOvertimePay = (decHoursWorked - 40) * decPayRate * 1.5D
            End If
```

ClearLabels
Sub procedure

Invokes the ClearLabels
Sub procedure

(Figure is continued on next page)

```
                    'calculate gross pay
                    decGrossPay = decRegularPay + decOvertimePay

                    'display regular pay, overtime pay, and gross pay
                    Me.lblRegularPay.Text = decRegularPay.ToString("N2")
                    Me.lblOvertimePay.Text = decOvertimePay.ToString("N2")
                    Me.lblGrossPay.Text = decGrossPay.ToString("N2")
                Else
                    MessageBox.Show("The hours worked and pay rate must be numeric.", _
                        "Gladis Antiques", MessageBoxButtons.OK, _
                        MessageBoxIcon.Information, MessageBoxDefaultButton.Button1)
                    Call ClearLabels()
                End If
            End Sub

            Private Sub btnExit_Click(ByVal sender As Object, _
                ByVal e As System.EventArgs) Handles btnExit.Click
                'ends the application
                Me.Close()
            End Sub
        End Class
```

Invokes the ClearLabels Sub procedure

FIGURE 7.4   Code for the Gladis Antiques application

TIP

When you enter a procedure below the last event procedure in the Code Editor window, be sure to enter it above the **End Class** statement.

In Figure 7.4, the ClearLabels procedure is entered above the event procedures in the Code Editor window. Rather than entering it in this area, it also could have been entered below the btnClear Click event procedure, or below the btnCalc Click event procedure, or below the btnExit Click event procedure. However, many programmers prefer to group together the procedures they create; they typically enter these procedures either above the first event procedure (as shown in Figure 7.4) or below the last event procedure. By organizing the code in this manner, the programmer can more easily locate the independent Sub and Function procedures in the Code Editor window.

As Figure 7.4 indicates, the Call statement that invokes the ClearLabels procedure appears in two places in the code; it appears in the btnClear Click event procedure and in the btnCalc Click event procedure. Study closely the code that appears in these two procedures. When the btnClear Click event procedure is processed, which is when the user clicks the Clear button in the interface, the computer processes the `Me.txtHours.Text = ""` and `Me.txtRate.Text = ""` statements. These two statements remove the contents of the two text boxes in the interface. When processing the next instruction, `Call ClearLabels()`, the computer temporarily leaves the btnClear Click event procedure to process the code in the ClearLabels procedure.

The first three statements in the ClearLabels procedure remove the contents of three label controls in the interface. After processing the assignment statements, the computer processes the ClearLabels procedure's `End Sub` statement, which ends the ClearLabels procedure. The computer then returns to the btnClear Click event procedure and processes the statement located immediately below the Call statement. The statement below the Call statement is `End Sub`, which ends the btnClear Click event procedure.

The btnCalc Click event procedure is processed when the user clicks the Calculate button in the interface. The first seven statements declare two String variables and five Decimal variables. The condition in the first If...Then...Else statement checks whether the txtHours and txtRate controls contain numbers. If either or both controls do not contain a number, the MessageBox.Show method in the first selection structure's false path displays an appropriate message. The computer then processes the `Call ClearLabels()` statement. Here again, the computer temporarily leaves the current procedure—in this case, the btnCalc Click event procedure—to process the code contained in the ClearLabels procedure.

As before, the first three statements in the ClearLabels procedure remove the contents of three label controls in the interface, and the `End Sub` statement ends the ClearLabels procedure. The computer then returns to the btnCalc Click event procedure and processes the statement located immediately below the Call statement. The statement below the Call statement is `End Sub`, which ends the btnCalc Click event procedure.

As mentioned earlier, an independent Sub procedure can contain one or more parameters in its procedure header. Each parameter stores data that is passed to the procedure when it is invoked. In the next section, you learn how to include parameters in a procedure header.

INCLUDING PARAMETERS IN AN INDEPENDENT SUB PROCEDURE

TIP

Visual Basic .NET allows you to specify that an argument in the Call statement is optional. If the argument is not provided, a default value is used for the corresponding parameter in the *parameterlist*. You learn more about optional arguments in Exercise 23 at the end of this chapter.

Recall that the Call statement has an optional *argumentlist*, which is a comma-separated list of arguments you want passed to the procedure being called. The number of arguments listed in the Call statement's *argumentlist* should agree with the number of parameters listed in the *parameterlist* in the procedure header. If the *argumentlist* includes one argument, then the procedure header should have one parameter in its *parameterlist*. Similarly, a procedure that is passed three arguments when called requires three parameters in its *parameterlist*. (Refer to the tip on this page for an exception to this general rule.)

In addition to having the same number of parameters as arguments, the data type and position of each parameter in the *parameterlist* must agree with the data type and position of its corresponding argument in the *argumentlist*. For instance, if the argument is an integer, then the parameter in which the integer will be stored should have a data type of Integer, Short, or Long, depending on the size of the integer. Likewise, if two arguments are passed to a procedure—the first one being a String variable and the second one being a Decimal variable—the first parameter should have a data type of String and the second parameter should have a data type of Decimal.

You can pass a literal constant, named constant, keyword, or variable to an independent Sub procedure; in most cases, you will pass a variable.

PASSING VARIABLES

Each variable you declare in an application has both a value and a unique address that represents the location of the variable in the computer's internal memory. Visual Basic .NET allows you to pass either the variable's value (referred to as **passing by value**) or its address (referred to as **passing by reference**) to the receiving procedure. The method you choose—*by value* or *by reference*—depends on whether you want the receiving procedure to have access to the variable in memory—in other words, whether you want to allow the receiving procedure to change the contents of the variable.

Although the idea of passing information *by value* and *by reference* may sound confusing at first, it is a concept with which you already are familiar. To illustrate, assume that you have a savings account at a local bank. During a conversation with a friend, you mention the amount of money you have in the account. Telling someone the amount of money in your account is similar to passing a variable *by value*. Knowing the balance in your account does not give your friend access to your bank account; it merely gives your friend some information that he or she can use—perhaps to compare to the amount of money he or she has saved.

The savings account example also provides an illustration of passing information *by reference*. To deposit money to or withdraw money from your account, you must provide the bank teller with your account number. The account number represents the location of your account at the bank and allows the teller to change the account balance. Giving the teller your bank account number is similar to passing a variable *by reference*. The account number allows the teller to change the contents of your bank account, similar to the way the variable's address allows the receiving procedure to change the contents of the variable passed to the procedure.

First, you learn how to pass a variable *by value*.

Passing Variables by Value

To pass a variable *by value* in Visual Basic .NET, you include the keyword `ByVal`, which stands for "by value", before the variable's corresponding parameter in the *parameterlist*. When you pass a variable *by value*, the computer passes only the contents of the variable to the receiving procedure. When only the contents are passed, the receiving procedure is not given access to the variable in memory, so it cannot change the value stored inside the variable. You pass a variable *by value* when the receiving procedure needs to *know* the variable's contents, but the receiving procedure does not need to *change* the contents. Unless specified otherwise, variables are passed *by value* in Visual Basic .NET.

Figure 7.5 shows two examples of passing variables *by value*. The *argumentlist* in each Call statement, and the *parameterlist* in each procedure header, are shaded in the figure.

TIP

The internal memory of a computer is like a large post office, where each memory cell, like each post office box, has a unique address.

Passing *by value*

Example 1

```
Private Sub btnGetInfo_Click(ByVal sender As Object, _
        ByVal e As System.EventArgs) Handles btnGetInfo.Click
        'gets pet information, then calls a Sub procedure
        'to display the information

        'declare variables
        Dim strName As String
        Dim strAge As String

        'assign input to variables
        strName = InputBox("Pet's name:", "Name")
        strAge = InputBox("Pet's age (years):", "Age")

        'call Sub procedure, passing it the pet information
        Call DisplayMessage(strName, strAge)
End Sub


Private Sub DisplayMessage(ByVal strPet As String, ByVal strYears As String)
        'displays the pet information passed to it
        Me.lblMessage.Text = "Your pet " & strPet & " is " _
        & strYears & " years old."
End Sub
```

Argumentlist — `strName, strAge`

Parameterlist — `ByVal strPet As String, ByVal strYears As String`

Example 2

```
Private Sub btnCalc_Click(ByVal sender As Object, _
        ByVal e As System.EventArgs) Handles btnCalc.Click
        'gets sales and rate information, then calls a Sub procedure
        'to calculate and display the bonus

        'declare variables
        Dim intRegion1 As Integer
        Dim intRegion2 As Integer
        Dim decBonusRate As Decimal

        'assign input to variables
        intRegion1 = Convert.ToInt32(Me.txtRegion1.Text)
        intRegion2 = Convert.ToInt32(Me.txtRegion2.Text)
        decBonusRate = Convert.ToDecimal(Me.txtBonusRate.Text)

        'call Sub procedure, passing it the sales amounts and bonus rate
        Call CalcAndDisplayBonus(intRegion1, intRegion2, decBonusRate)
End Sub
```

Argumentlist — `intRegion1, intRegion2, decBonusRate`

(Figure is continued on next page)

Parameterlist

```
Private Sub CalcAndDisplayBonus(ByVal intSale1 As Integer, _
                                ByVal intSale2 As Integer, _
                                ByVal decRate As Decimal)
    'calculates and displays a bonus amount, based on the
    'sales amounts and bonus rate passed to it

    'declare variable
    Dim decBonus As Decimal

    'calculate and display bonus amount
    decBonus = Convert.ToDecimal(intSale1 + intSale2) * decRate
    Me.lblBonus.Text = decBonus.ToString("C2")
End Sub
```

FIGURE 7.5   *Examples of passing variables* by value

Notice that, in both examples, the number, data type, and sequence of the arguments in the Call statement match the number, data type, and sequence of the corresponding parameters in the procedure header. Also notice that the names of the parameters do not need to be identical to the names of the arguments to which they correspond. In fact, for clarity, it usually is better to use different names for the arguments and parameters.

Study closely the code shown in Example 1 in Figure 7.5. The btnGetInfo control's Click event procedure first declares two String variables named strName and strAge. The next two statements in the procedure use the InputBox function to prompt the user to enter the name and age (in years) of his or her pet. Assume that the user enters "Spot" as the name and "4" as the age. The computer stores the string "Spot" in the strName variable and the string "4" in the strAge variable.

Next, the `Call DisplayMessage(strName, strAge)` statement calls the DisplayMessage procedure, passing it the strName and strAge variables *by value*, which means that only the contents of the variables—in this case, "Spot" and "4"—are passed to the procedure. You know that the variables are passed *by value* because the keyword `ByVal` appears before each variable's corresponding parameter in the DisplayMessage procedure header. At this point, the computer temporarily leaves the btnGetInfo Click event procedure to process the code contained in the DisplayMessage procedure.

The first instruction processed in the DisplayMessage procedure is the procedure header. When processing the procedure header, the computer creates the strPet and strYears variables (which are listed in the *parameterlist*) in its internal memory, and stores the information passed to the procedure in those variables. In this case, the computer stores the string "Spot" in the strPet variable and the string "4" in the strYears variable. The strPet and strYears variables (as well as any variables that appear in a procedure header) are procedure-level variables, which means they can be used only by the procedure in which they are declared. In this case, the strPet and strYears variables can be used only by the DisplayMessage procedure.

After processing the DisplayMessage procedure header, the computer processes the assignment statement contained in the procedure. The assignment statement uses the values stored in the procedure's parameters—strPet and strYears—to display the appropriate message in the lblMessage control. In this case, the statement displays the message "Your pet Spot is 4 years old."

TIP

You cannot determine by looking at the Call statement whether a variable is being passed *by value* or *by reference*. You must look at the procedure header to make the determination.

Next, the computer processes the DisplayMessage procedure footer (`End Sub`), which ends the DisplayMessage procedure. At this point, the strPet and strYears variables are removed from the computer's internal memory. (Recall that a procedure-level variable is removed from the computer's memory when the procedure in which it is declared ends.) The computer then returns to the btnGetInfo Click event procedure, to the statement immediately following the `Call DisplayMessage(strName, strAge)` statement. This statement, `End Sub`, ends the btnGetInfo Click event procedure. The computer then removes the procedure's procedure-level variables (strName and strAge) from its internal memory.

Now study closely the code shown in Example 2 in Figure 7.5. The btnCalc Click event procedure first declares two Integer variables named intRegion1 and intRegion2, and a Decimal variable named decBonusRate. The next three statements in the procedure assign the contents of three text boxes to the variables. Assume that the user entered the number 1000 in the txtRegion1 control, the number 3000 in the txtRegion2 control, and the number .1 in the txtBonusRate control. The computer stores the number 1000 in the intRegion1 variable, the number 3000 in the intRegion2 variable, and the number .1 in the decBonusRate variable.

Next, the `Call CalcAndDisplayBonus(intRegion1, intRegion2, decBonusRate)` statement calls the CalcAndDisplayBonus procedure, passing it three variables *by value*, which means that only the contents of the variables—in this case, 1000, 3000, and .1—are passed to the procedure. Here again, you know that the variables are passed *by value* because the keyword `ByVal` appears before each variable's corresponding parameter in the CalcAndDisplayBonus procedure header. At this point, the computer temporarily leaves the btnCalc Click event procedure to process the code contained in the CalcAndDisplayBonus procedure.

The first instruction processed in the CalcAndDisplayBonus procedure is the procedure header. When processing the procedure header, the computer creates the three procedure-level variables listed in the *parameterlist*, and stores the information passed to the procedure in those variables. In this case, the computer stores the number 1000 in the intSale1 variable, the number 3000 in the intSale2 variable, and the number .1 in the decRate variable.

After processing the CalcAndDisplayBonus procedure header, the computer processes the statements contained in the procedure. The first statement declares an additional procedure-level variable named decBonus. The next statement adds the value stored in the intSale1 variable (1000) to the value stored in the intSale2 variable (3000). It then multiplies the sum (4000) by the value stored in the decRate variable (.1), and assigns the result (400) to the decBonus variable. The third statement in the procedure displays the bonus, formatted with a dollar sign and two decimal places, in the lblBonus control; in this case, the statement displays $400.00.

Next, the computer processes the CalcAndDisplayBonus procedure footer, which ends the CalcAndDisplayBonus procedure. At this point, the procedure's procedure-level variables—intSale1, intSale2, decRate, and decBonus—are removed from the computer's internal memory. The computer then returns to the btnCalc Click event procedure, to the statement immediately following the Call statement. This statement, `End Sub`, ends the btnCalc Click event procedure. The computer then removes the intRegion1, intRegion2, and decBonusRate variables from its internal memory.

Next, you learn how to pass variables *by reference*.

Passing Variables by Reference

In addition to passing a variable's value to a procedure, you also can pass a variable's address—in other words, its location in the computer's internal memory. Passing a variable's address is referred to as passing *by reference*, and it gives the receiving procedure access to the variable being passed. You pass a variable *by reference* when you want the receiving procedure to change the contents of the variable.

To pass a variable *by reference* in Visual Basic .NET, you include the keyword `ByRef`, which stands for "by reference", before the name of the variable's corresponding parameter in the procedure header. The `ByRef` keyword tells the computer to pass the variable's address rather than its contents.

Figure 7.6 shows two examples of passing variables *by reference*. The *argumentlist* in each Call statement, and the *parameterlist* in each procedure header, are shaded in the figure.

Passing *by reference*

Example 1

```
Private Sub btnDisplay_Click(ByVal sender As Object, _
      ByVal e As System.EventArgs) Handles btnDisplay.Click
      'calls a Sub procedure to get the pet information, then
      'displays the information

      'declare variables
      Dim strName As String
      Dim strAge As String
```

Argumentlist

```
      'call Sub procedure, passing it the addresses
      'of two variables
      Call GetInfo(strName, strAge)

      'display the pet information
      Me.lblMessage.Text = "Your pet " & strName & " is " _
      & strAge & " years old."
End Sub
```

Parameterlist

```
Private Sub GetInfo(ByRef strPet As String, ByRef strYears As String)
      'gets the pet information
      strPet = InputBox("Pet's name:", "Name")
      strYears = InputBox("Pet's age (years):", "Age")
End Sub
```

Example 2

```
Private Sub btnBonus_Click(ByVal sender As Object, _
      ByVal e As System.EventArgs) Handles btnBonus.Click
      'calls a Sub procedure to calculate the bonus amount, then
      'displays the bonus amount
```

(Figure is continued on next page)

```
                    'declare variables
                    Dim intRegion1 As Integer
                    Dim intRegion2 As Integer
                    Dim decBonus As Decimal

                    'assign input to variables
                    intRegion1 = Convert.ToInt32(Me.txtRegion1.Text)
                    intRegion2 = Convert.ToInt32 (Me.txtRegion2.Text)

                    'call Sub procedure, passing it the sales amounts,
                    'bonus rate, and the address of the decBonus variable
                    Call CalcBonus(intRegion1, intRegion2, .05D, decBonus)

                    'display the bonus amount
                    Me.lblBonus.Text = decBonus.ToString("C2")
                End Sub

                Private Sub CalcBonus(ByVal intSale1 As Integer, _
                                      ByVal intSale2 As Integer, _
                                      ByVal decRate As Decimal, _
                                      ByRef decDollars As Decimal)
                    'calculates the bonus amount
                    decDollars = Convert.ToDecimal(intSale1 + intSale2) * decRate
                End Sub
```

Argumentlist

Parameterlist

FIGURE 7.6   Examples of passing variables *by reference*

Notice that, in both examples, the number, data type, and sequence of the arguments in the Call statement match the number, data type, and sequence of the corresponding parameters in the procedure header. Also notice that the names of the parameters do not need to be identical to the names of the arguments to which they correspond.

Study closely the code shown in Example 1 in Figure 7.6. The btnDisplay Click event procedure first declares two String variables named strName and strAge. The next statement in the procedure calls the GetInfo procedure, passing it the strName and strAge variables *by reference*, which means that each variable's address in memory, rather than its contents, is passed to the procedure. You know that the variables are passed *by reference* because the keyword `ByRef` appears before each variable's corresponding parameter in the GetInfo procedure header. At this point, the computer temporarily leaves the btnDisplay Click event procedure to process the code contained in the GetInfo procedure.

The first instruction processed in the GetInfo procedure is the procedure header. The `ByRef` keyword that appears before each parameter's name in the procedure header indicates that the procedure will be receiving the addresses of two variables. When you pass a variable's address to a procedure, the computer uses the address to locate the variable in memory. It then assigns the name appearing in the procedure header to the memory location. In this case, for example, the computer first locates the strName and strAge variables in memory; after doing so, it assigns the names strPet and strYears, respectively, to these locations. At this point, each of the two memory locations has two names: one assigned by the btnDisplay Click event procedure, and the other assigned by the GetInfo procedure.

TIP

In Example 1 in Figure 7.6, the procedure-level strName and strAge variables can be used only by the btnDisplay Click event procedure. The procedure-level strPet and strYears variables, on the other hand, can be used only by the GetInfo procedure.

After processing the GetInfo procedure header, the computer processes the two assignment statements contained in the procedure. Those statements prompt the user to enter the name and age of his or her pet, and then store the user's responses in the strPet and strYears variables. Assume that the user entered "Simba" as the name and "9" as the age. The computer stores the string "Simba" in the strPet variable and the string "9" in the strYears variable. Figure 7.7 shows the contents of memory after the GetInfo procedure header and the two assignment statements are processed. Notice that changing the contents of the strPet and strYears variables also changes the contents of the strName and strAge variables, respectively. This is because the names refer to the same locations in memory.

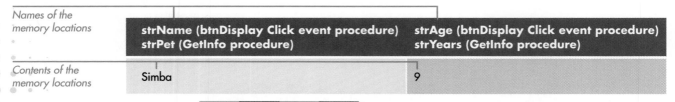

Names of the memory locations

strName (btnDisplay Click event procedure) strPet (GetInfo procedure)	strAge (btnDisplay Click event procedure) strYears (GetInfo procedure)

Contents of the memory locations

Simba	9

FIGURE 7.7   Contents of memory after the GetInfo procedure header and two assignment statements are processed

As Figure 7.7 indicates, the two memory locations belong to both the btnDisplay Click event procedure and the GetInfo procedure. Although both procedures can access the two memory locations, each procedure uses a different name to do so. The btnDisplay Click event procedure, for example, uses the names strName and strAge to refer to these memory locations. The GetInfo procedure, on the other hand, uses the names strPet and strYears.

The `End Sub` statement in the GetInfo procedure is processed next and ends the procedure. At this point, the computer removes the strPet and strYears names assigned to the memory locations. Now, each memory location shown in Figure 7.7 has only one name: the name assigned to it by the btnDisplay Click event procedure.

The computer then returns to the btnDisplay Click event procedure, to the statement located immediately below the Call statement. This statement displays the message "Your pet Simba is 9 years old." in the lblMessage control. Next, the computer processes the `End Sub` statement in the btnDisplay Click event procedure, which ends the procedure. The computer then removes the strName and strAge variables from its internal memory.

Now study the code shown in Example 2 in Figure 7.6. The btnBonus Click event procedure first declares two Integer variables named intRegion1 and intRegion2, and a Decimal variable named decBonus. The next two statements assign the contents of two text boxes to the intRegion1 and intRegion2 variables. Assume that the user enters the numbers 500 and 200 in the text boxes. The computer stores the number 500 in the intRegion1 variable and the number 200 in the intRegion2 variable.

Next, the `Call CalcBonus(intRegion1, intRegion2, .05D, decBonus)` statement calls the CalcBonus procedure. The CalcBonus procedure header indicates that the first three arguments in the Call statement are passed *by value*, whereas the last argument is passed *by reference*. The items passed *by value* will be stored in the intSale1, intSale2, and decRate variables. The item passed *by reference* will be stored in a variable named decDollars.

When the computer processes the CalcBonus procedure header, it first creates the intSale1, intSale2, and decRate variables in memory. It then stores the numbers 500, 200, and .05, respectively, in the variables. Next, the computer locates the decBonus variable (which is declared in the btnBonus Click event procedure) in memory, and assigns the name decDollars to the memory location.

After processing the CalcBonus procedure header, the computer processes the statement contained in the procedure. The statement adds the value stored in the intSale1 variable (500) to the value stored in the intSale2 variable (200). It then multiplies the sum (700) by the value stored in the decRate variable (.05), and assigns the result (35) to the decDollars variable. The `End Sub` statement in the CalcBonus procedure then ends the procedure. At this point, the computer removes the intSale1, intSale2, and decRate variables from its internal memory. It also removes the decDollars name assigned to the decBonus memory location.

When the CalcBonus procedure ends, the computer returns to the btnBonus Click event procedure, to the statement located immediately below the Call statement. This statement displays the number $35.00 in the lblBonus control. Finally, the computer processes the `End Sub` statement in the btnBonus Click event procedure, which ends the procedure. The computer then removes the intRegion1, intRegion2, and decBonus variables from its internal memory.

As you learned earlier, in addition to creating Sub procedures, you also can create Function procedures in Visual Basic .NET.

FUNCTION PROCEDURES

Like a Sub procedure, a **Function procedure** (typically referred to simply as a **function**) is a block of code that performs a specific task. However, unlike a Sub procedure, a function returns a value after completing its task. Some functions, such as the Pmt and InputBox functions, are built into Visual Basic .NET. Recall that the Pmt function returns the periodic payment on either a loan or an investment, and the InputBox function returns the user's response to a prompt that appears in a dialog box.

You also can create your own functions in Visual Basic .NET. After creating a function, you then can invoke it from one or more places in the application in which it is defined. You invoke a function that you create in exactly the same way as you invoke a built-in function—simply by including the function's name in a statement. Usually the statement will display the function's return value, or use the return value in a calculation, or assign the return value to a variable.

As is true with Sub procedures, you also can pass (send) information to a function that you create, and the information can be passed either *by value* or *by reference*. Figure 7.8 shows the syntax you use to create a Function procedure. It also includes an example of a Function procedure, and the steps you follow to enter a Function procedure in the Code Editor window.

HOW TO...

Procedure header

Procedure footer

Create a Function Procedure

Syntax
Private Function *procedurename*([*parameterlist*]) **As** *datatype*
    [*statements*]
    Return *expression*
End Function

Example
```
Private Function CalcNew(ByVal decOld As Decimal) As Decimal
    'calculates and returns a new price using the current
    'price passed to it and a 5% price increase rate

    Return decOld * 1.05D
End Function
```

Steps for entering a Function procedure in the Code Editor window

1. Open the Code Editor window.
2. Click a blank line in the Code Editor window. The blank line can be anywhere between the [Windows Form Designer generated code] entry and the End Class statement; however, it must be outside of any other Sub or Function procedure.
3. Type the Function procedure header and press the Enter key on your keyboard. When you press the Enter key, the Code Editor will automatically enter the Function procedure footer (End Function) for you.

FIGURE 7.8   How to create a Function procedure

TIP

The *datatype* of the value returned by the Pmt function is Double. The *datatype* of the value returned by the InputBox function is String.

Like Sub procedures, Function procedures have both a procedure header and procedure footer. The procedure header for a Function procedure is almost identical to the procedure header for a Sub procedure, except it includes the keyword Function rather than the keyword Sub. The keyword Function identifies the procedure as a Function procedure—one that returns a value after completing its task.

Also different from a Sub procedure header, a Function procedure header includes the **As** *datatype* clause. You use this clause to specify the data type of the value returned by the function. For example, if the function returns a string, you include As String at the end of the procedure header. Similarly, if the function returns a decimal number, you can include As Decimal, As Double, or As Single at the end of the procedure header. The *datatype* you use depends on the size of the number, and whether you want the number stored with a fixed decimal point or a floating decimal point.

The procedure footer in a Function procedure is always End Function. Between the procedure header and procedure footer, you enter the instructions you want the computer to process when the function is invoked. In most cases, the last statement in a Function procedure is `Return` *expression*, where *expression* represents the one and only value that is returned to the statement that called the function. The data type of the *expression* in the Return statement must agree with the data type specified in the **As** *datatype* clause in the procedure header. The **Return statement** alerts the computer that the function has completed its task. It also ends the function after returning the value of its *expression*.

In the example shown in Figure 7.8, the CalcNew function is passed the current price of an item. The current price is passed *by value* and stored in the decOld variable. The `Return decOld * 1.05D` statement in the function calculates the new price and then returns the new price to the statement that called the function.

Next, you view an application that creates and uses a function.

The Pine Lodge Application

The owner of the Pine Lodge wants an application that allows her to calculate an employee's new hourly pay, given the employee's current hourly pay and raise rate. Figure 7.9 shows a sample run of the Pine Lodge application, and Figure 7.10 shows the application's code.

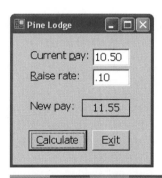

FIGURE 7.9   Sample run of the Pine Lodge application

```
'Project name:          Pine Lodge Project
'Project purpose:       The project calculates an employee's new hourly pay,
'                       given the current hourly pay and raise rate.
'Created/revised by:    Diane Zak on 2/1/2005

Option Explicit On
Option Strict On

Public Class frmPineLodge
    Inherits System.Windows.Forms.Form

[Windows Form Designer generated code]
```

(Figure is continued on next page)

GetNewPay
function

```
Private Function GetNewPay(ByVal decOldPay As Decimal, _
                          ByVal decRate As Decimal) As Decimal
    'calculates and returns an employee's new hourly pay
    'based on the current hourly pay and raise rate passed to it

    'declare variables
    Dim decRaise As Decimal
    Dim decNewPay As Decimal

    'calculate new hourly pay
    decRaise = decOldPay * decRate
    decNewPay = decOldPay + decRaise

    'return new hourly pay
    Return decNewPay
End Function

Private Sub btnCalc_Click(ByVal sender As Object, _
    ByVal e As System.EventArgs) Handles btnCalc.Click
    'calls a function to calculate an employee's new hourly
    'pay, then displays the new hourly pay

    'declare variables
    Dim decCurrentPay As Decimal
    Dim decRaiseRate As Decimal
    Dim decNewHourlyPay As Decimal

    If IsNumeric(Me.txtCurrentPay.Text) _
        AndAlso IsNumeric(Me.txtRaiseRate.Text) Then
        'assign input to variables
        decCurrentPay = Convert.ToDecimal(Me.txtCurrentPay.Text)
        decRaiseRate = Convert.ToDecimal(Me.txtRaiseRate.Text)

        'call function to calculate the new hourly pay, assign
        'the return value to the decNewHourlyPay variable
        decNewHourlyPay = GetNewPay(decCurrentPay, decRaiseRate)

        'display new hourly pay
        Me.lblNewPay.Text = decNewHourlyPay.ToString("N2")
    Else
        MessageBox.Show("The pay and rate must be numeric.", _
            "Pine Lodge", MessageBoxButtons.OK, _
            MessageBoxIcon.Information, _
            MessageBoxDefaultButton.Button1)
    End If
End Sub

Private Sub btnExit_Click(ByVal sender As Object, _
    ByVal e As System.EventArgs) Handles btnExit.Click
    'ends the application
    Me.Close()
End Sub

End Class
```

Invokes the
GetNewPay
function and
assigns the
function's return
value to the
decNewHourlyPay
variable

FIGURE 7.10   Code for the Pine Lodge application

Study closely the code shown in Figure 7.10. The btnCalc Click event procedure first declares three Decimal variables named decCurrentPay, decRaiseRate, and decNewHourlyPay. The condition in the selection structure determines whether the txtCurrentPay and txtRaiseRate controls contain numbers. If either or both controls do not contain a number, an appropriate message is displayed. However, if both controls contain numbers, the contents of the controls are converted to Decimal and assigned to the decCurrentPay and decRaiseRate variables. Assume that the user entered the numbers 10.50 and .10 in the text boxes. The computer stores the number 10.50 in the decCurrentPay variable and the number .10 in the decRaiseRate variable.

Next, the `decNewHourlyPay = GetNewPay(decCurrentPay, decRaiseRate)` statement calls the GetNewPay procedure, passing it the values 10.50 and .10. The computer stores the values in the decOldPay and decRate variables, which appear in the GetNewPay procedure header.

After processing the GetNewPay procedure header, the computer processes the statements contained in the function. The first two statements declare procedure-level variables named decRaise and decNewPay. The next statement multiplies the value stored in the decOldPay variable (10.50) by the value stored in the decRate variable (.10), and then assigns the result (1.05) to the decRaise variable. The next statement adds the value stored in the decOldPay variable (10.50) to the value stored in the decRaise variable (1.05), and assigns the sum (11.55) to the decNewPay variable. The `Return decNewPay` statement in the function returns the contents of the decNewPay variable (11.55) to the statement that called the function, which is the `decNewHourlyPay = GetNewPay(decCurrentPay, decRaiseRate)` statement in the btnCalc Click event procedure. After processing the Return statement, the GetNewPay function ends and the computer removes the decOldPay, decRate, decRaise, and decNewPay variables from its internal memory.

The `decNewHourlyPay = GetNewPay(decCurrentPay, decRaiseRate)` statement assigns the GetNewPay function's return value (11.55) to the decNewHourlyPay variable. The `Me.lblNewPay.Text = decNewHourlyPay.ToString("N2")` statement then displays 11.55 in the lblNewPay control, as shown earlier in Figure 7.9. Finally, the computer processes the `End Sub` statement in the btnCalc Click event procedure, which ends the procedure. The computer then removes the decCurrentPay, decRaiseRate, and decNewHourlyPay variables from its internal memory.

PROGRAMMING EXAMPLE

Rainfall Application

Create an application that allows the user to enter the monthly rainfall amounts for the previous year. The application should calculate and display the total rainfall amount and the average rainfall amount. Name the solution Rainfall Solution. Name the project Rainfall Project. Name the form file Rainfall Form.vb.

TOE Chart:

Task	Object	Event
1. Get monthly rainfall amounts for the year 2. Calculate total rainfall amount 3. Calculate average rainfall amount 4. Display total rainfall amount and average rainfall amount in lblTotal and lblAverage	btnCalc	Click
End the application	btnExit	Click
Display the total rainfall amount and the average rainfall amount (from btnCalc)	lblTotal, lblAverage	None

FIGURE 7.11

User Interface:

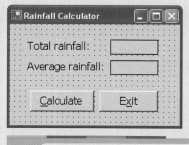

FIGURE 7.12

Objects, Properties, and Settings

Object	Property	Setting
frmRainfall	Name	frmRainfall (be sure to change the startup form to this name)
	Font	Tahoma, 12 point (be sure to change the form's font before adding the controls)
	Size	264, 192
	StartPosition	CenterScreen
	Text	Rainfall Calculator
Label1	AutoSize	True
	Text	Total rainfall:
Label2	AutoSize	True
	Text	Average rainfall:
lblTotal	Name	lblTotal
	BorderStyle	FixedSingle
	Text	(empty)
lblAverage	Name	lblAverage
	BorderStyle	FixedSingle
	Text	(empty)
btnCalc	Name	btnCalc
	Text	&Calculate
btnExit	Name	btnExit
	Text	E&xit

FIGURE 7.13

Tab Order:

FIGURE 7.14

Pseudocode:

btnExit Click event procedure

1. close application

btnCalc Click event procedure

1. call the CalcTotalAndAverage procedure to calculate the total and average rainfall amounts
2. display the total and average rainfall amounts in lblTotal and lblAverage

CalcTotalAndAverage procedure

1. initialize the month counter to 1
2. repeat while the month counter <= 12
> get a rainfall amount
> if the rainfall amount is numeric
>> add the rainfall amount to the total rainfall accumulator
>> add 1 to the month counter
> else
>> display a message informing the user to enter a number
> end if
> end repeat
3. calculate the average rainfall by dividing the total rainfall by 12

Code:

```
'Project name:          Rainfall Project
'Project purpose:       The project allows the user to enter the monthly rainfall amounts
'                       for 12 months. It calculates the total rainfall amount and the
'                       average rainfall amount.
'Created/revised by:    Diane Zak on 2/1/2005

Option Explicit On
Option Strict On

Public Class frmRainfall
    Inherits System.Windows.Forms.Form

[Windows Form Designer generated code]

    Private Sub CalcTotalAndAverage(ByRef decTotal As Decimal, ByRef decAvg As Decimal)
        'calculates the total and average rainfall amount

        'declare variables
        Dim strMonthlyRainfall As String
        Dim intMonthCounter As Integer = 1  'counter
        Dim decMonthlyRainfall As Decimal

        'get 12 valid rainfall amounts
        Do While intMonthCounter <= 12
            strMonthlyRainfall = InputBox("Enter the rainfall for month " _
                & intMonthCounter, "Rainfall Calculator")
            If IsNumeric(strMonthlyRainfall) Then
                decMonthlyRainfall = Convert.ToDecimal(strMonthlyRainfall)
                'update total accumulator
                decTotal = decTotal + decMonthlyRainfall
```

(Figure is continued on next page)

```
                'update month counter
                intMonthCounter = intMonthCounter + 1
            Else
                MessageBox.Show("The rainfall amount must be a number.", _
                    "Rainfall Calculator", MessageBoxButtons.OK, _
                    MessageBoxIcon.Information, MessageBoxDefaultButton.Button1)
            End If
        Loop

        'calculate average rainfall
        decAvg = decTotal / 12D
    End Sub

    Private Sub btnExit_Click(ByVal sender As Object, _
        ByVal e As System.EventArgs) Handles btnExit.Click
        'ends the application
        Me.Close()
    End Sub

    Private Sub btnCalc_Click(ByVal sender As Object, _
        ByVal e As System.EventArgs) Handles btnCalc.Click
        'calls a procedure to calculate the total rainfall _
        'amount and the average rainfall amount, then displays
        'both amounts

        'declare variables
        Dim decTotalRainfall As Decimal        'accumulator
        Dim decAverageRainfall As Decimal

        'call procedure to calculate the total and average rainfall amounts
        Call CalcTotalAndAverage(decTotalRainfall, decAverageRainfall)

        'display total and average rainfall amounts
        Me.lblTotal.Text = decTotalRainfall.ToString("N2")
        Me.lblAverage.Text = decAverageRainfall.ToString("N2")
    End Sub
End Class
```

FIGURE 7.15

Quick Review

- Procedures allow programmers to avoid duplicating code in different parts of a program. Procedures also allow a team of programmers to work on large and complex programs.
- The difference between a Sub procedure and a Function procedure is that a Function procedure returns a value, whereas a Sub procedure does not return a value.
- Event procedures are Sub procedures that are associated with a specific object and event.
- Independent Sub procedures and Function procedures are not associated with any specific object or event. The names of independent Sub procedures and Function procedures typically begin with a verb.

- You enter Sub and Function procedures in the Code Editor window.
- You can use the Call statement to invoke an independent Sub procedure. You invoke a Function procedure by including its name and any arguments in a statement.
- When calling a procedure, the number of arguments listed in the *argumentlist* should agree with the number of parameters listed in the *parameterlist* in the procedure header. Also, the data type and position of each parameter in the *parameterlist* must agree with the data type and position of its corresponding argument in the *argumentlist*.
- You can pass information to a Sub or Function procedure either *by value* or *by reference*.
- To pass a variable *by value*, you precede the variable's corresponding parameter with the keyword `ByVal`.
- To pass a variable *by reference*, you precede the variable's corresponding parameter with the keyword `ByRef`.
- The procedure header indicates whether a variable is being passed *by value* or *by reference*.
- When you pass a variable *by value*, only the contents of the variable are passed.
- When you pass a variable *by reference*, the variable's address is passed.
- Variables that appear in the *parameterlist* in a procedure header are procedure-level, which means that they can be used only by the procedure.

Key Terms

A **procedure** is a block of program code that performs a specific task.

A **Sub procedure** is a procedure that does not return a value after performing its assigned task.

An **independent Sub procedure** is a procedure that is not associated with any specific object or event, and is processed only when invoked (called) from code.

The memory locations listed in a procedure header are called **parameters**.

The **Call statement** is used to invoke an independent Sub procedure in a program.

When you pass a variable's contents to a procedure, you are **passing by value**.

When you pass a variable's address to a procedure, you are **passing by reference**.

A **Function procedure**, or **function**, is a procedure that returns a value after performing its assigned task.

You use the **Return statement** to return a value in a function.

Review Questions

1. Which of the following is false?
    a. A Function procedure can return one or more values to the statement that called it.
    b. A procedure can accept one or more items of data passed to it.
    c. The *parameterlist* in a procedure header is optional.
    d. At times, a memory location inside the computer's internal memory may have more than one name.

2. Each memory location listed in the *parameterlist* in the procedure header is referred to as _____.
   a. an address
   b. a constraint
   c. an event
   d. a parameter

3. To determine whether a variable is being passed *by value* or *by reference* to a procedure, you will need to examine _____.
   a. the Call statement
   b. the procedure header
   c. the statements entered in the procedure
   d. Either a or b.

4. Which of the following statements can be used to call the CalcArea Sub procedure, passing it two variables *by value*?
   a. `Call CalcArea(intLength, intWidth)`
   b. `Call CalcArea(ByVal intLength, ByVal intWidth)`
   c. `Call CalcArea ByVal(intLength, intWidth)`
   d. `Call ByVal CalcArea(intLength, intWidth)`

5. Which of the following procedure headers receives the value stored in a String variable?
   a. `Private Sub DisplayName(ByValue strName As String)`
   b. `Private Sub DisplayName(ByRef strName As String)`
   c. `Private Sub DisplayName ByVal(strName As String)`
   d. None of the above.

6. Which of the following is a valid procedure header for a procedure that receives an integer first and a number with a decimal place second?
   a. `Private Sub CalcFee(intBase As Integer, decRate As Decimal)`
   b. `Private Sub CalcFee(ByRef intBase As Integer, ByRef decRate As Decimal)`
   c. `Private Sub CalcFee(ByVal intBase As Integer, ByVal decRate As Decimal)`
   d. None of the above.

7. A Function procedure can return _____.
   a. one value only
   b. one or more values

8. The procedure header specifies the procedure's _____.
   a. name
   b. parameters
   c. type (either Sub or Function)
   d. All of the above.

9. Which of the following is false?
   a. In most cases, the number of arguments should agree with the number of parameters.
   b. The data type of each argument should match the data type of its corresponding parameter.
   c. The name of each argument should be identical to the name of its corresponding parameter.
   d. When you pass information to a procedure *by value*, the procedure stores the value of each item it receives in a separate memory location.

10. Which of the following instructs a function to return the contents of the decStateTax variable to the statement that called the function?
    a. `Return decStateTax`
    b. `Return decStateTax ByVal`
    c. `Return ByVal decStateTax`
    d. `Return ByRef decStateTax`

11. Which of the following is a valid procedure header for a procedure that receives the value stored in an Integer variable first, and the address of a Decimal variable second?
    a. `Private Sub CalcFee(ByVal intBase As Integer, ByAdd decRate As Decimal)`
    b. `Private Sub CalcFee(intBase As Integer, decRate As Decimal)`
    c. `Private Sub CalcFee(ByVal intBase As Integer, ByRef decRate As Decimal)`
    d   None of the above.

12 Which of the following is a valid procedure header for a procedure that receives the number 15?
    a. `Private Function CalcTax(ByVal intRate As Integer) As Decimal`
    b. `Private Function CalcTax(ByAdd intRate As Integer) As Decimal`
    c. `Private Sub CalcTax(ByVal intRate As Integer)`
    d. Both a and c.

13. If the statement `Call CalcNet(decNet)` passes the address of the decNet variable to the CalcNet procedure, the variable is said to be passed _____.
    a. *by address*
    b. *by content*
    c. *by reference*
    d. *by value*

14. If the statement `Call CalcNet(decNet)` passes the contents of the decNet variable to the CalcNet procedure, the variable is said to be passed _____.
    a. *by address*
    b. *by content*
    c. *by reference*
    d. *by value*

15. Which of the following is false?
    a. When you pass a variable *by reference*, the receiving procedure can change its contents.
    b. When you pass a variable *by value*, the receiving procedure creates a procedure-level variable that it uses to store the passed value.
    c. Unless specified otherwise, all variables in Visual Basic .NET are passed *by value*.
    d. To pass a variable *by reference* in Visual Basic .NET, you include the keyword `ByRef` before the variable's name in the Call statement.

16. Assume that a Sub procedure named CalcEndingInventory is passed four Integer variables named intBegin, intSales, intPurchases, and intEnd. The procedure's task is to calculate the ending inventory, based on the beginning inventory, sales, and purchase amounts passed to the procedure. The procedure should store the result in the intEnd memory location. Which of the following procedure headers is correct?

    a. `Private Sub CalcEndingInventory(ByVal intB As Integer, ByVal intS As Integer, ByVal intP As Integer, ByRef intE As Integer)`

    b. `Private Sub CalcEndingInventory(ByVal intB As Integer, ByVal intS As Integer, ByVal intP As Integer, ByVal intE As Integer)`

    c. `Private Sub CalcEndingInventory(ByRef intB As Integer, ByRef intS As Integer, ByRef intP As Integer, ByVal intE As Integer)`

    d. `Private Sub CalcEndingInventory(ByRef intB As Integer, ByRef intS As Integer, ByRef intP As Integer, ByRef intE As Integer)`

17. Which of the following statements should you use to call the CalcEndingInventory procedure described in Question 16?

    a. `Call CalcEndingInventory(intBegin, intSales, intPurchases, intEnd)`

    b. `Call CalcEndingInventory(ByVal intBegin, ByVal intSales, ByVal intPurchases, ByRef intEnd)`

    c. `Call CalcEndingInventory(ByRef intBegin, ByRef intSales, ByRef intPurchases, ByRef intEnd)`

    d. `Call CalcEndingInventory(ByVal intBegin, ByVal intSales, ByVal intPurchases, ByVal intEnd)`

18. The memory locations listed in the *parameterlist* in a procedure header are procedure-level and are removed from the computer's internal memory when the procedure ends.

    a. True

    b. False

19. Assume that the CalcTax function's procedure header is `Private Function CalcTax(ByVal decSales As Decimal) As Decimal`. Which of the following are valid Return statements for this function? (You can assume that decTax and decRate are declared in the function.)

    a. `Return decSales * .06D`

    b. `Return decTax`

    c. `Return decSales * decRate`

    d. All of the above.

20. Assume that the GetName function's procedure header is `Private Function GetPayRate() As Decimal`. Which of the following are valid Return statements for this function?

    a. `Return decPayRate`

    b. `Return strPayRate`

    c. `Return intPayRate`

    d. All of the above.

Exercises

1. Explain the difference between a Sub procedure and a Function procedure.

2. Explain the difference between passing a variable *by value* and passing it *by reference*.

3. Write the Visual Basic .NET code for a Sub procedure that receives an integer passed to it. The procedure, named HalveNumber, should divide the integer by 2, and then display the result in the lblNum control.

4. Write the Visual Basic .NET code for a Sub procedure that prompts the user to enter the name of a city, and then stores the user's response in the String variable whose address is passed to the procedure. Name the procedure GetCity.

5. Write the Visual Basic .NET code for a Sub procedure that receives four Integer variables: the first two *by value* and the last two *by reference*. The procedure should calculate the sum and the difference of the two variables passed *by value*, and then store the results in the variables passed *by reference*. (When calculating the difference, subtract the contents of the second variable from the contents of the first variable.) Name the procedure CalcSumAndDiff.

6. Write the Visual Basic .NET code for a Sub procedure that receives three Decimal variables: the first two *by value* and the last one *by reference*. The procedure should divide the first variable by the second variable, and then store the result in the third variable. Name the procedure CalcQuotient.

7. Write the Visual Basic .NET code for a Function procedure that receives the value stored in an Integer variable named intNumber. The procedure, named DivideNumber, should divide the integer by 2, and then return the result (which may contain a decimal place).

8. Write an appropriate statement to call the DivideNumber function created in Exercise 7. Assign the value returned by the function to the decAnswer variable.

9. Write the Visual Basic .NET code for a Function procedure that prompts the user to enter the name of a state, and then returns the user's response to the calling procedure. Name the procedure GetState.

10. Write the Visual Basic .NET code for a Function procedure that receives four integers. The procedure should calculate the average of the four integers, and then return the result (which may contain a decimal place). Name the procedure CalcAverage.

11. Write the Visual Basic .NET code for a Function procedure that receives two numbers that both have a decimal place. The procedure should divide the first number by the second number, and then return the result. Name the procedure CalcQuotient.

12. In this exercise, you modify this chapter's Programming Example.
    a. Create the Rainfall application shown in this chapter's Programming Example. Save the application in the VbDotNet\Chap07 folder.
    b. Modify the application so that it uses two function procedures rather than a Sub procedure to calculate the total and average rainfall amounts. Be sure to modify the pseudocode before modifying the code.
    c. Save the solution, then start and test the application. Click the Exit button to end the application, then close the solution.

13. In this exercise, you code an application that uses an independent Sub procedure to clear the label controls in an interface.
    a. Create the Gladis Antiques interface shown in Figure 7.3. Name the solution Gladis Antiques Solution. Name the project Gladis Antiques Project. Save the application in the VbDotNet\Chap07 folder.
    b. Use the code shown in Figure 7.4 to code the application.
    c. Save the solution, and then start the application. Test the application.
    d. Click the Exit button to end the application, then close the solution.

14. In this exercise, you code an application that uses an independent Sub procedure to display a message.
    a. Build an appropriate interface for the code shown in Example 1 in Figure 7.5. Name the solution Pet Solution. Name the project Pet Project. Save the application in the VbDotNet\Chap07 folder.
    b. Use the code shown in Figure 7.5's Example 1 to code the application.
    c. Save the solution, and then start the application. Test the application.
    d. Stop the application, then close the solution.

15. In this exercise, you code an application that uses an independent Sub procedure to calculate a bonus amount.
    a. Build an appropriate interface for the code shown in Example 2 in Figure 7.5. Name the solution Bonus Solution. Name the project Bonus Project. Save the application in the VbDotNet\Chap07 folder.
    b. Use the code shown in Figure 7.5's Example 2 to code the application.
    c. Save the solution, and then start the application. Test the application.
    d. Stop the application, then close the solution.

16. In this exercise, you code an application that uses an independent Sub procedure to display a message.
    a. Build an appropriate interface for the code shown in Example 1 in Figure 7.6. Name the solution Pet Solution 2. Name the project Pet Project 2. Save the application in the VbDotNet\Chap07 folder.
    b. Use the code shown in Figure 7.6's Example 1 to code the application.
    c. Save the solution, and then start the application. Test the application.
    d. Stop the application, then close the solution.

17. In this exercise, you code an application that uses an independent Sub procedure to calculate a 5% bonus amount.
    a. Build an appropriate interface for the code shown in Example 2 in Figure 7.6. Name the solution Bonus Solution 2. Name the project Bonus Project 2. Save the application in the VbDotNet\Chap07 folder.
    b. Use the code shown in Figure 7.6's Example 2 to code the application.
    c. Save the solution, and then start the application. Test the application.
    d. Stop the application, then close the solution.

18. In this exercise, you modify the application that you created in Exercise 17 so that it uses a function rather than a Sub procedure.
    a. Use Windows to make a copy of the Bonus Solution 2 folder, which is contained in the VbDotNet\Chap07 folder. Rename the copy Function Bonus Solution.
    b. Open the Bonus Solution 2 (Bonus Solution 2.sln) file, which is contained in the VbDotNet\Chap07\Function Bonus Solution folder.
    c. Modify the code so that it uses a function rather than a Sub procedure to calculate the bonus.
    d. Save the solution, and then start the application. Test the application.
    e. Stop the application, then close the solution.

19. In this exercise, you code an application that uses a function to calculate an employee's new pay.
    a. Create the Pine Lodge interface shown in Figure 7.9. Name the solution Pine Lodge Solution. Name the project Pine Lodge Project. Save the application in the VbDotNet\Chap07 folder.
    b. Use the code shown in Figure 7.10 to code the application.
    c. Save the solution, and then start the application. Test the application.
    d. Click the Exit button to end the application, then close the solution.

20. In this exercise, you modify the application that you created in Exercise 19 so that it uses a Sub procedure rather than a function.
    a. Use Windows to make a copy of the Pine Lodge Solution folder, which is contained in the VbDotNet\Chap07 folder. Rename the copy Modified Pine Lodge Solution.
    b. Open the Pine Lodge Solution (Pine Lodge Solution.sln) file, which is contained in the VbDotNet\Chap07\Modified Pine Lodge Solution folder.
    c. Modify the code so that it uses a Sub procedure rather than a function to calculate the new pay.
    d. Save the solution, and then start the application. Test the application.
    e. Click the Exit button to end the application, then close the solution.

21. In this exercise, you code an application that uses two independent Sub procedures: one to convert a temperature from Fahrenheit to Celsius, and the other to convert a temperature from Celsius to Fahrenheit.
    a. Build an appropriate interface. Name the solution Temperature Solution. Name the project Temperature Project. Save the application in the VbDotNet\Chap07 folder.
    b. Code the application.
    c. Save the solution, and then start the application. Test the application.
    d. Stop the application, then close the solution.

22. In this exercise, you modify the application that you created in Exercise 21 so that it uses two functions rather than two Sub procedures.
    a. Use Windows to make a copy of the Temperature Solution folder, which is contained in the VbDotNet\Chap07 folder. Rename the copy Modified Temperature Solution.
    b. Open the Temperature Solution (Temperature Solution.sln) file, which is contained in the VbDotNet\Chap07\Modified Temperature Solution folder.
    c. Modify the code so that it uses two functions rather than two Sub procedures to convert the temperatures.
    d. Save the solution, and then start the application. Test the application.
    e. Stop the application, then close the solution.

23. In this exercise, you learn how to specify that one or more arguments are optional in a Call statement.

   a. Open the Optional Solution (Optional Solution.sln) file, which is contained in the VbDotNet\Chap07\Optional Solution folder.

   b. Study the application's existing code. Notice that the btnCalc control's Click event procedure contains two Call statements. The first Call statement passes three variables (decSales, decBonus, and decRate) to the GetBonus procedure. The second Call statement, however, passes only two variables (decSales and decBonus) to the procedure. (Do not be concerned about the jagged line that appears below the second Call statement.) Notice that the decRate variable is omitted from the second Call statement. You indicate that the decRate variable is optional in the Call statement by including the keyword `Optional` before the variable's corresponding parameter in the procedure header; you enter the `Optional` keyword before the `ByVal` keyword. You also assign a default value that the procedure will use for the missing parameter when the procedure is called. You assign the default value by entering the assignment operator followed by the default value after the parameter in the function header. In this case, you will assign the number .1 as the default value for the decRate variable. (Optional parameters must be listed at the end of the procedure header.)

   c. Change the `ByVal decBonusRate As Decimal` in the procedure header appropriately.

   d. Save the solution, then start the application. Type the letter A in the Code text box, then type 1000 in the Sales text box. Click the Calculate button. When the Rate Entry dialog box appears, type .05 and press Enter. The `Call GetBonus(decSales, decBonus, decRate)` statement calls the GetBonus procedure, passing it the number 1000, the address of the decBonus variable, and the number .05. The GetBonus procedure stores the number 1000 in the decTotalSales variable. It also assigns the name decBonusAmount to the decBonus variable, and stores the number .05 in the decBonusRate variable. The procedure then multiplies the contents of the decTotalSales variable (1000) by the contents of the decBonusRate variable (.05), and assigns the result (50) to the decBonusAmount variable. The `Me.lblBonus.Text = decBonus.ToString("C2")` statement then displays the number $50.00 in the lblBonus control.

   e. Now type the letter B in the Code text box, then type 2000 in the Sales text box. Click the Calculate button. The `Call GetBonus(decSales, decBonus)` statement calls the GetBonus procedure, passing it the number 2000 and the address of the decBonus variable. The GetBonus procedure stores the number 2000 in the decTotalSales variable, and assigns the name decBonusAmount to the decBonus variable. Because the Call statement did not supply a value for the decBonusRate variable, the default value (.1) is assigned to the variable. The procedure then multiplies the contents of the decTotalSales variable (2000) by the contents of the decBonusRate variable (.1), and assigns the result (200) to the decBonusAmount variable. The `Me.lblBonus.Text = decBonus.ToString("C2")` statement then displays the number $200.00 in the lblBonus control.

   f. Click the Exit button to end the application, then close the solution.

24. In this exercise, you find and correct an error in an application. The process of finding and correcting errors is called debugging.
    a. Open the Debug Solution (Debug Solution.sln) file, which is contained in the VbDotNet\Chap07\Debug Solution folder.
    b. Open the Code Editor window. Review the existing code.
    c. Start the application. Click the Display Name button. When prompted to enter a name, type your name and press Enter. Notice that your name did not appear in the lblName control, which is incorrect. Click the Exit button to end the application.
    d. Modify the application's code appropriately.
    e. Save the solution, then start the application. Click the Display Name button. When prompted to enter a name, type your name and press Enter. This time, your name should appear in the lblName control.
    f. Click the Exit button to end the application, then close the solution.

Case Projects

Car Shoppers Inc.

Recently, in an effort to boost sales, Car Shoppers Inc. is offering buyers a choice of either a large cash rebate or an extremely low financing rate, much lower than the rate most buyers would pay by financing the car through their local bank. Jake Miller, the manager of Car Shoppers Inc., wants you to create an application that he can use to help buyers decide whether to take the lower financing rate from his dealership, or take the rebate and then finance the car through their local bank. Be sure to use one or more independent Sub or Function procedures in the application. (Payments are due at the beginning of the month.)

Wallpaper Warehouse

Last year, Johanna Liu opened a new wallpaper store named Wallpaper Warehouse. Business is booming at the store, and Johanna and her salesclerks are always busy. Recently, however, Johanna has received several complaints from customers about the store's slow service, and she has decided to ask her salesclerks for suggestions on how the service can be improved. The overwhelming response from the salesclerks is that they need a more convenient way to calculate the number of single rolls of wallpaper required to cover a room. Currently, the salesclerks perform this calculation manually, using pencil and paper. Doing this for so many customers, however, takes a great deal of time, and service has begun to suffer. Johanna has asked for your assistance in this matter. She would like you to create an application that the salesclerks can use to quickly calculate and display the required number of rolls. Be sure to use one or more independent Sub or Function procedures in the application.

Cable Direct

Sharon Barrow, the billing supervisor at Cable Direct (a local cable company) has asked you to create an application that she can use to calculate and display a customer's bill. The cable rates are as follows:

Residential customers:

Processing fee:	$4.50
Basic service fee:	$30
Premium channels:	$5 per channel

Business customers:

Processing fee:	$16.50
Basic service fee:	$80 for first 10 connections; $4 for each additional connection
Premium channels:	$50 per channel for any number of connections

Be sure to use one or more independent Sub or Function procedures in the application.

Harvey Industries

Currently, Khalid Patel, the payroll manager at Harvy Industries, manually calculates each employee's weekly gross pay, Social Security and Medicare (FICA) tax, federal withholding tax (FWT), and net pay—a very time-consuming process and one that is prone to mathematical errors. Mr. Patel has asked you to create an application that he can use to perform the payroll calculations both efficiently and accurately.

Employees at Harvey Industries are paid every Friday. All employees are paid on an hourly basis, with time and one-half paid for the hours worked over 40.

The amount of FICA tax to deduct from an employee's weekly gross pay is calculated by multiplying the gross pay amount by 7.65%.

The amount of FWT to deduct from an employee's weekly gross pay is based on the employee's filing status—either single (including head of household) or married—and his or her weekly taxable wages. You calculate the weekly taxable wages by first multiplying the number of withholding allowances by $55.77 (the value of a withholding allowance), and then subtracting the result from the weekly gross pay. For example, if your weekly gross pay is $400 and you have two withholding allowances, your weekly taxable wages are $288.46. You use the weekly taxable wages, along with the filing status and the weekly Federal Withholding Tax table, to determine the amount of FWT tax to withhold. The weekly tax tables are shown in Figure 7.16.

FWT Tables – Weekly Payroll Period

Single person (including head of household)

If the taxable wages are:		The amount of income tax to withhold is		
Over	**But not over**	**Base amount**	**Percentage**	**Of excess over**
	$ 51	0		
$ 51	$ 552	0	15%	$ 51
$ 552	$1,196	$ 75.15 plus	28%	$ 552
$1,196	$2,662	$ 255.47 plus	31%	$1,196
$2,662	$5,750	$ 709.93 plus	36%	$2,662
$5,750		$1,821.61 plus	39.6%	$5,750

Married person

If the taxable wages are:		The amount of income tax to withhold is		
Over	**But not over**	**Base amount**	**Percentage**	**Of excess over**
	$ 124	0		
$ 124	$ 960	0	15%	$ 124
$ 960	$2,023	$ 125.40 plus	28%	$ 960
$2,023	$3,292	$ 423.04 plus	31%	$2,023
$3,292	$5,809	$ 816.43 plus	36%	$3,292
$5,809		$1,722.55 plus	39.6%	$5,809

FIGURE 7.16

Be sure to use one or more independent Sub or Function procedures in the application.

Sequential Access Files and Error Handling

After studying Chapter 8, you should be able to:

- Declare StreamReader and StreamWriter variables
- Open a sequential access file
- Determine whether a sequential access file exists
- Write information to a sequential access file
- Align the text written to a sequential access file
- Read information from a sequential access file
- Test for the end of a sequential access file
- Close a sequential access file
- Handle exceptions using a Try/Catch block
- Write records to a sequential access file
- Read records from a sequential access file

FILE TYPES

In addition to getting information from the keyboard and sending information to the computer screen, an application also can get information from and send information to a file on a disk. Getting information from a file is referred to as "reading the file," and sending information to a file is referred to as "writing to the file." Files to which information is written are called **output files**, because the files store the output produced by an application. Files that are read by the computer are called **input files**, because an application uses the information in these files as input.

You can create three different types of files in Visual Basic .NET: sequential, random, and binary. The file type refers to how the information in the file is accessed. The information in a sequential access file is always accessed sequentially—in other words, in consecutive order from the beginning of the file through the end of the file. The information stored in a random access file can be accessed either in consecutive order or in random order. The information in a binary access file can be accessed by its byte location in the file. You learn about sequential access files in this chapter. Random access and binary access files are used less often in programs, so these file types are not covered in this book.

USING SEQUENTIAL ACCESS FILES

A **sequential access file** is often referred to as a **text file**, because it is composed of lines of text. The text might represent an employee list, as shown in Example 1 in Figure 8.1. Or, it might be a memo or a report, as shown in Examples 2 and 3 in Figure 8.1.

Example 1 — employee list
```
Bonnel, Jacob
Carlisle, Donald
Eberg, Jack
Hou, Chang
```

Example 2 — memo
```
To all employees:

Effective January 1, 2005, the cost of dependent coverage will
increase from $35 to $38.50 per month.

Jefferson Williams
Insurance Manager
```

Example 3 — report
```
ABC Industries Sales Report

State          Sales
California      15000
Montana         10000
Wyoming          7000
                -----
Total sales:   $32000
```

FIGURE 8.1   Examples of text stored in a sequential access file

Sequential access files are similar to cassette tapes in that each line in the file, like each song on a cassette tape, is both stored and retrieved in consecutive order (sequentially). In other words, before you can record (store) the fourth song on a cassette tape, you first must record songs one through three. Likewise, before you can write (store) the fourth line in a sequential access file, you first must write lines one through three. The same holds true for retrieving a song from a cassette tape and a line of text from a sequential access file. To listen to the fourth song on a cassette tape, you must play (or fast-forward through) the first three songs. Likewise, to read the fourth line in a sequential access file, you first must read the three lines that precede it.

Figure 8.2 shows the procedure you follow when using a sequential access file in an application.

HOW TO...

Use a Sequential Access File

1. declare either a StreamWriter or StreamReader variable
2. create a StreamWriter or StreamReader object by opening a file; assign the object's address to the variable declared in Step 1
3. use the StreamWriter object to write one or more lines of text to the file, or use the StreamReader object to read one or more lines of text from the file
4. use the StreamWriter or StreamReader object to close the file

FIGURE 8.2   How to use a sequential access file

Step 1 in Figure 8.2 is to declare either a StreamWriter or StreamReader variable. The appropriate variable to declare depends on whether you want to write information to the file or read information from the file.

DECLARING STREAMWRITER AND STREAMREADER VARIABLES

In Visual Basic .NET, you use a **StreamWriter object** to write a sequence of characters—referred to as a **stream of characters** or, more simply, a **stream**—to a sequential access file. Similarly, you use a **StreamReader object** to read a stream (sequence of characters) from a sequential access file. Before you create the appropriate object, you first declare a variable to store the address of the object in the computer's internal memory. You use a StreamWriter variable to store the address of a StreamWriter object, and a StreamReader variable to store the address of a StreamReader object. Figure 8.3 shows the syntax you use to declare StreamWriter and StreamReader variables. The figure also includes examples of declaring the variables.

HOW TO...

Declare StreamWriter and StreamReader Variables

Syntax
accessibility variablename **As IO.***objecttype*

Examples
`Dim swrStreamWriter As IO.StreamWriter`
declares a procedure-level StreamWriter variable named swrStreamWriter

`Private mswrStreamWriter As IO.StreamWriter`
declares a module-level StreamWriter variable named mswrStreamWriter

`Dim sreStreamReader As IO.StreamReader`
declares a procedure-level StreamReader variable named sreStreamReader

`Private msreStreamReader As IO.StreamReader`
declares a module-level StreamReader variable named msreStreamReader

FIGURE 8.3   How to declare StreamWriter and StreamReader variables

In the syntax, *accessibility* is usually either the keyword `Dim` or the keyword `Private`. The appropriate keyword to use depends on whether the variable is a procedure-level or module-level variable. *Variablename* in the syntax is the name of the variable, and *objecttype* is either `StreamWriter` or `StreamReader`. The `IO` in the syntax stands for "Input/Output".

After you declare the appropriate variable, you then create a StreamWriter or StreamReader object and assign the object's address to the variable; this is Step 2 in the procedure shown in Figure 8.2. You create a StreamWriter or StreamReader object by opening a sequential access file.

OPENING A SEQUENTIAL ACCESS FILE

When you open a sequential access file, the computer creates an object that represents the file in the program. You assign the object's address to a StreamWriter or StreamReader variable, and then use the variable to refer to the object, and therefore the file, in the program.

Figure 8.4 shows the syntax you use to open a sequential access file and assign the resulting object's address to a variable. The figure also describes the methods that are used to open a sequential access file. In addition, the figure includes several examples of using the syntax.

HOW TO...

Open a Sequential Access File and Assign the Object's Address to a Variable

Syntax
variablename = **IO.File**.*method*(*filename*)

Method	Object created	Description
OpenText	StreamReader	opens an existing sequential access file for input, which allows the computer to read the information stored in the file; if the file does not exist, the computer displays an error message
CreateText	StreamWriter	opens a sequential access file for output, which creates a new, empty file to which data can be written; if the file already exists, its contents are erased before the new data is written
AppendText	StreamWriter	opens a sequential access file for append, which allows the computer to write new data to the end of the existing data in the file; if the file does not exist, the file is created before data is written to it

Examples
```
sreStreamReader = IO.File.OpenText("a:\reports\pay.txt")
```
opens for input the pay.txt file contained in the reports folder on the A drive; creates a StreamReader object and assigns its address to the sreStreamReader variable

```
sreStreamReader = IO.File.OpenText("pay.txt")
```
opens the pay.txt file for input; creates a StreamReader object and assigns its address to the sreStreamReader variable

```
swrStreamWriter = IO.File.CreateText("memo.txt")
```
opens the memo.txt file for output; creates a StreamWriter object and assigns its address to the swrStreamWriter variable

```
mswrStreamWriter = IO.File.AppendText("sales.txt")
```
opens the sales.txt file for append; creates a StreamWriter object and assigns its address to the mswrStreamWriter variable

FIGURE 8.4 How to open a sequential access file and assign the object's address to a variable

TIP

You also can declare the appropriate variable and open a sequential access file in one statement. For example, you can use the statement **Dim sreStreamReader As IO.StreamReader = IO.File.OpenText ("pay.txt")** to declare the sreStreamReader variable and open the pay.txt file for input.

In the syntax, *filename* is the name of the file you want to open. When you open a sequential access file, the computer creates either a StreamReader or StreamWriter object, depending on the *method* specified in the syntax. The **OpenText method**, for example, opens an existing sequential access file for input and allows the computer to read the information stored in the file. If the file does not exist when the OpenText method is processed, the computer displays an error message in a message box. The OpenText method creates a StreamReader object and can be used to open input files only.

You use the **CreateText method** to create a new, empty sequential access file to which data can be written. If the file already exists, the computer erases the contents of the file before writing any data to it. You use the **AppendText method** when you want to add data to the end of an existing sequential access file. If the file does not exist, the computer creates the file for you. Unlike the OpenText method, the CreateText and AppendText methods create StreamWriter objects and are used to open output files only.

When the computer processes the statement shown in the first example in Figure 8.4, it first searches the reports folder on the A drive for a file named pay.txt. If it cannot locate the pay.txt file, the computer displays an error message in a message box; otherwise, it opens the file for input, creates a StreamReader object, and assigns the object's address to the sreStreamReader variable. Notice that the statement shown in the second example is identical to the statement shown in the first example, except the *filename* argument does not specify a folder path. If you do not include a folder path in the *filename* argument, the computer will search for the file in the current project's bin folder. For example, if the current project is stored in the VbDotNet\Chap08\Payroll Solution\Payroll Project folder, the computer will search for the pay.txt file in the VbDotNet\Chap08\Payroll Solution\Payroll Project\bin folder.

When processing the statement shown in the third example in Figure 8.4, the computer searches the current project's bin folder for a file named memo.txt. If the memo.txt file exists, its contents are erased and the file is opened for output; otherwise, a new, empty file is created and opened for output. In addition to opening the memo.txt file, the statement shown in the third example also creates a StreamWriter object and assigns the object's address to the swrStreamWriter variable.

When the computer processes the statement shown in the last example in Figure 8.4, it searches the current project's bin folder for a file named sales.txt. If it locates the sales.txt file, the computer opens the file for append, which allows new information to be written to the end of the file. If the computer cannot locate the sales.txt file, it creates a new, empty file and opens the file for append. The statement also creates a StreamWriter object and assigns the object's address to the mswrStreamWriter variable.

The computer uses a file pointer to keep track of the next character either to read in or write to a file. When you open a file for input, the computer positions the file pointer at the beginning of the file, immediately before the first character. When you open a file for output, the computer also positions the file pointer at the beginning of the file, but recall that the file is empty. (As you learned earlier, opening a file for output tells the computer to create a new, empty file or erase the contents of an existing file.) However, when you open a file for append, the computer positions the file pointer immediately after the last character in the file. Figure 8.5 illustrates the position of the file pointer when files are opened for input, output, and append.

Lines of text

File pointer is
positioned here

File pointer is
positioned here

Lines of text

File pointer is
positioned here

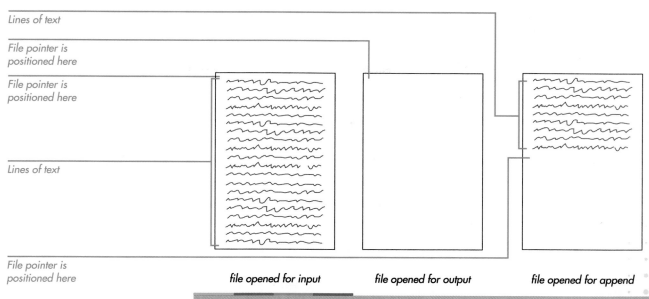

file opened for input   file opened for output   file opened for append

FIGURE 8.5   Position of the file pointer when files are opened for input, output, and append

Recall that the computer displays an error message if you use the OpenText method to open a file that does not exist. It is a good programming practice to verify that a file exists before you attempt to open the file for input.

Determining Whether a File Exists

You can use the **Exists method** to determine whether a file exists before you attempt to open it. Figure 8.6 shows the syntax of the Exists method and includes two examples of using the method. Both examples shown in Figure 8.6 produce the same result and simply represent two different ways of accomplishing the same task.

HOW TO...

Use the Exists Method to Determine Whether a File Exists

Syntax
IO.File.Exists(*filename*)

Examples
```
If IO.File.Exists("pay.txt") Then
     sreStreamReader = IO.File.OpenText("pay.txt")
     [instructions for processing the file]
Else
     MessageBox.Show("File does not exist", "Payroll", _
         MessageBoxButtons.OK, MessageBoxIcon.Information)
End If
```
opens and then processes the pay.txt file if the file exists; otherwise, displays the "File does not exist" message in a message box

```
If Not IO.File.Exists("pay.txt") Then
     MessageBox.Show("File does not exist", "Payroll",
         MessageBoxButtons.OK, MessageBoxIcon.Information)
Else
     sreStreamReader = IO.File.OpenText("pay.txt")
     [instructions for processing the file]
End If
```
displays the "File does not exist" message in a message box if the pay.txt file does not exist; otherwise, opens and then processes the file

FIGURE 8.6   How to use the Exists method to determine whether a file exists

TIP

You also can write the If clause shown in the first example as `If IO.File.Exists("pay.txt") = True Then`, and the If clause shown in the second example as `If IO.File.Exists("pay.txt") = False Then`.

In the syntax shown in Figure 8.6, *filename* is the name of the file whose existence you want to verify. The *filename* argument can include an optional folder path; if the folder path is omitted, the computer searches for the file in the current project's bin folder. The Exists method returns the Boolean value True if *filename* exists; otherwise, it returns the Boolean value False.

Step 3 in the procedure shown earlier in Figure 8.2 is to use the StreamWriter object to write one or more lines of text to the file, or use the StreamReader object to read one or more lines of text from the file. First, you learn how to write information to a sequential access file.

WRITING INFORMATION TO A SEQUENTIAL ACCESS FILE

You can use either the Write method or the WriteLine method to write information to a sequential access file. Figure 8.7 shows the syntax of both methods and includes examples of using the methods to write information to sequential access files. The figure also indicates the placement of the file pointer after the method in each example is processed.

HOW TO...

Use the Write and WriteLine Methods to Write Information to a Sequential Access File

Syntax
variablename.**Write**(*data*)
variablename.**WriteLine**(*data*)

Example 1
```
swrStreamWriter.Write("Hello")
```

Result

File pointer

```
Hello
```

Example 2
```
swrStreamWriter.WriteLine("Hello")
```

Result
```
Hello
```

File pointer

Example 3
```
swrStreamWriter.Write("The top salesperson is ")
swrStreamWriter.WriteLine(strName & ".")
swrStreamWriter.WriteLine()
swrStreamWriter.Write("ABC Sales")
```

Result (assuming strName contains "Carolyn")
```
The top salesperson is Carolyn.

ABC Sales
```

File pointer

Example 4
```
swrStreamWriter.Write("Total price: ")
swrStreamWriter.WriteLine(intPrice.ToString("C2"))
```

Result (assuming intPrice contains 25)
```
Total price: $25.00
```

File pointer

Example 5
```
swrStreamWriter.WriteLine(Space(10) & "A" & Space(5) & "B")
```

Result
```
          A     B
```

File pointer

FIGURE 8.7 How to use the Write and WriteLine methods to write information to a sequential access file

In each syntax shown in Figure 8.7, *variablename* is the name of a StreamWriter variable, and *data* is the information you want written to the file associated with the variable. The difference between the Write and WriteLine methods is the location of the file pointer after the *data* is written to the file. The **Write method** positions the file pointer at the end of the last character it writes to the file. The **WriteLine method**, on the other hand, positions the file pointer at the beginning of the next line in the file; it does so by appending a **line terminator character**, which is simply a carriage return followed by a line feed, to the end of the *data*.

The swrStreamWriter.Write("Hello") statement shown in Example 1 in Figure 8.7 writes the string "Hello" to the file and then positions the file pointer immediately after the last letter in the string, as indicated in the example. The swrStreamWriter.WriteLine("Hello") statement in Example 2 writes the string "Hello" and a line terminator character to the file. The line terminator character positions the file pointer at the beginning of the next line in the file, as indicated in the example.

The first statement shown in Example 3, swrStreamWriter.Write ("The top salesperson is "), writes the string "The top salesperson is " to the file and then positions the file pointer after the last character in the string (in this case, after the space character). The next statement, swrStreamWriter. WriteLine(strName & "."), first concatenates the contents of the strName variable with a period; it then writes the concatenated string and a line terminator character to the file. The line terminator character moves the file pointer to the next line in the file. The third statement in Example 3, swrStreamWriter. WriteLine(), writes only a line terminator character to the file; you can use this statement to insert a blank line in a file. The last statement in Example 3, swrStreamWriter.Write("ABC Sales"), writes the string "ABC Sales" to the file, and then positions the file pointer after the last character in the string, as indicated in the example.

The two statements shown in Example 4 write the string "Total price: " and the contents of the intPrice variable (formatted with a dollar sign and two decimal places) on the same line in the file. The file pointer is then positioned at the beginning of the next line in the file.

Example 5 in Figure 8.7 shows how you can use the **Space function** to write a specific number of spaces to a file. The syntax of the Space function is **Space(*number*)**, where *number* represents the number of spaces you want to write. The swrStreamWriter.WriteLine(Space(10) & "A" & Space(5) & "B") statement writes 10 spaces, the letter "A", five spaces, the letter "B", and the line terminator character to the file. After the statement is processed, the file pointer is positioned at the beginning of the next line in the file.

Next, you learn how to align columns of information in a sequential access file.

Aligning Columns of Information

In Chapter 6, you learned how to use the PadLeft and PadRight methods to pad a string with a character until the string is a specified length. Recall that the syntax of the PadLeft method is *string*.**PadLeft**(*length*[, *character*]), and the syntax of the PadRight method is *string*.**PadRight**(*length*[, *character*]). In each syntax, *length* is an integer that represents the desired length of the *string*, and *character* (which is optional) is the character that each method uses to pad the *string* until it reaches the desired *length*. If the *character* argument is omitted, the default *character* is the space character. Figure 8.8 shows examples of using the PadLeft and PadRight methods to align columns of information written to a sequential access file.

HOW TO...

Align Columns of Information in a Sequential Access File

Example 1

```
For intRegion = 1 To 3
      strSales = InputBox("Sales amount", "Sales")
      decSales = Convert.ToDecimal(strSales)
      strSales = decSales.ToString("N2")
      swrStreamWriter.WriteLine(strSales.PadLeft(8))
Next intRegion
```

Result (assuming the user enters the following sales amounts: 645.75, 1200, 40.80)

```
  645.75
1,200.00
   40.80
```

Example 2

```
swrStreamWriter.WriteLine("Name" & Space(11) & "Age")
strName = InputBox("Name:", "Name")
Do While strName <> ""
      strAge = InputBox("Age:", "Age")
      swrStreamWriter.WriteLine(strName.PadRight(15) & strAge)
      strName = InputBox("Name:", "Name")
Loop
```

Result (assuming the user enters the following names and ages: Janice, 23, Sue, 67)

```
Name           Age
Janice         23
Sue            67
```

FIGURE 8.8   How to align columns of information in a sequential access file

The code in Example 1 shows how you can align a column of numbers by the decimal point. First, you format each number in the column to ensure that each has the same number of digits to the right of the decimal point. You then use the PadLeft method to insert spaces at the beginning of the number; this right-aligns the number within the column. Because each number has the same number of digits to the right of the decimal point, aligning each number on the right will, in effect, align each by its decimal point.

The code in Example 2 in Figure 8.8 shows how you can align the second column of information when the first column contains strings whose lengths vary. To align the second column, you first use either the PadRight or PadLeft method to ensure that each string in the first column contains the same number of characters. You then concatenate the padded string to the information in the second column before writing the concatenated string to the file. The code shown in Example 2, for instance, uses the PadRight method to ensure that each name in the first column contains exactly 15 characters. It then concatenates the 15 characters with the age stored in the strAge variable, and then writes the concatenated string to the file. Because each name has 15 characters, each age will automatically appear beginning in character position 16 in the file.

In the next section, you learn how to read information from a sequential access file.

READING INFORMATION FROM A SEQUENTIAL ACCESS FILE

You use the **ReadLine method** to read a line of text from a sequential access file. A **line** is defined as a sequence of characters followed by the line terminator character. The string returned by the ReadLine method contains only the sequence of characters contained in the line; it does not include the line terminator character. Figure 8.9 shows the syntax of the ReadLine method and includes examples of using the method to read lines of text from a sequential access file. In the syntax, *variablename* is the name of a StreamReader variable.

HOW TO...

Use the ReadLine Method to Read Information From a Sequential Access File

Syntax
variablename.**ReadLine()**

Examples
```
strLine = sreStreamReader.ReadLine()
```
reads a line from a sequential access file, and then assigns the line (excluding the line terminator character) to the strLine variable

```
Do Until sreStreamReader.Peek() = -1
    strLine = sreStreamReader.ReadLine()
    MessageBox.Show(strLine, "Line", _
        MessageBoxButtons.OK, MessageBoxIcon.Information)
Loop
```
reads a sequential access file, line by line; assigns each line (excluding the line terminator character) to the strLine variable and displays each line in a message box

FIGURE 8.9   How to use the ReadLine method to read information from a sequential access file

In the first example shown in Figure 8.9, the `strLine = sreStreamReader.ReadLine()` statement reads a line of text from a sequential access file and assigns the line, excluding the line terminator character, to the strLine variable.

In most cases, an application will need to read each line of text contained in a sequential access file, one line at a time. You can do so using a repetition structure along with the Peek method, as shown in the second example in Figure 8.9. The syntax of the Peek method is *variablename*.**Peek()**, where *variablename* is the name of a StreamReader variable. The **Peek method** "peeks" into the file to see whether the file contains another character to read. If the file contains another character, the Peek method returns the character; otherwise, it returns the number -1. The `Do Until sreStreamReader.Peek() = -1` clause shown in the second example tells the computer to process the loop instructions, which read a line of text and then display the line (excluding the line terminator character) in a message box, until the Peek method returns the number -1, which indicates that there are no more characters to read.

The last step in the sequential access file procedure (shown earlier in Figure 8.2) is to use the StreamWriter or StreamReader object to close the file.

CLOSING A SEQUENTIAL ACCESS FILE

To prevent the loss of data, you should use the **Close method** to close a sequential access file as soon as you are finished using it. Figure 8.10 shows the syntax of the Close method and includes examples of using the method to close sequential access files. In the syntax, *variablename* is the name of either a StreamReader or StreamWriter variable.

HOW TO...

> **Use the Close Method to Close a Sequential Access File**
>
> **Syntax**
> *variablename*.**Close()**
>
> `sreStreamReader.Close()`
> closes the input file associated with the sreStreamReader object
>
> `swrStreamWriter.Close()`
> closes the output file associated with the swrStreamWriter object

FIGURE 8.10   How to use the Close method to close a sequential access file

TIP

Because it is so easy to forget to close the files used in an application, you should enter the statement to close the file as soon as possible after entering the one that opens it.

In the first example shown in Figure 8.10, the Close method closes the input file associated with the sreStreamReader variable. In the second example, the Close method closes the output file associated with the swrStreamWriter variable.

Next, you view an application that demonstrates most of what you have learned so far about files.

THE FRIENDS APPLICATION

Assume you want to create an application that allows the user to write the names of his or her friends to a sequential access file, and also read the names from the file. The user interface for this application is shown in Figure 8.11.

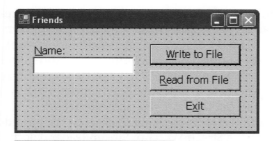

FIGURE 8.11   User interface for the Friends application

The user interface for the Friends application contains a text box for entering the names, and three buttons labeled Write to File, Read from File, and Exit. You use the Write to File button to write the name entered in the Name text box to a sequential access file named friends.txt. You use the Read from File button to read each name in the friends.txt file and display each name in a message box. You use the Exit button to end the application. Figure 8.12 shows the pseudocode for the Write to File and Read from File buttons, and Figure 8.13 shows the application's code.

Pseudocode for the Write to File button's Click event procedure
1. open a sequential access file named friends.txt for append
2. write the name entered in the Name text box to the file
3. close the file
4. clear the Name text box
5. send the focus to the Name text box

Pseudocode for the Read from File button's Click event procedure

1. if the friends.txt file exists
        open the file for input
        repeat until there are no more characters to read
                read a name from the file
                display the name in a message box
        end repeat
        close the file
    else
        display a message informing the user that the friends.txt file does not exist
    end if

FIGURE 8.12   Pseudocode for the Write to File and Read from File buttons

```
'Project name:        Friends Project
'Project purpose:     The project allows the user to write information
'                     to a sequential access file, and also read information
'                     from a sequential access file.
'Created/revised by:  Diane Zak on 2/1/2005

Option Explicit On
Option Strict On

Public Class frmFriends
    Inherits System.Windows.Forms.Form

[Windows Form Designer generated code]

    Private Sub btnExit_Click(ByVal sender As Object, ByVal e As System.EventArgs) _
        Handles btnExit.Click
        'ends the application
        Me.Close()
    End Sub

    Private Sub btnWrite_Click(ByVal sender As Object, ByVal e As System.EventArgs) _
        Handles btnWrite.Click
        'writes information to a sequential access file

        'declare a StreamWriter variable
        Dim swrStreamWriter As IO.StreamWriter

        'create a StreamWriter object by opening the file for append
        swrStreamWriter = IO.File.AppendText("friends.txt")

        'write the name entered in the Name text box
        'on a separate line in the file
        swrStreamWriter.WriteLine(Me.txtName.Text)

        'close the file
        swrStreamWriter.Close()

        'clear the Name text box, then send the focus to the text box
        Me.txtName.Text = ""
        Me.txtName.Focus()

    End Sub

    Private Sub btnRead_Click(ByVal sender As Object, ByVal e As System.EventArgs) _
        Handles btnRead.Click
        'reads information from a sequential access file

        'declare variables
        Dim strName As String
        Dim sreStreamReader As IO.StreamReader

        'determine whether the friends.txt file exists
        If IO.File.Exists("friends.txt") Then
            'create a StreamReader object by opening the file for input
            sreStreamReader = IO.File.OpenText("friends.txt")
```

(Figure is continued on next page)

```
            'process the loop instructions until there are
            'no more characters to read
            Do Until sreStreamReader.Peek() = -1
                'read a name from the file--each name
                'appears on a separate line in the file
                strName = sreStreamReader.ReadLine()
                'display the name in a message box
                MessageBox.Show(strName, "Friend", _
                    MessageBoxButtons.OK, MessageBoxIcon.Information)
            Loop

            'close the file
            sreStreamReader.Close()
        Else
            'display an appropriate message
            MessageBox.Show("The friends.txt file does not exist.", "Friend", _
                MessageBoxButtons.OK, MessageBoxIcon.Information)
        End If

    End Sub
End Class
```

FIGURE 8.13　　Code for the Friends application

Notice that the btnWrite Click event procedure declares a StreamWriter variable named swrStreamWriter. It then uses the AppendText method to open the friends.txt file; this creates a StreamWriter object. The procedure assigns the StreamWriter object's address to the swrStreamWriter variable. Next, the procedure uses the WriteLine method to write the contents of the Name text box on a separate line in the friends.txt file. The procedure then uses the Close method to close the friends.txt file. After closing the file, the procedure clears the contents of the Name text box and also sends the focus to the text box. If you start the Friends application and enter three names (Janice, Carl, and William), clicking the Write to File button after entering each name, the btnWrite Click event procedure will write each name on a separate line in the friends.txt file. You can verify that the records were written correctly by viewing the contents of the file in a separate window in the IDE. Figure 8.14 shows the procedure you follow to view the contents of a sequential access file, and Figure 8.15 shows the contents of the friends.txt file.

HOW TO...

View the Contents of a Sequential Access File

1. Click File on the menu bar.
2. Point to Open, then click File. The Open File dialog box opens.
3. Open the bin folder contained in the application's project folder.
4. Click the name of the sequential access file in the list of filenames.
5. Click the Open button to view the contents of the file in a separate window.
6. To close the window, click its Close button.

FIGURE 8.14　　How to view the contents of a sequential access file

FIGURE 8.15 Contents of the friends.txt file displayed in a window

The btnRead Click event procedure shown earlier in Figure 8.13 declares a StreamReader variable named sreStreamReader. It then uses the Exists method to determine whether the friends.txt file exists. If the file does not exist, the procedure displays the message "The friends.txt file does not exist." in a message box. However, if the file does exist, the procedure uses the OpenText method to open the file; this creates a StreamReader object. The procedure assigns the StreamReader object's address to the sreStreamReader variable. Next, the procedure uses a repetition structure, the Peek method, the ReadLine method, and the MessageBox.Show method to read each name in the file and display each name in a message box. After each name in the file has been displayed, the procedure uses the Close method to close the friends.txt file. Assuming the friends.txt file exists, Figure 8.16 shows the message box that will appear when the user clicks the Read from File button the first time.

FIGURE 8.16 Message box containing the first name read from the file

As you learned earlier, the computer displays an error message when the OpenText method tries to open an input file that does not exist. Recall that you can prevent this error from occurring by using the Exists method to verify that the file exists before you attempt to open it. Unfortunately, trying to open a non-existent input file is not the only error that can occur when using sequential access files. For example, the AppendText and CreateText methods will result in an error if the file you are trying to open is read-only, or if the folder path specified in the *filename* argument does not exist. You can handle these errors using a Try/Catch block.

USING A TRY/CATCH BLOCK

In Visual Basic .NET, an error that occurs while a program is running is called an **exception** and typically results in the program displaying an error message and then ending abruptly. You can use the **Try statement** to catch (or trap) an exception when it occurs in a program, and then use a **Catch statement** to have the computer take the appropriate action to resolve the problem. A block of code that uses both the Try and Catch statements is referred to as a **Try/Catch block**. Figure 8.17 shows the syntax of a Try/Catch block. It also lists common *exceptionTypes* and includes several examples of using a Try/Catch block to catch exceptions.

HOW TO...

Use a Try/Catch Block

Syntax
Try
> *one or more statements that might generate an exception*

Catch [*variablename As exceptionType*]
> *one or more statements that will execute when an exceptionType exception occurs*

[**Catch** [*variablename As exceptionType*]
> *one or more statements that will execute when an exceptionType exception occurs*]

End Try

Common *exceptionTypes*	Caused By
ArithmeticException	an error in a calculation
IO.DirectoryNotFoundException	an invalid folder path
IO.FileNotFoundException	a file that cannot be located
Exception	any error
FormatException	an argument that does not meet the specifications of the invoked method

Example 1
```
Try
    'calculate and display the average
    decAverage =
        Convert.ToDecimal(intTotalScores / intNumStudents)
    Me.lblAverage.Text = decAverage.ToString("N2")
Catch exArithmetic As ArithmeticException
    'processed when the average cannot be calculated
    Me.lblAverage.Text = "0.00"
End Try
```

Example 2
```
Try
    'open an output file
    swrStreamWriter = IO.File.AppendText("a:\reports\pay.txt")
Catch exDirectory As IO.DirectoryNotFoundException
    'processed when the folder path is invalid
    MessageBox.Show("Cannot locate the folder a:\reports.", _
        "Payroll Report", MessageBoxButtons.OK, _
        MessageBoxIcon.Information)
Catch exFile As IO.FileNotFoundException
    'processed when the file cannot be found
    MessageBox.Show("Cannot locate the pay.txt file.", _
        "Payroll Report", MessageBoxButtons.OK, _
        MessageBoxIcon.Information)
Catch ex As Exception
    'handles any other errors
    MessageBox.Show(ex.Message, "Payroll Report", _
        MessageBoxButtons.OK, MessageBoxIcon.Information)
End Try
```

(Figure is continued on next page)

Example 3
```
Try
        'assign input to a variable, then remove any dollar signs,
        'commas, or spaces from the input
        strSales = Me.txtSales.Text
        strSales = strSales.Replace("$", "")
        strSales = strSales.Replace(",", "")
        strSales = strSales.Replace(" ", "")

        'show modified input in the text box
        Me.txtSales.Text = strSales

        'convert input to a decimal
        decSales = Convert.ToDecimal(strSales)

        'calculate and display commission
        decCommission = decSales * .05
        Me.lblCommission.Text = decCommission.ToString("C2")

Catch exFormat As FormatException
        'processed when the input cannot be converted to a decimal
        MessageBox.Show("The sales amount must be numeric.", _
                "Sales", MessageBoxButtons.OK, _
                MessageBoxIcon.Information)
Catch ex As Exception
        'handles any other errors
        MessageBox.Show(ex.Message, "Sales", _
                MessageBoxButtons.OK, MessageBoxIcon.Information)
End Try
```

FIGURE 8.17 How to use a Try/Catch block

TIP

You can use any name for the variable in the Catch statement.

The Try statement begins with the keyword **Try** and ends with the keywords **End Try**. Within the Try statement you place the code that might generate an exception. You also list one or more Catch statements. Each Catch statement begins with the keyword **Catch**, followed by the name of a variable, the keyword **As**, and an exception type. A Catch statement ends when the computer reaches another Catch statement or the End Try clause.

A Try/Catch block can contain multiple Catch statements, with each Catch statement handling a different type of exception (error). When an exception occurs in the code included in the Try statement, only one of the Catch statements is processed; the appropriate Catch statement depends on the exception that occurred.

Study closely the examples shown in Figure 8.17. In Example 1, the Try section of the Try/Catch block contains two statements. The first statement, decAverage = Convert.ToDecimal(intTotalScores / intNumStudents), will generate an ArithmeticException if the intNumStudents variable contains the number zero, because division by zero is not mathematically possible. If an ArithmeticException does not occur, the computer calculates the average and stores the result in the decAverage variable. It then processes the Me.lblAverage.Text = decAverage.ToString("N2") statement, which displays the average in the lblAverage control. The computer then processes the End Try clause, which marks the end of the Try/Catch block. Notice that the computer skips over the Catch section of the Try/Catch block when an ArithmeticException does not occur.

If, on the other hand, an ArithmeticException does occur when processing the code shown in Example 1, the computer will process the `Me.lblAverage.Text = "0.00"` statement contained in the `Catch exArithmetic As ArithmeticException` section of the Try/Catch block. That statement displays 0.00 in the lblAverage control. After displaying the average, the computer processes the End Try clause, which marks the end of the Try/Catch block.

In Example 2 in Figure 8.17, the Try section contains the statement `swrStreamWriter = IO.File.AppendText("a:\reports\pay.txt")`. The statement will generate an IO.DirectoryNotFoundException if the folder path (a:\reports) is invalid. However, it will generate an IO.FileNotFoundException if the pay.txt file cannot be located in the a:\reports folder. Notice that the first Catch statement in Example 2 displays an appropriate message—in this case, "Cannot locate the folder a:\reports."—when the IO.DirectoryNotFoundException occurs. The second Catch statement also displays an appropriate message—in this case, "Cannot locate the pay.txt file."—when the IO.FileNotFoundException occurs.

Example 2's code also contains a third Catch statement: `Catch ex As Exception`. This Catch statement will catch any errors that are not handled by the previous, more specific Catch statements listed in the Try/Catch block. It is a good programming practice to include a general Catch statement as the last Catch statement in a Try/Catch block. The purpose of the general Catch statement is to handle any unexpected exceptions (errors) that may arise. You can access a description of the exception that occurred using the syntax *variablename*.**Message**, where *variablename* is the name of the variable used in the Catch statement. For example, if the variable's name is ex, as it is in Example 2, you can display a description of the error by using `ex.Message` as the *text* argument in the MessageBox.Show method.

In Example 3 in Figure 8.17, the first four statements in the Try section assign the contents of the txtSales text box to the strSales variable, and then remove any dollar signs, commas, or spaces from the variable's contents. The next statement displays the contents of the strSales variable in the txtSales text box. The `decSales = Convert.ToDecimal(strSales)` statement then attempts to convert the contents of the strSales variable to a Decimal number, and assign the result to the decSales variable. If the conversion and assignment can be made, the computer calculates and displays the commission and then skips to the End Try clause, which marks the end of the Try/Catch block.

If, on the other hand, the contents of the strSales variable cannot be converted to a number, a FormatException occurs. In this case, the computer does not process the instructions that calculate and display the commission; rather, it processes the MessageBox.Show method contained in the `Catch exFormat As FormatException` statement. The MessageBox.Show method displays the message "The sales amount must be numeric." After displaying the message, the computer processes the End Try clause, which marks the end of the Try/Catch block.

Notice that the last Catch statement in Example 3 is a general Catch statement. If an unexpected error occurs when processing the code shown in Example 3, the computer will process the MessageBox.Show method contained in this Catch statement.

Figure 8.18 shows the Friends application with a Try/Catch block in the btnWrite_Click and btnRead_Click procedures. Notice that this version of the btnRead_Click procedure does not use the Exists method to verify that the input file (friends.txt) exists before the OpenText method opens it. In this version of the btnRead_Click procedure, the Catch statement will handle the exception that occurs when the input file cannot be found. You also do not need to include a separate Catch statement for the DirectoryNotFoundException in the btnWrite_Click and btnRead_Click procedures, because the AppendText and OpenText methods do not specify a folder path in their *filename* argument.

```
'Project name:          Friends Project
'Project purpose:       The project allows the user to write information
'                       to a sequential access file, and also read information
'                       from a sequential access file.
'Created/revised by:    Diane Zak on 2/1/2005

Option Explicit On
Option Strict On

Public Class frmFriends
    Inherits System.Windows.Forms.Form

[Windows Form Designer generated code]

    Private Sub btnExit_Click(ByVal sender As Object, ByVal e As System.EventArgs) _
        Handles btnExit.Click
        'ends the application
        Me.Close()
    End Sub


    Private Sub btnWrite_Click(ByVal sender As Object, ByVal e As System.EventArgs) _
        Handles btnWrite.Click
        'writes information to a sequential access file

        'declare a StreamWriter variable
        Dim swrStreamWriter As IO.StreamWriter

        Try
            'create a StreamWriter object by opening the file for append
            swrStreamWriter = IO.File.AppendText("friends.txt")

            'write the name entered in the Name text box
            'on a separate line in the file
            swrStreamWriter.WriteLine(Me.txtName.Text)

            'close the file
            swrStreamWriter.Close()

            'clear the Name text box, then send the focus to the text box
            Me.txtName.Text = ""
            Me.txtName.Focus()
```

(Figure is continued on next page)

```
        Catch ex As Exception
            'handles any errors
            MessageBox.Show(ex.Message, "Friends", _
                MessageBoxButtons.OK, MessageBoxIcon.Information)

        End Try

    End Sub

    Private Sub btnRead_Click(ByVal sender As Object, ByVal e As System.EventArgs) _
        Handles btnRead.Click
        'reads information from a sequential access file

        'declare variables
        Dim strName As String
        Dim sreStreamReader As IO.StreamReader

        Try
            'create a StreamReader object by opening the file for input
            sreStreamReader = IO.File.OpenText("friends.txt")

            'process the loop instructions until there are
            'no more characters to read
            Do Until sreStreamReader.Peek() = -1
                'read a name from the file--each name
                'appears on a separate line in the file
                strName = sreStreamReader.ReadLine()
                'display the name in a message box
                MessageBox.Show(strName, "Friend", _
                    MessageBoxButtons.OK, MessageBoxIcon.Information)
            Loop

            'close the file
            sreStreamReader.Close()

        Catch exFile As IO.FileNotFoundException
            'processed when the file cannot be found
            MessageBox.Show("Cannot locate the friends.txt file.", _
                "Friends", MessageBoxButtons.OK, _
                MessageBoxIcon.Information)
        Catch ex As Exception
            'handles any other errors
            MessageBox.Show(ex.Message, "Friends", _
                MessageBoxButtons.OK, MessageBoxIcon.Information)

        End Try

    End Sub

End Class
```

FIGURE 8.18   Try/Catch blocks included in the Friends application

Finally, you learn how to write a record to and read a record from a sequential access file.

WRITING AND READING RECORDS

In some applications, a sequential access file is used to store fields and records. A **field** is a single item of information about a person, place, or thing—for example, a name, a salary, a Social Security number, or a price. A **record** is one or more related fields that contain all of the necessary data about a specific person, place, or thing. The college you are attending keeps a student record on you. Your student record might contain the following fields: your Social Security number, name, address, phone number, credits earned, grades earned, grade point average, and so on. The place where you are employed also keeps a record on you. Your employee record might contain your Social Security number, name, address, phone number, starting date, salary or hourly wage, and so on.

When writing records to a sequential access file, you typically write each record on a separate line in the file. If the records contain more than one field, programmers separate each field with a special character, such as a comma or the number symbol (#); this is done to distinguish one field from the next when reading the record later. Figure 8.19 shows examples of writing records to a sequential access file.

HOW TO...

Write a Record to a Sequential Access File

```
swrStreamWriter.WriteLine(Me.txtCity.Text & "," &
Me.txtState.Text)
```
assuming the txtCity and txtState controls contain Miami and Florida, respectively, the statement writes the following record on a separate line in the file associated with the swrStreamWriter variable: Miami,Florida

```
swrStreamWriter.WriteLine(strLast & "#" & strFirst)
```
assuming the strLast and strFirst variables contain Smithson and Carol, respectively, the statement writes the following record on a separate line in the file associated with the swrStreamWriter variable: Smithson#Carol

FIGURE 8.19   How to write a record to a sequential access file

The statement shown in the first example in Figure 8.19 writes a record that consists of two fields—a city field and a state field—separated by a comma. The comma indicates where the city field ends in the record and where the state field begins. The WriteLine method in the statement ensures that the record appears on a separate line in the file.

The statement shown in the second example also writes a record that contains two fields: a last name field and a first name field. In this example, however, the fields are separated by the # character, which indicates where the last name ends and the first name begins.

Figure 8.20 shows examples of reading records from a sequential access file. More specifically, the examples in Figure 8.20 can be used to read the records from Figure 8.19.

HOW TO...

Read a Record from a Sequential Access File

```
Do Until sreStreamReader.Peek() = -1
    'read a record from the file
    strRecord = sreStreamReader.ReadLine()
    'display the city name
    intIndex = strRecord.IndexOf(",")
    strCityName = strRecord.Substring(0, intIndex)
    MessageBox.Show(strCityName, "City Name", _
        MessageBoxButtons.OK, MessageBoxIcon.Information)
Loop
```
assuming the file contains the record *Miami,Florida*, the code displays *Miami* in a message box

```
Do Until sreStreamReader.Peek() = -1
    'read a record from the file
    strRecord = sreStreamReader.ReadLine()
    'display the first name
    intIndex = strRecord.IndexOf("#")
    strFirstName = strRecord.Substring(intIndex + 1)
    MessageBox.Show(strFirstName, "First Name", _
        MessageBoxButtons.OK, MessageBoxIcon.Information)
Loop
```
assuming the file contains the record *Smithson#Carol*, the code displays *Carol* in a message box

FIGURE 8.20   How to read records from a sequential access file

TIP

You learned about the IndexOf and Substring methods in Chapter 6.

The loop shown in the first example in Figure 8.20 processes its instructions until there are no more characters to read from the file. The first instruction in the loop uses the ReadLine method to read a line of text from the file, and it assigns the text to the strRecord variable. In this case, the line of text represents a record that contains a city name field, followed by a comma and a state name field. The next statement in the loop, `intIndex = strRecord.IndexOf (",")`, searches for the comma in the strRecord variable and assigns the comma's index to the intIndex variable. Assuming the strRecord variable contains *Miami,Florida*, the statement assigns the number five to the intIndex variable. The next statement in the loop, `strCityName = strRecord.Substring (0, intIndex)`, tells the computer to assign intIndex characters from the strRecord variable, beginning with the first character. Assuming the strRecord and intIndex variables contain *Miami,Florida* and *5*, respectively, the statement assigns *Miami* (the city name) to the strCityName variable. Lastly, the MessageBox.Show method displays the city name in a message box.

The loop shown in the second example in Figure 8.20 also processes its instructions until there are no more characters to read from the file. Here again, the first instruction in the loop uses the ReadLine method to read a line of text from the file, and it assigns the text to the strRecord variable. In this case, however, the line of text represents a record that contains a last name field, followed by the # character and a first name field. The next statement in the loop, `intIndex = strRecord.IndexOf("#")`, searches for the # character in the record and assigns the character's index to the intIndex variable. Assuming the strRecord variable contains *Smithson#Carol*, the statement assigns the number eight to the intIndex variable. The next statement in the loop, `strFirstName = strRecord.Substring(intIndex + 1)`, tells the computer to assign to the strFirstName variable all of the characters from the strRecord variable, beginning with the character immediately after the # character. Assuming the strRecord and intIndex variables contain *Smithson#Carol* and *8*, respectively, the statement assigns *Carol* (the first name) to the strFirstName variable. Lastly, the MessageBox.Show method displays the first name in a message box.

PROGRAMMING EXAMPLE

PAO Application

During July and August of each year the Political Awareness Organization (PAO) sends a questionnaire to the voters in their district. The questionnaire asks the voter to provide his or her political party (Democrat, Republican, or Independent) and age. From the returned questionnaires, the organization's secretary tabulates the number of Democrats, Republicans, and Independents in the district. Create an application that allows the organization's secretary to enter the political party and age, and also save this information to a sequential access file. The application also should calculate and display the number of voters in each political party. Name the solution PAO Solution. Name the project PAO Project. Name the form file PAO Form.vb.

TOE Chart:

Task	Object	Event
1. Open a sequential access file named pao.txt for append 2. If the political party is valid, write the political party and age to a sequential access file 3. If the political party is not valid, display an appropriate message 4. Close the sequential access file 5. Clear the text boxes 6. Send the focus to the txtParty control	btnWrite	Click
1. Open a sequential access file named pao.txt for input 2. Read each record in the sequential access file 3. If the current record begins with D, then add 1 to the Democrat counter 4. If the current record begins with R, then add 1 to the Republican counter 5. If the current record begins with I, then add 1 to the Independent counter 6. Close the sequential access file 7. Display the number of Democrats, Republicans, and Independents in lblTotalDem, lblTotalRep, and lblTotalInd	btnDisplay	Click
End the application	btnExit	Click

(Table is continued on next page)

Task	Object	Event
Display the total number of Democrats (from btnDisplay)	lblTotalDem	None
Display the total number of Republicans (from btnDisplay)	lblTotalRep	None
Display the total number of Independents (from btnDisplay)	lblTotalInd	None
Get the political party	txtParty	None
Get the age	txtAge	None

FIGURE 8.21

User Interface:

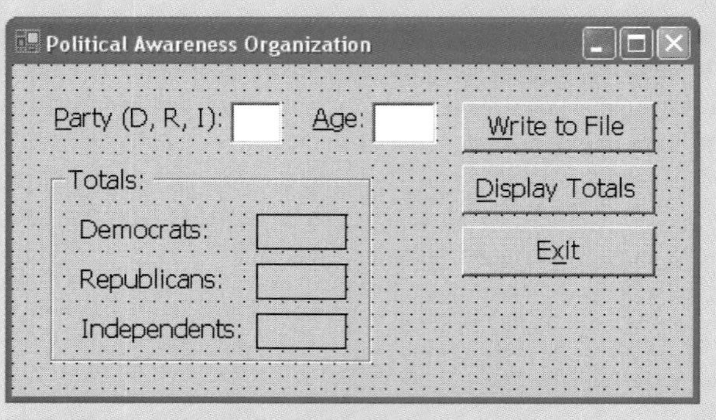

FIGURE 8.22

Objects, Properties, and Settings

Object	Property	Setting
frmPao	Name	frmPao (be sure to change the startup form to this name)
	Font	Tahoma, 12 point (be sure to change the form's font before adding the controls)
	Size	432, 248
	StartPosition	CenterScreen
	Text	Political Awareness Organization
GroupBox1	Text	Totals:
Label1	AutoSize	True
	Text	&Party (D, R, I):
Label2	AutoSize	True
	Text	&Age:
Label3	AutoSize	True
	Text	Democrats:

(Table is continued on next page)

Object	Property	Setting
Label4	AutoSize	True
	Text	Republicans:
Label5	AutoSize	True
	Text	Independents:
lblTotalDem	Name	lblTotalDem
	BorderStyle	FixedSingle
	Text	(empty)
lblTotalRep	Name	lblTotalRep
	BorderStyle	FixedSingle
	Text	(empty)
lblTotalInd	Name	lblTotalInd
	BorderStyle	FixedSingle
	Text	(empty)
btnWrite	Name	btnWrite
	Text	&Write to File
btnDisplay	Name	btnDisplay
	Text	&Display Totals
btnExit	Name	btnExit
	Text	E&xit
txtParty	Name	txtParty
	CharacterCasing	Upper
	MaxLength	1
	Text	(empty)
txtAge	Name	txtAge
	Text	(empty)

FIGURE 8.23

Tab Order:

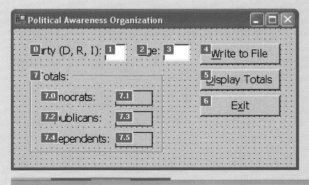

FIGURE 8.24

Pseudocode:

btnExit Click event procedure

1. close application

btnWrite Click event procedure

include the following in the Try section of a Try/Catch block:
1. open the pao.txt file for append
2. if the txtParty control contains D, R, or I
        write the contents of the txtParty control, a comma, and the contents of the txtAge control
        to the pao.txt file
    else
        display a message prompting the user to enter D, R, or I in the txtParty control
    end if
3. close the pao.txt file
4. clear the contents of the txtParty and txtAge controls
5. send the focus to the txtParty control

include the following in the Catch section of a Try/Catch block:
1. use a general Catch statement to handle any errors
        if an error occurs, display a description of the error in a message box

btnDisplay Click event procedure

include the following in the Try section of a Try/Catch block:
1. open the pao.txt file for input
2. repeat until there are no more characters to read
        read a record from the file
        if the first character in the record is the letter D
                add 1 to the Democrat counter
        else if the first character in the record is the letter R
                add 1 to the Republican counter
        else add 1 to the Independent counter
        end if
    end repeat
3. close the pao.txt file
4. display the Democrat counter value in lblTotalDem
5. display the Republican counter value in lblTotalRep
6. display the Independent counter value in lblTotalInd

include the following in the Catch section of a Try/Catch block:
1. use a Catch statement to handle the FileNotFoundException
        if a FileNotFoundException occurs, display the message "Cannot locate the pao.txt file." in a message box
2. use a general Catch statement to handle any other errors
        if an error occurs, display a description of the error in a message box

Code:

```vb
'Project name:          PAO Project
'Project purpose:       The project writes the party affiliation and age,
'                       which are entered by the user, to a sequential
'                       access file. It also displays the total number
'                       of Democrats, Republicans, and Independents
'                       stored in the file.
'Created/revised by:    Diane Zak on 2/1/2005

Option Explicit On
Option Strict On

Public Class frmPao
    Inherits System.Windows.Forms.Form

[Windows Form Designer generated code]

    Private Sub btnExit_Click(ByVal sender As Object, ByVal e As System.EventArgs) _
        Handles btnExit.Click
        'ends the application
        Me.Close()
    End Sub

    Private Sub btnWrite_Click(ByVal sender As Object, ByVal e As System.EventArgs) _
        Handles btnWrite.Click
        'writes information to a sequential access file

        'declare a StreamWriter variable
        Dim swrStreamWriter As IO.StreamWriter

        Try
            'create a StreamWriter object by opening the file for append
            swrStreamWriter = IO.File.AppendText("pao.txt")

            'write the party affiliation and age to the file, but only
            'if the party affiliation is D, R, or I
            If Me.txtParty.Text Like "[DRI]*" Then
                swrStreamWriter.WriteLine(Me.txtParty.Text & "," & Me.txtAge.Text)
            Else
                MessageBox.Show("Please enter D, R, or I in the Party box.", _
                    "PAO", MessageBoxButtons.OK, MessageBoxIcon.Information)
            End If


            'close the file
            swrStreamWriter.Close()

            'clear the text boxes
            Me.txtParty.Text = ""
            Me.txtAge.Text = ""

            'set the focus
            Me.txtParty.Focus()

        Catch ex As Exception
            'handles any errors
```

(Figure is continued on next page)

```
                    MessageBox.Show(ex.Message, "PAO", _
                        MessageBoxButtons.OK, MessageBoxIcon.Information)

            End Try

    End Sub

    Private Sub btnDisplay_Click(ByVal sender As Object, ByVal e As System.EventArgs) _
        Handles btnDisplay.Click
        'displays the total number of Democrats, Republicans, and Independents
        'stored in a sequential access file

        'declare variables
        Dim strRecord As String
        Dim sreStreamReader As IO.StreamReader
        Dim intTotalDem As Integer       'counter for total Democrats
        Dim intTotalRep As Integer       'counter for total Republicans
        Dim intTotalInd As Integer       'counter for total Independents

        Try
            'create a StreamReader object by opening the file for input
            sreStreamReader = IO.File.OpenText("pao.txt")

            'process the loop instructions until there are
            'no more characters to read
            Do Until sreStreamReader.Peek() = -1
                'read a record from the file
                strRecord = sreStreamReader.ReadLine()

                'update the appropriate counter
                If strRecord.StartsWith("D") Then
                    intTotalDem = intTotalDem + 1
                ElseIf strRecord.StartsWith("R") Then
                    intTotalRep = intTotalRep + 1
                Else
                    intTotalInd = intTotalInd + 1
                End If
            Loop

            'close the file
            sreStreamReader.Close()

            'display the totals
            Me.lblTotalDem.Text = Convert.ToString(intTotalDem)
            Me.lblTotalRep.Text = Convert.ToString(intTotalRep)
            Me.lblTotalInd.Text = Convert.ToString(intTotalInd)

        Catch exFile As IO.FileNotFoundException
            'processed when the file cannot be found
            MessageBox.Show("Cannot locate the pao.txt file.", _
                "PAO", MessageBoxButtons.OK, _
                MessageBoxIcon.Information)
        Catch ex As Exception
            'handles any other errors
            MessageBox.Show(ex.Message, "PAO", _
                MessageBoxButtons.OK, MessageBoxIcon.Information)

        End Try

    End Sub
End Class
```

FIGURE 8.25

Quick Review

- An application can write information to a file and also read information from a file.
- The information in a sequential access file is always accessed in consecutive order (sequentially) from the beginning of the file through the end of the file.
- In Visual Basic .NET, you use a StreamWriter object to write a sequence of characters (stream) to a sequential access file. You use a StreamReader object to read a stream (sequence of characters) from a sequential access file.
- When you open a sequential access file for input, the computer creates a StreamReader object. When you open a sequential access file for output or append, the computer creates a StreamWriter object.
- The Exists method returns the Boolean value True if a file exists; otherwise, it returns the Boolean value False.
- You use either the Write method or the WriteLine method to write data to a sequential access file.
- You use the ReadLine method to read a line of text from a sequential access file.
- You use the Peek method to determine whether a file contains another character to read. If the file contains another character, the Peek method returns the character; otherwise, it returns the number -1.
- The computer uses a file pointer to keep track of the next character either to read in or write to a file.
- You can use the Space function to write a specific number of spaces to a file.
- You can use the PadLeft and PadRight methods to align columns of information in a sequential access file.
- To prevent the loss of data, you should use the Close method to close a sequential access file as soon as you are finished using it.
- You can use a Try/Catch block to catch an exception when it occurs in a Visual Basic .NET program, and then have the computer take the appropriate action to resolve the problem.
- It is a good programming practice to use a general Catch statement to handle unexpected errors. The general Catch statement should be the last Catch statement in the Try/Catch block.
- You can access a description of an exception that occurred using the syntax *variablename*.**Message**, where *variablename* is the name of the variable used in the Catch statement.
- Sequential files are also used to store fields and records.
- Typically, each record in a sequential access file appears on a separate line in the file. You use a special character, such as a comma or the # character, to separate each field in the record.

Key Terms

An application writes information to an **output file**, and reads information from an **input file**.

A **sequential access file** is composed of lines of text that are both stored and retrieved sequentially. A sequential access file is often referred to as a **text file**.

A **StreamWriter object** is used to write a sequence of characters to a sequential access file.

A **StreamReader object** is used to read a sequence of characters from a sequential access file.

A sequence of characters is also called a **stream of characters** or, more simply, a **stream**.

The **OpenText method** opens an existing sequential access file for input.

The **CreateText method** creates a new, empty sequential access file to which data can be written.

The **AppendText method** opens a new or existing sequential access file for append.

You can use the **Exists method** to determine whether a file exists.

The **Write method** writes information to a sequential access file, and positions the file pointer at the end of the last character it writes.

The **WriteLine method** writes information to a sequential access file, and positions the file pointer at the beginning of the next line in the file.

The **line terminator character** written by the WriteLine method is a carriage return followed by a line feed.

You can use the **Space function** to write a specific number of spaces to a file.

The **ReadLine method** reads a line of text from a sequential access file.

A **line** is defined as a sequence of characters followed by the line terminator character.

You can use the **Peek method** to determine whether a sequential access file contains another character to read.

You use the **Close method** to close a sequential access file.

An **exception** is an error that occurs while a program is running.

A **Try/Catch block** is a block of code that contains the Try statement and one or more Catch statements.

The **Try statement** is used to trap an exception when it occurs in a program.

The **Catch statement** contains the instructions that tell the computer how to handle an exception.

A **field** is a single item of information about a person, place, or thing.

A **record** is one or more related fields that contain all of the necessary data about a specific person, place, or thing.

Review Questions

1. Which of the following creates a variable that can be used when reading a sequential access file?
   a. `Dim creCharReader As IO.CharReader`
   b. `Dim freFileReader As IO.FileReader`
   c. `Dim sreSequenceReader As IO.SequenceReader`
   d. `Dim sreStreamReader As IO.StreamReader`

2. Which of the following opens the states.txt file and allows the computer to write information to the end of the existing data in the file?
   a. `swrStreamWriter = IO.File.AddText("states.txt")`
   b. `swrStreamWriter = IO.File.AppendText("states.txt")`
   c. `swrSequenceWriter = IO.File.InsertText("states.txt")`
   d. `swrStreamWriter = IO.File.OpenText("states.txt")`

3. The OpenText method creates a _____.
   a. StreamReader object
   b. StreamReader variable
   c. StreamWriter object
   d. StreamWriter variable

4. If the file you want to open exists, the _____ method erases the file's contents.
   a. AppendText
   b. CreateText
   c. InsertText
   d. OpenText

5. If the file you want to open does not exist, the _____ method displays an error message in a message box.
   a. AppendText
   b. CreateText
   c. InsertText
   d. OpenText

6. Which of the following can be used to write the string "Your pay is $56" to a sequential access file? (Assume that the intPay variable contains the number 56.)
   a. `swrStreamWriter.Write("Your pay is $")`
      `swrStreamWriter.WriteLine(intPay)`
   b. `swrStreamWriter.WriteLine("Your pay is $" &`
      `intPay.ToString("N0"))`
   c. `swrStreamWriter.Write("Your ")`
      `swrStreamWriter.Write("pay is ")`
      `swrStreamWriter.WriteLine(intPay.ToString("C0"))`
   d. All of the above.

7. Which of the following can be used to write 15 space characters to a sequential access file?
   a. `swrStreamWriter.WriteLine(Blank(15, " "))`
   b. `swrStreamWriter.WriteLine(Chars(15, " "))`
   c. `swrStreamWriter.WriteLine(Space(15))`
   d. `swrStreamWriter.WriteLine(Space(15, " "))`

8. Which of the following reads a line of text from a sequential access file, and assigns the line (excluding the line terminator character) to the strText variable?
   a. `sreStreamReader.Read(strText)`
   b. `sreStreamReader.ReadLine(strText)`
   c. `strText = sreStreamReader.ReadLine()`
   d. `strText = sreStreamReader.Read(line)`

9. The Peek method returns _____ if the sequential access file does not contain any more characters to read.
   a. -1
   b. 0 (zero)
   c. the last character read
   d. the line terminator character

10. You can use the Close method to close files opened for _____.
    a. append
    b. input
    c. output
    d. All of the above.

11. Which of the following can be used to determine whether the "employ.txt" file exists?
    a. `If IO.File.Exists("employ.txt") Then`
    b. `If IO.File("employ.txt").Exists Then`
    c. `If IO.Exists("employ.txt") Then`
    d. `If IO.Exists.File("employ.txt") = True Then`

12. Which of the following can be used as a general Catch statement?
    a. `Catch exGeneral As General`
    b. `Catch ex As Exception`
    c. `Catch ex As GenException`
    d. `Catch exGeneral As GenException`

13. Which of the following assigns (to the strMsg variable) a description of the exception that occurred?
    a. `strMsg = ex.Message`
    b. `strMsg = ex.Description`
    c. `strMsg = ex.Exception`
    d. None of the above.

14. What type of exception occurs when the computer cannot process a statement that contains a calculation?
    a. ArithmeticException
    b. CalculationException
    c. MathException
    d. MathematicalException

15. What type of exception occurs when the Convert.ToDecimal method cannot convert a string to a number?
    a. ConversionException
    b. ConvertException
    c. FormatException
    d. NumericException

16. When a sequential access file is opened for _____, the file pointer is always positioned at the beginning of the file.
    a. append
    b. input
    c. output
    d. Both b and c.

17. Which of the following writes the contents of the strName variable to a sequential access file, and then positions the insertion point at the beginning of the next line in the file?
    a. `swrStreamWriter.Write(strName)`
    b. `swrStreamWriter.WriteLine(strName)`
    c. `swrStreamWriter.WriteToLine(strName)`
    d. `swrStreamWriter.WriteNextLine(strName)`

18. Which of the following can be used to write a record that contains two fields: a book title field and an author field?
    a. `swrStreamWriter.WriteLine(strTitle & "#" & strAuthor)`
    b. `swrStreamWriter.WriteLine(strTitle & "," & strAuthor)`
    c. `swrStreamWriter.WriteLine(strTitle & "$" & strAuthor)`
    d. All of the above.

19. Assume that each record stored in a sequential access file contains two fields separated by the # character. Which of the following can be used to read a record from the file?
    a. `strRecord = sreStreamReader.ReadLine()`
    b. `sreStreamReader.ReadLine(strRecord)`
    c. `strRecord = sreStreamReader.ReadLine("#")`
    d. None of the above.

20. The string returned by the ReadLine method contains the line terminator character.
    a. True
    b. False

Exercises

1. Write the statement to declare a procedure-level StreamReader variable named sreStreamReader.

2. Write the statement to open a sequential access file named jansales.txt for input. Assign the resulting StreamReader object to the sreStreamReader variable.

3. Write the statement to open a sequential access file named firstQtr.txt for append. Assign the resulting StreamWriter object to the swrStreamWriter variable.

4. Write the statement to open a sequential access file named febsales.txt for output. Assign the resulting StreamWriter object to the swrStreamWriter variable.

5. Assume you want to write the string "Employee" and the string "Name" to the sequential access file associated with the swrStreamWriter variable. Each string should appear on a separate line in the file. Write the Visual Basic .NET code to accomplish this task.

6. Assume you want to write the contents of the strCapital variable followed by 20 spaces, the contents of the strState variable, and the line terminator character to the sequential access file associated with the swrStreamWriter variable. Write the Visual Basic .NET code to accomplish this task.

7. Assume that the decSales variable contains the number 2356.75. Write the statement to assign the contents of the decSales variable, formatted with a dollar sign and two decimal places, to the strSales variable. The statement also should right-align the contents of the strSales variable, which should contain a total of 15 characters.

8. Assume you want the strAward variable to contain 10 characters, which should be right-aligned in the variable. Write the statement to accomplish this task. Use the asterisk character to pad the variable.

9. Write the statement that will ensure that the strName variable contains 30 characters, which should be left-aligned in the variable. Use the space character to pad the variable.

10. Write the statement to read a line of text from the sequential access file associated with the sreStreamReader variable. Assign the line of text (excluding the line terminator character) to the strText variable.

11. Assume you want to read a sequential access file, line by line, displaying each line in a message box. The file is associated with the sreStreamReader variable. Write the Visual Basic .NET code to accomplish this task.

12. Write the statement to close the jansales.txt file, which is associated with the swrStreamWriter variable.

13. Write the Visual Basic .NET code to determine whether the jansales.txt file exists. If it does, the code should display the string "File exists" in the lblMsg control; otherwise, it should display the string "File does not exist" in the lblMsg control.

14. Write a Try statement that contains an instruction to convert the contents of the txtAge control to an integer, and then assign the result to the intAge variable. Then write a Catch statement that contains an instruction to display the message "The age must be numeric." if the computer cannot convert the age to a number.

15. Write a general Catch statement that contains an instruction to display a description of the error that occurred.

16. In this exercise, you code an application that writes information to and reads information from a sequential access file.
    a. Create the Friends interface shown in Figure 8.11. Name the solution Friends Solution. Name the project Friends Project. Save the application in the VbDotNet\Chap08 folder.
    b. Use the code shown in Figure 8.13 to code the application.
    c. Save the solution, and then start the application. Test the Write to File button by writing the names Janice, Carl, and William to the file. Then test the Read from File button. Each name in the file should appear in a message box.
    d. Click the Exit button to end the application.
    e. Open the friends.txt file in a separate window in the IDE. The file should contain three names.
    f. Close the friends.txt window, then close the solution.

17. In this exercise, you modify the application you created in Exercise 16 so that it uses a Try/Catch block.
    a. Use Windows to make a copy of the Friends Solution folder, which is contained in the VbDotNet\Chap08 folder. Rename the copy TryCatch Friends Solution.
    b. Open the Friends Solution (Friends Solution.sln) file, which is contained in the VbDotNet\Chap08\TryCatch Friends Solution folder.
    c. Modify the code as shown in Figure 8.18.
    d. Save the solution, and then start the application. Test the Write to File button by writing your name to the file. Then test the Read from File button. Each name in the file should appear in a message box.
    e. Click the Exit button to end the application.
    f. Open the friends.txt file in a separate window in the IDE. The file should contain four names.

g. Close the friends.txt window.

h. Modify the OpenText method in the btnRead Click event procedure so that it tries to open a file named friends2.txt. Save the solution, and then start the application. Click the Read from File button. The "Cannot locate the friends.txt file." should appear in a message box. Close the message box, then click the Exit button to end the application.

i. Change the filename in the OpenText method back to "friends.txt".

j. Change the AppendText method in the btnWrite Click event procedure so that it tries to open the friends.txt file from a folder that does not exist on your computer's hard disk. Save the solution, and then start the application. Click the Write to File button. A description of the error should appear in a message box. Close the message box, then click the Exit button to end the application.

k. Change the filename argument in the AppendText method back to "friends.txt".

l. Save the solution.

18. In this exercise, you modify the application that you created in Exercise 16. The modified application allows the user to either create a new file or append information to the end of an existing file.

a. Use Windows to make a copy of the Friends Solution folder, which is contained in the VbDotNet\Chap08 folder. Rename the copy Modified Friends Solution.

b. Open the Friends Solution (Friends Solution.sln) file, which is contained in the VbDotNet\Chap08\Modified Friends Solution folder.

c. Change the filename in the btnRead Click event procedure from "friends.txt" to "pets.txt". (You will need to change the name in four places.)

d. Change the filename in the btnWrite Click event procedure from "friends.txt" to "pets.txt".

e. When the btnWrite Click event procedure is processed the first time, the procedure should determine whether the pets.txt exists before the file is opened. If the file exists, the procedure should use the MessageBox.Show method to ask the user if he or she wants to replace the existing file. Include Yes and No buttons in the message box. If the user clicks the Yes button, then replace the existing file; otherwise, append to the existing file.

f. Save the solution, then start the application. Type Bosco in the Name text box, and then click the Write to File button.

g. Click the Exit button to end the application, then start the application again. Type Ginger in the Name text box, and then click the Write to File button. The application should ask if you want to replace the existing file. Click the No button.

h. Click the Exit button to end the application, then use the File menu to open the pets.txt file in a window. The file should contain two names: Bosco and Ginger. Close the pets.txt window.

i. Start the application again. Type Spot in the Name text box, and then click the Write to File button. The application should ask if you want to replace the existing file. Click the Yes button.

j. Click the Exit button to end the application, then use the File menu to open the pets.txt file in a window. The file should contain one name: Spot. Close the pets.txt window, then close the solution.

19. In this exercise, you modify this chapter's Programming Example.
    a. Create the PAO application shown in this chapter's Programming Example. Save the application in the VbDotNet\Chap08 folder.
    b. Modify the application so that it also verifies that the age entered in the txtAge text box is at least 18. If the age is not valid, don't write the record; rather, display an appropriate error message.
    c. Modify the application so that it also displays the total number of voters in each of the following four age groups: 18-35, 36-50, 51-65, and Over 65. Be sure to modify the TOE chart and pseudocode before modifying the code.
    d. Save the solution, then start and test the application.
    e. Click the Exit button to end the application, then close the solution.

20. In this exercise, you create an application for Markus Industries. The application allows the product manager to enter a product number and price. The application should save the product information in a sequential access file named markus.txt. The application also should allow the user to enter a product number, and then display the price of the product. Display an appropriate message if the product number is not in the file.
    a. Name the solution Markus Solution. Name the project Markus Project. Save the application in the VbDotNet\Chap08 folder.
    b. Design an appropriate interface.
    c. Code the application. Save the product number (which should contain five characters) and price on separate lines in the sequential access file. In other words, save the first product's number on the first line in the file, and save its price on the second line.
    d. Save the solution, then start the application. Write the following product numbers and prices to the file.

Product number	Price
ABX23	5.45
CLN46	7.89
NNE59	9.67
ABC87	11.99
JKL12	25.89

    e. Use the application to display the prices of the following products: ABX23, NNE59, and JTT11.
    f. Stop the application, then close the solution.

21. In this exercise, you modify the application that you created in Exercise 20. The modified application saves a product's information on one line in the sequential access file.
    a. Use Windows to make a copy of the Markus Solution folder, which is contained in the VbDotNet\Chap08 folder. Rename the copy Modified Markus Solution.
    b. Use Windows to delete the markus.txt file, which is contained in the VbDotNet\Chap08\Modified Markus Solution\Markus Project\bin folder.
    c. Open the Markus Solution (Markus Solution.sln) file, which is contained in the VbDotNet\Chap08\Modified Markus Solution folder.
    d. Modify the application so that it saves the product number and price on the same line in the sequential access file. In other words, save the first product's number and price on the first line in the file. You also will need to modify the procedure that reads the product information from the file.

e. Save the solution, then start the application. Write the following product numbers and prices to the file.

Product number	Price
HRP21	16.50
ZSA13	22.25
OPO45	4.50
RST10	12.00
BVR09	3.45

f. Use the application to display the prices of the following products: OPO45, BVR09, and JTT11.

g. Stop the application, then close the solution.

22. In this exercise, you update the contents of a sequential access file.
   a. Open the Pay Solution (Pay Solution.sln) file, which is contained in the VbDotNet\Chap08\Pay Solution folder.
   b. Open the payrates.txt file and view its contents, then close the payrates.txt file.
   c. Code the Increase button's Click event procedure so that it increases each pay rate by 10%. Save the increased prices in a sequential access file named updated.txt.
   d. Save the solution, then start the application. Click the Increase button to update the pay rates.
   e. Click the Exit button to end the application.
   f. Open the payrates.txt file. Also open the updated.txt file. The pay rates contained in the updated.txt file should be 10% more than the pay rates contained in the payrates.txt file.
   g. Close the updated.txt and payrates.txt windows, then close the solution.

23. In this exercise, you find and correct an error in an application. The process of finding and correcting errors is called debugging.
   a. Open the Debug Solution (Debug Solution.sln) file, which is contained in the VbDotNet\Chap08\Debug Solution folder.
   b. Open the Code Editor window. Review the existing code.
   c. Start the application. Type your name in the Name text box, then click the Write to File button.
   d. Click the Exit button to end the application.
   e. Open the debug.txt file, which is contained in the VbDotNet\Chap08\ Debug Solution\Debug Project\bin folder. Notice that the file is empty. Close the debug.txt window.
   f. Start the application. Type your name in the Name text box, then click the Write to File button. Type your name again in the Name text box, then click the Write to File button. An error message appears in a message box. Close the message box, then click the Exit button to end the application.
   g. Correct the application's code, then save the solution and start the application. Type your name in the Name text box, then click the Write to File button. Type your name again in the Name text box, then click the Write to File button.
   h. Click the Exit button to end the application.
   i. Open the debug.txt file. Your name appears twice in the file.
   j. Close the debug.txt window, then close the solution.

Case Projects

Warren High School

This year, three students are running for senior class president: Mark Stone, Sheima Patel, and Sam Perez. Create an application that allows the current class president to keep track of the voting. Save the voting information in a sequential access file. The application also should display the number of votes per candidate.

WKRK-Radio

Each year, WKRK-Radio polls its audience to determine which Super Bowl commercial was the best. The choices are as follows: Budweiser, FedEx, MasterCard, and Pepsi. The station manager has asked you to create an application that allows him to enter a caller's choice. The choice should be saved in a sequential access file. The application also should display the number of votes for each commercial.

Shoe Circus

Shoe Circus sells 10 styles of children's shoes. The store manager has asked you to create an application that she can use to enter the following information for each shoe style: the style number and the price. The application should save the information in a sequential access file. It also should allow the user to enter a style number and then display the style's price.

Revellos

Revellos has stores located in several states. The sales manager has asked you to create an application that he can use to enter the following information for each store: the store number, the state in which the store is located, and the name of the store manager. The application should save the information in a sequential access file. Each store's information should appear on a separate line in the file. In other words, the first store's number, state name, and manager name should appear on the first line in the file. The application also should allow the sales manager to enter a store number, and then display the state in which the store is located and the store manager's name. Use the following data:

Number	State	Manager
1004	Texas	Jeffrey Jefferson
1005	Texas	Paula Hendricks
1007	Arizona	Jake Johansen
1010	Arizona	Henry Abernathy
1011	California	Barbara Millerton
1013	California	Inez Baily
1015	California	Sung Lee
1016	California	Lou Chan
1017	California	Homer Gomez
1019	New Mexico	Ingrid Nadkarni

CHAPTER

9

Arrays

After studying Chapter 9, you should be able to:

- Declare and initialize a one-dimensional array
- Store data in a one-dimensional array
- Display the contents of a one-dimensional array
- Code a loop using the For Each...Next statement
- Access an element in a one-dimensional array
- Search a one-dimensional array
- Compute the average of a one-dimensional array's contents
- Find the highest entry in a one-dimensional array
- Update the contents of a one-dimensional array
- Sort a one-dimensional array
- Enter code in the form's Load event procedure
- Create and manipulate parallel one-dimensional arrays
- Create and initialize a two-dimensional array
- Store data in a two-dimensional array
- Search a two-dimensional array

TIP

The variables in an array are stored in consecutive memory locations in the computer's internal memory.

TIP

It takes longer for the computer to access the information stored in a disk file, because the computer must wait for the disk drive to locate the needed information and then read the information into internal memory.

TIP

You also can visualize a one-dimensional array as a row of variables, rather than as a column of variables.

USING ARRAYS

All of the variables you have used so far have been simple variables. A **simple variable**, also called a **scalar variable**, is one that is unrelated to any other variable in memory. In many applications, however, you may need to reserve a block of variables, referred to as an array.

An **array** is a group of variables that have the same name and data type and are related in some way. For example, each variable in the array might contain an inventory quantity, or each might contain a state name, or each might contain an employee record (name, Social Security number, pay rate, and so on). It may be helpful to picture an array as a group of small, adjacent boxes inside the computer's memory. You can write information to the boxes and you can read information from the boxes; you just cannot *see* the boxes.

Programmers use arrays to temporarily store related data in the internal memory of the computer. Examples of data stored in an array would be the federal withholding tax tables in a payroll program, and a price list in an order entry program. Storing data in an array increases the efficiency of a program, because data can be both written to and read from internal memory much faster than it can be written to and read from a file on a disk. Additionally, after the data is entered into an array, which typically is done at the beginning of the program, the program can use the data as many times as desired. A payroll program, for example, can use the federal withholding tax tables stored in an array to calculate the amount of each employee's federal withholding tax.

The most commonly used arrays are one-dimensional and two-dimensional.

ONE-DIMENSIONAL ARRAYS

You can visualize a **one-dimensional** array as a column of variables. Each variable in a one-dimensional array is identified by a unique number, called a **subscript**, which the computer assigns to the variable when the array is created. The subscript indicates the variable's position in the array. The first variable in a one-dimensional array is assigned a subscript of 0 (zero), the second a subscript of 1 (one), and so on. You refer to each variable in an array by the array's name and the variable's subscript, which is specified in a set of parentheses immediately following the array name. For example, to refer to the first variable in a one-dimensional array named strStates, you use strStates(0)—read "strStates sub zero." Similarly, to refer to the third variable in the strStates array, you use strStates(2). Figure 9.1 illustrates this naming convention.

strStates(0)	Alaska
strStates(1)	Montana
strStates(2)	South Carolina
strStates(3)	Tennessee

FIGURE 9.1   Names of the variables in a one-dimensional array named strStates

Before you can use an array, you first must declare (create) it. Figure 9.2 shows two versions of the syntax you use to declare a one-dimensional array in Visual Basic .NET. The figure also includes examples of using each syntax.

HOW TO...

Declare a One-Dimensional Array

Syntax – Version 1
accessibility arrayname(*highestSubscript*) **As** *datatype*

Syntax – Version 2
accessibility arrayname() **As** *datatype* = {*initialValues*}

Examples
```
Dim strCities(3) As String
```
declares a four-element procedure-level array named strCities; each element is automatically initialized using the keyword `Nothing`

```
Private mintNumbers(5) As Integer
```
declares a six-element module-level array named mintNumbers; each element is automatically initialized to the number zero

```
Private mstrStates() As String = {"Hawaii", "Alaska",
"Maine"}
```

declares and initializes a three-element module-level array named mstrStates

```
Dim decSales() As Decimal = {75.30D, 9.65D, 23.55D, 6.89D}
```
declares and initializes a four-element procedure-level array named decSales

FIGURE 9.2 How to declare a one-dimensional array

In each syntax version, *accessibility* is usually either the keyword `Dim` or the keyword `Private`, depending on whether you are declaring a procedure-level array or a module-level array. *Arrayname* is the name of the array, and *datatype* is the type of data the array variables, referred to as **elements**, will store. Recall that each of the elements (variables) in an array has the same data type.

In Version 1 of the syntax, *highestSubscript* is an integer that specifies the highest subscript in the array. When the array is created, it will contain one element more than the number specified in the *highestSubscript* argument; this is because the first element in a one-dimensional array has a subscript of zero. For instance, the statement `Dim strCities(3) As String`, which is shown in the first example in Figure 9.2, creates a procedure-level one-dimensional array named strCities. The strCities array contains four elements with subscripts of 0, 1, 2, and 3; each element can store a string. Similarly, the statement shown in the second example, `Private mintNumbers(5) As Integer`, creates a module-level one-dimensional array named mintNumbers. The mintNumbers array contains six elements with subscripts of 0, 1, 2, 3, 4, and 5; in this case, each element can store an integer.

When you use the syntax shown in Version 1 to declare a one-dimensional array, Visual Basic .NET automatically initializes each element in the array when the array is created. If the array's data type is String, each element in the array is initialized using the keyword Nothing. As you learned in Chapter 3, variables initialized to Nothing do not actually contain the word "Nothing"; rather, they contain no data at all. Elements in a numeric array are initialized to the number zero, and elements in a Boolean array are initialized to the Boolean value False. Date array elements are initialized to 12:00 AM January 1, 0001.

You use the syntax shown in Version 2 in Figure 9.2 to declare an array and, at the same time, specify each element's initial value. You list the initial values in the *initialValues* section of the syntax, using commas to separate the values; you enclose the list of values in braces ({}). Notice that the syntax shown in Version 2 does not include the *highestSubscript* argument; rather, an empty set of parentheses follows the array name. Visual Basic .NET automatically calculates the highest subscript based on the number of values listed in the *initialValues* section. If the *initialValues* section contains five values, the highest subscript in the array is 4. Likewise, if the *initialValues* section contains 100 values, the highest subscript in the array is 99. Notice that the highest subscript is always one number less than the number of values listed in the *initialValues* section; this is because the first subscript in a one-dimensional array is the number zero.

The statement shown in the third example in Figure 9.2, Private mstrStates() As String = {"Hawaii", "Alaska", "Maine"}, declares a module-level one-dimensional String array named mstrStates. The mstrStates array contains three elements with subscripts of 0, 1, and 2. When the array is created, Visual Basic .NET assigns the string "Hawaii" to the mstrStates(0) element, "Alaska" to the mstrStates(1) element, and "Maine" to the mstrStates(2) element. Similarly, the statement shown in the last example, Dim decSales() As Decimal = {75.30D, 9.65D, 23.55D, 6.89D}, declares a procedure-level one-dimensional Decimal array named decSales. The decSales array contains four elements with subscripts of 0, 1, 2, and 3. Visual Basic .NET assigns the number 75.30 to the decSales(0) element, 9.65 to the decSales(1) element, 23.55 to the decSales(2) element, and 6.89 to the decSales(3) element.

After declaring the array, you can use an assignment statement to store data in the array.

STORING DATA IN A ONE-DIMENSIONAL ARRAY

In most cases, you use an assignment statement to enter data into an existing array. Figure 9.3 shows the syntax of such an assignment statement and includes several examples of using the syntax to enter data into the arrays declared in Figure 9.2. In the syntax, *arrayname*(*subscript*) is the name and subscript of the array variable to which you want the *value* (data) assigned.

HOW TO...

Store Data in a One-Dimensional Array

Syntax

arrayname(*subscript*) = *value*

Examples

```
strCities(0) = "Madrid"
strCities(1) = "Paris"
strCities(2) = "Rome"
```
assigns the strings "Madrid", "Paris", and "Rome" to the strCities array

```
Dim intX As Integer
For intX = 1 To 6
    mintNumbers(intX - 1) = intX * intX
Next intX
```
assigns the squares of the numbers from one through six to the mintNumbers array

```
Dim intX As Integer
Dim sreStreamReader As IO.StreamReader
sreStreamReader = IO.File.OpenText("numbers.txt")
Do Until intX > 5 OrElse sreStreamReader.Peek() = -1
    mintNumbers(intX) = _
        Convert.ToInt32(sreStreamReader.ReadLine())
    intX = intX + 1
Loop
sreStreamReader.Close()
```
assigns the numbers stored in a sequential access file named numbers.txt to the mintNumbers array

```
mstrStates(1) = "Virginia"
```
assigns the string "Virginia" to the second element in the mstrStates array

```
decSales(0) = Convert.ToDecimal(Me.txtSales.Text)
```
assigns the value entered in the txtSales control (converted to Decimal) to the first element in the decSales array

FIGURE 9.3　　　How to store data in a one-dimensional array

The three assignment statements shown in the first example in Figure 9.3 assign the strings "Madrid", "Paris", and "Rome" to the strCities array, replacing the values stored in the array elements when the array was created. The code shown in the second example assigns the squares of the numbers from one through six to the mintNumbers array, writing over the array's initial values. Notice that the number one must be subtracted from the value stored in the intX variable when assigning the squares to the array; this is because the first array element has a subscript of zero rather than one.

The code shown in the third example in Figure 9.3 reads the numbers from the numbers.txt file, assigning each number to an element in the mintNumbers array. In the fourth example, the statement `mstrStates(1) = "Virginia"` assigns the string "Virginia" to the second element in the mstrStates array, replacing the string "Alaska" that was stored in the element when the array was created. In the last example, the statement `decSales(0) = Convert.ToDecimal(Me.txtSales.Text)` replaces the value stored in the first element in the decSales array (75.30) with the value entered in the txtSales control (treated as a Decimal).

Now that you know how to declare and enter data into a one-dimensional array, you learn how to manipulate an array in an application.

MANIPULATING ONE-DIMENSIONAL ARRAYS

The variables (elements) in an array can be used just like any other variables. For example, you can assign values to them, use them in calculations, display their contents, and so on. In the next several sections, you view sample procedures that demonstrate how one-dimensional arrays are used in an application. More specifically, the procedures will show you how to perform the following tasks using a one-dimensional array:

1. Display the contents of an array.
2. Access an array element using its subscript.
3. Search the array.
4. Calculate the average of the data stored in a numeric array.
5. Find the highest value stored in an array.
6. Update the array elements.
7. Sort the array elements.

Begin by viewing a procedure that displays the contents of a one-dimensional array.

Displaying the Contents of a One-Dimensional Array

The btnDisplayMonths_Click procedure shown in Figure 9.4 demonstrates how you can display the contents of an array—in this case, the strMonths array—in a label control.

TIP

In most applications, the values stored in an array come from a file on the computer's disk, and are assigned to the array after it is declared. However, so that you can follow the code and its results more easily, most of the procedures you view in this chapter use the Dim statement to assign the appropriate values to the array.

Pseudocode
1. declare a String array named strMonths
2. declare an Integer variable named intX
3. repeat for each element in the strMonths array
display the contents of the current array element in the lblMonths control
end repeat
(Table is continued on next page)

Visual Basic .NET code

```
Dim strMonths() As String = {"JAN", "FEB", "MAR", "APR", _
        "MAY", "JUN", "JUL", "AUG", "SEP", "OCT", "NOV", "DEC"}
Dim intX As Integer

For intX = 0 To 11
    Me.lblMonths.Text = Me.lblMonths.Text & strMonths(intX) _
        & ControlChars.NewLine
Next intX
displays the contents of the strMonths array in the lblMonths control
```

FIGURE 9.4   btnDisplayMonths_Click procedure

The procedure shown in Figure 9.4 declares a 12-element String array named strMonths, using the names of the 12 months to initialize the array; it also declares an Integer variable named intX. The procedure uses a loop, along with the intX variable, to display the contents of each array element in the lblMonths control. The first time the loop is processed, the intX variable contains the number zero, and the statement `Me.lblMonths.Text = Me.lblMonths.Text & strMonths(intX) & ControlChars.NewLine` displays the contents of the strMonths(0) element—JAN—in the lblMonths control, and then advances the insertion point to the next line in the lblMonths control. The `Next intX` statement then adds the number one to the value stored in the intX variable, giving one. When the loop is processed the second time, the statement `Me.lblMonths.Text = Me.lblMonths.Text & strMonths(intX) & ControlChars.NewLine` adds the contents of the strMonths(1) element—FEB—to the lblMonths control, and so on. The computer repeats the loop instructions for each element in the strMonths array, beginning with the element whose subscript is zero and ending with the element whose subscript is 11. The computer stops processing the loop when the value contained in the intX variable is 12, which is one number more than the highest subscript in the array. Figure 9.5 shows the results of processing the btnDisplayMonths_Click procedure.

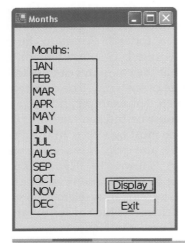

FIGURE 9.5   Result of processing the btnDisplayMonths_Click procedure

The btnDisplayMonths_Click procedure shown in Figure 9.4 uses the For...Next statement to display each array element. You also could use the Do...Loop statement (which you learned about in Chapter 5) or the For Each...Next statement (which you learn about next).

The For Each...Next Statement

You can use the **For Each...Next statement** to code a loop whose instructions you want processed for each element in a group—for example, for each array variable in an array. Figure 9.6 shows the syntax of the For Each...Next statement. It also shows how you can rewrite the btnDisplayMonths_Click procedure from Figure 9.4 using the For Each...Next statement.

HOW TO...

Use the For Each...Next Statement

Syntax
For Each *element* **In** *group*
    [*statements*]
Next *element*

Example
```
Dim strMonths() As String = {"JAN", "FEB", "MAR", "APR", _
        "MAY", "JUN", "JUL", "AUG", "SEP", "OCT", "NOV", "DEC"}
Dim strElement As String

For Each strElement In strMonths
        Me.lblMonths.Text = Me.lblMonths.Text & strElement _
            & ControlChars.NewLine
Next strElement
```
displays the contents of the strMonths array in the lblMonths control

FIGURE 9.6   How to use the For Each...Next statement

The For Each...Next statement begins with the For Each clause and ends with the Next clause. Between the two clauses you enter the instructions that you want the loop to repeat for each *element* in the *group*.

When using the For Each...Next statement to process an array, *element* is the name of a variable that the computer can use to keep track of each array variable, and *group* is the name of the array. The data type of the *element* must match the data type of the *group*. For example, if the *group* is an Integer array, then the *element*'s data type must be Integer. Likewise, if the *group* is a String array, then the *element*'s data type must be String. In the example shown in Figure 9.6, *group* is the strMonths array, and *element* is a String variable named strElement.

In the example shown in Figure 9.6, the `Me.lblMonths.Text = Me.lblMonths.Text & strElement & ControlChars.NewLine` statement, which displays the current array element in the lblMonths control, will be processed for each element in the strMonths array. The example will display the same result as shown earlier in Figure 9.5.

Next, you view a procedure that uses the array subscript to access the appropriate element in an array.

Using the Subscript to Access an Element in a One-Dimensional Array

Assume that XYZ Corporation pays its managers based on six different salary codes, 1 through 6. Each code corresponds to a different salary amount. You can use the btnDisplaySalary_Click procedure shown in Figure 9.7 to display the salary amount corresponding to the code entered by the user.

Pseudocode

1. declare an Integer array named intSalaries
2. declare an Integer variable named intCode
3. assign the code in the txtCode control to the intCode variable
4. if the code stored in the intCode variable is not 1 through 6
   display the message "Invalid code" in the lblSalary control
   else
   display, in the lblSalary control, the salary stored in the array element
   located in position (intCode − 1)
   end if

Visual Basic .NET code

```
Dim intSalaries() As Integer = {25000, 35000, 55000, _
                                70000, 80200, 90500}
Dim intCode As Integer

intCode = Convert.ToInt32(Me.txtCode.Text)
If intCode < 1 OrElse intCode > 6 Then
    Me.lblSalary.Text = "Invalid code"
Else
    Me.lblSalary.Text = _
        Convert.ToString(intSalaries(intCode - 1))
End If
```

Results (displayed in the lblSalary control)

55000   (assuming the user enters the number 3)
Invalid code   (assuming the user enters the number 8)

FIGURE 9.7   btnDisplaySalary_Click procedure

TIP

Before accessing an array element, a procedure always should verify that the subscript is valid—in other words, that it is in range. If the procedure uses a subscript that is not in range, Visual Basic .NET displays an error message and the procedure ends abruptly.

The procedure shown in Figure 9.7 declares an Integer array named intSalaries, using six salary amounts to initialize the array. The salary amount for code 1 is stored in intSalaries(0). Code 2's salary amount is stored in intSalaries(1), and so on. Notice that the code is one number more than its corresponding array subscript.

After creating and initializing the array, the procedure declares an Integer variable named intCode. It then assigns the salary code entered in the txtCode control to the intCode variable. The selection structure in the procedure determines whether the code entered by the user is invalid. In this case, invalid codes are numbers that are less than one or greater than six. If the code is not valid, the procedure displays an appropriate message; otherwise, it displays the corresponding salary from the intSalaries array. Notice that, to access the correct element in the intSalaries array, the number one must be subtracted from the contents of the intCode variable; this is because the code entered by the user is one number more than its associated array subscript. As Figure 9.7 indicates, the procedure displays the number 55000 if the user enters a code of 3. If the user enters a code of 8, the program displays the message "Invalid code".

In the next section, you learn how to search a one-dimensional array.

Searching a One-Dimensional Array

Assume that the sales manager at Jacobsen Motors wants a procedure that allows him to determine the number of salespeople selling above a certain amount, which he will enter. To accomplish this task, the procedure will need to search the array, looking for values that are greater than the amount entered by the sales manager. The btnSearchArray_Click procedure shown in Figure 9.8 shows you how to search an array.

Pseudocode

1. declare an Integer array named intSalesArray
2. declare Integer variables named intAmount, intCount, and intSearchFor
3. assign the sales amount in the txtSearch control to the intSearchFor variable
4. repeat for each element in the intSalesArray array
       if the value in the current array element is greater than the value in the intSearchFor variable
           add 1 to the intCount variable
       end if
     end repeat
5. display the contents of the intCount variable in the lblCount control

---

Visual Basic .NET code

```
Dim intSalesArray() As Integer = {45000, 35000, 25000, 60000, 23000}
Dim intAmount As Integer        'represents an array element
Dim intCount As Integer         'counter variable
Dim intSearchFor As Integer     'number to search for

intSearchFor = Convert.ToInt32(Me.txtSearch.Text)
For Each intAmount in intSalesArray
    If intAmount > intSearchFor Then
        intCount = intCount + 1
    End If
Next intAmount
Me.lblCount.Text = "Count: " & Convert.ToString(intCount)
```

Results (displayed in the lblCount control)

Count: 2   (assuming the user enters the number 40000)
Count: 0   (assuming the user enters the number 60000)

FIGURE 9.8   btnSearchArray_Click procedure

The btnSearchArray_Click procedure declares an Integer array named intSalesArray, using five sales amounts to initialize the array. The procedure also declares three Integer variables named intAmount, intCount, and intSearchFor. After declaring the array and variables, the procedure assigns the sales amount entered in the txtSearch control to the intSearchFor variable. The loop in the procedure then repeats its instructions for each element in the intSalesArray array. Notice that the loop uses the intAmount variable to represent each element in the array.

The selection structure in the loop compares the contents of the current array element with the contents of the intSearchFor variable. If the array element contains a number that is greater than the number stored in the intSearchFor variable, the selection structure's true path adds the number one to the value stored in the intCount variable. In the btnSearchArray_Click procedure, the intCount variable is used as a counter to keep track of the number of salespeople selling over the amount entered by the sales manager.

When the loop ends, which is when there are no more array elements to search, the procedure displays the contents of the intCount variable in the lblCount control. As Figure 9.8 indicates, the procedure displays the number two if the sales manager enters 40000 as the sales amount, and it displays the number zero if he enters 60000 as the sales amount.

Next, you learn how to calculate the average of the data stored in a numeric array.

Calculating the Average Amount Stored in a One-Dimensional Numeric Array

Professor Jeremiah wants a procedure that calculates and displays the average test score earned by his students on the final exam. The btnDisplayAverage_Click procedure shown in Figure 9.9 can be used to accomplish this task.

Pseudocode

1. declare an Integer array named intScores
2. declare Integer variables named intX and intTotal
3. declare a Decimal variable named decAvg
4. repeat for each element in the intScores array
      add the contents of the current array element to the intTotal variable
   end repeat
5. calculate the average score by dividing the contents of the intTotal variable by the number of array elements, and assign the result to the decAvg variable
6. display the contents of the decAvg variable in the lblAverage control

(Table is continued on next page)

Visual Basic .NET code

```
Dim intScores() As Integer = {98, 100, 56, 74, 35}
Dim intX As Integer      'keeps track of subscripts
Dim intTotal As Integer  'accumulator variable
Dim decAvg As Decimal    'average score

For intX = 0 To 4
     intTotal = intTotal + intScores(intX)
Next intX

decAvg = Convert.ToDecimal(intTotal / intScores.Length)
Me.lblAverage.Text = "Average: " & decAvg.ToString("N1")
```

Results (displayed in the lblAverage control)

Average: 72.6

FIGURE 9.9   btnDisplayAverage_Click procedure

TIP

You also can use the statement `decAvg = Convert.ToDecimal(intTotal / intX)` to calculate the average test score in the btnDisplayAverage_Click procedure shown in Figure 9.9.

TIP

You also can write the For clause shown in Figure 9.9 as `For intX = 0 To intScores.Length - 1`.

The procedure shown in Figure 9.9 declares an Integer array named intScores, using five test scores to initialize the array. It also declares two Integer variables named intX and intTotal, and a Decimal variable named decAvg. The loop in the procedure repeats its instruction for each element in the intScores array, beginning with the element whose subscript is zero and ending with the element whose subscript is four. The instruction in the loop adds the score contained in the current array element to the intTotal variable, which is used as an accumulator to add up the test scores. When the loop ends, which is when the intX variable contains the number five, the `decAvg = Convert.ToDecimal (intTotal / intScores.Length)` statement uses the array's Length property to calculate the average test score. An array's **Length property**, whose syntax is *arrayname*.**Length**, stores an integer that represents the number of elements in the array; in this case, it stores the number five, because the intScores array contains five elements. The btnDisplayAverage_Click procedure then displays the average test score in the lblAverage control. As Figure 9.9 indicates, the procedure displays the number 72.6.

In the next section, you learn how to determine the highest value stored in a one-dimensional array.

Determining the Highest Value Stored in a One-Dimensional Array

Sharon Johnson keeps track of the amount of money she earns each week. She would like a procedure that displays the highest amount earned in a week. Similar to the btnSearchArray_Click procedure shown earlier in Figure 9.8, the btnDisplayHighest_Click procedure will need to search the array. However, rather than looking in the array for values that are greater than a specific amount, the procedure will look for the highest amount in the array, as shown in Figure 9.10.

Pseudocode

1. declare a Decimal array named decDollars
2. declare a Decimal variable named decHigh, and initialize the variable to the contents of the first element in the decDollars array
3. declare an Integer variable named intX, and initialize the variable to 1 (the second subscript)
4. repeat while intX is less than the number of elements in the array
      if the value in the current array element is greater than the value in the decHigh variable
          assign the value in the current array element to the decHigh variable
     end if
     add 1 to the intX variable
   end repeat
5. display the contents of the decHigh variable in a message box

Visual Basic .NET code

```
Dim decDollars() As Decimal = {25.60D, 30.25D, 50D, 20D, 25.45D}
Dim decHigh As Decimal = decDollars(0)   'stores the highest value
Dim intX As Integer = 1   'begins search with second element

Do While intX < decDollars.Length
    If decDollars(intX) > decHigh Then
        decHigh = decDollars(intX)
    End If
    intX = intX + 1
Loop
Me.lblHighest.Text = "High: " & decHigh.ToString("C2")
```

Results (displayed in the lblHighest control)

High: $50.00

FIGURE 9.10   btnDisplayHighest_Click procedure

TIP

Notice that the loop shown in Figure 9.10 searches the second through the last element in the array. The first element is not included in the search because it is already stored in the decHigh variable.

The btnDisplayHighest_Click procedure declares a Decimal array named decDollars, and it initializes the array to the amounts that Sharon earned during the last five weeks. The procedure also declares an Integer variable named intX and a Decimal variable named decHigh. The decHigh variable is used to keep track of the highest value stored in the decDollars array, and is initialized using the value stored in the first array element. The intX variable is used to keep track of the array subscripts. Notice that the procedure initializes the intX variable to the number one, which is the subscript corresponding to the second element in the decDollars array.

The first time the loop in the btnDisplayHighest_Click procedure is processed, the selection structure within the loop compares the value stored in the second array element—decDollars(1)—with the value stored in the decHigh variable. (Recall that the decHigh variable contains the same value as the first array element at this point.) If the value stored in the second array element is greater than the value stored in the decHigh variable, then the statement decHigh = decDollars(intX) assigns the array element value to the decHigh variable. The statement `intX = intX + 1` then adds the number one to the intX variable, giving 2. The next time the loop is processed, the selection structure compares the value stored in the third array element—decDollars(2)—with the value stored in the decHigh variable, and so on. When the loop ends, which is when the intX variable contains the number five, the procedure displays the contents of the decHigh variable in the lblHighest control. As Figure 9.10 indicates, the procedure displays $50.00.

Next, you learn how to update the values stored in a one-dimensional array.

Updating the Values Stored in a One-Dimensional Array

The sales manager at Jillian Company wants a procedure that allows her to increase the price of each item the company sells. She also wants the procedure to display each item's new price in the lblNewPrices control. The btnUpdateArray_Click procedure shown in Figure 9.11 will perform these tasks.

Pseudocode

1. declare a Decimal array named decPrices
2. declare two Decimal variables named decElement and decIncrease
3. assign the increase amount in the txtIncrease control to the decIncrease variable
4. display the heading "New Prices" in the lblNewPrices control
5. repeat for each element in the decPrices array
      add the increase amount to the value stored in the current array element
      display the contents of the current array element in the lblNewPrices control
  end repeat

Visual Basic .NET code

```
Dim decPrices() As Decimal = {150.35D, 35.60D, 75.75D, 25.30D}
Dim decElement As Decimal        'represents an array element
Dim decIncrease As Decimal       'stores increase amount

decIncrease = Convert.ToDecimal(Me.txtIncrease.Text)
Me.lblNewPrices.Text = "New Prices" & ControlChars.NewLine
For Each decElement in decPrices
     decElement = decElement + decIncrease
     Me.lblNewPrices.Text = Me.lblNewPrices.Text _
          & decElement.ToString("C2") & ControlChars.NewLine
Next decElement
```

Results (displayed in the lblNewPrices control)

New Prices (assuming the user enters the number 5)
$155.35
$40.60
$80.75
$30.30

FIGURE 9.11   btnUpdateArray_Click procedure

The procedure shown in Figure 9.11 declares a Decimal array named decPrices, using four values to initialize the array. The procedure also declares two Decimal variables named decElement and decIncrease. The procedure stores the contents of the txtIncrease control, converted to Decimal, in the decIncrease variable. It then assigns the string "New Prices" and the newline character to the lblNewPrices control.

The loop in the procedure repeats its instructions for each element in the array. Notice that the procedure uses the decElement variable to represent each array element. The first instruction in the loop, `decElement = decElement + decIncrease`, updates the contents of the current array element by adding the increase amount to it. The second instruction in the loop then displays the updated contents in the lblNewPrices control. The loop ends when all of the array elements have been updated. Figure 9.11 shows the results of the procedure when the user enters the number five as the increase amount. Notice that each new price is five dollars more than the corresponding original price.

Next, you learn how to sort the data stored in a one-dimensional array.

Sorting the Data Stored in a One-Dimensional Array

At times, a procedure might need to arrange the contents of an array in either ascending or descending order. Arranging data in a specific order is called **sorting**. When an array is sorted in ascending order, the first element in the array contains the smallest value, and the last element contains the largest value. When an array is sorted in descending order, on the other hand, the first element contains the largest value, and the last element contains the smallest value.

You use the **Array.Sort method** to sort the elements in a one-dimensional array in ascending order. The method's syntax is **Array.Sort(*arrayname*)**, where *arrayname* is the name of the one-dimensional array to be sorted. The btnSortAscending_Click procedure shown in Figure 9.12 uses the Array.Sort method to sort the intNumbers array in ascending order.

Pseudocode

1. declare an Integer array named intNumbers
2. declare an Integer variable named intX
3. declare a StreamReader variable named sreStreamReader
4. if the numbers.txt sequential access file exists
    open the file for input
    repeat until the array is filled or there are no more numbers to read
        read a number from the file and assign it to the current array element
        add 1 to the contents of the intX variable
    end repeat
    close the numbers.txt file
    sort the intNumbers array in ascending order
    repeat for each element in the intNumbers array
        display the contents of the current array element in the lblSorted control
    end repeat
  else
    display an appropriate message
  end if

(Table is continued on next page)

Visual Basic .NET code

```
Dim intNumbers(5) As Integer
Dim intX As Integer 'keeps track of subscripts
Dim sreStreamReader As IO.StreamReader

'use the numbers.txt file to fill the array
If IO.File.Exists("numbers.txt") Then
    'open the file
    sreStreamReader = IO.File.OpenText("numbers.txt")
    'read each number in the file until the array is filled
    'or there are no more numbers to read
    Do Until intX > intNumbers.Length - 1 _
        OrElse sreStreamReader.Peek() = -1
            intNumbers(intX) = _
                Convert.ToInt32(sreStreamReader.ReadLine())
            intX = intX + 1
    Loop
    'close the file
    sreStreamReader.Close()

    'sort the array in ascending order
    Array.Sort(intNumbers)

    'display the contents of the array
    For intX = 0 To intNumbers.Length - 1
        Me.lblSorted.Text = Me.lblSorted.Text _
            & Convert.ToString(intNumbers(intX)) _
            & ControlChars.NewLine
    Next intX

Else
    'display an appropriate message
    MessageBox.Show("The numbers.txt file does not exist.", _
        "Numbers", MessageBoxButtons.OK, _
        MessageBoxIcon.Information)
End If
```

Results (displayed in the lblSorted control)

```
1        (assuming the numbers.txt file contains the numbers 75, 3, 400, 1, 16, and 7)
3
7
16
75
400
```

FIGURE 9.12 btnSortAscending_Click procedure

The procedure shown in Figure 9.12 declares an Integer array named intNumbers, as well as an Integer variable named intX and a StreamReader variable named sreStreamReader. The selection structure in the procedure verifies that the numbers.txt file, which is a sequential access file, exists. If the numbers.txt file does not exist, the computer processes the instruction in the selection structure's false path, which displays an appropriate message in a message box. However, if the numbers.txt file does exist, the computer processes the instructions in the selection structure's true path.

The first instruction in the selection structure's true path opens the numbers.txt file for input. Next, the computer processes the Do...Loop statement, which repeats its instructions until one (or both) of the following is encountered: the end of the array or the end of the numbers.txt file. The first instruction in the Do...Loop statement reads a number from the numbers.txt file and stores the number in the current element in the intNumbers array. The second instruction in the Do...Loop statement increases by one the value stored in the intX variable, which keeps track of the array subscripts. When the Do...Loop statement stops, which is when the value in the intX variable is six or when there are no more numbers to read in the numbers.txt file, the procedure closes the numbers.txt file.

The `Array.Sort(intNumbers)` statement in the procedure sorts the numbers in the intNumbers array in ascending order. The For...Next statement then displays the contents of the intNumbers array in the lblSorted control. As Figure 9.12 indicates, the For...Next statement displays the numbers 1, 3, 7, 16, 75, and 400. Notice that the numbers appear in ascending numerical order.

To sort a one-dimensional array in descending order, you first use the Array.Sort method to sort the array in ascending order, and then use the **Array.Reverse method** to reverse the array elements. The syntax of the Array.Reverse method is **Array.Reverse**(*arrayname*), where *arrayname* is the name of the one-dimensional array whose elements you want reversed. The btnSortDescending_Click procedure shown in Figure 9.13 sorts the contents of the strStates array in descending order, and then displays the contents of the array in the lblSorted control.

TIP

Recall that an array's Length property stores the number of elements in the array and is always one more than the highest subscript.

Pseudocode

1. declare a String array named strStates
2. declare a String variable named strElement
3. sort the strStates array in descending order
4. repeat for each element in the strStates array
        display the contents of the current array element in the lblSorted control
    end repeat

(Table is continued on next page)

Visual Basic .NET code

```
Dim strStates() As String = _
    {"Colorado", "Hawaii", "Alaska", "Florida"}
Dim strElement As String

Array.Sort(strStates)     'sort the array in ascending order,
Array.Reverse(strStates)  'then reverse the array elements

For Each strElement in strStates
    Me.lblSorted.Text = Me.lblSorted.Text _
         & strElement & ControlChars.NewLine
Next strElement
```

Results (displayed in the lblSorted control)

Hawaii
Florida
Colorado
Alaska

FIGURE 9.13   btnSortDescending_Click procedure

The procedure shown in Figure 9.13 declares a String array named strStates and a String variable named strElement. It then uses the Array.Sort and Array.Reverse methods to sort the array elements in descending order. The loop in the procedure displays the contents of the strStates array in the lblSorted control. As Figure 9.13 indicates, the loop displays Hawaii, Florida, Colorado, and Alaska. Notice that the state names appear in descending alphabetical order.

In all of the procedures you viewed so far in this chapter, the arrays were declared in a procedure and, therefore, had procedure scope. Arrays also can be declared in the form's Declarations section, which gives them module scope. An array with module scope can be used by all of the procedures in the form, including the procedures associated with the controls contained on the form.

TIP

You learned about scope in Chapter 3.

USING A MODULE-LEVEL ONE-DIMENSIONAL ARRAY

Assume that an application needs to display the names contained in a sequential access file. The application should give the user the choice of displaying the names in either ascending or descending order. Figure 9.14 shows the code for an application that performs this task, and Figure 9.15 shows a sample run of the application.

```vb
'Project name:          Names Project
'Project purpose:       The project sorts names in ascending and descending order.
'Created/revised by:    Diane Zak on 2/1/2005

Option Explicit On
Option Strict On

Public Class frmNames
    Inherits System.Windows.Forms.Form

[Windows Form Designer generated code]

    'declare module-level array
    Dim mstrNames(9) As String

    Private Sub frmNames_Load(ByVal sender As Object, ByVal e As System.EventArgs) _
        Handles MyBase.Load
        'fills the mstrNames array with data from a sequential access file

        'declare variables
        Dim intX As Integer 'keeps track of subscripts
        Dim sreStreamReader As IO.StreamReader

        'use the names.txt file to fill the array
        If IO.File.Exists("names.txt") Then
            'open the file
            sreStreamReader = IO.File.OpenText("names.txt")
            'read each name in the file until the array is filled
            'or there are no more names to read
            Do Until intX > mstrNames.Length - 1 OrElse sreStreamReader.Peek() = -1
                mstrNames(intX) = sreStreamReader.ReadLine()
                intX = intX + 1
            Loop
            'close the file
            sreStreamReader.Close()
        Else
            'display an appropriate message
            MessageBox.Show("The names.txt file does not exist.", _
            "Friend", MessageBoxButtons.OK, MessageBoxIcon.Information)
        End If
    End Sub

    Private Sub btnAscending_Click(ByVal sender As Object, _
        ByVal e As System.EventArgs) Handles btnAscending.Click
        'displays the mstrNames array in ascending order

        'declare variable
        Dim strElement As String

        'sort the array in ascending order
        Array.Sort(mstrNames)

        'clear the lblNames control, then display the contents of the array
        Me.lblNames.Text = ""
        For Each strElement In mstrNames
            Me.lblNames.Text = Me.lblNames.Text & strElement & ControlChars.NewLine
        Next strElement
    End Sub
```

The array is declared in the form's Declarations section

The array is filled in the form's Load event procedure

(Figure is continued on next page)

```
Private Sub btnDescending_Click(ByVal sender As Object, _
    ByVal e As System.EventArgs) Handles btnDescending.Click
    'displays the mstrNames array in descending order

    'declare variable
    Dim strElement As String

    'sort the array in descending order
    Array.Sort(mstrNames)
    Array.Reverse(mstrNames)

    'clear the lblNames control, then display the contents of the array
    Me.lblNames.Text = ""
    For Each strElement In mstrNames
        Me.lblNames.Text = Me.lblNames.Text & strElement & ControlChars.NewLine
    Next strElement
End Sub

Private Sub btnExit_Click(ByVal sender As Object, ByVal e As System.EventArgs) _
    Handles btnExit.Click
    'ends the application
    Me.Close()
End Sub
End Class
```

FIGURE 9.14   Code for the Names application

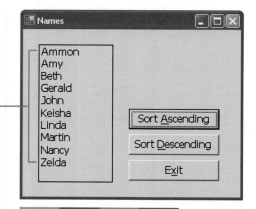

The names appear in ascending alphabetical order

FIGURE 9.15   Sample run of the Names application

TIP

When you start an application that contains more than one form, the start-up form's Load event occurs. The Load events of the other forms occur when those forms are first displayed.

   In the code shown in Figure 9.14, the mstrNames array is declared in the form's Declarations section, making it a module-level array. The array is filled with data in the form's Load event procedure. When you start an application that contains one form, the form's **Load event** occurs before the form is displayed the first time. In the Load event procedure, you can enter code that you want processed before the form appears. As Figure 9.14 shows, you can enter the code to fill an array with data.

To open a form's Load event procedure, you click the Class Name list arrow in the Code Editor window, and then click (*formname* Events) in the list. You also click the Method Name list arrow in the Code Editor window and then click Load in the list.

Notice that the module-level mstrNames array is used by three procedures in the application's code: the form's Load event procedure, the btnAscending_Click procedure, and the btnDescending_Click procedure.

Next, you learn about parallel one-dimensional arrays.

PARALLEL ONE-DIMENSIONAL ARRAYS

Takoda Tapahe owns a small gift shop named Treasures. She wants an application that allows her to display the price of the item whose product ID she enters. Figure 9.16 shows a portion of the gift shop's price list.

Product ID	Price
BX35	13
CR20	10
FE15	12
KW10	24
MM67	4

FIGURE 9.16   A portion of the gift shop's price list

Recall that all of the variables in an array have the same data type. So how can you store a price list, which includes a string (the product ID) and a number (the price), in an array? One way of doing so is to use two one-dimensional arrays: a String array to store the product IDs and an Integer array to store the prices. Both arrays are illustrated in Figure 9.17.

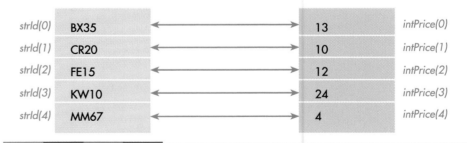

FIGURE 9.17   Illustration of a price list stored in two one-dimensional arrays

The arrays shown in Figure 9.17 are referred to as parallel arrays. **Parallel arrays** are two or more arrays whose elements are related by their position—in other words, by their subscript—in the arrays. The strId and intPrice arrays shown in Figure 9.17 are parallel because each element in the strId array corresponds to the element located in the same position in the intPrice array. For example, the first element in the strId array corresponds to the first element in the intPrice array. In other words, the item whose product ID is BX35 [strId(0)] has a price of $13 [intPrice(0)]. Likewise, the second elements in both arrays— the elements with a subscript of 1—also are related; the item whose product ID is CR20 has a price of $10. The same relationship is true for the remaining elements in both arrays. If you want to know an item's price, you simply locate the item's ID in the strId array and then view its corresponding element in the intPrice array. Figure 9.18 shows a procedure that displays the item's price based on the ID entered by the user.

Pseudocode

1. declare a String array named strId
2. declare an Integer array named intPrice
3. declare an Integer variable named intX
4. declare a String variable named strSearchFor
5. assign the product ID entered in the txtId control, converted to uppercase, to the strSearchFor variable
6. repeat while intX is less than the number of elements in the strId array and, at the same time, the value stored in the strSearchFor variable is not equal to the value stored in the current element in the strId array
      add 1 to intX
   end repeat
7. if the intX variable contains a number that is less than the number of elements in the strId array
      display, in the lblPrice control, the appropriate price from the intPrice array
   else
      display the message "Product ID is not valid" in the lblPrice control
   end if

(Table is continued on next page)

Visual Basic .NET code

```
Dim strId() As String = {"BX35", "CR20", "FE15", "KW10", "MM67"}
Dim intPrice() As Integer = {13, 10, 12, 24, 4}
Dim intX As Integer
Dim strSearchFor As String
strSearchFor = txtId.Text.ToUpper()


'search the array
Do While intX < strId.Length AndAlso strSearchFor <> strId(intX)
    intX = intX + 1
Loop


'determine whether the ID was located in the strId array
If intX < strId.Length Then
    Me.lblPrice.Text = "Price: $" & _
        Convert.ToString(intPrice(intX))
Else
    Me.lblPrice.Text = "Product ID is not valid"
End If
```

Results (displayed in the lblPrice control)

Price: $12   (assuming the user enters FE15 as the product ID)
Product ID is not valid   (assuming the user enters XX90 as the product ID)

FIGURE 9.18   btnDisplayPrice_Click procedure using parallel one-dimensional arrays

The procedure shown in Figure 9.18 declares and initializes two parallel one-dimensional arrays: a five-element String array named strId and a five-element Integer array named intPrice. Notice that each item's ID is stored in the strId array, and each item's price is stored in the corresponding location in the intPrice array. The procedure also declares an Integer variable named intX and a String variable named strSearchFor. After declaring the arrays and variables, the procedure assigns the contents of the txtId control, converted to uppercase, to the strSearchFor variable.

The loop in the procedure continues to add the number one to the intX variable as long as the intX variable contains a value that is less than the number of elements in the strId array and, at the same time, the product ID has not been located in the array. The loop stops when either of the following conditions is true: the intX variable contains the number five (which indicates that the loop reached the end of the array without finding the product ID) or the product ID is located in the array.

After the loop completes its processing, the selection structure in the procedure compares the number stored in the intX variable with the value stored in the array's Length property, which is 5. If the intX variable contains a number that is less than five, it indicates that the loop stopped processing because the product ID was located in the strId array. In that case, the procedure displays (in the lblPrice control) the corresponding price from the intPrice array. However, if the intX variable's value is not less than five, it indicates that the loop stopped processing because it reached the end of the array without finding the product ID; in that case, the message "Product ID is not valid" is displayed in the lblPrice control. As Figure 9.18 indicates, the procedure displays a price of $12 if the user enters FE15 as the product ID, and the message "Product ID is not valid" if the user enters XX90 as the product ID.

Finally, you learn about two-dimensional arrays.

TWO-DIMENSIONAL ARRAYS

Recall that you can visualize a one-dimensional array as a column of variables. A **two-dimensional array**, however, resembles a table in that the variables are in rows and columns. Figure 9.19 illustrates a two-dimensional array.

AC34	Shirt	Red
BD12	Coat	Blue
CP14	Blouse	White

FIGURE 9.19   Illustration of a two-dimensional array

Each variable (element) in a two-dimensional array is identified by a unique combination of two subscripts, which the computer assigns to the variable when the array is created. The subscripts specify the variable's row and column position in the array. Variables located in the first row in a two-dimensional array are assigned a row subscript of 0 (zero). Variables located in the second row are assigned a row subscript of 1 (one), and so on. Similarly, variables located in the first column in a two-dimensional array are assigned a column subscript of 0 (zero). Variables located in the second column are assigned a column subscript of 1 (one), and so on. You refer to each variable in a two-dimensional array by the array's name and the variable's row and column subscripts, which are separated by a comma and specified in a set of parentheses immediately following the array name. For example, to refer to the variable located in the first row, first column in a two-dimensional array named strProducts, you use strProducts(0, 0)—read "strProducts sub zero comma zero." Similarly, to refer to the variable located in the second row, third column in the strProducts array, you use strProducts(1, 2). Figure 9.20 illustrates this naming convention. Notice that the row subscript is listed first in the parentheses.

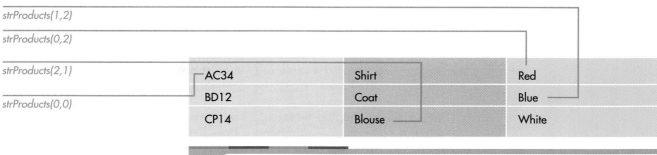

strProducts(1,2)

strProducts(0,2)

strProducts(2,1)

strProducts(0,0)

AC34	Shirt	Red
BD12	Coat	Blue
CP14	Blouse	White

FIGURE 9.20   Names of some of the variables contained in the strProducts array

Recall that, before you can use an array, you first must declare (create) it. Figure 9.21 shows two versions of the syntax you use to declare a two-dimensional array in Visual Basic .NET. The figure also includes an example of using each syntax.

HOW TO...

Declare a Two-Dimensional Array

Syntax - Version 1
accessibility arrayname(*highestRowSubscript, highestColumnSubscript*) **As** *datatype*

Syntax - Version 2
accessibility arrayname(,) **As** *datatype* = {{*initialValues*},…{*initialValues*}}

Examples
```
Dim strCities(5, 3) As String
```
declares a six-row, four-column array named strCities; each element is automatically initialized using the keyword `Nothing`

```
Dim intScores(,) As Integer = {{75, 90}, _
                              {9, 25}, _
                              {23, 56}, _
                              {6, 12}}
```
declares and initializes a four-row, two-column array named intScores

FIGURE 9.21   How to declare a two-dimensional array

In each syntax version, *accessibility* is usually either the keyword `Dim` (for a procedure-level array) or the keyword `Private` (for a module-level array). *Arrayname* is the name of the array, and *datatype* is the type of data the array variables (elements) will store. Recall that each of the elements in an array has the same data type.

In Version 1 of the syntax, *highestRowSubscript* and *highestColumnSubscript* are integers that specify the highest row and column subscripts, respectively, in the array. When the array is created, it will contain one row more than the number specified in the *highestRowSubscript* argument, and one column more than the number specified in the *highestColumnSubscript* argument; this is because the first row subscript in a two-dimensional array is zero, and the first column subscript also is zero. When you use the syntax shown in Version 1 to declare a two-dimensional array, Visual Basic .NET automatically initializes each element in the array when the array is created.

You use the syntax shown in Version 2 in Figure 9.21 to declare a two-dimensional array and, at the same time, specify each element's initial value. Using Version 2's syntax, you include a separate *initialValues* section, enclosed in braces, for each row in the array. If the array has two rows, then the statement that declares and initializes the array should have two *initialValues* sections. If the array has five rows, then the declaration statement should have five *initialValues* sections.

Within the individual *initialValues* sections, you enter one or more values separated by commas. The number of values to enter corresponds to the number of columns in the array. If the array contains 10 columns, then each individual *initialValues* section should contain 10 values.

In addition to the set of braces that surrounds each individual *initialValues* section, notice in the syntax that a set of braces also surrounds all of the *initialValues* sections. Also notice that a comma appears within the parentheses that follow the array name. The comma indicates that the array is a two-dimensional array. (Recall that a comma is used to separate the row subscript from the column subscript in a two-dimensional array.)

Study closely the two examples shown in Figure 9.21. The statement shown in the first example creates a two-dimensional String array named strCities; the array has six rows and four columns. Visual Basic .NET automatically initializes each element in the strCities array using the keyword Nothing. The statement shown in the second example creates a two-dimensional Integer array named intScores; the intScores array has four rows and two columns. The statement initializes the intScores(0, 0) variable to the number 75, and initializes the intScores(0, 1) variable to the number 90. The intScores(1, 0) and intScores(1, 1) variables are initialized to the numbers 9 and 25, respectively. The intScores(2, 0) and intScores(2, 1) variables are initialized to the numbers 23 and 56, respectively, and the intScores(3, 0) and intScores(3, 1) variables are initialized to the numbers 6 and 12, respectively.

After declaring the array, you can use an assignment statement to store data in the array.

STORING DATA IN A TWO-DIMENSIONAL ARRAY

As with one-dimensional arrays, you generally use an assignment statement to enter data into a two-dimensional array. Figure 9.22 shows the syntax of such an assignment statement and includes several examples of using the syntax to enter data into the arrays declared in Figure 9.21. In the syntax, *arrayname*(*rowSubscript*, *columnSubscript*) is the name and subscripts of the array variable to which you want the *value* (data) assigned.

HOW TO...

Store Data in a Two-Dimensional Array

Syntax
arrayname(*rowSubscript*, *columnSubscript*) = *value*

Examples
```
strCities(0, 0) = "Madrid"
strCities(0, 1) = "Paris"
strCities(0, 2) = "Rome"
strCities(0, 3) = "London"
```
assigns the strings "Madrid", "Paris", "Rome", and "London" to the
elements contained in the first row in the strCities array

```
For intRow = 0 To 3
    For intColumn = 0 To 1
        intScores(intRow, intColumn) = 0
    Next intColumn
Next intRow
```
assigns the number zero to each element in the intScores array

```
For Each intNum In intScores
    intNum = 0
Next intNum
```
assigns the number zero to each element in the intScores array

FIGURE 9.22   How to store data in a two-dimensional array

The code shown in the first example in Figure 9.22 uses four assignment
statements to assign values to the elements contained in the first row in the
strCities array. The code shown in the second and third examples assigns the
number zero to each element in the intScores array. The second example uses a
nested For...Next loop to make the assignments, while the third example uses a
For Each...Next statement.

Next, you view a procedure that searches a two-dimensional array.

SEARCHING A TWO-DIMENSIONAL ARRAY

Earlier, in the *Parallel One-Dimensional Arrays* section, you viewed a procedure
created for Takoda Tapahe, the owner of a small gift shop named Treasures. As
you may remember, the procedure allows Takoda to display the price of the item
whose product ID she enters. In that procedure, shown earlier in Figure 9.18,
you used two parallel one-dimensional arrays to store the gift shop's price list. In
the procedure shown in Figure 9.23, you use a two-dimensional array. To do so,
you will need to treat the price as a string rather than as an integer, because all of
the elements in an array must be of the same data type.

Pseudocode

1. declare a String array named strItems
2. declare an Integer variable named intRow
3. declare a String variable named strSearchFor
4. assign the product ID entered in the txtId control, converted to uppercase, to the strSearchFor variable
5. repeat while intRow is less than the number of rows in the strItems array and, at the same time, the value stored in the strSearchFor variable is not equal to the value stored in the first column of the current element in the strItems array
   add 1 to intRow
   end repeat
6. if the intRow variable contains a number that is less than the number of rows in the strItems array
   display, in the lblPrice control, the appropriate price from the second column of the current element in the strItems array
   else
   display the message "Product ID is not valid" in the lblPrice control
   end if

Visual Basic .NET code

```
Dim strItems(,) As String = {{"BX35", "13"}, _
                             {"CR20", "10"}, _
                             {"FE15", "12"}, _
                             {"KW10", "24"}, _
                             {"MM67", "4"}}

Dim intRow As Integer
Dim strSearchFor As String
strSearchFor = txtId.Text.ToUpper()

'search the array
Do While intRow < 5 AndAlso strSearchFor <> strItems(intRow, 0)
    intRow = intRow + 1
Loop

'determine whether the ID was located in the strItems array
If intRow < 5 Then
    Me.lblPrice.Text = "Price: $" & strItems(intRow, 1)
Else
    Me.lblPrice.Text = "Product ID is not valid"
End If
```

Results (displayed in the lblPrice control)

Price: $12   (assuming the user enters FE15 as the product ID)
Product ID is not valid   (assuming the user enters XX90 as the product ID)

FIGURE 9.23   btnDisplayPrice_Click procedure using a two-dimensional array

The procedure shown in Figure 9.23 declares and initializes a two-dimensional array named strItems; the array has five rows and two columns Notice that each item's ID is stored in the first column of the strItems array, and each item's price is stored in the corresponding row in the second column. The procedure also declares an Integer variable named intRow and a String variable named strSearchFor. After declaring the array and variables, the procedure assigns the contents of the txtId control, converted to uppercase, to the strSearchFor variable.

The loop in the procedure continues to add the number one to the intRow variable as long as the intRow variable contains a value that is less than the number five (which is the number of rows in the strItems array) and, at the same time, the product ID has not been located in the first column of the array. The loop stops when either of the following conditions is true: the intRow variable contains the number five (which indicates that the loop reached the end of the array without finding the product ID) or the product ID is located in the array.

After the loop completes its processing, the selection structure in the procedure compares the number stored in the intRow variable with the number five. If the intRow variable contains a number that is less than five, it indicates that the loop stopped processing because the product ID was located in the first column of the strItems array. In that case, the procedure displays (in the lblPrice control) the corresponding price from the second column in the array. However, if the intRow variable's value is not less than five, it indicates that the loop stopped processing because it reached the end of the array without finding the product ID; in that case, the message "Product ID is not valid" is displayed in the lblPrice control. As Figure 9.23 indicates, the procedure displays a price of $12 if the user enters FE15 as the product ID, and the message "Product ID is not valid" if the user enters XX90 as the product ID. The weekly FWT tables are shown in Figure 7.16 in Chapter 7.

PROGRAMMING EXAMPLE

Perrytown Gift Shop Application

Stanley Habeggar is the owner and manager of Perrytown Gift Shop. Every Friday afternoon, Mr. Habeggar calculates the weekly pay for his six employees. The most time-consuming part of this task, and the one prone to the most errors, is the calculation of the federal withholding tax (FWT). Create an application that Mr. Habeggar can use to quickly and accurately calculate the FWT. Name the solution Perrytown Solution. Name the project Perrytown Project. Name the form file Perrytown Form.vb.

TOE Chart:

Task	Object	Event
1. Calculate the federal withholding tax 2. Display the federal withholding tax in lblFwt	btnCalc	Click
End the application	btnExit	Click
Display the federal withholding tax (from btnCalc)	lblFwt	None
Get and display the taxable wages	txtTaxable	None
Get and display the marital status	txtStatus	None

FIGURE 9.24

User Interface:

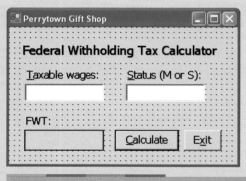

FIGURE 9.25

Objects, Properties, and Settings

Object	Property	Setting
frmPerrytown	Name	frmPerrytown (be sure to change the startup form to this name)
	AcceptButton	btnCalc
	Font	Tahoma, 12 point (be sure to change the form's font before adding the controls)
	Size	352, 248
	StartPosition	CenterScreen
	Text	Perrytown Gift Shop
Label1	AutoSize	True
	Font	Tahoma, 14 point
	Text	Federal Withholding Tax Calculator

(Table is continued on next page)

Object	Property	Setting
Label2	AutoSize Text	True &Taxable wages:
Label3	AutoSize Text	True &Status (M or S):
Label4	AutoSize Text	True FWT:
lblFwt	Name BorderStyle Text TextAlign	lblFwt FixedSingle (empty) MiddleCenter
btnCalc	Name Text	btnCalc &Calculate
btnExit	Name Text	btnExit E&xit
txtTaxable	Name Text	txtTaxable (empty)
txtStatus	Name CharacterCasing MaxLength Text	txtStatus Upper 1 (empty)

FIGURE 9.26

Tab Order:

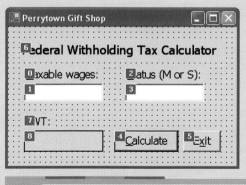

FIGURE 9.27

Pseudocode:

btnExit Click event procedure

1. close application

btnCalc Click event procedure

include the following in the Try section of a Try/Catch block:
1. remove any dollar signs and spaces from the txtTaxable control
2. assign the taxable wages stored in the txtTaxable control to a variable
3. assign the marital status entered in the txtStatus control to a variable
4. if the marital status is not either M or S
       display an appropriate message
   else
       if the marital status is M
          use the Married tax table, which is stored in an array
       else
          use the Single tax table, which is stored in an array
       end if
   end if
5. repeat while there are still rows in the tax table to search and the taxable wages have not been found
       if the taxable wages are less than or equal to the value stored in the first
       column of the current row in the tax table
          use the information stored in the second, third, and fourth columns in the
          tax table to calculate the federal withholding tax

          indicate that the taxable wages were found by assigning the value True
          to the blnFound variable
       else
          add 1 to the contents of the intRow variable to continue the search in the next
          row in the tax table
       end if
   end repeat
6. display the federal withholding tax in the lblFwt control

include the following in the Catch section of a Try/Catch block:
1. use a general Catch statement to handle any errors
       if an error occurs, display a description of the exception in a message box

Code:

```
'Project name:          Perrytown Project
'Project purpose:       The project calculates the federal withholding
'                       tax (FWT) based on the taxable wages and
'                       marital status entered by the user.
'Created/revised by:    Diane Zak on 2/1/2005

Option Explicit On
Option Strict On

Public Class frmPerrytown
    Inherits System.Windows.Forms.Form

[Windows Form Designer generated code]

    'declare and initialize module-level arrays
    Private mdecSingle(,) As Decimal = {{51D, 0D, 0D, 0D}, _
                                        {552D, 0D, 0.15D, 51D}, _
                                        {1196D, 75.15D, 0.28D, 552D}, _
                                        {2662D, 255.47D, 0.31D, 1196D}, _
                                        {5750D, 709.93D, 0.36D, 2662D}, _
                                        {99999D, 1821.61D, 0.396D, 5750D}}

    Private mdecMarried(,) As Decimal = {{124D, 0D, 0D, 0D}, _
                                         {960D, 0D, 0.15D, 124D}, _
                                         {2023D, 125.4D, 0.28D, 960D}, _
                                         {3292D, 423.04D, 0.31D, 2023D}, _
                                         {5809D, 816.43D, 0.36D, 3292D}, _
                                         {99999D, 1722.55D, 0.396D, 5809D}}

    Private Sub btnExit_Click(ByVal sender As Object, ByVal e As System.EventArgs) _
        Handles btnExit.Click
        'ends the application
        Me.Close()
    End Sub

    Private Sub btnCalc_Click(ByVal sender As Object, ByVal e As System.EventArgs) _
        Handles btnCalc.Click
        'calculates the FWT

        'declare array and variables
        Dim decTaxTable(5, 3) As Decimal
        Dim decTaxable As Decimal
        Dim strStatus As String
        Dim decFwt As Decimal
        Dim intRow As Integer
        Dim blnFound As Boolean
```

(Figure is continued on next page)

```
      Try
            'remove any dollar signs and spaces from the taxable wages
            Me.txtTaxable.Text = Me.txtTaxable.Text.Replace("$", "")
            Me.txtTaxable.Text = Me.txtTaxable.Text.Replace(" ", "")
            'assign taxable wages to a variable
            decTaxable = Convert.ToDecimal(Me.txtTaxable.Text)

            'verify that the status is either M or S
            strStatus = Me.txtStatus.Text
            If strStatus <> "M" AndAlso strStatus <> "S" Then
                  'if the status is invalid, display an appropriate message
                  MessageBox.Show("Please enter either M or S as the status.", _
                        "Perrytown Gift Shop", MessageBoxButtons.OK, _
                        MessageBoxIcon.Information, MessageBoxDefaultButton.Button1)
                  Me.txtStatus.Focus()
            Else
                  'if the status is valid, determine the appropriate array to use
                  If strStatus = "M" Then
                        'use Married tax table
                        decTaxTable = mdecMarried
                  Else      'use Single tax table
                        decTaxTable = mdecSingle
                  End If
            End If

            'search for the taxable wages in the first column in the array
            Do While intRow < 6 AndAlso blnFound = False
                  If decTaxable <= decTaxTable(intRow, 0) Then
                        'calculate the FWT
                        decFwt = decTaxTable(intRow, 1) + decTaxTable(intRow, 2) _
                        * (decTaxable - decTaxTable(intRow, 3))
                        blnFound = True
                  Else      'continue searching for the taxable wages
                        intRow = intRow + 1
                  End If
            Loop

            'display the FWT
            Me.lblFwt.Text = decFwt.ToString("C2")

      Catch ex As Exception
            MessageBox.Show(ex.Message, "Perrytown Gift Shop", _
                  MessageBoxButtons.OK, MessageBoxIcon.Information, _
                  MessageBoxDefaultButton.Button1)
      End Try

   End Sub
End Class
```

FIGURE 9.28

Quick Review

- Programmers use arrays to temporarily store related data in the internal memory of the computer.
- All of the variables in an array have the same name and data type.
- Each element in a one-dimensional array is identified by a unique subscript, which appears in parentheses after the array's name.
- Each element in a two-dimensional array is identified by a unique combination of two subscripts: a row subscript and a column subscript. The subscripts appear in parentheses after the array's name. You list the row subscript first, followed by a comma and the column subscript.
- The first subscript in a one-dimensional array is 0 (zero).
- The first row subscript in a two-dimensional array is 0 (zero). Likewise, the first column subscript also is 0 (zero).
- When declaring a one-dimensional array, you provide either the highest subscript or the initial values.
- When declaring a two-dimensional array, you provide either the highest row and column subscripts or the initial values.
- The number of elements in a one-dimensional array is one more than its highest subscript.
- The number of rows in a two-dimensional array is one more than its highest row subscript. Likewise, the number of columns is one more than its highest column subscript.
- You usually use an assignment statement to store data in an array.
- You refer to an element in a one-dimensional array using the array's name followed by the element's subscript.
- You refer to an element in a two-dimensional array using the array's name followed by the element's row and column subscripts, which are separated by a comma.
- You can use the For Each...Next statement to code a loop whose instructions you want processed for each element in an array. You also can use the For...Next statement or the Do...Loop statement.
- You can use the Length property to determine the number of elements in an array.
- You use the Array.Sort method to sort the elements in a one-dimensional array in ascending order.
- You use the Array.Reverse method to reverse the order of the elements in a one-dimensional array.
- The elements in parallel arrays are related by their subscript (or position) in the arrays.

Key Terms

A **simple variable** is a variable that is unrelated to any other variable in the computer's internal memory.

Scalar variable is another term for simple variable.

An **array** is a group of variables that have the same name and data type and are related in some way.

A **one-dimensional** array is a group of related variables; each variable is identified by a unique number, called a **subscript**.

The variables in an array are also called **elements**.

The **For Each...Next statement** can be used to code a loop whose instructions you want processed for each element in an array.

An array's **Length property** stores an integer that represents the number of elements in the array.

The **Array.Sort method** sorts the elements in a one-dimensional array in ascending order.

The **Array.Reverse method** reverses the order of the elements in a one-dimensional array.

Arrays whose elements are related by their subscript (position) in the arrays are called **parallel arrays**.

A **two-dimensional array** is a group of related variables. Each variable is identified by a unique combination of two numbers: a row subscript and a column subscript.

Review Questions

1. Which of the following statements declares a one-dimensional array named decPrices that contains five elements?
   a. `Dim decPrices(4) As Decimal`
   b. `Dim decPrices(5) As Decimal`
   c. `Dim decPrices(4) As Decimal = {3.55D, 6.70D, 8D, 4D, 2.34D}`
   d. Both a and c.

2. Assume that the strItem array is declared using the statement `Dim strItem(20) As String`. Also assume that the intX variable, which keeps track of the array subscripts, is initialized to the number zero. Which of the following Do clauses will process the loop instructions for each element in the array?
   a. `Do While intX > 20`
   b. `Do While intX < 20`
   c. `Do While intX >= 20`
   d. `Do While intX <= 20`

Use the intSales array to answer Questions 3 through 6. The array was declared with the following statement: `Dim intSales() As Integer = {10000, 12000, 900, 500, 20000}`.

3. The statement `intSales(3) = intSales(3) + 10` will _____.
   a. replace the 500 amount with 10
   b. replace the 500 amount with 510
   c. replace the 900 amount with 10
   d. replace the 900 amount with 910

4. Which of the following If clauses can be used to verify that the array subscript, named intX, is valid for the intSales array?
   a. `If intSales(intX) >= 0 AndAlso intSales(intX) < 4 Then`
   b. `If intSales(intX) >= 0 AndAlso intSales(intX) <= 4 Then`
   c. `If intX >= 0 AndAlso intX < 4 Then`
   d. `If intX >= 0 AndAlso intX <= 4 Then`

5. Which of the following will correctly add 100 to each variable in the intSales array? (You can assume that the intX variable was initialized to the number zero.)

   a. ```
   Do While intX <= 4
        intX = intX + 100
   Loop
   ```

   b. ```
   Do While intX <= 4
        intSales = intSales + 100
   Loop
   ```

   c. ```
   Do While intSales < 5
        intSales(intX) = intSales(intX) + 100
   Loop
   ```

   d. ```
   Do While intX < 5
        intSales(intX) = intSales(intX) + 100
        intX = intX + 1
   Loop
   ```

6. Which of the following statements sorts the intSales array in ascending order?

   a. `Array.Sort(intSales)`
   b. `intSales.Sort()`
   c. `Sort(intSales)`
   d. `SortArray(intSales)`

Use the intNum array to answer Questions 7 through 12. The array was declared with the following statement: `Dim intNum() As Integer = {10, 5, 7, 2}`. Assume that the intTotal, intX, and decAvg variables are initialized to the number zero.

7. Which of the following will correctly calculate the average of the elements included in the intNum array?

   a. ```
   Do While intX < 4
        intNum(intX) = intTotal + intTotal
        intX = intX + 1
   Loop
   decAvg = Convert.ToDecimal(intTotal / intX)
   ```

   b. ```
   Do While intX < 4
        intTotal = intTotal + intNum(intX)
        intX = intX + 1
   Loop
   decAvg = Convert.ToDecimal(intTotal / intX)
   ```

   c. ```
   Do While intX < 4
        intTotal = intTotal + intNum(intX)
        intX = intX + 1
   Loop
   decAvg = Convert.ToDecimal(intTotal / intX - 1)
   ```

   d. ```
   Do While intX < 4
        intTotal = intTotal + intNum(intX)
        intX = intX + 1
   Loop
   decAvg = Convert.ToDecimal(intTotal / (intX - 1))
   ```

8. The code in Question 7's answer a will assign _____ to the decAvg variable.

   a. 0
   b. 5
   c. 6
   d. 8

9. The code in Question 7's answer b will assign _____ to the decAvg variable.
   a. 0
   b. 5
   c. 6
   d. 8

10. The code in Question 7's answer c will assign _____ to the decAvg variable.
    a. 0
    b. 5
    c. 6
    d. 8

11. The code in Question 7's answer d will assign _____ to the decAvg variable.
    a. 0
    b. 5
    c. 6
    d. 8

12. Which of the following assigns to the intElements variable the number of elements included in the intNum array?
    a. `intElements = Len(intNum)`
    b. `intElements = Length(intNum)`
    c. `intElements = intNum.Len`
    d. `intElements = intNum.Length`

13. Which of the following statements creates a two-dimensional array that contains three rows and four columns?
    a. `Dim decTemps(2, 3) As Decimal`
    b. `Dim decTemps(3, 4) As Decimal`
    c. `Dim decTemps(3, 2) As Decimal`
    d. `Dim decTemps(4, 3) As Decimal`

Use the mdecSales array to answer Questions 14 through 16. The array was declared with the following statement:

```
Dim mdecSales(,) As Decimal = {{1000, 1200, 900, 500, 2000}, _
                              {350, 600, 700, 800, 100}}
```

14. The statement `mdecSales(1, 3) = mdecSales(1, 3) + 10` will _____.
    a. replace the 900 amount with 910
    b. replace the 500 amount with 510
    c. replace the 700 amount with 710
    d. replace the 800 amount with 810

15. The statement `mdecSales(0, 4) = mdecSales(0, 4 - 2)` will _____.
    a. replace the 500 amount with 1200
    b. replace the 2000 amount with 900
    c. replace the 2000 amount with 1998
    d. result in an error

16. Which of the following If clauses can be used to verify that the array subscripts named intRow and intCol are valid for the mdecSales array?
    a. `If mdecSales(intRow, intCol) >= 0 AndAlso`
       `mdecSales(intRow, intCol) < 5 Then`
    b. `If mdecSales(intRow, intCol) >= 0 AndAlso`
       `mdecSales(intRow, intCol) <= 5 Then`
    c. `If intRow >= 0 AndAlso intRow < 3 AndAlso intCol >= 0`
       `AndAlso intCol < 6 Then`
    d. `If intRow >= 0 AndAlso intRow < 2 AndAlso intCol >= 0`
       `AndAlso intCol < 5 Then`

17. Which of the following statements assigns the string "California" to the variable located in the third column, fifth row of a two-dimensional array named strStates?
    a. `strStates(3, 5) = "California"`
    b. `strStates(5, 3) = "California"`
    c. `strStates(2, 4) = "California"`
    d. `strStates(4, 2) = "California"`

18. Which of the following assigns the number one to each element in a one-dimensional Integer array named intCounters? The intCounters array contains five elements. You can assume that the intX variable was declared using the statement `Dim intX As Integer`.
    a.
    ```
    For intX = 0 To 4
        intCounters(intX) = 1
    Next intX
    ```
    b.
    ```
    Do While intX < 5
        intCounters(intX) = 1
        intX = intX + 1
    Loop
    ```
    c.
    ```
    For Each intX In intCounters
        intX = 1
    Next intX
    ```
    d. All of the above.

19. Which of the following assigns the number zero to each element in a two-dimensional Integer array named intSums? The intSums array contains two rows and four columns. You can assume that the intRow and intColumn variables were declared using the statement `Dim intRow, intColumn As Integer`. You also can assume that the intElement variable was declared using the statement `Dim intElement As Integer`.
    a.
    ```
    For intRow = 0 To 1
        For intColumn = 0 To 3
            intSums(intRow, intColumn) = 0
        Next intColumn
    Next intRow
    ```
    b.
    ```
    Do While intRow < 2
        intColumn = 0
        Do While intColumn < 4
            intSums(intRow, intColumn) = 0
            intColumn = intColumn + 1
        Loop
        intRow = intRow + 1
    Loop
    ```
    c.
    ```
    For Each intElement In intSums
        intElement = 0
    Next intElement
    ```
    d. All of the above.

20. If the elements in two arrays are related by their subscripts, the arrays are called _____ arrays.
    a. associated
    b. coupled
    c. matching
    d. parallel

Exercises

1. Write the statement to declare a procedure-level one-dimensional array named intNumbers. The array should have 20 elements.

2. Write the statement to store the value 7 in the second element contained in the intNumbers array.

3. Write the statement to declare a module-level one-dimensional array named mstrProducts. The array should have 10 elements.

4. Write the statement to store the string "Paper" in the third element contained in the mstrProducts array.

5. Write the statement to declare and initialize a procedure-level one-dimensional array named decRates that has five elements. Use the following numbers to initialize the array: 6.5, 8.3, 4, 2, 10.5.

6. Write the code to display, in the lblRates control, the contents of the decRates array. (The array has five elements.) Use the For...Next statement.

7. Rewrite the code from Exercise 6 using the Do...Loop statement.

8. Rewrite the code from Exercise 6 using the For Each...Next statement.

9. Write the statement to sort the decRates array in ascending order.

10. Write the statement to reverse the contents of the decRates array.

11. Write the code to calculate the average of the elements stored in the decRates array. (The array has five elements.) Display the average in the lblAvg control. Use the For...Next statement.

12. Rewrite the code from Exercise 11 using the Do...Loop statement.

13. Rewrite the code from Exercise 11 using the For Each...Next statement.

14. Write the code to display, in the lblLargest control, the largest number stored in the decRates array. (The array has five elements.) Use the Do...Loop statement.

15. Rewrite the code from Exercise 14 using the For...Next statement.

16. Rewrite the code from Exercise 14 using the For Each...Next statement.

17. Write the code to subtract the number one from each element in the decRates array. (The array has five elements.) Use the Do...Loop statement.

18. Rewrite the code from Exercise 17 using the For...Next statement.

19. Rewrite the code from Exercise 17 using the For Each...Next statement.

20. Write the code to multiply by two the number stored in the first element of a one-dimensional array named intNum. Store the result in the intDouble variable.

21. Write the code to add together the numbers stored in the first and second elements of a one-dimensional array named intNum. Display the sum in the lblSum control.

22. If the strState and strCapital arrays are parallel arrays, the capital of the state stored in the strState(0) element is contained in which element?

23. Write the statement to declare a two-dimensional Decimal array named decBalances. The array should have four rows and six columns.

24. Write a loop that stores the number 10 in each element in the decBalances array. The array has four rows and six columns. Use the For...Next statement.

25. Rewrite the code from Exercise 24 using a Do...Loop statement.

26. Rewrite the code from Exercise 24 using a For Each...Next statement.

27. Write the statement to assign the Boolean value True to the variable located in the third row, first column of the blnAnswers array.

28. Assume that a sequential access file contains 20 numbers; each number appears on a separate line in the file. Write the code to read the numbers into a two-dimensional array named intNumbers, which contains four rows and five columns. Use the For...Next statement.

29. Rewrite the code from Exercise 28 using the Do...Loop statement.

30. Rewrite the code from Exercise 28 using the For Each...Next statement.

31. In this exercise, you modify this chapter's Programming Example.
    a. Create the Perrytown Gift Shop application shown in this chapter's Programming Example. Save the application in the VbDotNet\ Chap09 folder.
    b. Open the Code Editor window. Remove any reference to the decTaxTable array from the btnCalc_Click procedure. Modify the selection structure so that it passes the taxable wages and the appropriate array—either mdecSingle or mdecMarried—to a function named CalcFwt.
    c. Create a function named CalcFwt. The function will need to accept the taxable wages and the array passed to it. Move the code that calculates the federal withholding tax from the btnCalc_Click procedure to the CalcFwt function.
    d. Save the solution, then start the application. Use the application to display the tax for a married employee with taxable wages of $288.46. The application should display $24.67 as the tax. Now use the application to display the tax for a single employee with taxable wages of $600. The application should display $88.59 as the tax.
    e. Click the Exit button to end the application, then close the solution.

32. In this exercise, you code an application that displays the number of days in a month.
    a. Open the Month Solution (Month Solution.sln) file, which is contained in the VbDotNet\Chap09\Month Solution folder.
    b. Open the Display Days button's Click event procedure. Declare a 12-element, one-dimensional array named intDays. Use the number of days in each month to initialize the array. (Use 28 for February.)
    c. Code the btnDisplay_Click procedure so that it displays (in a message box) the number of days in the month corresponding to the number entered by the user in the txtMonth control. For example, if the txtMonth control contains the number one, the procedure should display 31 in a message box, because there are 31 days in January. The procedure should display an appropriate message in a message box if the user enters an invalid number in the txtMonth control.
    d. Save the solution, then start the application. Enter the number 20 in the txtMonth control, then click the Display Days button. An appropriate message should appear in a message box. Close the message box.

e. Now test the application by entering numbers from 1 through 12 in the txtMonth control. Click the Display Days button after entering each number.

f. Click the Exit button to end the application, then close the solution.

33. In this exercise, you code an application that displays the lowest value stored in an array.

a. Open the Lowest Solution (Lowest Solution.sln) file, which is contained in the VbDotNet\Chap09\Lowest Solution folder.

b. Open the Display Lowest button's Click event procedure. Declare a 20-element, one-dimensional Integer array named intScores. Assign the 20 numbers contained in the scores.txt file to the array. The scores.txt file is a sequential access file located in the VbDotNet\Chap09\Lowest Solution\Lowest Project\bin folder.

c. Code the btnDisplay_Click procedure so that it displays (in a message box) the lowest score stored in the array.

d. Save the solution, then start the application. Click the Display Lowest button. A message containing the lowest score (13) should appear in a message box. Close the message box.

e. Click the Exit button to end the application, then close the solution.

34. In this exercise, you code an application that updates each value stored in an array.

a. Open the Prices Solution (Prices Solution.sln) file, which is contained in the VbDotNet\Chap09\Prices Solution folder.

b. Declare a module-level one-dimensional Decimal array named mdecPrices. The array should contain 10 elements.

c. Open the form's Load event procedure. Assign the 10 prices stored in the prices.txt file to the mdecPrices array. The prices.txt file is a sequential access file located in the VbDotNet\Chap09\Prices Solution\Prices Project\bin folder.

d. Open the Increase button's Click event procedure. The procedure should ask the user for a percentage amount by which each price should be increased. It then should increase each price by that amount, and then save the increased prices to a sequential access file named newprices.txt.

e. Save the solution, then start the application. Click the Increase button. Increase each price by 5%.

f. Click the Exit button to end the application.

g. Open the prices.txt and newprices.txt files. The prices contained in the newprices.txt file should be 5% more than the prices in the prices.txt file.

h. Close the prices.txt and newprices.txt windows, then close the solution.

35. In this exercise, you modify the application from Exercise 34. The modified application allows the user to update a specific price.

a. Use Windows to make a copy of the Prices Solution folder, which is contained in the VbDotNet\Chap09 folder. Rename the copy Prices2 Solution.

b. Open the Prices Solution (Prices Solution.sln) file, which is contained in the VbDotNet\Chap09\Prices2 Solution folder.

c. Open the Increase button's Click event procedure. Modify the procedure so that it also asks the user to enter a number from one through 10. If the user enters the number one, the procedure should update the first price in the array. If the user enters the number two, the procedure should update the second price in the array, and so on.

    d. Save the solution, then start the application. Click the Increase button. Increase the second price by 10%. Click the Increase button again. This time, increase the tenth price by 2%.

    e. Click the Exit button to end the application.

    f. Open the prices.txt and newprices.txt files. The second price contained in the newprices.txt file should be 10% more than the second price in the prices.txt file. The tenth price in the newprices.txt file should be 2% more than the tenth price in the prices.txt file.

    g. Close the prices.txt and newprices.txt windows, then close the solution.

36. In this exercise, you code an application that displays the number of students earning a specific score.

    a. Open the Scores Solution (Scores Solution.sln) file, which is contained in the VbDotNet\Chap09\Scores Solution folder.

    b. Open the Display button's Click event procedure. Declare a 20-element, one-dimensional Integer array named intScores. Assign the 20 numbers contained in the scores.txt file to the array. The scores.txt file is a sequential access file located in the VbDotNet\Chap09\Scores Solution\Scores Project\bin folder.

    c. Code the btnDisplay_Click procedure so that it prompts the user to enter a score from zero through 100. The procedure then should display (in a message box) the number of students who earned that score.

    d. Save the solution, then start the application. Use the application to answer the following questions.

    How many students earned a score of 72?
    How many students earned a score of 88?
    How many students earned a score of 20?
    How many students earned a score of 99?

    e. Click the Exit button to end the application, then close the solution.

37. In this exercise, you modify the application that you coded in Exercise 36. The modified application allows the user to display the number of students earning a score in a specific range.

    a. Use Windows to make a copy of the Scores Solution folder, which is contained in the VbDotNet\Chap09 folder. Rename the copy Scores2 Solution.

    b. Open the Scores Solution (Scores Solution.sln) file, which is contained in the VbDotNet\Chap09\Scores2 Solution folder.

    c. Open the Display button's Click event procedure. Modify the procedure so that it prompts the user to enter a minimum score and a maximum score. The procedure then should display (in a message box) the number of students who earned a score within that range.

    d. Save the solution, then start the application. Use the application to answer the following questions.

    How many students earned a score between 70 and 79, including 70 and 79?
    How many students earned a score between 65 and 85, including 65 and 85?
    How many students earned a score between 0 and 50, including 0 and 50?

    e. Click the Exit button to end the application, then close the solution.

38. In this exercise, you code an application that sorts (in ascending order) the values stored in a sequential access file.
    a. Open the Sort Solution (Sort Solution.sln) file, which is contained in the VbDotNet\Chap09\Sort Solution folder.
    b. Open the Sort button's Click event procedure. Code the procedure so that it stores the 10 integers contained in the unsorted.txt file in an array. The unsorted.txt file is a sequential access file contained in the VbDotNet\Chap09\Sort Solution\Sort Project\bin folder. The procedure should sort the numbers in ascending order, and then save the sorted numbers to a sequential access file named sorted.txt.
    c. Save the solution, then start the application. Click the Sort button.
    d. Click the Exit button to end the application.
    e. Open the sorted.txt file. The 10 integers should appear in ascending order in the file.
    f. Close the sorted.txt window, then close the solution.

39. In this exercise, you modify the application that you coded in Exercise 38. The modified application sorts (in descending order) the values stored in a sequential access file.
    a. Use Windows to make a copy of the Sort Solution folder, which is contained in the VbDotNet\Chap09 folder. Rename the copy Sort2 Solution.
    b. Open the Sort Solution (Sort Solution.sln) file, which is contained in the VbDotNet\Chap09\Sort2 Solution folder.
    c. Open the Sort button's Click event procedure. Modify the procedure so that it sorts the numbers in descending order.
    d. Save the solution, then start the application. Click the Sort button.
    e. Click the Exit button to end the application.
    f. Open the sorted.txt file. The 10 integers should appear in descending order in the file.
    g. Close the sorted.txt window, then close the solution.

40. In this exercise, you code an application that allows Professor Carver to display a grade based on the number of points he enters. The grading scale is shown in Figure 9.29.

Minimum points	Maximum points	Grade
0	299	F
300	349	D
350	399	C
400	449	B
450	500	A

FIGURE 9.29

    a. Open the Carver Solution (Carver Solution.sln) file, which is contained in the VbDotNet\Chap09\Carver Solution folder.
    b. Store the minimum points in a five-element, one-dimensional Integer array named mintPoints. Store the grades in a five-element, one-dimensional String array named mstrGrades. The arrays should be parallel arrays.

    c. Code the Display Grade button's Click event procedure so that it searches the mintPoints array for the number of points entered by the user, and then displays the corresponding grade from the mstrGrade array.

    d. Save the solution, and then start the application. Enter 455 in the Points text box, then click the Display Grade button. A grade of A appears in the interface.

    e. Enter 210 in the Points text box, then click the Display Grade button. A grade of F appears in the interface.

    f. Click the Exit button to end the application, then close the solution.

41. In this exercise, you modify the application that you coded in Exercise 40. The modified application allows the user to change the grading scale when the application is started.

    a. Use Windows to make a copy of the Carver Solution folder, which is contained in the VbDotNet\Chap09 folder. Rename the copy Carver2 Solution.

    b. Open the Carver Solution (Carver Solution.sln) file, which is contained in the VbDotNet\Chap09\Carver2 Solution folder.

    c. When the form is loaded into the computer's memory, the application should use the InputBox function to prompt the user to enter the total number of possible points—in other words, the total number of points a student can earn in the course. Modify the application's code to perform this task.

    d. Modify the application's code so that it uses the grading scale shown in Figure 9.30. For example, if the user enters the number 500 in response to the InputBox function, the code should enter 450, which is 90% of 500, as the minimum number of points for an A. If the user enters the number 300, the code should enter 270, which is 90% of 300, as the minimum number of points for an A.

Minimum points	Grade
Less than 60% of the possible points	F
60% of the possible points	D
70% of the possible points	C
80% of the possible points	B
90% of the possible points	A

FIGURE 9.30

    e. Save the solution, and then start the application. Enter 300 as the number of possible points, then enter 185 in the Points text box. Click the Display Grade button. A grade of D appears in the interface.

    f. Click the Exit button to end the application.

    g. Start the application again. Enter 500 as the number of possible points, then enter 363 in the Points text box. Click the Display Grade button. A grade of C appears in the interface.

    h. Click the Exit button to end the application, then close the solution.

42. In this exercise, you code an application that sums the values contained in a two-dimensional array.
    a. Open the Inventory Solution (Inventory Solution.sln) file, which is contained in the VbDotNet\Chap09\Inventory Solution folder.
    b. Code the Display Total button's Click event procedure so that it adds together the values stored in the intInventory array. Display the sum in the lblTotal control.
    c. Save the solution, and then start the application. Click the Display Total button to display the sum of the array values.
    d. Click the Exit button to end the application, then close the solution.

43. In this exercise, you code an application that displays the highest score earned on the midterm exam and the highest score earned on the final exam.
    a. Open the Highest Solution (Highest Solution.sln) file, which is contained in the VbDotNet\Chap09\Highest Solution folder.
    b. Code the Display Highest button's Click event procedure so that it displays (in the appropriate label controls) the highest score earned on the midterm exam and the highest score earned on the final exam.
    c. Save the solution, and then start the application. Click the Display Highest button to display the highest scores.
    d. Click the Exit button to end the application, then close the solution.

44. In this exercise, you learn about the ReDim statement.
    a. Display the Help screen for the ReDim statement. What is the purpose of the statement?
    b. What is the purpose of the keyword `Preserve`?
    c. Open the ReDim Solution (ReDim Solution.sln) file, which is contained in the VbDotNet\Chap09\ReDim Solution folder.
    d. Open the Code Editor window and view the btnDisplay_Click procedure. Study the existing code, then modify the procedure so that it stores any number of sales amounts in the intSales array.
    e. Save the solution, then start the application. Click the Display Sales button, then enter the following sales amounts: 700, 550, and 800. The button's Click event procedure should display each sales amount in a separate message box.
    f. Click the Display Sales button again, then enter the following sales amounts: 5, 9, 45, 67, 8, and 0. The button's Click event procedure should display each sales amount in a separate message box.
    g. Click the Exit button to end the application, then close the solution.

45. In this exercise, you learn about the Array.GetUpperBound method.
    a. Display the Help screen for the Array.GetUpperBound method. What is the purpose of the method?
    b. Write the statement to display (in a message box) the highest subscript included in a one-dimensional array named strItems.
    c. Write the statement to display (in a message box) the highest column subscript included in a two-dimensional array named strNames.
    d. Use the Array.GetUpperBound method to rewrite the conditions in the Do and If clauses shown in Figure 9.23.

46. In this exercise, you find and correct an error in an application. The process of finding and correcting errors is called debugging.
    a. Open the Debug Solution (Debug Solution.sln) file, which is contained in the VbDotNet\Chap09\Debug Solution folder.
    b. Open the Code Editor window. Review the existing code. Notice that the strNames array contains five rows and two columns. Column one contains five first names, and column two contains five last names. The btnDisplay_Click procedure should display the first and last names in the lblFirst and lblLast controls, respectively.
    c. Notice that a jagged line appears below some of the lines of code in the Code Editor window. Correct the code to remove the jagged lines.
    d. Save the solution, then start the application. Click the Display button. If an error message appears in a dialog box, click the Break button. Click Debug, then click Stop Debugging.
    e. Correct the errors in the application's code, then save the solution and start the application. Click the Display button to display the first and last names in the appropriate label controls.
    f. Click the Exit button to end the application, then close the solution.

Case Projects

JT Sales

JT Sales employs 10 salespeople. The sales made by the salespeople during the months of January, February, and March are stored in a sequential access file named sales.txt. You will need to create an appropriate sequential access file. The file should contain 10 records, one for each salesperson. Each salesperson's record should contain three fields. The first field is the January sales amount, the second field is the February sales amount, and the third field is the March sales amount. The sales manager wants an application that allows him to enter the current bonus rate. The application should save, to a sequential access file, a report that shows each salesperson's number (1 through 10), total sales amount, and bonus amount. The report also should show the total bonus paid. Be sure to use one or more arrays in the application.

Waterglen Horse Farms

Each year, Sabrina Cantrell, the owner of Waterglen Horse Farms, enters four of her horses in five local horse races. She uses the table shown in Figure 9.31 to keep track of how her horses performed in each race. In the table, a 1 means that the horse won the race, a 2 means that the horse finished in second place, and a 3 means that the horse finished in third place. A 0 means that the horse did not finish in the top three. Sabrina wants an application that she can use to display a summary of how each horse performed individually, as well as how all of the horses performed. For example, using the table shown in Figure 9.31, horse 1 won one race, finished second in one race, finished third in one race, and didn't finish in the top three in two races. Overall, Sabrina's horses won four races, finished second in three races, finished third in three races, and didn't finish in the top three in ten races. Be sure to use one or more arrays in the application.

Each column represents a race

Each row represents a horse

FIGURE 9.31

Conway Enterprises

Conway Enterprises has both domestic and international sales operations. The company's sales manager wants an application that she can use to display the total domestic, total international, and total company sales made during a six-month period. The sales are stored in a sequential access file named company.txt. You will need to create an appropriate sequential access file. The file should contain six records, one for each month. Each record should contain two fields: one for the domestic sales and the other for the international sales. Be sure to use one or more arrays in the application.

Parker Apparel

Marcus Washington, the inventory manager at Parker Apparel, wants an application that allows him to keep track of the quantity of each item in inventory. The inventory numbers and quantities in stock are stored in a sequential access file named inventory.txt. You will need to create an appropriate sequential access file. The file should contain 10 records, one for each inventory item. Each record should contain two fields: one for the inventory number and the other for the quantity in stock. The inventory numbers, number of items purchased, number of items sold, and number of items returned are stored in a sequential access file named changes.txt. You will need to create an appropriate sequential access file. The file should contain 10 records, one for each inventory item. Each record should contain four fields: one for the inventory number, the second for the number of items purchased, the third for the number of items sold, and the fourth for the number of items returned. The application also should allow Mr. Washington to enter an inventory number and then display the quantity in stock. The inventory.txt file should always contain the inventory numbers and current quantities in stock. Be sure to use one or more arrays in the application.

10

Structures and More Controls

- Create a structure
- Declare and manipulate a structure variable
- Differentiate between a structure variable and member variables
- Create an array of structure variables
- Include a radio button in an interface
- Include a check box in an interface
- Include a list box in an interface
- Code a text box's KeyPress event
- Code a text box's Enter event
- Associate a procedure with different events

STRUCTURES

In previous chapters, you used only the data types built into Visual Basic .NET, such as the Integer, Decimal, and String data types. You also can create your own data types in Visual Basic .NET using the **Structure statement**. Data types created using the Structure statement are referred to as **user-defined data types** or **structures**. Figure 10.1 shows the syntax of the Structure statement and includes an example of using the statement to create a structure (user-defined data type) named Employee.

HOW TO...

Create a Structure (User-Defined Data Type)

Syntax
Structure *structureName*
    Public *memberVariable1* **As** *datatype*
    [**Public** *memberVariableN* **As** *datatype*]
End Structure

Example
```
Structure Employee
     Public strNumber As String
     Public strFirstName As String
     Public strLastName As String
     Public decSalary As Decimal
End Structure
```

FIGURE 10.1   How to create a structure (user-defined data type)

The Structure statement begins with the Structure clause, which contains the keyword `Structure` followed by the name of the structure. In the example shown in Figure 10.1, the name of the structure is Employee. The Structure statement ends with the End Structure clause, which contains the keywords `End Structure`. Between the Structure and End Structure clauses, you define the members included in the structure. The members can be variables, constants, or procedures. However, in most cases, the members will be variables; such variables are referred to as **member variables**. In this book, you learn how to include only member variables in a structure.

As the syntax shown in Figure 10.1 indicates, each member variable's definition contains the keyword `Public` followed by the name of the variable, the keyword `As`, and the variable's *datatype*. The *datatype* identifies the type of data that the member variable will store and can be any of the standard data types available in Visual Basic .NET; it also can be another structure (user-defined data type). The Employee structure shown in Figure 10.1 contains four member variables: three are String variables and one is a Decimal variable.

In most applications, you enter the Structure statement in the form's Declarations section, typically below the `Windows Form Designer generated code` entry in the Code Editor window. After entering the Structure statement, you then can use the structure to declare a variable.

TIP

Most programmers use the Class statement rather than the Structure statement to create data types that contain procedures. You learn about the Class statement in Chapter 11.

TIP

Keep in mind that the Structure statement simply defines the structure. It does not actually create a structure variable.

USING A STRUCTURE TO DECLARE A VARIABLE

As you can with the standard data types built into Visual Basic .NET, you can use a structure (user-defined data type) to declare a variable. Variables declared using a structure are often referred to as **structure variables**. Figure 10.2 shows the syntax for creating a structure variable. The figure also includes examples of declaring structure variables using the Employee structure from Figure 10.1.

HOW TO...

Declare a Structure Variable

Syntax
accessibility structureVariableName **As** *structureName*

Examples
```
Dim empManager As Employee
```
declares a procedure-level Employee variable named empManager

```
Private mempSalaried As Employee
```
declares a module-level Employee variable named mempSalaried

FIGURE 10.2   How to declare a structure variable

In the syntax, *accessibility* is typically either the keyword `Dim` or the keyword `Private`, depending on whether you are creating a procedure-level or module-level variable. *StructureVariableName* is the name of the structure variable you are declaring and *structureName* is the name of the structure (user-defined data type).

Similar to the way the `Dim intAge As Integer` instruction declares an Integer variable named intAge, the `Dim empManager As Employee` instruction, which is shown in the first example in Figure 10.2, declares an Employee structure variable named empManager. However, unlike the intAge variable, the empManager variable itself contains four member variables. In code, you refer to the entire structure variable by its name—in this case, empManager. To refer to an individual member variable within a structure variable, however, you precede the member variable's name with the name of the structure variable in which it is defined. You use the dot member access operator (a period) to separate the structure variable's name from the member variable's name. For instance, the names of the member variables within the empManager structure variable are empManager.strNumber, empManager.strFirstName, empManager.strLastName, and empManager.decSalary.

The `Private mempSalaried As Employee` instruction shown in the second example in Figure 10.2 declares a module-level Employee structure variable named mempSalaried. The names of the members within the mempSalaried variable are mempSalaried.strNumber, mempSalaried.strFirstName, mempSalaried.strLastName, and mempSalaried.decSalary.

You can use an assignment statement to enter data into the member variables contained in a structure variable. Figure 10.3 shows the syntax of such an assignment statement and includes several examples of using the syntax to enter data into the member variables shown in Figure 10.2.

TIP

The dot member access operator indicates that strNumber, strFirstName, strLastName, and decSalary are members of the empManager and mempSalaried variables.

HOW TO...

Store Data in a Member Variable

Syntax

structureVariableName.memberVariableName = value

Examples

```
empManager.strNumber = "0477"
empManager.strFirstName = "Janice"
empManager.strLastName = "Lopenski"
empManager.decSalary = 34500D
```
assigns data to the member variables contained in the empManager variable

```
empManager.strNumber = sreStreamReader.ReadLine()
```
assigns the line read from a sequential access file to the empManager.strNumber member variable

```
mempSalaried.decSalary = mempSalaried.decSalary * 1.05D
```
multiplies the contents of the mempSalaried.decSalary member variable by 1.05, and then assigns the result to the member variable

```
mempSalaried.strFirstName = Me.txtFirst.Text
```
assigns the value entered in the txtFirst control to the mempSalaried.strFirstName member variable

FIGURE 10.3   How to store data in a member variable

TIP

The member variables contained in a structure variable can be used just like any other variables. For example, you can assign values to them, use them in calculations, display their contents, and so on.

In the syntax, *structureVariableName* is the name of a structure variable, and *memberVariableName* is the name of a member variable within the structure variable. *Value* is the data you want assigned to the member variable. The data type of the *value* must match the data type of the member variable.

In the first example shown in Figure 10.3, the first three assignment statements assign the strings "0477", "Janice", and "Lopenski" to the String members of the empManager variable. The fourth assignment statement in the example assigns a Decimal number to the Decimal member of the empManager variable.

The second example in Figure 10.3 reads a line of data from a sequential access file and stores the data in the strNumber member of the empManager variable. The third example multiplies the contents of the mempSalaried.decSalary member variable by 1.05, and then assigns the result to the member variable. The last example assigns the value entered in the txtFirst control to the mempSalaried.strFirstName member variable.

Programmers use structures (user-defined data types) to group related items into one unit. The advantages of doing so will become more apparent as you read through the next two sections.

Passing a Structure Variable to a Procedure

The personnel manager at Johnsons Lumber wants an application that he can use to save each manager's employee number, name, and salary in a sequential access file. Figure 10.4 shows a sample run of the Johnsons Lumber application, and Figure 10.5 shows how you can code the application without using a structure.

FIGURE 10.4   Sample run of the Johnsons Lumber application

```
'Project name:         Johnsons Project
'Project purpose:      The project writes employee information to
'                      a sequential access file.
'Created/revised by:   Diane Zak on 2/1/2005

Option Explicit On
Option Strict On

Public Class frmJohnsons
    Inherits System.Windows.Forms.Form

[Windows Form Designer generated code]

    Private Function GetData(ByRef strNum As String, _
                             ByRef strFirst As String, _
                             ByRef strLast As String, _
                             ByRef decPay As Decimal) As Boolean
        'gets the employee data and returns a Boolean value
        'indicating whether the data is OK

        'declare variable
        Dim blnDataOK As Boolean = True

        'assign input to variables
        strNum = Me.txtNumber.Text
        strFirst = Me.txtFirst.Text
        strLast = Me.txtLast.Text
        'remove any dollar signs from the salary
        Me.txtSalary.Text = Me.txtSalary.Text.Replace("$", "")

        Try
            decPay = Convert.ToDecimal(Me.txtSalary.Text)

        Catch exFormat As FormatException
            blnDataOK = False
            MessageBox.Show("The salary must be numeric.", _
                "Johnsons Lumber", MessageBoxButtons.OK, _
                MessageBoxIcon.Information)
        End Try

        Return blnDataOK
    End Function
```

*Receives four
variables by
reference, and
assigns data to
the variables*

(Figure is continued on next page)

```
Private Sub btnSave_Click(ByVal sender As Object, _
    ByVal e As System.EventArgs) Handles btnSave.Click
    'save the employee information to a sequential access file

    'declare variables
    Dim strNumber As String
    Dim strFirstName As String
    Dim strLastName As String
    Dim decSalary As Decimal
    Dim blnGoodData As Boolean
    Dim swrStreamWriter As IO.StreamWriter

    'call a function to get the data and return a Boolean
    'value indicating whether the data is OK
    blnGoodData = GetData(strNumber, strFirstName, _
        strLastName, decSalary)

    If blnGoodData Then
        Try
            'open the file for append
            swrStreamWriter = IO.File.AppendText("employees.txt")

            'write the employee information
            swrStreamWriter.WriteLine(strNumber _
                & "#" & strFirstName & "#" _
                & strLastName & "#" _
                & Convert.ToString(decSalary))

            'clear the text boxes
            'then send the focus to the Number text box
            Me.txtNumber.Text = ""
            Me.txtFirst.Text = ""
            Me.txtLast.Text = ""
            Me.txtSalary.Text = ""
            Me.txtNumber.Focus()

            'close the file
            swrStreamWriter.Close()

        Catch ex As Exception
            MessageBox.Show(ex.Message, "Johnsons Lumber", _
                MessageBoxButtons.OK, MessageBoxIcon.Information)
        End Try
    End If
End Sub

Private Sub btnExit_Click(ByVal sender As Object, _
    ByVal e As System.EventArgs) Handles btnExit.Click
    'ends the application
    Me.Close()
End Sub
End Class
```

Declares four variables to store the input data

Passes four variables to the GetData function

Writes the information stored in each variable to the file

FIGURE 10.5   Code for the Johnsons Lumber application (without a structure)

When the user clicks the Save button in the interface, the btnSave_Click procedure shown in Figure 10.5 declares the necessary variables. It then calls the GetData function, passing it four variables *by reference*. The GetData function is responsible for assigning to the variables the employee data entered by the user. Notice that the function also verifies that the salary entry can be converted to the Decimal data type. The function returns the Boolean value True if it does not find a problem with the conversion; otherwise, it returns the Boolean value False.

If the GetData function did not encounter a problem when assigning the employee data to the variables, the btnSave_Click procedure writes the contents of the variables to a sequential access file; otherwise, the btnSave_Click procedure ends.

Figure 10.6 shows a more convenient way of writing the code for the Johnsons Lumber application. In this version of the code, the Employee structure from Figure 10.1 is used to group together the employee data.

```
'Project name:          Johnsons Project
'Project purpose:       The project writes employee information to
'                       a sequential access file.
'Created/revised by:    Diane Zak on 2/1/2005

Option Explicit On
Option Strict On

Public Class frmJohnsons
    Inherits System.Windows.Forms.Form

[Windows Form Designer generated code]

    Structure Employee
        Public strNumber As String
        Public strFirstName As String
        Public strLastName As String
        Public decSalary As Decimal
    End Structure
```

Defines the
Employee
structure

(Figure is continued on next page)

```
Private Function GetData(ByRef empInfo As Employee) As Boolean
    'gets the employee data and returns a Boolean value
    'indicating whether the data is OK

    'declare variable
    Dim blnDataOK As Boolean = True

    'assign input to variables
    empInfo.strNumber = Me.txtNumber.Text
    empInfo.strFirstName = Me.txtFirst.Text
    empInfo.strLastName = Me.txtLast.Text
    'remove any dollar signs from the salary
    Me.txtSalary.Text = Me.txtSalary.Text.Replace("$", "")

    Try
        empInfo.decSalary = Convert.ToDecimal(Me.txtSalary.Text)

    Catch exFormat As FormatException
        blnDataOK = False
        MessageBox.Show("The salary must be numeric.", _
            "Johnsons Lumber", MessageBoxButtons.OK, _
            MessageBoxIcon.Information)
    End Try

    Return blnDataOK
End Function

Private Sub btnSave_Click(ByVal sender As Object, _
    ByVal e As System.EventArgs) Handles btnSave.Click
    'save the employee information to a sequential access file

    'declare variables
    Dim empManager As Employee
    Dim blnGoodData As Boolean
    Dim swrStreamWriter As IO.StreamWriter

    'call a function to get the data and return a Boolean
    'value indicating whether the data is OK
    blnGoodData = GetData(empManager)

    If blnGoodData Then
        Try
            'open the file for append
            swrStreamWriter = IO.File.AppendText("employees.txt")
```

Receives an Employee structure variable by reference, and assigns data to the members

Declares an Employee structure variable to store the input data

Passes the Employee structure variable to the GetData function

(Figure is continued on next page)

Writes the information stored in each member variable to the file

```
                        'write the employee information
                        swrStreamWriter.WriteLine(empManager.strNumber _
                            & "#" & empManager.strFirstName & "#" _
                            & empManager.strLastName & "#" _
                            & Convert.ToString(empManager.decSalary))

                        'clear the text boxes
                        'then send the focus to the Number text box
                        Me.txtNumber.Text = ""
                        Me.txtFirst.Text = ""
                        Me.txtLast.Text = ""
                        Me.txtSalary.Text = ""
                        Me.txtNumber.Focus()

                        'close the file
                        swrStreamWriter.Close()

                    Catch ex As Exception
                        MessageBox.Show(ex.Message, "Johnsons Lumber", _
                            MessageBoxButtons.OK, MessageBoxIcon.Information)
                    End Try
                End If
            End Sub

            Private Sub btnExit_Click(ByVal sender As Object, _
                ByVal e As System.EventArgs) Handles btnExit.Click
                'ends the application
                Me.Close()
            End Sub
        End Class
```

FIGURE 10.6   Code for the Johnsons Lumber application (with a structure)

In the code shown in Figure 10.6, the Structure statement that defines the Employee structure is entered in the form's Declarations section, immediately below the `Windows Form Designer generated code` entry. The `Dim empManager As Employee` statement in the btnSave_Click procedure uses the Employee structure to declare a structure variable named empManager. The `blnGoodData = GetData(empManager)` statement in the btnSave_Click procedure calls the GetData function, passing it the empManager structure variable *by reference*. When you pass a structure variable, all of the member variables are automatically passed.

The GetData function receives the address of the Employee structure variable passed to it, and it assigns the employee data entered by the user to each of the member variables. The function returns the Boolean value True if it did not encounter a problem when assigning the data; otherwise, it returns the Boolean value False. If the GetData function returns the Boolean value True, the btnSave_Click procedure writes the data stored in each member variable to a sequential access file; otherwise, the procedure ends.

Notice that the btnSave_Click procedure shown earlier in Figure 10.5 uses four scalar variables to store the input data; however, in Figure 10.6's code, the procedure uses only one structure variable for this purpose. The btnSave_Click

TIP

As you learned in Chapter 9, a scalar variable, also called a simple variable, is one that is unrelated to any other variable in memory.

TIP

Notice that there are many different ways to solve the same problem.

procedure in Figure 10.5 also must pass four scalar variables (rather than one structure variable) to the GetData function, which must use four scalar variables (rather than one structure variable) to accept the data. Imagine if the employee data consisted of 20 items rather than just four items! Passing a structure variable would be much less work than passing 20 individual scalar variables.

Another advantage of grouping related data into one unit is that the unit then can be stored in an array.

Creating an Array of Structure Variables

In Chapter 9, you learned how to use two parallel one-dimensional arrays to store a price list for Takoda Tapahe, the owner of a small gift shop named Treasures. (The code is shown in Figure 9.18 in Chapter 9.) As you may remember, you stored each product's ID in a one-dimensional String array, and stored each product's price in the corresponding location in a one-dimensional Integer array. Also in Chapter 9, you learned how to store the Treasures price list in a two-dimensional String array. (The code is shown in Figure 9.23 in Chapter 9.) In addition to using parallel one-dimensional arrays or a two-dimensional array, you also can use a one-dimensional array of structure variables.

Figure 10.7 shows a sample run of the Treasures application, and Figure 10.8 shows the application's code using an array of structure variables.

FIGURE 10.7   Sample run of the Treasures application

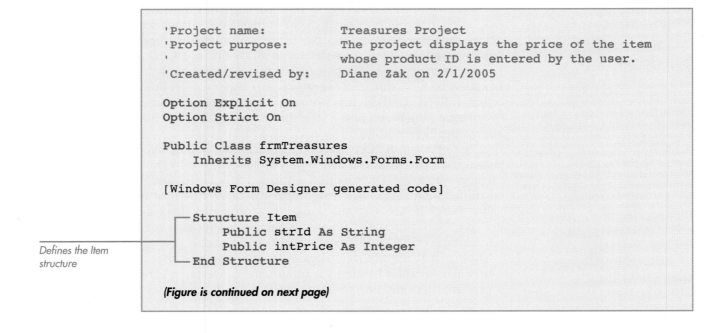

```
'Project name:         Treasures Project
'Project purpose:      The project displays the price of the item
'                      whose product ID is entered by the user.
'Created/revised by:   Diane Zak on 2/1/2005

Option Explicit On
Option Strict On

Public Class frmTreasures
    Inherits System.Windows.Forms.Form

[Windows Form Designer generated code]

    Structure Item
        Public strId As String
        Public intPrice As Integer
    End Structure
```

Defines the Item structure

(Figure is continued on next page)

```
Private Sub btnDisplayPrice_Click(ByVal sender As Object, _
    ByVal e As System.EventArgs) Handles btnDisplayPrice.Click
    'displays the price of an item

    'declare variables
    Dim strSearchFor As String
    Dim intX As Integer  'keeps track of the array subscripts

    'declare array of structure variables
    Dim iteGifts(4) As Item

    'assign product IDs and prices to the array
    iteGifts(0).strId = "BX35"
    iteGifts(0).intPrice = 13
    iteGifts(1).strId = "CR20"
    iteGifts(1).intPrice = 10
    iteGifts(2).strId = "FE15"
    iteGifts(2).intPrice = 12
    iteGifts(3).strId = "KW10"
    iteGifts(3).intPrice = 24
    iteGifts(4).strId = "MM67"
    iteGifts(4).intPrice = 4

    'assign input to variable
    strSearchFor = txtId.Text.ToUpper()

    'search the array for the product ID
    Do While intX < iteGifts.Length _
            AndAlso strSearchFor <> iteGifts(intX).strId
        intX = intX + 1
    Loop

    'determine whether the ID was located in the strId array
    If intX < iteGifts.Length Then
        'display the price
        Me.lblPrice.Text = _
            "Price: $" & Convert.ToString(iteGifts(intX).intPrice)
    Else
        Me.lblPrice.Text = "Product ID is not valid"
    End If
End Sub

Private Sub btnExit_Click(ByVal sender As Object, _
    ByVal e As System.EventArgs) Handles btnExit.Click
    'ends the application
    Me.Close()
End Sub
End Class
```

Declares an array of Item structure variables

Fills the structure variables with data

Accesses the length of the array and the contents of the strId member variable contained in the current array element

Accesses the contents of the intPrice member variable contained in the current array element

FIGURE 10.8   Code for the Treasures application

The btnDisplayPrice_Click procedure declares a String variable named strSearchFor and an Integer variable named intX. The strSearchFor variable will store the product ID entered by the user, and the intX variable will keep track of the array subscripts. The procedure uses the Item structure, which is defined in the form's Declarations section, to declare a five-element, one-dimensional array named iteGifts. Each element in the iteGifts array is a structure variable that contains two member variables: a String variable named strId and an Integer variable named intPrice. After declaring the array, the procedure assigns the appropriate IDs and prices to the array. Assigning initial values to an array is often referred to as **populating the array**. Notice that you refer to a member variable in an array element using the syntax *arrayname(subscript).memberVariableName*. For example, you use iteGifts(0).strId to refer to the strId member contained in the first element in the iteGifts array. Likewise, you use iteGifts(4).intPrice to refer to the intPrice member contained in the last element in the iteGifts array.

After populating the iteGifts array, the btnDisplayPrice_Click procedure assigns the contents of the txtId control, converted to uppercase, to the strSearchFor variable. The loop in the procedure then continues to add the number one to the intX variable as long as the intX variable contains a value that is less than the number of elements in the iteGifts array (in this case, 5) and, at the same time, the product ID has not been located in the strId member in the array. The loop stops when either of the following conditions is true: the intX variable contains the number five (which indicates that the loop reached the end of the array without finding the product ID) or the product ID is located in a strId member in the array.

After the loop completes its processing, the selection structure in the procedure compares the number stored in the intX variable with the value stored in the iteGifts array's Length property, which is 5. If the intX variable contains a number that is less than five, it indicates that the loop stopped processing because the product ID was located in a strId member in the array. In that case, the procedure displays (in the lblPrice control) the price from the corresponding intPrice member in the array. However, if the intX variable's value is not less than five, it indicates that the loop stopped processing because it reached the end of the array without finding the product ID; in that case, the message "Product ID is not valid" is displayed in the lblPrice control. As Figure 10.7 indicates, the procedure displays a price of $12 if the user enters FE15 as the product ID.

So far, most of the applications you created in this book used text boxes to get user input. An advantage of using a text box for user input is that it can accept any data the user enters. A disadvantage is that it requires the application to perform data validation to ensure that the data was entered in the required format. In applications where the user is expected to enter one or more specific values, it is better to use other controls—such as radio buttons, check boxes, or list boxes—to display the values. Then, rather than typing the desired value in a text box, the user can select the appropriate value from one of these other controls. You learn about radio buttons first.

ADDING A RADIO BUTTON TO THE FORM

You use the **RadioButton tool** in the toolbox to add a radio button to an interface. A **radio button** allows you to limit the user to only one choice in a group of two or more related and mutually exclusive choices. Figure 10.9 lists the names and uses of several properties of a radio button.

Use a Radio Button

Property	Use to
CheckAlign	indicate the location of the circle that appears on the button
Checked	indicate whether the button is checked or unchecked
ContextMenu	specify a shortcut menu that displays when the user right-clicks the radio button
Font	specify the font type and size to use for text (usually set to Tahoma)
Name	give the radio button a meaningful name that begins with "rad"
Text	specify the text that appears inside the radio button
TextAlign	indicate the alignment of the text that appears inside the radio button

FIGURE 10.9   How to use a radio button

Figure 10.10 shows the Gentry Supplies application's interface, which contains radio buttons.

Default radio button in the Delivery group

Default radio button in the State group

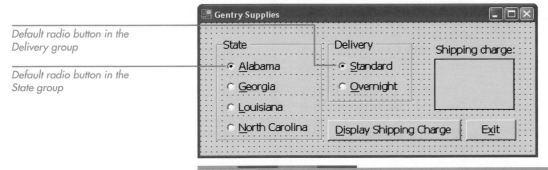

FIGURE 10.10   Gentry Supplies application's interface

Notice that each radio button in Figure 10.10 is labeled so that the user knows its purpose. You enter the label using sentence capitalization in the radio button's Text property. Each radio button also has a unique access key, which allows the user to select the button using the keyboard.

Radio buttons that are related should be grouped together. For example, two groups of radio buttons appear in the interface shown in Figure 10.10: one group contains the four state radio buttons, and the other contains the two delivery radio buttons. To include two groups of radio buttons in an interface, at least one of the groups must be placed within either a group box control or a panel control; otherwise, the radio buttons are considered to be in the same group and only one can be selected at any one time. In this case, the radio buttons pertaining to the state choice are contained in the GroupBox1 control, and the radio buttons pertaining to the delivery choice are contained in the GroupBox2 control. Placing each group of radio buttons in a separate group box control allows the user to select one button from each group.

TIP

If you have more than seven choices from which the user can choose, you should consider using a list box, checked list box, or combo box control rather than radio buttons.

The minimum number of radio buttons in a group is two, because the only way to deselect a radio button is to select another radio button. The recommended maximum number of radio buttons in a group is seven.

It is customary in Windows applications to have one of the radio buttons in each group of radio buttons already selected when the user interface first appears. The selected button is called the **default radio button** and is either the radio button that represents the user's most likely choice or the first radio button in the group. You designate a radio button as the default radio button by setting the button's Checked property to the Boolean value True. When you set the Checked property to True in the Properties window, a black dot appears inside the circle in the button, as shown in Figure 10.10.

When the user clicks the Display Shipping Charge button in the Gentry Supplies application's user interface, the btnDisplay Click event procedure should calculate and display the appropriate shipping charge. The shipping charges are shown in Figure 10.11.

State	Charge for standard delivery
Alabama	20
Georgia	35
Louisiana	30
North Carolina	28
Overnight delivery: add $10 to the charge for standard delivery	

FIGURE 10.11 Shipping charges

Figure 10.12 shows the code for the btnDisplay Click event procedure, and Figure 10.13 shows a sample run of the Gentry Supplies application. Notice that the code uses the Checked property to determine which radio button in the State group is selected. It also uses the Checked property to determine whether the Overnight radio button in the Delivery group is selected.

```
Private Sub btnDisplay_Click(ByVal sender As Object, _
        ByVal e As System.EventArgs) Handles btnDisplay.Click
        'displays a shipping charge

        'declare variable
        Dim intShipping As Integer

        'determine appropriate shipping charge based on the state
        If Me.radAlabama.Checked Then
            intShipping = 20
        ElseIf Me.radGeorgia.Checked Then
            intShipping = 35
        ElseIf Me.radLouisiana.Checked Then
            intShipping = 30
        Else
            intShipping = 28
        End If

        'add $10 for overnight delivery
        If Me.radOvernight.Checked Then
            intShipping = intShipping + 10
        End If

        'display shipping charge
        Me.lblShipping.Text = intShipping.ToString("C2")
End Sub
```

Determines which State radio button is selected

Determines whether the Overnight radio button is selected

FIGURE 10.12   Code for the btnDisplay Click event procedure

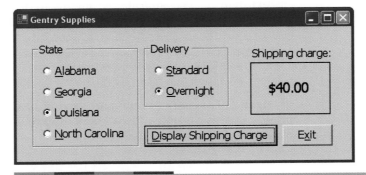

FIGURE 10.13   Sample run of the Gentry Supplies application

Next, you learn about check boxes.

ADDING A CHECK BOX CONTROL TO THE FORM

You use the **CheckBox tool** in the toolbox to add a check box to an interface. Check boxes work like radio buttons in that they are either selected or deselected only; but that is where the similarity ends. You use radio buttons when you want to limit the user to only one choice from a group of related and mutually exclusive choices. You use **check boxes**, on the other hand, to allow the user to select any number of choices from a group of one or more independent and nonexclusive choices. Unlike radio buttons, where only one button in a group can be selected at any one time, any number of check boxes on a form can be selected at the same time. Figure 10.14 lists the names and uses of several properties of a check box.

HOW TO...

Use a Check Box

Property	Use to
CheckAlign	indicate the location of the check box that appears on the control
Checked	indicate whether the check box is checked or unchecked
ContextMenu	specify a shortcut menu that displays when the user right-clicks the check box
Font	specify the font type and size to use for text (usually set to Tahoma)
Name	give the check box a meaningful name that begins with "chk"
Text	specify the text that appears inside the check box
TextAlign	indicate the alignment of the text that appears inside the check box

FIGURE 10.14 How to use a check box

Figure 10.15 shows a different version of the Gentry Supplies application's interface. This version uses a check box to indicate whether the user wants overnight delivery.

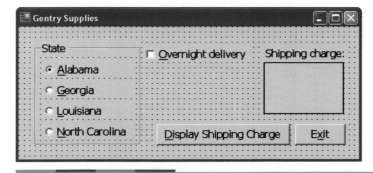

A different version of the Gentry Supplies application's interface

As with radio buttons, each check box in an interface should be labeled so that the user knows its purpose. You enter the label using sentence capitalization in the check box's Text property. Each check box also should have a unique access key.

Figure 10.16 shows the modified code for the btnDisplay Click event procedure, and Figure 10.17 shows a sample run of the Gentry Supplies application using the new interface. The modification made to the original code is shaded in Figure 10.16. Notice that the modified code uses the Checked property to determine whether the Overnight delivery check box is selected.

```
Private Sub btnDisplay_Click(ByVal sender As Object, _
        ByVal e As System.EventArgs) Handles btnDisplay.Click
    'displays a shipping charge

    'declare variable
    Dim intShipping As Integer

    'determine appropriate shipping charge based on the state
    If Me.radAlabama.Checked Then
        intShipping = 20
    ElseIf Me.radGeorgia.Checked Then
        intShipping = 35
    ElseIf Me.radLouisiana.Checked Then
        intShipping = 30
    Else
        intShipping = 28
    End If

    'add $10 for overnight delivery
    If Me.chkOvernight.Checked Then
        intShipping = intShipping + 10
    End If

    'display shipping charge
    Me.lblShipping.Text = intShipping.ToString("C2")
End Sub
```

Determines whether the Overnight delivery check box is selected

Modified code for the btnDisplay Click event procedure

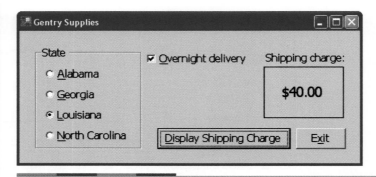

FIGURE 10.17   Another sample run of the Gentry Supplies application

Next, you learn how to add a list box to an interface.

ADDING A LIST BOX TO AN INTERFACE

You use the **ListBox tool** in the toolbox to add a list box to an interface. You can use a **list box** to display a list of choices from which the user can select zero choices, one choice, or more than one choice. Figure 10.18 lists the names and uses of several properties of a list box, and Figure 10.19 shows yet another version of the Gentry Supplies application's interface. This version allows the user to select the state from a list box rather than from radio buttons.

HOW TO...

Use a List Box

Property	Use to
ContextMenu	specify a shortcut menu that displays when the user right-clicks the list box
Font	specify the font type and size to use for text (usually set to Tahoma)
Name	give the list box a meaningful name that begins with "lst"
SelectedIndex	get or set the index of the selected item; not listed in the Properties window; only available in code
SelectedItem	get or set the value of the selected item; not listed in the Properties window; only available in code
SelectionMode	specify whether the user can select zero choices, one choice, or more than one choice; one choice is the default
Sorted	control whether the items in the list are sorted

FIGURE 10.18 How to use a list box

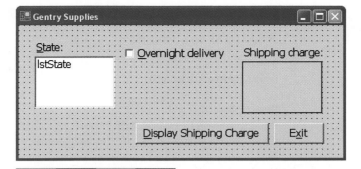

FIGURE 10.19   The Gentry application's interface using a list box

TIP

If you have only two options to offer the user, you should use two radio buttons instead of a list box.

You can make a list box any size you want. If you have more items than fit into the list box, the control automatically displays scroll bars that you can use to view the complete list of items. The Windows standard for list boxes is to display a minimum of three selections and a maximum of eight selections at a time. You should use a label control to provide keyboard access to the list box. Set the TabIndex property of the label control to a value that is one less than the list box's TabIndex value.

Next, you learn how to specify the items to display in a list box.

Adding Items to a List Box

The items in a list box belong to a collection called the **Items collection**. A **collection** is simply a group of one or more individual objects treated as one unit. The first item in the Items collection appears as the first item in the list box, the second item appears as the second item in the list box, and so on. Each item in a collection is identified by a unique number called an **index**. The first item in the Items collection—and, therefore, the first item in the list box—has an index of zero; the second item has an index of one, and so on.

You use the Items collection's **Add method** to specify each item you want displayed in a list box. You typically enter the Add methods in the form's Load event procedure. As you learned in Chapter 9, the form's Load event occurs before the form is displayed the first time.

Figure 10.20 shows the syntax of the Add method and includes examples of using the method to add items to a list box. In the syntax, *object* is the name of the control to which you want the item added, and *item* is the text you want displayed in the control.

HOW TO...

TIP

You also can use the Items collection's Insert method to add an item at a desired position in the list box. The syntax of the Insert method is *object*.**Items.Insert**(*position, item*). For example, the statement **Me.lstName.Items. Insert(0, "Carol")** inserts "Carol" as the first name in the lstName control.

TIP

As you learned in Chapter 4, ASCII stands for American Standard Code for Information Interchange and is the coding scheme used by microcomputers to represent the numbers, letters, and symbols on your keyboard.

TIP

If a list box's Sorted property is set to True, the items 1, 2, 3, and 10 will appear in the following order in the list box: 1, 10, 2, and 3. This is because items in a list box are sorted based on the ASCII value of the leftmost character in the item.

Add Items to a List Box

Syntax
object.**Items.Add**(*item*)

Examples
```
Me.lstAnimal.Items.Add("Dog")
```
displays the string "Dog" in the lstAnimal control

```
Me.lstAge.Items.Add(35)
```
displays the number 35 in the lstAge control

```
For decRate = 0D To 5D Step .5D
    Me.lstRate.Items.Add(decRate)
Next decRate
```
displays the numbers from 0 through 5, in increments of .5, in the lstRate control

FIGURE 10.20 How to add items to a list box

In the first example shown in Figure 10.20, the `Me.lstAnimal.Items. Add("Dog")` statement adds the string "Dog" to the lstAnimal control. In the second example, the `Me.lstAge.Items.Add(35)` statement adds the number 35 to the lstAge control. In the last example, the `Me.lstRate.Items.Add(decRate)` statement contained in the For...Next loop displays numbers from zero through five, in increments of .5, in the lstRate control.

When you use the Add method to add an item to a list box, the position of the item in the list depends on the value stored in the list box's Sorted property. If the Sorted property contains its default value, False, the item is added to the end of the list. However, if the Sorted property is set to True, the item is sorted along with the existing items, and then placed in its proper position in the list. Visual Basic .NET sorts the list box items in ascending ASCII order, which means that numbers are sorted first, followed by uppercase letters, and then lowercase letters.

Whether you display the list box items in sorted order, or display them in the order in which they are added to the list box, depends on the application. If several list items are selected much more frequently than other items, you typically leave the list box's Sorted property set to False, and then add the frequently used items first, so that the items appear at the beginning of the list. However, if the list box items are selected fairly equally, you typically set the list box's Sorted property to True, because it is easier to locate items when they appear in a sorted order.

When you select an item in a list box, the item appears highlighted in the list. Additionally, the computer stores the item's value in the list box's SelectedItem property, and stores the item's index in the list box's SelectedIndex property.

It is customary in Windows applications to have one of the items in the list box selected when the interface appears. The selected item, called the **default list box item**, should be either the most used selection or, if all of the selections are used fairly equally, the first selection in the list. You can use either the list box's SelectedItem property or its SelectedIndex property to select an item in a list box.

The SelectedItem and SelectedIndex Properties

A list box's SelectedItem property and its SelectedIndex property can be used both to determine the item selected in the list box and to select a list box item from code. Figure 10.21 shows examples of using these properties.

HOW TO...

Use the SelectedItem and SelectedIndex Properties

Example 1
```
Me.lblName.Text = Convert.ToString(Me.lstName.SelectedItem)
```
displays the contents of the lstName control's SelectedItem property in the lblName control

Example 2
```
If Convert.ToInt32(Me.lstHours.SelectedItem) > 40 Then
```
determines whether the value of the item selected in the lstHours control is greater than 40

Example 3
```
Me.lstRate.SelectedItem = 7
```
selects the number 7 in the lstRate control

Example 4
```
MessageBox.Show(Convert.ToString(Me.lstName.SelectedIndex))
```
displays the contents of the lstName control's SelectedIndex property in a message box

Example 5
```
If Convert.ToInt32(Me.lstHours.SelectedIndex) = 0 Then
```
determines whether the first item is selected in the lstHours control

Example 6
```
Me.lstRate.SelectedIndex = 2
```
selects the third item in the lstRate control

FIGURE 10.21 How to use the SelectedItem and SelectedIndex properties

---

The statement shown in Example 1 in Figure 10.21 assigns the contents of the lstName control's SelectedItem property to the lblName control. If the name "Jenny" is selected in the lstName control, the statement displays "Jenny" in the lblName control. In Example 2, the If clause compares the contents of the lstHours control's SelectedItem property with the number 40 to determine whether the employee worked more than 40 hours. You can use the `Me.lstRate.SelectedItem = 7` statement shown in Example 3 to select the item whose value is 7 in the lstRate control.

The statement shown in Example 4 in Figure 10.21 displays the contents of the lstName control's SelectedIndex property in a message box. If the second item is selected in the lstName control, the statement displays the number 1. However, if no item is selected in the 1stName control, the statement displays the number -1. In Example 5, the If clause compares the contents of the lstHours control's SelectedIndex property with the number 0 to determine whether the first item is selected in the control. You can use the `Me.lstRate.SelectedIndex = 2` statement shown in Example 6 to select the third item in the lstRate control.

Figure 10.22 shows the modified code for the Gentry Supplies application, and Figure 10.23 shows a sample run of the application using a list box in the interface.

```
'Project name:          Gentry Project
'Project purpose:       The project displays a shipping charge
'                       based on the state and method of delivery
'                       chosen by the user.
'Created/revised by:    Diane Zak on 2/1/2005

Option Explicit On
Option Strict On

Public Class frmGentry
    Inherits System.Windows.Forms.Form

[Windows Form Designer generated code]

    Private Sub frmGentry_Load(ByVal sender As Object, _
        ByVal e As System.EventArgs) Handles MyBase.Load
        'fill the list box with the state names

        Me.lstState.Items.Add("Alabama")
        Me.lstState.Items.Add("Georgia")
        Me.lstState.Items.Add("Louisiana")
        Me.lstState.Items.Add("North Carolina")


        'select the first item in the list
        Me.lstState.SelectedIndex = 0

    End Sub

    Private Sub btnExit_Click(ByVal sender As Object, _
        ByVal e As System.EventArgs) Handles btnExit.Click
        'ends the application
        Me.Close()
    End Sub

    Private Sub btnDisplay_Click(ByVal sender As Object, _
        ByVal e As System.EventArgs) Handles btnDisplay.Click
        'displays a shipping charge

        'declare variables
        Dim strState As String
        Dim intShipping As Integer
```

Fills the list box with state names — Me.lstState.Items.Add lines

Selects the first item in the list box — Me.lstState.SelectedIndex = 0

(Figure is continued on next page)

Assigns the
selected item to
a variable

```
'assign selected state to a variable
strState = Convert.ToString(Me.lstState.SelectedItem)

'determine appropriate shipping charge based on the state
If strState = "Alabama" Then
    intShipping = 20
ElseIf strState = "Georgia" Then
    intShipping = 35
ElseIf strState = "Louisiana" Then
    intShipping = 30
Else
    intShipping = 28
End If

'add $10 for overnight delivery
If Me.chkOvernight.Checked Then
    intShipping = intShipping + 10
End If

'display shipping charge
Me.lblShipping.Text = intShipping.ToString("C2")
End Sub

End Class
```

FIGURE 10.22   Modified code for the Gentry Supplies application

FIGURE 10.23   Sample run of the Gentry Supplies application using a list box

Notice that the form's Load event procedure in Figure 10.22 fills the lstState list box with the state names. It also selects the first state name in the list. The `strState = Convert.ToString(Me.lstState.SelectedItem)` statement in the btnDisplay_Click procedure uses the list box's SelectedItem method to access the state name selected by the user; it assigns the name to the strState variable.

If you do need to use a text box to get user input, you can use the text box's KeyPress event to prevent the user from typing unwanted characters.

USING THE KEYPRESS EVENT

A control's **KeyPress event** occurs when the user presses a key while the control has the focus. When the KeyPress event occurs, a character corresponding to the key that was pressed is sent to the KeyPress event's **e** parameter, which appears in the procedure header in every event procedure. For example, when you press the period (.) on your keyboard, a period is sent to the **e** parameter. Similarly, when you press the Shift key along with a letter key on your keyboard, the uppercase version of the letter is sent to the **e** parameter.

One popular use for the KeyPress event is to prevent users from entering inappropriate characters in a text box. For example, a text box for entering a person's age should contain numbers only; it should not contain letters or special characters, such as the dollar sign or percent sign. To prevent a text box from accepting inappropriate characters, you first use the **e** parameter's **KeyChar property** to determine the key that the user pressed. You then use the **e** parameter's **Handled property** to cancel the key if it is an inappropriate one. Figure 10.24 shows examples of using the KeyChar and Handled properties in the KeyPress event procedure.

TIP

KeyChar stands for "key character".

HOW TO...

Prevent a Text Box From Accepting Inappropriate Characters

Example 1
```
Private Sub txtSales_KeyPress(ByVal sender As Object, _
        ByVal e As System.Windows.Forms.KeyPressEventArgs) _
        Handles txtSales.KeyPress
    If e.KeyChar = "$" Then
            e.Handled = True
    End If
End Sub
```
prevents the text box from accepting the dollar sign

Example 2
```
Private Sub txtAge_KeyPress(ByVal sender As Object, _
        ByVal e As System.Windows.Forms.KeyPressEventArgs) _
        Handles txtAge.KeyPress
    If e.KeyChar < "0" OrElse e.KeyChar > "9" Then
            e.Handled = True
    End If
End Sub
```
allows the text box to accept only numbers

Example 3
```
Private Sub txtAge_KeyPress(ByVal sender As Object, _
        ByVal e As System.Windows.Forms.KeyPressEventArgs) _
        Handles txtAge.KeyPress
    If (e.KeyChar < "0" OrElse e.KeyChar > "9") _
            AndAlso e.KeyChar <> ControlChars.Back Then
            e.Handled = True
    End If
End Sub
```
allows the text box to accept only numbers and the Backspace key

FIGURE 10.24 How to prevent a text box from accepting inappropriate characters

The selection structure shown in Example 1 in Figure 10.24 prevents the txtSales control from accepting the dollar sign. The e.KeyChar = "$" condition in the selection structure compares the contents of the e parameter's KeyChar property with a dollar sign ($). If the condition evaluates to True, which means that a dollar sign is stored in the KeyChar property, the e.Handled = True instruction cancels the key before it is entered in the txtSales control.

You can use the selection structure shown in Example 2 in Figure 10.24 to prevent a text box from accepting a character that is not a number. However, keep in mind that Example 2's selection structure also prevents the text box from accepting the Backspace key. In other words, when entering text in the txtAge control, you will not be able to use the Backspace key to delete a character entered in the text box. You can, however, use the left and right arrow keys to position the insertion point immediately before the character you want to delete, and then use the Delete key to delete the character.

Like Example 2's selection structure, the selection structure shown in Example 3 in Figure 10.24 also prevents the txtAge control from accepting a character that is not a number. However, unlike Example 2's selection structure, Example 3's selection structure allows the user to employ the Backspace key, which is represented by the constant ControlChars.Back. Basically, Example 3's selection structure tells the KeyPress event to cancel a key if it is not a number and, at the same time, it is not the Backspace key.

You also can prevent some input errors by selecting the existing text when a text box receives the focus.

SELECTING THE EXISTING TEXT IN A TEXT BOX

When you select the existing text in a text box, the user can remove the text simply by pressing a key—for example, the letter "n" on the keyboard. The key that is pressed –in this case, the letter "n"—replaces the selected text in the text box.

You use the **SelectAll method** to select all of the text contained in a text box. Figure 10.25 shows the syntax of the SelectAll method and includes an example of using the method. In the syntax, *textbox* is the name of the text box whose text you want to select.

HOW TO...

Select the Existing Text in a Text Box

Syntax
textbox.**SelectAll()**

Example
```
Private Sub txtName_Enter(ByVal sender As Object, _
        ByVal e As System.EventArgs) Handles txtName.Enter
        'selects the existing text in the text box
        Me.txtName.SelectAll()
End Sub
```

FIGURE 10.25 How to select the existing text in a text box

In the example shown in Figure 10.25, the SelectAll method is entered in the txtName control's Enter event. A text box's **Enter event** occurs when the user tabs to the control, and when the Focus method is used in code to send the focus to the control. When the txtName control's Enter event occurs, the `Me.txtName.SelectAll()` statement selects (highlights) the existing text in the control.

Lastly, you learn how to associate a procedure with different events.

ASSOCIATING A PROCEDURE WITH DIFFERENT EVENTS

As mentioned in Chapter 1, you can associate the same procedure with more than one event. To do so, you list each event, separated by commas, in the `Handles` section of the procedure header. You can use the Gentry Supplies application to observe how this works.

Assume that, when the user clicks a different state name in the lstState control shown in Figure 10.23, or when he or she clicks the Overnight delivery check box, you want to clear the current contents of the lblShipping control, because the shipping charge displayed in the control is no longer valid. To clear the control, you can enter the `Me.lblShipping.Text = ""` statement in two event procedures: the lstState control's **SelectedValueChanged event**, which occurs when you select a different value in the list box, and the chkOvernight control's Click event procedure, which occurs when you click the check box. You also can create an independent Sub procedure, and then list the appropriate events after the Handles section in the procedure header, as shown in Figure 10.26.

```
Private Sub ClearShippingLabel(ByVal sender As Object, _
        ByVal e As System.EventArgs) _
        Handles lstState.SelectedValueChanged, chkOvernight.Click
        'clears the shipping charge from the lblShipping control
        Me.lblShipping.Text = ""
End Sub
```

FIGURE 10.26 Example of associating a procedure with different events

TIP

You can use a text box's TextChanged event to perform an action (such as cleaning a label control) when a change is made to the contents of the text box.

Notice that two events are listed in the Handles section of the ClearShippingLabel procedure: `lstState.SelectedValueChanged` and `chkOvernight.Click`. When either event occurs, the computer processes the `Me.lblShipping.Text` statement contained in the procedure; that statement clears the contents of the lblShipping control. Rather than using the list box's SelectedValueChanged event, you also can use its **SelectedIndexChanged event**, which also occurs when you select a different item in the list.

PROGRAMMING EXAMPLE

Glovers Application

Glovers Industries stores the item numbers, wholesale prices, and retail prices of the items it sells in a sequential access file named items.txt. Opal Jacoby, the company's sales manager, wants an application that allows her to enter an item number and then display either the wholesale price or the retail price. Open the Glovers Solution (Glovers Solution.sln) file, which is contained in the VbDotNet\Chap10\Glovers Solution folder. Open the items.txt sequential access file, which is contained in the VbDotNet\Chap10\Glovers Solution\Glovers Project\bin folder. Notice that the item numbers and prices appear on separate lines in the file. The item number is first, then the wholesale price, and then the retail price. Close the items.txt window, then create the Glovers Industries application.

TOE Chart:

Task	Object	Event
1. Search the mitmItems array for the item number selected in lstNumbers 2. Display (in lblPrice) the item's wholesale price if radWholesale is selected 3. Display (in lblPrice) the item's retail price if radRetail is selected	btnDisplay	Click
End the application	btnExit	Click
Display either the wholesale or retail price (from btnDisplay)	lblPrice	None
Get the item number	lstNumbers	None
1. Fill mitmItems array with data from items.txt file 2. Fill lstNumbers with item numbers 3. Select the first item in lstNumbers	frmGlovers	Load
Clear the contents of lblPrice	lstNumbers radWholesale radRetail	SelectedValueChanged Click Click

FIGURE 10.27

User Interface:

FIGURE 10.28

Objects, Properties, and Settings

Object	Property	Setting
frmGlovers	Name	frmGlovers (be sure to change the startup form to this name)
	AcceptButton	btnDisplay
	Font	Tahoma, 12 point (be sure to change the form's font before adding the controls)
	Size	408, 208
	StartPosition	CenterScreen
	Text	Glovers
Label1	AutoSize	True
	Text	Item &numbers:
Label2	AutoSize	True
	Text	Price:
lblPrice	Name	lblPrice
	BorderStyle	FixedSingle
	Text	(empty)
	TextAlign	MiddleCenter
radWholesale	Checked	True
	Name	radWholesale
	Text	&Wholesale
radRetail	Name	radRetail
	Text	&Retail
lstNumbers	Name	lstNumbers
	Sorted	True
btnDisplay	Name	btnDisplay
	Text	&Display Price
btnExit	Name	btnExit
	Text	E&xit

FIGURE 10.29

Tab Order:

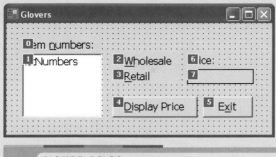

FIGURE 10.30

Pseudocode:

frmGlovers Load event procedure

include the following in the Try section of a Try/Catch block:
1. open the items.txt file for input
2. repeat until there are no more characters to read in the file or the end of the array is encountered
    read an item number, wholesale price, and retail price from the file, and assign to the mitmItems array
    add the item number to the lstNumbers control
    add 1 to the variable that keeps track of the array subscripts
   end repeat
3. close the items.txt file
4. select the first item in the lstNumbers control

include the following in the Catch section of a Try/Catch block:
1. use a general Catch statement to handle any errors
    if an error occurs, display a description of the exception in a message box

btnExit Click event procedure

1. close application

btnDisplay Click event procedure

1. assign the item number selected in the lstNumbers control to the strSearchForNumber variable
2. repeat until the item number is located in the mitmItems array
     add 1 to the variable that keeps track of the array subscripts
   end repeat
3. if the radWholesale control is selected
    display (in lblPrice) the wholesale price stored in the mitmItems array
  else
    display (in lblPrice) the retail price stored in the mitmItems array
  end if

radRetail and radWholesale Click event procedures, lstNumbers.SelectedIndexChanged procedure

1. clear the contents of the lblPrice control

Code:

```vbnet
'Project name:          Glovers Project
'Project purpose:       The project displays either the wholesale or
'                       retail price of an item.
'Created/revised by:    Diane Zak on 2/1/2005

Option Explicit On
Option Strict On

Public Class frmGlovers
    Inherits System.Windows.Forms.Form

[Windows Form Designer generated code]

    'define structure
    Structure Item
        Public strItemNumber As String
        Public decWholesalePrice As Decimal
        Public decRetailPrice As Decimal
    End Structure

    'declare module-level array
    Private mitmItems(4) As Item

    Private Sub frmGlovers_Load(ByVal sender As Object, ByVal e As System.EventArgs) _
        Handles MyBase.Load
        'fills the mitmItems array and lstNumbers control with data from a
        'sequential access file

        'declare variables
        Dim intSubscript As Integer
        Dim sreStreamReader As IO.StreamReader

        Try
            'create a StreamReader object by opening the file for input
            sreStreamReader = IO.File.OpenText("items.txt")

            'process the loop instructions until there are
            'no more characters to read or the end of the array is
            'encountered
            Do Until sreStreamReader.Peek() = -1 _
                OrElse intSubscript >= mitmItems.Length
                'read an item number, wholesale price, and retail price
                'from the file, and assign to the mitmItems array;
                'the information is stored on separate lines in the file
                mitmItems(intSubscript).strItemNumber = sreStreamReader.ReadLine()
                mitmItems(intSubscript).decWholesalePrice = _
                    Convert.ToDecimal(sreStreamReader.ReadLine())
                mitmItems(intSubscript).decRetailPrice = _
                    Convert.ToDecimal(sreStreamReader.ReadLine())
```

(Figure is continued on next page)

```
                        'add the item number to the lstNumbers control
                        Me.lstNumbers.Items.Add(mitmItems(intSubscript).strItemNumber)

                        'update the array subscript
                        intSubscript = intSubscript + 1
                    Loop

                    'close the file
                    sreStreamReader.Close()

                    'select a default item in the list box
                    Me.lstNumbers.SelectedIndex = 0

                Catch ex As Exception
                    MessageBox.Show(ex.Message, "Glovers", _
                        MessageBoxButtons.OK, MessageBoxIcon.Information)
                End Try

            End Sub

            Private Sub btnDisplay_Click(ByVal sender As Object, ByVal e As System.EventArgs) _
                Handles btnDisplay.Click
                'searches the mitmItems array for the item number selected
                'in the lstNumbers control, and then displays either its _
                'wholesale price or its retail price, depending on the selected
                'radio button

                'declare variables
                Dim strSearchForNumber As String
                Dim intSubscript As Integer

                'assign input to variable
                strSearchForNumber = Convert.ToString(Me.lstNumbers.SelectedItem)

                'add 1 to the array subscript until the item number is located
                'in the array
                Do Until mitmItems(intSubscript).strItemNumber = strSearchForNumber
                    intSubscript = intSubscript + 1
                Loop

                'when the item number is located in the array, display the
                'appropriate price in the lblPrice control, depending on the
                'selected radio button
                If Me.radWholesale.Checked Then
                    Me.lblPrice.Text = _
                        mitmItems(intSubscript).decWholesalePrice.ToString("C2")
                Else
                    Me.lblPrice.Text = _
                        mitmItems(intSubscript).decRetailPrice.ToString("C2")
                End If

            End Sub
```

(Figure is continued on next page)

```
    Private Sub btnExit_Click(ByVal sender As Object, ByVal e As System.EventArgs) _
        Handles btnExit.Click
        'ends the application
        Me.Close()
    End Sub

    Private Sub ClearPrice_Click(ByVal sender As Object, ByVal e As System.EventArgs) _
        Handles radRetail.Click, radWholesale.Click, lstNumbers.SelectedIndexChanged
        'clears the lblPrice control
        Me.lblPrice.Text = ""
    End Sub
End Class
```

FIGURE 10.31

Quick Review

- You can use the Structure statement to define a user-defined data type (or structure) in Visual Basic .NET. You typically enter the Structure statement in the form's Declarations section.
- After defining a structure, you can use the structure to declare a structure variable.
- A structure variable contains one or more member variables. You access a member variable using the structure variable's name, followed by the dot member access operator and the member variable's name.
- You usually use an assignment statement to assign a value to a member variable. The data type of the value must match the data type of the member variable.
- A structure variable can be passed to procedures.
- You can create a one-dimensional array of structure variables. You access a member variable in an array element using the array's name, followed by the element's subscript enclosed in parentheses, the dot member access operator, and the member variable's name.
- Use radio buttons when you want to limit the user to one of two or more related and mutually exclusive choices.
- The minimum number of radio buttons in a group is two, and the recommended maximum is seven.
- The label in the radio button's Text property should be entered using sentence capitalization.
- Assign a unique access key to each radio button in an interface.
- Use a group box control (or a panel control) to create separate groups of radio buttons. Only one button in each group can be selected at any one time.
- Designate a default radio button in each group of radio buttons.

- Use check boxes when you want to allow the user to select any number of choices from a group of one or more independent and nonexclusive choices.
- The label in the check box's Text property should be entered using sentence capitalization.
- Assign a unique access key to each check box in an interface.
- A list box should contain a minimum of three selections.
- A list box should display a minimum of three selections and a maximum of eight selections at a time.
- Use a label control to provide keyboard access to the list box. Set the label control's TabIndex property to a value that is one less than the list box's TabIndex value.
- List box items are either arranged by use, with the most used entries appearing first in the list, or sorted in ascending order.
- If a list box allows the user to make only one selection at a time, then a default item should be selected in the list box when the interface first appears. The default item should be either the most used selection or the first selection in the list.
- When an item is selected in a list box, the item appears highlighted in the list. The item's value is stored in the list box's SelectedItem property, and the item's index is stored in the list box's SelectedIndex property.
- When a control's KeyPress event occurs, a character corresponding to the key that was pressed is sent to the KeyPress event's e parameter.
- You can use the e parameter's KeyChar and Handled properties to prevent a text box from accepting inappropriate characters.
- It is customary in Windows applications to highlight, or select, the existing text in a text box when the text box receives the focus. To do so, you enter the SelectAll method in the text box's Enter event.
- You can enter more than one event after the `Handles` keyword in a procedure.
- When you select a different value in a list box, the list box's SelectedValueChanged and SelectedIndexChanged event occurs.

Key Terms

You use the **Structure statement** to create **user-defined data types** or **structures** in Visual Basic .NET.

The variables contained in a **structure variable**, which is a variable declared using a structure (user-defined data type), are called **member variables**.

When you assign initial values to an array, you are said to be **populating the array**.

You use the **RadioButton tool** to add a radio button to an interface.

A **radio button** allows you to limit the user to only one choice in a group of two or more related and mutually exclusive choices.

The **default radio button** is the radio button that is automatically selected when the interface first appears.

You use the **CheckBox tool** to add a check box to an interface.

Check boxes allow the user to select any number of choices from a group of one or more independent and nonexclusive choices.

You use the **ListBox tool** to add a list box to an interface.

A **list box** allows you to display a list of choices from which the user can select zero choices, one choice, or more than one choice.

The items in a list box belong to **Items collection**.

A **collection** is a group of one or more individual objects treated as one unit. Each item in a collection is identified by a unique number called an **index**.

You use the Items collection's **Add method** to specify the items you want displayed in a list box.

The **default list box item** is the item that is automatically selected when the interface first appears.

A control's **KeyPress event** occurs when the user presses a key while the control has the focus.

You can use the e parameter's **KeyChar property** to determine the key that the user pressed, and its **Handled property** to cancel the key.

ControlChars.Back is the Visual Basic .NET constant that represents the Backspace key on your keyboard.

A text box control's **Enter event** occurs when the user tabs to the control, and when the Focus method is used in code to send the focus to the control.

You can use the **SelectAll method** to select all of the text contained in a text box.

A list box's **SelectedValueChanged** and **SelectedIndexChanged events** occurs when a different value is selected in the list box.

Review Questions

1. You use the _____ statement to create a user-defined data type.
   a. Declare
   b. Define
   c. Structure
   d. UserType

2. Which of the following declares a Country variable named couSpain?
   a. `Private couSpain As Country`
   b. `Dim couSpain As Country`
   c. `Dim Country As couSpain`
   d. Both a and b.

3. Which of the following assigns the string "Madrid" to the strCity member of a Country variable named couSpain?
   a. `strCity.couSpain = "Madrid"`
   b. `Country.strCity = "Madrid"`
   c. `Country.couSpain.strCity = "Madrid"`
   d. `couSpain.strCity = "Madrid"`

4. Assume that an application uses a structure named Employee. Which of the following creates a five-element, one-dimensional array of Employee structure variables?
   a. `Dim empWorkers(4) As Employee`
   b. `Dim empWorkers(5) As Employee`
   c. `Dim empWorkers As Employee(4)`
   d. `Dim empWorkers As Employee(5)`

5. Assume that each structure variable in the invItems array contains two members: a String variable named strNumber and an Integer variable named intQuantity. Which of the following assigns the inventory number "123XY" to the first element in the array?
   a. `invItems(0).strNumber = "123XY"`
   b. `invItems(1).strNumber = "123XY"`
   c. `invItems.strNumber(0) = "123XY"`
   d. `invItems.strNumber(1) = "123XY"`

6. You use the _____ method to include items in a list box control.
   a. Add
   b. AddList
   c. Item
   d. ItemAdd

7. You use the _____ property to specify whether the user can select zero or more choices from a list box.
   a. Choices
   b. Number
   c. SelectionMode
   d. SelectionNumber

8. The items in a list box belong to the _____ collection.
   a. Items
   b. List
   c. ListBox
   d. Values

9. The _____ property stores the index of the item that is selected in a list box.
   a. Index
   b. SelectedIndex
   c. Selection
   d. SelectionIndex

10. When you select an item in a list box, the item is stored in the list box's _____ property.
    a. Item
    b. SelectedItem
    c. Selection
    d. SelectionItem

11. Which of the following adds the word DESK to a list box named lstOffice?
    a. `Me.lstOffice.AddItem("DESK")`
    b. `Me.lstOffice.AddItems("DESK")`
    c. `Me.lstOffice.Items.Add("DESK")`
    d. `Me.lstOffice.ItemAdd("DESK")`

12. The second item in a list box has an index of _____.
    a. 1
    b. 2
    c. 3

13. Which of the following selects the number 3, which is the first item in a list box named lstTerm?
    a. `Me.lstTerm.SelectedIndex = 0`
    b. `Me.lstTerm.SelectedIndex = 3`
    c. `Me.lstTerm.SelectedItem = 0`
    d. Both a and c.

14. The _____ event occurs when the user selects a different value in a list box.
    a. ChangeItem
    b. ChangeValue
    c. SelectNewItem
    d. SelectedValueChanged

15. The minimum number of radio buttons in a group is _____.
    a. one
    b. two
    c. three
    d. four

16. If a check box is selected, its _____ property contains the Boolean value True.
    a. Checked
    b. On
    c. Selected
    d. Value

17. A text box's _____ event occurs when the user tabs to the text box.
    a. Enter
    b. Focus
    c. Tab
    d. Tabbing

18. Which of the following tells the computer to select the contents of the txtName control?
    a. `txtName.Select()`
    b. `txtName.SelectAll()`
    c. `txtName.SelectText()`
    d. `txtName.TextSelect()`

19. When entered in a text box's KeyPress event, which of the following statements cancels the key pressed by the user?
    a. `Cancel = True`
    b. `e.Cancel = True`
    c. `e.Handled = True`
    d. `Handled = True`

20. Which of the following If clauses determines whether the user pressed the $ (dollar sign) key?
    a. `If ControlChars.DollarSign = True Then`
    b. `If e.KeyChar = "$" Then`
    c. `If e.KeyChar = Chars.DollarSign Then`
    d. `If KeyChar.ControlChars = "$" Then`

Exercises

1. Write a Structure statement that defines a structure named Book. The structure contains three member variables: strTitle, strAuthor, and decCost.

2. Write a Structure statement that defines a structure named Tape. The structure contains four member variables: strName, strArtist, intSong, and strLength.

3. Write a Private statement that declares a Book variable named mbooFiction.

4. Write a Dim statement that declares a Tape variable named tapBlues.

5. Assume that an application contains the following structure:

```
Structure Computer
        Public strModel As String
        Public decCost As Decimal
End Structure
```

   a. Write a Dim statement that declares a Computer variable named comHomeUse.
   b. Write an assignment statement that assigns the string "IB-50" to the strModel member variable.
   c. Write an assignment statement that assigns the number 2400 to the decCost member variable.

6. Assume that an application contains the following structure:

```
Structure Friend
        Public strLast As String
        Public strFirst As String
End Structure
```

   a. Write a Dim statement that declares a Friend variable named friSchool.
   b. Write an assignment statement that assigns the value in the txtFirst control to the strFirst member variable.
   c. Write an assignment statement that assigns the value in the txtLast control to the strLast member variable.
   d. Write an assignment statement that assigns the value in the strLast member variable to the lblLast control.
   e. Write an assignment statement that assigns the value in the strFirst member variable to the lblFirst control.

7. Assume that an application contains the following structure:

```
Structure Computer
        Public strModel As String
        Public decCost As Decimal
End Structure
```

   a. Write a Private statement that declares a 10-element, one-dimensional array of Computer variables. Name the array mcomBusiness.
   b. Write an assignment statement that assigns the string "HPP405" to the strModel member variable contained in the first array element.
   c. Write an assignment statement that assigns the number 3600 to the decCost member variable contained in the first array element.

8. Assume that an application contains the following structure:

```
Structure Friend
        Public strLast As String
        Public strFirst As String
End Structure
```

   a. Write a Private statement that declares a 5-element, one-dimensional array of Friend variables. Name the array mfriHome.
   b. Write an assignment statement that assigns the value in the txtFirst control to the strFirst member variable contained in the last array element.
   c. Write an assignment statement that assigns the value in the txtLast control to the strLast member variable contained in the last array element.

9. In this exercise, you code an application that writes data to a sequential access file.
   a. Create the Johnsons Lumber interface shown in Figure 10.4. Name the solution Johnsons Solution. Name the project Johnsons Project. Save the application in the VbDotNet\Chap10 folder.
   b. Use the code shown in Figure 10.5 to code the application.
   c. Save the solution, and then start the application. Test the application by writing the data for two employees to the employees.txt file.
   d. Click the Exit button to end the application.
   e. Open the employees.txt file in a separate window in the IDE. The file should contain the data for the two employees you entered.
   f. Close the employees.txt window, then close the solution.

10. In this exercise, you modify the application you created in Exercise 9 so that it writes the data contained in a structure to a sequential access file.
    a. Use Windows to make a copy of the Johnsons Solution folder, which is contained in the VbDotNet\Chap10 folder. Rename the copy Johnsons Structure Solution.
    b. Use Windows to delete the employees.txt file, which is contained in the VbDotNet\Chap10\Johnsons Structure Solution\Johnsons Project\ bin folder.
    c. Open the Johnsons Solution (Johnsons Solution.sln) file, which is contained in the VbDotNet\Chap10\Johnsons Structure Solution folder.
    d. Use the code shown in Figure 10.6 to modify the application.
    e. Save the solution, and then start the application. Test the application by writing the data for three employees to the employees.txt file.
    f. Click the Exit button to end the application.
    g. Open the employees.txt file in a separate window in the IDE. The file should contain the data for the three employees you entered.
    h. Close the employees.txt window, then close the solution.

11. In this exercise, you code an application that uses an array of structure variables.
    a. Create the Treasures interface shown in Figure 10.7. Name the solution Treasures Solution. Name the project Treasures Project. Save the application in the VbDotNet\Chap10 folder.
    b. Use the code shown in Figure 10.8 to code the application.
    c. Save the solution, and then start and test the application.
    d. Click the Exit button to end the application, then close the solution.

12. In this exercise, you code an application that uses radio buttons.
    a. Create the Gentry Supplies interface shown in Figure 10.10. Name the solution Gentry Radio Buttons Solution. Name the project Gentry Radio Buttons Project. Save the application in the VbDotNet\Chap10 folder.
    b. Code the application. Use the code shown in Figure 10.12 to code the btnDisplay_Click procedure.
    c. Save the solution, and then start and test the application.
    d. Click the Exit button to end the application, then close the solution.

13. In this exercise, you code an application that uses a check box.
    a. Create the Gentry Supplies interface shown in Figure 10.15. Name the solution Gentry Check Box Solution. Name the project Gentry Check Box Project. Save the application in the VbDotNet\Chap10 folder.
    b. Code the application. Use the code shown in Figure 10.16 to code the btnDisplay_Click procedure.

c. Save the solution, and then start and test the application.

d. Click the Exit button to end the application, then close the solution.

14. In this exercise, you code an application that uses a list box.

a. Create the Gentry Supplies interface shown in Figure 10.19. Name the solution Gentry List Box Solution. Name the project Gentry List Box Project. Save the application in the VbDotNet\Chap10 folder.

b. Use the code shown in Figure 10.22 to code the application.

c. Save the solution, and then start and test the application.

d. Click the Exit button to end the application, then close the solution.

15. In this exercise, you modify this chapter's Programming Example.

a. Create the Glovers application shown in this chapter's Programming Example. Save the application in the VbDotNet\Chap10 folder.

b. Use Windows to make a copy of the Glovers Solution folder. Rename the copy Glovers Check Box Solution.

c. Open the Glovers Solution (Glovers Solution.sln) file, which is contained in the VbDotNet\Chap10\Glovers Check Box Solution folder.

d. Modify the application so that it uses two check boxes rather than two radio buttons. If the Wholesale check box is selected, the application should display the wholesale price. If the Retail check box is selected, the application should display the retail price. If both check boxes are selected, the application should display the wholesale price and the retail price. If neither check box is selected, display a message prompting the user to make a selection.

e. Save the solution, then start and test the application.

f. Click the Exit button to end the application, then close the solution.

16. In this exercise, you modify this chapter's Programming Example.

a. Create the Glovers application shown in this chapter's Programming Example. Save the application in the VbDotNet\Chap10 folder.

b. Use Windows to make a copy of the Glovers Solution folder. Rename the copy Glovers Three Arrays Solution.

c. Open the Glovers Solution (Glovers Solution.sln) file, which is contained in the VbDotNet\Chap10\Glovers Three Arrays Solution folder.

d. Modify the application so that it uses three parallel one-dimensional arrays instead of a one-dimensional array of structure variables.

e. Save the solution, then start and test the application.

f. Click the Exit button to end the application, then close the solution.

17. In this exercise, you code an application that allows Professor Hansen to display a grade based on the number of points she enters. The grading scale is shown in Figure 10.32.

Minimum points	Maximum points	Grade
0	299	F
300	349	D
350	399	C
400	449	B
450	500	A

FIGURE 10.32

a. Open the Hansen Solution (Hansen Solution.sln) file, which is contained in the VbDotNet\Chap10\Hansen Solution folder.

b. Create a structure that contains two member variables: an Integer variable for the minimum points and a String variable for the grades.

c. Use the structure to declare a five-element, one-dimensional array. Store the grading scale in the array.

d. Code the Display Grade button's Click event procedure so that it searches the array for the number of points entered by the user, and then displays the corresponding grade from the array.

d. Save the solution, and then start the application. Enter 455 in the Points text box, then click the Display Grade button. A grade of A appears in the interface.

e. Enter 210 in the Points text box, then click the Display Grade button. A grade of F appears in the interface.

f. Click the Exit button to end the application, then close the solution.

18. In this exercise, you code an application that allows Mr. Laury to display a shipping charge based on the number of items ordered by a customer. The shipping charge scale is shown in Figure 10.33.

Minimum order	Maximum order	Shipping charge
1	10	15
11	50	10
51	100	5
101	99999	0

FIGURE 10.33

a. Name the solution Laury Solution. Name the project Laury Project. Save the application in the VbDotNet\Chap10 folder.

b. Design an appropriate interface.

c. Create an appropriate structure. Use the structure to declare a one-dimensional array. Store the shipping charge scale in the array.

d. Code the application so that it searches the array for the number of items ordered, and then displays the corresponding shipping charge from the array.

e. Save the solution, and then start and test the application.

f. Close the application, then close the solution.

19. In this exercise, you code an application that displays the telephone extension corresponding to the name selected in a list box. The names and extensions are shown here:

Smith, Joe	3388
Jones, Mary	3356
Adkari, Joel	2487
Lin, Sue	1111
Li, Vicky	2222

a. Open the Phone Solution (Phone Solution.sln) file, which is contained in the VbDotNet\Chap10\Phone Solution folder.

b. Set the list box's Sorted property to True.

c. Code the form's Load event procedure so that it adds the five names shown above to the lstNames control. Select the first name in the list.

d. Code the list box's SelectedValueChanged event procedure so that it assigns the item selected in the lstName control to a variable. The procedure then should use the Select Case statement to display the telephone extension that corresponds to the name stored in the variable.

e. Save the solution, then start the application. Test the application by clicking each name in the list box.

f. Click the Exit button to end the application, then close the solution.

20. In this exercise, you modify the application that you coded in Exercise 19. The application will now assign the index of the selected item, rather than the selected item itself, to a variable.

a. Use Windows to make a copy of the Phone Solution folder, which is contained in the VbDotNet\Chap10 folder. Rename the copy Modified Phone Solution.

b. Open the Phone Solution (Phone Solution.sln) file, which is contained in the VbDotNet\Chap10\Modified Phone Solution folder.

c. Modify the list box's SelectedValueChanged event procedure so that it assigns the index of the item selected in the lstName control to a variable. The procedure then should use the Select Case statement to display the telephone extension that corresponds to the index stored in the variable.

d. Save the solution, then start the application. Test the application by clicking each name in the list box.

e. Click the Exit button to end the application, then close the solution.

21. In Chapter 8's Exercise 19, you created an application for the Political Awareness Organization (PAO). In this exercise, you modify the application so that it uses two list boxes rather than two text boxes.

a. Use Windows to copy the PAO Solution folder, which is contained in the VbDotNet\Chap08 folder, to the VbDotNet\Chap10 folder. Rename the copy PAO List Boxes Solution.

b. Use Windows to delete the pao.txt file contained in the VbDotNet\Chap10\PAO List Boxes Solution\PAO Project\bin folder.

c. Open the PAO Solution (PAO Solution.sln) file, which is contained in the VbDotNet\Chap10\PAO List Boxes Solution folder.

d. Modify the application so that it uses a list box for the political party entry, and a list box for the age group entry. The age groups are as follows: 18–35, 36–50, 51–65, and Over 65. The application should display the number of voters in each political party and the number of voters in each age group.

e. Save the solution, then start and test the application.

f. Click the Exit button to end the application, then close the solution.

22. In Chapter 8's Exercise 19, you created an application for the Political Awareness Organization (PAO). In this exercise, you modify the application so that it uses two groups of radio buttons rather than two text boxes.

a. Use Windows to copy the PAO Solution folder, which is contained in the VbDotNet\Chap08 folder, to the VbDotNet\Chap10 folder. Rename the copy PAO Radio Buttons Solution.

b. Use Windows to delete the pao.txt file contained in the VbDotNet\Chap10\PAO Radio Buttons Solution\PAO Project\bin folder.

c. Open the PAO Solution (PAO Solution.sln) file, which is contained in the VbDotNet\Chap10\PAO Radio Buttons Solution folder.

d. Modify the application so that it uses two groups of radio buttons: one group for the political party entry, and the other group for the age group entry. The age groups are as follows: 18–35, 36–50, 51–65, and Over 65. The application should display the number of voters in each political party and the number of voters in each age group.

      e. Save the solution, then start and test the application.

      f. Click the Exit button to end the application, then close the solution.

23. In this exercise, you modify this chapter's Programming Example.

      a. Create the Glovers application shown in this chapter's Programming Example. Save the application in the VbDotNet\Chap10 folder.

      b. Use Windows to make a copy of the Glovers Solution folder. Rename the copy Glovers Two Arrays Solution.

      c. Open the Glovers Solution (Glovers Solution.sln) file, which is contained in the VbDotNet\Chap10\Glovers Two Arrays Solution folder.

      d. Modify the application so that it uses a one-dimensional array to store the item number, and a parallel two-dimensional array to store the wholesale and retail prices.

      e. Save the solution, then start and test the application.

      f. Click the Exit button to end the application, then close the solution.

24. In this exercise, you find and correct an error in an application. The process of finding and correcting errors is called debugging.

      a. Open the Debug Solution (Debug Solution.sln) file, which is contained in the VbDotNet\Chap10\Debug Solution folder.

      b. Open the Code Editor window. Review the existing code.

      c. Notice that a jagged line appears below some of the lines of code in the Code Editor window. Correct the code to remove the jagged lines.

      d. Save the solution, then start and test the application. If an error message appears in a dialog box, click the Break button. Click Debug, then click Stop Debugging.

      e. Correct the errors in the application's code, then save the solution and start the application. Test the application.

      f. Click the Exit button to end the application, then close the solution.

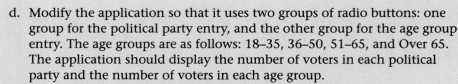

Case Projects

Glasgow Health Club

Each member of the Glasgow Health Club must pay monthly dues that consist of a basic fee and, optionally, one or more additional charges. The basic fee for a single membership is $50 per month. The basic fee for a family membership is $90 per month. If the member has a single membership, the additional charges are $30 per month for tennis, $25 per month for golf, and $20 per month for racquetball. If the member has a family membership, the additional charges are $50 per month for tennis, $35 per month for golf, and $30 per month for racquetball. The application should calculate and display a member's monthly dues.

Swanee Grade School

Susan Chen, the principal of Swanee Grade School, needs an application that the first and second grade students can use to practice both adding and subtracting numbers. The application should display the addition or subtraction problem on the screen, then allow the student to enter the answer, and then verify that the answer is correct. If the student's answer is not correct, the application should give him or her as many chances as necessary to answer the problem correctly.

The problems displayed for the first grade students should use numbers from 1 through 10 only. The problems for the second grade students should use numbers from 10 through 99. Because the first and second grade students have not learned about negative numbers yet, the subtraction problems should never ask them to subtract a larger number from a smaller one. To generate the random numbers for the math problems, first use the `Dim ranGenerator As Random` statement to create a variable that represents the Visual Basic .NET random number generator. You then can use the statement *variableName* = `ranGenerator.Next(1, 11)` to generate a random integer from 1 through 10, and the statement *variableName* = `ranGenerator.Next(10, 100)` to generate a random integer from 10 through 99.

Ms. Chen also wants the application to keep track of how many correct and incorrect responses the student makes; this information will help her assess the student's math ability. Finally, she wants to be able to control the display of this information to keep students from being distracted or pressured by the number of right and wrong answers.

Smoke Shack Barbeque

Smoke Shack Barbecue offers the following items on its lunch menu: rib plate ($5.50), chicken plate ($4.50), hot dog ($1.25), hamburger ($2.50), pulled pork sandwich ($3.00), sweet tea ($1.00), and soft drinks ($1.25). Create an application that allows the user to enter a customer's lunch order. (Keep in mind that the customer might be ordering for more than one person.) The application should display the price of the order without sales tax, the sales tax amount (use a 5% sales tax rate), and the total price of the order.

Harvey Industries

In the Chapter 7 Case Projects, you created an application for Khalid Patel, the payroll manager at Harvey Industries. Mr. Patel has asked you to modify the application so that it allows him to select the marital status using radio buttons. He also wants to select the hours, rate, and allowances from list boxes. Use hours from 1 through 50, rates from $6 to $12 in increments of $.50, and allowances of 1 through 10. Use two arrays of structure variables for the FWT tables. (The tables are shown in Figure 7.16 in Chapter 7.)

11

Creating Classes and Objects

CLASSES AND OBJECTS

As you learned in Chapter 1, object-oriented programs are based on objects, which are created, or instantiated, from classes. A text box, for example, is created from the TextBox class. Similarly, buttons and label controls are created from the Button class and Label class, respectively.

Recall that a class contains (encapsulates) the properties (attributes) that describe the object it creates, and the methods (behaviors) that allow the object to perform tasks. The TextBox class, for instance, contains the Name, CharacterCasing, and Text properties. Examples of methods contained in the TextBox class include Focus (which allows a text box to send the focus to itself) and SelectAll (which allows a text box to select its existing text).

In previous chapters, you created objects using classes that are built into Visual Basic .NET, such as the TextBox and Label classes. The objects created from the classes were used in a variety of ways in many different applications. For example, in some applications a text box was used to enter a name, while in other applications it was used to enter a sales tax rate. Similarly, label controls were used to identify text boxes and also display the result of calculations. The ability to use an object for more than one purpose saves programming time and money—an advantage that contributes to the popularity of object-oriented programming.

In addition to using the Visual Basic .NET classes, you also can define your own classes, and then create objects from the classes. The classes that you define can represent something encountered in real life—such as a credit card receipt, a check, and an employee.

TIP

Recall from Chapter 1 that each tool in the toolbox represents a class. When you drag a tool from the toolbox to the form, Visual Basic .NET uses the class to instantiate the appropriate object.

DEFINING A CLASS

Like the Visual Basic .NET classes, your classes must specify the properties and methods of the objects they create. The properties describe the characteristics of the objects, and the methods specify the tasks that the objects can perform.

You use the **Class statement** to define a class in Visual Basic .NET. Figure 11.1 shows the syntax of the Class statement and includes an example of using the statement to create a class named TimeCard.

HOW TO...

Define a Class

Syntax
Public Class *classname*
    properties section
    methods section
End Class

Example
```
Public Class TimeCard
    variables and Property procedures appear in the properties section
    Sub and Function procedures appear in the methods section
End Class
```

FIGURE 11.1   How to define a class

The Class statement begins with the keywords `Public Class`, followed by the name of the class; it ends with the keywords `End Class`. Although it is not required by the syntax, the convention is to capitalize the first letter in a class name, as well as the first letter in any subsequent words in the name. The names of Visual Basic .NET classes—such as String and TextBox—also follow this naming convention.

Within the Class statement, you define the properties and methods of the class. The properties are represented by variables and Property procedures, and the methods are represented by Sub and Function procedures. You learn various ways of defining the properties and methods later in this chapter.

You enter the Class statement in a class file. Figure 11.2 shows how to add a class file to the current project, and Figure 11.3 shows an example of a completed Add New Item – *projectname* dialog box.

HOW TO...

Add a Class File to the Current Project

1. Click Project on the menu bar.
2. Click Add Class. The Add New Item – *projectname* dialog box opens with Class selected in the Templates list box.
3. Type the name of the class followed by a period and the letters vb in the Name box.
4. Click the Open button.

FIGURE 11.2   How to add a class file to the current project

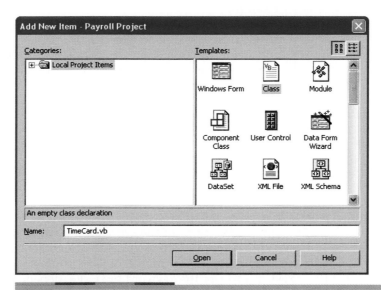

FIGURE 11.3   Completed Add New Item – *projectname* dialog box

When you click the Open button in the Add New Item – Payroll Project dialog box shown in Figure 11.3, the computer adds a file named TimeCard.vb to the current project. It also opens the file in the Code Editor window, as shown in Figure 11.4.

Form file

Class file

FIGURE 11.4   TimeCard.vb file opened in the Code Editor window

Notice that Visual Basic .NET automatically enters the Class statement in the TimeCard.vb file. You complete the Class statement by entering the properties and methods of the class. (Recall that you learn how to enter the properties and methods later in this chapter.)

After you define a class, you then can use the class to create objects. Figure 11.5 shows two versions of the syntax you use to create objects from a class. It also includes an example of using each syntax.

HOW TO...

Create an Object From a Class

Syntax - Version 1
accessibility objectVariable **As** *class*
objectVariable = **New** *class*

Syntax - Version 2
accessibility objectVariable **As New** *class*

Examples
```
Private mobjTimeCard As TimeCard
mobjTimeCard = New TimeCard
```
the first instruction creates a TimeCard variable named mobjTimeCard; the second instruction creates a TimeCard object and assigns its address to the mobjTimeCard variable

```
Dim objTimeCard As New TimeCard
```
the instruction creates a TimeCard variable named objTimeCard and a TimeCard object, and assigns the object's address to the variable

FIGURE 11.5   How to create an object from a class

In both versions of the syntax for creating an object, *class* is the name of the class the computer will use to create the object, and *objectVariable* is the name of a variable that will store the object's address. *Accessibility* is typically either the keyword `Dim` or the keyword `Private`, depending on whether the *objectVariable* has procedure or module scope.

Study closely the two examples shown in Figure 11.5. The first example uses Version 1 of the syntax shown in the figure. In the example, the `Private mobjTimeCard As TimeCard` statement creates a variable named mobjTimeCard that can store the address of a TimeCard object. (The "m" indicates that the variable has module scope, and the "obj" stands for "object.") The `mobjTimeCard = New TimeCard` statement in the example then creates a TimeCard object and assigns its address to the mobjTimeCard variable.

Example 1 — Using a Class That Contains Properties Only 419

The second example shown in Figure 11.5 uses Version 2 of the syntax. In the example, the `Dim objTimeCard As New TimeCard` statement creates both a variable named objTimeCard and a TimeCard object, and it assigns the object's address to the variable. Notice that the difference between both versions of the syntax used to create an object relates to when the object is actually created. In Visual Basic .NET, the object is created by the statement that contains the `New` keyword.

The easiest way to learn how to define classes and create objects is to view a few examples. You begin with a simple example that uses a class containing properties only.

EXAMPLE 1 — USING A CLASS THAT CONTAINS PROPERTIES ONLY

In Chapter 10, you learned that you can use the Structure statement to group together related data; you also can use the Class statement. For example, assume that the sales manager at Sweets Unlimited wants an application that allows him to save each salesperson's name, quarterly sales amount, and quarterly bonus amount in a sequential access file. The bonus amount is calculated by multiplying the sales amount by 5%. Figure 11.6 shows a sample run of the Sweets Unlimited application, and Figure 11.7 shows the Salesperson class defined in the Salesperson.vb file. Notice that the Salesperson.vb file contains the `Option Explicit On` and `Option Strict On` statements. As is true when coding a form, it's a good programming practice to enter both statements when coding a class.

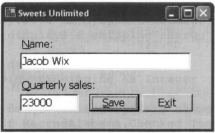

FIGURE 11.6   Sample run of the Sweets Unlimited application

Defines the Salesperson class

FIGURE 11.7   Salesperson class defined in the Salesperson.vb file

The Salesperson class contains three properties; each property is represented by a variable. Notice that the variable names (Name, Sales, and Bonus) do not begin with a three-character ID, which you used in previous chapters to identify the variable's data type. This is because the rules for naming properties differ slightly from the rules for naming variables. Properties should be assigned a name composed of one or more words, with the first letter of each word being capitalized. You should use nouns and adjectives to name a property, as in Bonus, TotalIncome, and FirstQuarterEarnings.

Notice that each variable (property) declaration in the Salesperson class begins with the keyword `Public`. When a property is declared using the `Public` keyword, it can be accessed by any application that uses an object created from the class. Figure 11.8 shows how you use the Salesperson class to code the Sweets Unlimited application.

```
'Project name:          Sweets Unlimited Project
'Project purpose:       The project writes the salesperson's name,
'                       quarterly sales amount, and a 5% quarterly bonus
'                       amount to a sequential access file.
'Created/revised by:    Diane Zak on 2/1/2005

Option Explicit On
Option Strict On

Public Class frmSweets
    Inherits System.Windows.Forms.Form

[Windows Form Designer generated code]

    Private Sub btnSave_Click(ByVal sender As Object, _
        ByVal e As System.EventArgs) Handles btnSave.Click
        'saves the sales information to a sequential access file

        'declare variables
        Dim objSalesperson As New Salesperson
        Dim swrStreamWriter As IO.StreamWriter

        Try
            'assign values to properties
            objSalesperson.Name = Me.txtName.Text
            objSalesperson.Sales = Convert.ToDecimal(Me.txtSales.Text)
            objSalesperson.Bonus = objSalesperson.Sales * 0.05D

            'open the file for append
            swrStreamWriter = IO.File.AppendText("sales.txt")

            'write the sales information
            swrStreamWriter.WriteLine(objSalesperson.Name _
                & "#" & objSalesperson.Sales.ToString("F2") & "#" _
                & objSalesperson.Bonus.ToString("F2"))

            'inform user that the record was written
            MessageBox.Show("The record was written.", _
                            "Sweets Unlimited", MessageBoxButtons.OK, _
                            MessageBoxIcon.Information)

            'clear the text boxes
            'then send the focus to the Name text box
            Me.txtName.Text = ""
            Me.txtSales.Text = ""
            Me.txtName.Focus()
```

Creates a Salesperson object and assigns its address to the objSalesperson variable

Assigns values to the object's properties

Writes the contents of the object's properties to a sequential access file

(Figure is continued on next page)

Example 1 — Using a Class That Contains Properties Only

421

```
                    'close the file
                    swrStreamWriter.Close()

            Catch exFormat As FormatException
                MessageBox.Show("The sales amount must be numeric.", _
                    "Sweets Unlimited", MessageBoxButtons.OK, _
                    MessageBoxIcon.Information)
            Catch ex As Exception
                MessageBox.Show(ex.Message, "Sweets Unlimited", _
                    MessageBoxButtons.OK, MessageBoxIcon.Information)
            End Try
        End Sub

        Private Sub btnExit_Click(ByVal sender As Object, _
            ByVal e As System.EventArgs) Handles btnExit.Click
            'ends the application
            Me.Close()
        End Sub
    End Class
```

FIGURE 11.8 Code for the Sweets Unlimited application

TIP

When you type **objSalesperson.** in the Code Editor window, the properties of a Salesperson object appear in a list. You then can select the appropriate property from the list.

TIP

Recall that "OOP" stands for "object-oriented programming."

In the btnSave_Click procedure shown in Figure 11.8, the `Dim objSalesperson As New Salesperson` statement uses the Salesperson class to create a Salesperson object; the statement assigns the object's address to the objSalesperson variable. After the object is created and its address assigned to a variable, you can access its properties using the syntax *objectVariable.property*, where *objectVariable* is the name of the variable that stores the object's address, and *property* is the name of the property you want to access. For example, you use `objSalesperson.Name` to access the Name property of the Salesperson object created in Figure 11.8. Likewise, you use `objSalesperson.Sales` and `objSalesperson.Bonus` to access the Sales and Bonus properties, respectively.

Notice that the btnSave_Click procedure shown in Figure 11.8 uses three assignment statements to assign values to the properties of the Salesperson object. The `objSalesperson.Name = Me.txtName.Text` statement assigns the contents of the txtName control to the object's Name property. Similarly, the `objSalesperson.Sales = Convert.ToDecimal(Me.txtSales.Text)` statement assigns the contents of the txtSales control, converted to Decimal, to the Sales property. Finally, the `objSalesperson.Bonus = objSalesperson.Sales * 0.05D` statement multiplies the contents of the Sales property by 5%, and then stores the result in the Bonus property. The procedure uses the WriteLine method to write the contents of the Name, Sales, and Bonus properties to a sequential access file named sales.txt.

Although you can define a class that contains properties only—like the Salesperson class shown in Figure 11.7—that is rarely done. This is because the purpose of a class in OOP is to encapsulate both the properties that describe an object and the methods that allow the object to perform tasks.

EXAMPLE 2 — USING A CLASS THAT CONTAINS PROPERTIES AND METHODS

In this example, you create a class named Square and then use the class in the Area application. The Square class creates an object that can calculate and return the area of a square, using the side measurement provided by the application. Figure 11.9 shows a sample run of the Area application, and Figure 11.10 shows the Square class defined in the Square.vb file.

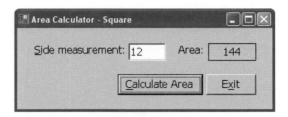

FIGURE 11.9   Sample run of the Area application

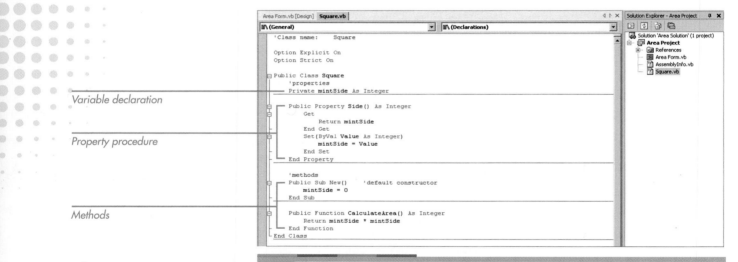

Variable declaration

Property procedure

Methods

FIGURE 11.10   Square class defined in the Square.vb file

The Square class contains the `Private mintSide As Integer` statement, which declares a Private variable named mintSide. The class will use the mintSide variable to store the side measurement of the square whose area is to be calculated. As in previous chapters, the letter "m" in the variable's name indicates that the variable has module scope, which means that it can be used only by the class in which it is defined. In this case, for example, the mintSide variable can be used only by the code entered in the Square class. The "int" in the variable's name identifies the variable's data type, which is Integer.

When you use a class to create an object in an application, only the variables and procedures declared using the `Public` keyword are exposed (made available) to the application; the variables and procedures declared using the `Private` keyword are hidden. When an application needs to assign data to or retrieve data from a Private variable in a class, it must use a Public property to do

Example 2 — Using a Class That Contains Properties And Methods   **423**

so. In other words, an application cannot refer, directly, to a Private variable in a class. Rather, it must refer to the variable indirectly, through the use of a Public property. You create a Public property using a **Property procedure**. Figure 11.11 shows the syntax of a Property procedure; it also includes the Property procedure entered in the Square class.

HOW TO...

Create a Property Procedure

Syntax
Public Property *propertyName*( ) **As** *datatype*
   Get
      [*instructions*]
      instruction to return the contents of the privateVariable
   End Get
   Set(ByVal Value As *datatype*)
      [*instructions*]
      instruction to assign, to the privateVariable, either the contents
      of the Value parameter or a default value
   End Set
End Property

Example
```
Public Property Side() As Integer
    Get
        Return mintSide
    End Get
    Set(ByVal Value As Integer)
        mintSide = Value
    End Set
End Property
```

FIGURE 11.11 How to create a Property procedure

A Property procedure begins with the keywords `Public Property`, followed by the name of the property, a set of parentheses, the keyword `As`, and the property's *datatype*. The data type of the property must match the data type of the *privateVariable* associated with the Property procedure. A Public Property procedure creates a property that is visible to any application that creates an object from the class.

A Property procedure ends with the keywords `End Property`. Within the Property procedure you define a Get block of code and a Set block of code. The code contained in the **Get block** allows an application to retrieve the contents of the *privateVariable* associated with the property. The code in the **Set block**, on the other hand, allows the application to assign a value to the *privateVariable*.

The Get block uses the **Get statement**, which begins with the keyword `Get` and ends with the keywords `End Get`. Most times, you will enter only one instruction in the Get statement. The instruction—typically, **Return** *privateVariable*—directs the computer to return the contents of the *privateVariable*.

The Set block uses the **Set statement**, which begins with the keyword `Set` and ends with the keywords `End Set`. As shown in Figure 11.11, the `Set` keyword is

TIP

As you learned earlier, properties should be assigned a name composed of one or more words, with the first letter of each word being capitalized. You should use nouns and adjectives to name a property.

followed by a parameter enclosed in parentheses. The parameter begins with the keywords `ByVal Value As`, followed by a *datatype*, which must match the data type of the *privateVariable* associated with the Property procedure. The Value parameter temporarily stores the value that the application wants assigned to the *privateVariable*.

You can enter one or more instructions within the Set statement. For example, you can enter the code to validate the value received from the application before assigning it to the *privateVariable*. If the value is valid, the last instruction in the Set statement should assign the contents of the Value parameter to the *privateVariable*; you can use the *privateVariable* = `Value` statement to do so. However, if the value received from the application is not valid, the last instruction in the Set statement should assign a default value—for example, the number zero—to the *privateVariable*.

In the example shown in Figure 11.11, the property's name is Side, and its data type is Integer to agree with the Private variable, named mintSide, associated with the Property procedure. The Get block in the Side property tells the computer to return the contents of the mintSide variable. The Set block, on the other hand, tells the computer to assign the contents of the Value parameter to the mintSide variable. An application that uses a Square object uses the Side property to assign values to and retrieve values from the mintSide variable.

As shown earlier in Figure 11.10, the Square class also contains two methods named New and CalculateArea. The New method is the default constructor for the class.

Constructors

A **constructor** is a method whose instructions the computer processes, automatically, each time an object is created (instantiated) from the class. The sole purpose of a constructor is to initialize the class's variables. Figure 11.12 shows the syntax of a constructor; it also includes the constructor entered in the Square class.

HOW TO...

How to Create a Constructor

Syntax
Public Sub New([*parameterlist*])
   instructions to initialize the class's variables
End Sub

Example
```
Public Sub New()
     mintSide = 0
End Sub
```

FIGURE 11.12 How to create a constructor

TIP

All constructors are Sub procedures rather than Function procedures; this is because a constructor never returns a value.

A constructor begins with the keywords `Public Sub New`, followed by a set of parentheses that contains an optional *parameterlist*. A constructor ends with the keywords `End Sub`. Within the constructor you enter the code to initialize the class's variables.

Example 2 — Using a Class That Contains Properties And Methods **425**

Every class should have at least one constructor. Each constructor included in a class has the same name, New, but its parameters (if any) must be different from any other constructor in the class. If a constructor contains one or more parameters, the values of the parameters are used to initialize the class's variables. A constructor that has no parameters is called the **default constructor**.

The Square class contains one constructor, which is shown in the example in Figure 11.12. The constructor is the default constructor, because it has no parameters. When you use the Square class to create a Square object, the computer automatically processes the class's default constructor, which, in this case, initializes the mintSide variable to the number zero.

A class also can contain methods other than constructors. The Square class, for example, contains a method named CalculateArea.

Methods Other Than Constructors

Except for constructors, which must be Sub procedures, the methods included in a class can be either Sub procedures or Function procedures. As you learned in Chapter 7, the difference between both types of procedures is that a Function procedure returns a value after performing its assigned task, whereas a Sub procedure does not return a value.

Figure 11.13 shows the syntax of a method that is not a constructor; it also includes the CalculateArea method entered in the Square class.

HOW TO...

How to Create a Method That Is Not a Constructor

Syntax
Public {Sub|Function} *methodname([parameterlist])* **As** *datatype*
    instructions
End {Sub|Function}

Example
```
Public Function CalculateArea() As Integer
     Return mintSide * mintSide
End Function
```

FIGURE 11.13 How to create a method that is not a constructor

The {**Sub | Function**} in the syntax shown in Figure 11.13 indicates that you can select only one of the keywords appearing within the braces. In this case, you can choose either the keyword `Sub` or the keyword `Function`.

The rules for naming methods are similar to the rules for naming properties. Like property names, method names should be composed of one or more words, with the first letter of each word being capitalized. However, unlike property names, the first word in a method name should be a verb; any subsequent words in the name should be nouns and adjectives. The name CalculateArea follows this naming convention.

The CalculateArea method in the Square class (shown earlier in Figure 11.10) is represented by a Function procedure. The `Return mintSide * mintSide` statement within the procedure uses the contents of the class's Private variable, mintSide, to calculate the area of a square. The statement then returns the area to the application that called the procedure.

Figure 11.14 shows how you can use the Square class to code the Area application.

```
'Project name:          Area Project
'Project purpose:       The project calculates the area of a square.
'Created/revised by:    Diane Zak on 2/1/2005

Option Explicit On
Option Strict On

Public Class frmArea
    Inherits System.Windows.Forms.Form

[Windows Form Designer generated code]

    Private Sub btnCalc_Click(ByVal sender As Object, _
        ByVal e As System.EventArgs) Handles btnCalc.Click
        'calculates the area of a square

        'declare variables
        Dim objSquare As New Square
        Dim intArea As Integer

        'assign input value to the property
        objSquare.Side = Convert.ToInt32(Me.txtSide.Text)

        'calculate and display the area
        intArea = objSquare.CalculateArea()
        Me.lblArea.Text = Convert.ToString(intArea)
    End Sub

    Private Sub btnExit_Click(ByVal sender As Object, _
        ByVal e As System.EventArgs) Handles btnExit.Click
        'ends the application
        Me.Close()
    End Sub
End Class
```

Creates a Square object and assigns its address to the objSquare variable

Assigns a value to the Side property

Uses the CalculateArea method to calculate the area of the Square object

FIGURE 11.14   Code for the Area application

The `Dim objSquare As New Square` statement shown in Figure 11.14 tells the computer to create a Square object, and then assign the object's address to a variable named objSquare. When creating the Square object, the computer uses the class's default constructor to initialize the Private variable (named mintSide) contained in the class.

The `objSquare.Side = Convert.ToInt32(Me.txtSide.Text)` statement shown in Figure 11.14 assigns the user's input to the Square object's Side property. The `intArea = objSquare.CalculateArea()` statement tells the computer to use the Square object's CalculateArea method to calculate and return the area of the object; the statement assigns the result to the intArea variable.

Next, you view an example of a class that contains more than one constructor. The class also performs some data validation.

EXAMPLE 3 — USING A CLASS THAT CONTAINS TWO CONSTRUCTORS AND DATA VALIDATION

In this example, you create a class named MyDate and then use the class in the Personnel application. The MyDate class creates an object that returns a month number, followed by a slash, and a day number. Figure 11.15 shows a sample run of the Personnel application, and Figure 11.16 shows the MyDate class defined in the MyDate.vb file.

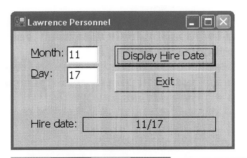

FIGURE 11.15   Sample run of the Personnel application

```
'Class name:     MyDate

Option Explicit On
Option Strict On

Public Class MyDate
    'properties
    Private mstrMonth As String
    Private mstrDay As String
```

(Figure is continued on next page)

The Set block in the Month Property procedure validates the month number

```
Public Property Month() As String
    Get
        Return mstrMonth
    End Get
    Set(ByVal Value As String)
        'verify that the Value parameter contains
        'a number from 1 through 12

        Try
            'declare variable
            Dim intMonth As Integer
            'assign value to variable
            intMonth = Convert.ToInt32(Value)
            'validate month number
            If intMonth >= 1 AndAlso intMonth <= 12 Then
                'assign Value to variable
                mstrMonth = Value
            Else   'assign empty string to variable
                mstrMonth = ""
            End If

        Catch ex As Exception
            MessageBox.Show("The Month must be numeric.", _
                "Month", MessageBoxButtons.OK, _
                MessageBoxIcon.Information)
        End Try
    End Set
End Property

Public Property Day() As String
    Get
        Return mstrDay
    End Get
    Set(ByVal Value As String)
        mstrDay = Value
    End Set
End Property

'methods
Public Sub New()      'default constructor
    mstrMonth = ""
    mstrDay = ""
End Sub
```

(Figure is continued on next page)

```
    Public Sub New(ByVal strM As String, ByVal strD As String)
        'assign month number to property
        Month = strM
        'assign day number to property
        Day = strD
    End Sub

    Public Function GetNewDate() As String
        'declare variable
        Dim strNewDate As String
        'format the date
        strNewDate = mstrMonth & "/" & mstrDay
        'return the formatted date
        Return strNewDate
    End Function

End Class
```

FIGURE 11.16   MyDate class defined in the MyDate.vb file

The MyDate class contains two Private variables named mstrMonth and mstrDay. It also contains two Property procedures named Month and Day. The Month Property procedure is associated with the mstrMonth variable, and the Day Property procedure is associated with the mstrDay variable.

Notice that the Set block in the Month Property procedure checks whether the Value parameter contains a number in the range of one through 12. If the month number is within the range, the Set block assigns the contents of the Value parameter to the mstrMonth variable; otherwise, it assigns the empty string to the variable.

In addition to the Private variables and Property procedures, the MyDate class also contains three methods: two named New and one named GetNewDate. Both New methods are constructors. The first constructor is the default constructor, because it does not have any parameters. The computer processes the default constructor when you use a statement such as `Dim objPayDate As MyDate` to create a MyDate object. Notice that assignment statements in the default constructor shown in Figure 11.16 initialize the two Private variables to the empty string.

The second constructor in the MyDate class allows you to specify the initial values for a newly created MyDate object. In this case, the initial values must be strings, because the constructor's *parameterlist* contains two String variables. You enter the initial values in the statement that creates the object. You enclose the initial values in parentheses because they are arguments. For example, the statement `Dim objPayDate As MyDate(strMonthNumber, strDayNumber)` creates a MyDate object and passes two String variables (arguments) to the MyDate class. The computer determines which class constructor to use by matching the number and data type of the arguments with the number and data type of the parameters listed in each constructor's *parameterlist*. In this case, the computer uses the constructor that contains two String variables in its *parameterlist*.

The GetNewDate method in the MyDate class is a Function procedure. Its purpose is to return the month and day numbers, separated by a slash. The month and day numbers are stored in the class's Private variables.

The methods in a class can reference the class's Private variables either directly (by name) or indirectly (through the Public properties). For example, in the

TIP

When two or more methods have the same name but different parameters, the methods are said to be overloaded. You can overload any methods contained in a class. However, if the methods are not constructors, you must use the keyword **Overloads** after the **Public** keyword in the first line of the method. The **Overloads** keyword is not used when overloading constructors.

MyDate class shown in Figure 11.16, both the default constructor and the GetNewDate method use the names of the Private variables to reference the variables directly. The second New constructor, on the other hand, uses the Public properties to reference the Private variables indirectly. You should always use a Public property to assign a value received from a program, because doing so ensures that the Set block, which typically contains validation code, is processed.

Figure 11.17 shows how you can use the Date class to code the Personnel application.

```
'Project name:          Personnel Project
'Project purpose:       The project displays the month number and day number,
'                       separated by a slash.
'Created/revised by:    Diane Zak on 2/1/2005

Option Explicit On
Option Strict On

Public Class frmPersonnel
    Inherits System.Windows.Forms.Form

[Windows Form Designer generated code]

    Private Sub btnDisplay_Click(ByVal sender As Object, _
        ByVal e As System.EventArgs) Handles btnDisplay.Click
        'displays a formatted date

        'declare variable and assign input
        Dim objHireDate As New MyDate(Me.txtMonth.Text, Me.txtDay.Text)

        'display the formatted date
        Me.lblDate.Text = objHireDate.GetNewDate()
    End Sub

    Private Sub btnExit_Click(ByVal sender As Object, _
        ByVal e As System.EventArgs) Handles btnExit.Click
        'ends the application
        Me.Close()
    End Sub
End Class
```

Creates a MyDate object and provides the initial values

Uses the GetNewDate method to get the formatted date

FIGURE 11.17   Code for the Personnel application

The `Dim objHireDate As New MyDate(Me.txtMonth.Text, Me.txtDay.Text)` statement creates a MyDate object, using the contents of the text boxes in the interface to initialize the Private variables in the class. The statement assigns the MyDate object's address to the objHireDate variable. The statement is equivalent to the following three lines of code:

```
Dim objHireDate As New MyDate
objHireDate.Month = Me.txtMonth.Text
objHireDate.Day = Me.txtDay.Text
```

The `Me.lblDate.Text = objHireDate.GetNewDate()` statement uses the MyDate object's GetNewDate method to return the month and day numbers, separated by a slash. The statement displays the formatted date in the lblDate control.

PROGRAMMING EXAMPLE

Kessler Landscaping Application

Monica Kessler, the owner of Kessler Landscaping, wants an application that she can use to estimate the cost of laying sod. In this application, you will use a MyRectangle class. Name the solution Kessler Solution. Name the project Kessler Project. Name the form file Kessler Form.vb. Name the class file MyRectangle.vb. Save the application in the VbDotNet\Chap11 folder.

TOE Chart:

Task	Object	Event
1. Calculate the area of the rectangle 2. Calculate the total price 3. Display the total price in lblTotalPrice	btnCalc	Click
End the application	btnExit	Click
Display the total price (from btnCalc)	lblTotalPrice	None
Get the length in feet	txtLength	None
Get the width in feet	txtWidth	None
Get the price of the sod per square yard	txtPrice	None
Clear the contents of lblTotalPrice	txtLength, txtWidth, txtPrice	TextChanged

FIGURE 11.18

User Interface:

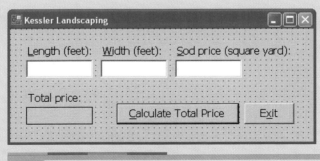

FIGURE 11.19

Objects, Properties, and Settings

Object	Property	Setting
frmKessler	Name	frmKessler (be sure to change the startup form to this name)
	AcceptButton	btnCalc
	Font	Tahoma, 12 point (be sure to change the form's font before adding the controls)
	Size	464, 208
	StartPosition	CenterScreen
	Text	Kessler Landscaping
Label1	AutoSize	True
	Text	&Length (feet):
Label2	AutoSize	True
	Text	&Width (feet):
Label3	AutoSize	True
	Text	&Sod price (square yard)):
Label4	AutoSize	True
	Text	Total price:
lblTotalPrice	Name	lblTotalPrice
	BorderStyle	FixedSingle
	Text	(empty)
txtLength	Name	txtLength
	Text	(empty)
txtWidth	Name	txtWidth
	Text	(empty)
txtPrice	Name	txtPrice
	Text	(empty)
btnCalc	Name	btnCalc
	Text	&Calculate Total Price
btnExit	Name	btnExit
	Text	E&xit

FIGURE 11.20

Tab Order:

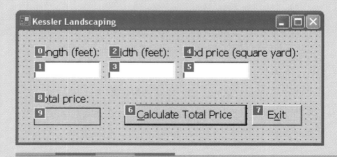

FIGURE 11.21

Pseudocode:

btnExit Click event procedure

1. close application

btnCalc Click event procedure

1. declare a MyRectangle object
2. assign the length and width to the MyRectangle object's properties
3. assign the sod price to a variable
4. calculate the area of the rectangle
5. calculate the total price of the sod
6. display the total price of the sod in lblTotalPrice

txtLength, txtWidth, and txtPrice TextChanged event procedures

1. clear the contents of the lblTotalPrice control

Code (MyRectangle.vb file):

```
'Class name:     MyRectangle

Option Explicit On
Option Strict On

Public Class MyRectangle
    'properties
    Private mdecLength As Decimal
    Private mdecWidth As Decimal

    Public Property Length() As Decimal
        Get
            Length = mdecLength
        End Get
        Set(ByVal Value As Decimal)
            mdecLength = Value
        End Set
    End Property

    Public Property Width() As Decimal
        Get
            Width = mdecWidth
        End Get
        Set(ByVal Value As Decimal)
            mdecWidth = Value
        End Set
    End Property
```

(Figure is continued on next page)

```
        'methods
        Public Sub New()      'default constructor
            mdecLength = 0D
            mdecWidth = 0D
        End Sub

        Public Function CalculateArea() As Decimal
            Return mdecLength * mdecWidth
        End Function

    End Class
```

FIGURE 11.22

Code (Kessler Form.vb file):

```
'Project name:          Kessler Project
'Project purpose:       The project calculates the cost of laying sod.
'Created/revised by:    Diane Zak on 2/1/2005

Option Explicit On
Option Strict On

Public Class frmKessler
    Inherits System.Windows.Forms.Form

[Windows Form Designer generated code]

    Private Sub btnExit_Click(ByVal sender As Object, ByVal e As System.EventArgs) _
        Handles btnExit.Click
        'ends the application
        Me.Close()
    End Sub

    Private Sub btnCalc_Click(ByVal sender As Object, ByVal e As System.EventArgs) _
        Handles btnCalc.Click
        'calculates the cost of laying sod
```

(Figure is continued on next page)

```
        'declare variables
        Dim recLawn As New MyRectangle
        Dim decSodPrice As Decimal
        Dim decArea As Decimal
        Dim decTotalPrice As Decimal

        Try
            'assign input to properties and variable
            recLawn.Length = Convert.ToDecimal(Me.txtLength.Text)
            recLawn.Width = Convert.ToDecimal(Me.txtWidth.Text)
            decSodPrice = Convert.ToDecimal(Me.txtPrice.Text)

            'calculate the area (in square yards)
            decArea = recLawn.CalculateArea() / 9D

            'calculate and display the total price
            decTotalPrice = decArea * decSodPrice
            Me.lblTotalPrice.Text = decTotalPrice.ToString("C2")

        Catch ex As Exception
            MessageBox.Show(ex.Message, "Kessler Landscaping", _
                MessageBoxButtons.OK, MessageBoxIcon.Information)
        End Try

    End Sub

    Private Sub ClearTotalPrice(ByVal sender As Object, ByVal e As System.EventArgs) _
        Handles txtLength.TextChanged, txtWidth.TextChanged, txtPrice.TextChanged
        'clears the total price
        Me.lblTotalPrice.Text = ""
    End Sub
```

FIGURE 11.23

Quick Review

- The objects used in an object-oriented program are created, or instantiated, from classes.
- A class contains (encapsulates) the properties (attributes) that describe the object it creates, and the methods (behaviors) that allow the object to perform tasks.
- In Visual Basic .NET, you can create objects from classes that you define with the Class statement.
- You enter the class definition in a class file, which you can add to the current project using the Project menu.
- It is a good programming practice to enter the Option Explicit On and Option Strict On statement in both the form file and the class file.
- The first letter in the class name, as well as the first letter in any subsequent words in the name, should be capitalized.
- The properties in a class should be assigned a name composed of one or more words, with the first letter of each word being capitalized. You should use nouns and adjectives to name a property.

- The methods in a class should be assigned a name composed of one or more words, with the first letter of each word being capitalized. You should use a verb for the first word in the name, and nouns and adjectives for any subsequent words in the name.
- Variables declared using the `Public` keyword in a class definition can be accessed by any application that uses an object created from the class.
- Most classes contain properties and methods.
- When an application needs to assign data to or retrieve data from a Private variable in a class, it must use a Public property to do so. You create a Public property using a Property procedure.
- The Get block in a Property procedure allows an application to access the contents of the class's Private variables.
- The Set block in a Property procedure allows an application to assign values to the class's Private variables.
- A class can have one or more constructors. All constructions are Sub procedures.
- The default constructor is automatically processed when an object is created from the class.

Key Terms

The **Class statement** allows you to define a class in Visual Basic .NET.

You use a **Property procedure** to create a Public property that allows the user to access the Private variables in a class.

The **Get block** in a Property procedure contains the **Get statement**. Within the Get statement, you enter the code that allows an application to retrieve the contents of the class's Private variables.

The **Set block** in a Property procedure contains the **Set statement**. Within the Set statement, you enter the code that allows an application to assign values to the class's Private variables.

A **constructor** is a method whose instructions are processed, automatically, each time you use the class to create (instantiate) an object.

A constructor that has no parameters is called the **default constructor**.

Review Questions

1. Which of the following statements is false?
   a. An example of an attribute is the intMinutes variable in a Time class.
   b. An example of a behavior is the SetTime method in a Time class.
   c. An object created from a class is referred to as an instance of the class.
   d. A class is considered an object.

2. In Visual Basic .NET, you enter the Class statement in _____.
   a. a class file that has a .vb extension on its filename
   b. a class file that has a .cls extension on its filename
   c. a form file that has a .cla extension on its filename
   d. a form file that has a .cls extension on its filename

3. The properties of an object are represented by _____ in a class.
   a. constants
   b. methods
   c. procedures
   d. variables

4. A Private variable in a class can be accessed directly by a Public method in the same class.
   a. True
   b. False

5. If a variable in a class is declared using the `Public` keyword, the variable can be accessed by any application that uses an object created from the class.
   a. True
   b. False

6. An application can access the Private variables in a class _____.
   a. directly
   b. using properties created by Property procedures
   c. through Private procedures contained in the class
   d. None of the above.

7. To expose a variable or method contained in a class, you declare the variable or method using the keyword _____.
   a. `Exposed`
   b. `Private`
   c. `Public`
   d. `Viewed`

8. The name of the default constructor for a class named Animal is _____.
   a. Animal
   b. AnimalConstructor
   c. Constructor
   d. None of the above.

9. A constructor can return a value.
   a. True
   b. False

10. A constructor _____.
    a. is a Function procedure
    b. is a Property procedure
    c. is a Sub procedure
    d. can be either a Function procedure or a Sub procedure

11. Which of the following creates an Animal object and assigns the object's address to the objDog variable?
    a. `Dim objDog As Animal`
    b. `Dim objDog As New Animal`
    c. `Dim objDog As Animal`
       `objDog = New Animal`
    d. Both b and c.

12. Assume an application creates an Animal object and assigns its address to the objDog variable. Which of the following calls the DisplayBreed method, which is contained in the Animal class?
    a. `Animal.DisplayBreed()`
    b. `DisplayBreed.Animal()`
    c. `DisplayBreed().objDog`
    d. `objDog.DisplayBreed()`

13. Before a class assigns values to its Private variables, it should validate the values. You enter the validation code in the _____ block in a Property procedure.
    a. Assign
    b. Get
    c. Set
    d. Validate

14. Following the naming convention discussed in the chapter, which of the following would be considered a good name for a method contained in a class?
    a. Bonus
    b. SalesIncome
    c. Setdate
    d. None of the above.

15. Following the naming convention discussed in the chapter, which of the following would be considered a good name for a property contained in a class?
    a. CalcBonus
    b. decSales
    c. FirstName
    d. Both b and c.

16. A class cannot contain more than one constructor.
    a. True
    b. False

17. Most classes contain only properties.
    a. True
    b. False

18. The `Option Explicit On` and `Option Strict On` statements can be entered in a form file only; they cannot be entered in a class file.
    a. True
    b. False

19. Assume an application creates a Date object and assigns its address to the objPayDate variable. Also assume that the Date class contains a Month property, which represents a String variable named strMonth. Which of the following assigns the number 12 to the Month property?
    a. `objPayDate.Month = "12"`
    b. `objPayDate.Month.strMonth = "12"`
    c. `objPayDate.strMonth = "12"`
    d. `Date.strMonth = "12"`

20. In a Property procedure, the Return statement is entered in the _____.
    a. Get block
    b. Set block

Exercises

1. Write a Class statement that defines a class named Book. The class contains three Public variables named Title, Author, and Cost.

2. Write a Class statement that defines a class named Tape. The class contains four Public variables named Name, Artist, SongNumber, and Length.

3. Use the syntax shown in Version 1 in Figure 11.5 to declare a variable named mobjFiction that can store the address of a Book object. Create the Book object and assign its address to the mobjFiction variable.

4. Use the syntax shown in Version 2 in Figure 11.5 to create a Tape object and assign its address to a variable named objBlues.

5. Assume that an application contains the class definition shown in Figure 11.24.

```
Public Class Computer
    'properties
    Private mstrModel As String
    Private mdecCost As Decimal

    Public Property Model() As String
        Get
            Return mstrModel
        End Get
        Set(ByVal Value As String)
            mstrModel = Value
        End Set
    End Property

    Public Property Cost() As Decimal
        Get
            Return mdecCost
        End Get
        Set(ByVal Value As String)
            mdecCost = Value
        End Set
    End Property

    'methods
    Public Sub New()
        mstrModel = ""
        mdecCost = 0D
    End Sub

    Public Function IncreasePrice() As Decimal
        Return mdecCost * 1.2D
    End Function
End Class
```

FIGURE 11.24

a. Write a Dim statement that creates a Computer object and assigns its address to a variable named objHomeUse.

b. Write an assignment statement that uses the Computer object created in Step a to assign the string "IB-50" to the mstrModel variable.

    c. Write an assignment statement that uses the Computer object created in Step a to assign the number 2400 to the mdecCost variable.

    d. Write an assignment statement that uses the Computer object created in Step a to call the IncreasePrice function. Assign the function's return value to a variable named decNewPrice.

6. Write the class definition for a class named Employee. The class should include Private variables and Property procedures for an Employee object's name and salary. (The salary may contain a decimal place.) The class also should contain two constructors: the default constructor and a constructor that allows an application to assign values to the Private variables.

7. Add another method to the Employee class you defined in Exercise 6. The method should calculate an Employee object's new salary, based on a raise percentage provided by the application using the object. Before calculating the new salary, the method should verify that the raise percentage is greater than or equal to zero. If the raise percentage is less than zero, the method should assign the number 0 as the new salary.

8. In this exercise, you use the Employee class from Exercise 7 to create an object in an application.

    a. Open the Salary Solution (Salary Solution.sln) file, which is contained in the VbDotNet\Chap11\Salary Solution folder.

    b. Open the Employee.vb class file in the Code Editor window, then enter the class definition from Exercise 7.

    c. View the Salary Form.vb file in the Code Editor window. Use the comments that appear in the code to enter the missing instructions.

    d. Save the solution, and then start the application.

    e. Test the application by entering your name, a current salary amount of 54000, and a raise percentage of 10 (for 10%). The application should display the number $59,400.

    f. Click the Exit button to end the application, then close the solution.

9. In this exercise, you create an application that uses a class.

    a. Create the Sweets Unlimited interface shown in Figure 11.6. Name the solution Sweets Unlimited Solution. Name the project Sweets Unlimited Project. Save the application in the VbDotNet\Chap11 folder.

    b. Add a class file to the project. Name the class file Salesperson.vb. Use the code shown in Figure 11.7 to define the class.

    c. Use the code shown in Figure 11.8 to code the Sweets Unlimited application.

    d. Save the solution, and then start and test the application.

    e. Click the Exit button to end the application, then close the solution.

10. In this exercise, you create an application that uses a class.

    a. Create the Area application's interface, which is shown in Figure 11.9. Name the solution Area Solution. Name the project Area Project. Save the application in the VbDotNet\Chap11 folder.

    b. Add a class file to the project. Name the class file Square.vb. Use the code shown in Figure 11.10 to define the class.

    c. Use the code shown in Figure 11.14 to code the Area application.

    d. Save the solution, and then start and test the application.

    e. Click the Exit button to end the application, then close the solution.

11. In this exercise, you create an application that uses a class.
    a. Create the Personnel application's interface, which is shown in Figure 11.15. Name the solution Personnel Solution. Name the project Personnel Project. Save the application in the VbDotNet\Chap11 folder.
    b. Add a class file to the project. Name the class file MyDate.vb. Use the code shown in Figure 11.16 to define the class.
    c. Use the code shown in Figure 11.17 to code the Personnel application.
    d. Save the solution, and then start and test the application.
    e. Click the Exit button to end the application, then close the solution.

12. In this exercise, you modify the application that you created in Exercise 11.
    a. Use Windows to make a copy of the Personnel Solution folder, which is contained in the VbDotNet\Chap11 folder. Rename the folder Modified Personnel Solution.
    b. Open the Personnel Solution (Personnel Solution.sln) file contained in the Modified Personnel Solution folder.
    c. Modify the interface to allow the user to enter the year number.
    d. The MyDate class should create an object that returns a month number, followed by a slash, a day number, a slash, and a year number. Modify the class appropriately.
    e. Modify the MyDate class to validate the day number, which should be from 1 through 31.
    f. Make the necessary modifications to the Personnel application's code.
    g. Save the solution, and then start and test the application.
    h. Click the Exit button to end the application, then close the solution.

13. In this exercise, you modify this chapter's Programming Example.
    a. Create the Kessler Landscaping application shown in this chapter's Programming Example. Save the application in the VbDotNet\Chap11 folder.
    b. Modify the MyRectangle class so that it verifies that the length and width entries are valid. To be valid, the entries must be greater than zero. If an entry is not valid, assign the number zero to the corresponding Private variable, and display an appropriate message.
    c. Modify the application so that it verifies that the sod price text box has been completed. If it hasn't been completed, assign the number zero to the decSodPrice variable.
    d. Save the solution, then start and test the application.
    e. Click the Exit button to end the application, then close the solution.

14. In this exercise, you modify the MyRectangle class, which you created in this chapter's Programming Example, and then use the class in a different application.
    a. Assume that Jack Sysmanski, the owner of All-Around Fence Company, wants a program that he can use to calculate the cost of installing a fence. Create an interface that allows the user to enter the length and width (both in feet) of a rectangle, as well as the fence cost per linear foot. Name the solution Fence Solution. Name the project Fence Project. Save the application in the VbDotNet\Chap11 folder.
    b. Use Windows to copy the MyRectangle.vb file from the VbDotNet\Chap11\Kessler Solution\Kessler Project folder to the VbDotNet\Chap11\Fence Solution\Fence Project folder.
    c. Use the Project menu to add the existing MyRectangle.vb class file to the Fence project.

d. Modify the MyRectangle class so that it calculates the perimeter of a rectangle. To calculate the perimeter, the class will need to add together the length and width measurements, and then multiply the sum by two.

e. Code the Fence application so that it displays the cost of installing the fence.

f. Save the solution, and then start the application. Test the application using 120 as the length, 75 as the width, and 10 as the cost per linear foot. The application should display $3,900.00 as the installation cost.

g. End the application, then close the solution.

15. In this exercise, you modify the MyRectangle class, which you created in this chapter's Programming Example, and then use the class in a different application.

a. The manager of Pool-Time, which sells in-ground pools, wants an application that the salespeople can use to determine the number of gallons of water required to fill an in-ground pool—a question commonly asked by customers. (Hint: To calculate the number of gallons, you need to find the volume of the pool. You can do so using the formula length * width * depth.) Create an appropriate interface. Name the solution Pool Solution. Name the project Pool Project. Save the application in the VbDotNet\Chap11 folder.

b. Use Windows to copy the MyRectangle.vb file from the VbDotNet\Chap11\Kessler Solution\Kessler Project folder to the VbDotNet\Chap11\Pool Solution\Pool Project folder.

c. Use the Project menu to add the existing MyRectangle.vb class file to the Pool project.

d. Modify the MyRectangle class appropriately.

e. Code the Pool application so that it displays the number of gallons. To calculate the number of gallons, you divide the volume by .13368.

f. Save the solution, and then start the application. Test the application using 25 feet as the length, 15 as the width, and 6.5 feet as the depth. The application should display 18,233.84 as the number of gallons.

g. Click the Exit button to end the application, then close the solution.

16. In this exercise, you define a Triangle class. You also create an application that uses the Triangle class to create a Triangle object.

a. Create an interface that allows the user to display either the area of a triangle or the perimeter of a triangle. (Hint: The formula for calculating the area of a triangle is ½ * base * height. The formula for calculating the perimeter of a triangle is a + b + c, where a, b, and c are the lengths of the sides.) Name the solution Math Solution. Name the project Math Project. Save the application in the VbDotNet\Chap11 folder.

b. Add a class file to the project. Name the class file Triangle.vb. The Triangle class should verify that the dimensions are greater than zero before assigning the values to the Private variables. The class also should include a method to calculate the area of a triangle and a method to calculate the perimeter of a triangle.

c. Save the solution, and then start and test the application.

d. Stop the application, then close the solution.

17. In this exercise, you learn how to create a region of code. The Code Editor window uses a region to hide the code generated by the Windows Form Designer. You also can create a region to hide sections of your code.

a. Use Windows to make a copy of the Kessler Solution folder, which you created in this chapter's Programming Example. Rename the copy Kessler Region Solution.

b. Open the Kessler Solution (Kessler Solution.sln) file, which is contained in the VbDotNet\Chap11\ Kessler Region Solution folder.

c. Use the Help menu to research the #Region statement.

d. Modify the application so that it uses a region to hide the properties contained in the MyRectangle class, and a region to hide the methods contained in the class.

e. Save the solution, then start and test the application.

f. Click the Exit button to end the application, then close the solution.

18. In this exercise, you find and correct an error in an application. The process of finding and correcting errors is called debugging.

a. Open the Debug Solution (Debug Solution.sln) file, which is contained in the VbDotNet\Chap11\Debug Solution folder.

b. Open the Code Editor window. Review the existing code.

c. Notice that a jagged line appears below some of the lines of code in the Code Editor window. Correct the code to remove the jagged lines.

d. Save the solution, then start the application.

e. Correct the errors in the application's code, then save the solution and start the application. Test the application.

f. Click the Exit button to end the application, then close the solution.

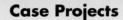

Case Projects

Glasgow Health Club

In Chapter 10's Case Projects, you created an application for the Glasgow Health Club. As you may remember, each member of the Glasgow Health Club must pay monthly dues that consist of a basic fee and, optionally, one or more additional charges. The basic fee for a single membership is $50 per month. The basic fee for a family membership is $90 per month. If the member has a single membership, the additional charges are $30 per month for tennis, $25 per month for golf, and $20 per month for racquetball. If the member has a family membership, the additional charges are $50 per month for tennis, $35 per month for golf, and $30 per month for racquetball. The application should calculate and display a member's monthly dues. Copy the solution's folder from the VbDotNet\Chap10 folder to the VbDotNet\Chap11 folder, then modify the application so that it uses a class.

Franklin University

In Chapter 5's Case Projects, you created an application for Franklin University. The application allows the user to enter a student's gender (either F or M) and GPA. The application should calculate the average GPA for all students, the average GPA for male students, and the average GPA for female students. Copy the solution's folder from the VbDotNet\Chap05 folder to the VbDotNet\Chap11 folder, then modify the application so that it uses a class.

Political Awareness Organization

In Chapter 8's Programming Example, you created an application for the Political Awareness Organization. The application allows the organization's secretary to enter a voter's political party and age, and also save this information to a sequential access file. The application also calculates and displays the number of voters in each political party. Copy the PAO Solution folder from the VbDotNet\Chap08 folder to the VbDotNet\Chap11 folder, then modify the application so that it uses a class.

Pennington Book Store

Shelly Jones, the manager of Pennington Book Store, wants an application that she can use to calculate and display the total amount a customer owes. Create the interface shown in Figure 11.25. Assume that a customer can purchase one or more books at either the same price or different prices. The application should keep a running total of the amount the customer owes, and display the total in the Total Due control. For example, a customer might purchase two books at $6 and three books at $10. To calculate the total due, Shelly will need to enter 2 in the Quantity box and 6 in the Price box, and then click the Add to Sale button. The Total Due control should display $12.00. To complete the order, Shelly will need to enter 3 in the Quantity box and 10 in the Price box, and then click the Add to Sale button. The Total Due control should display $42.00. Before calculating the next customer's order, Shelly will need to click the New Order button.

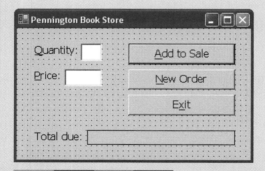

FIGURE 11.25

Using ADO.NET

- Define the terms used when talking about databases
- Explain the purpose of the DataAdapter, Connection, and DataSet objects
- Explain the role of the provider
- Create and configure an OleDbDataAdapter object
- Write SQL SELECT statements
- Create a dataset
- Display a dataset in various controls in an interface
- Position the record pointer in a dataset

DATABASE TERMINOLOGY

In order to maintain accurate records, most businesses store information about their employees, customers, and inventory in files called databases. In general, a **database** is simply an organized collection of related information stored in a file on a disk.

Many computer products exist for creating databases; some of the most popular are Microsoft Access, Oracle, and SQL Server. You can use Visual Basic .NET to access the data stored in databases created by these products. This allows a company to create a standard interface in Visual Basic .NET that employees can use to access database information stored in a variety of formats. Instead of learning each product's user interface, the employee needs to know only one interface. The actual format the database is in is unimportant and will be transparent to the user.

In this chapter, you learn how to access the data stored in a Microsoft Access database. Databases created by Microsoft Access are relational databases. A **relational database** is one that stores information in tables, which are composed of columns and rows. Each column in a table represents a field, and each row represents a record. As you learned in Chapter 8, a field is a single item of information about a person, place, or thing—such as a name, address, or phone number—and a record is a group of related fields that contain all of the necessary data about a specific person, place, or thing. A **table** is a group of related records. Each record in the group pertains to the same topic, and each contains the same type of information—in other words, the same fields.

A relational database can contain one or more tables. A one-table database would be a good choice for storing the information regarding the college courses you have taken. An example of such a table is shown in Figure 12.1.

ID	Title	Hours	Grade
CIS100	Intro to Computers	5	A
Eng100	English Composition	3	B
Phil105	Philosophy	5	C
CIS201	Visual Basic .NET	5	A

FIGURE 12.1   Example of a one-table relational database

Notice that each record in the table contains four fields: an ID field that indicates the department name and course number, a course title field, a number of credit hours field, and a grade field. In most tables, one of the fields uniquely identifies each record and is called the **primary key**. In the table shown in Figure 12.1, you could use either the ID field or the Title field as the primary key, because the data in those fields will be unique for each record.

If you were storing information about your CD (compact disc) collection, you typically would use a two-table database: one table to store the general information about each CD (such as the CD's name and the artist's name) and the other table to store the information about the songs on each CD (such as their title and track number). You then would use a common field—for example, a CD number—to relate the records contained in both tables. Figure 12.2 shows an example of a two-table database that stores CD information.

The two tables are related by the Number field

Number	Name	Artist
01	Western Way	Dolly Draton
02	Midnight Blue	Paul Elliot

Number	Song title	Track
01	Country	1
01	Night on the Road	2
01	Old Times	3
02	Lovely Nights	1
02	Colors	2
02	Heavens	3

FIGURE 12.2   Example of a two-table relational database

The first table shown in Figure 12.2 is often referred to as the **parent table**, and the second table as the **child table**. In the parent table, the Number field is the primary key, because it uniquely identifies each record in that table. In the child table, the Number field is used solely to link the song title and track information to the appropriate CD in the parent table. In the child table, the Number field is called the **foreign key**.

Storing data in a relational database offers many advantages. The computer can retrieve data stored in that format both quickly and easily, and the data can be displayed in any order. For example, the information in the CD database shown in Figure 12.2 can be arranged by artist name, song title, and so on. A relational database also allows you to control how much information you want to view at a time. You can view all of the information in the CD database, or you can view only the information pertaining to a certain artist, or only the names of the songs contained on a specific CD.

In Visual Basic .NET, you use ADO.NET to access the data stored in a database.

ADO.NET

The previous version of Visual Basic (Version 6.0) used a technology called **ADO (ActiveX Data Objects)** to connect an application to a database. The connection allows the application to read information from and write information to the database. The technology used in Visual Basic .NET to perform the same task is called **ADO.NET**.

ADO.NET works differently from its predecessor, ADO. Using ADO, the connection between an application and a database remains open the entire time the application is running. This does not pose a problem when only a few applications are connected to the database. However, when many applications are connected, at some point the demands on the database will exceed its ability to respond in a timely fashion.

With ADO.NET, the connection between an application and a database is only a temporary one. For example, when an application first connects to a database, it makes a copy of the records and fields it wants to access; the copy, called a **dataset**, is stored in the computer's internal memory. The application then closes both the database and the connection to the database. The application reconnects to the database when any changes made to the dataset (which is in internal memory) need to be saved. After saving the changes, the application again closes the database and the connection to the database. Unlike ADO, ADO.NET allows multiple users to access the same database without tying up limited resources. ADO.NET also was designed to better operate with the Web.

You use three ADO.NET objects (DataAdapter, Connection, and DataSet), as well as a provider, to access a database from a Visual Basic .NET application. Figure 12.3 illustrates the relationships among an application, the ADO.NET objects, a provider, and a database.

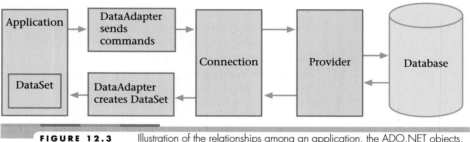

FIGURE 12.3   Illustration of the relationships among an application, the ADO.NET objects, a provider, and a database

When an application needs to access the data stored in a database, it submits the appropriate request using a **DataAdapter object**. The DataAdapter object, in turn, contacts the **Connection object**, which is responsible for establishing the connection to the database, and then submitting the request for data. The Connection object communicates with the database using one of several different providers, depending on the type of database. For example, the Connection object uses a provider named Microsoft Jet 4.0 OLE DB Provider to communicate with a Microsoft Access database. However, it uses a provider named Microsoft OLE DB Provider for Oracle to communicate with an Oracle database. A provider is like a translator in that it allows communication between two entities that do not speak the same language. In this case, the **provider** translates the Connection object's request for data into a language that the database can understand.

The database sends the requested data back to the provider, which translates the data into a language that the Connection object can understand. The Connection object sends the data to the DataAdapter object, which stores the data in a DataSet object. The data in the DataSet object is then made available to the application.

In the remainder of this chapter, you learn how to access the data stored in a Microsoft Access database named Employees.mdb. Figure 12.4 shows the database opened in Microsoft Access.

Table name

Field names

Records

Number	Last	First	Hired	Rate	Status	Code
100	Benton	Jack	3/5/1996	$15.00	F	2
101	Jones	Carol	4/2/1996	$15.00	F	2
102	Ismal	Asaad	1/15/1997	$10.00	P	1
103	Rodriguez	Carl	5/6/1997	$12.00	P	3
104	Iovanelli	Sam	8/15/1997	$20.00	F	1
105	Nyugen	Thomas	10/20/1997	$8.00	P	3
106	Vine	Martha	2/5/1997	$9.50	P	2
107	Smith	Paul	5/14/1998	$17.50	F	2
108	Gerber	Wanda	9/24/1998	$21.00	F	3
109	Zonten	Mary	12/4/1998	$13.50	F	4
110	Sparrow	John	12/4/1998	$9.00	P	4
111	Krutchen	Jerry	12/15/1998	$9.00	P	4
0				$0.00		0

FIGURE 12.4   Employees.mdb database opened in Microsoft Access

The Employees.mdb database has one table, named tblEmploy, that contains seven fields and 12 records. The Number, Last, First, Hired, and Rate fields store employee numbers, last names, first names, hire dates, and rates of pay, respectively. The Status field contains the employment status, which is either the letter F (for fulltime) or the letter P (for parttime). The Code field identifies the employee's department: 1 for Accounting, 2 for Advertising, 3 for Personnel, and 4 for Inventory. In the tblEmploy table, the Number field is the primary key, because it uniquely identifies each record.

Recall that the DataAdapter object is one of the three ADO.NET objects you use to connect an application to a database. In the next section, you learn how to create a DataAdapter object, and then configure the object.

CREATING AND CONFIGURING A DATAADAPTER OBJECT

As illustrated earlier in Figure 12.3, the DataAdapter object is the link between the application and the Connection object. Its purpose is to contact the Connection object whenever the application needs to read data from or write data to a database. Figure 12.5 shows the procedure you follow to create and configure a DataAdapter object for an application that connects to a Microsoft Access database.

HOW TO...

TIP

The procedure shown in Figure 12.5 is only one way of creating and configuring a DataAdapter object; there are other ways.

Create and Configure a DataAdapter Object for a Microsoft Access Database

1. Drag the OleDbDataAdapter tool from the Data tab on the Toolbox window to the form. This adds an OleDbDataAdapter object to the component tray and also displays a Welcome screen. (See Figure 12.6.)
2. Click the Next > button on the Welcome screen to display the Choose Your Data Connection screen. (See Figure 12.7.)
3. Click the New Connection button on the Choose Your Data Connection screen.
4. Click the Provider tab on the Data Link Properties dialog box, then click Microsoft Jet 4.0 OLE DB Provider in the OLE DB Provider(s) list box. (See Figure 12.8.)
5. Click the Connection tab on the Data Link Properties dialog box, then click the ... (ellipsis) button that appears next to the "Select or enter a database name" text box.
6. Locate and then click the name of the database in the Select Access Database dialog box.
7. Click the Open button, and then click the Test Connection button. (See Figure 12.9.)
8. Click the OK button to close the Microsoft Data Link dialog box, and then click the OK button to close the Data Link Properties dialog box; this displays the Choose Your Data Connection screen. (See Figure 12.10.)
9. Click the Next > button on the Choose Your Data Connection screen; this displays the Choose a Query Type screen. (See Figure 12.11.)
10. Verify that the Use SQL statements radio button is selected on the Choose a Query Type screen, and then click the Next > button; this displays the Generate the SQL statements screen. (See Figure 12.13.)
11. Click the Query Builder button on the Generate the SQL statements screen; this displays the Query Builder and Add Table dialog boxes. (See Figure 12.14.)
12. Click the name of the table on the Tables tab in the Add Table dialog box. Click the Add button, and then click the Close button; this displays the Query Builder dialog box. (See Figure 12.15.)
13. Select the check boxes next to the desired fields. (See Figure 12.16.)
14. Click the OK button in the Query Builder dialog box; this displays the Generate the SQL statements screen. (See Figure 12.17.)
15. Click the Next > button on the Generate the SQL statements screen to display the View Wizard Results screen. (See Figure 12.18.)
16. Click the Finish button on the View Wizard Results screen. If the "Do you want to include the password in the connection string?" dialog box opens, click the Don't include password button. Visual Basic .NET adds an OleDbConnection object to the component tray.
17. Assign meaningful names to the OleDbDataAdapter and OleDbConnection objects. In this book, you use the prefix "oledb_adap" when naming OleDbDataAdapter objects, and the prefix "oledb_con" when naming OleDbConnection objects.

FIGURE 12.5   How to create and configure a DataAdapter object for a Microsoft Access database

TIP

"OleDb" stands for "Object Linking and Embedding for Databases."

When you drag the OleDbDataAdapter tool to the form, which is the first step in the procedure shown in Figure 12.5, Visual Basic .NET creates a DataAdapter object; more specifically, it creates an OleDbDataAdapter object named OleDbDataAdapter1. It places the object in the component tray in the Form Designer window, as shown in Figure 12.6. The **component tray** stores the objects that do not appear in the interface when an application is running. Additionally, the Welcome screen for the Data Adapter Configuration Wizard appears. As the Welcome screen shown in Figure 12.6 indicates, the wizard helps you specify the connection and commands that will be used to access the data in the database.

This tool creates a DataAdapter object for a Microsoft Access database

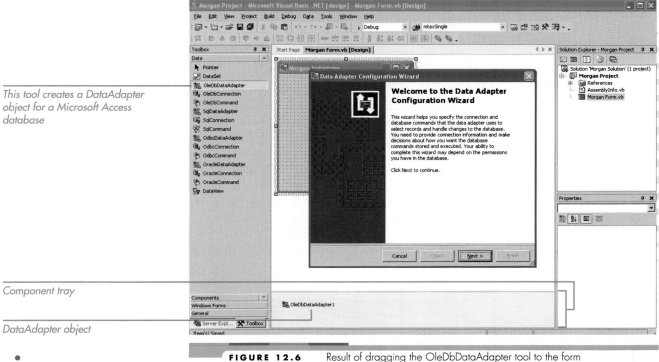

Component tray

DataAdapter object

FIGURE 12.6   Result of dragging the OleDbDataAdapter tool to the form

TIP

The Data tab on the Toolbox window contains four tools that you can use to create DataAdapter objects; the appropriate tool depends on the type of database used by the application.

When you click the Next > button on the Welcome screen, the Choose Your Data Connection screen appears, as shown in Figure 12.7. You can use this screen to create a new connection to a database, or to select an existing connection.

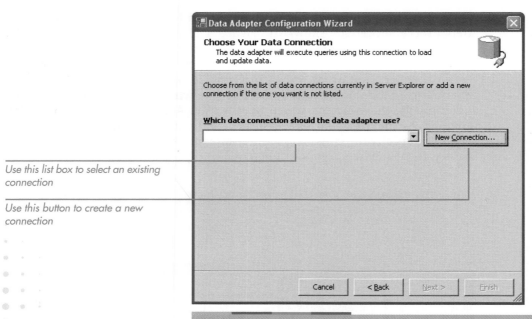

Use this list box to select an existing connection

Use this button to create a new connection

FIGURE 12.7   Choose Your Data Connection screen

Clicking the New Connection button on the Choose Your Data Connection screen opens the Data Link Properties dialog box. You use the Provider tab on the dialog box to specify the name of the provider. Recall that the provider facilitates the communication between the Connection object and the database. The provider for all Microsoft Access databases is named Microsoft Jet 4.0 OLE DB Provider. Figure 12.8 shows an example of a completed Provider tab. (Your list of providers may differ from the list shown in Figure 12.8.)

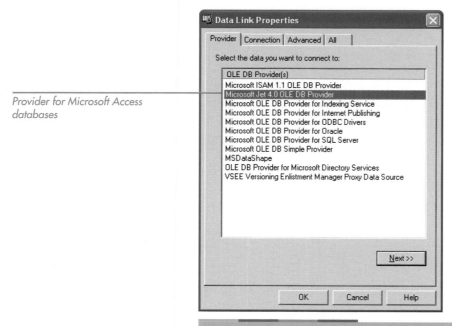

Provider for Microsoft Access databases

FIGURE 12.8   Provider tab

You use the Connection tab on the Data Link Properties dialog box to specify the name of the database to which you want to connect. The tab also contains the Test Connection button, which allows you to test the connection to the database. If the connection is successful, the message "Test connection succeeded." appears in the Microsoft Data Link dialog box; otherwise, the dialog box displays an error message. Figure 12.9 shows an example of a completed Connection tab. The figure also shows the Microsoft Data Link dialog box that appears when the connection is successful.

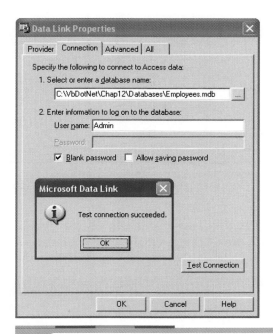

FIGURE 12.9   Connection tab and Microsoft Data Link dialog box

When you close the Microsoft Data Link and Data Link Properties dialog boxes, the connection you created appears in the "Which data connection should the data adapter use?" list box on the Choose Your Data Connection screen, as shown in Figure 12.10.

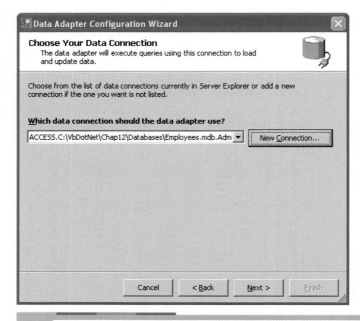

FIGURE 12.10   Connection shown on the Choose Your Data Connection screen

Clicking the Next > button on the Choose Your Data Connection screen displays the Choose a Query Type screen, as shown in Figure 12.11.

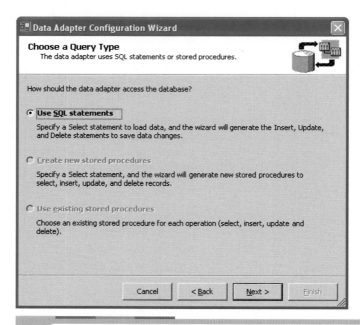

FIGURE 12.11   Choose a Query Type screen

You use the Choose a Query Type screen to specify how the DataAdapter object should access the database. Notice that the Use SQL statements radio button is selected in Figure 12.11. You learn about SQL in the next section.

SQL

SQL, pronounced like the word *sequel*, stands for **Structured Query Language**. **SQL** is a set of commands that allows you to access and manipulate the data stored in many database management systems on computers of all sizes, from large mainframes to small microcomputers. You can use SQL commands to perform database tasks such as storing, retrieving, updating, deleting, and sorting data.

The SELECT statement is the most commonly used command in SQL. The **SELECT statement** allows you to specify the fields and records you want to view, as well as control the order in which the fields and records appear when displayed. Figure 12.12 shows the basic syntax of the SELECT statement and includes several examples of using the statement to access the data stored in the Employees.mdb database (shown earlier in Figure 12.4). As you may remember, the database contains one table (named tblEmploy) and seven fields. The Number, Rate, and Code fields contain numeric data. The Last, First, and Status fields contain text data, and the Hired field contains dates.

HOW TO...

Use the SELECT Statement

Syntax
SELECT *fields* **FROM** *table* [**WHERE** *condition*] [**ORDER BY** *field*]

Example 1
```
SELECT Code, First, Hired, Last, Number, Rate, Status
FROM tblEmploy
```
selects all of the fields and records in the table

Example 2
```
SELECT * FROM tblEmploy
```
selects all of the fields and records in the table

Example 3
```
SELECT Number, First, Last FROM tblEmploy
```
selects the Number, First, and Last fields from each record in the table

Example 4
```
SELECT * FROM tblEmploy WHERE Status = 'F'
```
selects the records for full-time employees

Example 5
```
SELECT Number, Rate FROM tblEmploy WHERE Code = 3
```
selects the Number and Rate fields for employees in the Personnel department

(Figure is continued on next page)

> **Example 6**
> `SELECT * FROM tblEmploy ORDER BY Hired`
> selects all of the fields and records in the table, and sorts the records in ascending order by the Hired field
>
> **Example 7**
> `SELECT * FROM tblEmploy WHERE Status = 'p' ORDER BY Code`
> selects the records for part-time employees, and sorts the records in ascending order by the Code field

FIGURE 12.12 How to use the SELECT statement

In the SELECT statement's syntax, *fields* is one or more field names (separated by commas), and *table* is the name of the table containing the fields. Notice that the syntax contains two clauses that are optional: the WHERE clause and the ORDER BY clause. The **WHERE clause** allows you to limit the records that will be selected, and the **ORDER BY clause** allows you to control the order in which the records appear when displayed.

Study closely the examples shown in Figure 12.12. The SELECT statement in Example 1 selects all of the fields and records from the tblEmploy table. The SELECT statement in Example 2 produces the same result and shows you a simpler way of selecting all of the fields in a table. Rather than entering each field name in the *fields* portion of the SELECT statement, you simply enter an asterisk (*). When the computer processes the SELECT statement, it replaces the asterisk with the names of the fields in the table; the field names appear in alphabetical order.

The SELECT statement in Example 3 selects only three of the fields from each record in the tblEmploy table. The SELECT statement in Example 4 uses the WHERE clause to limit the records that will be selected; in this case, the statement indicates that only records for full-time employees should be selected. Notice that, when comparing the contents of the Status field (which contains text) with a string, you enclose the string in single quotation marks rather than in double quotation marks.

The SELECT statement in Example 5 in Figure 12.12 selects only the Number and Rate fields for employees working in the Personnel department. Example 6's SELECT statement selects all of the fields and records from the tblEmploy table, and then uses the ORDER BY clause to sort the records in ascending order by the Hired field. To sort the records in descending order, you use `SELECT * FROM tblEmploy ORDER BY Hired DESC`. The "DESC" stands for "descending".

The last SELECT statement shown in Figure 12.12 selects the records for part-time employees, and it sorts the records in ascending order by the Code field. Notice that the statement compares the contents of the Status field (which contains uppercase letters) with a lowercase 'p'. The statement works correctly because the SQL commands are not case-sensitive.

Now that you know how to write SELECT statements, you can continue learning how to configure the DataAdapter object.

Using the Query Builder to Enter a SELECT Statement

When you click the Next > button on the Choose a Query Type screen (shown earlier in Figure 12.11), the Generate the SQL statements screen appears, as shown in Figure 12.13.

TIP

You do not have to capitalize the keywords SELECT, FROM, WHERE, and ORDER BY in a SELECT statement; however, many programmers do so for clarity.

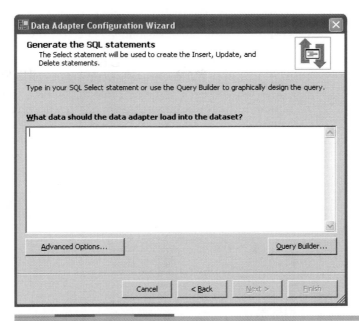

FIGURE 12.13 Generate the SQL statements screen

You enter the appropriate SELECT statement in the "What data should the data adapter load into the dataset?" box. You can enter the SELECT statement yourself, or you can have the Query Builder enter it for you. To use the Query Builder, you click the Query Builder button. After doing so, the Query Builder and Add Table dialog boxes open, as shown in Figure 12.14.

Tables tab

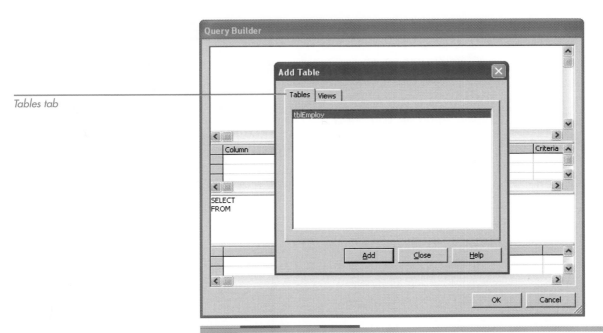

FIGURE 12.14 Query Builder and Add Table dialog boxes

Notice that tblEmploy, which is the name of the table contained in the Employees.mdb database, appears on the Tables tab in the Add Table dialog box. The tblEmploy table contains the employee information that you want to access. You add the tblEmploy table to the Query Builder dialog box by clicking the Add button. You then click the Close button to close the Add Table dialog box.

When you close the Add Table dialog box, the names of the seven fields contained in the tblEmploy table appear in a list box in the Query Builder dialog box, as shown in Figure 12.15. Notice that the field names are listed in ascending alphabetical order (which is not the order in which the fields appear in the table). Additionally, the Query Builder begins entering a SELECT statement for you.

Scroll the list box to view the remaining field names

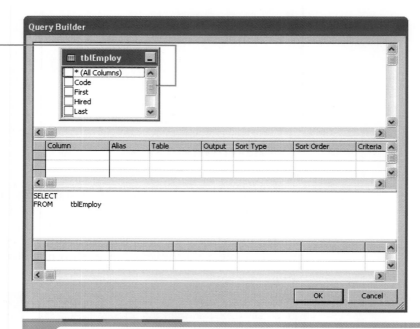

FIGURE 12.15   Query Builder dialog box showing the fields and SELECT statement

Assume you want to display each employee's number, name, and rate of pay. To do so, you select the check boxes next to the Number, First, Last, and Rate fields, as shown in Figure 12.16. When you select a check box, the corresponding field name appears in the SELECT statement. Notice that the Number field, which is the primary key, appears in brackets in the SELECT statement; it also appears in bold text in the listing of field names.

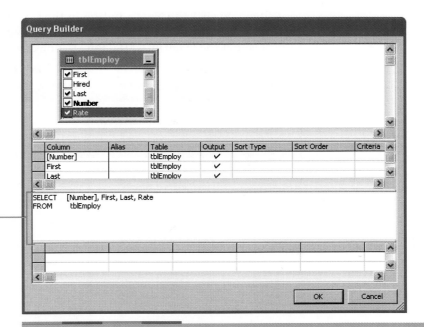

The field names appear in the order in which they were selected

FIGURE 12.16   Completed SELECT statement in the Query Builder dialog box

The SELECT statement shown in Figure 12.16 tells the DataAdapter object to select only four of the seven fields from all of the records in the tblEmploy table. When you click the OK button to close the Query Builder dialog box, the Generate the SQL statements screen appears and displays the SELECT statement created by the Query Builder, as shown in Figure 12.17.

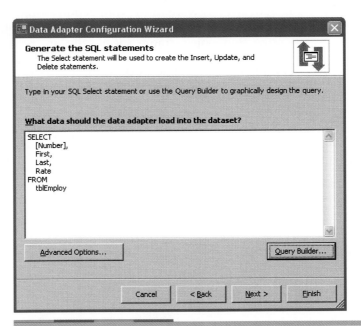

FIGURE 12.17   SELECT statement entered in the Generate the SQL statements screen

When you click the Next > button in the Generate the SQL statements screen, the View Wizard Results screen appears, as shown in Figure 12.18. The screen indicates that the "OleDbDataAdapter1" object was configured successfully.

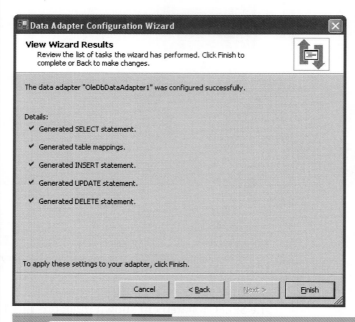

FIGURE 12.18   View Wizard Results screen

Finally, you click the Finish button in the View Wizard Results screen to close the Data Adapter Configuration Wizard dialog box. If the "Do you want to include the password in the connection string?" dialog box opens, you click the Don't include password button. At this point, Visual Basic .NET creates a Connection object; more specifically, it creates an OleDbConnection object named OleDbConnection1. It places the object in the component tray in the Form Designer window, as shown in Figure 12.19.

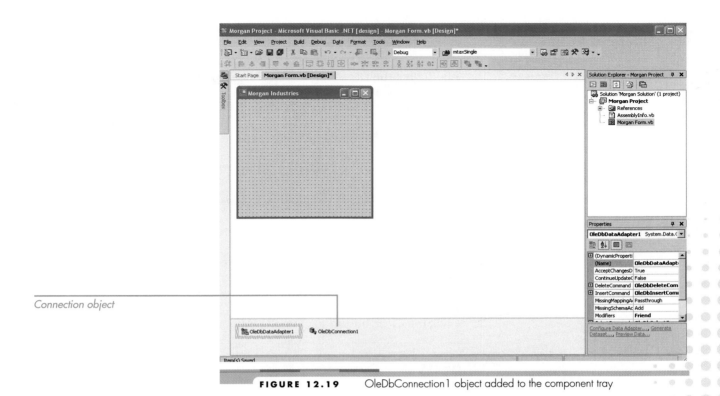

Connection object

FIGURE 12.19 OleDbConnection1 object added to the component tray

You can use the Properties window to assign different names to the OleDbDataAdapter1 and OleDbConnection1 objects. In this book, you will use the prefix "oledb_adap" when naming OleDbDataAdapter objects, and the prefix "oledb_con" when naming OleDbConnection objects. Good names for the OleDbDataAdapter1 and OleDbConnection1 objects shown in Figure 12.19 are oledb_adapEmployees and oledb_conEmployees. The names remind you that the objects are associated with the Employees database.

You have now finished creating and configuring the DataAdapter object. The next step in accessing the data stored in a Microsoft Access database is to create a dataset.

CREATING A DATASET

A dataset contains the data you want to access from the database, as specified in the SELECT statement associated with the DataAdapter object. In this case, the dataset will contain each employee's number, name, and rate of pay. Figure 12.20 shows the procedure you follow to create a dataset, and Figure 12.21 shows a completed Generate Dataset dialog box.

HOW TO...

Create a Dataset

1. Right-click the DataAdapter object in the component tray, then click Generate Dataset.
2. Verify that the New radio button is selected in the Generate Dataset dialog box.
3. Assign a meaningful name to the dataset. In this book, you use the prefix "dst" when naming datasets.
4. Select the appropriate table(s) from the Choose which table(s) to add to the dataset list box.
5. Verify that the Add this dataset to the designer check box is selected. (See Figure 12.21.)
6. Click the OK button to close the Generate Dataset dialog box. (See Figure 12.22.)
7. To preview the contents of the dataset, right-click the DataAdapter object in the component tray. Click Preview Data, and then click the Fill Dataset button in the Data Adapter Preview dialog box. (See Figure 12.23.)
8. Click the Close button to close the Data Adapter Preview dialog box.

FIGURE 12.20 How to create a Dataset

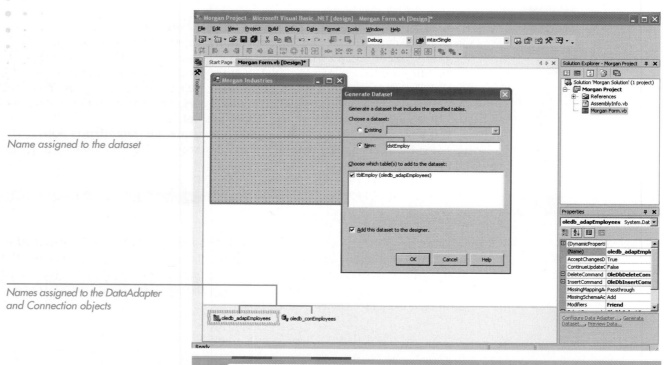

Name assigned to the dataset

Names assigned to the DataAdapter and Connection objects

FIGURE 12.21   Generate Dataset dialog box

When you close the Generate Dataset dialog box in Step 6, a DataSet object appears in the component tray, as shown in Figure 12.22. Notice that Visual Basic .NET names the object using the dataset's name (with the first letter capitalized) followed by the number one. The number one indicates that the DstEmploy1 object is the first DataSet object created using the dstEmploy dataset. Also notice that the Solution Explorer window contains a new file named dstEmploy.xsd. The .xsd extension on the filename indicates that the file is an XML schema definition file. **XML**, which stands for **Extensible Markup Language**, is a text-based language used to store and share data between applications and across networks and the Internet. An **XML schema definition file** defines the tables and fields that make up the dataset. (You view the contents of the dstEmploy.xsd file in Exercise 6 at the end of this chapter.)

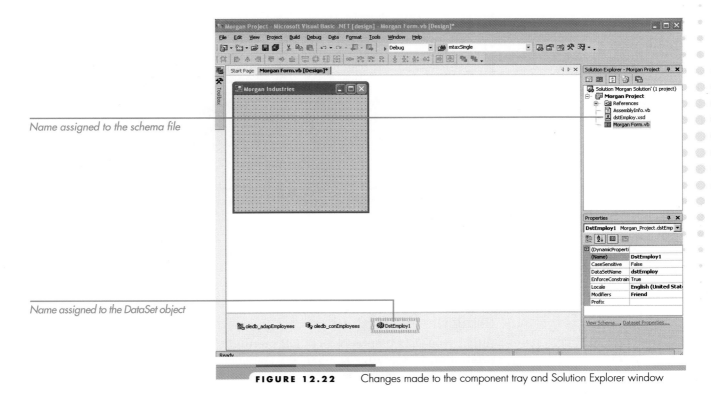

Name assigned to the schema file

Name assigned to the DataSet object

FIGURE 12.22   Changes made to the component tray and Solution Explorer window

Once you have created the dataset, you can preview its contents by right-clicking the DataAdapter object in the component tray, and then clicking Preview Data. When the Data Adapter Preview dialog box opens, you click the Fill Dataset button. Figure 12.23 shows the dstEmploy dataset displayed in the Data Adapter Preview dialog box.

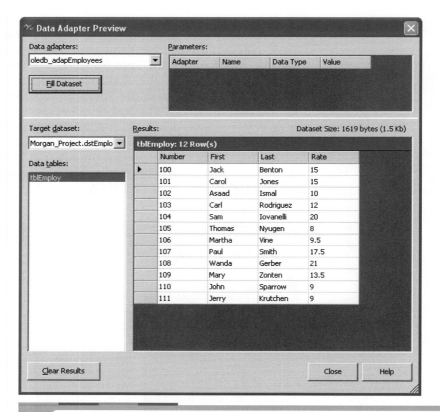

FIGURE 12.23   Data Adapter Preview dialog box

The Data Adapter Preview dialog box allows you to preview the dataset while you are designing the application. To fill the dataset with data when the application is running, you use the DataAdapter object's Fill method.

Using the Fill Method

You use the DataAdapter object's **Fill method** to fill a dataset with data while an application is running. The SELECT statement you entered when configuring the DataAdapter object determines the appropriate data. Figure 12.24 shows the syntax of the Fill method and includes an example of using the method.

HOW TO...

Use the Fill Method

Syntax
dataAdapter.**Fill**(*dataSet*)

Example
```
Me.oledb_adapEmployees.Fill(Me.DstEmploy1)
```

FIGURE 12.24 How to use the Fill method

In the Fill method's syntax, *dataAdapter* is the name of a DataAdapter object, and *dataSet* is the name of a DataSet object. The example shown in Figure 12.24 will fill the dataset associated with the DstEmploy1 object with the data specified in the oledb_adapEmployees object's SELECT statement. In most cases, you enter the Fill method in the form's Load event procedure, because you typically want to fill the dataset when the application first starts.

For the user to view the dataset in an application, you need to bind the DataSet object to one or more controls in the interface. First you learn how to bind the DataSet object to a DataGrid control.

BINDING THE DATASET OBJECT TO A DATAGRID CONTROL

You view the data contained in a dataset by connecting its DataSet object to one or more controls in the interface. Connecting a DataSet object to a control is called **binding**, and the connected controls are referred to as **bound controls**. You bind a control using one or more properties listed in the Properties window. The appropriate property (or properties) to use depends on the control you are binding. For example, you use the DataSource and DataMember properties to bind a DataGrid control. However, you use the DataSource and DisplayMember properties to bind a ListBox control. To bind label and text box controls, you use the DataBindings/Text property. Figure 12.25 shows the procedure you follow to bind a DataSet object to a DataGrid control.

HOW TO...

Bind a DataSet Object to a DataGrid Control

1. Set the DataGrid control's DataSource property to the name of the DataSet object.
2. Set the DataGrid control's DataMember property to the name of a table.

FIGURE 12.25 How to bind a DataSet object to a DataGrid control

When bound to a DataSet object, the **DataGrid control** displays the data from the dataset in a row and column format, similar to a spreadsheet. Each field in the dataset appears in a column in the DataGrid control, and each record appears in a row. The intersection of a row and a column in the DataGrid control is called a cell. Figure 12.26 lists the names and uses of several properties of a DataGrid control.

HOW TO...

Use a DataGrid Control

Property	Use to
CaptionText	specify the caption that appears at the top of the control
ColumnHeadersVisible	control the display of the column headings
ContextMenu	specify a shortcut menu that displays when the user right-clicks the control
DataMember	specify the table to associate with the control
DataSource	specify the DataSet object to associate with the control
Font	specify the font type and size to use for text (usually set to Tahoma)
Name	give the DataGrid control a meaningful name that begins with "dgd"
ReadOnly	specify whether changes can be made to the data displayed in the control
RowHeadersVisible	control the display of the row headings

Note: The DataGrid control also has an Auto Format link that appears in the Properties window when the control is selected. You can use the link to display a dialog box that allows you to select from a list of predefined formats for displaying data.

FIGURE 12.26 How to use a DataGrid control

TIP

You also could have set the DataGrid control's DataSource property to DstEmploy1.tblEmploy, and then left the DataMember property empty.

Figure 12.27 shows a sample run of an application that contains a DataGrid control, and Figure 12.28 shows the code entered in the form's Load event procedure. In the application, the DataGrid control's Name property is set to dgdEmployees, its CaptionText property to "Employee Records", its ReadOnly property to True, and its RowHeadersVisible property to False. Additionally, the control's DataSource and DataMember properties are set to DstEmploy1 (the name of the DataSet object) and tblEmploy (the name of the table within the DataSet object), respectively.

FIGURE 12.27   Sample run of an application that contains a DataGrid control

```
Private Sub frmMorgan_Load(ByVal sender As Object, ByVal e As System.EventArgs) _
    Handles MyBase.Load
    'fills the dataset with data
    Me.oledb_adapEmployees.Fill(Me.DstEmploy1)
End Sub
```

FIGURE 12.28   Form's Load event procedure

When you start the application, the Fill method in the form's Load event procedure fills the dataset associated with the DstEmploy1 object with data. Because the DstEmploy1 object is bound to the DataGrid control, the records from the dataset appear in the control, as shown in Figure 12.27. You can use the arrow keys on your keyboard to access a different field and/or record in the DataGrid control. Notice that scroll bars appear when there is more data than will fit into the control.

Now assume that you want to display (in the DataGrid control) the number, name, pay rate, and department code of employees working in the Personnel department. Additionally, you want the records displayed in ascending last name order. To accomplish this task, you need to reconfigure the DataAdapter object.

RECONFIGURING THE DATAADAPTER OBJECT

Figure 12.29 shows the procedure you follow to reconfigure an existing DataAdapter object.

HOW TO...

Reconfigure an Existing DataAdapter Object

1. Right-click the DataAdapter object in the component tray, and then click Configure Data Adapter.
2. Click the Next > button on the Welcome to the Data Adapter Configuration Wizard screen.
3. Click the Next > button on the Choose Your Data Connection screen.
4. Click the Next > button on the Choose a Query Type screen.
5. Click the Query Builder button on the Generate the SQL statements screen.
6. Make the desired modifications to the SELECT statement in the Query Builder dialog box.
7. Click the OK button to close the Query Builder dialog box.
8. Click the Next > button on the Generate the SQL statements screen.
9. Click the Finish button on the View Wizard Results screen.
10. Right-click the DataAdapter object in the component tray, then click Generate Dataset.
11. Click the OK button in the Generate Dataset dialog box.
12. To preview the contents of the dataset, right-click the DataAdapter object in the component tray. Click Preview Data, and then click the Fill Dataset button in the Data Adapter Preview dialog box. Click the Close button to close the Data Adapter Preview dialog box.

FIGURE 12.29 How to reconfigure an existing DataAdapter object

Figure 12.30 shows the modifications made to the SELECT statement in the Query Builder dialog box, and Figure 12.31 shows the new dataset displayed in the DataGrid control.

The funnel symbol indicates that the Code field is used in the WHERE clause

This symbol indicates that the dataset is sorted in ascending alphabetical order by the Last name field

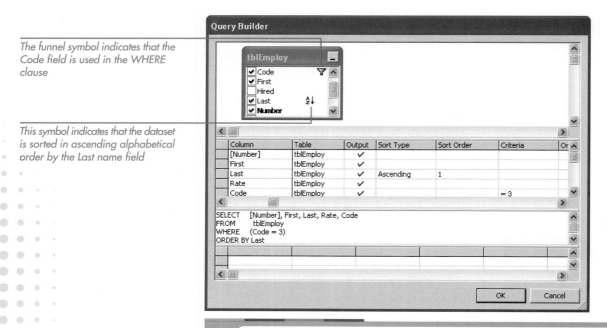

FIGURE 12.30   Modifications made to the SELECT statement in the Query Builder dialog box

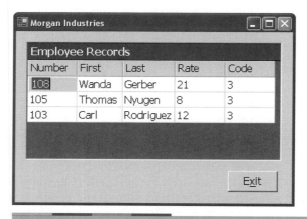

FIGURE 12.31   New dataset displayed in the DataGrid control

Rather than displaying all of the records in a DataGrid control, you may want to display each record individually in label controls or text boxes in the interface.

BINDING THE DATASET OBJECT TO A LABEL CONTROL OR TEXT BOX

Figure 12.32 shows the procedure you follow to bind a DataSet object to a label control or text box, and Figure 12.33 shows an example of setting the DataBindings/Text property in the Properties window.

HOW TO...

Bind a DataSet Object to a Label Control or Text Box

1. Select the label control or text box.
2. Click (DataBindings), in the Properties list.
3. Click the plus box that appears to the left of (DataBindings).
4. Click Text in the Properties list.
5. Click the list arrow in the Settings box, and then click the plus box that appears next to the name of the DataSet object.
6. Click the plus box that appears next to the table name, and then click the name of the field. (See Figure 12.33.)

FIGURE 12.32 How to bind a DataSet object to a label control or text box

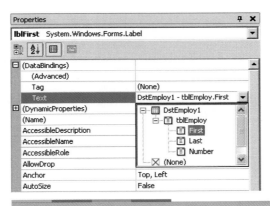

FIGURE 12.33   DataBindings/Text property shown in the Properties window

Figure 12.34 shows a sample run of an application that uses label controls to display the data contained in the dataset, and Figure 12.35 shows the application's code.

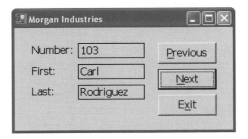

FIGURE 12.34   Sample run of an application that uses label controls to display the dataset

```
'Project name:          Morgan Project
'Project purpose:       The project displays information from the
'                       Employees.mdb database.
'Created/revised by:    Diane Zak on 2/1/2005

Option Explicit On
Option Strict On

Public Class frmMorgan
    Inherits System.Windows.Forms.Form

[Windows Form Designer generated code]

    Private Sub btnExit_Click(ByVal sender As Object, _
        ByVal e As System.EventArgs) Handles btnExit.Click
        'ends the application
        Me.Close()
    End Sub

    Private Sub frmMorgan_Load(ByVal sender As Object, _
        ByVal e As System.EventArgs) Handles MyBase.Load
        'fills the dataset with data
        Me.oledb_adapEmployees.Fill(Me.DstEmploy1)
    End Sub

    Private Sub btnNext_Click(ByVal sender As Object, _
        ByVal e As System.EventArgs) Handles btnNext.Click
        'moves the record pointer to the next record in the dataset
        Me.BindingContext(Me.DstEmploy1, "tblEmploy").Position = _
            Me.BindingContext(Me.DstEmploy1, "tblEmploy").Position + 1
    End Sub

    Private Sub btnPrevious_Click(ByVal sender As Object, _
        ByVal e As System.EventArgs) Handles btnPrevious.Click
        'moves the record pointer to the previous record in the dataset
        Me.BindingContext(Me.DstEmploy1, "tblEmploy").Position = _
            Me.BindingContext(Me.DstEmploy1, "tblEmploy").Position - 1
    End Sub
End Class
```

FIGURE 12.35 Code for the application shown in Figure 12.34

Notice that the interface shown in Figure 12.34 contains two buttons labeled "Previous" and "Next". You use the Previous and Next buttons to display the previous and next records, respectively, from the dataset.

To display the next record, you need to move the record pointer, which keeps track of the current record, to the next position in the dataset. You can move the record pointer using the syntax **Me.BindingContext(***datasetObject***,** *tablename***)** **.Position** = *value*. In the syntax, *datasetObject* is the name of the DataSet object associated with the dataset, and *tablename* (which must be enclosed in quotation marks) is the name of the table within the dataset. *Value* is the value you want assigned to the BindingContext.Position property. For example, to move the record pointer to the next record in the database, you use the statement `Me.BindingContext(Me.DstEmploy1, "tblEmploy").Position = Me.BindingContext(Me.DstEmploy1, "tblEmploy").Position + 1`, as shown in the btnNext_Click procedure in Figure 12.35. Similarly, to move the record pointer to the previous record in the database, you use the statement `Me.BindingContext(Me.DstEmploy1, "tblEmploy").Position = Me.BindingContext(Me.DstEmploy1, "tblEmploy").Position - 1`, as shown in the btnPrevious_Click procedure in Figure 12.35. To move the record pointer to the first record in the dataset, you use the number 0 as the *Value*, because the first record is in position 0 (zero). To move the record pointer to the last record in the dataset, you use `Me.DstEmploy1.tblEmploy.Rows.Count - 1` as the *Value*.

PROGRAMMING EXAMPLE

Cartwright Industries Application

Carl Simons, the sales manager at Cartwright Industries, records the item number, name, and price of each product the company sells in a database named Items.mdb. The database is contained in the VbDotNet\Chap12\Databases folder. Mr. Simons wants an application that the sales clerks can use to enter an item number and then display the item's price. Name the solution Cartwright Solution. Name the project Cartwright Project. Name the form file Cartwright Form.vb. Save the application in the VbDotNet\Chap12 folder.

Figure 12.36 shows the Items.mdb database opened in Microsoft Access. The database contains one table named tblItems. The Number and Name fields contain text, and the Price field contains numbers.

Number	Name	Price
ABX12	Chair	$45.00
CSR14	Desk	$175.00
JTR23	Table	$65.00
NRE09	End Table	$46.00
OOE68	Bookcase	$300.00
PPR00	Coffee Table	$190.00
PRT45	Lamp	$30.00
REZ04	Love Seat	$700.00
THR98	Side Chair	$33.00
WKP10	Sofa	$873.00
*		$0.00

tblItems : Table

FIGURE 12.36

TOE Chart:

Task	Object	Event
End the application	btnExit	Click
Display the price from the dataset	lblPrice	None
Get the item number	lstItemNumber	None
Fill the dataset with the item numbers and prices from the Items.mdb database	frmCartwright	Load
Access the data in the Items.mdb database	oledb_adapItems, oledb_conItems, DstItems1	None

FIGURE 12.37

User Interface:

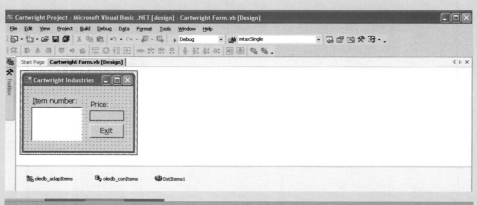

FIGURE 12.38

Objects, Properties, and Settings

Object	Property	Setting
frmCartwright	Name	frmCartwright (be sure to change the startup form to this name)
	Font	Tahoma, 12 point (be sure to change the form's font before adding the controls)
	Size	248, 184
	StartPosition	CenterScreen
	Text	Cartwright Industries
Label1	AutoSize	True
	Text	&Item number:
Label2	AutoSize	True
	Text	Price:
lblPrice	Name	lblPrice
	BorderStyle	FixedSingle
	DataBindings/Text	DstItems1 - tblItems.Price
	Text	(empty)
lstItemNumber	Name	lstItemNumber
	DataSource	DstItems1
	DisplayMember	tblItems.Number
btnExit	Name	btnExit
	Text	E&xit

FIGURE 12.39

Tab Order:

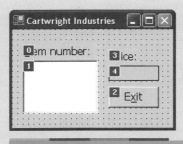

FIGURE 12.40

Pseudocode:

btnExit Click event procedure

1. close application

frmCartwright Load event procedure

1. fill the dataset with the item numbers and prices from the Items.mdb database

Code:

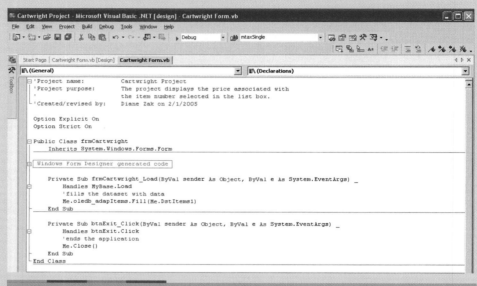

FIGURE 12.41

Quick Review

- Companies and individuals use databases to organize information.
- You can use Visual Basic .NET to access the data stored in many different types of databases.
- Databases created by Microsoft Access are relational databases. A relational database can contain one or more tables.
- Most tables contain a primary key that uniquely identifies each record.
- The data in a relational database can be displayed in any order, and you can control the amount of information you want to view.
- Visual Basic .NET uses a technology called ADO.NET to access the data stored in a database.
- The connection between a database and an application that uses ADO.NET is only temporary.
- To access the data stored in a database, you first create and configure a DataAdapter object, which is the link between the application and the Connection object.

- You use an OleDbDataAdapter object and an OleDbConnection object in applications that access Microsoft Access databases.
- The DataAdapter, Connection, and DataSet objects are stored in the component tray.
- You use a SQL SELECT statement to specify the fields and records for a dataset.
- The Query Builder provides a convenient way to create a SELECT statement.
- A dataset contains the data you want to access from the database. The data you want to access is specified in the SELECT statement associated with the DataAdapter object.
- You use the DataAdapter object's Fill method to fill a dataset with data while an application is running.
- Users view the data stored in a dataset through controls that are bound to the DataSet object.
- You can use the DataGrid control to display the records contained in a dataset.
- When you change the SELECT statement associated with a DataAdapter object, you must regenerate the dataset.

Key Terms

A **database** is an organized collection of related information stored in a file on a disk.

A **relational database** is a database that stores information in tables, which are composed of columns and rows.

A **table** is a group of related records.

A **primary key** is the field that uniquely identifies each record in a table.

A **parent table** is a table to which another table, called a **child table**, links. The tables are linked using a common field. The common field is called the primary key in the parent table, but the **foreign key** in the child table.

ADO stands for **ActiveX Data Objects** and refers to the technology used in Visual Basic 6.0 to connect an application to a database.

ADO.NET refers to the technology used in Visual Basic .NET to connect an application to a database.

A **dataset** is a copy of some or all of the records and fields stored in a database. A dataset is stored in the computer's internal memory.

The **DataAdapter object** submits requests for data from the application to the Connection object.

The **Connection object** establishes a connection to the database, and then submits the request for data.

A **provider** translates the Connection object's request for data into a language that the database can understand.

The **component tray** stores the objects that do not appear in the interface when an application is running.

SQL stands for **Structured Query Language**.

SQL is a set of commands that allows you to access and manipulate the data stored in databases.

The **SELECT statement** is the most commonly used SQL command. It allows you to specify the fields and records you want to access from a database, as well as control the order in which the fields and records appear when displayed.

You use the **WHERE clause** in a SELECT statement to limit the records that will be selected.

You use the **ORDER BY clause** in a SELECT statement to control the order in which the records appear when displayed.

XML, which stands for **Extensible Markup Language**, is a text-based language used to store and share data between applications and across networks and the Internet.

An **XML schema definition file** defines the tables and fields that make up the dataset.

You use the DataAdapter object's **Fill method** to fill a dataset with data while an application is running.

Binding refers to the process of connecting a DataSet object to a control.

Controls that are bound to a DataSet object are called **bound controls**.

The **DataGrid control** displays the data from a dataset in a row and column format, similar to a spreadsheet.

Review Questions

1. A(n) _____ is an organized collection of related information stored in a file on a disk.
   a. database
   b. field
   c. object
   d. record

2. A _____ database is one that stores information in tables.
   a. columnar
   b. relational
   c. sorted
   d. tabular

3. A group of related records in a database is called a _____.
   a. column
   b. field
   c. row
   d. table

4. Which of the following statements are true about a relational database?
   a. Data stored in a relational database can be retrieved both quickly and easily by the computer.
   b. Data stored in a relational database can be displayed in any order.
   c. A relational database stores data in a column and row format.
   d. All of the above are true.

5. When binding a DataSet object to a control, you set the control's _____ property to the name of the DataSet object.
   a. Data
   b. Dataset
   c. DataMember
   d. DataSource

6. _____ is a set of commands that allow you to access the data stored in many databases.
   a. ADO.NET
   b. DB .NET
   c. OLE .NET
   d. SQL

Use the following database table, named tblState, to answer Questions 7 through 9.

Field name	Data type
State	Text
Capital	Text
Population	Numeric

7. Which of the following statements allows you to view all of the records in the table?
   a. `SELECT ALL records FROM tblState`
   b. `SELECT * FROM tblState`
   c. `VIEW ALL records FROM tblState`
   d. `VIEW * FROM tblState`

8. Which of the following statements allows you to retrieve only the record whose State field contains the two letters "NY"?
   a. `SELECT * FROM tblState FOR "NY"`
   b. `SELECT * FROM tblState WHERE State = "NY"`
   c. `SELECT * FROM tblState WHERE State = 'ny'`
   d. `SELECT "NY" FROM tblState`

9. Which of the following statements allows you to retrieve all records having a population that exceeds 5,000,000?
   a. `SELECT ALL FROM tblState FOR Population > 5000000`
   b. `SELECT * FROM tblState WHERE Population > "5000000"`
   c. `SELECT * FROM tblState WHERE Population > '5000000'`
   d. None of the above.

10. A field that uniquely identifies each record in a table is called a _____.
    a. foreign field
    b. foreign key
    c. primary field
    d. primary key

11. The _____ contains the SELECT statement, which specifies the data the application wants to access.
    a. DataAdapter object
    b. Connection object
    c. DataSet object
    d. Provider

12. A _____ allows the database to communicate with the Connection object.
    a. DataAdapter object
    b. DataSet object
    c. Provider
    d. Translator object

13. In a SELECT statement, the _____ clause is used to limit the records that will be selected.
    a. LIMIT
    b. ORDER BY
    c. SET
    d. None of the above.

14. Controls connected to a DataSet object are called _____ controls.
    a. bound
    b. connected
    c. data
    d. None of the above.

15. You can use the _____ to build a SELECT statement.
    a. Query Builder
    b. Select Builder
    c. SQL Builder
    d. SQL Helper

16. If a funnel symbol appears next to a field's name in the Query Builder, it indicates that the field is _____.
    a. used in an ORDER BY clause in a SELECT statement
    b. used in a WHERE clause in a SELECT statement
    c. the primary key
    d. the foreign key

17. Objects that do not appear in the interface when an application is running are stored in the _____.
    a. component tray
    b. control tray
    c. object tray
    d. None of the above.

18. You use the _____ tool to create a DataAdapter object for a Microsoft Access database.
    a. OleDataAdapter
    b. OleDbAdapter
    c. OleDbDataAdapter
    d. OleDataDbAdapter

19. Which of the following tells the oledb_adapState object to load the dstState dataset with data? The dataset is associated with the DstState1 object.
    a. `Me.oledb_adapState(dstState)`
    b. `Me.oledb_adapState.Fill(Me.dstState)`
    c. `Me.oledb_adapState.Fill(DstState1)`
    d. `Me.oledb_adapState.Load(Me.dstState)`

20. The SQL SELECT statement is case-sensitive.
    a. True
    b. False

Exercises

1. In this exercise, you create an application that accesses the data stored in a database.
    a. Create the Morgan Industries interface shown in Figure 12.22. Name the solution Morgan Solution. Name the project Morgan Project. Save the solution in the VbDotNet\Chap12 folder.
    b. Add the DataAdapter, Connection, and DataSet objects shown in Figure 12.22 to the application. The Employees.mdb database is contained in the VbDotNet\Chap12\Databases folder.
    c. Use the application to test each of the SELECT statements shown in Figure 12.12. Enter each SELECT statement, one at a time, on the Generate the SQL statements screen (see Figure 12.13). After entering each statement, regenerate the dataset and then preview the data to verify that the statement selects the appropriate records.
    d. Write the SELECT statement to select only records with a hire date of 12/4/1998.
    e. Save the solution.

2. In this exercise, you create an application that displays a dataset in a DataGrid control.
    a. Use Windows to make a copy of the Morgan Solution folder, which you created in Exercise 1. Rename the folder Morgan DataGrid Solution.
    b. Open the Morgan Solution (Morgan Solution.sln) file contained in the Morgan DataGrid Solution folder.
    c. Add an Exit button to the interface. Code the button appropriately.
    d. Add a DataGrid control to the interface. The control should display each employee's number, name, and pay rate, as shown in Figure 12.27. Use the code shown in Figure 12.28 to code the form's Load event procedure.
    e. Save the solution, and then start and test the application.
    f. Click the Exit button to end the application.
    g. Modify the application so that it displays the fields and records shown in Figure 12.31.
    h. Save the solution, and then start and test the application.
    i. Click the Exit button to end the application, then close the solution.

3. In this exercise, you modify this chapter's Programming Example.
    a. Create the Cartwright Industries application shown in this chapter's Programming Example. Save the application in the VbDotNet\Chap12 folder.
    b. Modify the application so that it also displays the name of the item associated with the item number selected in the list box.
    c. Save the solution, then start and test the application.
    d. Click the Exit button to end the application, then close the solution.

4. In this exercise, you create an application that displays a dataset in label controls.
    a. Create the interface shown in Figure 12.34. Name the solution Morgan Labels Solution. Name the project Morgan Labels Project. Save the application in the VbDotNet\Chap12 folder.
    b. Add DataAdapter, Connection, and DataSet objects to the application.
    c. Use the code shown in Figure 12.35 to code the application.
    d. Save the solution, and then start and test the application.

    e.   Click the Exit button to end the application.

    f.   Add two buttons to the interface. One of the buttons should display the first record in the dataset, and the other should display the last record.

    g.   Save the solution, and then start and test the application.

    h.   Click the Exit button to end the application, then close the solution.

5.   In this exercise, you create an application that displays a dataset in label controls.

    a.   Create a Microsoft Access database named Friends.mdb that keeps track of the names and addresses of your friends. (Or, use the Friends.mdb database contained in the VbDotNet\Chap12\Databases folder.)

    b.   Create an application that allows you to display (in label controls) the records contained in the Friends.mdb database. Name the solution Friends Solution. Name the project Friends Project. Save the application in the VbDotNet\Chap12 folder.

    c.   Save the solution, and then start and test the application.

    d.   End the application, then close the solution.

6.   In this exercise, you learn about the XML schema definition file.

    a.   Open the Cartwright Solution (Cartwright Solution.sln) file, which is contained in the VbDotNet\Chap12\Cartwright Solution folder. (You created the solution in this chapter's Programming Example and, optionally, modified it in Exercise 3.)

    b.   Right-click the XML schema definition file in the Solution Explorer window, and then click Open. What information appears in the window?

    c.   Click the XML tab at the bottom of the window. Explain the following line: `<xs:element name="Number" type="xs:string" />`.

    d.   Close the solution.

7.   In this exercise, you find and correct an error in an application. The process of finding and correcting errors is called debugging.

    a.   Open the Debug Solution (Debug Solution.sln) file, which is contained in the VbDotNet\Chap12\Debug Solution folder.

    b.   Open the Code Editor window. Review the existing code.

    c.   Notice that a jagged line appears below one of the lines of code in the Code Editor window. Correct the code to remove the jagged line.

    d.   Save the solution, then start and test the application. Notice that the application is not working correctly. Click the Exit button to end the application.

    e.   Correct the errors in the application's code, then save the solution and start the application. Test the application.

    f.   Click the Exit button to end the application, then close the solution.

Case Projects

Addison Playhouse

Create a Microsoft Access database that contains one table named tblReservations. The table should contain three fields: a numeric field named Seat and two String fields named Name and Phone. The database should contain 20 records. (If you cannot create your own database, you can use the Play.mdb database contained in the VbDotNet\Chap12\Databases folder.) Create an application that allows the user to enter a seat number in the playhouse. The application should display the Name and Phone number of the person who reserved the seat.

College Courses

Create a Microsoft Access database that you can use to keep track of the courses you have taken in college. (Or, use the Courses.mdb database contained in the VbDotNet\Chap12\Databases folder.) The database should have one table named tblCourses and four fields. The four fields should store the course ID, course title, credit hours, and grade. The credit hours field should be numeric; the other fields should be text. Create an application that allows you to display the course title, credit hours, and grade associated with a course ID.

Sports Action

Create a Microsoft Access database that you can use to record the basketball scores for your favorite team. (Or, use the Sports.mdb database contained in the VbDotNet\Chap12\Databases folder.) The database should have one table named tblScores and four fields. The four fields should store the name of the opposing team, the date of the game, your favorite team's score, and the opposing team's score. Create an application that allows you to enter the game date and then display the name of the opposing team, your favorite team's score, and the opposing team's score.

The Fiction Bookstore

Jerry Schmidt, the manager of the Fiction Bookstore, uses a Microsoft Access database named Books.mdb to keep track of the books in his store. The database has one table named tblBooks. The table has three fields: a numeric field named BookNumber and two text fields named Title and Author. (You can either create your own Microsoft Access database, or use the Books.mdb database contained in the VbDotNet\Chap12\Databases folder.) Mr. Schmidt wants an application that he can use to select an author's name, and then display only the titles of books written by the author. (*Hint*: In this application, you need to allow the user to specify the records he or she wants to select while the application is running. You can use a parameterized query to accomplish this task. A parameterized query is simply a SELECT statement that contains a question mark in the WHERE clause; the question mark is a placeholder for the missing data—in this case, the author name. You will need to research the SelectCommand, Parameters, and Value properties of the DataAdapter object, and the Clear method of the DataSet object.)

13

Creating Web Applications Using ASP.NET

After studying Chapter 13, you should be able to:

- Define the terms used when talking about the Web
- Create a Web application
- Add controls to a Web form
- Start a Web application
- Use the validator controls
- Include a list box on a Web form
- Determine whether a postback has occurred
- Include a DataGrid control on a Web form

WEB TERMINOLOGY

The **Internet** is the world's largest computer network, connecting millions of computers located all around the world. One of the most popular features of the Internet is the **World Wide Web**, often referred to simply as **WWW** or the **Web**. The Web consists of documents called **Web pages** that are stored on Web servers. A **Web server** is a computer that contains special software that "serves up" Web pages in response to requests from clients. A **client** is a computer that requests information from a Web server. The information is requested and subsequently viewed through the use of a program called a **Web browser** or, more simply, a **browser**. Currently, the two most popular browsers are Microsoft Internet Explorer and Netscape Communicator. Figure 13.1 illustrates the relationship between a client, a browser, and a Web server.

FIGURE 13.1   Illustration of the relationship between a client, a browser, and a Web server

Many Web pages are static. A **static Web page** is a document whose purpose is merely to display information to the viewer. You can create a static Web page by opening a document in a text editor (such as Notepad) and then saving the document using a filename extension of .htm or .html. Within the document you enter the information you want displayed on the Web page. You then use **HTML (Hypertext Markup Language)** tags to tell the browser how to display the information. Figure 13.2 shows a static Web page created for the Greenview toy store, and Figure 13.3 shows the contents of the greenview.html file, which contains the instructions to create the Web page.

FIGURE 13.2   Example of a static Web page

```
greenview.html - Notepad
File  Edit  Format  View  Help
<!greenview.html>
<HTML>
    <HEAD><TITLE>Greenview Toy Store</TITLE></HEAD>
    <BODY>
        <H1 ALIGN=center>Greenview Toy Store</H1>
        <H3 ALIGN=center>333 Main Street<BR>
        Chicago, IL 60611<BR>
        (111) 555-5555</H3>

        <BR>
        <H2 ALIGN=center>
            <I>Please visit us during these hours:</I><BR><BR>
            <FONT COLOR=green>
            Monday - Friday 8am - 10pm<BR>
            Saturday        9am - 6pm<BR>
            Closed Sunday
            </FONT>
        </H2>
    </BODY>
</HTML>
```

FIGURE 13.3   Contents of the greenview.html file

TIP

To view the Web page shown in Figure 13.2, you first need to create the greenview.html file shown in Figure 13.3, and save it in the public_html folder.

Displayed on the Web page shown in Figure 13.2 are the toy store's name, address, telephone number, and business hours. The <I> and </I> tags in the greenview.html file tell the browser to display the text "Please visit us during these hours:" in italics. The <FONT COLOR=green> and </FONT> tags direct the browser to use green text when displaying the business hours.

Every Web page has a unique address that indicates its location on the Web. The address is called a **URL**—an acronym for **Uniform Resource Locator**. To view a Web page, you simply enter the page's URL in the appropriate box of a Web browser. For example, to view the Greenview toy store's Web page, you enter the URL http://localhost/public_html/greenview.html in the Address box in Internet Explorer, as shown in Figure 13.2.

A URL consists of four parts. The first part of the URL shown in Figure 13.2, http://, refers to the **HTTP communication protocol**, which is the protocol used to transmit Web pages on the Web. A **protocol** is simply an agreement between a sender and a receiver regarding how data are sent and interpreted. If you do not enter the communication protocol in a URL, Web browsers assume the HTTP protocol.

The second part of the URL is the name of the Web server where the document resides; the Web server is also referred to as the **host**. A Web server can be a remote computer, or you can make your local machine a Web server by installing and configuring Microsoft IIS (Internet Information Services). In the URL shown in Figure 13.2, the Web server's name is localhost and refers to your local machine.

The third part of the URL is the **path**, which specifies the location of the document on the Web server. The URL shown in Figure 13.2 indicates that the document is located in the public_html folder on the localhost server. It is important that the path you enter in the URL is exact; otherwise, the browser will not be able to locate the document. If you do not specify a path, the Web server assumes that the document is contained in a default location on the server. The network administrator defines the default location when the Web server is configured.

The last part of the URL specifies the name of the document—in this case, greenview.html. If you do not specify the name, most Web servers send a default home page to the Web browser.

When you type a URL in the Address box and then press the Enter key, the browser looks for the Web server specified in the URL. If the browser is able to locate the Web server, it submits your request. When the Web server receives a request for a static Web page, it locates the file, opens it, and then transfers its contents to the browser. The browser interprets the HTML instructions it receives and renders the Web page on the client's screen.

One drawback of static Web pages is that they are not interactive. The only interaction that can occur between a static Web page and the user is through links that allow the user to "jump" from one Web page to another.

To do business on the Web, a company must be able to do more than just list information on static Web pages. Rather, the company needs to be able to interact with customers through its Web site. The Web site should allow customers to submit inquiries, select items for purchase, provide shipping information, and submit payment information. It also should allow the company to track customer inquiries and process customer orders. Tasks such as this can be accomplished using dynamic Web pages.

Unlike a static Web page, a **dynamic Web page** is interactive; it can accept information from the user and also retrieve information for the user. If you have ever completed an online form—say, for example, to purchase merchandise or submit a resume—then you have used a dynamic Web page. Figure 13.4 shows an example of a dynamic Web page that converts American dollars to British pounds. To use the Web page, you enter the number of American dollars in the American dollars box and then click the Convert button. The button displays the corresponding number of British pounds on the Web page.

FIGURE 13.4   Example of a dynamic Web page

You use a Web form, rather than a Windows form, to create a Web page in Visual Basic .NET. You create (or design) the Web page in the **Web Form Designer window**. (Recall that Windows forms are created in the Windows Form Designer window.) Figure 13.5 shows the Currency Converter Web page in the Web Form Designer window.

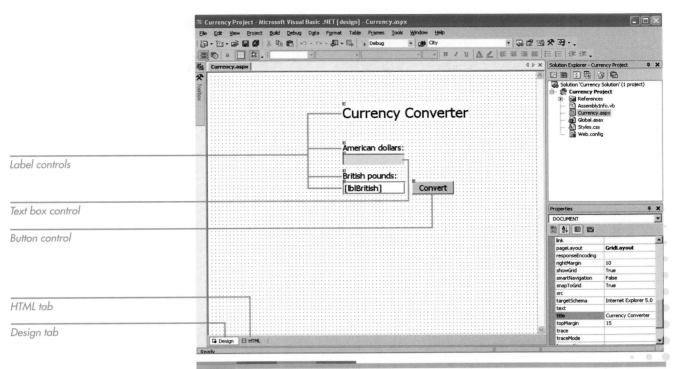

Label controls

Text box control

Button control

HTML tab

Design tab

FIGURE 13.5 Currency Converter Web page in the Web Form Designer window

Notice that two tabs—labeled Design and HTML—appear at the bottom of the Web Form Designer window. The Design tab shows the controls included on the Web page. For example, the Design tab in Figure 13.5 indicates that the Currency Converter Web page contains six controls: four labels, one text box, and one button. The HTML tab, on the other hand, contains the HTML tags that tell the browser how to render the Web page. Figure 13.6 shows the HTML tab for the Currency Converter Web page.

This file contains the information shown on the Design and HTML tabs

Indicates the location of the Visual Basic .NET code

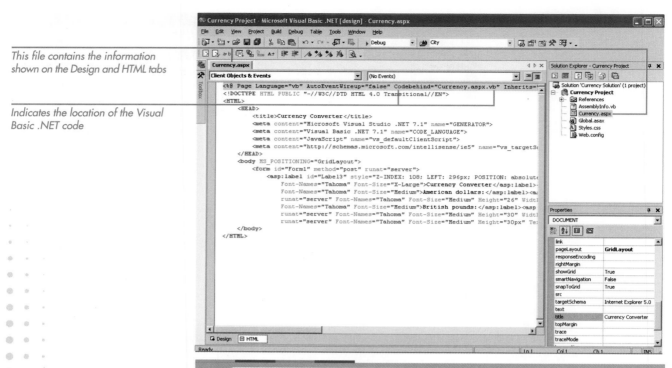

FIGURE 13.6 HTML tab for the Currency Converter Web page

Notice the `Codebehind="Currency.aspx.vb"` text that appears in the first line of code in Figure 13.6. Whereas a static Web page is simply an HTML file, a dynamic Web page usually requires two files: one of the files has an .aspx extension on its filename, while the other has an .aspx.vb extension. The .aspx file contains the controls and HTML that define the Web page's interface; in other words, it contains the information shown on the Design and HTML tabs on the Web Form Designer window. As indicated in Figure 13.6, the controls and HTML for the Currency Converter Web page is stored in a file named Currency.aspx. The .aspx.vb file, on the other hand, contains program code. The code tells the computer how to process the data submitted by or retrieved for the user, and is referred to as the "code behind the Web page." The `Codebehind="Currency.aspx.vb"` text indicates that the code behind the Currency Converter Web page is contained in a file named Currency.aspx.vb. Figure 13.7 shows the contents of the Currency.aspx.vb file.

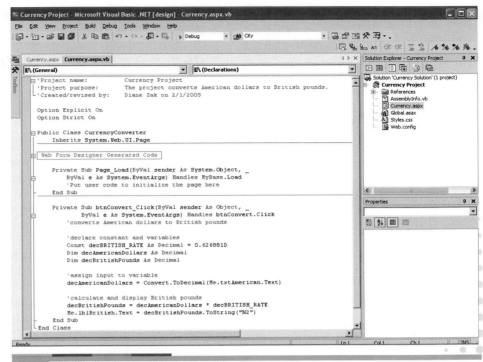

FIGURE 13.7   Currency.aspx.vb file

Notice that the btnConvert_Click procedure contains the instructions to convert the American dollars entered in the txtAmerican control to British pounds, and then display the result in the lblBritish control.

In the remainder of this chapter, you learn how to create Web applications that contain dynamic Web pages.

CREATING WEB APPLICATIONS

Figure 13.8 shows the procedure you follow to create a Web application.

HOW TO...

Create a Web Application

1. Click File on the menu bar, point to New, and then click Blank Solution. The New Project dialog box opens with Visual Studio Solutions selected in the Project Types box, and Blank Solution selected in the Templates box.
2. Enter an appropriate name in the Name box.
3. In the Location box, enter the path to the folder that stores your Web applications. (See Figure 13.9.)
4. Click the OK button to close the New Project dialog box.
5. Click File on the menu bar, point to Add Project, and then click New Project. The Add New Project dialog box opens.
6. Verify that Visual Basic Projects is selected in the Project Types list box, then click ASP.NET Web Application in the Templates list box.
7. In the Location text box, enter the URL of the Web server and folder where you want to create your project, followed by the project name. (See Figure 13.10.)
8. Click the OK button to close the Add New Project dialog box. (See Figure 13.11.)
9. Assign a more meaningful name to the Web form file; however, be sure to keep the .aspx extension on the name.
10. Click the Design tab on the Web Form Designer window, then use the Properties window to assign a more meaningful value to the DOCUMENT object's title property. (See Figure 13.12.)

FIGURE 13.8   How to create a Web application

Steps 1 through 3 in Figure 13.8 tell you how to open and complete the New Project dialog box. You use the dialog box to create a blank solution for your Web application. Figure 13.9 shows an example of a completed New Project dialog box.

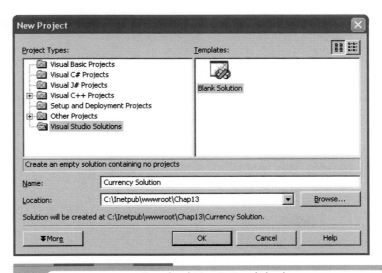

FIGURE 13.9   Completed New Project dialog box

Steps 5 through 7 in Figure 13.8 tell you how to open and complete the Add New Project dialog box. You use this dialog box to add an ASP.NET Web Application project to the blank solution. **ASP.NET** is Microsoft's newest technology for creating Web applications containing dynamic (interactive) Web pages. ("ASP" stands for "Active Server Pages.") Figure 13.10 shows an example of a completed Add New Project dialog box.

Use this template to create a Web application

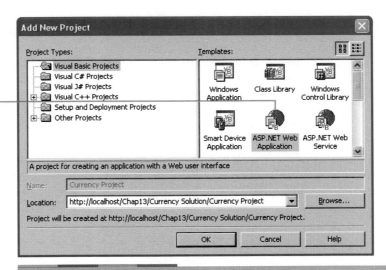

FIGURE 13.10   Completed Add New Project dialog box

When you close the Add New Project dialog box, the Create New Web message box appears momentarily, and then a new Web application appears on the screen, as shown in Figure 13.11. Notice that the default name for the Web form file in the application is WebForm1.aspx.

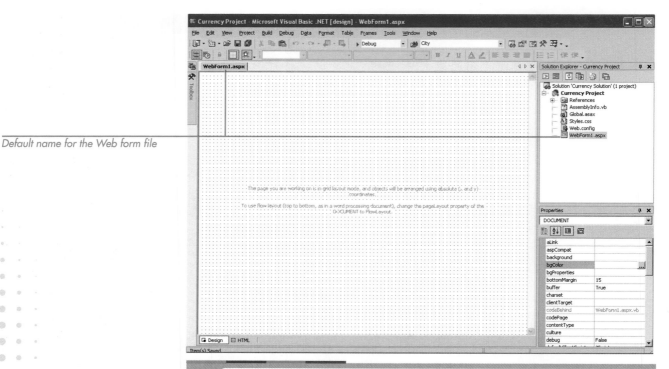

Default name for the Web form file

FIGURE 13.11 New Web application

Step 9 in the procedure shown earlier in Figure 13.8 is to assign a more meaningful name to the Web form file. You can use the Properties window to assign the name; or, you can right-click WebForm1.aspx in the Solution Explorer window and then click Rename. Be sure to keep the .aspx extension on the new name; otherwise, the Web application will not work correctly. A good name for the Web form file shown in Figure 13.11 is Currency.aspx.

The last step in the procedure for creating a Web application is to assign a more meaningful value to the title property of the DOCUMENT object, which is the Web form itself. In the current application, you will set the title property to Currency Converter. When the Web form is displayed in a browser, the contents of its title property appears in the browser's title bar. (You can look back at Figure 13.4 to see where the title property appears.) Figure 13.12 shows the changes made to the form file's name and the DOCUMENT object's title property.

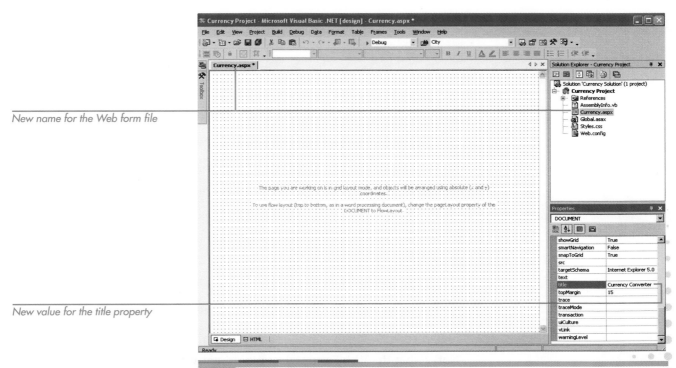

New name for the Web form file

New value for the title property

FIGURE 13.12 Changes made to the Web application

Next, you learn how to add controls to a Web form.

Adding Controls to a Web Form

Similar to the way you add controls to a Windows form, you use the tools contained in the Toolbox window to add controls to a Web form. However, the tools for a Web form are located on the Web Forms tab in the toolbox rather than on the Windows Forms tab. The Web Forms tab is shown in Figure 13.13. You can add a control to a Web form by simply dragging the corresponding tool from the Web Forms tab to the form.

Web Forms tab

FIGURE 13.13 Web Forms tab on the toolbox

Notice that the Web Forms tab contains many of the same tools found on the Windows Forms tab—such as the Label, TextBox, and Button tools. You can use these tools to create label, text box, and button controls for your Web applications. Although Web controls operate in a manner similar to their Windows counterparts, they are not identical to the Windows controls. For example, Web controls have an ID property rather than a Name property.

Figure 13.14 lists the names and uses of several properties of Web label, text box, and button controls.

HOW TO...

Use Web Label, Text Box, and Button Controls

Property	Use to
BackColor	specify the background color for the control
BorderStyle	specify whether the control has a visible border
Font/Name	specify the name of the font to use for text (usually set to Tahoma); you will need to expand the Font node to set the name
Font/Size	specify the size of the font to use for text; you will need to expand the Font node to set the size
ForeColor	specify the color of the text that appears in the control
Height	specify the height of the control; measured in px (pixels)
ID	give the control a meaningful name (labels begin with "lbl", text boxes with "txt", and buttons with "btn")
Text	specify the caption that appears inside the control
Width	specify the width of the control; measured in px (pixels)

FIGURE 13.14 How to use Web label, text box, and button controls

Figure 13.15 lists the property settings for the label, text box, and button controls included in the Currency Converter application shown earlier in Figure 13.5.

Object	Property	Setting
Label1	Font/Name	Tahoma
	Font/Size	Medium
	Text	American dollars:
Label2	Font/Name	Tahoma
	Font/Size	Medium
	Text	British pounds:
Label3	Font/Name	Tahoma
	Font/Size	X-Large
	Text	Currency Converter
lblBritish	ID	lblBritish
	BorderStyle	Groove
	Font/Name	Tahoma
	Font/Size	Medium
	Height	30px
	Text	(empty)
	Width	138px
txtAmerican	ID	txtAmerican
	BackColor	Beige (on the Web tab)
	BorderStyle	Inset
	Font/Name	Tahoma
	Font/Size	Medium
	Height	26px
	Text	(empty)
	Width	137px
btnConvert	ID	btnConvert
	Font/Name	Tahoma
	Font/Size	Medium
	Height	30px

FIGURE 13.15 Property settings for the controls in the Currency Converter application

After creating the Web application's interface, you then code the application. You can open the Code Editor window by right-clicking the Web form and then clicking View Code. Figure 13.16 shows the code for the Currency Converter application. As the figure indicates, the name of the class was changed from its default value (WebForm1) to CurrencyConverter, which is a more meaningful name.

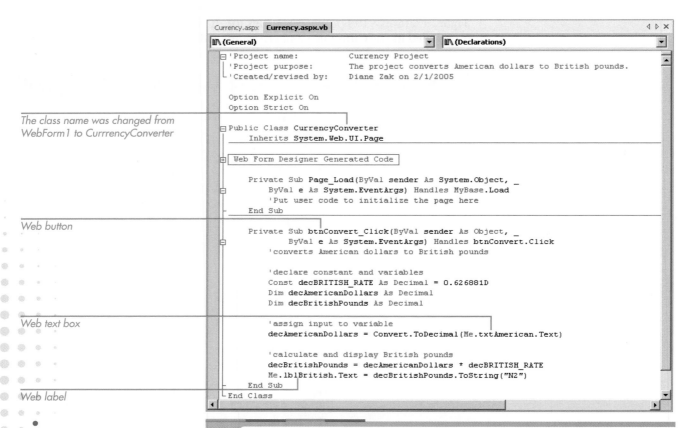

The class name was changed from WebForm1 to CurrrencyConverter

Web button

Web text box

Web label

```
Currency.aspx   Currency.aspx.vb                                          ◁ ▷ ×
(General)                                  ▼     (Declarations)            ▼
'Project name:            Currency Project
'Project purpose:         The project converts American dollars to British pounds.
'Created/revised by:      Diane Zak on 2/1/2005

Option Explicit On
Option Strict On

Public Class CurrencyConverter
    Inherits System.Web.UI.Page

 Web Form Designer Generated Code

    Private Sub Page_Load(ByVal sender As System.Object, _
        ByVal e As System.EventArgs) Handles MyBase.Load
        'Put user code to initialize the page here
    End Sub

    Private Sub btnConvert_Click(ByVal sender As Object, _
        ByVal e As System.EventArgs) Handles btnConvert.Click
        'converts American dollars to British pounds

        'declare constant and variables
        Const decBRITISH_RATE As Decimal = 0.626881D
        Dim decAmericanDollars As Decimal
        Dim decBritishPounds As Decimal

        'assign input to variable
        decAmericanDollars = Convert.ToDecimal(Me.txtAmerican.Text)

        'calculate and display British pounds
        decBritishPounds = decAmericanDollars * decBRITISH_RATE
        Me.lblBritish.Text = decBritishPounds.ToString("N2")
    End Sub
End Class
```

FIGURE 13.16 Code for the Currency Converter Web application

TIP

If an application contains more than one Web form, the Web form designated as the start page appears in the browser window when the application is started. You designate the start page by right-clicking the name of the Web form file in the Solution Explorer window, and then clicking Set As Start Page. Recall that Web form files have an .aspx extension on their filenames.

Notice that, like a Windows button control, a Web button control has a Click event. Also notice that you can refer to the property of a Web control in an assignment statement.

As you do with a Windows application, you need to start a Web application to determine whether it is working correctly.

Starting a Web Application

You can use either of the four methods shown in Figure 13.17 to start a Web application. When a Web application is started, the Web form in the application appears in a browser window. You use the browser window to verify that the form appears and works as intended.

HOW TO...

Start a Web Application

- Click Debug on the menu bar, and then click Start.
- Press the F5 key on your keyboard.
- Right-click the Web form, and then click View in Browser.
- Click File on the menu bar, and then click View in Browser.

FIGURE 13.17 How to start a Web application

The first two methods shown in Figure 13.17 display the Web form in your default browser, which typically is Microsoft Internet Explorer. The last two methods display the Web form in the internal Web browser built into Visual Studio .NET. Figure 13.18 shows the Currency Converter Web form displayed in Microsoft Internet Explorer, and Figure 13.19 shows the form displayed in Visual Studio .NET's internal browser. When you are finished viewing the form, you close the browser window using its Close button.

Use the Close button to close the Microsoft Internet Explorer browser window

FIGURE 13.18 Currency Converter Web form displayed in Microsoft Internet Explorer

Use this Close button to close the internal browser window

TIP

To change the browser used by the last two methods shown in Figure 13.17, click File on the menu bar, and then click Browse With. Select the name of the browser in the Browser list, and then click the Set as Default button. Click the Close button to close the Browse With dialog box.

FIGURE 13.19 Currency Converter Web form displayed in the internal browser built into Visual Studio .NET

The Web Forms tab in the toolbox contains five tools that allow you to validate user input. These tools are referred to as the validator tools.

USING THE WEB VALIDATOR TOOLS

Figure 13.20 lists the names, uses, and several properties of the validator tools found on the Web Forms tab in the toolbox.

HOW TO...

Use the Validator Tools

Name	Use to	Properties
RequiredFieldValidator	verify that a control contains data	ControlToValidate ErrorMessage
RangeValidator	verify that an entry is within the specified minimum and maximum values	ControlToValidate ErrorMessage MinimumValue MaximumValue Type
RegularExpressionValidator	verify that an entry matches a specific pattern	ControlToValidate ErrorMessage ValidationExpression
CompareValidator	compare an entry with a constant value or the property value stored in a control	ControlToValidate ControlToCompare ErrorMessage Type ValueToCompare
CustomValidator	verify that an entry passes the specified validation logic	ControlToValidate ErrorMessage ClientValidationFunction

FIGURE 13.20 How to use the validator tools

Figure 13.21 shows the RequiredFieldValidator and RangeValidator controls added to the Currency Converter Web form. The RequiredFieldValidator control verifies that the txtAmerican control contains data, and the RangeValidator control determines whether the data is a number within the 1 through 100,000 range.

RequiredFieldValidator control

RangeValidator control

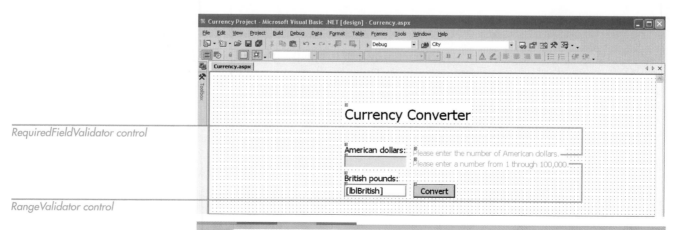

FIGURE 13.21 Validator controls added to the Currency Converter Web form

The ControlToValidate property for each validator control is set to txtAmerican, and the Font/Name and Font/Size properties are set to Tahoma and Small, respectively. The RequiredFieldValidator control's ErrorMessage property is set to "Please enter the number of American dollars." The message will appear on the Web page only if the user clicks the Convert button before entering any data in the txtAmerican control.

The RangeValidator control's MinimumValue and MaximumValue properties are set to 1 and 100000, respectively, and its Type property is set to Currency. Additionally, the ErrorMessage property for the RangeValidator control is set to "Please enter a number from 1 through 100,000." The message will appear on the Web page only if the user clicks the Convert button after entering (in the txtAmerican control) a value that is not within the 1 through 100,000 range.

As you learned in Chapter 10, in applications where the user is expected to enter one or more specific values, it is better to use other controls—such as list boxes, radio buttons, or check boxes—to display the values. Then, rather than typing the desired value in a text box, the user can select the appropriate value from one of these other controls. In the next section, you learn how to include a list box on a Web form.

INCLUDING A LIST BOX ON A WEB FORM

You use the ListBox tool on the Web Forms tab to add a list box to a Web form. You can use a list box to display a list of choices from which the user can select one or more choices. Figure 13.22 lists the names and uses of several properties of a Web list box.

HOW TO...

Use a Web List Box

Property	Use to
BackColor	specify the background color for the control
DataMember	specify the database table to bind to
DataSource	specify the data set to bind to
Font/Name	specify the name of the font to use for text (usually set to Tahoma); you will need to expand the Font node to set the name
Font/Size	specify the size of the font to use for text; you will need to expand the Font node to set the size
ForeColor	specify the color of the text that appears in the control
Height	specify the height of the control; measured in px (pixels)
ID	give the control a meaningful name that begins with "lst"
Rows	specify the number of visible rows to display
SelectedIndex	get or set the index of the selected item; not listed in the Properties window; only available in code
SelectedValue	get or set the value of the selected item; not listed in the Properties window; only available in code
SelectionMode	specify whether the user can select one or more choices
Width	specify the width of the control; measured in px (pixels)

FIGURE 13.22 How to use a Web list box

For this next example, assume that Stovall Pharmacies is located in five stores in southern Florida. The pharmacists have asked for an application that allows them to display the names of the manager and assistant manager at each of the stores. You will use a list box to display the store numbers, and label controls to display the names of the manager and assistant manager. Figure 13.23 shows the Web form for the Stovall application.

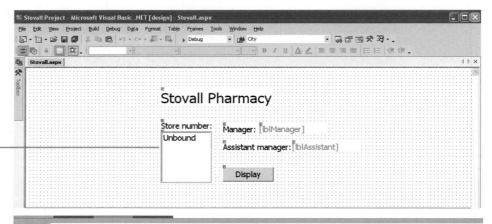

FIGURE 13.23 Web form for the Stovall application

Web list box

The Stovall Web form contains six labels, one button, and one list box. The list box's ID property is set to lstNumber, its Rows property to 5, and its Width property to 112px. Additionally, its Font/Name and Font/Size properties are set to Tahoma and Medium, respectively. Figure 13.24 shows the Stovall application's code.

TIP

The word "Unbound" that appears in the list box indicates that the list box is not bound to a dataset.

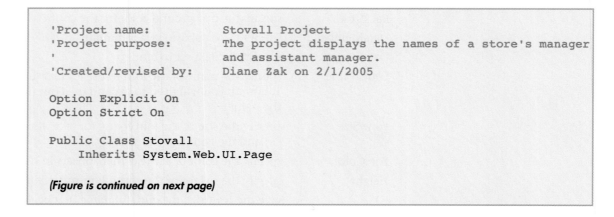

```
'Project name:          Stovall Project
'Project purpose:       The project displays the names of a store's manager
'                       and assistant manager.
'Created/revised by:    Diane Zak on 2/1/2005

Option Explicit On
Option Strict On

Public Class Stovall
    Inherits System.Web.UI.Page
```

(Figure is continued on next page)

```
[Web Form Designer Generated Code]

    Private Sub Page_Load(ByVal sender As System.Object, _
        ByVal e As System.EventArgs) Handles MyBase.Load
        'Put user code to initialize the page here
        'fills the list box with data, then selects the first item

        If Not Me.IsPostBack Then
            Me.lstNumber.Items.Add("1001")
            Me.lstNumber.Items.Add("1002")
            Me.lstNumber.Items.Add("1005")
            Me.lstNumber.Items.Add("1007")
            Me.lstNumber.Items.Add("1010")
            Me.lstNumber.SelectedIndex = 0
        End If
    End Sub

    Private Sub btnDisplay_Click(ByVal sender As Object, _
        ByVal e As System.EventArgs) Handles btnDisplay.Click
        'displays the names of the manager and assistant manager

        'declare variable
        Dim strNumber As String

        'assign input to variable
        strNumber = Convert.ToString(Me.lstNumber.SelectedValue)

        'display names
        Select Case strNumber
            Case "1001"
                Me.lblManager.Text = "Jeffrey Jefferson"
                Me.lblAssistant.Text = "Paula Hendricks"
            Case "1002"
                Me.lblManager.Text = "Barbara Millerton"
                Me.lblAssistant.Text = "Sung Lee"
            Case "1005"
                Me.lblManager.Text = "Inez Baily"
                Me.lblAssistant.Text = "Homer Gomez"
            Case "1007"
                Me.lblManager.Text = "Lou Chan"
                Me.lblAssistant.Text = "Jake Johansen"
            Case "1010"
                Me.lblManager.Text = "Henry Abernathy"
                Me.lblAssistant.Text = "Ingrid Nadkarni"
        End Select
    End Sub

End Class
```

The Page_Load procedure is processed only when the Web form is first displayed in the browser window

FIGURE 13.24 Stovall application's code

The Page_Load procedure in the code fills the lstNumber control with the five store numbers, and then selects the first store number in the list. The Page_Load event occurs the first time the Web form is displayed. It also occurs each time the user selects a store number from the list box, as well as each time he or she clicks the Display button. This is because those actions cause a post-back to occur. A **postback** refers to the client requesting data from the server, and the server responding. Each time a postback occurs, the Web page is redis-played on the client's screen. You can use the Web form's **IsPostBack property** to determine whether the Web form is being displayed for the first time or as a result of a postback. The property contains the Boolean value False the first time the form is displayed; otherwise, it contains the Boolean value True. The `If Not Me.IsPostBack Then` clause in the Page_Load procedure tells the computer to process the six instructions contained in the selection structure's True path only the first time the Web form is displayed, and to ignore the instructions when it is a postback.

When the user clicks a store number in the lstNumber control, the btnDisplay_Click procedure displays the names of the store's manager and assis-tant manager in the lblManager and lblAssistant controls. Figure 13.25 shows a sample run of the Stovall application.

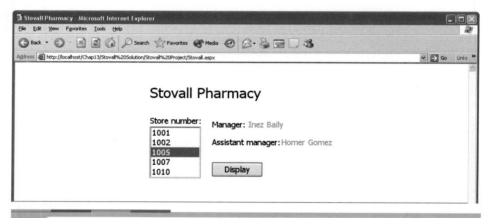

FIGURE 13.25 Sample run of the Stovall application

In Chapter 12, you learned how to display information in a DataGrid control on a Windows form. You also can display information in a DataGrid control on a Web form.

INCLUDING A DATAGRID CONTROL ON A WEB FORM

Recall that a DataGrid control displays the data from a dataset in a row and col-umn format, similar to a spreadsheet. Each field in the dataset appears in a col-umn in the DataGrid control, and each record appears in a row. Figure 13.26 lists the names and uses of several properties of a Web DataGrid control.

HOW TO...

Use a Web DataGrid Control

Property	Use to
BackColor	specify the background color for the control
Columns	specify the columns to display in the control
DataMember	specify the table to associate with the control
DataSource	specify the DataSet object to associate with the control
Font/Name	specify the name of the font to use for text (usually set to Tahoma); you will need to expand the Font node to set the name
Font/Size	specify the size of the font to use for text; you will need to expand the Font node to set the size
GridLines	specify which (if any) gridlines appear in the control
Height	specify the height of the control; measured in px (pixels)
ID	give the DataGrid control a meaningful name that begins with "dgd"
ShowHeader	specify whether the column headings should be shown or hidden
Width	specify the width of the control; measured in px (pixels)

Note: The Web DataGrid control also has an Auto Format link that appears in the Properties window when the control is selected. You can use the link to display a dialog box that allows you to select from a list of predefined formats for displaying data.

FIGURE 13.26 How to use a Web DataGrid control

For this example, assume that Jack Benton, the Personnel Manager at Fairview Industries, has asked you to create a Web application that displays the names of the company's 12 employees, as well as their employee numbers, hourly pay rates, and status (either F for full-time or P for part-time). The employee information is stored in a Microsoft Access database named Employees.mdb. The Employees.mdb file is contained in the Inetpub\wwwroot\Chap13\Databases folder. Figure 13.27 shows the Web form for the Fairview application.

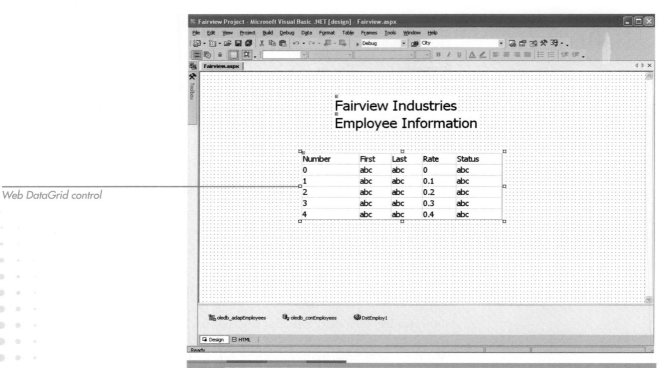

Web DataGrid control

FIGURE 13.27 Web form for the Fairview application

The Fairview Web form contains an OleDbDataAdapter object, an OleDbConnection object, and a DataSet object; you learned how to use these objects in Chapter 12. The Web form also contain two labels and a DataGrid control. The DataGrid control's ID property is set to dgdEmploy, its DataMember property to tblEmploy, its DataSource property to DstEmploy1, and its Width property to 440px. Additionally, its Font/Name and Font/Size properties are set to Tahoma and Medium, respectively. Figure 13.28 shows the Fairview application's code.

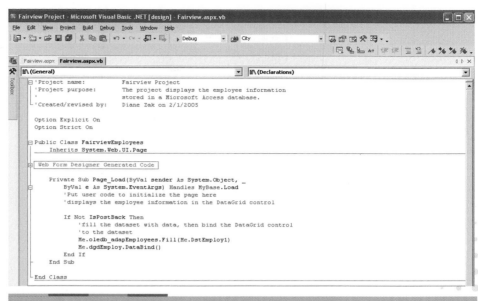

FIGURE 13.28 Fairview application's code

TIP

The DataBind method is necessary to bind a Web DataGrid control to a dataset; however, it is not used when binding a Windows DataGrid control to a dataset.

In the Page_Load procedure, the two instructions in the selection structure's True path will be processed only once, which is when the Web form first appears in the browser. The first instruction fills the dataset with the employee data. The second instruction uses the DataGrid control's **DataBind method** to bind the control to the dataset.

Finally, you learn how to customize the appearance of the data displayed in a Web DataGrid control.

Customizing the Appearance of the Web DataGrid Control's Data

The DataGrid control provides many properties that you can use to control the appearance of its output. For example, the ShowHeader property allows you to specify whether the column headings should be shown or hidden. The BackColor property allows you to select the background color for the control. The DataGrid control also provides an Auto Format dialog box that allows you to select from a list of predefined formats, or schemes, for displaying data. You can open the dialog box by right-clicking the DataGrid control and then clicking Auto Format. Or, you can click the DataGrid control and then click the Auto Format link that appears below the Properties list in the Properties window. The Auto Format dialog box is shown in Figure 13.29.

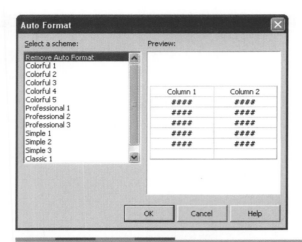

FIGURE 13.29 Auto Format dialog box

Figure 13.30 shows a sample run of the Fairview application with the DataGrid control formatted using the Professional 2 scheme.

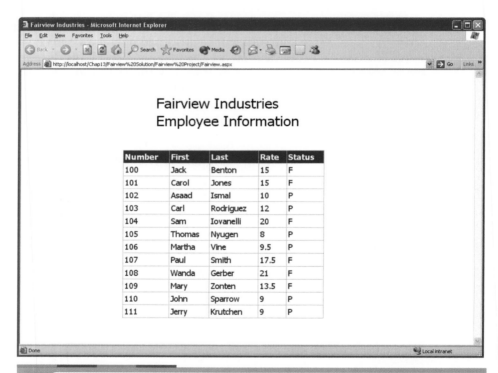

FIGURE 13.30 Sample run of the Fairview application

PROGRAMMING EXAMPLE

Monthly Payment Calculator Application

Fred Pierce has been shopping for a new car and has asked you to create an application that he can use to calculate and display his monthly car payment, using annual interest rates of 5%, 6%, 7%, 8%, 9%, and 10%, and terms of two, three, four, and five years. Name the solution Payment Solution. Name the project Payment Project. Name the Web form file Payment.aspx. Save the application in the inetpub\wwwroot\Chap13 folder.

TOE Chart:

Task	Object	Event
1. Calculate the monthly payment 2. Display the monthly payment in lblPayment	btnCalc	Click
1. Fill the lstRate and lstTerm controls with data 2. Select the first item in each list box	Page	Load
Display the monthly payment (from btnCalc)	lblPayment	None
Get and display the interest rates	lstRate	None
Get and display the terms	lstTerm	None
Verify that the principal is from 0 through 50,000	RangeValidator1	None
Verify that the principal was entered	RequiredFieldValidator	None
Get and display the principal	txtPrincipal	None

FIGURE 13.31

User Interface:

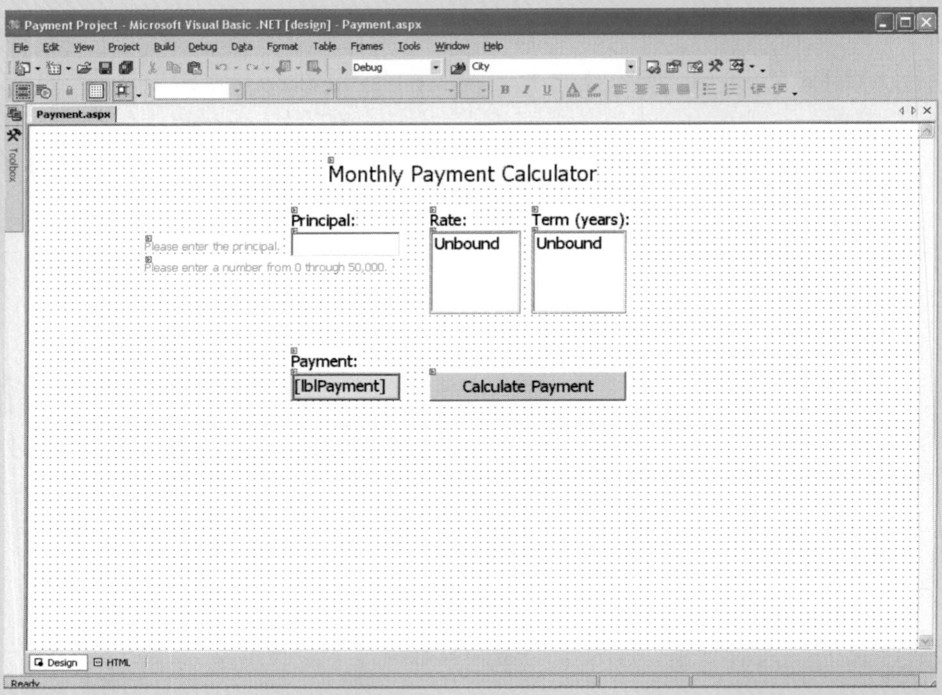

FIGURE 13.32

Objects, Properties, and Settings

Object	Property	Setting
DOCUMENT	title	Payment Calculator
RangeValidator1	ControlToValidate	txtPrincipal
	ErrorMessage	Please enter a number from 0 through 50,000.
	Font/Name	Tahoma
	Font/Size	X-Small
	MaximumValue	50000
	MinimumValue	0
	Type	Currency
RequiredFieldValidator1	ControlToValidate	txtPrincipal
	ErrorMessage	Please enter the principal.
	Font/Name	Tahoma
	Font/Size	X-Small

(Table is continued on next page)

Object	Property	Setting
Label1	Font/Name Font/Size Text	Tahoma Large Monthly Payment Calculator
Label2	Font/Name Font/Size Text	Tahoma Medium Principal:
Label3	Font/Name Font/Size Text	Tahoma Medium Rate:
Label4	Font/Name Font/Size Text	Tahoma Medium Term (years):
Label5	Font/Name Font/Size Text	Tahoma Medium Payment:
lblPayment	ID BackColor BorderStyle Font/Name Font/Size Height Text Width	lblPayment Beige (on the Web tab) Ridge Tahoma Medium 32px (empty) 120px
lstRate	ID Font/Name Font/Size Width	lstRate Tahoma Medium 100px
lstTerm	ID Font/Name Font/Size Width	lstTerm Tahoma Medium 104px
txtPrincipal	ID BorderStyle Font/Name Font/Size Text Width	txtPrincipal Inset Tahoma Medium (empty) 120px
btnCalc	ID Font/Name Font/Size Text	btnCalc Tahoma Medium Calculate Payment

FIGURE 13.33

Pseudocode:

Page Load event procedure

1. if it's the first time the Web form is displayed
       fill the lstRate control with data
       fill the lstTerm control with data
       select the first item in each list box
  end if

btnCalc Click event procedure

1. calculate the monthly payment
2. display the monthly payment in lblPayment

Code:

```
'Project name:          Payment Project
'Project purpose:       The project calculates a monthly payment on a loan.
'Created/revised by:    Diane Zak on 2/1/2005

Option Explicit On
Option Strict On

Public Class PaymentCalculator
    Inherits System.Web.UI.Page

[Web Form Designer Generated Code]

    Private Sub Page_Load(ByVal sender As System.Object, _
        ByVal e As System.EventArgs) Handles MyBase.Load
        'Put user code to initialize the page here
        'fills the list boxes with data

        If Not Me.IsPostBack Then
            'declare variable
            Dim intX As Integer

            'fill the lstRate control with interest rates
            For intX = 5 To 10
                Me.lstRate.Items.Add(intX.ToString() & "%")
            Next intX

            'fill the lstTerm control with terms
            For intX = 2 To 5
                Me.lstTerm.Items.Add(intX.ToString())
            Next intX

            'select first item in each list box
            Me.lstRate.SelectedIndex = 0
            Me.lstTerm.SelectedIndex = 0
        End If
    End Sub

    (Figure is continued on next page)
```

```
        Private Sub btnCalc_Click(ByVal sender As Object, _
            ByVal e As System.EventArgs) Handles btnCalc.Click
            'calculates and displays the monthly payment

            'declare variables
            Dim decPrincipal As Decimal
            Dim decRate As Decimal
            Dim decTerm As Decimal
            Dim decPayment As Decimal

            'assign input to variables
            decPrincipal = Convert.ToDecimal(Me.txtPrincipal.Text)
            decRate = _
                Convert.ToDecimal(Me.lstRate.SelectedValue.TrimEnd("%"c)) / 100D
            decTerm = Convert.ToDecimal(Me.lstTerm.SelectedValue)

            'calculate and display monthly payment
            decPayment = _
                Convert.ToDecimal(-Pmt(decRate / 12D, decTerm * 12D, decPrincipal))
            Me.lblPayment.Text = decPayment.ToString("C2")
        End Sub

End Class
```

FIGURE 13.34

Quick Review

- The Web consists of Web pages that are stored on Web servers.
- A client uses a browser to request a Web page from a Web server.
- Web pages can be either static or dynamic (interactive).
- Static Web pages contain the information to display, as well as the HTML tags that control the appearance of the information. Static Web pages are not interactive.
- Every Web page has a unique address, called a URL, that indicates its location on the Web.
- A URL consists of four parts: the protocol, the name of the Web server, the path to the Web page, and the name of the Web page.
- A Web server can be a remote computer or your local machine. To make your local machine a Web server, you must install and configure Microsoft IIS (Internet Information Services).
- A dynamic Web page requires two files: one ending with .aspx and the other with .aspx.vb. The .aspx file contains the controls and HTML that define the Web page's interface, and the .aspx.vb file contains program code.
- You add controls to a Web form in the same way that you add controls to a Windows form.
- The Web Forms tab in the toolbox contains the Web tools. Web tools are similar but not identical to their Windows counterparts.

- You test a Web application using a browser.
- The Web Forms tab on the toolbox contains five validator tools. The validator tools allow you to validate user input.
- You can use a Web form's IsPostBack method to determine whether the form is being displayed for the first time.

Key Terms

The **Internet** is a computer network that connects millions of computers located all around the world.

The **World Wide Web**, also called **WWW** or the **Web**, consists of documents called **Web pages** that are stored on Web servers.

A **Web server** is a computer that contains special software that "serves up" Web pages in response to requests from clients.

A **client** is a computer that requests information from a Web server.

A **Web browser**, or **browser**, is a program that allows a client to access and view Web pages.

A **static Web page** is a non-interactive document whose only purpose is to display information to the viewer.

HTML stands for **Hypertext Markup Language**, which is a language that uses tags to tell a browser how to display the information on a Web page.

URL stands for **Uniform Resource Locator** and is the unique address assigned to each Web page on the Web.

The **HTTP communication protocol** is the protocol used to transmit Web pages on the Web.

A **protocol** is an agreement between a sender and a receiver regarding how data are sent and interpreted.

The **path** in a URL specifies the location of the document on the Web server.

A **dynamic Web page** is an interactive document that can accept information from the user and also retrieve information for the user.

You create a Web page in the **Web Form Designer window**.

ASP.NET stands for "Active Server Pages .NET" and is Microsoft's newest technology for creating Web applications containing dynamic Web pages.

A **postback** occurs when a server responds to a request from a client.

The first time a Web form is displayed in a browser, the form's **IsPostBack property** contains the Boolean value False; otherwise, the property contains the Boolean value True.

You use the **DataBind method** to bind a Web DataGrid control to a dataset.

Review Questions

1. Every Web page is identified by a unique address called _____.
   a. an AP
   b. an ASP
   c. a ULR
   d. a URL

2. A computer that requests information from a Web server is called a client.
   a. True
   b. False

3. A _____ is a program that requests and then displays a Web page.
   a. browser
   b. client
   c. server
   d. requester

4. An online form that you use to purchase a product is an example of a _____.
   a. dynamic Web page
   b. static Web page

5. When using ASP.NET to create a dynamic Web page, the _____ file contains the controls and HTML that define the interface.
   a. .asp
   b. .aspx
   c. .aspx.vb
   d. .vb

6. When using ASP.NET to create a dynamic Web page, the _____ file contains the program code.
   a. .asp
   b. .aspx
   c. .aspx.vb
   d. .vb

7. Which of the following Web validator controls allows you to verify that a text box contains data?
   a. DataValidator
   b. RangeValidator
   c. TextValidator
   d. None of the above.

8. Which of the following Web validator controls allows you to verify that the data entered in a text box is between 1 and 5?
   a. DataValidator
   b. RangeValidator
   c. TextValidator
   d. None of the above.

9. _____ occurs when a server responds to a request from a client.
   a. An AnswerBack
   b. A CallBack
   c. A ReturnBack
   d. None of the above.

10. You use the DataBind method to bind Web DataGrid controls and Windows DataGrid controls to a dataset.
    a. True
    b. False

11. The first time a Web form is displayed in a browser, its _____ property contains the Boolean value False.
    a. IsBack
    b. IsBackPost
    c. IsPostBack
    d. PostBack

12. The _____ event occurs each time a Web form is displayed in the browser window.
    a. Load_Page
    b. Page_Load
    c. Web_Page_Load
    d. None of the above.

13. "URL" is an acronym for "Universal Resource Locator".
    a. True
    b. False

14. "ASP" is an acronym for "Active Server Pages".
    a. True
    b. False

15. "HTML" is an acronym for "Hypertext Markup Language".
    a. True
    b. False

16. _____ is the communication protocol used to transmit Web pages on the Web.
    a. ASP
    b. HTML
    c. HTTP
    d. URL

17. You can use a _____ to display a list of choices from which the user can select one or more choices.
    a. DataGrid
    b. Data
    c. List
    d. ListBox

18. A client computer is also referred to as a host.
    a. True
    b. False

19. You test a Web application using a browser.
    a. True
    b. False

20. A URL contains the communication protocol, the name of the Web server, the path to the Web page, and the name of the Web page.
    a. True
    b. False

Exercises

1. In this exercise, you create a Web application that converts American dollars to British pounds.
   a. Use Figures 13.15, 13.16, and 13.21 to create the Currency Converter application. Name the solution Currency Solution. Name the project Currency Project. Name the Web form file Currency.aspx. Save the application in the inetpub\wwwroot\Chap13 folder.
   b. Modify the application so that it also displays the number of Canadian dollars and the number of Japanese yen. Use the following conversion rates:

      1 American dollar = 1.3874 Canadian dollar
      1 American dollar = 118.24 Japanese yen

   c. Save the solution, then start and test the application.
   d. Close your browser and the solution.

2. In this exercise, you create a Web application that allows the user to select a store number from a list box. The application then displays the names of the store's manager and assistant manager.
   a. Use Figures 13.23 and 13.24 to create the Stovall Pharmacy application. Name the solution Stovall Solution. Name the project Stovall Project. Name the Web form file Stovall.aspx. Save the application in the inetpub\wwwroot\Chap13 folder.
   b. Save the solution, then start and test the application.
   c. Close your browser and the solution.

3. In this exercise, you create a Web application that displays employee information stored in a Microsoft Access database named Employees.mdb. The database is contained in the inetpub\wwwroot\Chap13\Databases folder.
   a. Use Figures 13.27 and 13.28 to create the Fairview Industries application. Name the solution Fairview Solution. Name the project Fairview Project. Name the Web form file Fairview.aspx. Save the application in the inetpub\wwwroot\Chap13 folder.
   b. Use the Auto Format dialog box to format the DataGrid control.
   c. Save the solution, then start and test the application.
   d. Close your browser and the solution.

4. In this exercise, you create a Web application that calculates and displays a bonus amount.
   a. Create a Web application that allows the user to enter a sales amount and a bonus rate. The user must enter the sales amount, which should be from $1 through $100,000. Use a list box to display bonus rates of 2% through 10%. The application should calculate and display the bonus amount. Name the solution Bonus Solution. Name the project Bonus Project. Name the Web form file Bonus.aspx. Save the application in the inetpub\wwwroot\Chap13 folder.
   b. Save the solution, then start and test the application.
   c. Close your browser and the solution.

5. In this exercise, you create a Web application that calculates and displays a food's fat calories and its fat percentage. It also displays a message informing the user whether the food is high in fat.
   a. In Chapter 4's Programming Example, you created a Windows application named Fat Calculator Application. Create a similar Web application. Use list boxes for the calories and grams of fat. The calories can be from 0 through 500. The grams of fat can be from 0 through 100. Name the solution Fat Solution. Name the project Fat Project. Name the Web form file Fat.aspx. Save the application in the inetpub\wwwroot\Chap13 folder.
   b. Save the solution, then start and test the application.
   c. Close your browser and the solution.

6. In this exercise, you create a Web application that allows the user to enter a voter's political party, and also save the information to a sequential access file. The application also calculates and displays the number of voters in each political party.
   a. Create a Web application that uses a list box for entering a voter's political party—Democrat, Republican, or Independent. The application should save the information to a sequential access file named pao.txt. It also should display the number of voters in each political party. Name the solution PAO Solution. Name the project PAO Project. Name the Web form file PAO.aspx. Save the application in the inetpub\wwwroot\Chap13 folder. Save the pao.txt file in the inetpub\wwwroot\Chap13\PAO Solution\PAO Project folder.
   b. Save the solution, then start and test the application.
   c. Close your browser and the solution.

7. In this exercise, you create a Web application that allows the user to enter a customer's name and address, as well as the number of pounds of regular coffee ordered and the number of pounds of decaffeinated coffee ordered. The application should calculate and display the total number of pounds of coffee ordered and the total price of the order.
   a. In Chapter 2's Programming Example, you created a Windows application named Moonbucks Coffee. Create a similar Web application. Name the solution Moonbucks Solution. Name the project Moonbucks Project. Name the Web form file Moonbucks.aspx. Save the application in the inetpub\wwwroot\Chap13 folder.
   b. Code the application appropriately. Assume that a pound of coffee costs $8.50.
   c. Save the solution, then start and test the application.
   d. Close your browser and the solution.

8. In this exercise, you create a Web application that allows the user to convert a temperature from Fahrenheit to Celsius, and from Celsius to Fahrenheit.
   a. Create an appropriate Web application. Name the solution Temperature Solution. Name the project Temperature Project. Name the Web form file Temperature.aspx. Save the application in the inetpub\wwwroot\Chap13 folder.
   b. Save the solution, then start and test the application.
   c. Close your browser and the solution.

9. In this exercise, you create a Web application that allows the user to enter an item number and then display the item's name and price. The item numbers, names, and prices are stored in a Microsoft Access database named Items.mdb. The database is contained in the inetpub\wwwroot\ Chap13\Databases folder. Figure 13.35 shows the Items.mdb database opened in Microsoft Access. The database contains one table named tblItems. The Number and Name fields contain text, and the Price field contains numbers.

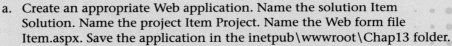

Number	Name	Price
ABX12	Chair	$45.00
CSR14	Desk	$175.00
JTR23	Table	$65.00
NRE09	End Table	$46.00
OOE68	Bookcase	$300.00
PPR00	Coffee Table	$190.00
PRT45	Lamp	$30.00
REZ04	Love Seat	$700.00
THR98	Side Chair	$33.00
WKP10	Sofa	$873.00
*		$0.00

tblItems : Table

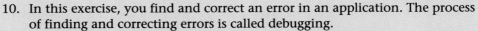

FIGURE 13.35

a. Create an appropriate Web application. Name the solution Item Solution. Name the project Item Project. Name the Web form file Item.aspx. Save the application in the inetpub\wwwroot\Chap13 folder.
b. Save the solution, then start and test the application.
c. Close your browser and the solution.

10. In this exercise, you find and correct an error in an application. The process of finding and correcting errors is called debugging.
a. Click Start on the Windows Taskbar, and then click Run to open the Run dialog box.
b. Type inetmgr.exe in the Open box, and then click the OK button. The Internet Information Services window opens.
c. Expand the nodes until you see the Debug Solution folder in the left pane, then click the Debug Solution folder.
d. Right-click the Debug Project folder in the right pane, and then click Properties. The Debug Project Properties dialog box opens.
e. Click the Create button in the Application Settings section on the Directory tab. Debug Project appears in the Application name box.
f. Click the OK button, then close the Internet Information Services window.
g. Open the Debug Solution (Debug Solution.sln) file, which is contained in the inetpub\wwwroot\Chap13\Debug Solution folder.
h. Open the Code Editor window. Review the existing code.
i. Start and then test the application. Notice that the application is not working correctly.
j. Close your browser. Correct the errors in the application's code, then save the solution and start the application. Test the application.
k. Close your browser and the solution.

Case Projects

Cable Direct

Sharon Barrow, the billing supervisor at Cable Direct (a local cable company) has asked you to create a Web application that a customer can use to calculate and display his or her bill. The cable rates are as follows:

Residential customers:

Processing fee:	$4.50
Basic service fee:	$30
Premium channels:	$5 per channel

Business customers:

Processing fee:	$16.50
Basic service fee:	$80 for first 10 connections; $4 for each additional connection
Premium channels:	$50 per channel for any number of connections

WKRK-Radio

Each year, WKRK-Radio polls its audience to determine which Super Bowl commercial was the best. The choices are as follows: Budweiser, FedEx, MasterCard, and Pepsi. The station manager has asked you to create a Web application that allows him to enter a caller's choice. The choice should be saved in a sequential access file. The application also should display the number of votes for each commercial.

Skate-Away Sales

Skate-Away Sales sells skateboards by phone. The skateboards are priced at $100 each and are available in two colors—yellow and blue. The company employs 20 salespeople to answer the phones. Create a Web application that allows the salespeople to enter the customer's name, address, and the number of blue and yellow skateboards ordered. The application should calculate the total number of skateboards ordered and the total price of the skateboards, including a 5% sales tax.

Perrytown Gift Shop

In Chapter 9's Programming Example, you created a Windows application for Stanley Habeggar, the owner and manager of Perrytown Gift Shop. The application allows Mr. Habeggar to quickly and accurately calculate the weekly federal withholding tax (FWT) for each of his six employees. Mr. Habeggar has asked you to create a Web application that calculates and displays the employee's gross pay, FWT, Social Security and Medicare (FICA) tax, and net pay. Use 7.65% as the FICA tax rate. Use $55.77 as the value of a withholding allowance. Employees receive time and one-half for hours worked over 40. The weekly FWT tables are shown in Figure 13.36.

FWT Tables – Weekly Payroll Period

Single person (including head of household)

If the taxable wages are:		The amount of income tax to withhold is		
Over	**But not over**	**Base amount**	**Percentage**	**Of excess over**
	$ 51	0		
$ 51	$ 552	0	15%	$ 51
$ 552	$1,196	$ 75.15 plus	28%	$ 552
$1,196	$2,662	$ 255.47 plus	31%	$1,196
$2,662	$5,750	$ 709.93 plus	36%	$2,662
$5,750		$1,821.61 plus	39.6%	$5,750

Married person

If the taxable wages are:		The amount of income tax to withhold is		
Over	**But not over**	**Base amount**	**Percentage**	**Of excess over**
	$ 124	0		
$ 124	$ 960	0	15%	$ 124
$ 960	$2,023	$ 125.40 plus	28%	$ 960
$2,023	$3,292	$ 423.04 plus	31%	$2,023
$3,292	$5,809	$ 816.43 plus	36%	$3,292
$5,809		$1,722.55 plus	39.6%	$5,809

FIGURE 13.36

A Tour of the Visual Studio .NET IDE

STARTING VISUAL STUDIO .NET

Visual Studio .NET is Microsoft's newest integrated development environment. An integrated development environment, or IDE, is an environment that contains all of the tools and features you need to create, run, and test your programs. For example, an IDE contains an editor for entering your program instructions, and a compiler for running and testing the program.

Included in Visual Studio .NET are the Visual Basic .NET, Visual C++ .NET, Visual C# .NET, and Visual J# .NET programming languages. You can use the languages available in Visual Studio .NET to create programs, called applications; however, before you can do so, you first must start Visual Studio .NET.

To start Visual Studio .NET:

1. Click the **Start** button on the Windows taskbar to open the Start menu.
2. Point to **All Programs**, then point to **Microsoft Visual Studio .NET 2003**, and then click **Microsoft Visual Studio .NET 2003**. The Microsoft Visual Studio .NET copyright screen appears momentarily, and then the Microsoft Development Environment window opens.
3. If the Start Page window is not open, click **Help** on the menu bar, and then click **Show Start Page**.
4. Click the **My Profile** tab on the Start Page window. The My Profile pane appears in the Start Page window, as shown in Figure A.1. (Your screen might not look identical to Figure A.1.)

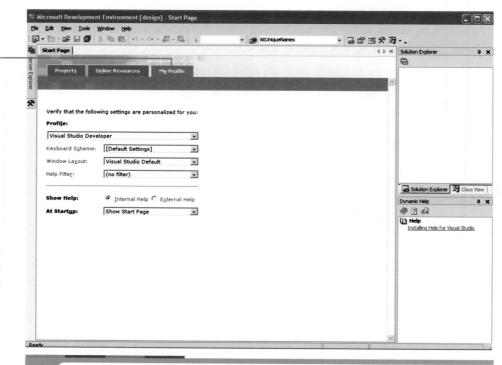

My Profile tab

FIGURE A.1   My Profile pane in the Start Page window

The My Profile pane allows you to customize various program settings in the IDE, such as the keyboard scheme, window layout, and help filter. A collection of customized preferences is called a profile. Visual Studio .NET provides a set of predefined profiles for your convenience.

5. If necessary, click the **Profile** list arrow, and then click **Visual Studio Developer** in the list.
6. If necessary, change the Keyboard Scheme, Window Layout, Help Filter, and At Startup list box selections on your screen to match those shown in Figure A.1.
7. If necessary, click the **Internal Help** radio button to select it. If the "Changes will not take effect until Visual Studio is restarted" message appears in a dialog box, click the **OK** button to close the dialog box.
8. Click the **Projects** tab on the Start Page window.

After starting Visual Studio .NET, you can create a Visual Basic .NET application, which can be Windows-based or Web-based. In this appendix, you learn how to create a Windows-based application.

CREATING A VISUAL BASIC .NET WINDOWS-BASED APPLICATION

A Windows-based application has a Windows user interface and runs on a desktop computer. A user interface is what you see and interact with when using an application.

Applications created in Visual Basic .NET are composed of solutions, projects, and files. A solution is a container that stores the projects and files for an entire application. A project also is a container, but it stores files associated with only a specific piece of the solution.

To create a Visual Basic .NET Windows-based application:

1. Click **File** on the Visual Studio .NET menu bar, point to **New**, and then click **Project**. The New Project dialog box opens.
2. If necessary, click **Visual Basic Projects** in the Project Types list box.
3. If necessary, click **Windows Application** in the Templates list box.
4. Type **First Project** in the Name text box.
5. Use the **Browse** button, which appears to the right of the Location text box, to open the **VbDotNet\AppA** folder.
6. If necessary, click the **More** button.
7. Select the **Create directory for Solution** check box.
8. Type **First Solution** in the New Solution Name text box. See Figure A.2.

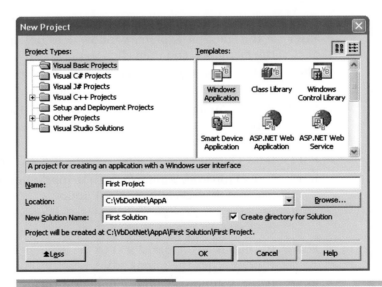

FIGURE A.2   Completed New Project dialog box

9. Click the **OK** button to close the New Project dialog box.

When you click the OK button in the New Project dialog box, Visual Studio .NET creates a solution and adds a Visual Basic .NET project to the solution, as shown in Figure A.3.

Windows Form Designer window

Start Page window

Server Explorer window

Toolbox window

Solution Explorer window

Class View window

Properties window

Dynamic Help window

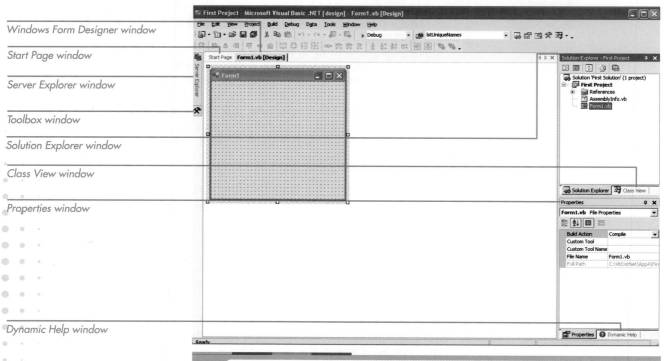

FIGURE A.3   Solution and project created by Visual Studio .NET

HELP?   If the Solution Explorer window does not appear in the IDE, click View on the menu bar, and then click Solution Explorer.

HELP?   If the Server Explorer window does not appear in the IDE, click View on the menu bar, and then click Server Explorer.

HELP?   If the Windows Form Designer window does not appear in the IDE, click Form1.vb in the Solution Explorer window, if necessary. Then click View on the menu bar, and then click Designer.

HELP?   If the Output window appears in the IDE, click the Close button on its title bar.

HELP?   If the Properties window does not appear in the IDE, click View on the menu bar, and then click Properties Window.

HELP?   If a plus box appears next to the project name in the Solution Explorer window, click the plus box.

HELP?   If a minus box appears next to the References folder in the Solution Explorer window, click the minus box.

HELP?   If the Solution Explorer window displays more folders and files than are shown in Figure A.3, click the Show All Files button on the Solution Explorer window's toolbar.

HELP?   If a Misc row appears in the Properties window, click the Alphabetic button on the Properties window's toolbar.

As Figure A.3 indicates, the IDE contains eight windows: Server Explorer, Toolbox, Start Page, Windows Form Designer, Solution Explorer, Class View, Properties, and Dynamic Help. In the next section, you learn how to manage the windows in the IDE.

MANAGING THE WINDOWS IN THE IDE

In the next set of steps, you learn how to close, auto-hide, and display the windows in the IDE.

To close, auto-hide, and display the windows in the IDE:

1. Place your mouse pointer on the **Server Explorer** tab. When the Server Explorer window slides into view, which may take several moments, click the **Close** button on its title bar.

Now close the Start Page, Class View, and Dynamic Help windows.

2. Click the **Start Page** tab to make the Start Page window the active window, and then click the **Close** button on its title bar.
3. Click the **Class View** tab to make the Class View window the active window, and then click the **Close** button on its title bar.
4. Click the **Dynamic Help** tab to make the Dynamic Help window the active window, and then click the **Close** button on its title bar.

Next, auto-hide the Solution Explorer window.

5. Click the **Auto Hide** button (the vertical pushpin) on the Solution Explorer window's title bar, then move the mouse pointer away from the window. The Solution Explorer window is minimized and appears as a tab on the right edge of the IDE.

HELP?   If the Solution Explorer window remains on the screen when you move your mouse pointer away from the window, click another window's title bar.

Now temporarily display the Solution Explorer window.

6. Place your mouse pointer on the **Solution Explorer** tab. The Solution Explorer window slides into view.
7. Move your mouse pointer away from the Solution Explorer window. The window is minimized and appears as a tab again.

Next, use the Auto Hide button to permanently display the Toolbox window.

8. Place your mouse pointer on the **Toolbox** tab. When the Toolbox window slides into view, click the **Auto Hide** button (the horizontal pushpin) on its title bar. The vertical pushpin button replaces the horizontal pushpin button. Figure A.4 shows the current status of the windows in the development environment.

HELP?   If the Toolbox window does not appear in the IDE, click View on the menu bar, and then click Toolbox.

Vertical pushpin

Form

The Solution Explorer window is auto-hidden

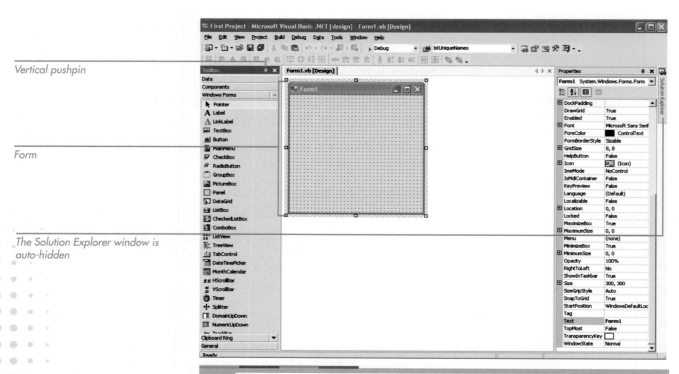

FIGURE A.4   Current status of the windows in the development environment

Only a form appears in the Windows Form designer window shown in Figure A.4. A form is the foundation for the user interface in a Windows-based application. You create the user interface by adding other objects, such as buttons and text boxes, to the form. You add the objects using the Toolbox window.

USING THE TOOLBOX WINDOW TO ADD OBJECTS TO A FORM

The Toolbox window, or toolbox, contains the tools and other components you use when creating your application. The contents of the toolbox vary depending on the designer in use. The toolbox shown earlier in Figure A.4, for example, appears when you are using the Windows Form designer. You use the tools to add objects, called controls, to a form. In the next set of steps, you add a label control and two button controls to the current form. You also learn how to size, move, delete, and undelete a control.

To add and manipulate a control:

1. Click the **Label** tool in the toolbox, but do not release the mouse button. Hold down the mouse button as you drag the mouse pointer to the form. (You do not need to worry about the exact location.) As you drag the mouse pointer, both an outline of a rectangle and a plus box follow the mouse pointer.
2. Release the mouse button. A label control appears on the form, as shown in Figure A.5. Notice that sizing handles appear around the label control. The sizing handles indicate that the control is selected. You can use the sizing handles to make a control bigger or smaller.

The asterisk indicates that the form has been changed since the last time it was saved

Sizing handle

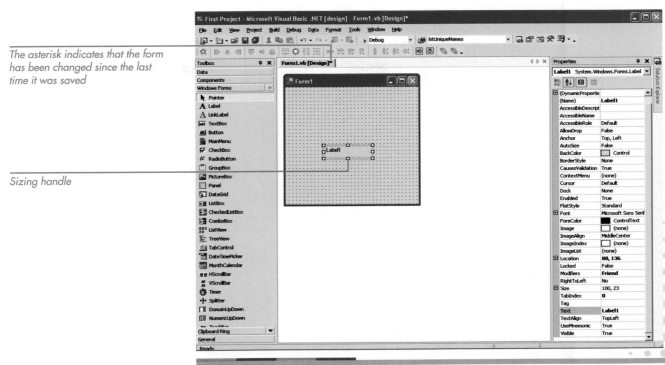

FIGURE A.5   Label control added to the form

Notice that an asterisk (*) appears on the Form1.vb [Design] tab in the Windows Form designer window. The asterisk indicates that the form has been changed since the last time it was saved.

3. Practice using the sizing handles to make the label control bigger and smaller.

Now reposition the label control on the form.

4. Place your mouse pointer on the center of the label control, then press the left mouse button and drag the control to another area of the form. Release the mouse button.

Next, delete and then undelete the label control.

5. Press the **Delete** key on your keyboard to delete the control.

6. Click **Edit** on the menu bar, and then click **Undo** to reinstate the label control.

You also can add a control to a form by clicking the appropriate tool and then clicking the form.

7. Click the **Button** tool in the toolbox, then click the **form**. (You do not need to worry about the exact location.)

Additionally, you can click the appropriate tool, then place the mouse pointer on the form, and then press the left mouse button and drag the mouse pointer until the control is the desired size.

8. Click the **Button** tool in the toolbox, and then place the mouse pointer on the form. Press the left mouse button and drag the mouse pointer until the control is the desired size, then release the mouse button. (You do not need to worry about the exact location and size.) See Figure A.6.

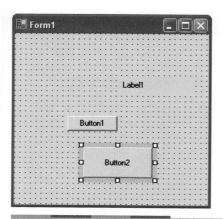

FIGURE A.6   Button controls added to the form

9. Auto-hide the Toolbox window.

Next, you learn how to use the Properties window to change the properties of an object.

USING THE PROPERTIES WINDOW TO CHANGE AN OBJECT'S PROPERTIES

Each object in Visual Basic .NET has a set of attributes that determine its appearance and behavior; the attributes are called properties. When an object is selected in the interface, its properties appear in the Properties window.

Every property has a default value assigned to it. However, you can use the Properties window to assign a different value to the property.

To assign values to some of the properties of the form:

1. Click the **form** (but not a control on the form). Sizing handles appear around the form, and the form's properties appear in the Properties window, as shown in Figure A.7.

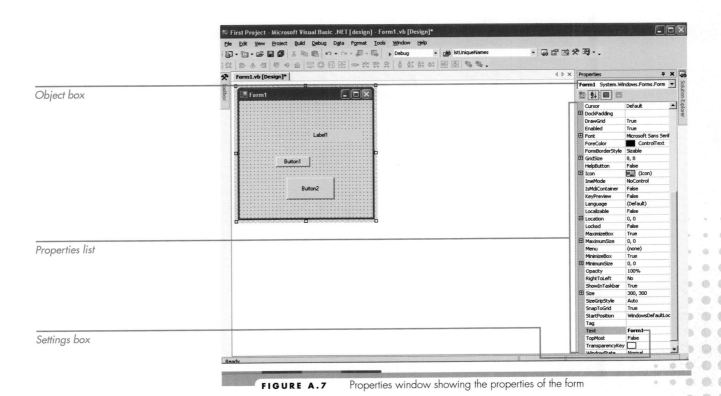

FIGURE A.7 Properties window showing the properties of the form

As indicated in Figure A.7, the Properties window includes an Object box and a Properties list. The Object box contains the name of the selected object; in this case, it contains Form1. The Properties list has two columns. The left column displays the names of the properties associated with the selected object, and the right column (called the Settings box) displays the current value, or setting, of each of the properties.

First, change the type and size of the font used to display text on the form.

2. Click **Font** in the Properties list, then click the **...** (ellipsis) button in the Settings box. When the Font dialog box opens, click **Tahoma** in the Font list box and **12** in the Size list box, and then click the **OK** button. (Notice that this change affects the text displayed in the controls on the form.)

A form's StartPosition property specifies where the form is positioned when the application is run and the form first appears on the screen.

3. Click **StartPosition** in the Properties list. Click the **list arrow** in the Settings box, and then click **CenterScreen**.

A form's Text property specifies the text to display in the form's title bar.

4. Click **Text** in the Properties list. Type **First Application** and press **Enter**. Notice that you do not have to erase the old value in the Settings box before entering the new value; as you type the new value, it replaces the old value.

Next, change the form's name from Form1 to frmFirst. The name is stored in the form's Name property.

5. Use the scroll bar in the Properties window to scroll to the top of the Properties list, then click **(Name)** in the Properties list.

6. Type **frmFirst** and press **Enter**. See Figure A.8.

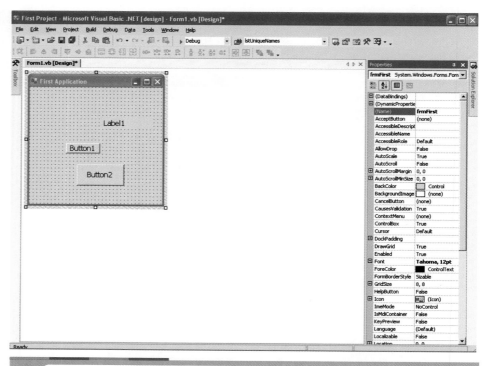

FIGURE A.8   Current status of the form

Next, assign values to some of the properties of the Label1 control. In this application, the Label1 control will be used to display a message.

To assign values to some of the properties of the Label1 control:

1. Click the **Label1** control in the form. Sizing handles appear around the control, and the control's properties appear in the Properties window.

First, change the label control's name from Label1 to lblMessage.

2. Click **(Name)** in the Properties list. Type **lblMessage** and press **Enter**.

Next, put a border around the lblMessage control.

3. Click **BorderStyle** in the Properties list. Click the **list arrow** in the Settings box, and then click **FixedSingle**.

Now remove the text that appears inside the lblMessage control. The text is stored in the control's Text property.

4. Click **Text** in the Properties list. Press the **Backspace** key on your keyboard, and then press **Enter**.

Now set the lblMessage control's Location and Size properties.

5. Click **Location** in the Properties list. Type **86, 40** and press **Enter**. (The first number is the horizontal location; the second number is the vertical location.)

6. Click **Size** in the Properties list. Type **120, 23** and press **Enter**. (The first number is the width; the second number is the height.)

Finally, assign values to some of the properties of the button controls.

To assign values to some of the properties of the button controls:

1. Click the **Button1** control in the form. Sizing handles appear around the control, and the control's properties appear in the Properties window.

First, change the button's name from Button1 to btnDisplay.

2. Click **(Name)** in the Properties list. Type **btnDisplay** and press **Enter**.

Next, change the location and size of the btnDisplay control.

3. Set the btnDisplay control's **Location** property to **80, 176**.
4. Set the btnDisplay control's **Size** property to **80, 32**.

The Text property determines the caption that appears on a button control.

5. Set the btnDisplay control's **Text** property to **Display**.

Next, set the Name, Location, and Text properties of the Button2 control.

6. Click the **Button2** control in the form. Sizing handles appear around the control, and the control's properties appear in the Properties window.
7. Set the Button2 control's **Name** property to **btnExit**.
8. Set the btnExit control's **Location** property to **176, 176**.
9. Set the btnExit control's **Text** property to **Exit**.

Now assume that you want to make the Exit button the same size as the Display button. You can do so by setting the Exit button's Size property to 80, 32; or, you can use the Format menu.

USING THE FORMAT MENU

The Format menu provides options that allow you to manipulate the controls in the user interface. The Align option, for example, allows you to align two or more controls by their left, right, top, or bottom borders. You can use the Make Same Size option to make two or more controls the same width and/or height. The Format menu also has a Center in Form option that centers one or more controls either horizontally or vertically on the form.

Before you can use the Format menu to make both button controls the same size, you first must select both controls. The last control you select should always be the one whose size and/or location you want to match. In this case, for example, you want the size of the Exit button to match the size of the Display button. Therefore, the Display button should be the last control you select. The last control selected is referred to as the reference control.

To make the Exit button the same size as the Display button:

1. Click the **Exit** button in the form. Press and hold down the Control (Ctrl) key as you click the **Display** button. Both buttons are now selected. Notice that the sizing handles on the reference control (the Display button) are black, whereas the sizing handles on the Exit button are white.
2. Click **Format** on the menu bar. Point to **Make Same Size**, and then click **Both**. The Exit button is now the same size as the Display button, as shown in Figure A.9.

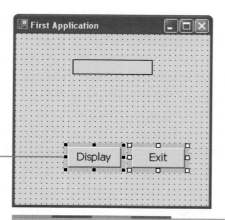

The last control selected is the reference control

FIGURE A.9   Completed user interface

3. Click the **form** to deselect the buttons.
4. Auto-hide the Properties window.

Now use the Format menu to lock the controls in place on the form. (You also can lock the controls by right-clicking the form and then clicking Lock Controls.) Locking the controls prevents them from being inadvertently moved as you work in the IDE.

To lock the controls on the form:

1. Click **Format** on the menu bar.
2. Click **Lock Controls**. Try dragging one of the controls to a different location on the form. You will not be able to.

If you need to move a control after you have locked the controls in place, you can either change the control's Location property setting in the Properties list or unlock the controls by selecting the Lock Controls option again. The Lock Controls option is a toggle option: selecting it once activates it, and selecting it again deactivates it.

It is a good practice to save the current solution every 10 or 15 minutes so that you will not lose a lot of work if the computer loses power.

SAVING A SOLUTION

One way to save the current solution is to click File on the menu bar, and then click Save All. Doing so saves any changes made to the files included in the solution. You also can click the Save All button on the Standard toolbar.

To save the current solution:

1. Click **File** on the menu bar.
2. Click **Save All**. Notice that an asterisk (*) no longer appears on the Form1.vb [Design] tab. This indicates that the form has not been changed since the last time it was saved.

Now that the user interface is complete, you can start the application to see how it will look to the user.

STARTING AND ENDING AN APPLICATION

You can start an application by clicking Debug on the menu bar, and then clicking Start; or you can simply press the F5 key on your keyboard.

To start and stop an application:

1. Temporarily display the Solution Explorer window. Right-click **First Project** in the Solution Explorer window, and then click **Properties**. The First Project Property Pages dialog box opens. If necessary, click the **Common Properties** folder to open it, and then click **General**.

When the application is started, the frmFirst form should be the first form that appears on the screen.

2. Click the **Startup object** list arrow, and then click **frmFirst** in the list. See Figure A.10.

This form will automatically appear when the application is started

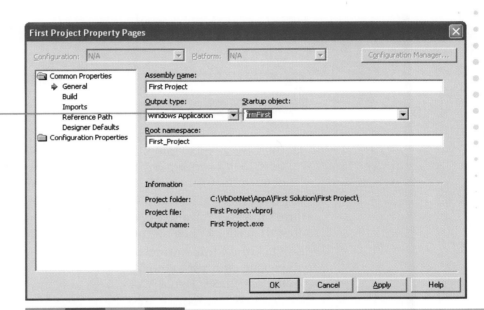

FIGURE A.10 First Project Property Pages dialog box

3. Click the **OK** button to close the First Project Property Pages dialog box.

Now save the solution and then start the application. (You should always save the solution before starting the application.)

4. Click **File** on the menu bar, and then click **Save All**. Click **Debug** on the menu bar, and then click **Start**. See Figure A.11. (Do not be concerned about the windows that appear at the bottom of the screen.)

Close button

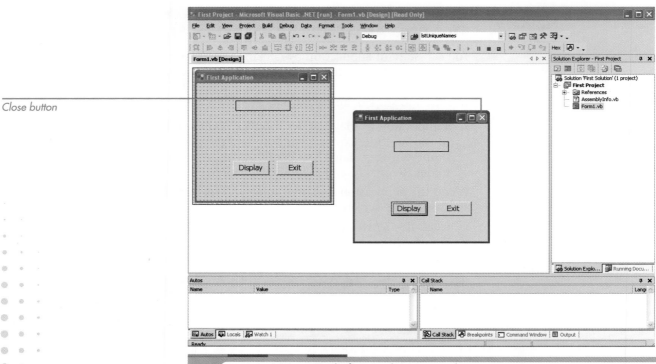

FIGURE A.11   Result of starting the current application

5. Click the **Display** button, and then click the **Exit** button. Currently, the buttons do not perform any tasks when clicked. This is because you have not yet entered the instructions that tell them what tasks to perform.

At this point, you can stop the application by clicking the Close button on the form's title bar. You also can click the designer window to make it the active window, then click Debug on the menu bar, and then click Stop Debugging.

6. Click the **Close** button on the form's title bar. When the application ends, you are returned to the IDE, and an Output window appears at the bottom of the screen. See Figure A.12.

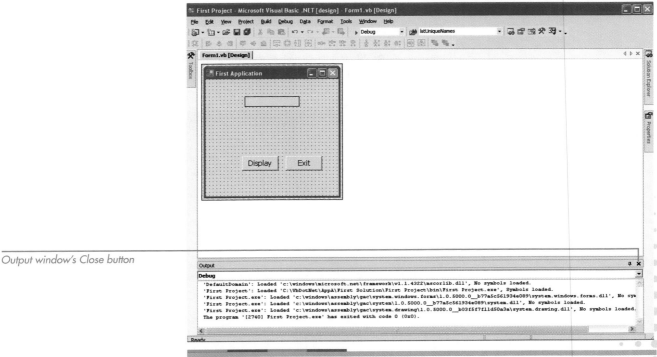

Output window's Close button

FIGURE A.12   Output window shown in the IDE

7. Close the Output window by clicking the **Close** button on its title bar.

You use Visual Basic .NET code to tell a button how to respond when the user clicks it.

WRITING VISUAL BASIC .NET CODE

Think about the Windows environment for a moment. Did you ever wonder why the OK and Cancel buttons respond the way they do when you click them? The answer to the question is very simple: a programmer gave the buttons explicit instructions on how to respond to the actions of the user. Those actions—such as clicking, double-clicking, and scrolling—are called events. The set of Visual Basic .NET instructions, or code, that tells an object how to respond to an event is called an event procedure.

At this point, the Display and Exit buttons on the form do not know what tasks they are expected to perform. You tell a button what to do by writing an event procedure for it. You write the event procedure in the Code Editor window, which is a window you have not yet seen. You can use various methods to open the Code Editor window. For example, you can right-click anywhere on the form (except the form's title bar), and then click View Code on the context menu. You also can click View on the menu bar, and then click Code; or you can press the F7 key on your keyboard. (To use the View menu or the F7 key, the designer window should be the active window.)

To open the Code Editor window:

1. Right-click the **form**.
2. Click **View Code**. The Code Editor window opens in the IDE, as shown in Figure A.13. Notice that the Code Editor window already contains some Visual Basic .NET code (instructions).

Method Name list box

Class Name list box

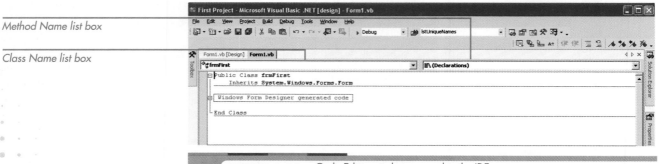

FIGURE A.13   Code Editor window opened in the IDE

HELP?   If a minus box appears next to the `Windows Form Designer generated code` entry, click the minus box.

As Figure A.13 indicates, the Code Editor window contains a Class Name list box and a Method Name list box. The Class Name list box lists the names of the objects included in the user interface. The Method Name list box, on the other hand, lists the events to which the selected object is capable of responding. You use the Class Name and Method Name list boxes to select the object and event, respectively, that you want to code.

In this application, you will have the Display button display the message "Good morning!" when the user clicks it. You will have the Exit button, on the other hand, end the application when it is clicked.

To code the Display button's Click event procedure:

1. Click the **Class Name** list arrow, and then click **btnDisplay** in the list. Click the **Method Name** list arrow, and then click **Click** in the list. See Figure A.14.

Insertion point

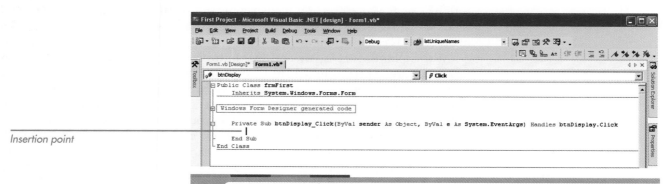

FIGURE A.14   btnDisplay control's Click event procedure shown in the Code Editor window

Notice that, when you select an object and event, additional code automatically appears in the Code Editor window. To help you follow the rules of the Visual Basic .NET programming language, called syntax, the Code Editor provides you with a code template for every event procedure.

The insertion point located in the event procedure indicates where you enter your code for the object. In this case, you want to instruct the button to display the "Good morning!" message in the lblMessage control. You can do so using the following assignment statement: `Me.lblMessage.Text = "Good morning!"`. An assignment statement is simply an instruction that assigns a value to something. In this case, for example, the assignment statement assigns the "Good morning!" message to the Text property of the lblMessage control. You can type the assignment statement on your own; or you can use the IntelliSense feature that is built into Visual Basic .NET. In this set of steps, you will use the IntelliSense feature.

2. Type **me.** (but don't press Enter). When you type the period, the IntelliSense feature displays a list of choices from which you can select. See Figure A.15.

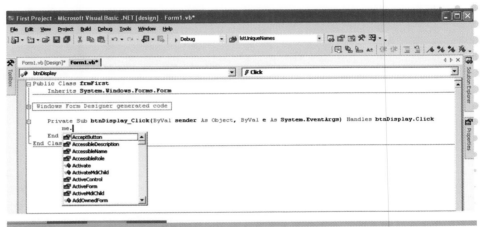

FIGURE A.15   IntelliSense feature displays a list of choices

HELP?   If the list of choices does not appear, the IntelliSense feature may have been turned off on your computer. To turn it on, click Tools on the menu bar, and then click Options. Open the Text Editor folder in the Options dialog box, and then open the Basic folder. Click General in the Basic folder, then select the Auto list members check box. Click the OK button to close the Options dialog box.

3. Type **lb** (but don't press Enter). The IntelliSense feature highlights the lblMessage choice in the list, as shown in Figure A.16.

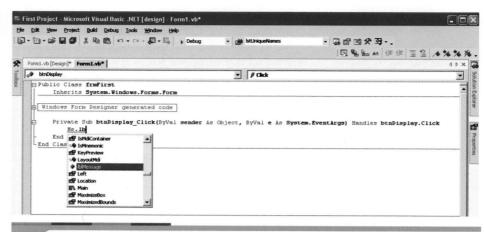

FIGURE A.16   lblMessage choice highlighted in the list

4. Press the **Tab** key on your keyboard to select the lblMessage choice, then type . (a period). The IntelliSense feature highlights the Text property in the list, as shown in Figure A.17.

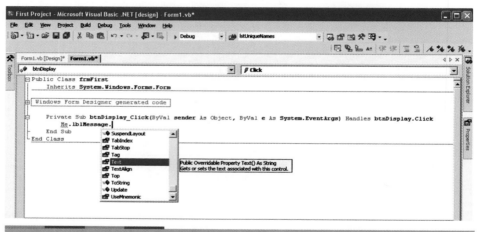

FIGURE A.17   Text property highlighted in the list

5. Press the **Tab** key on your keyboard to select the Text property, then type = **"Good morning!"** and press **Enter**. See Figure A.18.

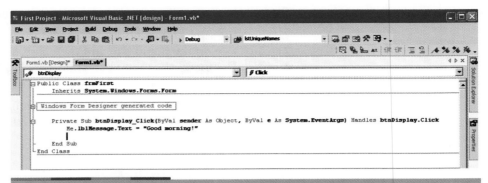

FIGURE A.18 Completed Click event procedure for the btnDisplay control

When the application is started and the user clicks the Display button, the assignment statement in the button's Click event procedure will display "Good morning!" in the lblMessage control.

In the next set of steps, you code the Exit button's Click event procedure. Recall that the procedure should end the application. You end an application using the `Me.Close()` statement.

To code the Exit button's Click event procedure:

1. Click the **Class Name** list arrow in the Code Editor window, and then click **btnExit** in the list. Click the **Method Name** list arrow, and then click **Click** in the list.
2. Type **me.close()** and then press **Enter**. See Figure A.19.

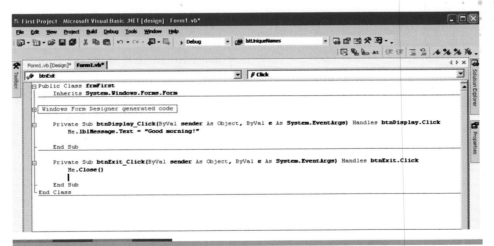

FIGURE A.19 Completed Click event procedure for the btnExit control

When the application is started and the user clicks the Exit button, the statement contained in the button's Click event procedure will terminate the application.

Now close the Code Editor window, then save the solution and start the application.

To close the Code Editor window, then save the solution, and start the application:

1. Click the **Close** button on the Code Editor window's title bar.
2. Click **File** on the menu bar, and then click **Save All**.
3. Click **Debug** on the menu bar, and then click **Start**.

Verify that the Display button is working correctly.

4. Click the **Display** button. The "Good morning!" message appears in the lblMessage control, as shown in Figure A.20.

Message displayed by the Display button's Click event procedure

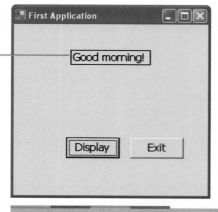

FIGURE A.20   Result of clicking the Display button

Now verify that the Exit button ends the application.

5. Click the **Exit** button. The application ends and you are returned to the designer window.
6. Close the Output window.

When you are finished working on a solution, you should close the solution.

CLOSING THE CURRENT SOLUTION

You close a solution using the Close Solution option on the File menu. When you close a solution, all projects and files contained in the solution also are closed. If unsaved changes were made to the solution, project, or form, a dialog box opens and prompts you to save the appropriate files. The dialog box contains Yes, No, Cancel, and Help buttons. You click the Yes button to save the files before the solution is closed. You click the No button to close the solution without saving the files. You click the Cancel button to leave the solution open, and you click the Help button to display Help pertaining to the dialog box.

To close the current solution:

1. Click **File** on the menu bar.
2. Click **Close Solution**.

You can use the Solution Explorer window to verify that the solution is closed.

3. Temporarily display the Solution Explorer window to verify that no solutions are open in the IDE.

Next, you learn how to open a solution that was saved previously.

OPENING AN EXISTING SOLUTION

If you want to open an existing solution, you simply click File on the menu bar, and then click Open Solution. You then select the appropriate solution file in the Open Solution dialog box. You can recognize a solution file by the .sln extension on its filename. If a solution is already open in the IDE, it is closed before another solution is opened. In other words, only one solution can be open in the IDE at any one time.

To open the First Solution:

1. Click **File** on the menu bar, and then click **Open Solution**. The Open Solution dialog box opens.
2. Locate and then open the **VbDotNet\AppA\First Solution** folder.
3. If necessary, click **First Solution** (First Solution.sln) in the list of filenames, and then click the **Open** button.
4. If the Windows Form Designer window is not displayed, click **View** on the menu bar, and then click **Designer**.
5. Temporarily display the Solution Explorer window to verify that the solution is open.

PRINTING YOUR CODE

You always should print a copy of the code entered in the Code Editor window, because the printout will help you understand and maintain the application in the future. To print the code, the Code Editor window must be the active, or current, window.

To print the current application's code:

1. Right-click the **form**, then click **View Code** to open the Code Editor window.

Only the code that is not collapsed will be sent to the printer for printing.

2. Verify that the only plus box in the Code Editor window appears next to the `Windows Form Designer generated code` entry. If a plus box appears anywhere else in the Code Editor window, click the plus box. (You typically do not need to print the code generated by the designer.)
3. Click **File** on the menu bar, then click **Print**. The Print dialog box opens.
4. If your computer is connected to a printer, click the **OK** button to begin printing; otherwise, click the **Cancel** button. If you clicked the OK button, your printer prints the code.
5. Close the Code Editor window.

Lastly, you learn how to exit Visual Studio .NET.

EXITING VISUAL STUDIO .NET

As in most Windows applications, you exit an application using either the Close button on the application window's title bar, or the Exit option on the File menu.

To exit Visual Studio .NET:

1. Click **File** on the menu bar, and then click **Close Solution** to close the current solution.
2. Click **File** on the menu bar, and then click **Exit** to exit Visual Studio .NET.

GUI Design Rules

The following list summarizes the GUI design guidelines you have learned. You can use this list to verify that the interfaces you create in the Exercises and Case Projects adhere to the GUI standards outlined in the book.

- A splash screen should not have a Minimize, Maximize, or Close button, and its borders should not be sizable.
- A form that is not a splash screen should always have a Minimize button and a Close button. Usually, it also contains a Maximize button. In most cases, the FormBorderStyle property is set to Sizable.
- If the form is a dialog box, it should have a Close button, but no Minimize or Maximize buttons, and its FormBorderStyle property should be set to FixedDialog.
- Set the form's StartPosition property; in most cases, you will set it to CenterScreen.
- Graphics and color should be used sparingly in an interface.
- If you use a graphic in the interface, use a small one and place it in a location that will not distract the user.

- Build the interface using black, white, and gray first, then add color only if you have a good reason to do so.
- Use white, off-white, or light gray for an application's background, and black for the text.
- Limit the number of colors in an interface to three, not including white, black, and gray. The colors you choose should complement each other.
- Never use color as the only means of identification for an element in the user interface.
- It is recommended that you use the Tahoma font for applications that will run on systems running Windows 2000 or Windows XP.
- Use 8-, 9-, 10-, 11-, or 12-point fonts for the text in an interface. Use no more than two different font sizes.
- Avoid using italics and underlining in an interface, and limit the use of bold text to titles, headings, and key items that you want to emphasize.
- Use only one font type, which should be a sans serif font, in the interface.
- You can use the form's AcceptButton property to designate an optional default button, and its CancelButton property to designate an optional cancel button. The default button should be the button that is most often selected by the user, except in cases where the tasks performed by the button are both destructive and irreversible. The default button typically is the first button.
- The information in an interface should flow either vertically or horizontally, with the most important information always located in the upper-left corner of the screen.
- When positioning the controls on a form, you should maintain a consistent margin from the edge of the form; two or three dots is recommended.
- Align the borders of the controls wherever possible to minimize the number of different margins used in the interface.
- Try to create a user interface that no one notices.
- Related controls should be grouped together using white space, a GroupBox control, or a Panel control.
- Related controls typically are placed on succeeding dots. Controls that are not part of any logical grouping may be positioned from two to four dots away from other controls.
- You can use a text box control to give the user an area in which to enter data.
- You use a label control to display information that you don't want the user to change while the application is running.
- In Windows applications, a button control is used to perform an immediate action when clicked.
- Labels that identify text boxes should be left-aligned and positioned either above or to the left of the text box. They also should end with a colon and be entered using sentence capitalization.
- Identifying labels and button captions should be from one to three words only, and each should appear on one line.
- Identifying labels and button captions should be meaningful.
- Labels that identify controls should have their BorderStyle property set to None.
- Labels that display program output, such as the result of a calculation, usually have their BorderStyle property set to FixedSingle.
- Button captions should be entered using book title capitalization.
- When buttons are positioned horizontally on the screen, all the buttons should be the same height; their widths, however, may vary if necessary. When buttons are stacked vertically on the screen, all the buttons should be the same height and the same width. The most commonly used button should be placed first.

- Use radio buttons when you want to limit the user to one of two or more related and mutually exclusive choices.
- The minimum number of radio buttons in a group is two, and the recommended maximum is seven.
- The label in the radio button's Text property should be entered using sentence capitalization.
- Use a group box control (or a panel control) to create separate groups of radio buttons. Only one button in each group can be selected at any one time. Use sentence capitalization for the optional identifying label in a group box control.
- Designate a default radio button in each group of radio buttons.
- Use check boxes when you want to allow the user to select any number of choices from a group of one or more independent and nonexclusive choices.
- The label in the check box's Text property should be entered using sentence capitalization.
- A list box should display a minimum of three selections and a maximum of eight selections at a time.
- Use a label control to provide keyboard access to the list box. Set the label control's TabIndex property to a value that is one less than the list box's TabIndex value.
- List box items are either arranged by use, with the most used entries appearing first in the list, or sorted in ascending order.
- If a list box allows the user to make only one selection at a time, then a default item should be selected in the list box when the interface first appears. The default item should be either the most used selection or the first selection in the list. However, if a list box allows more than one selection at a time, you do not select a default item.
- Assign a unique access key to each control (in the interface) that can receive user input (text boxes, buttons, and so on).
- When assigning an access key to a control, use the first letter of the caption or identifying label, unless another letter provides a more meaningful association. If you can't use the first letter and no other letter provides a more meaningful association, then use a distinctive consonant. Lastly, use a vowel or a number.
- Set each control's TabIndex property to a number that represents the order in which you want the control to receive the focus (begin with 0).
- A text box's TabIndex value should be one more than the TabIndex value of its identifying label.
- A list box's TabIndex value should be one more than the TabIndex value of its identifying label.
- Lock the controls in place on the form.
- In the InputBox function, use sentence capitalization for the *prompt*, and book title capitalization for the *title*.
- Use sentence capitalization for the *text* argument in the MessageBox.Show method, but book title capitalization for the *caption* argument. The name of the application typically appears in the *caption* argument.
- Avoid using the words "error," "warning," or "mistake" in the MessageBox.Show method's message, as these words imply that the user has done something wrong.
- Display the Warning Message icon in a message box that alerts the user that he or she must make a decision before the application can continue. You can phrase the message as a question.

- Display the Information Message icon in a message box that displays an informational message along with an OK button only.
- Display the Stop Message icon when you want to alert the user of a serious problem that must be corrected before the application can continue.
- The default button in a message box should be the one that represents the user's most likely action, as long as that action is not destructive.
- You can use the KeyPress event to prevent a text box from accepting inappropriate keys.
- If appropriate, format an application's numeric output so that it displays special characters (such as dollar signs and percent signs) and the desired number of decimal places.
- You can use the Focus method to move the focus to a control while the application is running.
- Highlight, or select, the existing text in a text box when the text box receives the focus.

C

Basic Tools Included in the Windows Form Designer Toolbox

Tool icon	Tool name	Purpose
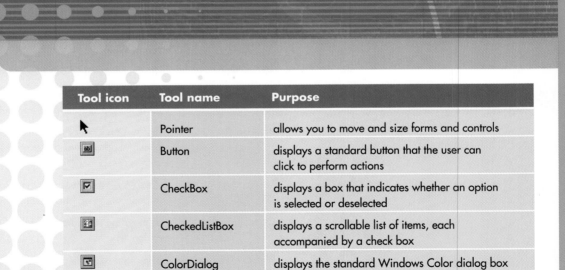	Pointer	allows you to move and size forms and controls
	Button	displays a standard button that the user can click to perform actions
	CheckBox	displays a box that indicates whether an option is selected or deselected
	CheckedListBox	displays a scrollable list of items, each accompanied by a check box
	ColorDialog	displays the standard Windows Color dialog box
	ComboBox	displays a drop-down list of items

(Table is continued on next page)

Tool icon	Tool name	Purpose
	ContextMenu	implements a menu that appears when the user right-clicks an object
	CrystalReport Viewer	allows a Crystal Report to be viewed in an application
	DataGrid	displays data in a series of rows and columns
	DateTimePicker	allows the user to select a single item from a list of dates or times
	DomainUpDown	displays a list of text items that users can scroll through, using the up and down arrow buttons
	ErrorProvider	displays error information to the user in a nonintrusive way
	FontDialog	displays the standard Windows Font dialog box
	GroupBox	provides a visual and functional container for controls; similar to the Panel control, but can display a caption but no scroll bars
	HelpProvider	associates an HTML Help file with a Windows application
	HScrollBar	displays a horizontal scroll bar
	ImageList	stores images
A	Label	displays text that the user cannot edit
A	LinkLabel	adds a Web style link to a Windows Forms application
	ListBox	displays a list from which a user can select one or more items
	ListView	displays items in one of four views (text only, text with small icons, text with large icons, or report view)
	MainMenu	displays a menu while an application is running
	MonthCalendar	displays an intuitive graphical interface for users to view and set date information
	NotifyIcon	displays an icon for a process that runs in the background and would not otherwise have a user interface
	NumericUpDown	displays a list of numerals that users can scroll through, using up and down arrow buttons
	OpenFileDialog	displays the standard Windows Open File dialog box
	PageSetupDialog	displays the standard Windows Page Setup dialog box

(Table is continued on next page)

Tool icon	Tool name	Purpose
	Panel	provides a visual and functional container for controls; similar to a GroupBox control, but can display scroll bars but no caption
	PictureBox	displays graphics in bitmap, GIF, JPEG, metafile, or icon format
	PrintDialog	displays the standard Windows Print dialog box
	PrintDocument	prints a document within a Windows application
	PrintPreview Control	allows you to create your own Print Preview dialog box
	PrintPreviewDialog	displays the standard Windows Print Preview dialog box
	ProgressBar	indicates the progress of an action by displaying an appropriate number of rectangles arranged in a horizontal bar
	RadioButton	displays a button that indicates whether an option is selected or deselected
	RichTextBox	allows users to enter, display, and manipulate text with formatting
	SaveFileDialog	displays the standard Windows Save As dialog box
+|+	Splitter	allows the user to resize a docked control while an application is running
	StatusBar	displays status information related to the object that has the focus
	TabControl	displays multiple tabs
	TextBox	accepts and displays text that the user can edit
	Timer	performs actions at specified time intervals
	ToolBar	displays menus and bitmapped buttons that activate commands
	ToolTip	displays text when the user points to an object
	TrackBar	allows a user to navigate through a large amount of information, or to visually adjust a numeric setting
	TreeView	displays a hierarchy of nodes that can be expanded or collapsed
	VScrollBar	displays a vertical scroll bar

Creating Reports Using Crystal Reports

CREATING A CRYSTAL REPORT

Assume that Mike Warren, the owner of Warren Sporting Goods, uses a Microsoft Access database to store each salesperson's name and annual sales amount. The database contains one table, which is named tblSales. It also contains two fields: Name and Sales. Figure D.1 shows the tblSales table opened in Microsoft Access.

Name	Sales
Carol Abdul	$14,300.00
Hilda Johnson	$4,675.00
Inez Williams	$14,250.00
Jake Hendrick	$35,000.00
John Materson	$13,400.00
Kate Baland	$40,000.00
Ned Iber	$25,000.00
Opal Smith	$23,000.00
Paula Smith	$40,000.00
Phil Jones	$36,000.00
	$0.00

FIGURE D.1 tblSales table opened in Microsoft Access

Mike would like a report that lists each salesperson's name and sales amount. You can create the report using the Crystal Reports designer, which is built into Visual Studio .NET. However, before you can create the report, you need to open the Warren Sporting Goods application.

To open the Warren Sporting Goods application:

1. If necessary, start Visual Studio .NET.
2. Open the Warren Solution (Warren Solution.sln) file, which is contained in the VbDotNet\AppD\Warren Solution folder. The user interface is shown in Figure D.2.

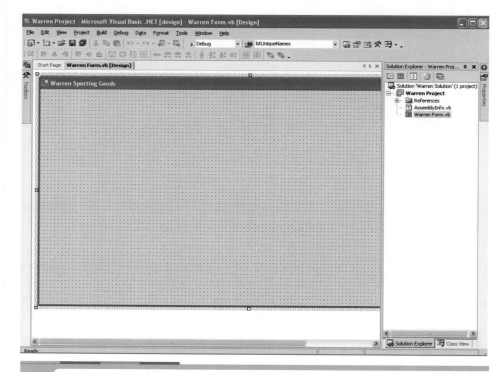

FIGURE D.2 Warren Sporting Goods application

In the next set of steps, you learn how to open the Crystal Reports designer and create a report.

To open the Crystal Reports designer and create a report:

1. Click **File** on the menu bar, and then click **Add New Item**. The Add New Item – Warren Project dialog box opens.
2. The Local Project Items folder should be selected in the Categories box. Scroll the Templates box until you see Crystal Report, then click **Crystal Report**.
3. Type **SalesReport.rpt** in the Name box. (Be sure to include the .rpt extension on the filename. The .rpt stands for "report".) See Figure D.3.

Select Crystal Report in the Templates list

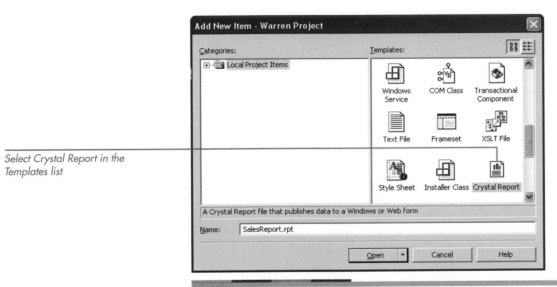

FIGURE D.3   Completed Add New Item – Warren Project dialog box

4. Click the **Open** button to close the dialog box. The Crystal Report Gallery dialog box opens. Notice that the Using the Report Expert radio button is selected, and so is the Standard entry. See Figure D.4.

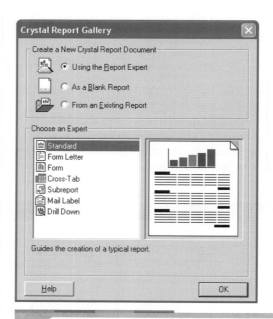

FIGURE D.4   Crystal Report Gallery dialog box

HELP? If the Crystal Decisions Registration Wizard dialog box opens, click the Register Later button.

5. Click the **OK** button to use the Report Expert to create a Standard report. The Standard Report Expert dialog box opens and displays the information on the Data tab.

6. Click the **plus box** next to the Database Files folder. The Open dialog box opens.

7. Open the VbDotNet\AppD\Warren Solution\Warren Project folder, then click **Sales.mdb** in the list of filenames.

8. Click the **Open** button to close the Open dialog box. The Data tab on the Standard Report Expert dialog box appears.

9. Click **tblSales** in the Available data sources list, and then click the **Insert Table** button. See Figure D.5.

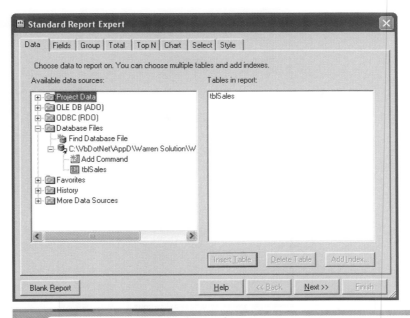

FIGURE D.5   Completed Data tab

10. Click the **Fields** tab, and then click the **Add All ->** button to display the Name and Sales fields in the report. See Figure D.6.

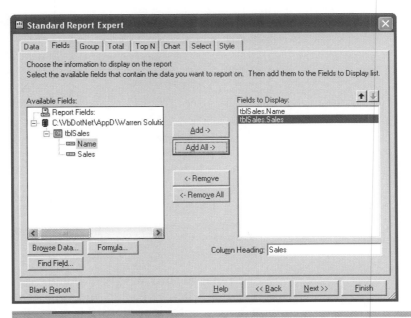

FIGURE D.6   Completed Fields tab

You can use the remaining tabs on the Standard Report Expert dialog box to create sophisticated, presentation-quality reports. In this case, however, the Warren application requires only a simple report.

11. Click the **Style** tab. Standard should be selected in the Style box. Type **Sales Report** in the Title box. See Figure D.7.

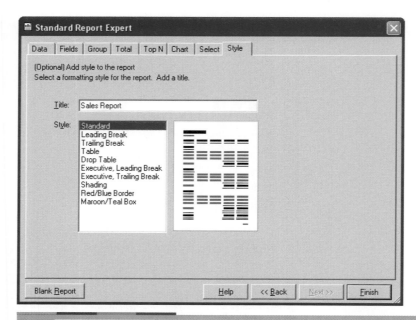

12. Click the **Finish** button. The Crystal Reports designer appears in the IDE, as shown in Figure D.8.

PrintDate element

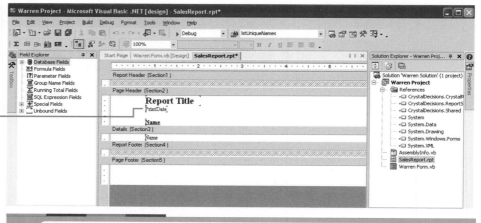

The Crystal Reports designer contains five sections: Report Header, Page Header, Details, Report Footer, and Page Footer. You can add, edit, or delete information from these sections. For example, in the next set of steps, you format the PrintDate element in the Page Header so that it displays the month number, followed by a slash and the day number.

To format the PrintDate element:

1. Auto-hide the Solution Explorer window.
2. Right-click **PrintDate** in the Page Header section, then click **Format**. The Format Editor dialog box opens and displays the Date tab.
3. Click **3/1** in the Style list. See Figure D.9.

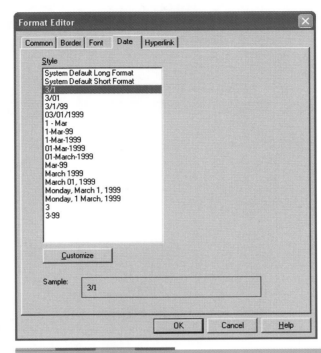

FIGURE D.9   Completed Date tab

4. Click the **OK** button to close the Format Editor dialog box.
5. Click **File** on the menu bar, and then click **Save All** to save the solution.
6. Close the Crystal Reports designer by clicking its **Close** button.

You use the CrystalReportViewer tool to view a Crystal Report while a Visual Basic .NET application is running. Usually, the CrystalReportViewer tool is the last tool on the Windows Forms tab in the toolbox.

To add a CrystalReportViewer tool to the current form:

1. Drag the CrystalReportViewer tool to the form. When you release the mouse button, a CrystalReportViewer control appears on the form.

Now set the CrystalReportViewer control's ReportSource property to the name of the Crystal Report—in this case, SalesReport.rpt.

2. Click **ReportSource** in the Properties window. Click the **list arrow** in the Settings box, and then click **Browse** in the list. The Open an Existing Crystal Report dialog box opens.
3. Open the VbDotNet\AppD\Warren Solution\Warren Project folder, then click **SalesReport.rpt** in the list of filenames.
4. Click the **Open** button to close the Open an Existing Crystal Report dialog box.

Now set the CrystalReportViewer control's DisplayGroupTree, Location, and Size properties.

5. Set the **DisplayGroupTree** property to **False**.
6. Set the **Location** property to **24, 24**.
7. Set the **Size** property to **872, 392**.
8. Click the **form's title bar** to select the form. Figure D.10 shows the CrystalReportViewer control in the form.

CrystalReportViewer control

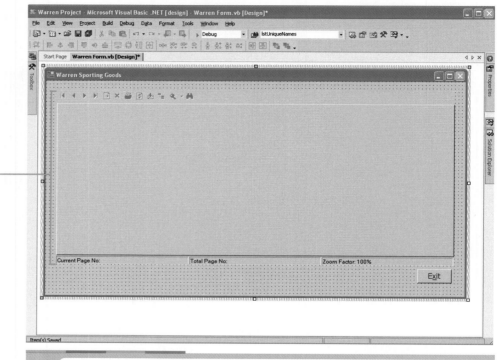

FIGURE D.10   CrystalReportViewer control shown in the form

Next, save the solution and then start and test the application.

To save the solution, and then start and test the application:

1. Click **File** on the menu bar, and then click **Save All**.
2. Click **Debug** on the menu bar, and then click **Start**. The Sales Report appears on the form, as shown in Figure D.11.

Print button

FIGURE D.11   Sales Report displayed on the form

You can use the Print button that appears on the CrystalReportViewer control to print the report.

3. If your computer is connected to a printer, click the **Print** button.
4. Click the **Exit** button to end the application.
5. Close the solution, then exit Visual Studio .NET.

Glossary

A

abstraction Refers to the hiding of the internal details of an object from the user.

AcceptButton property The form property that specifies the default button.

access key The underlined character in an object's caption. An access key allows the user to select the object using the Alt key in combination with the character.

accumulator A numeric variable used for accumulating (adding together) something; it allows you to answer the question "How much?".

Add method A method of the Items collection; used to specify the items you want displayed in a list box.

ADO Stands for **ActiveX Data Objects** and refers to the technology used in Visual Basic 6.0 to connect an application to a database.

ADO.NET Refers to the technology used in Visual Basic .NET to connect an application to a database.

AppendText method Opens a new or existing sequential access file for append.

application Another name for program.

array A group of variables that have the same name and data type and are related in some way.

Array.Reverse method Reverses the order of the elements in a one-dimensional array.

Array.Sort method Sorts the elements in a one-dimensional array in ascending order.

ASP.NET Stands for "Active Server Pages .NET", which is Microsoft's newest technology for creating Web applications containing dynamic Web pages.

assembler A program that converts assembly instructions into machine code.

assembly languages These languages were developed after machine languages. They allow the programmer to use mnemonics in place of the 0s and 1s in a program.

assignment operator The equal sign (=) in an assignment statement.

assignment statement An instruction that assigns a value to something, such as a property of a control, while an application is running.

attributes The characteristics that describe an object. Attributes are also called properties.

B

base class The original class from which another class is created.

behaviors The operations (actions) that an object is capable of performing; also called methods.

binding Refers to the process of connecting a DataSet object to a control.

block-level scope Refers to the scope of block-level variables.

block-level variable A variable declared within a specific block of code; can be used only within the statement block in which it is declared.

book title capitalization When using this form of capitalization, you capitalize the first letter in each word, except for articles, conjunctions, and prepositions that do not occur at either the beginning or the end of the caption.

Boolean operators The operators that allow you to combine two or more *conditions* into one compound *condition*; also called logical operators.

bound controls Controls that are bound to a DataSet object.

browser A program that allows a client to access and view Web pages; also referred to as a Web browser.

bug An error in a program.

button control The control used in a Windows application to perform an immediate action when clicked.

button tool The tool used to instantiate a button control.

C

Call statement The statement used to invoke an independent Sub procedure in a program.

cancel button The button on a form that can be selected by pressing the Esc key.

CancelButton property The form property that specifies the cancel button.

Catch statement Contains the instructions that tell the computer how to handle an exception.

check box The control that allows the user to select any number of choices from a group of one or more independent and nonexclusive choices.

CheckBox tool The tool used to instantiate a check box.

child table The table linked by a common field to a parent table.

class A pattern or blueprint used to create an object.

class definition A block of code that specifies (or defines) the attributes and behaviors of an object.

Class Name list box In the Code Editor window, this list box lists the names of the objects included in the user interface.

Class statement Used to define a class.

client A computer that requests information from a Web server.

Close method Closes a sequential access file.

code Another name for program instructions.

collection A group of one or more individual objects treated as one unit.

comparison operators The operators that allow you to compare values; also called relational operators.

compiler A program that translates all of a program's high-level instructions into machine code before running the program.

component tray Stores the objects that do not appear in the interface when an application is running.

concatenation operator The operator used to concatenate strings; the ampersand (&).

condition Specifies the decision you are making and must be phrased so that it results in either a true or false answer only.

Connection object Establishes a connection to a database, and then submits a request for data.

constructor The method whose instructions are processed, automatically, each time you use the class to create (instantiate) an object.

Const statement The statement used to create a named constant.

control An object displayed on a form.

ControlChars.Back The constant that represents the Backspace key on your keyboard.

ControlChars.NewLine constant The constant used to advance the insertion point to the next line in a control.

Convert class This class contains methods that return the result of converting a value to a specified data type.

counter A numeric variable used for counting something; allows you to answer the question "How many?".

CreateText method Creates a new, empty sequential access file to which data can be written.

D

DataAdapter object Submits requests for data from an application to the Connection object.

database An organized collection of related information stored in a file on a disk.

DataBind method The method used to bind a Web DataGrid control to a dataset.

DataGrid control The control that displays the data from a dataset in a row and column format, similar to a spreadsheet.

dataset A copy of some or all of the records and fields stored in a database.

data type Determines the type of data a variable can store.

data validation The process of verifying that a program's input data is within the expected range.

debugging The process of locating errors in the program.

decision structure Allows a program to make a decision or comparison and then select the appropriate path, depending on the result of that decision or comparison; also called the selection structure.

default button The button on a form that can be selected by pressing the Enter key when the button does not have the focus.

default constructor A constructor that has no parameters.

default list box item The item that is automatically selected when the interface first appears.

default radio button The radio button that is automatically selected when the interface first appears.

derived class The class that inherits from a base class.

dialog box A window that supports and supplements a user's activities in a primary window.

Do...Loop statement Can be used to code both a pretest loop and a posttest loop.

dot member access operator The period used to indicate a hierarchy of namespaces.

Dynamic Help window A context-sensitive system that is constantly being updated as you are working in the IDE.

dynamic Web page An interactive document that can accept information from the user and also retrieve information for the user.

E

element A variable in an array.

Else clause Contains the instructions that are processed when the condition in an If...Then...Else statement evaluates to False.

empty string A set of quotation marks with nothing between them; also called a zero-length string.

encapsulate An OOP term that means "contain"; for example, a class encapsulates (contains) all of the attributes and behaviors that describe the object the class creates.

EndsWith method Returns the Boolean value True if a specific sequence of characters occurs at the end of a string; otherwise, it returns the Boolean value False.

Enter event Occurs when the user tabs to a control, and when the Focus method is used in code to send the focus to the control.

event procedure A set of Visual Basic .NET instructions that tells an object how to respond to an event.

events Actions (such as clicking and double-clicking) performed by a user and recognized by an object.

exception An error that occurs while a program is running.

executable file A file that can be run outside the Visual Studio .NET IDE.

Exists method Used to determine whether a file exists.

exposed An OOP term that refers to the accessible attributes and behaviors of an object.

extended selection structures The If/ElseIf/Else and Case forms of the selection structure; also called multiple-path selection structures, because they have several alternatives from which to choose.

Extensible Markup Language XML; a text-based language used to store and share data between applications and across networks and the Internet.

F

false path Contains the instructions that are processed when the condition in a selection structure evaluates to False.

field A single item of information about a person, place, or thing.

Fill method Used to fill a dataset with data while an application is running.

floating-point number A number that is expressed as a multiple of some power of 10.

flowchart Uses standardized symbols to show the steps a procedure needs to take to accomplish its goal.

flowlines The lines connecting the symbols in a flowchart.

focus When a control has the focus, it can accept user input.

Focus method Moves the focus to a control while an application is running.

font The general shape of the characters in the text.

Font property Allows you to change the type, style, and size of the font used to display the text in an object.

For Each...Next statement Can be used to code a loop whose instructions you want processed for each element in a group (such as an array).

foreign key The field in the child table that links the child table to a parent table.

form The foundation for the user interface in a Windows-based application; also called a Windows Form object.

format specifier Determines the special characters that will appear in a formatted number.

formatting Refers to the process of specifying the number of decimal places and the special characters to display in a number.

FormBorderStyle property Allows you to specify the border style of a form.

form file Contains the code associated with a Windows Form object.

For...Next statement Can be used to code a pretest loop whose instructions must be processed a precise number of times.

function A predefined procedure that performs a specific task and then returns a value after completing the task.

Function procedure A procedure that returns a value after performing its assigned task.

G

Get block One of the blocks in a Property procedure; the Get block contains the Get statement.

Get statement Within the Get statement, you enter the code that allows an application to retrieve the contents of a class's Private variables.

GUI Stands for graphical user interface.

H

Handled property A property of the e parameter; allows you to cancel the key that the user pressed.

hidden Refers to the inaccessible attributes and behaviors of an object.

high-level languages These languages were developed after assembly languages; they allow the programmer to use computer instructions that more closely resemble the English language.

HTML Stands for Hypertext Markup Language, which is a language that uses tags to tell a browser how to display the information on a Web page.

HTTP communication protocol The protocol used to transmit Web pages on the Web.

Hypertext Markup Language HTML; a language that uses tags to tell a browser how to display the information on a Web page.

I

IDE Stands for "integrated development environment", which is an environment that contains all of the tools and features you need to create, run, and test your programs.

If selection structure Contains only one set of instructions, which are processed when the condition is true.

If/ElseIf/Else A form of the selection structure; commonly referred to as an extended selection structure or multiple-path selection structure, because it has several alternatives from which to choose.

If/Else selection structure Contains two sets of instructions: one set is processed when the condition is true and the other set is processed when the condition is false.

If...Then...Else statement Used to code the If, If/Else, and If/ElseIf/Else forms of the selection structure.

implicit type conversion The process by which a value is automatically converted to fit the memory location to which it is assigned.

incrementing Adding a number to the value stored in a counter or accumulator variable; also called updating.

independent Sub procedure A procedure that is not associated with any specific object or event, and is processed only when invoked (called) from code.

index The unique number assigned to each character in a string, and each item in a collection.

IndexOf method Searches a *string* for a *value*, and returns the number –1 if the *value* is not found in the *string*; otherwise, it returns the index of the starting position of *value* within *string*.

inheritance Refers to the fact that you can create one class from another class.

initializing Assign a beginning value to a variable.

InputBox function Displays a dialog box that contains a message, OK and Cancel buttons, and an input area.

input file A file from which an application reads information.

input/output symbol The parallelogram in a flowchart.

Insert method Returns a string with the appropriate characters inserted.

instances The objects created from a class.

integer A whole number; that is, a number without any decimal places.

integer division operator The backslash (\); divides two integers, and then returns the result as an integer.

integrated development environment IDE; an environment that contains all of the tools and features you need to create, run, and test your programs.

internal documentation The comments in a program.

Internet A computer network that connects millions of computers located all around the world.

interpreter A program that translates high-level instructions into machine code, line by line, as the program is running.

Invalid data Data that an application is not expecting.

IsNumeric function Checks whether an *expression* can be converted to a number, and then returns either the Boolean value True or the Boolean value False.

IsPostBack property A property of a Web form; the first time a Web form is displayed in a browser, the IsPostBack property contains the Boolean value False; otherwise, the property contains the Boolean value True.

Items collection Contains the items in a list box.

K

KeyChar property A property of the e parameter; used to determine the key that the user pressed.

KeyPress event Occurs when the user presses a key while a control has the focus.

keyword A word that has a special meaning in a programming language.

L

label control Displays text that the user is not allowed to edit while the application is running.

Label tool The tool used to instantiate a label control.

Length property Stores an integer that represents the number of characters contained in a string, or the number of elements in an array.

lifetime Indicates how long a variable remains in the computer's internal memory.

Like operator Allows you to use pattern-matching characters to determine whether one string is equal to another.

line A sequence of characters followed by the line terminator character.

line continuation character A space followed by an underscore; used to enter a long instruction on two or more physical lines in the Code Editor window.

line terminator character A carriage return followed by a line feed.

list box A control that allows you to display a list of choices from which the user can select zero choices, one choice, or more than one choice.

ListBox tool Used to instantiate a list box.

literal constant An item of data whose value does not change while an application is running.

literal type character A character used to convert a literal constant to a different data type.

logical operators Allow you to combine two or more *conditions* into one compound *condition*; also referred to as Boolean operators.

logic error Occurs when you enter an instruction that is syntactically correct, but does not give you the expected results.

loop Another name for a repetition structure; used to repeatedly process one or more program instructions until some condition is met, at which time the loop ends.

M

machine code Computer instructions written in 0s and 1s; also called machine language.

machine language Computer instructions written in 0s and 1s; also called machine code.

Me.Close method Instructs the computer to terminate the current application.

member variables The variables contained in a structure variable.

MessageBox.Show method Displays a message box that contains text, one or more buttons, and an icon.

method A predefined Visual Basic .NET procedure that you can call (or invoke) when needed.

Method Name list box In the Code Editor window, it lists the events to which the selected object is capable of responding.

methods The operations (actions) that an object is capable of performing; also called behaviors.

Mid statement Replaces a portion of a string with another string.

mnemonics The alphabetic abbreviations used to represent instructions in assembly languages.

module-level variables Variables declared in the form's Declarations section.

module scope The scope of module-level variables.

modulus arithmetic operator Mod; returns the remainder of a division.

multiple-path selection structures The If/ElseIf/Else and Case forms of the selection structure; also referred to as extended selection structures, because they have several alternatives from which to choose.

N

Name property Used to refer to an object in code.

named constant A computer memory location whose contents cannot be changed while the application is running; created with the Const statement.

namespace An area in the computer's internal memory that contains the code definitions for a group of related classes.

negation operator A hyphen (-); reverses the sign of a number.

O

object Anything that can be seen, touched, or used.

Object box In the Properties window, it contains the name of the selected object.

object-oriented program When writing this type of program, the programmer concentrates on the objects that the program can use to accomplish its goal.

one-dimensional array A group of related variables, with each variable identified by a unique number, called a subscript.

OOD An acronym for object-oriented design, which is the design methodology used to plan object-oriented programs.

OOP An acronym for object-oriented programming, which means that you are using an object-oriented language to create a program that contains one or more objects.

OpenText method Opens an existing sequential access file for input.

ORDER BY clause In a SELECT statement, it controls the order in which the records appear when displayed.

output file The type of file to which an application writes information.

P

PadLeft method Returns a string with the appropriate characters inserted at the beginning of the string.

PadRight method Returns a string with the appropriate characters inserted at the end of the string.

parallel arrays Arrays whose elements are related by their subscript (position) in the arrays.

parameters The memory locations listed in a procedure header.

parent table A table to which another table, called a child table, links.

Pascal-case When using this case to enter a variable name, you capitalize the first letter in each word in the name.

passing by reference Passing a variable's address to a procedure.

passing by value Passing a variable's contents to a procedure

path In a URL, it specifies the location of the document on the Web server.

Peek method Determines whether a sequential access file contains another character to read.

Pmt function Calculates a periodic payment on either a loan or an investment.

point A font measurement that is equal to $\frac{1}{72}$ of an inch.

Polymorphism The object-oriented feature that allows the same instruction to be carried out differently depending on the object.

populating the array The process of assigning initial values to an array.

postback Occurs when a server responds to a request from a client.

posttest loop The type of repetition structure where the condition is evaluated after the instructions within the loop are processed.

precedence numbers Indicate the order in which Visual Basic .NET performs an operation (such as an arithmetic operation) in an expression.

pretest loop The type of repetition structure where the condition is evaluated before the instructions within the loop are processed.

primary decision In a nested selection structure, this decision is always made by the outer selection structure.

primary key The field that uniquely identifies each record in a table.

primary window A window in which the primary viewing and editing of your application's data takes place.

priming read The read operation that prepares a loop for processing.

procedure A block of program code that performs a specific task.

procedure footer The last line in a procedure.

procedure header The first line in a procedure.

procedure-level variables Variables that are declared in a procedure.

procedure-oriented program In this type of program, the programmer concentrates on the major tasks that the program needs to perform.

procedure scope The scope of procedure-level variables.

process symbol The rectangle symbol in a flowchart.

programmers The people who write programs.

programming languages The languages that programmers use to communicate with the computer.

programs The directions given to computers.

project A container that stores files associated with a specific piece of a solution.

properties The characteristics that describe an object; also called attributes.

Properties list The left column in the Properties window; displays the names of the properties associated with the selected object.

Properties window The window that lists an object's attributes (properties).

Property procedure Used to create a Public property that allows the user to access the Private variables in a class.

protocol An agreement between a sender and a receiver regarding how data are sent and interpreted.

provider Translates a Connection object's request for data into a language that a database can understand.

pseudocode Uses English phrases to describe the steps a procedure needs to take to accomplish its goal.

R

radio button A control that allows you to limit the user to only one choice in a group of two or more related and mutually exclusive choices.

RadioButton tool The tool used to instantiate a radio button control.

ReadLine method Reads a line of text from a sequential access file.

record One or more related fields that contain all of the necessary data about a specific person, place, or thing.

references Addresses of memory cells within the computer's internal memory; each reference points to a namespace.

relational database A database that stores information in tables, which are composed of columns and rows.

relational operators These operators allow you to compare values in a condition.

Remove method Removes one or more characters from a string, and then returns a string with the appropriate characters removed.

repetition structure Another name for a loop; allows you to repeatedly process one or more program instructions until some condition is met, at which time the loop ends.

Replace method Returns a string with all occurrences of a sequence of characters replaced with another sequence of characters.

Return statement Used to return a value in a function.

S

scalar variable Another term for simple variable.

scope Indicates where in the application's code a variable can be used.

secondary decision In a nested selection structure, this decision depends on the result of the primary decision and is always made by the inner (nested) selection structure.

SelectAll method Used to select all of the text contained in a text box.

Select Case statement Used to code the Case selection structure.

SelectedValueChanged event Occurs when a different value is selected in a list box.

selection/repetition symbol The diamond in a flowchart.

selection structure Allows a program to make a decision or comparison and then select the appropriate path, depending on the result of that decision or comparison; also called the decision structure.

SELECT statement The most commonly used SQL command; it allows you to specify the fields and records you want to access from a database, as well as control the order in which the fields and records appear when displayed.

sentence capitalization Using this form of capitalization, you capitalize only the first letter in the first word and in any words that are customarily capitalized.

sequence structure Refers to the fact that the computer processes a procedure's instructions, one after another, in the order in which they appear in the procedure; also called sequential processing.

sequential access file A file composed of lines of text that are both stored and retrieved sequentially; often referred to as a text file.

sequential processing Refers to the fact that the computer processes a procedure's instructions, one after another, in the order in which they appear in the procedure; also called the sequence structure.

serif A light cross stroke that appears at the top or bottom of a character.

Set block In a Property procedure, this block contains the Set statement.

Set statement Contains the code that allows an application to assign values to the class's Private variables.

Settings box The right column in the Properties window; displays the current value (setting) of each of the properties.

short-circuit evaluation Refers to the fact that the AndAlso and OrElse logical operators do not always evaluate the second condition in a compound condition.

simple variable A variable that is unrelated to any other variable in the computer's internal memory.

solution A container that stores the projects and files for an entire application.

Solution Explorer window Displays a list of the projects contained in the current solution, and the items contained in each project.

source file A file that contains code.

Space function Used to write a specific number of spaces to a file.

splash screen The first image that appears when an application is started. It is used to introduce the application and hold the user's attention while the application is being read into the computer's internal memory.

SQL Acronym for Structured Query Language, which is a set of commands that allows you to access and manipulate the data stored in databases.

StartPosition property Determines where the form is positioned when the application is run and the form first appears on the screen.

start/stop symbol The oval symbol in a flowchart.

StartsWith method Returns the Boolean value True if a specific sequence of characters occurs at the beginning of a string; otherwise, it returns the Boolean value False.

startup form The form that is automatically displayed when an application is started.

statement block A set of statements terminated by an Else, End If, Loop, or Next statement.

static Web page A non-interactive document whose only purpose is to display information to the viewer.

stream A sequence of characters; also called a stream of characters.

stream of characters A sequence of characters; also called a stream.

StreamReader object Used to read a sequence of characters from a sequential access file.

StreamWriter object Used to write a sequence of characters to a sequential access file.

string A group of characters enclosed in quotation marks.

Structured Query Language SQL; a set of commands that allows you to access and manipulate the data stored in databases.

structures User-defined data types created using the Structure statement.

Structure statement Used to create structures (user-defined data types).

structure variable A variable declared using the Structure statement.

Sub procedure A procedure that does not return a value after performing its assigned task.

subscript A unique number that identifies each element in an array.

Substring method Returns characters from a string.

syntax errors Typing errors that occur when entering instructions.

T

TabIndex property Determines the order in which a control receives the focus when the user presses either the Tab key or an access key while the application is running.

table A group of related records in a database.

text box A control that gives the user an area in which to enter data.

TextBox tool The tool used to instantiate a text box.

text file Another name for a sequential access file.

Text property The Text property of a form displays in the form's title bar and on the taskbar while the application is running. The Text property of a control appears inside the control.

ToLower method Temporarily converts a string to lowercase.

toolbox Refers to the Toolbox window.

ToUpper method Temporarily converts a string to uppercase.

Toolbox window Contains the tools and other components you use when creating your application; each tool represents a class.

Trim method Removes one or more characters from the beginning and end of a string, and then returns a string with the appropriate characters removed.

TrimEnd method Removes one or more characters from the end of a string, and then returns a string with the appropriate characters removed.

TrimStart method Removes one or more characters from the beginning of a string, and then returns a string with the appropriate characters removed.

true path In a selection structure, it contains the instructions that are processed when the condition evaluates to True.

truth tables Summarize how Visual Basic .NET evaluates the logical operators in an expression.

Try statement Used to trap an exception when it occurs in a program.

Try/Catch block A block of code that contains the Try statement and one or more Catch statements.

two-dimensional array A group of related variables, with each variable identified by a unique combination of two numbers: a row subscript and a column subscript.

U

Uniform Resource Locator URL; the unique address assigned to each Web page on the Web.

Updating Adding a number to the value stored in a counter or accumulator variable; also called incrementing.

URL Stands for Uniform Resource Locator and is the unique address assigned to each Web page on the Web.

user-defined data types Data types created using the Structure statement; also called structures.

user interface What you see and interact with when using an application.

V

valid data Data that the application is expecting.

variable A computer memory location where programmers can temporarily store data.

W

Web Consists of documents called Web pages that are stored on Web servers; also referred to as WWW or the World Wide Web.

Web-based application An application that has a Web user interface and runs on a server.

Web browser A program that allows a client to access and view Web pages; also called a browser.

Web Form Designer window The window in which you create a Web page.

Web pages The documents that are stored on Web servers.

Web server A computer that contains special software that "serves up" Web pages in response to requests from clients.

WHERE clause Used in a SELECT statement to limit the records that will be selected.

Windows-based application An application that has a Windows user interface and runs on a desktop computer.

Windows Form Designer window The window in which you create your Windows application's GUI.

Windows Form object The foundation for the user interface in a Windows-based application; also called a form.

World Wide Web Consists of documents called Web pages that are stored on Web servers; also called WWW or the Web.

Write method Writes information to a sequential access file, and positions the file pointer at the end of the last character it writes.

WriteLine method Writes information to a sequential access file, and positions the file pointer at the beginning of the next line in the file.

WWW Stands for World Wide Web.

X

XML Stands for Extensible Markup Language, which is a text-based language used to store and share data between applications and across networks and the Internet.

XML schema definition file Defines the tables and fields that make up a dataset.

Z

zero-length string A set of quotation marks with nothing between them; also called an empty string.

Index